Saving One's Own

The Jewish Publication Society expresses its gratitude for the generosity of the following sponsors of this book:

JPS BENEFACTOR

Alan and Gittel Hilibrand, in honor of the many members of our families who were killed during the Holocaust.

JPS FRIEND

The Kroloff, Segal, Rose, and Youdovin Families, and Temple Emanu-El of Westfield, New Jersey, in memory of our beloved Lisbeth Brodie (z"l), for her heroism in Warsaw and her work to raise the next generation of Jews in America.

Joshua Landes and Bryna Shuchat and Family, in honor of our beloved parents and grandparents, Rabbi Aaron (z"l) and Sora Landes and Rabbi Wilfred and Miriam (z"l) Shuchat.

Harvey Schulweis, in support of Mr. Paldiel's much-needed exploration of a subject not adequately addressed in the study of the Holocaust.

Rabbi Barry L., Linda, Amy, and Laine Weinstein, in loving memory of Eliyahu "Eddie" Weinstein (z"l), for his lifelong remembrance of all the Shoah's Jewish victims and ceaseless support of Eretz Yisrael.

University of Nebraska Press
Lincoln

Saving One's Own

Jewish Rescuers during the Holocaust

MORDECAI PALDIEL

The Jewish Publication Society
Philadelphia

Published by the University of Nebraska Press as a
Jewish Publication Society book. Manufactured in
the United States of America. ∞

Library of Congress Cataloging-in-Publication Data
Names: Paldiel, Mordecai, author.
Title: Saving one's own: Jewish rescuers during the
Holocaust / Mordecai Paldiel.
Description: Lincoln: University of Nebraska Press,
[2016] | "Published by the University of Nebraska Press
as a Jewish Publication Society book"—Title page
verso. | Includes bibliographical references and index.
Identifiers: LCCN 2016039133 (print)
LCCN 2016039297 (ebook)
ISBN 9780827612617 (cloth: alk. paper)
ISBN 9780827612952 (epub)
ISBN 9780827612969 (mobi)
ISBN 9780827612976 (pdf)
Subjects: LCSH: World War, 1939–1945—
Jews—Rescue. | Righteous Gentiles in the
Holocaust—Biography. | Holocaust, Jewish
(1939–1945)—Biography. | World War, 1939–1945—
Jewish resistance.
Classification: LCC D804.6 .P35 2016 (print) | LCC
D804.6 (ebook) | DDC 940.53/1835—dc23
LC record available at https://lccn.loc.gov/2016039133

Set in Minion Pro by Rachel Gould.

To Haim Roet, founder of the
private citizens' JRJ—
Jewish Rescuers of Jews project

Contents

Photographs

Preface

I was born in Antwerp, Belgium, in 1937 into a Jewish family that had left Poland to seek a better life. In May 1940, in the wake of the German invasion, we fled to France and were constantly on the move, first in the Vichy zone and then in the Italian zone. Finally, in September 1943, we crossed illegally into Switzerland with the help of a Catholic priest, Simon Gallay, who was later honored as a Righteous Among the Nations by Yad Vashem, the museum in Jerusalem and Israel's national memorial to the victims of the Holocaust. At the end of the war my family returned to Belgium, and then in 1950 we left for the United States. I made *aliyah* in 1962; earned a BA degree in economics and political science at the Hebrew University, Jerusalem, saw action in the 1967 Six-Day War, and married and raised three children. In 1982 I received a PhD in Holocaust studies from Temple University, Philadelphia.

From 1982 to 2007, I headed the Righteous Among the Nations Department at Yad Vashem, whose mission it is to identify and honor non-Jewish rescuers of Jews during the Holocaust. In that capacity I was instrumental in adding some 18,000 names to the Righteous roster, and I have written books and articles on the subject. It is while I was doing that work that I came across many stories of Jewish rescuers who worked in tandem with non-Jewish ones. While the non-Jewish rescuers were duly acknowledged and justifiably honored by the Jewish people through Yad Vashem, the Jewish ones were left out in the cold, as there was no program similar to the Righteous Gentiles to praise and honor their courageous deeds.

Having retired from Yad Vashem in 2007 and begun teaching at Stern College and Touro College, both in New York, I decided to devote my time to writing a book about these brave Jews, based on material at Yad Vashem and elsewhere. I feel that the worldwide Jewish community needs to know about its own Holocaust heroes—people who did not necessarily take a gun to fight the Nazis (although a number of them did, the Jewish partisans), but rather felt that the greatest immediate need was to save the lives of as many Jews as possible. They did this mostly by creating rescue and escape networks, some in collaboration with non-Jews whose names adorn the roster of Righteous Gentiles.

It is important to know that non-Jewish rescuers need only to have saved one Jew to have his or her name listed among the Righteous, but here, writing about Jewish rescuers, I have included principally persons who were active in saving a great number of Jews, not just one or a few. Let me also point out that many Jewish rescuers in this book had the opportunity to flee and save themselves, such as Gisi Fleischmann in Slovakia, yet they chose to stay behind in locations where Jews were in great jeopardy, risking their own lives in order to carry out clandestine operations for the sole purpose of saving their brethren. These Jewish rescuers, and those that were active in countries not under German control—such as George Mandel-Mantello and Recha Sternbuch in Switzerland, and Peter Bergson in the United States—worked to save as many Jews as they possibly could. They too need to be acknowledged and have an honorable place in the Jewish pantheon. I hope that this book will help promote and further that endeavor.

Acknowledgments

To start, I would like to thank Haim Roet and his fellow private citizens' team workers, the JRJ–Jewish Rescuers of Jews Committee in Jerusalem. Since 1995 they have worked diligently to highlight the role of Jewish rescuers during the Holocaust and to make it an integral part of the Yad Vashem and Israeli schools' educational program. The JRJ team, to which I also belong, inspired me to do something to make the role of Jewish rescuers more generally known, and I thank them for this. Included in this committed team are Yuval Alpan, Chana Arnon, Margot Cohen, Ilana Drukker, David Gur, Tsilla Hershko, Shoshana Langerman, Eliezer Lev Zion, Genia Markon, Judith Reifen-Ronen, Esther Reiss, Alan Schneider, Joel Shachar, and Mirjam Wartman. Also the departed Efraim Agmon, Emeric Deutsch, Eitan Ginat, Ester Golan, Marianne Picard and Denis Skirsky.

My appreciation also to JPS director Barry Schwartz, who accepted the manuscript on behalf of JPS and suggested some structural changes, with which I graciously complied. And to Carol Hupping, managing editor at JPS, who patiently worked with me over a period of several weeks to trim the manuscript and make it more readable.

To Michael Berenbaum and Samuel Oliner, who read the original manuscript and made several editorial suggestions. Rafael Medoff, of the David S. Wyman Institute for Holocaust Studies, for suggesting a few changes in the Bergson and Hecht story, and Menachem Rosensaft, son of Hadassah and Josef Rosensaft, for providing additional source material. They both also sent me photos for the book. Special thanks also to Irene Frisch, originally from Drohobych (Poland-Ukraine), for making known to me the story of Nafatali Backenroth. And to Hadassa Carlebach, daughter of Rabbi Zalman Schneerson, for additional information on her father's rescue activity.

I am grateful to the following for providing photos: Judith Cohen and Nancy Hartman, U.S. Holocaust Memorial Museum, Washington DC;

Emanuel Saunders, Yad Vashem Archives, Jerusalem; and Lior Smadja, Mémorial de la Shoah, Paris; Anton Kras, Jewish Historical Museum, Amsterdam; Zvi Oren, Beit Lohamei Hagetaot–Ghetto Fighters House; Anat Banin, Zionist Archives, Jerusalem; Daniel and Noémi Mattis and daughter Olivia Mattis; Avery Peleg; and Netty Segal.

It is my sincere hope that this book, which contains so many stories from numerous sources, is error-free. But should there be some, hopefully only minor ones, the responsibility for them is either in the sources' accounts or my own.

Introduction

Jewish youth, do not be led astray. Of the 80,000 Jews in the "Jerusalem
of Lithuania" [Vilna] only 20,000 have remained. . . . All those who were
taken away from the ghetto never came back. All the roads of the Gestapo
lead to Ponary. And Ponary is death! . . . Cast off all illusions. . . . Ponary
is not a camp—all are shot there. Hitler aims to destroy all the Jews of
Europe. . . . Let us not go as sheep to slaughter! It is true that we are weak
and defenseless, but resistance is the only reply to the enemy! Brothers! It
is better to fall as free fighters than to live by the grace of the murderers.
Resist! To the last breath.

—Proclamation by the JEWISH ZIONIST YOUTH
   GROUP, Vilna ghetto, January 1, 1942

According to information that we have received from a reliable source, the
Germans are going to carry out a massive roundup of Jews in view of their
deportation. . . . Closing the eyes in the face of this tragic reality is equal
to committing suicide! Opening the eyes, recognizing the danger, leads to
salvation, to resistance, to life! Do not wait for these bandits in your home.
Take all necessary measures to hide, and hide first of all your children with
the aid of sympathetic French people. . . . If you fall into the hands of these
bandits, resist in any way you can. Barricade the doors, call for help, fight
the police. You have nothing to lose. You can only save your life. Seek to
flee at every moment. . . . Every Jew that remains alive and free constitutes
a victory over our enemy: we must not, we may not, we will not allow ourselves to be exterminated.

—Tract distributed by SOLIDARITÉ (Jewish communists) in Paris
   on the eve of the massive roundup of Jews on July 16, 1942

This decree of the government to deport the Jews to Poland . . . we must
know that . . . this time, however, we shall be expelled as slaves to a foreign
land, and who knows if we shall return and see our loved ones again. To

begin with, we shall lose our daughters, and after them, our sons . . . What did our forefathers do before they went into exile? . . . They tried to flee to neighboring countries where this danger did not threaten, they hid, they went underground and disappeared, they did not register in any census and did not report to any authorities. . . . My dear ones! Perhaps you do not fathom my words; perhaps I have caused you heartbreak; perhaps your illusions have been dashed by the bleak picture which I have presented you. . . . You might say . . . it is inconceivable that this will happen to us. Would that I be mistaken, would that I be proven wrong. Act prudently and instead of criticizing, take action today and tomorrow! We are speaking of saving lives, saving human beings. . . . Therefore, save yourselves, each and every individual. . . . Therefore choose life—follow the path of salvation and redemption, for life and not, God forbid, for death.

—RABBI ABBA AVRAHAM FRIEDER, sermon at Nové
   Mesto synogogue, Slovakia, March 14, 1942

You other Poles are fortunate. You are suffering, too. Many of you will die, but at least your nation goes on living. . . . From this ocean of tears, pain, rage, and humiliation, your country will emerge again, but the Polish Jews will no longer exist. We will be dead. . . . The Jewish people will be murdered. Our entire people will be destroyed. A few may be saved, perhaps, but three million Polish Jews are doomed. . . . You ask me what plan of action I suggest to the Jewish leaders. Tell them to go to all the important English and American offices and agencies. Tell them not to leave until they have obtained guarantees that a way has been decided upon to save the Jews. Let them accept no food or drink. Let them die a slow death while the world is looking on. Let them die. This may shake the conscience of the world.

—LEON FEINER (Bund) and MENACHEM KIRSZENBAUM (Zionists)
   to Jan Karski (Polish underground activist) in Warsaw, summer 1942

In Auschwitz . . . starting from yesterday, 12,000 Jewish souls—men, women, children, the old, the sick, and the healthy—will be taken daily to be choked, to be burned, and to be manure for the fields. And you, brother Jews! And you, ministers of state in all countries! How can you keep quiet at this murder? . . . . Surely, you can do something to object and stop it—now! . . . We beg you, we plead with you, we claim and demand of you: do something immediately! ... We demand, absolutely, and in the strongest terms: The destruction of all roads leading from Hungary to Poland or Germany, in particular the following roads: Kosice-Kysak-Presov-Orlova; Legene-Laborce, Cadca-Zilina. . . .

Now we ask: how can you eat, sleep, live? How guilty will you feel in your hearts if you fail to move heaven and earth to help us in the only ways that are available to our own people and as quickly as possible? Consider that every day 13,000 of your brothers and sisters, old and young, women and children, are destroyed. Do you not fear the day of judgment and reckoning in this world and in the world to come? . . . For God's sake, do something now and quickly.

—RABBI MICHAEL DOV-BER WEISSMANDL,
Slovakia, secret letters, May 16 and 31, 1944

The above excerpts ought to put to rest the widely held assertion that all Jewish leaders and organizations within Nazi-dominated Europe wore blinders and did little or close to nothing to stem the Nazi avalanche on their brethren Jews. On the contrary, many took action against threats to the Jewish people during the Holocaust years. Many Jews and Jewish organizations saved thousands of their fellow Jews by superhuman efforts never before seen in Jewish history. How, then, can one explain the assumption that Jews, whether fully conscious or not of the Nazi extermination scheme, went passively like sheep to their own slaughter?

In a 2002 publication about the role of non-Jewish rescuers of Jews, Holocaust historian Nechama Tec, who earlier wrote on Polish rescuers of Jews, lamented, "Why had I overlooked the rescue of Jews by Jews? . . . Historically Jews have been viewed as victims, and not as rescuers, not as heroes. Had I unconsciously assimilated these perceptions?"[1] As also pointed out by Marion van Binsbergen Pritchard, a celebrated non-Jewish Dutch rescuer in Holland and a recipient of Yad Vashem's Righteous title, in a private communication with me in 1997: "Not recognizing the moral courage, the heroism of the Jewish rescuers, who if caught were at much higher risk of the most punitive measures than the gentiles, is a distortion of history. It also contributes to the widespread fallacious impression that the Jews were cowards, who allowed themselves to be led like 'lambs to the slaughter.'"

While it is true that in many instances Jews failed to take adequate contingency measures to meet the Nazi threat, there are dozens of documented cases of Jews who took great risks to safeguard the lives of fellow Jews, and most of their names still remain unknown to the public at large. I've written this book to finally have their stories told, and in so doing counter the general, erroneous impression that only the Righteous Gentiles saved Jews.

There are more stories that one book can contain, so I've chosen the most remarkable accounts of Jews going out of their way to establish rescue networks in most of the countries occupied by the Germans. There were also efforts by Jewish activists in countries not under German domination, such as Switzerland, England, and the United States. Many of these Jewish rescuers remained anonymous in the postwar period. Why was this? Some have argued that it was because Jews are morally obligated to help fellow Jews and hence they merit no special acknowledgment. In contrast, gentiles helping Jews were engaged in behavior not expected of them, and so they merit special recognition. I find this argument fallacious: who is to say that the Jews who were themselves in great danger were obligated to risk greater danger in order to create clandestine networks to save others?

A more compelling reason, however, for trivializing the role of Jewish rescuers has to do with the Zionist ethos that led to the creation of the State of Israel. It was part of the Zionist teaching before and during the formative years of Jewish state to minimize, and some would say to dismiss, accounts of Diaspora Jewry assertiveness. It was furthermore argued to justify historical Jewish impassiveness that in order to survive the ongoing explosions of anti-Jewish rage in countries inhabited by Jews, Jewish leaders counseled a passive and submissive response to local authority, so as to minimize physical harm by outside forces. This is best borne out in the records of Jewish behavior during the Holocaust: a mixture of confusion, helplessness, and submissiveness, because European Jews were not conditioned to fight for their rights and their safety. The sole exception to this hapless situation, so goes the argument, were those who took up arms against the Germans in the ghettos and the forests. It was only in the State of Israel that Jewish assertiveness came to full bloom, as the country stood off numerous powerful enemies bent on the destruction of the new nation.[2]

Ironically, when survivors of the Holocaust arrived in Israel to help build the new nation and wished to tell the stories of their heroism in saving fellow Jews during the Holocaust, they were quickly silenced because their stories were at odds with the negative Diaspora image of passive Jews.[3]

The Righteous Among the Nations program, to honor non-Jewish rescuers of Jews, launched by Yad Vashem in 1962, is based on the Yad Vashem 1953 law passed by the Knesset, Israel's parliament, which stipulates that the honoring of non-Jews who risked their lives to save Jews during the Holocaust was one of the basic obligations of the newly founded national memorial institution. In my twenty-four years as head of the Righteous Among the Nations Department at Yad Vashem, I dealt with thousands of such cases, and I take pride that during my stewardship of the Righteous Department (1982–2007) some 18,000 names were added to the original 4,000 names. As I write this, there are more than 25,000 on the list, and several hundred more are added each year, as additional requests are received at Yad Vashem, sent in by survivors who were helped by non-Jewish rescuers. At the same time, in my work of processing these cases, I noted many stories in which non-Jewish rescuers worked in tandem with Jewish rescuers, and in some cases the Jewish rescuers played the dominant role in the rescue operation. In truth, one cannot properly speak of rescue undertakings during the Holocaust, especially in Belgium and France, but also in other countries, without mentioning the role of Jewish rescuers.

The stories of Jewish rescuers in the Diaspora need to be told: persons and organizations who displayed not submissiveness and resignation to a bitter fate but initiative, inventiveness, and courage, in a superhuman attempt to outwit the enemy and rouse fellow Jews to self-asserted rescue acts, and who succeeded in saving literally thousands of Jews. These Jews deserve an honorable place in the Jewish pantheon. Hopefully, this book of Jewish rescuers will help to fill this void and to instill in the Jewish people pride in the role many of their brethren played in saving their own.

Saving One's Own

1 Germany and Austria

Outwitting the Nazis in Their Home Base

Germany

Jews have lived in Germany since Roman days primarily in what is today the city of Cologne.[1] Starting with the Crusaders in 1096, persecutions, pogroms, mass killings, and expulsions followed the Jews from one German region to another, and later the great Protestant religious reformer Martin Luther fulminated against the Jews and actually called for the utmost violence against them if they persisted in maintaining their separate religion.[2] But at the dawn of the modern age, with the unification of Germany in 1871, Jews were fully emancipated, and they prospered and shared in the country's economic, political, scientific, and cultural life.[3] This gave birth to antisemitism, a modern term coined by the German publicist Wilhelm Marr. However, through World War I and into the Weimar Republic that followed, Jews continued to rise in prominence in all spheres of the country's life, including journalism, the theater, music, philosophy, and science. The integration of the Jews proceeded here much further and deeper than in many other European countries. This was especially so in the big cities of Berlin, Frankfurt, Munich, and Hamburg, where Jews and non-Jews intermingled with each other daily, to the extent that three out of ten marriages of Jews in 1932 were to non-Jewish partners.[4]

Hitler's assumption of power on January 30, 1933, sounded the death knell for German Jews, who numbered 566,000 (a bit less than 1 percent of the population). It must, however, be stated at the outset that Hitler's regime initially favored a policy of forced emigration through increased anti-Jewish measures, and indeed many left if they could get a visa. Thus the Zionist movement was able to carry on with relative freedom and with little interference as it, like the Nazis, urged Jews to leave—and as fast as possible.[5]

Under Nazi rule one more repressive law after another and one more restrictive regulation after another were designed to deny Jews a proper and normal human existence. It began with the one-day boycott of Jewish stores on April 1, 1933, which was soon followed by two new laws, one that dismissed Jews from work in the civil service and one that drastically reduced the number of Jewish pupils who were allowed to attend public schools.[6] Then came laws restricting Jews from the practice of law and medicine and Jewish exclusion from cultural life—the media, theater, and cinema.[7] All Jewish organizations had to close their doors and were subsumed under one Gestapo-controlled Jewish umbrella organization, the Reich Representation of German Jews (Reichsvertretung der Deutschen Juden), a Judenrat-type precursor, later applied in other countries under German domination.[8]

In September 1935 came the infamous Nuremberg laws, which stripped Jews of their citizenship and forbade marriage and intimate relations between Jews and non-Jews. An adjunct to this law also defined who was fully Jewish (one with three or four Jewish grandparents) and created a new category known as Mischlinge—non-Jewish and non-Aryan (those with one or two Jewish grandparents).[9] This was meant to create a so-called pure Aryan society. Jews were eliminated from commerce by being forced to sell out their business at a below-market value, under a program known as Aryanization.[10] Jews were forced to add a Jewish middle name on the id cards (Israel for men; Sarah for women), and their passports were marked with a large *J* (Jude-Jew).

On November 9, 1938, the Nazis launched a massive pogrom in every German city (this included Austria and the Sudeten region of Czechoslovakia, both annexed to Germany), known as Kristallnacht (Night of Broken Glass), causing the destruction of hundreds of synagogues, the vandalizing of thousands of Jewish homes and small businesses, the murder of close to 100 Jews, and the detention in concentration camps of some 30,000 Jewish men. On January 30, 1939, Hitler in a public address warned that in the event of a war, all Jews in Europe would face "annihilation" (Vernichtung).[11] With the start of the war on September 1, 1939, Jews were moved to specially designated Jewish homes (with as many as eight persons to a room) and required to perform menial labor. They had to hand over their jewelry, radios, cameras, electrical appliances, and pets. In September 1941 Jews ages seven and above were ordered to wear the Jewish Star and were no longer permitted to use public transportation, but were still required to perform menial labor.

Deportations had begun earlier, in October 1940, when 7,500 Jews from the Baden/Palatinate/Saar districts were expelled to German-occupied France. In September 1941 thousands of Jews began to be deported eastward to Polish ghettos and concentration camps and to Soviet-occupied areas, where they were murdered by the Einsatzgruppen mobile killing units. Some 42,000 mostly elderly people and others were sent to the Theresienstadt ghetto in former Czechoslovakia.[12] In July 1943 the Nazi regime proudly announced that Germany was "clean" of Jews (Judenrein).[13] In fact, up to 20,000 Jews still remained in Germany, most in hiding, including partners in mixed marriages as well as so-called half-Jews.[14]

Jews in hiding inside Germany were referred as U-Boaters, "submariners," as they were mostly in hiding or passing as non-Jews with the help of false credentials.[15] More than half of all those in hiding in Germany were in Berlin, given the demographic concentration of the Jewish population in wartime Berlin and the better prospects for hiding that the anonymity of the big city offered to Jews going underground.[16] Of the approximately 150,000 Jews remaining in Germany in October 1941 (at the start of the mass deportations), some 12,000 to 15,000 (8–10 percent) opted for an illegal way of existence, mostly in hiding. Of these, about 75 percent were seized by the Gestapo, according to one estimate. Altogether, some 3,500 to 4,000 (25–28 percent) survived while the rest were caught and deported.[17]

In summary, of the 566,000 Jews in Germany when Hitler came to power, some 300,000 were able to save themselves, mostly by emigrating (an option until November 1941) or by avoiding apprehension while in hiding. Of the rest, some 200,000 were deported, including German Jews deported from German-occupied countries to where they had earlier fled, and 160,000–180,000 of them died in the Holocaust.[18] Now to stories of some of the Jewish rescue activists who worked to get Jews out of Germany while this was still possible

Recha Freier

She worked tirelessly to get thousands of German Jewish youth out of danger's path by helping them to emigrate to Palestine through the organization she founded, Youth Aliyah.

On the eve of the Nazi takeover in 1932, five Jewish youths asked to see Recha Freier in her Berlin home.[19] These sixteen-year-old boys of Eastern European Jewish background had been told that she, a rabbi's wife, could assist them. In her words, "There they stood, thinking, excited, gloomy, despair on their pale faces. They told me that they had been sacked from their jobs for no other reason than that they were Jews. They were looking for a way out. Could I help them to get to Western Germany?" That year, the Nazi party, not yet in power, had garnered more votes than any other single party and was attracting many people to its ranks. Standing before Freier, the boys wondered whether there were any chances of finding employment in the coal mines or perhaps she had other advice for them? At that time, Freier, a rabbi's wife, was engaged in research on folklore, and she did not understand why these boys had come to her. However, that visit disturbed her peace of mind. As she stated, "The right to work, that is, the right to exist, had been taken from these boys and this—because they were Jews. . . . The utter senselessness of Jewish life in the Diaspora stood palpably before my eyes."[20]

The following day, still unsure how she could be of help to these distraught boys, she went to the Jewish Labor Exchange in Berlin, the director of which was a member of Poalei Zion, a Socialist-Zionist organization, to seek his advice. She was shocked by the man's dismissal of the boys' concern. As she related, "He shrugged his shoulders. 'This state of affairs is undoubtedly due to the general unemployment in the country,' he said. 'As soon as this comes to an end, the Jewish boys will get work again.'" He advised Freier to let matters take their course, but his response left her disturbed. "The way that director shrugged his shoulders made me shudder."[21]

Youth Aliyah

After some further thought, she got an idea: the predicament of these boys could be resolved through the creation of a movement of youngsters for work in Palestine, where they would strengthen their self-confidence and simultaneously help build up the Jewish community there. The boys responded enthusiastically. Thus was born the idea of Youth Aliyah— one year before the Nazi assumption of power, but with increasing dark clouds hovering over the Jewish community in Germany, as the Nazis continued to gain electoral strength.

Enzo Sereni, a kibbutz emissary, was then passing through Berlin, and Freier explained her idea to him. "Do it," he said, "and revolutionize the entire German Zionist Movement!" To help put the Youth Aliyah idea into action, he advised her to get in touch with the Histadrut, the Zionist Labor Federation in Palestine. Freier suggested to that organization that German Jewish youths aged fifteen and sixteen be educated and trained in the kibbutzim with a view to their settling in the country. The reply was positive, but doubts and opposition to Freier's idea soon sprouted, and they threatened to undo the whole undertaking before it had taken root.[22]

When she approached Zionist leaders in Germany with her idea, she was greeted with laughter and derision. "'Fantastic! Impossible!' they cried." Instead, "'Send the lads to German farmers where they will really learn something and where the money will be properly spent.'" In a Palestinian kibbutz, they claimed, the boys would be spoiled. Freier was thunderstruck at the blindness of these leaders to the signs of impending disaster. She also encountered resistance from parents and Jewish organizations, who felt that the situation in Germany wasn't that bad. But Freier received encouragement from the Histadrut when it sent her a list of Jewish settlements prepared to accept youth groups, such as Ein Harod, Geva, and Nahalal, and an estimate of the costs involved.[23]

She then began to approach people one on one, and she organized public meetings. She offered to create a special unit within the German Federation of the Women's Zionist Organization (WIZO), but was turned down. A "Children's crusade!" (recalling the tragic conscription of children for a holy crusade to the Holy Land by the Crusaders in the eleventh century), they disdainfully scoffed at this idea. Appealing to Ezra, the religious youth organization, she was also rebuffed, but for a different reason. Ezra's leadership refused to be a partner to the education of Jewish boys in Palestinian kibbutzim, owing to the nonobservance of Jewish rituals and lack of traditional Jewish education in many of these places. "The youth would become Communists there," they warned her. The Ezra organization, nevertheless, agreed to place its bank account at Freier's disposal for holding all funds collected for her Youth Aliyah purposes.[24] But this is as far as it would go.

Undeterred, Freier decided to appeal directly to the Jewish youth in Germany, and the response proved widespread and affirmative. This in turn led the German Zionist organization to view her plan favorably, provided that the Jewish community in Palestine created a satisfactory organ to supervise the necessary arrangements for settling the children and look after their education, as well as undertake responsibility for financial matters that might arise. It was suggested that she contact Henrietta Szold, who headed the social department in the Vaad Leumi, the Palestinian Jewish National Council. The American-born Szold was a notable Zionist leader, having established the Hadassah Women Organization and settled in Palestine. Freier did write to her about her Youth Aliyah idea, but she received a negative reply; she was told that, for the moment, no children could be brought over.[25] Although Szold later changed her mind and assumed the leadership of the Youth Aliyah operation, she simultaneously carried on a vindictive campaign against Freier, based it seems on a personal dislike for reasons unclear. This was coupled with an attempt to undercut Freier's work and claim for herself the authorship of the Youth Aliyah idea and leadership.[26]

But Freier did not relent. As she related: "My faith in the ultimate success of my mission was likewise becoming stronger and stronger. I was convinced that the task I had taken upon myself was a vital necessity and that it was up to me to fulfill it." She contacted Kibbutz Ein Harod, and they agreed to take the boys. The kibbutz's emissaries, then in Berlin, contacted her to arrange the journey of the first group.[27] Freier was also encouraged when she learned in June 1932 that the founder and director of the Ben Shemen children's village in Palestine was about to visit Berlin and had asked to meet her. This took place in Freier's home, in the presence of a group of forty youths. Ben Shemen offered her twelve immigration certificates and places in its youth village. The Königsberg Zionist Women undertook to cover the cost of immigration and training of five boys, and seven other places were reserved for Berliner youths.[28]

Department store head Wilfrid Israel also helped by offering equipment from his store for the trip, and the Aid Association of German Jews (Hilfsverein der Deutschen Juden) defrayed the cost of the journey. Now all that was needed was the consent of the boys' parents in writing, and they dutifully signed. Departure date was set for October 12, 1932. At the train station, the boys sang Hebrew songs, excited about this, their first big journey. Wilfried Israel whispered to Freier reassuringly: "'This is an historic moment!' . . . The work had begun; no one could interfere with it anymore."[29] Another group of twenty-five young immigration candidates was formed in the summer of 1932, with six arriving in November 1932 and directed to the youth village of Ben Shemen.[30]

This led to another religious organization, the Union of Religious Pioneers, known as Bachad, to get in touch with Freier on the aliyah of a youth group to the religious settlements.[31] Szold again rejected Freier's request for assistance and gave an additional reason: kibbutzim in Palestine were not the right places for the education of youth, since vocational schools on a par with those in Germany did not exist in Palestine.[32] In addition, there was no reason to be in a hurry, as the Nazis had not yet obtained power (although in the parliamentary election of July 31, 1932, they had doubled their representation in the Reichstag and emerged as the most powerful political party).

Recha Freier dreamed of ultimately sending 10,000 boys to Palestine, but she was satisfied to start with very small groups. She created a committee of seven members, whom she picked from the leaders of the Zionist youth organizations. On January 30, 1933, the day Hitler assumed power, Freier's committee's first official meeting took place at the office of a notary. The new organization's name was Aid Committee for Jewish Youth (Hilfskomitee für Jüdische Jugend), but among themselves they preferred to call it Youth Aliyah, or Children's Aliyah. As they left the notary's office and turned onto Unter den Linden Boulevard, they could not help but witness the torchlight procession of thousands of Nazi Storm Troopers (SA) celebrating Hitler's accession to power. The bell of doom had just rung for German Jews.[33]

Some months later, in May 1933, with the Nazis already in power, Freier sailed for Palestine to inspect the various colonies in the Galilee and take a firsthand look at the German youth enrolled in the Ben Shemen children's village. She also met Henrietta Szold in Jerusalem, but the two could not agree on working together to further the Youth Aliyah program. (Szold eventually took over its leadership on November 27, 1933.)[34]

During the second half of 1933, about 1,000 children came to Palestine under Youth Aliyah auspices. More would come in the following years, most placed with private families as well as in kibbutzim and other settlements. A total of 4,000 had arrived by the end of 1938, many of them thanks to Freier's dedicated work.[35] As German schools began to dismiss their Jewish pupils under Nazi pressure, Freier's Youth Aliyah office in Berlin created special classes for ninth graders, with Hebrew, Jewish history, and Zionism as the bedrock of the curriculum, together with practical studies linked to agricultural work in Palestine.[36]

When Kristallnacht erupted in Germany in November 1938, and with immigration possibilities restricted by the British administration in Palestine, Freier tried to divert Jewish emigrants to England. Learning that there was a great shortage of farmworkers there, she tried to get permits for over 1,000 Zionist Hechalutz pioneering members for temporary sojourns in England until they were cleared for travel to Palestine. For this purpose, Freier sought out the help of Rebecca Sieff, a prominent Jewish and Zionist activist whose family owned the Marks and Spencer department store. In the event, about 2,000 obtained entry permits before the outbreak of hostilities in 1939. There were also Youth Aliyah camps in other European countries, including Belgium, Holland, and Scandinavia, where youths from Germany were placed with private families or in special homes. In 1939 Freier began to make arrangements for sending a shipload of children to Palestine for whom no Palestine immigration certificates were available, but the plans had to be abandoned.[37]

Not relenting, Freier tried to set up children's camps in other places far from the approaching war zones of Europe, such as Cyprus, Greece, and Turkey. Dr. Chaim Weizmann, head of the World Zionist Organization, tried to help by writing to Roland Storrs, the former governor of Cyprus, and he also asked Mrs. Blanche Dugdale (secretary to British Foreign Secretary Arthur Balfour during World War I) to intercede with the British ambassador in Turkey. When all these requests failed, Freier suggested that several islands off the Greek mainland be placed at the disposal of children's camps, but this too was turned down.[38]

Crossing Borders into Safety

In her efforts to get as many Jewish teenagers out of danger's path, Freier was not beyond working in a semilegal gray zone. For instance, she procured passages with shipping companies, deceptively stipulating that she had the needed documents for immigration. When she claimed that she was able to secure at first 30 and later another 100 emigration permits, men were released from concentration camps and left for Palestine. She then was ordered to appear before ss officer Adolf Eichmann who, in her words, "threw my passport at my head and ordered me to surrender it" on the following day.[39] Many Jewish women appealed to her to help liberate their husbands who had been incarcerated during Kristallnacht. "As I look at the pinched, pale faces of the [men's] children," she recalled, "I vowed solemnly that I would free them, the children at least, although at the moment I did not know how to do it."[40]

In 1941, warned of possible arrest, she took her eleven-year-old daughter Maayan and a group of children and crossed the border illegally into Yugoslavia, where she awaited the arrival of another group of children who had journeyed there via Vienna. While in Zagreb, Freier kept busy teaching Hebrew to the youngsters. "They love Recha," a witness testified; "who else cared for their children at a time when everybody else had abandoned them? She was in control, but she didn't boss. They felt drawn to her, their shield, their refuge."[41]

From Zagreb, she cabled her affiliates in Berlin to bring as many children and youths as possible to Zagreb via border smuggling points from Austria (then annexed to Germany), as she herself and her daughter had done. The Jewish Federation leaders in Germany, however, hesitated to place children at such risk. The smugglers sent by her went time and again, but came back empty-handed. "So I had to do something," Freier recalled. "In desperate situations I was afraid of nothing, not even trickery and lies. I sent a telegram to Berlin: 'Hundreds of immigration certificates lie here and if the children do not come, I will make a world-wide scandal of the situation.'" This proved effective. Smugglers brought the first group of German children to Zagreb—orphans of fathers who had died in concentration camps, a total of 120. They were allowed to leave with the approval of the Gestapo, who then still followed a policy of forced emigration of Jews in legal or illegal ways. The children were housed with Yugoslavian Jewish families.[42] The Yugoslav authorities gave the children exit visas, but it remained uncertain how many immigration certificates would be made available by the British authorities in Palestine. At first the British declined because the children originated in a country that was at war with England. Freier then interceded with Chaim Barlas, the Jewish Agency representative in Turkey, and he effected British permission for 90 of the children to be admitted. They left just days ahead of the German invasion of Yugoslavia in April 1941.

Freier had also left days ahead of the German attack with her daughter, joining an illegal Palestine transport together with Youth Aliyah children, steaming down the Danube River to the Black Sea. Another group of 43 illegal children was left behind under the care of Youth Aliyah leader Josef-Joshko Indig (later Itai), a story told in chapter 6.[43]

Here is testimony by Kalman Givon (formerly Karl Kleinberger), one of those lucky children who made it safely out of Germany.

Recha saved thousands of children from Nazi Germany. I was one of those children. I was born in 1924 in Frankfurt. My mother died when I was 4½ years. Father had to flee for political reasons. I was raised by my uncle's family. . . . [At the] end of 1940 I learned that there was a possibility for Polish descendant orphans to be illegally spirited across into Yugoslavia. I was told that Recha is organizing such a group for Yugoslavia, and we should present ourselves before the Jewish community in Frankfurt. Two days later we were already on a train heading to Vienna. We were 16 children, aged 12 to 16. The Palestine Office in Vienna organized a larger group of 100 children from four cities, Berlin, Leipzig, Frankfurt, and Vienna. We continued to Graz, where . . . with the help of smugglers we crossed into Yugoslavia. . . . We arrived in Zagreb where we stayed . . . for several months with Recha and her daughter, Maayan, about 100 children. Recha was constantly close to us. Recha then succeeded to bring us all to Belgrade. From there we left on the last train to Greece, and then Turkey. Arriving in Istanbul, we continued by boat to the Asian side; then by train to Eretz Israel, where we arrived on April 17, 1941. After a short stay in Atlit, we were taken to Kfar Hanoar Hadati, a religious children's home near Haifa. . . . We thank Recha Freier for saving our lives. We will always be thankful to her.[44]

Thus an undertaking that began innocently in a chance meeting with a group of Jewish teenagers in 1932 led a rabbi's wife to the creation of an organization that evolved into a large rescue operation, saving the lives of many Jewish youth. Safely in Palestine, Freier wanted to continue her work for the Youth Aliyah, but the differences she had with Henrietta Szold proved an insurmountable obstacle. In Freier's words, "A short time after my arrival in Palestine Miss Szold informed me in the name of Youth Aliyah in Jerusalem that there was no place for me in Youth Aliyah. Thus my services on behalf of the movement were terminated."[45]

Later, in the new state of Israel, Freier found solace in various educational activities, such as the founding of an Agricultural Training Center for Israeli children and a Composer's Fund to encourage musical creativity. She also wrote poetry and prose, and in 1981 she was awarded the Israel Prize. She died in 1984. There are no reliable statistics on how many children she helped save; some claim that the number runs into the thousands.[46]

Wilfrid Israel

> He helped hundreds of Jews leave Germany for Palestine, Shanghai, and elsewhere, but his greatest accomplishment was his participation in the Kindertransport, the exodus of close to 10,000 children from Nazi Germany to England.

In 1902 the Nathan Israel family department store, one of the largest chain stores in Berlin, supplied linen and furnishings to hotels, clubs, and theaters, to hospitals and churches, as well as to military barracks and officers' messes. Starting with 250 employees, it produced one of the first mail-order catalogs on the American pattern, and by the early 1930s it employed more than 2,000 people. The huge store was closed on Saturdays and the Jewish High Holy days, as its head, Jacob Israel, was an observant Jew, and his son Berthold held a position in a prominent synagogue. The first of the great Jewish business houses in Berlin (without any other branches), it was the last to close its doors during Hitler's reign.[47]

Wilfrid Israel, Berthold's son, the store's general manager in the 1920s, had Zionist aspirations, and he managed to persuade his father to contribute a substantial sum to the Jewish National Fund (JNF) to help in the construction of the Ben Shemen youth village in Palestine. In fact, Israel became the "godfather" of the village. Earlier, in the summer of 1932, Recha Freier, founder of Youth Aliyah, had sought Israel's help for adolescent Jews wishing to emigrate to Palestine, and together they organized the emigration of a group of twelve Berlin boys, the pilot project for thousands of German-Jewish children who were soon to leave their sheltered lives in middle-class homes in Germany for the unknown rigors of life in Palestine. Wilfrid Israel supplied the Berlin boys with tweed overcoats and velvet collars. The group left on October 12, 1932. It was the beginning of Israel's work for the rescue of thousands of fellow Jews. When the capacity of the Palestinian orphanages and Ben Shemen village was exhausted, Israel and his colleagues decided, together with the Zionist pioneering movement Hechalutz, to send groups of children to other kibbutzim: sixty children left for Ein Harod in the Jezreel Valley in 1934, and another group was sent to Mishmar HaEmek a little later.[48]

With the Nazis already in power, on February 27, 1933, Wilfrid Israel was arrested by Storm Troopers, released, and rearrested on March 30. After a stiff interrogation, he was again freed. About 20 percent of the employees of the N. Israel firm were registered members of the Nazi Party. But in this early period of Nazi rule, of the 500 Jews in the firm, only 2 are known to have lost their jobs while the firm was under the Israel family management. In the meantime, Israel was commuting constantly between Berlin and London, soliciting funds from German Jewry's benefactors in England, such as the Central British Fund. Although he was never to become a religious observant Jew, he began to adopt certain Jewish practices, in particular the Friday evening ritual of lighting candles and saying blessings over wine and bread, a practice he continued until his death.[49]

On November 14, 1935, Wilfrid Israel was served with a notice that he was officially removed from his position as head of the N. Israel department store, now to be formally filled by the non-Jewish Paul Krentz. Israel still made all the operative decisions, but henceforth he was in a peculiar position: the heir, but not the master, of N. Israel. Then in April 1936 the Nazi regime withdrew the trade school's license, and Nazi members inside the firm were instigated to harass other employees with threats of reprisals if they did not join the party. Gone were the outings to the river or to the country, and no more celebrations or anniversaries, theater groups, or debating societies.[50] Sensing that the curtain was coming down for Jews in Germany, Israel began working intensively in the Jewish community's Hilfsverein in 1937, an organization that helped Jews leave Germany, something that Israel had been slowly helping his Jewish employees do already.

The Israel-Pollack-Foley Conspiracy

Zionist activists repeatedly appealed to Wilfrid Israel to leave, but he refused, always assuring them that eventually he would join them in Palestine. The sole British official in Berlin who was unabashedly active on behalf of Jews in distress was Frank Foley, the diplomat in charge of passports and visas. He was responsible for issuing all the immigration

certificates for Palestine, and he bent over backward to overlook his country's immigration laws in order to facilitate the exit of Jews from Nazi
Germany. Foley and Israel knew each other well, and they maintained
contact for the rest of their lives. Foley's double role in Germany, as diplomat and also master spy for the British intelligence, and his links with
Israel were to be of great importance for both the British government
and the Jews of Germany.[51]

Hubert Pollack, a Jewish associate of Foley's, was another teammate of
Israel helping Jews anxious to leave the country. The two profited from
each other's expertise: Pollack had contacts in the Gestapo; Israel had
money. A specialist in public finance, Pollack began working with the
statistical office of the German government in 1927. Pollack held clandestine meetings with Gestapo officials in cafes and backstreets, where
money could change hands smoothly, much of it supplied by Israel. He
swiftly built up a network of contacts among policemen and officials who
would produce virtually any document for suitable payment, either in
cash or in valuables.

In his postwar testimony, Pollack wrote, "Besides my superior and
friend Wilfrid Israel, no one knew of my activities." In testimony written
in 1944, he stated that Germans Jews owed an unrecognized debt to Wilfrid Israel. When people came to Israel pleading for his help in releasing
their relatives from the camps, he provided the necessary funds to Pollack. Pollack obtained the documents, and Foley granted visas to those
who Israel and Pollack told him were honest people whose names had
been unjustly blackened by the Gestapo. This appears to have become
standard procedure well before the Kristallnacht pogrom.[52]

On November 9, 1938, at about 2 p.m. (the eve of Kristallnacht), the
police guard usually stationed around the N. Israel department store
was suddenly withdrawn. Then the assault began. Young men in work
clothes, armed with sticks and iron bars, followed by ss men in uniform,
pushed their way past the workers. They smashed display cases, tore
down lengths of silk from the stands, and trampled clothes and materials underfoot. They hurled furniture into the main stairwell from the
galleries. The Jewish employees were hauled off for arrest. According to
one account, Israel negotiated to have them released from the Sachsenhausen concentration camp. The camp commander agreed after Israel
promised him he could shop for Christmas at the department store for

free. The remaining 200 Jews in the firm were given the equivalent of two years' salary in cash, coupled with efforts by Israel to find them jobs abroad. The Nazis now decreed that all Jewish firms were to be Aryanized by the end of the year, in other words, to be forcibly sold at a fraction of their worth. Indeed, on February 6, 1939, a parting message was handed to all N. Israel employees that the store had been Aryanized, and a poster appeared all over Berlin, stating: "All are cordially invited to the inauguration of the renamed Das Haus im Zentrum.[53]

Kindertransport

Wilfrid Israel was now free to dedicate himself fully, with the help of the Quakers and leading British Jews, in the transport of close to 10,000 children to England. The Quakers, Israel's longtime fellow social activists, selected five people to go to Berlin and meet with Israel, and under his direction they set out for Jewish communities all over Germany. In each community, they made contact with Jewish leaders to urge them to send their children to England under the Kindertransport program. They also met with Protestant pastors who were involved in helping baptized Jews, who were considered "fully" Jewish under Nazi law.[54]

To activate this large-scale exodus of children, Wilfrid Israel had prepared an emigration plan for submission to the British government. An Anglo-Jewish deputation led by Lord Herbert Samuel and including Chaim Weizmann, Lionel de Rothschild, and the chief rabbi hastily put together a petition incorporating Israel's cable and went to see Prime Minister Neville Chamberlain, who at first remained noncommittal. On November 21, 1938, Samuel led another delegation to meet with Home Secretary Samuel Hoare. Speaking in the House of Commons that evening, Hoare announced that the government had agreed to the admission of refugee children. Passports and visa requirements were waived, and 1,000 applications a day were being received at the Home Office. Professor Dennis Cohen, head of the Emigrant Department of the Council for German Jewry, was sent to Berlin, where he worked with Wilfrid Israel in organizing the first transport of children to Britain. The first group—200 in all—arrived in England on December 2, 1938. They had left at twenty-four hours' notice, bringing only a few personal belongings with them. The British Home Office had agreed to admit 5,000 children as a first batch, and this was eventually enlarged to close to 10,000.[55]

Since Kristallnacht, Wilfrid Israel did not sleep in his own bed, as he was closely watched by the Gestapo and was told that he was not to visit the British embassy without a special permit. Together with his colleagues, he continued ransoming people from the Gestapo and placing them on boats leaving Germany for Shanghai, where no formalities were needed to disembark. On May 15, 1939, he left for London with a few Reich marks in his pocket, as the law prescribed, but was back in Berlin in August, where he worked frantically, dispatching what were to be the last of the children's transports across Holland to England. He then left Germany for good.[56]

Rescue Missions to Palestine

In January 1943 the Jewish Agency enlisted Israel for another rescue mission. This took him to Portugal, where he was to plan a route and means of transportation to Palestine for Jewish refugees in Portugal and Spain and to look for possibilities of rescue for others, including 1,000 children trapped in Vichy France (their departure had been approved the previous year). With the North African campaign at its zenith, the escape route through the Mediterranean was quite risky. Not knowing what was in store for him, on March 25, 1943, on the eve of his departure for Lisbon, he wrote his will, leaving his art collection to Kibbutz Hazorea.[57]

In Lisbon Wilfrid Israel learned of Isaac Weissman, a one-man operator who tried to get many illegal Jewish refugees out of detention and into the less restrained residence of refugee villages. Working alone, Israel decided to distribute the largest number of his Palestine certificates to Jews who were in greater danger in Fascist Spain, for whom he gathered information on escape routes to safer havens. He even thought of diverting refugees for travel across central Africa. As he wrote to Richard Lichtheim, the Zionist Jewish Agency representative in Switzerland: "I have decided to find a new way across Central Africa. This would lead to the Congo, up the river to Stanleyville, from there across Juba to the Nile. I am consulting with doctors, the Tropical Institute, and through the Federation of South Africa to get a clear view."[58]

On April 29, 1943, he left for Madrid. What he found in the camps and prisons of Spain was worse than anything he had seen in Portugal. In Miranda del Ebro, the largest camp, refugees from Nazi-occupied France slept on stone floors, and washing facilities were so primitive that most refugees had skin diseases, with many cases of tuberculosis. He worked out of the British embassy preparing detailed lists of those eligible for certificates to Palestine, with the backing of the British ambassador. On May 25 he returned to Lisbon, where he learned that the Congo route was impassable at this time of the year because of heavy rains. Only after November, six months later, he was told, would it be possible to send a party through the jungle. He was now besieged by refugees to whom he had no more certificates to offer. All he could do was promise that once back in London, he would press for a larger allocation.[59] He prepared to fly back there.

Unbeknownst to Wilfrid Israel, the German air force (Luftwaffe) had orders to attack every plane flying the route between Portugal and Britain within the next few days, in the hope of shooting down a plane carrying Winston Churchill back from North Africa, through Gibraltar, and across the Bay of Biscay. On June 1, 1943, Israel and other passengers, including actor Leslie Howard, boarded a British plane heading for London. Over the Bay of Biscay, the plane was intercepted and shot down by a German war plane, with the loss at sea of all passengers.[60]

Israeli journalist Ofer Aderet credits Wilfrid Israel with saving thousands of Jews. He portrays him as a multifaceted figure: a capitalist who believed in Communism; a lover of mankind who spent much of his time alone; a pacifist and timid person who became a selfless hero, taking great risks to save fellow Jews.[61] His signature achievement was in getting thousands of Jewish children out of Nazi Germany to England in time, on the eve of World War II.

David Glick

David negotiated the release of prisoners from the Dachau concentration camp and facilitated the emigration of German Jews to South America.

A Jewish lawyer in Pittsburgh who spoke German fluently, David Glick left for Germany several times in 1936 and 1937, at the urging of Max Warburg of Berlin and his brother, Felix Warburg of the Joint Distribution Committee (JDC) in New York. Glick was to serve as a liaison between the German Jews and the authorities of large German cities on immigration issues.[62] Arriving in Berlin, Glick met with the U.S. ambassador, William

E. Dodd, the U.S. consul general in Berlin, George S. Messersmith, and his first assistant, and Consul Raymond H. Geist. The latter arranged for Glick to meet with (incredibly) ss head Heinrich Himmler, accompanied by Geist for Glick's protection. Geist and Glick assured Himmler that they would not make public Glick's activity in Germany, especially not what he was doing to facilitate Jewish emigration to distant lands.[63] During this meeting, Himmler called in his second in command, Reinhard Heydrich, who took the two visitors to the office of Dr. Karl Haselbacher, in charge of Jewish questions in the Gestapo. Glick reported that Haselbacher showed them a filing cabinet that contained the names, addresses, activities, and occupations of thousands of important Jews. Again, Glick and Geist assured their Gestapo interlocutor that they would withhold news of their meetings and activities from foreign journalists in Berlin.[64]

Glick remained in Germany a full month, then returned to the United States and reported to Felix Warburg and Paul Baerwald of the JDC. They asked him to return, and he left again in 1937. Upon meeting again with Heydrich, the latter introduced Glick to Dr. Werner Best, the deputy leader in the Gestapo (later of ill fame when in 1943 he represented the ss in Denmark). At Glick's request, he was given a letter granting him permission to visit various German cities without hindrance. In October 1937 Glick reportedly negotiated for the release of 120 of the 200 Jews then held at Dachau concentration camp. The Gestapo released them on the condition that they leave the country immediately. Glick worked with the main Jewish Federation, Reichsvertretung der Juden in Deutschland, and its director, Frederick Borchardt, visiting every South American country to facilitate the emigration of German Jews there. One contact alone, a German émigré to Argentina and tin mine millionaire, Don Mauricio Hochschild, financed the settlement of 3,000 refugees in Bolivia.[65]

David Glick's story, "Some Were Rescued," which he published in 1960, still requires further substantive research with regard to precise details of places and number of persons aided. But it is added proof of the extent of Nazi policy in the early years of the Nazi regime to openly encourage and even facilitate Jewish emigration from Germany. Glick does not mention what exactly he did in Germany, with whom he met in each Jewish community, what he told them, and how he helped facilitate their exit from Germany other than that it was done in tandem with the Reichsvertretung. Glick's story does not appear in Holocaust literature dealing with emigration of German Jews before the war, such as the studies of Yehuda Bauer and Henry Feingold. The question remains why Himmler would give this unknown Jewish American, presumably representing the Joint Distribution Committee, carte blanche to move freely throughout Germany and meet with Jewish representatives on the matter of immigration.[66] Whatever the explanation, David Glick should be commended for his efforts in trying to get Jews out of Germany by staying for a long period in a country where, as a Jew, he risked being exposed to ridicule and the possibility of mistreatment and physical injury by Nazi officials.

Erich Klibansky

> He gave up the opportunity to flee Germany with his family so that he could arrange safe haven in England for 127 of his own pupils.

Dr. Erich Klibansky, the scion of a long line of Lithuanian rabbis, headed the Jewish religious Jawne high school in Cologne. As Jewish pupils were evicted from German public schools, their number in Jewish day schools was on the rise.[67] Some came to the Jawne school from distant towns, and they lodged in Cologne during the weekdays. During the Kristallnacht pogrom of November 1938, the school and synagogue suffered serious damage. Benches and equipment were destroyed, documents torn up, books thrown into the yard, and two of the teachers were arrested and sent to Dachau camp.

Klibansky then decided to try moving all his students to England, under the terms of the Kindertransport, for which he had the approval of the children's parents and for which he visited England twice, with Gestapo approval, to make the necessary arrangements. The first transport departed from Cologne on January 17, 1939, with about 30 boys; the second, in February 1939, the third, on May 9, 1939, and the fourth, in June 1939—all together 127 boys and girls. With most of his students safe and secure, Klibansky made plans to move to England with his family, but the war intervened and he remained stranded. He lived with his family in a small disabled room of the former Jawne school until teachers and pupils were "evacuated" to the east. Klibansky and his family were deported on July 20, 1942. Several days later, they were shot before pits in the Minsk, Belarus, region.[68] Erich Klibansky had managed to get 127 of his pupils out in time, but that left no time for himself and his family, who were murdered by his own countrymen for the "sin" of having been born.

Austria

In March 1938 Austria was annexed to Nazi Germany. Jews had lived there since Roman days (third century CE). As in nearby Germany, the Middle Ages saw many riots against Jews, fanned mostly on religious grounds, and in the years that followed Jews managed through good and bad days at the hands of the non-Jewish authorities: princes, kings, and bishops. In the mid-nineteenth century things began to improve. Emperor Franz Joseph I granted them full civic rights, and in the following years their contributions to the country's culture and politics were substantial, such as music (Gustav Mahler), literature (Arthur Schnitzler), psychiatry (Sigmund Freud), philosophy (Karl Popper), theater and film (Max Reinhardt and Fritz Lang), politics (Victor Adler), and Zionism (Theodor Herzl). In 1897 Karl Lueger was elected mayor of Vienna on an antisemitic platform, but the conditions of Jews were not adversely affected. That was to change dramatically after the Nazi takeover on March 12, 1938.

There were more than 180,000 Jews in Austria, with some 170,000 concentrated in Vienna alone, as Hitler rode triumphantly into that city and was received in a tumultuous and rousing welcome by the inhabitants.[69] To everyone's surprise, Vienna, which was known for its *gemütlichkeit* (warm cordiality) and its cheerful Strauss waltzes, erupted in antisemitic violence in a way not anticipated even in German cities. Many Austrian civilians enthusiastically joined the German Nazis in terrorizing Jews. Jewish men and women were forced to scrub the street sidewalks and pavements with toothbrushes and others with their bare hands, to the delight of onlookers. Some pulled religious Jewish men around by their beards.[70] New anti-Jewish laws were passed at a speed unparalleled in Nazi Germany, laws returning the status of Jews to what it was during the Middle Ages. Jewish organizations and newspapers were shut down, and Jews were fired from state and municipal posts, followed by public school teachers and bank employees. Jews could no longer use public baths, swimming pools, or park benches. Signs forbade their entrance at theaters, concerts, sporting events, and businesses.

By December 1938 the Nazis had seized 44,000 out of 70,000 Jewish apartments, forcing as many as five or six families to live together in one apartment.[71] The Nazi regime was still committed to its policy of driving the Jews out of the country by making their lives as miserable as they could and assisting them to leave by whatever means possible, legal or illegal. By 1942, 128,500 Jews had left. But when in November 1941 the Nazi regime forbade further emigration and switched to a policy of extermination, some 67,500 Jews had not made it out in time, and they perished when deported to labor and death camps or were shot over pits in Poland and other Eastern Europe locations.

Because of the fervent antisemitism of Austrian society, it was very difficult for people to help Jews. Austrians who rescued Jews or the relatives of such rescuers were often blacklisted by their immediate environment. Some 7,000 Jews tried to remain in Vienna throughout the war, most of whom had non-Jewish spouses or were of mixed ethnic origin, and most of them were eventually deported. Out of an estimated 700 Jews who chose a life in hiding, only a handful were to be found in Vienna when the war ended.[72]

Aaron Menczer

> He found semilegal or illegal ways for hundreds of Jews to escape Austria across the Yugoslav border and elsewhere.

Born in 1917, Aaron Menczer came from a religious family and was a member of the Gordonia Zionist youth organization.[73] His parents and brothers left for Palestine before the start of the war, but Aaron remained behind in Vienna, where he took over the direction of the Vienna Youth Aliyah. In February 1939 he accompanied a group of Viennese children to Palestine, but he returned to Vienna because of the many other Jewish children there who needed his help and supervision.[74] In the summer of 1940, with Vienna under tight Nazi control, the Youth Aliyah Schools (Ju-Al Schule) managed by Menczer, and tolerated by the authorities, had 600 boarders and 100 day pupils. In that capacity, he was able to send a few of the older children aboard the *Sakaria*, one of the many illegal boats that plied the Mediterranean on the way to Palestine.

Menczer learned of Josef Schleich, who owned a small restaurant with his wife in the southern Austrian city of Graz and a pig farm on the outskirts of the city. In return for substantial payments, Schleich spirited hundreds of people across the border into Yugoslavia. This, it should be noted, was done with the blessings of the Gestapo, who, still adhering to the policy of forced emigration, looked the other way. Erich Profesorsky (later, Ezra Peri) was with a group of fourteen or fifteen children who left Vienna for the Yugoslav border on November 21, 1940. "Aaron Menczer went with us by train to Graz, where he turned us over to a man named Schleich. He was not Jewish and acted in return for payment." In Schleich's home, Menczer met many other Jews, adults and children, hoping to cross the Yugoslav border.[75]

Throughout this time, Menczer rejected all offers to leave Austria (now part of Nazi Germany) and join the many youths that he had sent over to Yugoslavia who were planning their further journey to Palestine. Thus, on December 14, 1940, Nathan Schwalb, the Zionist Hechalutz representative in Geneva, wrote to him, urging him to join Recha Freier, who had recently arrived in Yugoslavia with a group of youngsters, and assured him that an immigration certificate for him would be ready, making possible his continued legal journey to Palestine, but Menczer declined this gracious offer. He would not leave Vienna as long as his Zionist youth colleagues were waiting to leave the country. He felt a moral responsibility to care for them and make possible their escape before his own. Like the captain of a sinking boat, he would be the last to leave. Robert Weiss, one of his benefactors, wrote that on February 4, 1941, he paid Menczer 600 Marks, the money that Robert had on him, to be forwarded to Schleich. It was meant for Robert's mother's younger sister and her son, Pauli, for journeying to Poland. Weiss urged Menczer to come with his group to Yugoslavia, but Menczer said, "As long as there are still other children here [in Vienna] who need me, I cannot leave."[76]

Aaron Menczer stayed on until it was no longer possible to leave, as the Nazi regime forbade further emigration of Jews in November 1941 and instead switched to a policy of mass extermination. Menczer bided his time, but on September 24, 1942, he was deported to Theresienstadt camp, and in September 1943, together with a group of children from Białystok, he was sent to Auschwitz-Birkenau, where he and the children were gassed on November 7, 1943. He was twenty-six years of age.[77]

Much more needs to be told of Vienna and how it became the principal jumping-off point for thousands of Jews trying to escape the Nazi clutches. Jews helped fellow Jews reach Palestine through devious ways, crisscrossing other countries along the Danube River basin. These escapes, surprisingly, were done in collusion with the Nazi authorities who were interested in getting rid of as many Jews under their control as possible through forced emigration—at least until they switched to a policy of mass extermination. The story of these endeavors are told in chapter 10.

2 Poland

Rescue in the Deadliest Place in Europe

Poland had the dubious honor of being chosen by the Germans as the killing center of Europe's Jews during the so-called Final Solution. The Holocaust claimed 6 million lives, of which close to 3 million were Polish Jews, about 10 percent of that country's population.[1] Jews had lived in Poland since the tenth century, and the population kept growing, exceeding 300,000 by the seventeenth century. Jewish life centered around two self-regulated organizations: the Kehillah and the Council of the Four Lands (Great Poland, Lesser Poland, Ruthenia, and Lithuania), which was an autonomous institution that managed Jewish life in Poland and collected on their behalf the special taxes imposed on the Jews. Polish Jewry became a stronghold of great Talmudic scholars, commentators, rabbinical authorities, and famous yeshivas. Hasidism emerged there in the eighteenth century.[2] Sadly, the massacres of 1648 and 1649 by the Cossack leader Bogdan Khmelnytsky, originally directed against their Polish overlords but also targeting the Jews, obliterated many Jewish communities. The Jewish population nevertheless kept growing, despite the rise of antisemitism among wide segments of the non-Jewish population.[3]

In the newly independent Poland that emerged after World War I, Jews constituted 10 percent of the population and as high as 30 percent in the major cities. Jews were a visible minority, distinguished by language, behavior, and appearance, and the presence of such a large minority was a constant source of tension and of periodic violence of Poles against Jews.[4] Between the two world wars, the government favored a so-called Polonization of economic life in the country's cities and towns. This meant restricting Jewish participation in various sectors of the economy and in the professions, followed with an economic boycott of Jewish businesses and barring Jews from the civil service. This eventually led to a pauperization of large segments of the Jewish population. The government, which favored accelerated emigration of its Jews, proposed to remove most to the distant island of Madagascar, an idea later taken up by the Germans but not acted upon. Remarkably, in spite of all this, Polish Jews continued to enjoy a large measure of freedom, and Jewish cultural life continued to thrive. In the 1930s Poland was the world center of Jewish national, social, and political activities.[5]

The German invasion on September 1, 1939, and with it the start of World War II, resulted in the division of Poland between Germany and the Soviet Union. Parts of western and northern Poland were annexed to Germany. The rest of German-occupied Poland was placed under a civil administration, known as the General Government, with headquarters in Kraków and ruled by Nazi governor Hans Frank. Over 2 million Jews found themselves under tight German control, and close to 1 million Jews lived in the Soviet zone.[6] After the German attack on the Soviet Union in June 1941, hundreds of thousands of Jews were added to German control, while several hundred thousand managed to flee into the interior of Russia. The conquest of Poland in 1939 began with a wave of riots and murders, followed by the stripping of the Jews of their valuables and property and the ordering of all Jews ages ten and older to wear a Star of David armband on the right sleeve of their inner and outer garments. Up to 1942, some 112,000 Jewish-owned businesses and shops and 115,000 workshops were confiscated, with many placed under German trusteeship management.[7]

The pauperization of the Jews went hand in hand with imprisoning them in Middle Age–style ghettos, such as the Łódż ghetto in May 1940, followed by the Warsaw ghetto in November 1940. Both held at the start a combined 600,000 imprisoned Jews.[8] In the Warsaw ghetto, historian Emanuel Ringelblum created a secret cell, code-named Oneg Shabbat Archive, to collect data and accounts of life in the Warsaw ghetto and other ghettos. Soon starvation set in, as the official daily food rations for Jews was cut down to 184 calories, compared with 2,613 for ethnic Germans and 669 for Poles.[9] Starvation, typhus, and tuberculosis in the Łódż and Warsaw ghettos took the lives of 54,616 Jews in 1941.[10]

German-appointed Jewish councils, known as Judenrats, were forced to administer the ghettos and especially to supply the Germans with a fixed quota of workers for various purposes. Judenrat elders held to a self-perceived conviction that Jewish slave labor was indispensable to the Germans and hence the Germans would keep them alive—a belief that proved tragically wrong when the systematic extermination of Polish Jewry began in the summer months of 1942. Six major extermination camps were created, all on Polish soil—Auschwitz, Bełżec, Chełmno, Majdanek, Sobibór, and Treblinka—in which the mass murder of millions of Jews from Poland and other countries was carried out between 1942 and 1944. The usual method of death was suffocation inside gas chambers. Mobile gas vans were chosen as the asphyxiation instrument for hundreds of thousands in the Chełmno extermination site, beginning on December 8, 1941. Auschwitz alone consumed over a million Jewish victims; Treblinka, over 800,00; and hundreds of thousands in the other extermination camps.[11]

The attitude of the Polish population, themselves suffering under the heavy boot of the Germans, is still a subject fraught with passionate debates. Few question that the spirit of antisemitism that was widespread in the country in the 1930s had an impact on the behavior of the Polish population when they witnessed their next-door neighbors being slaughtered, in many cases literally before their eyes.[12] Not a few Poles made a living by exacting payment from Jews caught on the run (popularly known as *Szmalcownicy*—"fat" seekers), then turning them over to the German authorities for an additional reward. Jews could usually be recognized by their facial appearance, the color of their hair and eyes, and their Yiddish language. Jewish boys and men were given away by the fact that they were circumcised. Hardly a single Jew in hiding outside the Warsaw ghetto avoided falling into the hands of extortionists at one point or another.[13] As for the main Polish underground resistance, the Home Army (Armia Krajowa, AK), it was known for its unfriendly attitude toward Jews and its reluctance to admit Jews into its ranks. It did not undertake any military action to help the Jews or to sabotage the Nazi deportation and murder operations. One wing within the AK, the NSZ (National Armed Forces), was notorious for hunting down and killing Jews on the run while offering resistance to the Germans.[14]

In September 1942 the Council for Aid to Jews (Rada Pomocy Żydom), later code-named Żegota, was founded by the Polish underground on the initiative of Zofia Kossak-Szczucka, an outspoken prewar antisemite who, under the impact of the Nazi murderous onslaught on the Jews, turned into an advocate of Polish help to Jews on the run. It is not known how many Jews were helped by Żegota, but at one point in 1943 it had 2,500 Jewish children under its care in Warsaw alone. By late 1944 an estimated 4,000 Jews were aided by Żegota; it found them hiding places and gave them monthly allowances with funds secretly funneled from abroad by Jewish sources.[15] Two Jewish deputy chairmen worked for Żegota: Leon Feiner (code name "Mikolaj"), a Jewish attorney from Kraków and leader in the Bund (Jewish Socialist) movement, and Dr. Adolf Abraham Berman (code name "Borowski"), who filled the post of secretary-general. Berman also headed the separate Jewish National Committee (together with Feiner) that helped thousands of Jews on the run.[16] There is much more about these two later in this chapter.

Flight from the ghettos was usually only possible for those who had social and professional connections with Poles on the outside and were able to obtain false papers once on the non-Jewish, so-called Aryan side. Such persons had to have a reliable Polish address and money or valuables to cover living expenses. An estimated 15,000 to 20,000 Jews succeeded in hiding on the Polish side of Warsaw and environs. Probably close to half of them received help from Żegota and other Jewish underground organizations.[17] Across the country, an estimated 5,000 children were saved in private homes and educational and religious institutions.[18] Also meriting mention were the thousands of Poles who risked their lives to help Jews and later were officially recognized as Righteous Among the Nations by Yad Vashem.[19] We should not forget that Poles faced death at the hands of the Germans if found offering any kind of help to a fleeing Jew, and they were reminded on large posters throughout the major cities.

Survival estimates of Jews on Polish soil during the German occupation vary, but most reliable sources place it within the range of 50,000 (30,000 to 35,000 thanks to direct help by non-Jewish rescuers), with over 20,000 hiding in the Warsaw metropolitan region. Altogether an estimated 380,000 Polish Jews survived, mostly by fleeing Poland in time. Approximately 165,000 of these were repatriated to Poland under the Polish-Soviet Repatriation Agreement, with some 20,000 more joining them a bit later, raising the number of registered Jews in June 1946 to 240,500. Sadly, Poland is the only country liberated from the Germans where surviving Jews were waylaid, ambushed, and killed soon after the war by marauding vigilantes, such as the notorious Kielce pogrom of June 1946, claiming at least 2,000 lives. This prompted a panicky exodus of surviving Jews.

By the end of 1947, only 70,000 to 80,000 Jews remained in Poland. A renewed anti-Jewish campaign, begun in 1967, led to a further reduction of Jews, with only a few thousand, mostly elderly people, remaining but taking precautions not to make their presence known and noticeable. The Polish Jewish landscape, once filled with a large and vibrant community, is now a desert, with only gutted synagogues, cemeteries, and tombstones as grim reminders.[20]

Vladka Peltel Meed

> She was a secret wartime courier who helped dozens of Jews
> in hiding and on the run with safe havens, false documents,
> and by outwitting blackmailers and informants.

By 1942 all Jews in Poland were incarcerated in ghettos or guarded labor camps. They were prohibited, under pain of death, to be outside these restricted areas without permission. Each ghetto was isolated and cut off from the world. In order to know a little of what was happening on the other side of the ghetto gate and in other ghettos, a courier system was created by the Zionist youth movements to transmit news and messages from one ghetto to another. It was much easier for women to act as couriers and stroll the streets, especially those who had received a relatively good Polish education and spoke the language well. Men could be ordered to drop their pants, and the telltale circumcision sign would give them away.[21] Many couriers lost their lives in these undertakings, such as Gusta Davidson Draenger ("Justyna"), a courier in Kraków, arrested, imprisoned, and shot. She left a diary written on toilet paper smuggled into her cell. The couriers also helped smuggle Jews out of the ghetto, arranging hiding places on the Aryan side and providing false identity cards and money to support those in hiding. Such a courier was Vladka Meed.

Born Feigele Peltel in 1921, she joined the Bund, a Jewish socialist and non-Zionist movement that bolstered the Yiddish language and culture and a secular Jewish nationalism in the Diaspora. As a secret wartime courier, she took the name Vladka when she was assigned dangerous errands outside the Warsaw ghetto and will be referred to in her story under that name.[22] Following are some episodes of her missions.

Helping Jews in Hiding

A certain Mrs. Riba, a gentile, in Miedzeszyn, a summer resort near Warsaw, was hiding Clara Falk and her ten-year-old son, Adash. At the request of the Jewish Underground in Warsaw, Vladka visited Mrs. Riba to see how they were managing. Arriving there, she was confronted by Mrs. Riba's request to move the Jews elsewhere. Vladka insisted on speaking to them first. She related: "She escorted me to an isolated wooden shed. I strained my eyes in the semi-darkness. The landlady then pointed to a corner, littered with debris and twigs. A woman and boy crouched side by side on the bare earthen floor so as to take up as little space as possible. They were skin and bones. The two appeared to be specters—they seemed no longer human. They asked me to close the door, because the daylight hurt their eyes." They had not taken a bath or even washed during the past few months. The son, lying on the earthen floor, had contracted a severe cold and had run a high temperature for several days. His coughing it was feared could betray the hiding place; his fever could mean death. Vladka, thereupon, decided to move them to another hideaway in Warsaw. Vladka happily added: "Falk and her son survived and are now (viz., 1972) living in Canada."[23]

Vladka pointed out that she had to carry out most of her activities, such as distributing money and providing forged documents, out in the open street, because there simply was no other place to meet fellow Jews. She related that once she was accosted by a man: "Are you by any chance the Vladka who distributes money to the Jews? I am Jewish myself. My bunker is in a bombed-out house not far from here. I am living in those ruins together with four other Jews who managed to escape from the ghetto. The group consisted of ten men, but the Germans had already caught five of them. We subsist on the *groszen* [pennies] I beg from kindhearted Poles." The tattered garments, the pale, emaciated face, and the constant nervous glancing around to see if anyone was watching—all these confirmed his words; he was indeed a Jew, and a Jew who needed help. Vladka arranged for this man and his comrades in hiding to be supported by the Warsaw Ghetto Coordinating Committee, a group representing all existing political parties set up to help fellow Jews on the run.[24]

All Jewish life on the non-Jewish, the so-called Aryan, side could be summarized in one word: fear. Fear of the Germans and fear of the Polish betrayers, known in Polish as *szmalcownicy*—meaning those who "fattened" themselves by robbing Jews on the run of whatever they possessed under threat of turning them over to the Germans. To avoid being recognized as Jews, persons passing as Aryans had to blend in with their surroundings, adopt Polish customs and mannerisms, celebrate the Christian festivals, and of course go to church. Worst of all were the eyes, the mute melancholy, the haunted look of fear. As Vladka was cautioned by a gentile friend: "Your eyes give you away. Make them livelier, merrier— you won't attract so much attention then."[25]

For a long time in late 1943, Vladka Peltel occupied a small room in a Gentile household where she was regarded as a smuggler—a common practice of many Poles trying to eke out a living. She frequently found it expedient to spend the night elsewhere to create the impression that she had to be away on "business." As a smuggler, she went under the name of Stanislawa Wonchalska, equipped with an appropriate false ID card.[26]

One of the best ploys open to Jewish women passing as non-Jews outside the ghetto was to find work as a maidservant. A servant was assured living quarters and food, together with good chances of concealment. A certain Marie Silberberg came across an advertisement in the newspaper that a small German family was looking for a maidservant with good references. Germans were not so adept as Poles in detecting Jewish traits and were not likely to identify her at once. Marie ventured to answer the advertisement, and she was hired. One morning while she was busy cleaning and dusting, the only daughter of the family entered the room and, after watching the maidservant for a minute or so, suddenly addressed her. "Marie, tell me something about the Warsaw ghetto!" Marie broke out into a cold sweat. What could have impelled the little girl to ask about the ghetto? Had she, by some chance, recognized her identity? She had to escape, and Vladka furnished her with new forged documents so she could find sanctuary elsewhere.[27]

Vladka was not always so successful. She gave funds to a Polish family that was hiding a large group of Jews under a garden hothouse in Warsaw. Thirty people crowded there, including the famed Jewish historian Emanuel Ringelblum and his young son. Tragically, the place was betrayed to the Germans, who shot all of the bunker's occupants, including their Polish rescuers.[28]

Outwitting Informers and Blackmailers

Blackmailers were to be found everywhere, lying in wait for all Jews on the Aryan side of the city. Without these Polish informers, Vladka asserted, the Germans would never have caught so many Jews. Not all Poles, of course, were of this sort, and some even evinced compassion, but these were few in number and their assistance was meager. Vladka was on several occasions close to becoming a victim herself. Once on an outing she became aware of footsteps behind her. Three men were trailing her, obviously blackmailers. Suddenly someone grabbed her by the shoulders. "You are from the ghetto. . . . If you want us to release you, let's have three thousand *zloty*—one thousand for each of us. . . . Hand over the money or else we'll go straight to the Germans." Vladka continued to deny she was Jewish and walked away. They followed her a bit, not sure about her. She began to mingle with the crowd, and luckily for her, she managed to elude the blackmailers. In another close call, Meed talked herself free from arrest after her Jewish confederates had bribed the police, but she was urged to change her name again for added security.[29]

Assisting the Jews on the Run

At the end of the summer of 1943, Vladka Peltel was asked by her underground affiliates to undertake a particularly dangerous mission. A group of Jewish insurgents from the Częstochowa ghetto who had found shelter among some peasants in Koniecpol, Kielce region, were desperately poor, and it was critical that they be supplied with money. Setting out on her journey, she found the train swarming with smugglers. "I too was disguised as a smuggler, with a big bag of 'merchandise' under my arm; the money and the letter I had concealed under my belt." In Częstochowa she switched to a train going to Kielce. She finally made it to the insurgents' home, where she collected the photographs of those who needed forged documents and letters to fellow insurgents. "Don't forget us!" they pleaded as Vladka climbed down the ladder of their hiding place. "I left the barn feeling as though I had taken leave of my own family."[30]

On one return visit to this group, she had to jump off the train to avoid inspection by German guards and cover the last 27 kilometers to Kielce on foot. It was dusk by the time she arrived at the barn, exhausted and grimy with sore feet (she had walked without shoes to avoid noise). The moment the landlady saw her she began wringing her hands in despair. Apparently something terrible had happened. Her neighbors had become suspicious of the barn and had spread the rumor that the old woman had Jews staying with her. In the meantime her tenants had run out of money and she had ordered them out. Several Jews had managed to find asylum with another peasant, while the rest took to the woods. That woman then referred Vladka to a peasant named Romanov who knew of the fugitive Jews' whereabouts. He told Vladka that some Jews came to him out of the forest under cover of darkness to beg for food. Vladka stayed over at the farmer's house, and late at night there was a scraping on the window pane, followed by a low but distinct tapping against the glass. It was two of the hidden Jews. When they saw Vladka, they told her about a group of Polish partisans who had arrived in the area. At first they were friendly, but then one night they attacked the Jewish encampment and felled several Jews. When Vladka met the surviving Jews in their forest lair, she saw living skeletons, bags of bones that could hardly stand up. She secured a document from the Polish underground claiming that these particular Jews were under the protection of the Armia Krajowa, the mainline Polish military underground, in order to safeguard them from further molestations by other Polish partisan groups.[31]

Vladka Peltel Meed did not keep a record of the people she helped, but their number runs into the dozens. Constantly on the move as a courier, passing as a non-Jewish woman, and appearing several times under different identities, she braved the dangers of arrest and death. She survived the horrors of the Holocaust, but not so her parents, sister, and brother, who perished.

After the war she married Benjamin Miedzyrzecki, one of those helped by her, who changed his name to Meed, and both moved to the United States and were active in the Jewish Labor Committee. In 1985 Vladka Meed initiated the annual summer American Teachers' Seminars on the Holocaust and Jewish Resistance, which included visits to Poland and Israel. She and her husband established a registry and database of Jewish Holocaust survivors and their families. When stopping off with her educators at Yad Vashem, she always made it a point to invite me to speak before her group on the role of Polish rescuers of Jews honored by Yad Vashem as Righteous Among the Nations. I remember how irritated I used to feel when in introducing me she cautioned her listeners not to be too impressed by what I was going to say, since the rescuers represented a tiny and insignificant group from the vast majority of Poles. I felt she had taken the wind out of my sails. After reading her memoirs, I came to understand her feelings on this still hotly debated subject. She had reached the ripe old age of ninety when she died in 2012.

Adolf-Avraham and Basia-Barbara Berman and Leon Feiner

Through their underground organizations, they saved the lives of 11,000 to 12,000 Jews by providing them with false documents, food, shelter, and financial and medical aid.

Adolf (later in Israel, Avraham) Berman and his wife, Basia, were rescue associates of Vladka Meed. A psychologist of children and orphans inside the Warsaw ghetto, Adolf Berman headed Centos (Centralne Towarzystwo Opieki Nad Sierotami—Central Society of Care for Orphans), together with Józef Gitler and Rachel Stein. This was a charitable welfare organization, supported by the U.S.-based Joint Distribution Committee, that cared for abandoned Jewish children, including the orphanage of Janusz Korczak.[32] Basia (later in Israel, Batya), a librarian, was initially a member of the Zionist-Socialist Hashomer Hatzair youth movement, and she joined her husband in the more extreme socialist Zionist Poalei-Zion Left. During the ghetto period, she went to endless trouble to open a public library for children in the ghetto; this was integrated into Centos and organized book exchanges between the tenants. She wrote that the hunger for books was felt with particular force among the children, who hadn't attended school for several years, and it helped them forget their hunger pangs.[33]

During the massive liquidation of the Warsaw ghetto, starting in July 1942, Adolf's associates decided it was best for the two Bermans to be outside the ghetto, where they would be able to seek and arrange hiding places for fleeing Jews. In her diary, Basia wrote disconsolately of that decision as "the greatest and the most dangerous journey of our life; we set out without saying goodbye to anyone and without believing in the success of our adventure." One reason for her concern was that Basia's features were characteristically Jewish, which could make it difficult for her to move freely in the city streets.[34] But responding to the appeal of duty, they snuck out of the ghetto on September 5, 1942, to an uncertain existence on the forbidden side, just as the Germans were in the midst of what they termed the "Great [liquidation] Action" of Warsaw Jews.[35] A bribe paid through a Jewish policeman opened one of the gates. Once outside the ghetto, the Bermans were assaulted by blackmailers, but they finally got to the city's public library, shocked beyond belief and almost unconscious, where they were met by their non-Jewish friend, Zofia Rodziewicz.

Going Underground with Żegota

On the Aryan side of the city, Adolf Berman became one of the principals in the Council for Aid to Jews, better known by its code name, Żegota, created by the Polish underground.[36] Żegota had two basic goals: material aid to Jews living on the Aryan side and obtaining false documents for the Jews in hiding. For this purpose it obtained a "factory" to forge thousands of birth and baptismal certificates, marriage documents, prewar identity documents, wartime German IDs, and various work permits. A special department dealt with children, headed by Irena Sendlerowa of the Social Welfare Department of the Warsaw municipality. In late 1943, some 600 Jewish children were smuggled out of the ghetto and placed in various institutions around Warsaw. Żegota also established a special medical department to ensure assistance to sick Jews.

In all these life-saving activities, Berman, appearing under the code name Adam (later changed to Jozef, then Ludwik, then Michał) Borowski, was assisted by Leon Feiner of the Jewish non-Zionist Socialist Bund movement, who left the ghetto with the same objectives as those of the Bermans. He specialized in contacts with Polish socialists.[37] Berman and Feiner were the only Jewish representatives in Żegota, with Berman acting as treasurer and later secretary-general, and Feiner as vice president and then president.[38] In July 1943 Żegota was able to expand its scope when it received funds from the Jewish National Committee and the Bund, who received it secretly from abroad, mainly from the Joint Distribution Committee (JDC). At first Żegota restricted its activities to the Warsaw region, but within months it opened a branch in Kraków, where it gave aid to Jews on the run.[39] Jewish sources assert that in 1943–44, slightly over 4,000 Jews in hiding in Warsaw received direct assistance from Żegota. To this may be added small numbers of Jews aided by Żegota in Kraków, Lwów, Lublin, and Zamość.[40]

The National Jewish Committee

Before joining Żegota, Adolf and Basia were involved in the creation of the Jewish National Committee, a clandestine umbrella organization of six Zionist parties formed to assist Jews on the run. It was aided by elements of the non-Jewish Polish underground and, a bit later, by the Żegota organization, and it was secretly funded by the JDC through its Warsaw agent, David Guzik.[41] Berman coordinated rescue activities mostly with Feiner and with Vladka Peltel (later, Meed). Meetings took place in a convent soup kitchen; this was also a regular meeting place for various Jewish clandestine operatives as well as Żegota.[42] Feiner, who did not look obviously Jewish and was armed with excellent forgeries, was able to move around Warsaw with relative ease under the code name of Mikolaj Berezowski.[43]

As for the role of the National Jewish Committee—the largest Jewish relief organization in Warsaw—in the rescue of Jews, Berman stated that 5,500 to 6,000 Jews were aided through the operation of more than 100 secret cells. To this number must be added those aided by Feiner's Bund organization separately, some 1,500 to 2,000 Jews, making for a grand total of at least 11,000 to 12,000 Jews receiving assistance.

The National Jewish Committee also dealt with aid to Jews incarcerated in the camps, such as secretly smuggling in crucifixes, religious medallions, prayer books, and New Testaments in order to help Jews planning to flee from the camps prepare themselves with the help of fabricated identities. The famed Jewish historian Dr. Emanuel Ringelblum was one of those smuggled out of a camp before going into hiding in Warsaw, where he and others were later discovered. The National Jewish Committee was also in constant contact with a group of Jewish partisans active in Koniecpol, near Kielce Częstochowa, and it also aided Jews hiding in several other cities.[44] In his postwar accounts, Berman credited several dozen Jews who participated in the efforts of the National Jewish Committee to find hiding places, to move Jews from one place to another, to arm them with false credentials, and to offer financial assistance, medical attention, and assistance to children.[45]

On the Aryan side of the city, the Bermans appeared as brother and sister and under assumed identities.[46] In her wartime diary Basia described what it meant for Jews to be living in wartime Poland.

> I would like to describe this state within a state, or rather city within a city, this most underground of all underground communities, whose members met with each other. . . . Every name was false, every word that was uttered carried a double meaning, and every telephone conversation was more encrypted than the secret diplomatic documents of embassies. I wanted to describe the history of those contemporary marranos, hunted down and persecuted with cruelty unknown in history.[47] . . . If we had to meet in some coffee shop, we greeted each other solemnly like strangers and made the conversation as minimal as possible. We almost never went out together during the day, and no matter where we went back to, each of us returned alone, whereas in the streetcar we took seats at the opposite ends of the car.[48]

Józef Zysman-Ziemian, another of the Bermans' conspiratorial confederates, attested:

> Every step had to be calculated, every word thought out, and every new contact summed up immediately. . . . Sometimes, in order to avoid someone's eyes, one had to blow one's nose, pretend to tie a shoelace, or study a shop window. . . . If he lost his self-confidence for a fraction of a second, he was done for. In this ocean of hostility, any false move could prove fatal. . . . I had a false *Kennkarte* (German identification), a false *Ausweis* (certificate of employment), and a fabricated life history. . . . It didn't do any harm, either, to suggest that one had contacts with the Polish Resistance. . . . I was a member of the Resistance movement, in fact, but only with the Jewish one. This, however, I could never admit.[49]

Basia further described how she masked her identity:

> I pretended I was a poor woman, part of an impoverished intelligentsia, refugee from eastern Poland. . . . I was walking round dressed

very shabbily, patched up shoes and a terrible, worn-out dark-red coat . . . torn from all directions, worn during the worst rains without an umbrella, it was shredded into strips. After a lot of patching and stitching it looked like unregulated peasant lots seen from the train windows. To this one should add the briefcase, torn up on one side, stitched together with gray thread and bound by a cord instead of the missing strap. . . . I am convinced that thanks to this uniform I avoided many blackmail attempts. . . . No self-respecting blackmailer would risk getting involved with a wretch like me.[50]

Rachela Auerbach, another Jewish rescue activist, related after the war that Basia would be seen running through the city with her double-bottom briefcase, where under apples, onions, rolls, cucumbers, and potatoes lay packets of *Kenkarten* and various other documents, forged baptism certificates, and fictitious marriage certificates. While scurrying back and forth on various rescue missions, Basia learned of the death of her sister, Mania Temkin-Majer, in the ghetto. Adolf learned that his elder brother, Dr. Mieczysław (Mietek) Szmuel Berman, a surgeon, had been murdered in the Treblinka camp.[51]

The plague of blackmailers and informers made the underground movements' work even harder, and how to thwart them became a principal concern of Żegota and the National Jewish Committee. Retribution from Polish underground sources did not meet expectations. Those punished were announced only in underground publications, not in fliers or bulletin boards for the public at large.[52] On January 4, 1944, Adolf was accosted by three secret agents who screamed at him: "You are Dr. Berman. We are from the Security Police." They dragged him to a police station and threatened to take him to Szucha Boulevard, where the Gestapo was headquartered. This was followed with a tense and dramatic blackmail negotiation that lasted for an hour; Berman was released after the payment of a large ransom. Afterward Adolf and Basia abandoned their "burned" home and wandered from place to place.[53]

False Identities, Avoiding Detection

When providing false papers for needy people, one had to try not to arouse suspicions. After obtaining someone's photograph, one had to invent personal data befitting the face shown. As explained by Basia, some first names and family names were associated with a certain social background; the person's profession somehow had to be closely related to one's appearance and, to the extent possible, to one's actual qualifications. As for places of birth, usually one gave localities that the given person knew well, at least from description:

> In the case of most Warsawians I gave Łódź as a place of birth, because almost every Jew knew it, or at least heard of it. I was reluctant to write localities from the eastern territories as place of birth, except for people who really originated from there. For example, for Genia Sylkes, who hails from Brest and has a terrible accent, I made a birth certificate with Białystok as the place of birth and the first and last name which would make it possible for her to pass off as a Belorussian.[54]

New names were also sometimes related to the true ones, either by duplicating the initial sounds or simply by translating Jewish first and last names. Hersz Berlinski became Jelenski; Rozenfeld—Różycki. Reason? Deer in German and Hirsh in Yiddish were Jelen in Polish— Rozenfeld means rose field in German, Różycki means rosy in Polish.[55]

The Bermans were especially aided by the non-Jewish Janina Bucholtz-Bukolska, who as a certified translator of German, French, and English operated a little office on 11 Miodowa Street for translation and application petitions.[56] She provided Basia with various forged documents, such as certifying a copy of Basia's forged birth certificate. As it was necessary to have a place for people to contact the Bermans, Janina agreed for her office to become a "post office box" for people wishing to pass secret messages. Thanks to her, the Bermans were able to arrange hiding places for others. Janina also helped change dollars that arrived from abroad into local currency.[57]

Basia Berman carefully noted in her diary the anguished travails she and Adolf experienced as they moved from one apartment to the next one to avoid detection. In her May 6, 1944, entry, she wrote: "This is our seventh apartment." She then described her earlier peregrinations. At first, after three near-denunciations, nervous and bewildered, the Bermans ended up in a bar on the corner of Furmanska and Karowa Streets. "I am still accompanied by the last blackmailer." She phoned a friend for help, but she didn't answer. "I felt as if the earth was slipping out from under our feet. I dismissed the blackmailer.... He parted from me politely, paid for my phone call (he did!), and went away." That was an incredibly lucky break![58]

Shortly afterward, their non-Jewish colleague Zofia Rodziewicz arrived. Unfortunately, she didn't have an apartment to offer, but she told the Bermans to follow her to the Mokotów section of Warsaw. "I also asked her to get for me some headwear, because my hat, my briefcase, and the coat were taken from me by blackmailers on Chłodna Street.... Zofia went out again and returned shortly afterward with a beret and a black veil. Then she told us to follow her," with Adolf trailing from behind.[59] Traveling on foot, then by tram to a closed library that they managed to enter, they spent the night alone sleeping on benches. The next morning another non-Jewish colleague, Irena Sawicka, took them to an apartment outside the city. The landlord there, who agreed to a two-week stay, didn't know the true identity of his tenants. The Bermans then inhabited a long series of apartments, moving from one to another to avoid detection.

Previously, in the second place, the Bermans stayed for three months, but then the money ran out. So Basia started working: one week as a cook's assistant in a bar, then two weeks as a charwoman with a cosmetician, "an anti-Semite, but a decent person who didn't know who I was until today." Finally they had to leave the workplace as well as the apartment for lack of payment. The next place was a bit below standard. As the Bermans introduced themselves as brother and sister, when the landlady, a conservative person, caught them together in bed (to keep warm during fierce frosts), she was shocked and evicted them. The fourth apartment was the most disgusting. The landlord, a physician but also a simpleton, was a very decent man. But his wife's cousin turned out to be not only an antisemite but also a thief. On one occasion, being in a rush, Basia left the key in her suitcase. The cousin opened the suitcase and saw the false documents and money. "A serious scandal ensued, and we were told to leave the apartment immediately because we were Jews. We claimed innocence.... True, the material and money were kept by us as we take care of Jews, but we ourselves? Heaven forbid!"[60] Nothing doing.

In the fifth apartment the Bermans were warned from the start that the place was dangerous, because a woman who lived above them had informed on the previous tenants—not Jews, but political activists, and they were arrested. The Bermans took the risk. "It was like a paradise there. The informant didn't suspect anything," and she was later killed by the Polish underground. The Bermans stayed there for seven months. Then, on January 4, 1944, Adolf returned home with a thuggish-looking man. Obviously this could mean only one thing—blackmail. "We had to open 'Krysia' [secret cache] and remove nearly all the money deposited with us."[61] The blackmailer took what was his, gave his "word of honor" that he and his friend who stood guard outside would not return, and left. That place was definitely "burnt," and had to be immediately vacated. To their landlady the Bermans concocted a story that a friend had come to warn them about a possible Gestapo visit, and they had to flee. It was nearly 10 p.m. when the landlady led them out through the picket fences to her neighbor, a seamstress.

This led to the sixth temporary apartment for a stay of three weeks. That was too much for Basia. "I was losing my self-confidence," and they decided for an "open" apartment; that is, to live openly as non-Jewish Poles and free to come and go as they pleased.[62] Many other Jews on the run had to run similar gauntlets and go through similar hair-raising apartment runs and flights. But one had to bear with it if one wished to survive.

Aid for Those under Cover

In addition to food and shelter, some of those in hiding desperately needed medical help, and the Bermans were able to engage a few trustworthy Polish and Jewish doctors to come to their aid. Whenever possible, the patients paid the doctors, and when not, Żegota paid the bill. However, doctors' visits had to be carefully planned in advance. It took several days before a doctor came to the patient, because the Żegota secretariat had to be given the address, and sometimes a password as well, through an intermediary.

Complicating matters was the fear by illegal residents and unregistered tenants to disclose their addresses directly to the doctor, which could lead perhaps to the tenants' exposure and arrest. In Basia's words, "Simply put, the doctor had to be forewarned if only to avoid a situation in which he would enter an apartment where the neighbors, and often co-tenants, were not aware of the existence of people in hiding, and then betray their presence by the obvious question: Who is the sick person here?"[63] In addition, there was concern, not so much that the doctor would become an informer but that he simply would not be able to restrain himself and go on to tell someone the story of a mysterious visit.

There were also doctors who performed cosmetic surgery—in most cases operations of the nose and operations aimed at disguising circumcision, and these proved very expensive and not free from injurious side effects. "However," Basia noted, "if someone requested a special allowance for such surgery, I didn't refuse, taking into consideration the possible positive psychological effect, namely, strengthening the patient's self-confidence."[64]

Unlikely as it might seem, the Bermans also had to deal with care for Jewish newborns. In spite of the terrible conditions for Jews, some women in hiding got pregnant, sometimes by accident, with no proper means to terminate the pregnancy. "However, in some cases women decided to give life to new Jews deliberately and despite everything, in the belief that these children would live to see better times." Basia Berman recalled three such cases, the second of which was the result of a conscious decision to bring new Jewish life into the world. Halina Bajer wanted to make up for the loss of her two children, murdered by the Germans in the fall of 1942 during the Aktion in Ciechanowiec. The Bermans arranged an apartment for the Bajers and their newborn son in some lodging house, where the child was apparently healthy and well cared for. The Bajers took comfort in their newborn child and gradually stopped talking about their murdered children. There were also several pregnancies due to rape, such as a certain Wanda, who was raped by her landlord. "It goes without saying that we covered the costs of the [abortion] procedure," Basia underlined.[65]

A Gestapo Trap

An additional danger lurked in early 1943 when, in their efforts to lure Jews from their hiding places, the Germans spread news of the arrival of a large quantity of passports from South America for Polish Jews, assuring them that they would be concentrated in a special camp in France (it was to be Vittel) or a German camp (such as Bergen-Belsen, which served as a transit camp for the exchange of prisoners)—both, so people were told, were under the supervision of the International Red Cross. Many Jews fell into that trap, and in spite of the warnings of Adolf Berman's National Jewish Committee, they left their hiding places and revealed their presence. They were first accommodated in the Warsaw hotels Royal and Polski and allowed a large measure of freedom, including buying provisions for their voyage to freedom. At this point, a conflict arose between the majority of the National Jewish Committee members and David Guzik, representing the JDC, who naively approved the Gestapo plan and set aside money for the purchase of these passports. He claimed that whenever there was the slightest chance of rescue, one must take it, even if it involved making a deal with the devil. This Gestapo gambit, sadly, claimed over 3,000 Jewish lives.[66]

Adolf and Basia Berman suffered with other Poles during the Warsaw uprising of August–October 1944 and, still posing as non-Jews, were exiled from Warsaw to outlying towns and villages with thousands of other Poles and luckily survived to witness liberation. After the war, the Bermans remained for a while in Poland, and Adolf was a member of the Polish parliament as well as head of the Central Committee of Jews in Poland. Basia returned to her beloved profession as a librarian. She wrote: "In the Ghetto I was the director of the central children's library of Centos . . . till the deportation. After the war I collected books in Hebrew and Yiddish which survived, and organized a central library with the help of the committee of Polish Jews. I collected 120,000 books, 80,000 of which we donated to the Hebrew University in Jerusalem."[67] The two immigrated to Israel in 1950 with their newborn son, Emanuel. Basia died in 1953, age forty-five, after a long illness. Adolf survived her for many years and was active both in left-wing politics as well as writing and recording events in Warsaw during the Holocaust. He died in 1978.[68]

In a preface to his mother's diary, Emanuel Berman wrote that his parents negated the Zionist ideology of "negating the Diaspora," the stereotypic image of the weak and easily victimized Diaspora Jew. They were the very opposite of the mythological Israeli-born Sabra, "the New Jew," who was supposedly fearless and always courageous.[69] A no less amount of courage was displayed by Adolf-Abraham and Basia Berman and dozens of Jewish rescue colleagues, who all operated under difficult conditions that no Israeli Sabra ever experienced.

As for Leon Feiner of the Bund, less than a year after the war ended, he was hospitalized and died of cancer. When the former Jewish underground leader Marek Edelman went to visit him the day before he died, Feiner whispered to him that under his pillow were the money receipts of people aided by Żegota, and he asked Edelman to ensure that they got to someone responsible, and he dutifully obliged.[70]

Józef Zysman-Ziemian

Through Centos he aided hundreds of Jewish orphans, including a group of enterprising street urchins who had lost their parents in the Warsaw ghetto.

The story of Józef (Jódzio) Zysman-Ziemian is intimately linked to the stories of Jewish children who survived by selling cigarettes in a Warsaw center town location, bustling with passers-by, including Germans—the Three Crosses Square. Born in 1922, Zysman-Ziemian (henceforth only Józef Ziemian), a member of the Zionist-Socialist Hashomer Hatzair, worked for Centos, which cared for orphaned Jewish children. Fleeing to the Aryan side of Warsaw, he was a liaison person for the National Jewish Committee and consequently in close contact with Adolf and Basia Berman.[71] Basia portrayed him in the following terms:

There was nothing special about his looks, an average Częstochowian [code word for Jewish] boy. . . . Plenty of self-confidence and boldness, which saved him. . . . He was impoverished, poorly dressed: ragged trousers, worn out jacket and shoes with wooden soles. . . . Kinder people let him sleep in basements. . . . He had a caretaker, an old woman from a tiny store . . . who cared for him like his own mother.[72] There he was receiving his numerous clients, hiding documents of other people, even brochures and leaflets, under her vegetables. . . . One could leave there for him letters, instructions, and parcels. . . . He distributed money among many of his old aid clients. . . . Józio was ready to take up any assignment. He was tenacious and obstinate like a mule, and there wasn't a mission he refused to take.[73]

Adolf Berman met Józef Ziemian once a month in a certain coffee shop on Marszałkowska Street; sometimes Basia came instead of her husband.[74] Ziemian accomplished a lot, eventually caring for several hundred people as needy aid recipients, including youth and children. He was also involved in finding jobs and apartments, providing false papers, and caring for miscellaneous needs, such as clothing and even toys for children. Then, quite coincidentally, in October 1943 he met a group of more than a dozen children, cigarette sellers at the Three Crosses Square, and kept watch over them.[75] In his postwar account, Józef described the initial encounter with these Jewish street boys:

One October day I was going down Nowy Swiat [street] toward Jerozolimskie Avenue. On the first floor, at number 23, there was an RGO [*Rada Glowna Opiekuncza*, Social Welfare Organization] soup kitchen.[76] I used to eat my dinners there almost daily. It was getting late and I was in a hurry to arrive before the place closed. The street was crowded. Suddenly I noticed two boys, one about 16, the other perhaps 13, the face of the elder boy seemed vaguely familiar from ghetto days. Jewish children? Is it possible, I wondered? No, I must be wrong. Several months had passed since the complete destruction of the ghetto. Nearly every day Jews found on the Aryan side were being executed. . . . Suddenly our eyes met and that was enough. I had no more doubts. It seems there is some truth in the saying that "Jews can smell each other at a distance." I decided to establish contact with the boys, but had to proceed with great care, without disclosing my identity or plans. . . . [In those days] every Jew was afraid of his own shadow.[77]

The Children of Three Crosses Square

Józef Ziemian learned that after their escape from the ghetto, the children who congregated mostly in the busy Three Crosses Square led an adventurous and independent existence on the Aryan side of Warsaw. They lived at first by begging, by singing in the streets, or by casual labor and selling cigarettes. Some of them used to smuggle food and arms to the ghetto in preparation for the uprising of April 1943. These street urchins, whose only possessions were their meager clothes, did not attract any special attention from the blackmailers and were therefore in less danger than the adults.[78] At his second meeting with the boys (there were also several girls), a trust relationship evolved. As told by Ziemian:

Entering the house, I turned my head and our eyes met again. The ice was broken. Probably the boys craved contact with a kindred soul. They followed me inside and when I sat down at a table they took the next one. . . . I looked at the boys. The elder of the two had a round face, wise blue eyes, and thick, wavy dark-blond hair. In a word, he looked Aryan. He seemed energetic and sure of himself. . . . The younger boy looked more Semitic. . . . The boys looked around the room, and I felt their eyes on me. I sensed that they wanted to approach me. I finished my meal quickly and left, imperceptibly beckoning them to follow. In the street the elder boy began: "Excuse me, but didn't you work in Placowska at the Ostbahn?"[79] Placowska was a workplace, outside the ghetto, for Jews only. . . . "If you want, you can sleep with us at a Polish women's place," offered the elder boy. I was dumbfounded. A voluntary offer of a "den" was in those times an extremely rare phenomenon. "And you? What do you do?" . . . I asked. "We work at the Three Crosses Square. There are many more of us. We stick together and we're doing all right," said the younger boy. . . . I couldn't believe my ears. . . . No one would have believed it then. . . . I made an arrangement to meet them at the same place together with one of my "charges," a Jew in hiding who was being helped by our underground organization.[80]

Józef Ziemian met the group's leader, Ignacy, known as "Bull," and was introduced to the others by their nicknames. They repeated to Józef that they sold cigarettes at the Three Crosses Square. "Business is booming. Come with us and see for yourself." The Square resounded with the voices of tram drivers gathered at the terminus, the cries of newspaper boys, and the patter of cigarette sellers trying to attract customers, the gabble of German soldiers waiting for Tram No. 0—Nur für Deutsche [only for Germans]. The Square, indeed, lay in the heart of the German district with a German gendarmerie and an ss barracks nearby. As Józef and the boys arrived on the Square, a detachment of ss was marching by. To Józef's utter surprise, rather shock, in a twinkling of the eye the whole group had surrounded an approaching German soldier. Each wanted to sell his cigarettes or to exchange them for tinned food or sardines. "Sir, Egyptian cigarettes. How much, how much, sir? These are originals. The lot for only 30 zlotys." The boys bargained and traded with all their might. There was also a transit camp for Hungarian soldiers, who were allies of the Germans. Using sign language the boys somehow managed to understand each other and make a sale.[81]

Józef was introduced to the other children. "Toothy," because of his buckteeth, was thirteen, but looked younger. There was "Frenchy," because he came from Paris; a twelve-year-old Jewish boy nicknamed "Burek" (the Peasant); and "Little Stasiek." He was not selling anything, the others explained, but helped them by carrying their supplies. He was their walking storehouse. A girl, Teresa, wore a torn dress and a dirty sweater. "This is not all," Bull added; "there are others, in other places."[82] Many of the children had begun their errands on the Aryan side by smuggling food to their starving families inside the ghetto. Józef was beside himself with disbelief. Jewish children in their early teens surviving in such a brazen way and challenging the risks to themselves with so much Jewish chutzpah!

A few days later, the National Jewish Committee discussed the matter of the street children with the participation of Adolf and Basia Berman, Helena Merenholc, Bela Elster-Rotenberg, Klima Fuswerk-Krymko, and Józef Ziemian. Before that, on the agenda, was the matter of the distribution of money to Jews in hiding. It was decided that 500 zlotys per month was sufficient, except for persons considered essential for the restoration of a viable Jewish community, such as scientists, intellectuals, artists, former public personalities, and escaped fighters from the ghetto, who were allotted a higher rate.[83] In Ziemian's care of 300-odd people were few well-known names; the majority were artisans and young intellectual workers and people whom Józef had met accidentally and identified as Jews.

Then, "I informed the meeting of my discovery: the cigarette sellers of Three Crosses Square. . . . We had found children alone, existing without anyone's help." Two separate plans emerged during the ensuing discussion. Some felt that the children should be taken away from the Square and placed in so-called "dens." In the end, it was decided otherwise—to leave the children where they were but help them financially and provide them with clothes and documents. Józef was assigned to take the children on as his additional personal charges.[84]

The following morning Józef Ziemian headed to his "office," the little grocery at 5 Sedziowska Street. The 65-year-old owner of the shop, Mrs. Ewa Brzostak, or "Grandma" as she was known to all her customers, helped Jews in full knowledge of their true identity and stored Jewish underground literature, false documents, printing machinery, and blank forms for birth certificates. Here Ziemian sometimes met his "clients." When told the news about the children, Brzostak offered to let them sleep at her place, but only from time to time. Józef Ziemian continued to see Bull, the boys' leader, and told him that some documents might soon be on hand for the children, who were bereft of any papers.[85]

In addition, Ziemian managed to establish contact with Mrs. Dargielowa, director of the Polish welfare RGO bureau at 10 Widok Street, who agreed to help the children once they obtained Aryan documents and to register them with the RGO as Polish orphans. Ziemian gave the children coupons for midday meals and helped out with clothes. "I bought suits of underwear, shoes, and as much as clothing as I could."[86]

Józef was an almost daily visitor at the Square. Gradually he came to know all the children well. Some of them sold cigarettes in the Square, or near the train station, or on trains and trams; others sold the *Nowy Kurier Warszawski* (New Warsaw Courier) newspaper, while still others stood on sidewalks or inside tramways and sang and so earned some money. A few boys found additional income by selling theater tickets. They bought them an hour before the performance and sold them for a much higher price when all the others were gone.[87] Most of these children, it is well to remember, had lost their parents and many of their siblings, some dying of diseases, such as typhus, or taken during the massive deportations of the Warsaw ghetto between July and September 1942.

Ziemian answered to the appeal to find a safe place for one of the boys elsewhere. As fifteen-year-old Bull pleaded with Józef, "If someone really wants to help, then let him take young Bolus [Berl Fiks, born 1936, the youngest of the group] away. Almost everyone at the Square knows he is Jewish. We can all get caught because of him." Ziemian found a widow, living in extreme poverty with her five small children, who agreed to take the seven-year-old Bolus for a suitable fee.[88]

Some of the children participated in the Polish uprising of August 1944, and some managed to cross over to the Russian lines in September 1944 and witness liberation. Others were evacuated with the rest of the Polish population to labor camps inside Germany after the suppression of the Polish uprising that ended on October 2, 1944. More than twenty of these street-running children, the majority, survived. As for Józef

Zysman-Ziemian, he moved to Israel, where he died in 1971, but not before writing about the Jewish street children in the Three Crosses Square.[89]

Miriam Hochberg-Mariańska

> She devoted herself to helping Jews under cover and those on the run wherever she found them—on the street, in trams, trains, orphanages, and in labor camps in and around Kraków.

Before the war, Miriam Hochberg (Peleg, later in Israel) edited the children's supplement of a daily newspaper in Kraków and was active in the Polish Socialist Party's youth organization. When the war broke out, she happened to be on her parents' farm in Przybyszów, near Pilzno, some 20 kilometers from Tarnów. In the summer of 1941, they were evicted and forced into the Pilzno ghetto. Miriam left the ghetto and went to Kraków, where she was aided by her prewar Socialist friends to register under a new name and a corresponding identity card. Translating her German-sounding family name, Hochberg, into Polish, she now appeared as Maria Górska, supposedly born in Równe Wołyńskie (then in the Soviet zone and not accessible for verification purposes), a Roman Catholic by faith and a clerk by occupation.

From announcements plastered on house walls, she found and rented a small room. To further conceal her Jewish traces, she enrolled in a German-language course to make it appear that she was looking for office work for which knowledge of German was necessary in a city filled with German administrative offices, for Kraków was the seat of the German administration during the occupation. While out on the street she took care to carry her German-language instruction books with her. She found employment, indeed, in firms run by German supervisors or ethnic Germans, known as Volksdeutsch.[90] She felt safe and secure—for the moment.

At this early point in the German occupation, she met Mordecai Kurz, her future husband. Then known by the first and middles names of Józef Mieczyslaw (Mietek), he at first stayed in Tarnów, under the family name of Piotrowski, with a corresponding prewar identity document that he received from the Polish Socialist operative Józef Cyrankiewicz. Mietek's blue eyes helped cover up his Jewish identity. He stated in a postwar book that he coauthored with Miriam that early in the German occupation he pledged to dedicate himself to helping anybody in need, disregarding all dangers. "I kept repeating this dozens of times on the Aryan side, when it seemed that the ground was on fire under my feet."[91]

As for Miriam, her Socialist operatives assigned her work on the editorial staff of an underground paper, *Wilność* (Liberty). Miriam's task was to transmit dispatches by a certain "Piotrus" of news that he secretly heard at night on the British BBC and translated into Polish. Miriam deposited it in a certain undercover store mailbox every morning. She also typed out bulletins for underground newspapers. "I used to carry with me a shopping basket as if I was going shopping. Matrices, notes to be typed, or papers already published were at the bottom, and on top I put a few bundles of firewood."[92] At this early stage of her clandestine life she divided her activity into two parts: work in the Polish Socialist Party, and keeping in touch with her family 100 kilometers from Kraków.[93]

Concerned with the safety of her and Mietek's families, Miriam left for Pilzno in June 1942 to urge her family no longer to stay put but to think about escaping in order to save themselves. Stopping first in Tarnów, she headed to the house where Mietek's father lived. He was completely resigned to his fate and did not attempt to flee or hide. He said he had already lost his wife, Mietek's stepmother, and small daughter; he did not know what had happened to his sons, and he would not try to save himself; he had nothing to live for. Miriam hurriedly left as the Germans were already only two houses away rounding up Jews. Arriving in Pilzno, she went to her parents' house. "I found the atmosphere almost idyllic. I had an attack of hysteria. I was shouting and crying. They looked at me as if I was crazy. 'What is the matter with you?' said my father. 'What is happening in Tarnów does not concern us at all. There are plenty of Jews there, but here? It is different. Nothing will happen to us.'" It was impossible to convince them otherwise. "I felt impotent, distraught, exhausted. It was they who tried to comfort and reassure me."

She argued at length with her sister for her to flee. "My sister, who looked Aryan, talked about escaping [the ghetto] and living on the Aryan side as if [it were] something impossible, like a trip to the moon. Her husband's looks did not augur well for his survival. Her two daughters aged seventeen and nine lived a more or less normal life in Pilzno and it seemed that they would be in more danger on the Aryan side." Even after Miriam told them how she witnessed the deportation of Jews in Tarnów that same day, they would not believe that the same fate awaited them.[94]

"I begged my sister to let at least her older daughter, Litka, come with me. She was seventeen. She had excellent Polish looks, and she knew German. 'I won't part with the children,' said my sister. 'Come what may, we shall stay together.'" Miriam left Pilzno the following day at dawn, unaware that she had said good-bye to her family forever, and returned to Kraków by train. Six weeks later, the night before their deportation to Bełżec extermination camp, Miriam's sister snuck out of the ghetto at night while her younger sister, Hania, was left with a Polish friend. Miriam's father and the other Jews of Pilzno were gassed upon arrival in the Bełżec death camp.[95]

Working alongside the Polish Socialist Party

Returning to Kraków, Miriam (under her pseudonym, Mariańska) devoted herself to helping Jews on the run in collaboration with her associates in the Polish Socialist Party. There the three leading activists engaged in helping Jews were Józef Cyrankiewicz (who was eventually captured by the Gestapo and spent time in Nazi camps, which he survived, and after the war served as prime minister), Zygmunt Klopotowski (also arrested), and Adam Rysiewicz (murdered in 1944). After the arrest of Cyrankiewicz, Klopotowski sent Miriam and Mietek on various help missions to Jews in hiding or about to go into hiding. It was still the period long before the emergence of Żegota, the official Warsaw-based organization that aided Jews.

Klopotowski found Miriam and Mietek a flat and legal employment. Miriam was to be a gardener with a family living in a village near Kraków. She would ostensibly leave in the morning for her job and return to Kraków in the evening. It was a large village and, in her words, the work was a good cover, since no one in Poland would suspect that a Jew was able to plant cabbages with such expertise. Still, passing as a non-Jew was a risky undertaking in those days, and no one could ever be sure they wouldn't be uncovered. Everybody knew about the way Gestapo interrogations were carried out. To make sure this would never happen to her, Miriam carried with her a portion of cyanide poison in a test-tube made of very thin glass, which could be easily crunched, just in case. "Fortunately I never had to use it." Miriam also had to be careful of run-ins with some Jews who were in the pay of the Gestapo and on the prowl at the railway station, capturing Jews who were trying to make their escape. She sadly added: "One had to live through such infamy."[96]

For added protection, even though she always carried an official work document under her assumed name, she frequented churches quite regularly; it was also a good place for couriers to meet. She stated that she was blessed with looks which were impeccably Aryan and an unshakable self-confidence. Even her Jewish charges did not detect her real identity and saw her as but a noble Pole. However, she had to be careful, for in Kraków many Jews and Poles knew her, and even the best gentile looks would be of no avail if someone reported her to the Gestapo. Klopotowski never told Miriam's Jewish clients that she was Jewish.[97]

Hiding from Antisemitism

Miriam told of a Polish family who agreed to take in a woman as a servant, but without revealing her Jewish identity, who needed a safe place for political reasons. As she was to appear as a non-Jewish Pole, the woman had to be coached in the Catholic religion. Strangely Miriam had been assigned to be her coach, and she was able to manage it, having learned about the rituals of the Catholic religion from Polish maidservants in her family home before the war, including the traditional Christmas Eve dishes. For instance, for the Easter holiday she remembered watching how food was prepared in a basket and taken to church to be blessed, how a blessed egg was shared on Easter, etc.

Passing as non-Jewish, Miriam was to teach Mrs. Helena Zając how to behave during holidays so as not to reveal her true Jewish origins. "I told her to remember that Good Friday was a day of fast and of visits to church; that on Saturday the food was taken to church to be blessed, and on Easter Day there was a special service in church and then everybody returned home for an equally special and big meal during which a 'blessed egg' was shared." The woman then said, "I know all this, just tell me about breaking the wafer with others." Miriam cut her short very sternly: "Heaven forbid that you should get religious holidays mixed up. A wafer is broken on Christmas Eve, not at Easter. Such a mistake may have dire results." To which Helena angrily shot back, not knowing of Miriam's Jewish identity: "All you have told me is not that important. If I started teaching you about our celebrations of Passover, you would never learn it!" Miriam had to quietly swallow this retort.[98]

Miriam, or Mariańska, was indeed lucky that no one gave her away during the more than five years of the occupation, when she walked the streets or traveled by train. Kraków was not as contaminated as Warsaw by the plague of informers and *szmalcownicy*—the notorious blackmailers and extortionists who preyed on people whom they suspected were Jewish. Still one had to be cautious. Once a girl approached her at a tram stop and asked in a low voice about the fate of Miriam's brother, who had been studying with her at the Commercial Academy.

"I didn't know her. I had never seen her before, and I didn't want to blow my cover. 'I don't know who you mean,' I said.

The young girl shot back, 'Are you not Morycek Hochberg's sister?'

'I don't know who you mean,' Miriam responded a bit sharply this time.

'I am sorry,' the girl said."

In Miriam's words, "I sensed that she did not believe me, but I think she understood why I was lying. Kraków was already [declared] *Judenrein*, free of Jews, by then."[99]

It was best not to take risks. It could prove fatal, for many in Kraków as elsewhere were imbued with antisemitism, including Miriam's landlady. She had hostile opinions of Jews and used to declare that she would immediately denounce to the police any Jew who came her way. One day, while dusting a painting of Jesus, she started talking to the painting, telling it that Jews were finally reaping their just rewards for their crimes and that this should be consolation to Him who suffered so much at their hands.

Miriam, or rather Mariańska, told her: "'Do you know that if Jesus could get one leg off the cross, he would kick you for what you are saying now?'

'Why?'

'Because he proclaimed "love thy neighbor," and he probably meant the innocent Jews who are being murdered now.'

'I can see that you are on the side of the Jews,' the landlady responded.

'No,' I said, 'I am on the side of Jesus Christ.'"

The landlady had no suspicion of her interlocutor's belonging to this "vile" people.[100]

The Żegota Phase

Miriam was probably the only Jewish woman who under the cover of her non-Jewish name worked for the Żegota branch organization in the Kraków region, established by Marek Arczyński in April 1943. She was to work closely with Adam Rysiewicz and Stanislaw Dobrowolski right up to the end of the occupation. Miriam's job was to find Jews in need of help and provide them with documents and financial assistance.[101]

"Dobrowolski was my godfather," Miriam explained, and it was he who chose for Miriam the pseudonym "Mariańska" (officially she was Maria, or Marysia) when she worked for Żegota. "It has remained my second surname to this day."[102] Miriam was the sole Jew in the Kraków branch of Żegota, an identity only known to her closest associates.[103] She traveled to Warsaw several times to meet members of the organization, including the two principal Jewish ones: Dr. Adolf-Avraham Berman and Leon Feiner. The Kraków Żegota funds were supported to a large extent by the Warsaw-based secret National Jewish Committee, headed by Berman and Feiner. According to Miriam's estimate, more than 1,000 people were being helped during this period in Kraków, its surroundings, and in the labor camps.[104]

Miriam visited one of these labor camps in the company of Teresa Lasocka, who worked with the Central Care Council, an official organization for helping Polish prisoners and their families. After leaving the camp, Teresa asked Miriam about her family. "I have no family," Miriam responded. Teresa began to suspect that Miriam-Mariańska was Jewish. Miriam later learned that what prompted Teresa were the saddened eyes of Miriam while visiting the Polish camp. "Yes, but it looks as if your tears were Jewish ones and Teresa found you out," Rysiewicz told her later. "Teodor [his pseudonym] was probably right, these tears were of a kind by which a Jew can be recognized," a fact known only too well by Miriam.[105]

But appearances were not all that mattered. "In those days I learned to believe in simple human luck. Neither a good appearance nor the best papers meant as much as that mysterious ounce of luck." She added in a somewhat religious tone: "In spite of all the disasters and horror of those days, more miracles used to happen than in the Old and New Testaments."[106] But not to everyone. In June 1944 Adam Rysiewicz was arrested while returning from a meeting with his Auschwitz prisoner contacts, where a plan for Cyrankiewicz's escape from Auschwitz was being worked out. Rysiewicz was murdered by the Germans.[107]

In those days hundreds of Poles, mainly women, traveled to Warsaw with all sorts of foodstuffs. They supplied everything to the capital, butter, bacon, sausage, eggs, and liquor. It was a dangerous occupation, and many frequently ended up in camp or prison as a result, but not killed, as happened when Jews were apprehended. Sometimes the smugglers would query Miriam when they noticed that her luggage consisted of nothing more than one small suitcase. "Is this all you are carrying? Maybe you will say that you bought this goose. For I have got two of them, and they are bound to take one of them away." Miriam readily agreed to such a deception. "This is my goose, a present for my family," she would say to the policeman. "This is a kilogram of butter for my sister in Warsaw. I am not going to sell it. And in my small suitcase I had photographs and cards containing details necessary for making ID cards."[108]

One day Miriam ran into a young man (a Jew) who was falsely appearing as a non-Jewish Jackowski, an official in the German sub-prefecture, the so-called Kreishauptmannschaft. She found it astonishing how a Jew found the courage to take on such a job without having such a totally non-Jewish appearance. (Later in Israel he was a famous lawyer by the name of Henryk Margulies.) Miriam would often meet him in the sub-prefecture to obtain various documents from him for use by Jews in hiding or non-Jews doing clandestine work. "I used to carry these forms out just under the nose of the German gendarme guarding the gate, hiding them in the capacious pockets of my coat, which were deliberately torn in such a way that the papers immediately fell through inside the lining."[109]

While Miriam obtained all of her aid addresses from Żegota, she sometimes attempted to make contacts based on her instincts. One day while riding the tram she noticed two women, probably a mother and daughter judging by their appearance. "They both seemed 'suspect' to me. Both were clearly depressed, and it was their behavior rather than their external appearance that indicated to me that they were Jewish." The elder woman wanted to get off at the next stop; the younger one was trying to hold her back. Miriam decided to join them as they got off at the next stop and followed them. Catching up with them, she said: "Excuse me, is there anything I can do to help you? Perhaps you need—" The younger one would not let Miriam finish. "Why are you picking on us?" she shouted in fear. "What do you want from us? Leave us alone!" At that moment a passer-by turned and stared at them. There was a danger that this incident could have a completely different ending from the one Miriam intended and that she could be exposing these two women to immediate danger instead of helping them. She immediately turned around and went off in the opposite direction. "I was devastated when I thought that these two people perhaps thought me a blackmailer and were probably glad that they got rid of me so easily."[110]

Not all her efforts, however, were in vain. One day she came upon a woman she had known before the war. She was Elza Matusowa from Vienna, married to a Jew. She had embraced Judaism, given birth to two children, and was known in Kraków as a Jewess fastidiously observing the Jewish traditions. Her husband and son had left Kraków at the start of the war and set off eastward. He had sent her formal divorce papers in order to protect her. She was doing business with Germans soldiers who were selling stolen goods to her, primarily all kinds of drink and cigarettes. Miriam met Elza in a public swimming pool. An immediate trust arose between the two women, and Elza organized a meeting in her flat. This is how Miriam managed to reach several people who, from that point onward, received an allowance and all kinds of required documents.[111]

In autumn 1944, Miriam met the non-Jewish Jadwiga Strzalecka. She was a director of a Warsaw orphanage, and following the Polish uprising there, she and the forty children in her care, including ten young Jews, found themselves in Poronin. Miriam visited the orphanage every month, helping out the Jewish children with money from Żegota. She asked that the Jews not be treated in any special way so they would not stand out. She also brought them a Jewish child for safekeeping.[112]

Miriam also helped some Jewish resistance fighters with false credentials, such as Stefan Grajek. After the Warsaw uprising in the fall of 1944, he found himself with two other members of a Jewish underground cell in Suchedniów, a little town in the Kielce region. Miriam was instructed to bring them documents and money. Upon meeting the group of Jewish fugitives, it was decided that Miriam would take two of them, Symcha Rathajzer (known as Każik) and Irena Gelblum, with her on her return voyage to Kraków.

In Kielce the Germans stopped the train and evacuated all the passengers to check everyone's documents. Miriam carried a work card and an exemption from forced labor work, and Irena had some sort of Warsaw certificate. The Germans let both of them go. Rathajzer (Każik), however, was stopped. He was immediately taken behind an enclosure where a group of young men was already gathered; they were destined to be deported for hard labor. Irena and Miriam went on the attack. Miriam told the German that Każik and Irena were recently married. The German immediately responded that he would then include Irena in the work group. That way they would be together. Miriam did not let it go. "I continued to pester that German until he got fed up with me. He pointed 'Każik' out to one of his group, and we were all together again."

The young couple decided that this good German should be repaid in some way, and Miriam consented to this kindly mission. They waited until the end of work selection process, when Miriam put 500 zlotys into an envelope and together with Irena headed to the hotel where the Germans were living. Finding her German, Miriam handed him the envelope. She was about to go when he grabbed her with one hand. With his other hand he opened the envelope and gave it back to her with indignation. "If you want to repay me, give me your address in Kraków. I am an old man and I don't like hotels. If I am passing through Kraków, I would like a room in a private house to rest and to eat a homemade meal." Realizing her mistake in approaching the man, Miriam did not lose her cool. Without hesitation, Miriam dictated a false street address and number, then quickly left. Once in Kraków she found a room in the flat of a lonely lady for Kazik and Irena.[113] It had been a close call with that German, foolishly initiated by Miriam and Irena. It could have proved fatal for both.

After the war, Miriam cared for surviving children under the aegis of the Jewish Committee. In 1949 she left for Israel, where she appeared as Miriam Peleg (the Hebraized family name of her husband, the former Mordecai Kurz). I knew her well when she worked as a member of the Tel Aviv branch of the Commission for the Designation of the Righteous, whose meetings I regularly attended during the 1980s. When Stanislaw Dobrowolski visited Yad Vashem, she helped me to organize the ceremony in his honor, which she and her husband attended. I remember how moved she was as she spoke of the man with whom she worked closely during the war years to save Jews. She also worked strenuously to have as many of her non-Jewish colleagues within Żegota honored with the Righteous title by Yad Vashem. She never spoke of her own wartime ordeals and heroic rescue activities, only of her Żegota colleagues. She remained a self-effacing woman, never asking for honors for herself. She died in 1996.

Abraham Bankier

> He was instrumental in expanding Oskar Schindler's manufacturing business, which provided jobs, food, and medical care to Jews in Schindler's factory and profits with which to bribe Nazi authorities.

Steven Spielberg's 1993 film *Schindler's List* spoke a lot about Isaac Stern, Oskar Schindler's major partner, but never mentioned another principal in his rescue operation, the Jewish Abraham Bankier. Without him, Schindler couldn't have possibly carried out his monumental rescue operation because he couldn't have amassed the necessary funds to pay off Nazi officials. Schindler depended on Isaac Stern, whom he often consulted on general business matters. But Stern was incarcerated in the Płaszów camp during the initial phase of Schindler's rescue operation. It was Abraham Bankier who took Stern's place, running the enamel business for Schindler in a way that made it a very profitable undertaking and, doubly important, expanded the business so that it could hire hundreds of Jewish workers and thus ensure their survival.

In 1935 Bankier founded the Rekord enamel factory in the Podgorze suburb of Kraków, together with his brother-in-law, Wolf Lazer Gleitmann, and Michal Gutman. When the German occupation began in September 1939, the factory was in the process of liquidation due to severe financial losses. Oskar Schindler was persuaded by Bankier (and also by Isaac Stern, who then was employed in another firm) that the Rekord factory could be salvaged with secret money that Bankier and some fellow Jews had stashed away. Schindler saw the benefits for him in such a deal and accepted the proposition and appointed Abraham Bankier factory manager. In early 1942 Schindler contrived to pass from a German occupation paid trustee of the firm (*treuhänder*) to owner with money raised by Bankier and his confederates, and the firm's name was changed to Deutsche Emailwarenfabrik (DEF).

At first Schindler hired mainly Polish workers. However, absenteeism was rampant among these workers, to as much as a third of the labor force. It was common practice for a Polish worker to work four days a week at his regular job and spend the rest of his time plugging away at other private money ventures in order to make ends meet for his family. Trying to save Jews from German atrocities, Bankier pointed out to Schindler the advantage of hiring Jewish workers from the nearby Kraków ghetto.

This idea pleased Schindler, since he had to pay 5 German Marks per day to the ss for a Jewish worker, much less than he was paying the Polish workers. At first Bankier brought a group of twenty Jewish workers from the ghetto to the factory each day and trained them in the production of metal sheets into enamel pots. He became indispensable to Schindler.[114]

It is important not to forget that initially Oskar Schindler was in Kraków for one reason only, and that was to make a lot of money. And it was the black market that afforded him this luxury, and this is where Bankier's intervention proved handy. Bankier financed the initial production costs, using materials he had kept hidden in various stores. Then, at Bankier's prodding, Schindler requested from the German authorities the proper raw material needed for filling orders for mess kits for the German army. Bankier knew how to contrive things so that as much as possible of the raw metal remained unused, and from this metal he manufactured additional pots and pans, which he then sold on the black market. This was the money that Schindler could spend for daily parties of high-ranking officers and generals and for bribing them when needed, in return for lightening the restrictions on his Jewish workers and providing them with extra food and medicine. Schindler could wine, dine, and bribe influential people, but he knew nothing about running a factory, and here he was totally dependent on Abraham Bankier's expertise. In the words of historian David Crowe, Bankier became the Gray Eminence behind Schindler.[115]

Milton S. Hirschfeld, of the New Cracow Friendship Society in the United States, one of the Schindlerjuden (Schindler Jews), stated emphatically that it was the money supplied from the business by Abraham Bankier that allowed Schindler to save over 1,000 Jewish workers.[116] Or, as further attested by one of Schindler's Jewish workers, Victor Dortheim: "Schindler was our savior. But in the Emalia factory Bankier was the key figure. Without Bankier there would have been no Schindler."[117] Bankier had an office next door to Schindler's where he received Polish businessmen. Almost 80 percent of Schindler's business dealings were on the black market, and it was Bankier who did most of the trading and provided Schindler with the vast resources he needed to bribe officials and hire, house, feed, transfer, and save hundreds of Jewish workers.

When Schindler secretly met Rudolf-Rezső Kasztner of the Jewish Rescue Committee in Budapest in 1943, he confided to him: "I can, without worrying, go away for four weeks, and know that he [Bankier] will faithfully substitute for me."[118] In the 1944–45 Brünnlitz phase of Schindler's rescue activity, Bankier helped out in making possible hard-to-get bread for the 1,200 Jewish factory workers. He did this by risking traveling back and forth to Kraków to fetch some hidden $2,000 that was largely used to pay the mill owners for providing bread to all the factory workers.[119]

Former workers in Schindler's factory in Kraków had only words of praise for Bankier. In 1998 Bronia Gross-Guns confirmed that Bankier was instrumental in employing hundreds of Jews and in a few cases whole families, and he was the actual liaison between Schindler and the workers. "He had a great influence on Mr. Schindler, who in turn, out of friendship with him, made a commitment to save his Jewish workers. Thanks to Abraham Bankier and Mr. Schindler, myself, my father, and my sister were saved."[120] Similarly Sol Urbach stated that his work in Schindler's factory brought him regularly to Bankier's office. His impression of the man was that of a father figure, and it was Bankier who "used his imagination and benevolence to help transform Oskar Schindler into a Righteous person."[121] Finally Rena Fagen-Schontal confirmed in 1998 that it was Abraham Bankier who was instrumental in employing hundreds of Jewish people and was Schindler's advisor on business affairs as well as in human matters. "Thanks to Bankier and Schindler, my mother, my future husband, and many members of our families were saved." She added that as one of Schindler's survivors, "I must say that it was immensely disappointing and unjust the way Abram Bankier was deprived of the credit due to him and hardly mentioned at all [in Spielberg's film]." She correctly explained this omission as probably due to the fact that testimonies forwarded to Steven Spielberg were by people who arrived at Schindler's Brünnlitz factory, in former Czechoslovakia, in late 1944, rather than those employed for a longer period in Schindler's pots and pans factory in Kraków some years earlier.[122]

In his film, Spielberg chose to make a composite of three people: Abraham Bankier, Isaac Stern, and Mietek Pemper. But Stern and Pemper, Jewish prisoners in the Płaszów labor camp (located a few kilometers from Kraków), never worked in Schindler's DEF factory with Bankier.[123]

After the war, Abraham Bankier returned to Kraków and tried to reopen the enamel factory, but it was confiscated by the newly established Communist regime. He stayed in Kraków and remained active in

Jewish communal affairs. In November 1956, during the tense period that accompanied the rise of the Władysław Gomułka regime, Abraham fled to Vienna with his second wife (his first wife died in the Holocaust) and daughter, Miriam, but he suffered a stroke upon arrival there and died.

Naftali Backenroth

> He shrewdly organized a forced labor force of over 1,000
> farmers, mechanics, cleaners, carpenters, engineers,
> and others, ostensibly for the benefit of the German
> war machine, but in reality to save their lives.

Jews had lived in Drohobych (for many years part of Poland, today in Ukraine) as far back as the fifteenth century.[124] They were instrumental in developing the ancient salt mines in the area into a modern industry. Jews gradually spread out to nearby towns and villages, and they especially prospered after the discovery of petroleum in the early nineteenth century in Boryslav, some 9 kilometers away. This led to an "oil rush," and inventors, entrepreneurs, wealthy investors, laborers, and adventurers flooded into the region, all trying to get rich fast. Most of the crude oil from Boryslav was transferred for processing to refineries in Drohobych, many of whom were under Jewish ownership. As a result, Drohobych and Boryslav became more urban and more prosperous. In 1918, with the demise of the Austro-Hungarian Empire, which had ruled this region, Drohobych became part of Ukraine; a year later it was annexed to Poland. By 1930 some 13,000 Jews lived in Drohobych and over 7,000 in Boryslav—44 percent of the total population. Jewish cultural life flourished with its theater, synagogues, yeshiva, and religious educational institutions. It also claimed the famous painter Maurycy Gottlieb and author and artist Bruno Schultz.[125]

Top of Form

With the start of World War II, the Germans briefly occupied Drohobych, then turned it over to the Russians as part of the Molotov-Ribbentrop treaty for the division of Poland. The Soviets took steps to integrate the new region into the Communist system and economy. They nationalized Jewish businesses and targeted Jewish intellectuals for expulsion to Siberia. This ended suddenly with the German attack on the Soviet Union on June 22, 1941. The German occupation of Drohobych eight days later prompted a three-day pogrom by Ukrainians (who welcomed the Germans as liberators) that claimed several hundred Jewish lives and was accompanied with much looting of Jewish homes.[126] At first the German military was in command, but within days the Gestapo and ss took charge of Drohobych and began to bear down on the Jews with a heavy hand.

As in other places in occupied Europe, a Judenrat (a German-appointed Jewish council) was created, and it set up workshops and small factories for the benefit of the new masters, dealing in carpentry, sewing, and the manufacture of baskets, brushes, brooms, and bricks, that employed hundreds of Jews. Many others were employed in factories related to the petroleum industry. The Judenrat also established workshops for shoemakers, tailors, furriers, and other craftsmen who were forced to work to fill German work orders.[127]

The German goal from the start was the total liquidation of all Jews, and they carried it out in stages, code-named "actions." Most Drohobych Jews were murdered in the nearby Bronica forest, shot over pits, or deported to the Bełżec death camp by train, where they were gassed. None were exempt—men and women of all ages, as well as children. By June 1943 most of the ghetto Jews were dead, including the Judenrat leaders and the Jewish ghetto police. The labor camps were also gradually liquidated. On July 15, 1943, the Germans proudly declared Drohobycz to be *Judenrein* (cleaned of Jews), although in practice hundreds were still there, assigned various labor duties, many of them organized and directed by the Jewish Naftali Backenroth.

Putting Jews to Work, Not to Death

Under these unprecedented horrific conditions, Naftali Backenroth stood out with the determination to try to save as many as possible with his scheming. His ancestors had wandered into Drohobych in the fourteenth century from Bavaria. With the discovery of oil on land owned by the Backenroths in the mid-nineteenth century near Dohobych, the elder Abraham Backenroth founded the Nafta Petroleum company, and the family's fortune was born. When in 1930 his father, Israel, died, Naftali Backenroth was summoned home from France, where he had studied agriculture, chemistry, geology, and engineering to run the drilling operations of the family oil business, Nafta Ltd. He had by then developed into a tall, sturdy, and forceful man with blue eyes, a fair mustache, and quick reflexes.[128] Earlier, at age twenty-three, he had become a lecturer at the Ecole Polytechnique, the most prestigious academy for engineering and science in France, and he had a knack for thinking up inventions and better ways to do things.

On the eve of World War II, Backenroth was busy building a mobile drilling machine and supervising a drill at a new site, but his work was halted by the Soviet takeover of eastern Poland and seizure of the family's oil business. He decided to deal in agriculture. When Stalin ordered Nikita Khrushchev, the first secretary of the Ukrainian Communist Party (and future leader of the Soviet Union), to tour the region and carry out a program for doubling agricultural production, Backenroth toured the countryside as Krushchev's guide. He made a positive impression on the leader and was appointed district agronomist; he recruited a group of Jewish engineers (many of them Communists) to help him . Khrushchev placed his confidence in this once prosperous businessman; this was highly unusual for a stalwart Communist leader.[129]

Under German rule, starting July 4, 1941, Backenroth at first declined to join the German-created Drohobych Judenrat. However, when the German military demanded that the Judenrat provide workers to gather the equipment the Soviets had left behind when they fled, Backenroth agreed to be in charge of such an ad hoc group. He repeated that when he organized a group of twelve Jews for a labor assignment in nearby Stryj. Like other Jewish leaders in German-occupied lands, during the initial phase of the German occupation, Naftali believed that it was important to show the new masters the aptitude and readiness of Jews to perform whatever work was demanded of them. When Gestapo man Felix Landau was in need of such labor, Naftali selected workers and brought them to his headquarters in the Villa Himmel and told Landau to prepare a list of tasks and the instructions so that he could assign workers to him. [130]

The Germans soon took notice of Backenroth's special talents; he was a hard worker, and when they discovered he was an agricultural expert, he was sent to work in the garden of a Gestapo officer. Backenroth then began forming permanent work groups, and he organized a handyman service and technical leadership for new construction projects. That's how he got the idea of suggesting the construction of an indoor horse riding ring to the ss men. The idea struck a chord, especially with Landau. When the building was inaugurated in May 1942, his superior put him in charge of the horses, and soon there were about 200 Jews working under his supervision, which kept them away from the death squads—at least temporarily.[131]

The Gestapo also needed chambermaids, janitors, cleaners, gardeners, and handymen, and the army needed technicians and engineers to operate and maintain the oil wells and the refining facilities. Backenroth created a group of skilled and diligent workers and tradesmen, independent from the Judenrat, and supplied the Germans with whatever services they needed, thereby making his workers indispensable and possibly saving their lives and those of their families. With the Gestapo's consent, he obtained 700 workers and 100 administrative officers. He involved nearly 25 percent of all the ghetto Jews and established workshops where children could learn various skills.[132] Backenroth also was granted permission to set up a kitchen, separate from the Judenrat one, for his Jewish workers. In order to get better rations for his teams, Backenforth's office reported directly to the German agricultural department, headed by Major Eberhard Helmrich. That supply department gave Naftali generous quantities of food.[133]

A Farm Run by Jews for Germans

One of Naftali Backenroth's notable achievements was setting up a farm and producing agricultural products for the benefit of the Germans, with the help of Helmrich. The two met one day when the Ukrainian mayor of nearby Stryj came to see Backenroth in the company of a tall, smiling, and aristocratic German in civilian clothes. That man introduced himself. "My name is Helmrich, and I am in charge of agriculture in this region." As they exchanged words, Backenroth told the affable German how he had organized the agriculture during the Russian occupation, so Helmrich proposed that Backenroth join him in his agricultural administration. "You surely cannot want to stay with these murderers," meaning the Gestapo, Major Helmrich told the surprised Naftali, who feared that this could be a setup." Backenroth replied, "I do not want to work with you and to be considered a collaborator." At which Helmrich cut in: "But Mr. Backenroth, I want to be your friend. I have no interest in forcing you."[134] At that point Backenroth felt that the German meant what he said, and it was the start of an official employer-employee work relationship and a deep friendship that benefited many Jews.

Their joint venture was the setting up of a dairy, fruit, vegetable, and poultry farm in nearby Hyrawka to supply the German military in the region with agricultural products. Later they added a rabbit breeding facility. About 250 Jews were stationed there, including many women. Employment there, it goes without saying, afforded many Jews an opportunity to survive. They exchanged vital information among themselves, and Helmrich was often able to warn Backenroth of impending "actions." When there were killing raids by the Gestapo and ss, Helmrich usually stayed on the Hyrawka farm camp day and night and was thus able to prevent any arrests. Hyrawka also served as a hiding place for the relatives of the men and women who worked there. They would leave the ghetto and stay at the farm overnight or longer. With the help of Backenroth and the consent of Helmrich, they built a room that could be loosely sealed off with rocks so that it couldn't be discovered easily.[135]

In their boldness, their sober reflection, and their readiness to help, these two men became soulmates and kindred spirits. Insofar as Naftali Backenroth was concerned, "only one thing was on my mind, how to survive, and how to expand the work group. I devoted all my energies to that."[136] The farm ceased operations after nine months, and some of its workers were mass-murdered in the Bronica forest. But Eberhard Helmrich managed to send some of the women to his wife Donata, in Berlin in the guise of non-Jewish Ukrainians, for domestic assignments in faraway Germany. The friendship between Backenroth and the Helmrichs lasted for many years after the war.[137]

Hyrawka was not the only farm undertaking spearheaded by Naftali Backenroth. One day a group of six Jewish farmers asked him for jobs. They owned about twenty-five acres of farmland on the outskirts of Drohobych. Backenroth arranged a deal with the Gestapo's Landau, who managed the Jewish labor assignments. Together they set up an agricultural ss unit to supply the Gestapo headquarters with fixed quotas of agricultural produce, particularly butter, vegetables, and fruit. Helmrich helped to create the farms, as he was in charge of agriculture in the district. Fifty years later, Backenroth described the creation of the new ss agricultural entity with relish: "It was a Jewish ss unit, can you believe it? Jewish ss. Of course, we put more than those six families onto the farms by combining families that were linked by marriage."[138] He was so successful in his management that the village Jews, outside Drohobycz, were allowed to remain on their property. They had to produce a good harvest, but they were permitted to keep part of it, and Backenroth saw to it that some of the food was distributed among the Jewish workers in Drohobycz. Soon all the Jews in the vicinity came to Backenroth with their problems, and he helped everyone whatever he could.[139]

Conniving to Save Jews

Until March 1943 all the people working with Naftali Backenroth were relatively secure and safe. Living conditions were a bit better, and the food was adequate. He did all that he could to protect the seven hundred souls, all of them his workers. He had mastered the art of organizing a forced labor force, ostensibly for the benefit of the German war machine, but in reality to save them. He also took pains to supply hard-to-get amenities to enrich the stark lives of Gestapo and Wehrmacht officers—for instance, fresh vegetables for their meals and fresh flowers in their quarters. The carpentry workshop that Backenroth set up was busy building office furniture. Officers uniforms were washed, the rooms of the police and the military encampments thoroughly cleaned, broken machines fixed, and army and police cars maintained.

Backenroth's strength also came from his manly appearance. Most Gestapo personnel saw in him the characteristics that they had been conditioned to attribute to the Aryan type: tall and strong, blue eyes, and a brilliant brain. In face-to-face talks with Germans, Backenroth never groveled or spoke to them in a frightened and slavish way. He stood erect and looked Gestapo officers straight in the eye, and they were a bit mesmerized by this.[140] The Germans went so far as to invite Naftali Backenroth to live in the Gestapo compound, but he preferred to stay with his engineers' group in a cellar at the Nafta company's oil fields because, as he stated, "that's where I was born, and I knew the territory. I could move freely between the refinery and the Gestapo headquarters."[141] This freedom afforded Backenroth the advantage of trying to save Jews outside of his workforce. When, for instance, he learned that some Jews had been imprisoned in the cellar of the Gestapo building, to be shot the following day, he managed to get some of them freed.[142] With the passage of time, Backenroth came to know about a dozen safe hiding places where he directed fellow Jews fleeing for their lives.

Other Gestapo staff members acted respectfully toward Backenroth, especially when they saw Gestapo chief Nicolaus Tolle speaking to him in a friendly way. When their long conversation ended, the German extended his hand to him, saying, "Auf Wiedersehen, Herr Backenroth." But Naftali did not take Tolle's outstretched hand. "You are refusing to shake the hand of a Gestapo officer?" Tolle asked in wonderment.

"My hands have not killed Jews," Backenroth replied. "Herr Hauptman [Mr. Officer], it is not for me that I refuse but for you. What will the Germans here think if they see the chief of the Gestapo shaking hands with a Jew?"

"Thank you for worrying about me," Tolle replied. "If you need any aid, I would be happy to help."[143]

When Gestapo man Karl Günther, who replaced Landau, wished to reduce Backenroth's workforce, Naftali began to look for other essential jobs. He assigned some of the people to set up a brick-making plant and then went to the German in charge of construction at the Kolomiya refineries and persuaded him to take over an entire Jewish technical team. Dozens of engineers, architects, and draftsmen moved over to the refineries—all this while the extermination process in Drohobych continued apace. When he saved Jews, he did not ask for any compensation or even thanks, and he declined gifts of any kind. Helmrich's daughter, Cornelia Schmalz-Jacobsen, recalled that her mother and father often spoke of Backenroth as a "terrific fellow" and a "hell of a guy." He never allowed the unending horrors all around him to paralyze him; on the contrary, they seemed to mobilize his ingenuity and his energy. He tried to organize the Judeneinsatz (Jewish workforce) in such a way that as many as possible of his Jewish protégés could have a better chance of surviving. By March 1944 Backenroth's work groups numbered more than 1,000 Jews. He must have been an impressive man—one who radiated authority and imperturbability. He was respected even by the Gestapo; they felt it was too bad that this strapping man with the gleaming blue eyes was a Jew! But here, too, the Germans were in for a surprise.[144]

A Jew to Gentile Masquerade

In spite of the strength of his position, and despite his special stature, Naftali's situation was becoming increasingly more worrisome. Would the Gestapo allow him to survive when they evacuated the region and thereby risk making it possible for him to witness the crimes they committed? Something phenomenal had to be devised to ensure his safety, now that the curtain of German rule was coming down. This gave birth to an incredible and audacious idea—to reinvent him not as a Jew but as a gentile, mistakenly considered a Jew. It all happened by coincidence when a bundle of old documents from 1917 was found, addressed to Naftali's parents, that included a large sum of money. Naftali then came up with the ingenious idea that this old bundle of letters and money had to do with him being a bastard child of a certain non-Jewish Katya Bronicki and Doctor Bronislaw Kozlowski, an old bachelor, womanizer, and antisemite.

The story concocted by Naftali was that in 1905, two babies were born a few days apart: one the Jewish Naftali Backenroth and the other, the gentile Mikola Bronicki. A forged document was presently drawn up, according to which the true Naftali had died at birth, and in order to spare the distraught mother from this terrible news and spare as well Katya Bronici from the stigma of being an unwed mother, it was decided that Katya's baby would be presented to Naftali's mother as her own son, and he was immediately circumcised with his mother's consent. Katya was compensated with a sum of money by Naftali's father, Israel Backenroth, so she would not reveal the identity of the infant. This explained the envelope with 2,000 crowns (meant for delivery to Naftali-Mikola, when he came of age) with the incriminating documents. All the principal actors of this farce were conveniently dead.[145]

Naftali Backenroth placed the forged papers among the heap of old documents and contrived for one of his non-Jewish workers to find them accidentally. At first Backenroth assumed the innocent role of doubting the authenticity of these documents, but then arranged for others to attest to the truth of the birth of the boy to Katya Bronicki. Backenroth then found himself congratulated by his non-Jewish friends for not really being Jewish. As one such woman, a devout Catholic, told him, "Look, you are not a Jew, and we have been insulting you. We thought you were Jewish. You are the son of the doctor, Kozlowski." A naïve priest was found to confirm the story. Soon the rumor began to circulate that Naftali Backenroth wasn't really Jewish. The Gestapo at first doubted the story and sent two men to interrogate him. They asked him, "Do you want to be an Aryan?" to which Backenroth hesitatingly replied, "Do you think it's possible?" They said, "Well, you know how the Jews kidnapped Christian children in order to convert them." Then they examined him closely, studied his profile, and scrutinized him from all angles, checking the shape of his head. Finally they showed him the forged document and asked, "And what do you say about this?" Backenroth perused the document that he himself had produced and said that if the documents were forged, then "I can tell you one thing, the copy of my father's signature is excellent, but I don't believe that it's real." The atmosphere during the interview was pleasant as Backenroth joked with the Gestapo agents.[146]

The Gestapo eventually swallowed the story. After all, they'd known all along that he couldn't be a Jew—"You with your blue eyes!" A ceremony was organized to mark Naftali Backenroth's new identity. They proudly proclaimed him to be a 100 percent Aryan, while his son Lucien was classified as half-Jewish, and his wife remained Jewish but under her husband's protection. The German regional governor then handed Backenroth a document stating, "The man known as Naftali Backenroth is Mikola Bronicki." Backenroth now received an apartment with three rooms and a kitchen on the upper story. He used his new identity to save not only himself but hundreds of other Jews as well. Backenroth never reverted to his original name, and after the war he retained the name of Bronicki—also in memory of the thousands murdered in the forest of the nearly similar-sounding Bronica.[147]

For himself, the risks were not yet over, as he faced a new challenge—standing up to the Russians who entered Drohobych on August 6, 1944, and accused him of having been a German collaborator, a charge that led to his arrest. The interrogators claimed that they had evidence that Backenroth had been seen in the company of the heads of the Gestapo. "During one of the *aktzias*," they said, "you were seen talking to the Nazis." Backenroth explained that he walked through the streets with the mayor, trying to save as many people as possible. The Soviets took their time, as the interrogations and the inquiries stretched over five long months. But he was eventually freed, and he moved to France with his wife and son.[148] Backenroth eventually settled in Israel, where he died in 1993.[149] In closing, out of up to 12,000 Jews who dwelled in Drohobych in 1939, an untold hundreds were left, thanks to the rescue efforts of Naftali Bronicki-Backenroth.[150]

Yeshayahu Drucker

He worked ceaselessly for the release of Jewish children
from their temporary Polish homes, mostly in return
for substantial payment to the host families.

This chapter of Jewish rescuers of Jews in Poland closes with a different type of rescue, one that took place as soon as the war ended and involved the search for Jewish children turned over to non-Jewish hands and the efforts to reclaim them for the Jewish people, as their parents (living or departed) would have wanted. It is the story of Yeshayahu Drucker.[151] Born in 1914, he lost all his family during the Holocaust. Originally arrested by the Soviets, he was expelled to forced labor near the North Pole. In 1943 he enlisted in the newly formed Polish Kosciuszko division and participated in the division's advance to Berlin. After the war Rabbi David Kahana, himself a survivor and then chief chaplain for Jewish soldiers in the Polish army, appointed Drucker as his aide and assigned him to retrieve Jewish children hidden with non-Jewish Poles.

Kahana's organization, Vaad Kehilot, acted separately from the mainline Coordination, a Zionist secular organization, representing the various Socialist pioneering parties in Palestine. Another organization, the Central Jewish Committee, where Dr. Adolf Berman was active, established children's homes, but only for orphans who were repatriated from Russia There, the education was mostly of a radical socialism, very close to Communism, and it naturally earned the full support of the new pro-Soviet authorities in the country. "We did not want to place any of our children there," exclaimed the traditionally religious Drucker. "So we opened up our own children's home in Zabrze, Upper Silesia."

The government-supported Jewish Committee's mission was to educate the repatriated children on strictly socialist values, with a minimum emphasis on Jewish studies. Former Bundists (non-Zionist socialists) were assigned as teachers for more than 3,800 children. The Zionist parties established their separate homes (called "kibbutz" homes), giving the children there a Zionist and Hebrew education, in preparation for their emigration to Palestine. About 3,300 children, mostly orphans, were admitted into some fifty kibbutz homes. The various Zionist organizations in Palestine established an umbrella organization, the Zionist Coordination for the Redemption of Children—in short, the Coordination. Barred from the Coordination were the religious Zionist Mizrahi and its Bnei Akiva youth movement, after their demand for the inclusion of religious instruction in the Coordination schools was rejected.

Drucker was basically a one-man operator. In a letter to the Jewish Agency in Palestine, he wrote, "Here in Poland there is hardly a village without a Jewish child, boy or girl, in some Christian home." And every effort was to be made, he added, to retrieve these lost children and return them to their people and their Jewish faith.[152] A certain Devorah (then Marisha) Silber scoured the Polish countryside, on Drucker's behalf, dressed as a peasant woman, gathering information from farmers on Jewish children in their midst. Then, appearing in Polish army uniform with the rank of captain, Drucker worked ceaselessly for the release of Jewish children mostly in return for substantial payment to the host families. But some also needed to be forcefully removed. Two homes were set up in Upper Silesia for retrieved children—in Geszcze and Zabrze (near Katowice), where they received a religious Zionist education. Eventually, as the Communists gained the upper hand in Poland with the open support of the Soviet regime, they clamped down on the activities of all Jewish organizations dealing with orphans. The children had consequently to be reclaimed as fast as possible.

Extricating the children from the host families proved an arduous and at times risky undertaking. To begin with, the child's response to the attempt to separate it from the new family was understandably mostly negative. "I don't want to go. I feel good here. I will not go" was the common response. Some Poles, victims to the stereotyped belief that Jews had lots of money, kept raising the price in return for the release of the children. Drucker did not judge them too harshly. "I felt that these people had risked tremendously in saving a Jewish child. Now we were forcing them to part with the child. The least we could do to reduce the separation pain was to reward them financially for the child's upkeep." They did this with funds from the Joint Distribution Committee and the Orthodox Vaad Hatzalah organization in the United States. Drucker's military uniform also helped, as many mistakenly thought he was an official assigned by the authorities for the purpose of reclaiming children.

Altogether, through the efforts of Drucker's organization and the Coordination Committee, some 2,000 to 3,000 children were found, of which some 600 to 700 were cared for by Rabbi Kahana's Vaad Kehilot, according to Drucker's estimate.[153] These religiously oriented children were quickly moved out of Poland to Palestine (soon to be Israel), or other countries: France, England, Canada, and the United States. During the visit of Rabbi Yitzhak Herzog from Palestine in 1946, he took back with him more than 500 of these children. Rabbi Solomon Schoenfeld, the son-in-law of a British chief rabbi, Dr. Joseph Herz (whose story appears in chapter 13), also took with him to England 120 to 130 children during his several visits in late 1946 and early 1947.[154]

Challenges in Returning the Children

In his postwar testimony, Drucker described some of the obstacles that inhibited non-Jewish rescuers from returning Jewish children to their families or Jewish organizations. The religious motivation played an important role, such as in the story of Moshe Helman, who had left for Palestine in 1939, leaving behind a married daughter with two children, a son and daughter. The son was killed, and the daughter (Marysia) was turned over to the house maidservant, who in turn placed the girl in a convent. Drucker went to see the Mother Superior. He brought her greetings from the Holy Land and added that the child's grandfather wanted very much to see his granddaughter. The Mother Superior remained unmoved, reminding Drucker that Jews justifiably suffer for having caused the death of Jesus. Drucker returned for a second visit and assured her that the child would not be lured away from her Christian observance when visiting her grandfather. But the child refused to leave.

Drucker decided to concoct a story. On an empty telegram that he himself wrote and that supposedly came from the child's grandfather, the elderly man stated that he was close to death and simply wished to see the only remnant of his family before dying. She could then return to Poland if she so wished. The child was eventually receptive to the idea of leaving the convent for a brief overseas visit. But once in Israel she decided to stay on. Settling in Tel Aviv, she continued to attend Catholic services in nearby Jaffa. During the Israeli Independence War, she was a soldier. Eventually she married and became a teacher. It is told that during the early period of her marriage, she would occasionally slip away and go to Jaffa to attend mass in the Catholic church there.

Both religious and monetary considerations played a part in the story taking place in Częstochowa, known for its shrine of the Black Madonna. There a man, himself rich, asked that in return for the release of the ten-year-old Jewish girl held by him, he wanted to receive the four buildings owned by the child's family (and relatives in Palestine) and some fields. Responding to Rabbi Herzog's appeal to intercede, Drucker went to speak to the bishop and appeal for him to intercede so that the girl could be united with her relative in Tel Aviv. This otherwise friendly bishop said he could not do it, for the child had already been baptized. Sacraments are holy, and if the girl was released, she would probably not continue to observe Christianity. Undeterred by this decision, the uncle arrived from Palestine and took the matter right up to the Polish Supreme Court, which ruled in his favor. Before returning to Tel Aviv with the ransomed girl, the uncle turned over to the Pole part of his family's property. The girl received a warm and tender rearing and was later happily married.

In a money-extortion scheme, a woman and her two daughters came to see Drucker, saying that in return for money she was ready to release a Jewish boy age seven or eight in her care. She claimed that her family had found him during the evacuation of Warsaw in 1944, after the German suppression of the Polish uprising, when he had wandered into their home. He claimed he was an orphan, but they understood he was Jewish, and they treated him well. Meeting the rescuer in her home, Drucker and the woman agreed on a sum of ransom money. Suddenly the boy opened the door and saw her counting the money. He cried, "Mom! You're selling me in return for money?" Taken aback, she changed her mind, but after a lengthy give-and-take, she agreed to release the boy. To calm the boy's fears, Drucker told him that he was his uncle.

Not satisfied with the boy's release, Drucker decided to investigate further about the boy's past. He only knew that his identity was linked to the name Baranowicz, and he came from the town of Milanowak. "I took him there and rode through the streets in a tram; he pointed to a certain house. I went to see the resident. I told him I am not from the police, just wanted more information." To Drucker's surprise, the man recognized the boy and said that the boy had a large inheritance waiting for him in America, and that whoever saved the boy would receive it from the Joint organization (Joint Distribution Committee). "Why do you think you deserve it?" Drucker queried this stranger. "Because I saved the boy" was the curt response. "How come he wound up on the street?" The man had no answer. It turned out that the boy's mother was the Joint representative in Warsaw before the war, and trying to save her son, she had turned the boy over to that man, but he was afraid to keep the child and threw him out. The boy, renamed Avigdor Baranowicz, was taken to Israel.

We follow with the story of a Jewish man from Hungary who came back to Poland to look up his son. He had lost his wife and daughter during the war, but the son was saved by a woman who took him with her to the women's Ravensbrück concentration camp and miraculously managed to save him in that hellish place—so goes Drucker's account. Returning to Warsaw, she registered him in the reconstituted Jewish committee, then worked as a prostitute, continuing to love and dote on the boy. Drucker and the boy's father went to court, which surprisingly decided in the woman's favor, arguing that the woman who raised the child deserved to keep him. Supreme Court overturned the lower court's decision and ruled in favor of the boy's father, but the woman refused to release him. Drucker's men then kidnapped the boy from his school. During that dramatic encounter, the woman appeared and created a scene but could not prevent the boy from being taken away. He was sent to Israel.

Up against Antisemism

One needs to take into account some of the risks faced by people like Drucker while on the road to locate and release children from their host families. They had to be wary of being accosted by antisemitic vigilantes, still roaming the countryside. One of Drucker's stories involved Hinda Zorkowska, daughter of rabbis, from Warsaw, who was kept in a priest's home in a village in the Kielce region. Four of Drucker's colleagues had lost their lives to the vigilantes there. Drucker, nevertheless, decided to try reaching the rabbi's daughter and arranged for himself a false ID under the name of Jerzy Trotsky and a letter from the army that said he was accompanying an American journalist, equipped with a proper journalist certificate, in a car sporting an American flag. On the way, as expected, the two were stopped by armed men. They consulted among themselves and finally decided to let Drucker and the fake journalist proceed. Drucker owed his life to his companion, for "myself, they would have shot since I represented what these vigilantes considered a Jewish-led Communist regime."

When they arrived at the priest's home, the little girl was brought in, but as in most instances, she refused to leave. Drucker showed her a picture of her grandfather (he was previously a rabbinical judge in Warsaw) and softly asked, "Hinde'le, do you recognize your grandfather?" She suddenly burst out in hysterical weeping and said she wanted to leave immediately. The priest released her with, according to Drucker, some anti-Jewish allegations. She eventually settled in Israel and became the mother of three.

In a similar dangerous confrontation with hostile people, a colleague of Drucker fought in court to have a Jewish girl released from a farmer in a village near Skarzysko, but the court decided in the farmer's favor. Drucker appealed to the Supreme Court and won, but the farmer refused to release girl. "One day I took two Jewish soldiers with me and left for the village. The man's wife sneaked out and alerted the villagers, and they soon assembled with knives and pitchforks." The farmer would only release the girl in return for payment. He also claimed to be emotionally attached to the child. "We ran for our lives. We went to the police, but they refused to get involved. After a few months, we made another try; came in the dead of the night; at 3 a.m.; knocked on the door, grabbed the girl from her bed, and ran." She eventually wound up in Israel in the religious kibbutz Hafetz Hayim; she then left to study at the Hebrew University and married the son of the state comptroller.

When he looked back, Drucker had mixed feelings about what he had done.[155] Was it all worth it, all this effort, he asked himself? To have these children torn away from people with whom in many cases they felt warmly ensconced and pass such torment at a tender age? In Drucker's words, the children wanted to belong to a specific family, not to a people, not to everyone, but to someone. Yet Drucker remained convinced that this operation had to be undertaken, painful as it was to the children. Their families, survivors of one of history's most horrific genocides, also had to be taken into consideration. The Jewish people, moreover, cruelly deprived of millions of its sons and daughters, had every right to make up, however moderate in numbers, the tremendous loss sustained and reclaim these embers from the fire that had engulfed their loved ones.

After the newly installed Communist regime took full control in Poland and closed all Zionist-affiliated offices, including those dealing with ransoming Jewish children, Yeshayahu Drucker left for Israel, where he continued to check on the welfare of the liberated children brought there. He died in 2004. At his funeral, Michal Hefer, one of the Zabrze children, eulogized him: "You did rightly, Captain Drucker. You acted out of national responsibility and nobility of spirit. You were our personal Korczak [referring to the legendary child educator Janusz Korczak, who perished in Treblinka], a symbolic and miraculous person."[156]

3 Lithuania and Belarus

Getting Out in Time, Refuge in Forest Lairs

Lithuania

As early as the eighth century, Jews lived in what later constituted Lithuania. A later and much larger influx of Jewish immigrants led to over 100,000 Jews at the start of World War I, when the country was part of the Russian Empire.[1] By then Lithuanian Jewry had achieved a reputation for the high standard of its Talmudic academies. In the late eighteenth century, for instance, Rabbi Eliyah ben Solomon, known as the Vilna Gaon (1720–97), who lived in Vilnius, was considered one of the greatest rabbinical scholars of his period.[2] In 1918 Lithuania was reconstituted as an independent country, but it lost Vilnius in a war with Poland in 1920, and the country's capital was moved to Kaunas-Kovno. The Jewish population counted 155,000.

By 1934 a nationalist trend that reflected throughout Europe led to the rise of antisemitism in the country. When the Russians occupied eastern Poland at the start of World War II, they handed back Vilnius to still-independent Lithuania. The Jewish population in the country consequently rose to between 250,000 and 263,000 (80,000 in Vilna, plus 15,000 Jewish refugees fleeing from German-occupied Poland). Then the Russians occupied Lithuania in June 1940 and made it part of the Soviet Union, in stark opposition to the feelings of most of the country's population. The Soviet occupation lasted a full year, ending with Germany's invasion of the Soviet Union on June 22, 1941. Before that, cadres of Communist Jews—mostly secular with little attachment to Judaism—had assumed significant positions in the Soviet administration. Other Jews, particularly religious Jews and Zionists, were treated harshly by the Soviet-imposed local Communist government. The Soviets also confiscated privately owned businesses, and this affected especially the Jewish population. The teaching of Hebrew was abolished, as were the renowned Talmudic academies.[3]

The following story takes place during the 1939–40 interlude, as the Germans invaded one country after another but spared Lithuania until it too was attacked as part of the Soviet Union on June 22, 1941. Those who had already left were spared one of the worst massacres perpetrated on Jews during the Holocaust, with the active participation of many Lithuanians. Between June 25 and July 8, thousands of Jews from Kovno were rounded up by Lithuanian militiamen under the watchful eyes of the Germans. They were taken to the Seventh Fort, an old military base on the outskirts of the city, and brutally beaten, raped, and then murdered. By the end of 1941, some 180,000 of the country's 230,000 Jews had been massacred by combined German Einsatzgruppen and Lithuanian militiamen. Only 40,000 Jews (those who were able to perform labor) were left, and they were concentrated in four main ghettos: Vilnius-Vilna, Kaunas-Kovno, Šiauliai-Shavli, and Švenčionys-Sventsian.

By the fall of 1943, these ghettos were liquidated and their inhabitants either shot or sent to other camps, where most perished. At the end of the war, no more than 8,000 Jews on Lithuanian soil and in concentration and labor camps survived, 3 percent of the Jewish population under Nazi occupation. Some were in hiding with compassionate non-Jews; others were members of partisan groups. The huge fatality toll is due to the large-scale participation of Lithuanian civilians and militiamen in the murder of Jews.[4]

Zerach Warhaftig

He helped more than 1,000 Jewish refugees emigrate to
Palestine and other places of refuge by a variety of methods
and circuitous routes, mostly via Russia, Japan, and China.

Before the war, Zerach Warhaftig was active in the religious Zionist Mizrahi movement in Poland as vice president of the Palestine office there, the unit that regulated immigration permits to Palestine from Poland. While the British government, leaning to the Arab side, sought ways to reduce and hamper Jewish immigration to Palestine, the Polish government, in its frantic efforts to remove 3 million Jews living in that country, encouraged all steps designed to foster Jewish emigration, including the release of potential immigrants from army service, speeding up the issuance of passports, transportation, and so forth. "All my applications met with a positive response," Warhaftig recalled. "I had ready access to every official when seeking to facilitate the transfer of Jews out of Poland."[5]

The problem, however, arose from the fact that there were very few open venues for the tens of thousands of Jews wishing to leave Poland. The American immigration quota for Poland amounted to a bare 6,524 yearly, and in 1939 it had already filled its quota for the next five years. As for Palestine, the quota for Poles slowed down to a trickle as a result of the British White Paper of 1939. Then came the war, which began with the German attack on Poland on September 1, 1939. Six days later Warhaftig fled with his wife, first on foot, then by horse and wagon, ahead of the swiftly advancing German army, passing through several cities and stopping at Lutsk to observe the Yom Kippur fast. He then continued with his brother to Lwów (today, Lviv) hoping to cross into Romania. But since that border was closed, he switched course and headed north to Vilnius, which had reverted from Polish to Lithuanian control. There, in February 1940, Warhaftig's wife gave birth to their first son.[6]

Large numbers of refugee Jews, estimated at 15,000, had also fled from ravaged Poland to Lithuania—hopefully as a stepping-stone to more distant lands. Twenty-three Talmudic institutions (yeshivot)— 2,336 principals, teachers, and students—managed to slip out of occupied Poland to the relative peace of Lithuania.[7] Public opinion in Vilna was divided. Most hoped for a prolonged and secure stay in Lithuania. Such was the position adopted by the highly secular and socialist Bund leaders as well as their diametrical opponents, the ultrareligious Agudath Israel. Most yeshiva deans, as well as the celebrated Rabbi Haim Ozer Grodzinski and some Zionist leaders, fondly hoped that Lithuania would succeed in maintaining its neutrality and that the Jews there would find a safe haven until the war ended.

Warhaftig, however, sided with the minority opinion—that the country would soon be engulfed in the war and squeezed to political oblivion by its two giant and aggressive neighbors, Nazi Germany and the Soviet Union. Hence no effort was to be spared to try to get as many Jews out of this vise in time through emigration, legal or not. For Warhaftig, emigration meant helping fellow Jews reach Palestine. He especially tried to sway the leaders of the main yeshiva strongholds in that direction, in particular, the Talmudic academies of Ponevezh, Slobodka, Telz, and Mir.[8]

Saving a Yeshiva

Having little faith in neutral Lithuania's survival as an independent nation and fearing for the fate of the yeshivot and their Talmudic students, Warhaftig sought to impress upon them his concern and awaken them to the need for action. As a first step, he urged Jews to acquire passports for themselves immediately so that in the event of an emergency they could make a quick try for a visa for leaving Lithuania. This was still possible for most yeshiva students who had fled from Poland without possessing a Polish passport, as the Lithuanian government still allowed nonexistent Poland to retain a diplomatic office in its country.

For this purpose Warhaftig called on Rabbi Grodzinski, who served as president of the Yeshivot Association (Vaad Hayeshivot). In a conversation lasting several hours, Warhaftig reported trying to impress upon the rabbi the need of the students to acquire a passport. To Grodzinski's objection, Warhaftig spoke up: "But we are sitting on a volcano between Nazi Germany and the Soviet Union, and we need to escape. At the least, to try for them to have passports, to try to get visas." Grodzinski objected: "What do you mean to do with documents and visas, and run around in the streets, as the refugees do, gathering in front of every consulate and every other place? This will mean a great amount of wasted time with doing nothing." A waste of time, he thought, for Talmudic students who needed to be constantly immersed in the study of religious texts.

After further pleadings by Warhaftig, Grodzinski said he was willing to convene the heads of the yeshivot to ask for their opinion on the passports issue. At that meeting, the other yeshiva heads agreed with Grodzinski's estimation that (1) there was no need to panic since every other place was dangerous and, paradoxically, Lithuania might be able to stay out of the storm, and (2) it was not justified to distance the yeshivot from the proximity of nearby Poland, as the war might soon end, and how then could Jewish life in Poland be rehabilitated and sustained without the teaching of Torah voiced by these yeshiva students?[9] Warhaftig's proposals for either leaving for Palestine on British certificates or finding ways to leave by other routes were ultimately rejected.

Still, not dismayed by these rebuttals, Warhaftig decided to seek out the Mir yeshiva head, Rabbi Eliezer Yehuda Finkel, and try to persuade him of the necessity of preparing travel documents and visas for as many students as possible, just in case they might be needed in unforeseen emergency situations. "I strove to transmit to him my grave forebodings and the urgency for action, for procuring travel documents and visas for the entire student body—whatever their immediate use. Rather than relying on miracles, I insisted that we had to go forward to meet the miracle and prepare ourselves for the Almighty's salvation." Rabbi Finkel listened attentively, but wanted to withhold any action until he was assured of obtaining Palestine immigration permits for the entire yeshiva, so as to prevent the dispersion of his students. Warhaftig could not give him such a guarantee, but insisted that this should not delay getting the travel documents.

Finally, after a long and tortuous conversation, the rabbi agreed to Warhaftig's plan; he allotted the necessary travel and other funds.[10] The Mir yeshiva was the only one of its kind that acted as a unit for all its students, and it was the only yeshiva that, thanks to this intervention by Warhaftig, was saved in its entirety just in time. In June 1940 the Russians took over, and the Polish consulate was shut down. There was no longer an office to hand out passports, and without a passport, one could not obtain a visa.[11]

Phantom Curaçao Visas

For those with passports in their hands, or a comparable document in lieu of a passport, the problem now was how to obtain a visa. There were the Palestine certificates, approved by the British. But these were few in number, and it meant passage through Turkey, a country that still refused travel through its territory except for a few isolated cases. "We went from consulate to consulate in Kaunas," Warhaftig recalled. "Although there was no possibility of passage, we thought that if we obtained a visa to a certain country, perhaps later we could obtain a transit visa" to get to our final destination.[12] Then, almost miraculously, Warhaftig learned from two Dutch yeshiva students that the Dutch consul, Jan Zwartendijk, was willing to stamp on passports that the Dutch-held Caribbean island of Curaçao and nearby Surinam could be reached without a visa. However, he left out the additional crucial stipulation that placed these two locations off-limits unless the Dutch governor there gave his prior written approval. Warhaftig inquired whether the Dutch consul would be willing to stamp only the Curaçao no-visa statement on passports, not only to Dutch nationals but to everyone demanding it.

Receiving a positive response from the Dutch consul, Warhaftig realized that the Curaçao visa could be the crack through which escape from
Lithuania would work. But how was one to get to that distant island? "I
looked on the map and saw that the road to Curaçao passes through the
Soviet Union and Japan. One could not travel through the Soviet Union
without first having a Japanese visa. So we went to the Japanese consul together with the map and said to him: 'You see. We have a visa to
Curaçao. We have to get to Curacao via Japan and sail on a Japanese boat.
Give us a transit visa to travel through Japan.'"[13] Disregarding instructions from his superiors, Chiune-Sempo Sugihara, the Japanese consul
general, agreed to issue Japanese transit visas to anyone producing a
Curaçao no-visa statement on his passport or other travel document.
Realizing the miraculous gambit this afforded him, Warhaftig launched
a frantic campaign to publicize news of the Curaçao possibility among
the refugees, and thousands applied for this phantom visa. As the former yeshiva student Nathan Gutwirth wrote to Warhaftig after the war:
"You were the first person to realize the significance of the Curaçao visas:
you were the main driving force and man of action who put the whole
idea into practice and thereby saved thousands of lives."[14] None of the
several thousands who availed themselves of the Curaçao visa bluff ever
made it to that distant island, preferring instead to head to Shanghai and
the Philippines or other temporary safe havens. The Dutch and Japanese
diplomats involved in this scheme, Jan Zwartendijk and Chiune-Sempo
Sugihara, were eventually awarded the Righteous title by Yad Vashem.[15]

While working on the Curaçao scheme Warhaftig, as the officially designated head of the Palestine office, also tried tirelessly to make possible
the exit of Jews who had already obtained British immigration certificates
to Palestine. He himself could have left, as he was afforded safe passage
to Palestine, but he decided to stay on because he felt a personal responsibility to help others leave as well. He would not follow the example of
many of other Jewish community leaders who took flight, leaving the
rank and file to fend for themselves.[16]

Long Road to Palestine

On the eve of the Russian takeover in June 1940, Warhaftig learned that
several hundred certificates earmarked for his Palestine office were sitting at the British consulate in Kaunas. To Warhaftig's request to stamp

the visa on the travel documents held by those confirmed for travel to Palestine, British consul Thomas Preston responded that, after one of the illegal immigrant boats (the *Salvador*) had sunk on its way to Turkey with a considerable loss of life, he had been instructed not to issue visas unless safe passage was ensured through Turkey, even if the Soviet authorities allowed them to travel to the Turkish border. Despite Warhaftig's pleadings, the British consul stood firm in his refusal. Then, without warning, on the morning of June 15, Russian tanks rumbled into Lithuania, and soon thereafter the country was incorporated into the Soviet Union. Under Soviet rule, Polish Jewish refugees in Lithuania were faced with the choice of either acquiring Soviet citizenship or suffering exile in labor settlements deep in the Russian hinterland or, even worse, be forced to return to their homes in German-occupied Poland.[17]

After the initial shock of the Soviet takeover, Warhaftig picked up the pieces of his work, but as a known Zionist activist (forbidden in the Soviet Union) he took care not to show himself in his office. Instead, work was carried out in private apartments, in hotels, or under open skies. As told by him: "We began holding our meeting in the streets or in the municipal garden. I would sit down on a garden bench with [the Russian Communist newspaper] *Izvestia* spread on my lap. Next to me would sit two or three of my colleagues, similarly perusing the paper, and in this manner we would exchange information and plan our activities."[18]

Warhaftig first concentrated on activating the 700–800 immigration certificates that had accumulated at the British consulate earmarked for travel to Palestine. While the British consulate continued to prevaricate, the Soviet authorities ordered all consulates in Kaunas closed by the end of August 1940. Henceforth all arrangements could only be made via the British embassy in Moscow, quite a distance from Kaunas. One morning as Warhaftig was reading the *Izvestia*, searching for a way to break out of the vise, his eyes fell on a rather unobtrusive report about a highway that had been constructed between the Turkish border town of Erzerum and another town on the Russian side of the border. He rushed over to the still functioning British envoy and asked for the British visa. Preston again proved obdurate. "So suddenly I took out the newspaper item and said to him: We don't have to go through the Black Sea. We will go through Turkey by land. There is another route. You see, a new road has been paved. We will go to this place in Russia, and from there continue through Turkey; then proceed to Istanbul, and continue further—but no longer through the Black Sea. I think he knew it was a joke, but since it ostensibly appeared a fine idea, or perhaps he wished to help us, he said, 'Good, it's a good plan. I will give you the visas.'"[19]

Unfortunately, only four days were left before the consulate was to close down permanently. Normally it would issue only twenty to thirty visas a day, for each certificate had to be carefully checked because visas were divided into several categories: young pioneers, relatives, businessmen, rabbis. With Preston's cooperation, Warhaftig summoned his two assistants to help clear up the backlog, and working overtime 200 passports were duly endorsed, signed, and stamped by the consul. There were still some 500 visas to be stamped the day Preston left. He agreed to allow Warhaftig's team to prepare a written confirmation on official stationery, endorsing the fact that entry permits to Palestine were in order for each of the applicants in question. Warhaftig's team then appended the consul's signature after he had already left—"May he forgive the impertinence!"[20]

The upshot? Between 700 and 800 visas or warrants for entry permits for Palestine were processed in those few days and delivered to the passport holders.[21] Warhaftig quipped: "When required, we had our own 'consul' who issued passports, transit visas, and a variety of permits." Justifying this unusual sleight of hand, the religiously minded Warhaftig noted: "It was a matter of life and death, which, according to the Torah, overrides all other considerations."[22] All holders of these fabricated documents arrived safely in Palestine. Paradoxically, none of these Palestine visa holders took the alleged Russian–Turkish land route but received Japanese transit visas, after telling the Japanese consul that one could reach Palestine by sea via Japan.[23]

Having obtained both Japanese and British-Palestine visas, one had to face the Soviet authorities, in command of Lithuania, for a Soviet visa to allow travel to Vladivostok, on the eastern fringe of that vast country, so as to be able to board a Japanese boat there. With the help of third parties, he was able to arrange a meeting with the communist deputy prime minister of Lithuania, Pius Glovacki. Warhaftig argued before him that it was in the best interest of the new Communist regime to let go of Polish Jewish refugees, who were unlikely to find employment in the region. "Why hold onto this foreign element? We ask you only to allow us to pass through your country so that we may eventually reach Palestine."[24]

Glovacki promised to contact Moscow, but in the meantime he asked Warhaftig to submit a list of refugees requesting transit through Russia. This, Warhaftig feared, could be a trap to expel the whole group to labor camps in Siberia. But could one dare return to Glovacki without such a list? After much searing discussion, Warhaftig's group decided to take a chance and submit the requested list, but only names without addresses, as well as his own name and that of his family. The list included some 700 Zionist pioneers and the whole student body of the famed Mir yeshiva. Within a short time, transit visas were granted to all of them. Eventually Turkey relaxed its visa restrictions, and in January 1941 began to allow passage for Jews with legal visas to Palestine. Warhaftig had by then already left for Japan.[25]

Gradually, nearly the entire Mir yeshiva (some 300) left Lithuania between December 1940 and January 1941 on a twelve-day journey to Vladivostok, followed by a two-day voyage to Tsuruga, Japan, and from there to Kobe, and then to Shanghai, China. The Mir yeshiva was the only Talmudic academy to have been rescued in almost its entirety.

A bit earlier, Warhaftig, who as a known Zionist leader was closely watched by the Soviet authorities, was invited to receive his Soviet transit visa on September 20, 1940. He was to cross Russia on October 1, 1940, and leave the country via Vladivostok on the Pacific within fifteen days. His family's passports were duly endorsed, and the tickets were in their hands.[26] However, a short time before leaving, he was returning from the synagogue on a Sabbath morning when his landlady told him that the NKVD, the much-feared Soviet secret police, had been to his flat to deliver a summons. Fearing for the worst (Zionist functionaries were then being arrested), he decided not to return home but instead roamed the streets until the Sabbath was over and then took a detour by traveling directly to Vilna.

Together with his wife, their baby son, and several dozen refugees, he rushed to board a Moscow-bound train, to continue from there on the Moscow–Vladivostok route as planned before the Soviet secret agents had time to figure out his possible whereabouts. An eighteen-day journey through the vast Soviet Union ensued. In Vladivostok, after a six-day wait, the Warhaftigs boarded a Japanese boat sailing to Tsuruga, Japan. Continuing to Kobe, Warhaftig joined the 1,000-member Jewish community there.[27] Warhaftig noted in his memoirs that between July

1940 and the end of May 1941, 4,664 refugees reached or passed through Japan, including 2,166 from Lithuania—rabbis, Talmudic students, and Polish Jewish refugees anxious to get out of war-torn Europe before the avalanche caught up with them. In Japan, the refugees depended for its funds entirely on the U.S.-based Joint Distribution Committee.[28]

To counter Japanese pressure for the Jews to leave, after having overstayed their stay, on February 28, 1941, Warhaftig set out for Shanghai to explore how many Jews could be rerouted to that city, which had already absorbed close to 20,000 European Jews, but since mid-1939, the Japanese who controlled the city had severely limited further Jewish ingress. As an accredited representative of the Palestine-based Jewish Agency, Warhaftig informed the Shanghai Municipal Council, in charge of the International Settlement quarter where the Jewish refugees were housed, that his refugee committee would assume personal responsibility for the upkeep of the incoming Polish refugees from Japan or Russia and for their continued travel expenses to Palestine. Warhaftig immediately drew up three lists, each with 100 names, and consequently the permits were issued without any further delay, which also included people in distant Lithuania who had their travel documents in order. No exact figures are available of how many rushed to leave Lithuania before the German invasion on June 22, 1941. But more than a few lives were surely saved, thanks to the timed intervention by Warhaftig.[29]

Postwar Rescue Attempts

As for himself, Warhaftig was granted an entry visa to the United States as a "political refugee," and he stayed there with his family until the war's end. Soon thereafter, as part of a delegation, Warhaftig left for a four-month tour of Europe, including the former German concentration camps that were converted into refugee displacement camps (DPs). Continuing to Poland and its devastated Jewish communities, he participated in the effort to retrieve Jewish children from non-Jewish hands, at times with the assistance of the aforementioned Yeshayahu Drucker, as both drove to various locations in that desperate effort. An estimated 5,000 Jewish children in Poland survived the war in convents or among Christian families, representing less than 1 percent of the Jewish child population of prewar Poland, and Warhaftig felt that every effort had to be done to ransom these embers of the great conflagration. Years later, in 1952, upon his appointment as deputy minister for religions in the Israeli cabinet, Warhaftig tried to revive the children's rescue campaign. His ministry sent out feelers and collected information, addresses, and any possible leads, but the results proved meager and disappointing.[30]

Earlier, in August 1947, the Warhaftigs (with their now four children) immigrated to Palestine, soon to become Israel. Zerach Warhaftig was nominated a member of the Vaad Leumi Executive, the soon-to-be provisional government of the newborn Jewish state. On the boat taking him to the Promised Land, he was still troubled by pangs of conscience as the images of the Holocaust came to haunt him. He agonized over the question whether greater efforts at rescue could have made a difference and more Jewish lives saved, and whether such opportunities had been overlooked. These pangs were slightly overcome by his role in the saving of over 1,000 Jews. On May 14, 1948, he was privileged to be one of the signatories to Israel's Declaration of Independence.[31] Finally, after a long career as a civic leader, political figure, government minister, lecturer, and author, Zerach Warhaftig died peacefully in 2002 at the ripe old age of ninety-six.

Belarus

Before its annexation by Russia in 1795, the area known today as Belarus was part of Poland. Jewish communities existed there as early as the fourteenth century, and in 1921 it was split in two, with the western part annexed to Poland and the eastern part becoming one of the Soviet Union's republics, Belorussia. On September 17, 1939, the Soviets retook the western part, and then after the German invasion of the USSR on June 22, 1941, all of present-day Belarus fell under direct German control.[32]

On the eve of the German invasion, the Jewish population of the whole of Belarus numbered between 670,000 and 700,000, plus some 65,000 refugees who had escaped from Poland. An estimated 160,000 Jews succeeded in fleeing the German advance to the Soviet interior. This left some 600,000 Jews to face the Germans and their special mobile killing units known as Einsatzgruppen. Thus began the murder of thousands of Jews—usually shot over pits and ravines—that lasted well into 1942. In some places the Germans created temporary ghettos; in other places, Jewish men were sent to compulsory labor and subjected to harsh treatment. The Germans carried out the killings with the assistance of collaborating units, Belorussian auxiliary police as well as Lithuanians and Ukrainians, who also took part in the mayhem.[33]

Before the war Minsk counted 53,686 Jews (40.8 percent of the population). It now became the largest ghetto in the region (in fact, one of the largest of its kind), counting over 100,000 Jews, which included some 35,500 brought over from Germany and the Czech protectorate. Starting November 7, 1941, and into July 1942, the Germans shot 37,000 of the Minsk ghetto, and tens of thousands more were killed at other times, with the final liquidation of the ghetto in October 1943. Some 10,000 Jews nevertheless were able to make their escape to the nearby forests, where partisan activity was widespread.[34] Some local non-Jews tried to save Jews, and as of January 1, 2016, Yad Vashem had honored 618 such Belarusians as Righteous Gentiles.

In light of the widespread German killings, many Jews sought survival in self-contained so-called family camps in some of the vast forests that extend far and wide in the interior of Belarus and included men, women, and children. Understandably, to keep themselves safe from German killing raids, family camps were only possible in heavily forested regions. Thus in the ghetto of Lachva, during a German *Aktion* (killing raid) in September 1942, some 600 men broke out of the ghetto, but only 120 reached the forests; others were murdered along the way by local collaborators. The two largest family camps were in the Naliboki forest: the camp headed by Anatoly-Tuvia Bielski, which counted approximately 1,200 inhabitants, and the camp by Shlomo Zorin, where about 800 people found shelter.[35]

From 1942 through 1944, the Germans conducted large-scale anti-guerrilla operations in the forests, with the participation of thousands of German soldiers, to ensure that no one would escape. According to historian Yitzhak Arad, thousands of Jews from the family camps were murdered during these continuous manhunt raids. The local population was generally hostile toward the family camps, due to the combination of traditional anti-Jewish sentiments and the fact that in order to survive, the forest Jews were compelled to use force in taking food from the peasants. There were also various Polish partisan groups (such as the NSZ) who viewed the Jews in the forests as pro-Soviet elements, and therefore they were open to attacks and elimination. In the southern regions of Belarus, Jewish family camps suffered from attacks by Ukrainian nationalists.[36]

The situation of the Jews in the forests changed a bit for the better, beginning in early 1943 with the arrival of the Russian general Vasily Chernyshev (code-named Platon), who brought order and discipline to the various partisan units. Still, the friction continued. The goal of the Jews in the family camps was not only to fight the Germans but also to rescue the thousands of Jews who had survived the massacres and found refuge in the forest. Priority was therefore given to the rescue of women, children, and other noncombatant elements. On the other hand, Soviet partisans considered fighting the Germans their exclusive aim, and all available manpower, weapons, and equipment had to be devoted to this effort, leaving no room for noncombative family matters.[37]

There are no exact statistics on the number of Jews who survived in the family camps and who found refuge in the Belarus forest lairs. Arad estimates that the number of Jews saved in the family camps did not exceed 10,000. Based on German figures, only 30,000 Jews were left in the whole of Belarus by the end of 1942, about 10 percent of the original Jewish population .[38]

The Bielski Brothers

> Jewish partisans who took in every Jew who asked, some
> 1,200, those who could fight and those who couldn't:
> women, children, the elderly, and the infirm.

During the initial German occupation period, close to 8,000 Jews in Lida (formerly part of Poland) were imprisoned in a ghetto, but on May 7, 1942, the Germans murdered 6,000 Jews next to ready-made grave pits. The rest of the Jewish community was exterminated on September 18, 1943, with the exception of a small group who earlier, in May 1943, had escaped from the Lida ghetto and wandered into the nearby forest. As they continued their aimless wandering, suddenly they saw armed men coming toward them. They were Jewish partisans led by Tuvia Bielski and his brothers, Asael, Zus, and Aharon (Arczyk), who were followed by others, about fourteen altogether. The ghetto escapees noticed tears in Tuvia's eyes as he addressed them: "*Chaverim* (comrades), this is the most beautiful day of my life because I lived to see such a big group come out of the ghetto! I don't promise you anything; we may be killed while we try to live. But we will do all we can to save more lives. This is our way, we don't select, and we don't eliminate the old, the children, and the women. Life is difficult, we are in danger all the time, but if we perish, if we die, we die like human beings."[39] This was something unheard of in partisan parlance. Only the young and able-bodied were generally admitted into partisan units, and sometimes they too were required to come with weapons in hand, or else they were sent away. In Tuvia's partisans there was to be no selection based on sex, age, health, and fighting qualifications. Every Jew was admitted. Tuvia and his brothers had committed themselves to save as many Jews as possible, without distinction, while simultaneously fighting the Germans in outings from the partisan forest lairs.

Another runaway ghetto resident related: "The man walking toward us was tall, graceful, with a smile that seduced all of us. The warmth and the way he received us was touching. . . . Tuvia was like a magnet that pulled us toward him. I had a feeling that with him I was totally secure, that danger could not reach me, and that around him all will be well. . . . We called him Yehuda HaMaccabee."[40] Still another arrival: "When we came we saw the camp; men, women, children, all without yellow patches, smiling . . . something I had not seen in the ghetto. . . . Tears of joy ran down my cheeks. People surrounded us, friends and family members hugged and kissed, they cried."[41]

Earlier, on July 1, 1941, the three Bielski brothers happened to be in their native village of Stankiewicze when they witnessed the entry of the German army, a week after the start of the German invasion of the Soviet Union. The Bielski family included the parents, David and Beila, ten sons, and two daughters. Two sons had left for America before the war. Drafted into the Polish army, son Tuvia had obtained the military know-how that years later would prove valuable when he became a partisan fighter. When the Germans invaded, he was married to Sonia. Presently, feeling threatened, Tuvia and Zus returned to their respective homes in Lida and Nowogródek, where they saw themselves conscripted with other Jews for some forced labor assignment. The two brothers made their escape at night. When the Bielski brothers learned that they were sought by the authorities, they fled in separate directions. Tuvia and Zus worked as farmhands in return for food and lodging, constantly moving from one place to another, while Asael worked as a mason.

In October 1941, the Bielski younger brothers Avremale and Jacob were shot trying to run away from prison in Nowogródek, while their thirteen-year-old brother, Aharon-Arczyk, witnessed the arrest of his parents from his hiding place in a barn in Nowogródek. The Bielski parents were shot on December 7, 1941, during a German execution of thousands of Jews that also claimed Tuvia's first wife, Rifka, and Zus's wife, Cyrl, and their baby daughter.[42] In the meantime Tuvia and Asael managed to acquire a pistol and submachine gun from two Belorussian peasants, and they decided to head to the forests, where they eventually formed an all-Jewish partisan unit.[43]

Essie Shor, a newcomer to Tuvia's group, related how she joined up with the Bielskis, to whom she was related. On a cold, snowy December night (probably in 1941), sixteen-year-old Essie with three other companions sneaked out of the Nowogródek ghetto and walked 15 miles in total darkness. A partisan met them on the way, and with his help they finally reached a clearing deep in the woods. She wrote: "I discerned people sitting around an open fire shielded by the trees. They were singing hopeful songs of freedom in low voices. The blurry figures stepped forward out from the fog, and I recognized my cousins Tuvia, Asael, and Zus. We hugged each other tightly." Essie was proud to join that first group of twenty-five members that became the kernel of the Bielski Partisan Brigade. It ultimately grew to over 1,000 Jews over a period of nearly three years. "I am so proud that I was among the original members," she said.[44]

To offset the high number of older people, they decided to encourage young people from the still existing Nowogródek ghetto to join them. With the assistance of a Belorussian peasant who acted as a guide, Tuvia led a group of seven young men out of the ghetto to a forest lair, increasing their size to thirty. It was now time to organize the group into a fighting detachment, known as *otriad* in Russian, with Tuvia as commander and brothers Asael and Zus as his closest aides. Tuvia had a commander's bearing and knew how to give orders. As told by a former partisan, he also knew how to be a diplomat. He would simply tell them, "If you want to live, follow me and do as I say. . . . If you stay with me, you must obey me." Essie remembered him as a handsome man with dark curly hair and keen, thoughtful eyes. He stood tall and erect and was bold and courageous. When he spoke, people listened, and when he gave a command, people obeyed. He was charismatic, and in her eyes he had the noble bearing of a biblical hero.[45]

In the winter of 1943, the Bielski group counted over 200 people; only a few who joined came with weapons. A local farmer named Gramov gave them some rifles.[46] They sometimes had to raid the homes of local farmers and force them at gunpoint to hand over food. There was no other alternative if the people in the forest were not to starve. At the same time, care was taken not to leave the farmers bereft of food for their own sustenance.[47]

Tuvia's people had also to be on the lookout for other partisan groups, known to be antisemitic. For instance, during the summer of 1942, Tuvia learned that a Russian partisan unit led by Victor Panchenko had decided to do away with the Bielski camp, charging it with robbing local peasants. In a tense meeting with Panchenko, Tuvia defended his actions: "We are not robbers. It is in the interest of our homeland to fight the German enemy together. Our homeland does not differentiate between Jews and non-Jews." The two visited one of the farmers who complained that the Bielski group took from him all the bread he had. As Victor was about to draw his gun to shoot Tuvia, he detected from the peasant's words that he was lying, and he held back. This led to a territorial division between the two partisan groups of the farms in the Lida and Nowogródek regions from which they would continue to fetch food. The Bielskis also punished anyone who betrayed Jews to the Germans. Some were eliminated with a sign posted on the door with the Bielski signature in Russian: "This family was annihilated because it cooperated with the Germans and pursued Jews."[48]

Saving Jews over Killing Germans

It should be pointed out that in the Bielski *otriad*, those who bore arms enjoyed a higher prestige; the nonfighters were derisively nicknamed *malbush* (probably meaning someone only interested in being clothed). But Tuvia kept reminding his men: "Don't rush to fight and die. So few of us are left. . . . To save a Jew is much more important than to kill Germans." He at times made it clear that it was better to save one Jew than to kill twenty Germans. He never strayed from this position, in spite of the seemingly increasing danger to his people, many of whom objected that the presence of too many children, women, and unarmed men would jeopardize everyone else. In the words of a former partisan, Tuvia "devoted his soul, his brains, and everything else to the rescue of Jews. He was grateful that he could save Jews. For him it was a privilege."

As further underlined by a former Bielski forest fighter, "Heroism was to save a child, a woman, a human being. To keep Jews in the forest for two years and save them, this was heroism."[49]

In a debate between Tuvia Bielski and the Jewish partisan Baruch Levin on what should be given first priority—struggle against the Germans or the defense of the family camps—Bielski reportedly said: "I would like you to know one thing. Since so few of us are left, it is important for me that Jews should remain alive. I see this as the essence of the matter."[50]

Still there was no letup on attacks on German military convoys. In the period 1942 to 1944, armed combatants within the Bielski camp bombed 19 bridges, blew up 800 meters of railroad tracks, damaged other German facilities, and killed 261 German and collaborating police officers. Tuvia divided his group into units of twenty to twenty-five people, with each unit balanced to include armed men as well as noncombatant older people, women, and children, so that in times of emergency, everyone could be swiftly moved. Each unit was self-sufficient as much as possible—its own space, cooking, and other functions.[51] Bunkers, known as *ziemlanka*, were constructed, with two-thirds underground, and one-third above ground, and covered with sheets of bark, leaves, and other materials that kept the bunker warm and well camouflaged. A properly built *ziemlanka* could hold up to forty people. *Ziemlankas* became their homes, their sleeping quarters, and places of refuge. Ultimately, twenty were built, dug deep into the ground, with low log walls resting on the surrounding forest floor and a wooden ladder leading down to the packed earth below. Branches were strewn across the simple log roofs, effectively hiding the bunkers from view. "We slept on wooden planks," Essie Shor recalled, "one alongside the next, with our heads to the wall and our feet to the wide aisle that ran down the center of the rectangular structure. . . . We slept on mattresses made of straw under blankets taken from nearby farmers. I went to sleep to the sound of twenty-four people breathing, snoring, and gossiping in low voices."[52]

One *ziemlanka* was transformed into a bakery. A partisan named Oppenheim, a locksmith, was kept busy fixing guns, while another man was repairing horseshoes. A special bunker served as a hospital. Some runaway Jews were accommodated while they passed through the Bielski camp, and then they proceeded to link up with other partisan groups, such as in the nearby Lipiczanska forest. Tuvia Bielski did not insist that they stay, and he noted sadly that many of them were killed by collaborating armed men. Tuvia would send out special scouts to find fugitive Jews on the run; persons who were hiding alone or in small groups in the forest would be invited to come over to his partisan unit. One of these lone wanderers, Abraham Viner, related: "I arrived in torn clothes without shoes. I had rags around my feet. . . . People around us said, 'Here we have more '*malbushim*.' They were annoyed. But Asael's and Tuvia's attitude was very warm. Tuvia turned to me with: 'You will live in our place.' This made a deep impression and stayed with me all the time. What did I think? I thought that I had met the Messiah." Others who left to link up with other partisans were told that they would always be welcomed back—an unheard of thing among partisan units those days.[53]

On the Run

When, in December 1942, news reached of a German raiding party approaching, the Bielski camp hurriedly packed up and moved in the middle of night to a nearby forest close to the town of Iwje. In another close call, informed that the Germans were about to liquidate that ghetto, Tuvia decided to save the Jews from there, and many made their escape to the Bielski camp, now ensconced in the Zabielowo forest. From there they had to flee again, this time a distance of 15 kilometers, to Boczkowicze, where they improvised primitive tents. With his then 300 men, the next move in April 1943 was to Stara Huta, then to the Jasinowo forest. In mid-1943, expecting a German attack, Tuvia moved his people again—to the Naliboki forest, an area with many marshes and swamps and with poorly built roads. His *otriad* now numbered some 700, as more and more people joined them.[54]

Then came the most frightening phase for the Bielski group, as well as other partisan units, when in August 1943 the Germans launched a big drive to clean out the partisans from their forest lairs. People began to panic as Tuvia and his brothers tried to restore order, going so far as to threaten to shoot panic mongers. Tuvia accepted the advice of two of his men who urged him to head to a certain island deep inside a big swamp area, where one could hide and wait for the Germans to depart.[55] To reach that wetland island, they could carry their weapons and food but would have to abandon their horses and cows. People were told to fill their pockets with nonperishable food, such as bread, grains, beans, and all kinds of groceries. Children were carried on the shoulders of adults.

As they entered the swamp region, the mud began to thicken and stick to the marchers' feet. In some spots the mud reached their navels. It was a slow march, covering a mile per hour. Reaching a dry spot, they sat down to rest and catch some sleep. Suddenly they were awakened by shots. Bullets flew over their heads. They could distinguish Germans shouting: "Hurrah, catch the Jews! Catch! Catch! Catch!" Tuvia roused his people for a quick escape into even deeper muddy terrain. To avoid getting lost, the marchers attached themselves to each other with belts or ropes, desperately holding on to passing bushes and trees, so as not to drown when wading through marshes. As Tuvia had correctly calculated, the Germans did not follow them there.[56]

Back in the Nowogródek ghetto, many of the 500 Jews remaining decided to make a run to the forest and join the Bielski camp. They planned the breakout for April 15, 1943, but someone betrayed them to the Germans, who proceeded to shoot many on that day, reducing the ghetto population to less than 300. These survivors planned another escape by the digging of a tunnel. It was set for September 26, and some 100 to 150 succeeded in fleeing, and most reached the Bielski camp. The following March, 95 Jewish workers in a labor camp in the Baranowicze region also made their escape, and most were admitted into the Bielski *otriad*—a welcome addition, as most of these newcomers were skilled craftsmen.[57]

More Shtetl than Base Camp

Toward the end of 1943, Tuvia's camp returned to its original base in the Naliboki forest. With the winter of 1943–44 approaching, and the Germans having given up on large-scale operations to destroy the partisan forest nests, it was time to prepare more solid bunkers. Rectangular foundations were dug, two-thirds deep in the ground, and lined with tree trunks that were wired together, with moss filled in between, and the roof camouflaged with tree branches. Wooden bunks along both sides of the walls served as beds for up to forty people. A stove in the middle, fetched from a demolished home, provided heat.

The compound also contained workshops for gun repair, tailoring, shoe repairs, and a smithy. Tailors were patching up clothes, and seamstresses with sewing machines were kept busy sewing shirts from locally woven linen. People came to order boots and have their shoes mended. A tannery supplied the shoemakers with leather, from which saddles and harnesses for the horses and belts for partisans were made. The Bielski camp also included a watch repair shop, and carpenters created wooden parts for weapons. Blacksmiths in the smithy attended to the horses and repaired wagon wheels. There was a sausage factory, a flour mill to bake bread, and even a barber shop, so everyone could look presentable even under those harsh conditions.[58] There was a clinic, served by a physician, a dentist, nurses, and a fenced-in area holding cows and horses.[59]

Soon the Bielski group resembled a *shtetl*, a small Jewish town. People were always busy. Partisans from other units often came over to have things repaired. There was a musical trio—with a guitar, a violin, and a mandolin—and a cultural club to discuss literature, philosophy, and social issues, with a historian lecturing on current events. A professional *shochet* (kosher ritual slaughterer) was allowed to kill animals in the traditional way. Everyone was fed three times a day. In the words of a female member: "Tuvia always worried if people had enough to eat. He would come where they were distributing food and look on if people had adequate food."[60]

Those who wanted to be excused from working on the Sabbath were usually permitted to do so. For Passover 1944, matzah was baked and made available to all requesting. As told by one participant: "We had a Seder with children asking the traditional questions. Instead of talking about the departure from Egypt, we spoke about our departures from the ghettos."[61] In fact, during that period, the Bielski camp with its now 1,200 people even took time to arrange a wedding, with the forest, in Essie Shor's words, serving as the covering *chuppah*. But the illusion of normal life never lasted. Suddenly it would all come back in full force— the war, the Nazis, antisemitic farmers and partisans, and the need to be suddenly on the run again.[62]

Only one-quarter of those in the Bielski *otriad* were armed with weapons and sent on various combat missions; the other three-quarters were mostly older people, women, and children.[63] When the Russian overall regional commander Vasily "Platon" Chernyshev came for an inspection tour and asked the meaning of several older Jews who happened to be immersed in prayer, he was told by Tuvia in a feigned serious mien: "They are studying the fourth chapter of the history of the Communist movement [written by Stalin]," to the smiling satisfaction of the Russian commander.[64] Tuvia persevered until the end in his policy of unconditional acceptance of every Jew, whether capable of fighting or not. Tuvia would say: "I want to be surrounded by thousands of Jews!" He was especially eager to save children, particularly orphans, and a woman was assigned to look after them. People in Tuvia's *otriad* accused of serious crimes, such as collaboration with the enemy, were severely dealt with, but not always without compassion. As often repeated by Tuvia: "I don't like to kill Jews." For severe offenses, a person usually would be expelled from the group.[65]

After Disbanding, Overlooked and Ignored

On June 23, 1944, the Red Army opened its great summer offensive that led it within a month to the final ousting of all German forces from Soviet territory and their advancement into prewar eastern Poland. At the Bielski camp, one could hear the echoes of the approaching artillery shells. Some of his men encountered retreating Germans, and in close combat most of these soldiers were shot; so were eleven Jews. Soon thereafter, the first Red Army soldiers arrived at the Bielski camp, and the following month Tuvia was ordered to evacuate the forest base and lead his people into Nowogródek. Some 1,200 made this 2-kilometer trek, of which some 70 percent were women, the elderly, and children.[66] On the way they passed a village and could hear the peasants murmuring among themselves, "So many Jews! So many Jews!" Before entering Nowogródek, the Bielski partisans celebrated with a last official parade, then disbanded.

According to one estimate, fifty people died in the Bielski group, including four who were condemned to death, one suicide, and one accidental death. In addition, forty-nine died in combat with the enemy. This represents an attrition rate of less than 5 percent, when compared with the figure of one-third to half of Jewish fatalities among other Jewish partisans.[67] That is quite an achievement for a partisan group that included over half noncombatant members! According to historian Nechama Tec, the Bielski brothers' saga is the single most massive rescue operation of Jews by Jews, having probably in mind those operating out of forest lairs.[68]

Soon after liberation, Tuvia Bielski faced a new danger, this time from the direction of the NKVD, the Soviet secret police, as several former partisans denounced him on various trumped-up charges. Together with their wives, Tuvia and Zus escaped to Romania, then headed to Palestine, and after a stint in the Israeli army, they left for the United States.[69] There, in New York, Tuvia joined his older and well-to-do brother, Chaim Velvel, who had emigrated to America before the war. Tuvia operated a moving truck and struggled for the rest of his life to make ends meet. Mostly forgotten, disillusioned, and overlooked by the Jewish community, while other Jewish partisans (all combat persons) were hailed and celebrated, Tuvia Bielski, who with his brothers saved 1,200 mostly noncombative Jews, died in 1987 at age eighty-one. His brother Zus died in 1995.[70]

Shalom-Simcha Zorin

> He formed his own Jewish-based fighting unit, which
> eventually grew to 800 participants, defending itself against
> attacks by the Germans and local collaborating militia

Shalom-Simcha Zorin was a Jewish Soviet partisan commander in the Minsk region, which included 800 Jews and was active in the Lipiczany forest. Before that, Zorin was interned with other Jews in the Minsk ghetto, where he was assigned work at a nearby Russian prisoner of war camp and there befriended a captured Soviet officer named Semyon Ganzenko. In late 1941 Zorin and Ganzenko fled to the forests in the Staroe Selo region, about 19 miles southwest of Minsk, and established their own partisan unit, named Parkhomenko, consisting of 150 members, including many Jews. As more escaping Jews joined this unit, conflicts arose between the Jewish and non-Jewish fighters, leading Zorin to split off and create his own Jewish-based fighting unit called "Unit 106" but better known as the Zorin unit, which eventually grew to 800 participants. Defending itself against attacks by the Germans and local collaborating militia, the unit moved its base into the Naliboki forest. The command of Zorin's unit was shared by Zorin and two associate commanders, Chaim Feigelson and Anatoly Wertheim. By July 1943 the Zorin detachment included 45 men of fighting capability and 270 women, elderly, and children. A year later, the numbers had risen to 137 fighting men and 270 others.[71]

From his forest lair, Zorin maintained contact with the Minsk Ghetto through some teenagers who helped Jews to escape and reach the forest. When more Jews realized that the ghetto was slated for full liquidation, they too attempted to flee into nearby forests in the hope of joining up with some partisans. But at times they ran into wild and undisciplined bands of partisans who robbed them and in some instances even murdered them. Even when Jews encountered organized and disciplined Soviet partisan units, they were not allowed to join them, as many of these new arrivals came accompanied by women, children, and old people who were of little combat use. At one point, Zorin went to speak about this with General "Platon," the supreme Soviet partisan leader in his area. Zorin suggested that a family camp of noncombative Jews be established, an idea to which "Platon" surprisingly agreed.

Zorin admitted all who came to him, counting some 100 fighters but also many noncombatants as well, such as artisans who created workshops in the forest: a sewing workshop, a shoemaker's workshop, a flour mill, a bakery, a sausage factory, a weapons repair shop, and a large hospital with doctors from Minsk. The camp also claimed an improvised school that served 70 students and a school for adults, and the camp inhabitants celebrated both Soviet and Jewish holidays. Deep in the forest refuge, there were medical facilities for orthopedic, gynecological, and internal medicine treatments that served the entire partisan force in the area.[72] Zorin's camp also included a warehouse for building bombs—understandably, a primitive facility, but whose bombs functioned well. An improvised school took care of about seventy children, and Jewish holidays were celebrated as much as possible.

A Minsk native and a carpenter by trade, Zorin was a simple man with no formal education, but he had strong leadership qualities. He felt that as a Jew, in these trying times for the Jewish people, all his energy had to be focused on saving fellow Jews and combating the Germans. Some units of saboteurs placed explosives on the train tracks and in the train stations. Taking part in such sabotage operations also entailed confiscating ammunition from slain German soldiers. In a confrontation with retreating Germans, in July 1944, on the eve of liberation by the advancing Red Army, Zorin sustained leg wounds and lost seven of his men. In 1971 Shalom-Simcha Zorin immigrated to Israel, where he died in 1974.[73]

Daniel Rufeisen

He used his special position in a German police
station to pass on vital information to his fellow Jews
in the ghetto and steal weapons for them.

On November 27, 1941, Oswald Rufeisen arrived in German-occupied Mir holding forged papers that identified him as a Pole as well as an ethnic German. Thanks to his command of the German language, he was employed as a translator for the commander of the Belarus regional police, Semion Serafinowicz. He was also assistant to the commandant of the security police and gendarmerie in Mir, the German Reinhold Hein, who dressed Rufesein in the uniform of a Belorussian policeman. The two police chiefs failed to detect that this new recruit was a Jew.

He was born in 1922 in Zadziele, Poland, and during his youth Oswald Rufeisen belonged to Akiba, a religious Zionist youth movement. In the early war years he fled from place to place, finally arriving in Mir. Aided by his fluent Polish and German, he passed himself off as an ethnic German.[74] In the meantime, in May 1942 the 800 Jews remaining in Mir had been herded into a makeshift ghetto in the ramshackle mansion of a former Polish noble.

One day a Jewish electrician from the ghetto, Dov Reznik, was sent to the Mir police station to fix an electrical problem, and he recognized Rufeisen from their days in a Zionist pioneering organization in Vilnius. Another Mir ghetto resident, Shlomo Charchas, also ran into Rufeisen: "I was walking to work with my friend Laizer Breslin. Coming toward us was the commandant of the Mir gendarmerie, accompanied by a Belarusian policeman. The commandant was leading the policeman in a friendly manner, with their arms tucked one under the other. I recognized the policeman as Rufeisen. He also recognized me. He broke away from the commandant, held back for a moment as if he were fixing his shoe, and when the commandant moved on a few steps he whispered to me, 'Shlomo, I will come to you today.'"[75]

Rufeisen made use of his job and special position in the German police station to pass on vital information to his fellow Jews in the ghetto. He warned them of planned attacks by the police and also stole weapons for the ghetto underground. In his words, "In Meister [Superior] Hein's room was a locked cupboard full of arms—rifles, pistols, and hand grenades. Each time I took one of them and placed it among the plants in the garden, and when evening fell I brought it to Yisrael Reznik at the ghetto gates. In this way I handed over twelve rifles." Leibel Itzkowicz, a member of the underground who worked in the German stables in Mir, would come to the police headquarters every day after work, and when he left, his bag was full of rounds of bullets covered with a small amount of food.[76]

One day Rufeisen overheard Hein speaking on the telephone with an ss officer in nearby Baranowicze on a planned liquidation of the Mir ghetto on August 13, 1942. Hein cautioned Rufeisen, "It's a secret, and nobody but you knows about it." On August 6 Rufeisen slipped over to the ghetto in the large mansion where the remaining Jews were kept and told Dov Reznik the bitter news. Rufeisen advised the underground to give up on their hopeless dream of battle, which would only end in the slaughter of all the remaining Jews of Mir. Instead he urged them to escape to the nearby forest and join the partisans. On the day of the escape, Rufeisen promised that he would distract the German and Belarus collaborator forces by leading them out of Mir and in the opposite direction of those fleeing the ghetto.

The members of the underground then broke the secret to Rabbi Schulman, the Judenrat head, that Rufeisen was actually a Jew and would cooperate in their escape. The ghetto people were not sure whether to trust Rufeisen, who after all worked as a Belorussian policeman inside the German police station. During a stormy special gathering, Rabbi Schulman declared that those wishing to escape should not be prevented from doing so, but as for himself, he would stay put. Members of the underground and the youth in the ghetto decided to flee, with many leaving their elderly family members behind.[77] And so, on the night of August 9, some 200 Jews made their escape, including all 80 members of the underground. As Rufeisen foretold, that night the policemen were busy on a false chase after "partisans" in the opposite direction of the escapees, leaving only four policemen behind at the Mir police headquarters.

The following day the policemen discovered that the Jews had fled. None of them yet connected the escape to Rufeisen. However, later, in a confrontation with Hein, who was told by a Jewish informant that Rufeisen was not an ethnic German as he claimed but a Pole, Rufeisen not only confessed his actions in favor of Jews but actually revealed to the startled German that he was a Jew. Hein thereupon ordered him jailed, but Rufeisen ingeniously managed to make his escape and hid for a year in a monastery close to the police headquarters in Mir.[78]

"A Jew of the Catholic Religion"
During his year in the convent of the Sisters of the Resurrection, Rufeisen immersed himself in the Christian literature he found there. In December 1943 he left the monastery and joined the partisans operating in the

Naliboki forest. His stay in the monastery had a profound impact on him, and after the war he decided to convert to Catholicism and become a monk in the Carmelite Monastery in Kraków. The Polish provincial of the Order suggested that Rufeisen take the name Daniel, because "he had been like Daniel in the lions' den and survived." He took his priestly vows in 1949 at the age of twenty-seven.

A few years later he applied to the Polish government for permission to leave for permanent residence in Israel, explaining it was "on the ground of my belonging to the Jewish people, which I have continued to do although I embraced the Catholic faith . . . and joined a monastic order. . . . I chose an order [Carmelite] which has a chapter in Israel, having regard to the fact that I would receive leave from my superiors to travel to the land for which I have yearned since my childhood when I was a member of the Zionist Youth Organization."[79] He arrived in Israel in July 1959 and moved into the Haifa Carmelite Stella Maris Monastery, where he introduced himself to the other startled monks as "a Jew of the Catholic religion."

In the 1950s Rufeisen applied for Israeli citizenship under the Law of Return, which grants Jews automatic Israeli citizenship. He claimed that although he was not a religious Jew, he identified with his Jewish ancestry and the Zionist aspirations of the Jewish people, and hence he continued to consider himself a Jew—an attachment that he never severed. When the Israeli Interior Ministry denied Rufeisen's request, he appealed to the Supreme Court of Israel, which upheld the government's decision, claiming that any Jew who in full conscience converted to another religion and went on to choose a ministerial role in that religion had severed ties with his Judaism. He eventually acquired Israeli citizenship through the process of naturalization. In the 1980s, as a licensed tourist guide, he guided groups of Christian tourists to holy sites in Israel as well as Yad Vashem, where I met him on several occasions. I remember him as a kindly and soft-spoken man. He died in 1998.[80] I felt that whatever one's position with regard to his conversion, when he helped the Jews in the Mir ghetto to escape, he did that as a Jewish rescuer and should be regarded as such.

4 Slovakia

Negotiating to Stop Deportations

Until 1918 Slovakia was part of Hungary, and in the interwar years it was part of the Czechoslovak republic. Some 70 percent of the Slovak population was Roman Catholic, and the rest were of other Christian denominations as well as Jewish. In 1930, 136,000 Jews lived in Slovakia.[1] On October 6, 1938, when Slovakia declared itself an autonomous region within the still existing Czecho-Slovak state (no longer called Czechoslovakia as one word), it was forced to cede some of its southern portions to Hungary. Later, in the so-called Vienna accord of March 14, 1939, stage-managed by Hitler, when Slovakia declared its independence, it was forced to cede to Hungary the eastern Carpathian Ruthenia region. Both these two regions contained between 30,000 and 40,000 Jews who now passed under Hungarian control, including the cities of Košice-Kassa, Uzhorod-Ungvár, and Mukacheve-Munkács, which held a sizable Jewish population. Some 89,000 Jews remained in independent Slovakia.[2]

The president of the newborn country, now closely tied to Nazi Germany, was Jozef Tiso, a Catholic priest, and the two other principal leaders at his side were Prime Minister Vojtech Tuka and Minister of the Interior Alexander (Sano) Mach, who also seconded as head of the Fascist militia, the Hlinka Guards, which was patterned after the German ss and sa.[3] The country with a population of 2,600,000, headed by a priest, prided itself as a stalwart Catholic bastion, but this did not prevent it from siding with Hitler in all respects, including the harsh treatment of its Jewish population, two-thirds of whom were followers of the Orthodox wing of Judaism.[4]

In August 1940 ss officer Dieter Wisliceny was dispatched to Slovakia as an "adviser" to the Slovak government on Jewish affairs.[5] But the Slovaks needed no prodding from their German overlords to start harassing the Jews, as the regime encouraged street attacks, the looting of property, and the forced removal of Jews holding Hungarian citizenship to the no-man's-land between Slovakia and Hungary. And this was followed by systematic anti-Jewish legislation. On September 26, 1940, a Nazi-modeled Judenrat, the *Ústredňa Židov* (Jewish Center), or UZ, was created as the sole authority representing Jews of Slovakia, to replace all separate Jewish organizations and institutions. It was first headed by Heinrich Schwarz and then in April 1941 by Arpad Sebestyen, a former principal of an Orthodox high school. The creation of the UZ was followed on September 9, 1941, by a series of anti-Jewish laws, known as the Jewish Code, which included the obligation of wearing a six-pointed yellow star and the expropriation of Jewish property, with non-Jewish trustees appointed to run large Jewish enterprises.[6]

A Central Economic Office, known as UHU, was created to oust Jews from participation in any commerce and oversee the confiscation of Jewish property; 10,025 Jewish businesses were consequently liquidated, and 2,233 were transferred to non-Jewish hands. In addition, Jews were forced to hand in their stocks and shares, as well as personal valuables such as jewels, furs, and even textiles.[7] Additional humiliations included prohibition from possession or use of private telephones and from admittance to public parks, entertainment places, and public washing places, as well as restrictive shopping hours. Dr. Anton Vašek, head of Section 14 of the Slovak Ministry of Interior, was made responsible for enforcing anti-Jewish legislation enacted by his superior, the violently antisemitic interior minister, Dr. Alexander Mach.[8]

In addition, persons aged sixteen to sixty were obliged to perform work in labor camps, the most notable being Sered, Vyhne, and Novaky. Facilities in these camps included about 130 workshops, producing textiles, furniture, toys, and chemical products for the country.[9] December 1941 saw the expulsion of 7,600 Jews from the country's capital, Bratislava, more than half of the Jewish population of 15,000 there.[10] Then things got even worse.

When in January 1942 Germany demanded from Slovakia 20,000 workers to be employed in various German economic enterprises, the Slovak leadership suggested sending over Jews instead. At first demurring, but later realizing that the Jews could help build up and expand the Auschwitz concentration camp, the Germans agreed to take 20,000 young Jews and, after at first hesitating, also agreed to include their families. The Slovaks added that they wished to be rid of all its Jews, not merely

20,000. The German side again vacillated, mainly for logistical reasons, but then accepted the Slovak offer, but on the condition that the Slovaks pay 500 German Marks for every Jew handed over to them. The Slovak regime acceded to this request but attached one of its own requests— that the Jews thus delivered should never be sent back to their former homes, thus hoping to "kill two birds with one stone," getting rid of the Jews and looting their still-remaining property.[11]

Deportations began on March 26, 1942, with ss "adviser" Wisliceny in charge of coordinating the transports with the Slovak regime. Deportations continued in the following seven months, netting close to 58,000 persons, and were stopped in late September 1942, for reasons to be further explained.[12] To avoid deportation, 7,000 to 8,000 or more fled to nearby Hungary, where Jews were still relatively safe. Slovakia, a nation headed by a Catholic priest, had the dubious distinction of being the only country in Europe that not only initiated but actually beseeched and appealed to Nazi Germany to rid it of its Jews and even paid it for this favor.[13]

Within the Jewish orthodox camp, one of the more radical leaders was Rabbi Shmuel David Ungar, head of a reputable yeshiva in Nitra, while Rabbi Abraham-Abba (Armin) Frieder represented the traditional Jeshurun community. Upon learning of the deportation decree, both Orthodox and traditional rabbis submitted a written appeal to Tiso, begging him as a priest and a human being to stay the deportation decree, but to no avail.[14] The Slovak bishops had already shown their true colors when in September 1941 they refused to take a stand against the antisemitic Jewish Code and in April 1942 repeated the traditional accusation of deicide, adding that the Jews were a malicious and harmful people. Jews desperate to save themselves believed that conversion to Christianity would exempt them from deportation, and an estimated 6,000 persons tried that course. The Slovak regime, however, attached no importance to these conversions after March 14, 1939, the date of Slovakia's independence.[15]

The Working Group

The real Jewish governing council, made up of Jews of all persuasions, had a singular goal: to aid and rescue their brethren.

Something happened on the Jewish front in Slovakia that had no counterpart in any other European country allied to Nazi Germany. Side by side with the government-appointed UZ Judenrat, a special confidential group was formed in the summer of 1941 that became known as the Working Group (*Pracovná skupina*), or the Parallel Government, or, in the words of Rabbi Michael Dov-Ber Weissmandl, one of its members, the Hidden Committee (*Havaad Hamistater*). It eventually came to overshadow the UZ as the true and effective representative Jewish governing council.

The Working Group (hereafter, WG) leadership spanned a wide spectrum—ultraorthodox, assimilationists, and Zionists.[16] The ultraorthodox Rabbi Weissmandl, who joined in early 1942, at first strongly criticized the secular composition of the WG in a country where most Jews were Orthodox. But in consideration of the overriding interest of saving the Jews, he quieted the protests of his fellow Orthodox: "This is not the time for schisms and arguments," he countered. He even stood fast in opposition with the revered Rabbi Ungar, his father-in-law and mentor, who upbraided him for collaborating with nonpracticing Jews.[17]

Gisi Fleischmann was the acknowledged leader of the WG. A mother of two and a cousin of Rabbi Ungar, she was in charge of the emigration department in the UZ. She also headed WIZO, the Women's Zionist Organization, and the Bratislava branch of HICEM (a merger of three Jewish migration associations, principally with HIAS), an organization that dealt with immigration other than to Palestine. She was the local representative of the U.S.-based Joint Distribution Committee (JDC or simply Joint).[18] The WG established secret contacts with Jewish organizations in Switzerland and Hungary and maintained a secret channel with the friendly Slovak minister of education and culture, Dr. Jozef Sivák, to keep abreast of new antisemitic measures contemplated by the government.[19]

The WG tried to keep in touch with the deported Jews and succeeded in sending parcels to those in the Lublin, Poland, region. It hired couriers who reported that many of the deportees had been removed to somewhere "beyond the Bug" River and ominously were never heard from again. In a letter penned on August 27, 1942, Fleischmann warned: "The information that the couriers brought last week had no precedent in history. I hardly believe we shall see any of our comrades again."[20] This was further underlined in a letter of December 1, 1942, by Weissmandl and Frieder to Saly Mayer, the JDC representative in Switzerland, one of the earliest documents on the organized killings.[21]

Attempts to Stop Deportations

The year 1943 was marked by several attempts by the Slovak regime to renew the deportations that had ceased the previous October, and these were foiled by a combination of circumstances, including pressures from within the Jewish community and foreign sources.[22] In this effort the WG managed, through third parties in Budapest, to contact Catholic Sister Margit Slachta, alerting her to the Slovak government's nefarious plan. She reportedly informed Vatican nuncio Angelo Rotta in Budapest, who then passed it on to his superiors in the Vatican. Slachta, moreover, took it upon herself to speak with the U.S. cardinal Francis Spellman, who happened to be on a visit to the Vatican in March 1943. Also, the Vatican apostolic delegate in Istanbul, Angelo Roncalli (future Pope John XXIII), cabled the Vatican to intercede to prevent the planned renewed deportation. The result of these interventions led the Slovak regime in March 1943 to shelve plans for further deportations.[23]

On April 21, 1944, Alfred Wetzler and Rudolf Vrba (a.k.a. Walter Rosenberg) made their legendary escape from Auschwitz camp and arrived in Žilina three days later. Oskar Krasniansky (later Karmi, in Israel), also of the WG, was dispatched to Žilina to interview the two escapees. He sat with them for two days and wrote down their detailed report, known henceforth as the Auschwitz Protocols, which included maps of the camp and roads leading to it. The report was translated into several languages, with one copy handed to Dr. Rudolf-Rezső Kasztner, one of the leaders of the Budapest-based Zionist Aid and Rescue Committee, when he visited Bratislava.[24] Copies also circulated to the Vatican nuncio Giuseppe Burzio, who transmitted it to the Vatican. Other copies made their way secretly to Switzerland.[25] Following the German invasion of Hungary on March 19, 1944, Jews fleeing from Poland via Slovakia to Hungary had now reversed course—not to Poland, but back to Slovakia, which now, due to the stoppage of deportations, appeared a haven against deportations.[26]

However, the Slovak revolt in September 1944 led to the direct intervention of German forces in Slovakia, and this put a damper on further rescue efforts.[27] The WG had now a more important item on its agenda: its own survival and that of the remaining Jewish community.[28] Deportation of Slovak Jews resumed in late 1944. Fleischmann offered valuable merchandise to SS officer Alois Brunner in exchange for allowing 7,000 Jews to leave for Switzerland, but this effort failed.[29]

On September 28, 1944, the Germans staged a big raid on the remaining Jews in Bratislava, capturing close to 1,900, including Oskar Neumann and Rabbi Frieder, who were then hauled to Sered labor camp. On September 30, the first renewed transport to Auschwitz left with 1,860 persons. This was followed by the deportation of others, for a total of up to 13,000 Jews deported mostly to Auschwitz. Between 4,000 and 5,000 managed to save themselves by going into hiding with compassionate non-Jews or in isolated mountainous forest lairs.[30] Soviet forces finally liberated the whole of Slovakia in early April 1945. Some 10,000 of the deported Jews survived, but most, together with the hidden Jews, later left the country.[31]

Rabbi Michael Dov-Ber Weissmandl

He attempted what was considered unthinkable: bribing Nazis to end deportations of Jews to concentration camps.

Rabbi Michael Dov-Ber Weissmandl (sometimes spelled Weissmandel) remains, by all accounts, one of the most extraordinary, controversial, and tragic Jewish figures in the history of the Holocaust. He was born in 1903 in Debrecen, Hungary, and his family later moved to Trnava, Slovakia. At the age of seventeen, Weissmandl was already recognized for his Talmudic erudition when he published three short volumes of novellae (Talmudic interpretations) he had heard from his teacher. He also became an expert at deciphering ancient manuscripts, for which purpose he journeyed three times to Oxford. In 1937 he married Bracha Rachel, the daughter of his mentor, Rabbi Shmuel David Ungar, and was ordained a rabbi.[32] Soon thereafter, he launched his first rescue activity.

On April 19, 1938, a month after the Nazi takeover of Austria, some of a group of sixty rabbis from the Burgenland region, bordering Hungary, known as the Seven Communities (*Sheva Kehillos*), were placed on a boat and sent down the Danube River, while others were dumped into no-man's-land between Hungary and Czechoslovakia, but the Czech authorities refused to let them in. Rabbi Weissmandl wrote to his Nitra yeshiva colleague, Rabbi Solomon Schonfeld, in London and asked for his intervention with highly placed Englishmen, and as a result, the archbishop of Canterbury, Gordon Lang, helped obtain British visas for them.[33]

On April 6, 1939, Weissmandl arrived in England on another rescue mission. He had a list of 200 families from Nitra he wanted to send to Canada. With British help, including the intervention of the archbishop of Oxford, Dr. William Temple, he obtained Canadian approval of this plan. The Canadian officials, however, conditioned their consent provided that the people were farmers. Weissmandl thereupon telegraphed back to Slovakia, urging the prospective immigrants to speedily take a course in agriculture. Unfortunately, when the Canadian delegate arrived to examine the future immigrants, what was left of Czecho-Slovakia (earlier known as Czechoslovakia) fell apart, and Slovakia gained full independence, with German blessing, and the Canadian proposition fell through.[34]

Negotiations with Wisliceny

In 1942, with news from secret paid emissaries on the fate of the deported Jews from Slovakia, Weissmandl and Fleischmann, both senior WG members, sent confidential messages to Jewish organizations in Switzerland, alerting them to the killing of the deportees by the Germans.[35] As the UZ proved unable to stop the deportations, the WG activists, driven to despair, began to explore other rescue possibilities. At this critical juncture, Weissmandl learned that Dr. Anton Vašek, director of Section 14 in the Interior Ministry, who was responsible for implementing the deportations, was rumored to be open to bribery, as was Dieter Wisliceny, the SS "Jewish advisor" dispatched to Slovakia.[36] Weissmandl then asked UZ member Aaron Grünhut to arrange a meeting with the Jewish Karl Hochberg, who had been installed by Wisliceny in the UZ as a stool pigeon and was charged with preparing lists of deportees.

When the two met, Weissmandl decided to gamble on a totally new tactic—to negotiate with the Nazis. He presented himself to Hochberg as a person with connections to high-powered Jews representing the Nazi-propagated "World Jewry," which included the Joint, an organization that the Nazis believed was part of the secret Protocols-of-the-Elders-of-Zion type Jewish network controlling the affairs of the Western powers from behind the scenes through the power of money. He also told Hochberg that he was in touch with nonexistent Ferdinand Roth, representing that conspiratorial Jewish government and stationed in Switzerland, who had been sent to explore the possibility of saving Slovakian Jewry by offering a ransom payment and wanted to know what Hochberg thought the price for this would be. Weissmandl came prepared with forged letters supposedly written by this fictitious Roth from a first-class hotel in Switzerland. In fact, Weissmandl had obtained an old English typewriter and, with the help of stationery and envelopes printed with the Swiss hotel's logo, had written letters to himself with a purported Roth signature, which he produced, and asked Hochberg to show to Wisliceny.

Hochberg evidently swallowed the bait and, falling for Weissmandl's contrived stratagem, went to see Wisliceny. He returned on June 16 or 17, 1942, in great excitement, with the news that Wisliceny had agreed to the proposal and was prepared to stop the deportations in return for only $50,000! Wisliceny reportedly had told Hochberg: "You have a swine's luck. [ss officer] Eichmann agrees."[37] Wisliceny's conditions were as follows: (1) first of all, as a good sign gesture, the three transports scheduled soon to leave with 3,000 persons were to be suspended without any prepayments. (2) Then on the coming second Friday, the first installment of $25,000 was to be remitted; (3) to be followed by a continuous seven-week cessation of deportations; and (4) the remaining $25,000 was to be paid at the end of this period. Also, adding a sarcastic note, Wisliceny suggested that the Jews ask the Slovak authorities, who also needed to be bribed, to stop begging the Germans to resume the deportations.[38]

Weissmandl and his colleagues in the WG could not believe their ears at the news that an ss officer responsible for the deportations of tens of thousands of Jews agreed to such a plan, and this caused them to be gripped by a euphoric sense of hope. It seemed to them that the ransom gamble had paid off and that the sword of Damocles hanging over the remaining 24,000 Jews of the country had been removed. But there remained one problem: where to find even this paltry sum, especially the first installment? After some difficulties, Weissmandl received the first $25,000 from Solomon Stern, a wealthy Orthodox businessman in Slovakia. The bank notes were steam ironed to give the impression that they were newly issued and had come from an overseas bank, and then given to Hochberg for delivery to Wisliceny in the name of the fictitious Ferdinand Roth. This first payment stopped the deportations for seven weeks, from August 1 to September 18, 1942.[39]

The problem then arose with the second installment, the additional $25,000. To stay Wisliceny's hands, Weissmandl forged a letter in Ferdinand Roth's name, saying that the messenger who was to have brought the money to Slovakia had broken his leg and was in the hospital, and this caused a slight postponement of the second payment. When Wisliceny agreed to a short grace period, Weissmandl, still without the additional $25,000, forged another Roth letter announcing that the messenger's convalescence was taking a bit longer than expected and that he needed approximately two more weeks. Wisliceny again agreed to a further postponement.[40] In the meantime, WG head Gisi Fleischmann, in a private message to Saly Mayer, the Swiss representative of the JDC, pleaded for $100,000 for bribes of all sorts, to start with an immediate $21,000, evidently for Wisliceny's second installment. Mayer's response on August 28 was disappointing: only $5,000 was immediately available and another $5,000, later in September.[41] In desperation Weissmandl wrote to Switzerland, asking that tens of thousands of dollars be sent immediately by the quickest possible route because it was a life-or-death situation. He followed this up with two urgent letters to Josef Blum, the Joint representative in Budapest, and to Gyula Link, of the Orthodox community there. Weissmandl pleaded: "Please do not delay even a minute doing this good deed which, in my opinion, takes precedence over the Shabbat and Yom Kippur."[42] On the eve of Yom Kippur, he also sent messengers in Rabbi Ungar's name, without the latter's knowledge, to the head of the Orthodox community in relatively peaceful Budapest, promising that the Joint would refund him the money.

But the money did not arrive on time, and Wisliceny, furious at what he perceived was an intentional Jewish delaying tactic, ordered the resumption of deportation a day after Yom Kippur with a complement of 3,000 more victims.[43] Two more transports were scheduled to leave, but on the morrow of Yom Kippur, a day after the second transport had left, Weissmandl had obtained the money from his Hungarian sources. When Hochberg, who handed Wisliceny the money, asked that the transport be stopped before reaching its horrific destination, Wisliceny refused and shot back: "That is the way of you pitiful Jews! Until I pushed you against the wall, there was no money. You thought you could stall us with excuses about the messenger's broken leg and such like excuses. . . . From now on, observe the agreement and so will we."[44] No further transports took place for two full years, other than an October 10 transport of mentally ill persons, and Rabbi Weissmandl was convinced that the $50,000 bribe was to be credited for this.[45] In other words, in his mind, bribe money had been the strongest weapon to dissuade the Nazis from continuing the deportations, and consequently more deportations, not limited to Slovakia, might be aborted for larger and more astronomical sums of money. He remained convinced of this to the end of his life.[46]

Some writers and historians, such as Abraham Fuchs and David Kranzler, accept Weissmandl's assessment of the power of ransom payments.[47] On the other hand, historian Gila Fatran wrote that part of the reason for the deportation stoppage may have had to do with the lack of information on the fate of the deportees that began to trouble the Slovak government, now under pressure from the Vatican, as well as the growing disapproval of the deportations by the churches. Thus she questioned Weissmandl's assertion that the payment is what caused the stoppage of the deportations.[48] Yehuda Bauer concurred that, based on the available data, the cessation of the deportations from late July until September 18 had nothing to do with bribing Wisliceny but for other reasons, including the Vatican intervention.[49]

It should be noted that in late July 1942, Slovak prime minister Tuka began to pester Wisliceny with requests to allow a Slovak delegation to visit the deportees in their supposed workplace, so as to dispel the rumors of massacres. To relieve this pressure, Adolf Eichmann had the editor of a local Nazi paper write a false report. The Nazi leadership decided—so goes the argument by some historians—that due to the mounting pressure from both the Slovak government and the Vatican (and not necessarily the $50,000 bribe received), it became "diplomatically correct" for the time being to postpone further deportations from Slovakia, and instead continued deportations from other European countries.

Bauer adds another interesting observation—that this paltry bribe may have served ss chief Heinrich Himmler, who agreed to this arrangement, as a vehicle for possible negotiations with "World Jewry," represented by the Joint, for high political stakes, an opinion not dismissed by Weissmandl.[50] Perhaps through linkage with the fictitious Ferdinand Roth, the German side would establish contact with the mysterious World Jewry conspiratorial government so as to break up the three-power military alliance at war with Nazi Germany.[51] We may never know what really transpired in Himmler's mind, but insofar as Weissmandl was concerned, the cessation of the deportation of Slovak Jews spawned a more audacious plan: a gambit to try to save all of Europe's Jews.

Convinced that the ransom payment stopped the deportations, Rabbi Weissmandl decided that the time had come for him to try something on a vaster scale: the possibility of stopping the Holocaust everywhere dead in its tracks through the same tactic—bribery. This became known as the Europa Plan, and it was meant to stop all deportations heading to Polish concentration camps and stop the killings themselves. When he suggested this to his colleagues in the WG, most thought it far-fetched— with the exception of a few, including Gisi Fleischmann. Ultimately all came around to give it a try.[52]

For this purpose, Weissmandl decided on a repeat of the forged letter tactic from the fictitious Ferdinand Roth, written on a Swiss luxury hotel stationery where the "representative of World Jewry" was supposedly staying. Weissmandl then typed a letter by Roth addressed to himself, in coded conspiratorial language, suggesting a monetary deal in return for some grandiose agreement benefiting both parties. Sometime in late October 1942, Hochberg turned the letter over to Wisliceny, who was truly impressed, seeing in it an indication that "World Jewry" was coming to its senses and was changing its policy vis-à-vis Germany. On this occasion Wisliceny hinted that Germany expected that "World Jewry," which the Nazis claimed had pushed the major powers into a war, would presently change its tactics and influence the Western Allies to sign a peace treaty with Germany.

A few days later, Wisliceny summoned Hochberg and told him that, in principle, his superiors were willing to open negotiations with World Jewry and asked how much they were willing to pay in return for stopping the Holocaust. This was followed by a feverish exchange of letters between the WG and representatives of Jewish organizations in Switzerland and Turkey. The JDC representative in Switzerland, Saly Mayer, basically responded that any sort of payment to Nazi Germany was contrary to Allied laws of not trading with an enemy country. To this Weissmandl countered that only bribes could ensure that deportations would cease. As to U.S. foreign-currency laws, Weissmandl suggested that the Joint keep the money in the account of a trustworthy person in Switzerland (probably a certain Meshullam Lebowitz) to be held there until after the war. After consulting with SS head Himmler in November 1942, Wisliceny reported that the SS was interested in starting negotiations, evidently in their quest to know the actual strength of what they termed World Jewry.[53] Andrej Steiner of the WG was told to suggest to Wisliceny that in return for an initial payment of $150,000, a first children's transport was to be diverted to Switzerland. After that they would discuss additional payments and releases.

In his letter to Swiss Jewish organizations, Weissmandl hinted that the negotiations for stopping the deportations throughout Europe had been cleared by "the head man in charge of the Jewish questions [i.e., Eichmann]" and that person's superior, "the official of the evil man [i.e., Himmler]." The Germans, according to Weissmandl, wished that a special representative of the JDC (Joint) would come to Slovakia or that a representative of the WG would travel to Switzerland to jump-start the negotiations. Added to this was a particularly enticing message, that deportations would stop fifteen days after the conclusion of an agreement, with the exception of deportations from Germany and the Czech provinces.[54] Weissmandl ended his letter with a renewed emotional appeal for the procurement of money for the expected ransom payment:

> We adjure you! Give this matter the consideration fitting for the matter of life and death of thousands, for the salvation of a single individual from expulsions is his salvation from certain death. . . . There is a power that can save and that power is money. . . . Money is nothing compared to life. . . . Thousands upon thousands are throwing themselves at your feet and pleading and begging you: 'Please save us from this bitter death! We do not have the money that can save—you do!' Please do not stand by the blood of your brothers and sisters among who are old men and women, pregnant women and infants. . . . Their eyes are lifted onto you to save them from this great evil."[55]

In a separate letter, on December 23, 1942, addressed to Nathan Schwalb of the Zionist Hechalutz office in Geneva, Weissmandl mixed rage and accusation with pleading:

> We cannot understand how you can eat and drink, how you can rest in your beds, how you can stroll in the streets—and I am sure you are doing all those things—while this responsibility rests upon

you. We have been crying out for months, and you have done nothing. . . . We demand deeds! Not great deeds and not acts of sacrifice. Just money—and thousands and hundreds of thousands depend on that money.[56]

In the meantime, Wisliceny seemed not to be in a hurry for a response, for he suddenly headed to Greece, where he helped Alois Brunner of the SS with the roundup and deportation of Jews in Thessaloniki (Salonika). He reappeared in Bratislava on approximately May 10, 1943, and happily announced that his superiors had sanctioned the Holocaust stoppage plan. Initially the sum of $2 to $3 million was mentioned by Wisliceny to Andrej Steiner of the WG. Weissmandl immediately wrote to Switzerland and reported that in return for this money, the Germans would cease deportations throughout continental Europe, including the possibility that exterminations would also cease in Poland, saving the lives of approximately 1 million Jews. As in previous communications, he peppered his words with accusations "against the heads and leaders of the Jewish people who, by the grace of the Almighty, are not able—even with the imagination of a crazed lunatic—to imagine what is being done to the Jews in these bloody lands."[57]

The JDC, through its European office in Lisbon, headed by Joseph Schwartz, was suspicious, believing it to be nothing but an extortion trick, and told its Swiss-based representative, Saly Mayer, not to deliver any money for this purpose.[58] Mayer decided instead on another ploy: the promise of a monthly allocation of 120,000 Swiss Francs to the WG, most of which, however, would be in a blocked account, only to be paid off after the war (a so-called *après*—"after" scheme). Then, in March 1943, Wisliceny after further consultations with his superiors, and presumably with Himmler's consent, decided to press home the point of payments by asking for a $200,000 down payment on a grand $2 million sum. Again Mayer hedged, willing to guarantee only $100,000 on the après scheme. Fleischmann kept pressuring Mayer to be more forthcoming, but with no results. Receiving no definite answer, she asked Wisliceny for a postponement of the payment until July 1. He agreed, while at the same time excluding Belgium and Holland from the deportation cessation. But the $2 million, he added graciously, could be extended and paid in fourteen installments.[59]

On June 18, 1943, Mayer wrote again to Fleischmann that he might keep $200,000 frozen in the United States, on the condition that Poland be included in the agreement and that all killing of Jews by the Germans should cease. Fleischmann wrote back in frustration: "The unique event in history will have taken place, that there was a possibility to save the lives of doomed people, and that this chance was passed by."[60] Mayer was skeptical: he felt that the Wisliceny offer was a mere bluff, since the deportations of Jews had continued throughout the negotiations.[61]

Weissmandl repeated the contents of the deal with Wisliceny in a May 31, 1943, letter to Switzerland, namely, all transports to Poland would be suspended until June 10, followed by the cancellation of all deportations in return for $2 to $3 million, to be paid in installments—the first one $150,000 by June 10. Upon receipt of this initial sum, expulsions would be suspended until August 10, during which time negotiations between the parties would decide on the schedule of further payments. The killings in Poland, however, would necessitate separate negotiations and a separate schedule of payments.[62] Weissmandl warned that if payment was not received by June, deportations from all countries under their control would continue. Therefore, immediate action was required, and Weissmandl again pleaded unashamedly:

> We beg you with tear-filled eyes. You only have one obligation—to raise money and money and money. Please do all you can and more. . . . All we are asking from you is that you give this money to save at least those who remain in Poland and those remaining who are to be taken there. If these letters had souls, that is what they would say to you, but they have no souls, and this pitiful writer does not have the strength to write, because his ideas are confused and his eyes are dark from tears.[63]

As no money was forthcoming on the stated deadline, Wisliceny again extended the time limit to July 1, but no money was on hand even then, all the additional pleadings by Fleischmann to Mayer notwithstanding. Negotiations were then discontinued, and finally the whole plan was scrapped on September 3, 1943, with Wisliceny claiming that the Jewish leaders had foregone an opportunity to save their brethren, a charge with which Weissmandl sadly agreed.[64] The people in the WG were stunned by the Nazi retreat from the Europa Plan. They had been taken in by Wisliceny's smooth talk and gentlemanly affectations. Weissmandl, Fleischmann, and Steiner remained convinced that the plan would have worked had the money been sent. A historical opportunity had been missed, so they felt.[65]

The question debated by historians, and still not settled, is whether millions of lives could really have been saved by what for Germany was a negligible amount of money compared with the huge expenses of the war. Were Fleischmann and Weissmandl "credulous" and "gullible" in this fantastic belief? On the other hand, is it possible that Wisliceny and Himmler may have speculated on the payment as merely a stepping-stone for something more grandiose for Nazi Germany—as a ploy to reach some sort of accord with what they believed was a Jewish inspired anti-German alliance? Let us not forget that after the stupendous German defeat at Stalingrad, it was clear to most sober Nazi observers that Germany might not win the war and most likely would lose it. Himmler seems to have approved of Wisliceny's talks with the WG heads and to have watched them with interest. So it is just possible that had Fleischmann and Weissmandl been given more room to bargain, the outcome of the Europa Plan talks might have been very different. "Alas, we shall never know," lamented one observer.[66]

Livia Rotkirchen is one of the historians who believes that the Europa Plan was doomed from the start. While acknowledging Weissmandl's courage, Rothkirchen sharpens her critique of the man and labels the description of events in his book *Min Hametsar* (From the depths) as redundant and lacking in coherence; his belief in Wisliceny's sincerity as "naïve assumptions," his faith in the ransom scheme as the only means to stop the Holocaust as unrealistic and delusional.[67]

Yehuda Bauer also questions Weissmandl's position, though somewhat less sharply than Rotkirchen. He states that it is clear that Himmler originally sanctioned the talks, but later forbade any further discussions. As for his motives? Not money, since even $2 to $3 million was a comparatively pitiful sum, and the earlier $50,000 was an even more ridiculous amount. In Bauer's estimation, some in the WG were misled into thinking that the Holocaust could be prevented, crippled, or at least restricted by bribing the SS.[68]

However, other factors may have gone into the SS thinking, such as Himmler's estimation by late 1942 that Germany could lose the war and that to avoid a catastrophic outcome for the country, negotiations needed to be secretly opened with the Western powers (principally the United

States) through their Nazi-imagined Jewish overlords. What then stopped Himmler from going through with the negotiations? Bauer writes that it was due to one of Himmler's character flaws. He was in the habit of prevaricating, swinging from one position to another, and never able to make up his mind, especially in this case, since it meant working behind Hitler's back, an unimaginable sin for the head of the ss. In the meantime, the Final Solution was to continue.[69] Unwilling to forego dealing with Jewish representatives, the fainthearted Himmler sought to protect himself against a possible charge of treason in an indirect manner. As he noted in a December 12, 1942, memorandum: "I have asked the Führer about the releasing [Loslösung] of Jews against hard currency. He had authorized me to approve such cases, provided they bring in genuinely substantial sums from abroad."[70] This gave him the green light, but only for a short-term negotiations with Jewish representatives—not for any Nazi radical shift on the Jewish question.[71]

As for Weissmandl, he was nobody's fool, and he did not place his full trust in Nazi promises. It is possible that he did not feel, despite his letters to the contrary, that money alone would save the Jews of Europe, but it could be an opening to other designs. The indications are that he vacillated. As he wrote in one of his dispatches, "We must accept premise No. 1, in theory and practice—that their intentions are honest in this matter. . . . Premise No. 2: . . . All this is a plot, a maneuver, a gesture of camouflage which they have undertaken to win our confidence, to undermine our already meager and paltry power to resist them. . . . Though we must operate on the basis of premise No. 1 in our posture and money, we must also in theory and practice confront premise No. 2."[72] Also, as he wrote in the summer of 1944, the Germans may have felt that by releasing multitudes of Jews, their compatriots within the Allied countries (whom the Nazis believed were at the Jews' beck and call) would cause the Allies to refrain from bombing the roads on which the Jews would be traveling to distant safe borders. Finally, according to Weissmandl, "Perhaps a faction within the ss hopes through this negotiation to make amends, in order to save themselves [in postwar trials], and therefore wishes to annul all the deportations."[73]

It remains an open question whether Weissmandl's gamble to stem the Holocaust would have paid off, had he possessed a greater authority and the funds to go along with it. Writing in 1991, Yehuda Bauer praised these efforts: "For once, a group of Jewish activists representing all factions in a divided Jewish community—from assimilationists through Neologs [religious conservatives though not Orthodox] and Zionists of all hues to the ultraorthodox leaders—united to rescue Jews outside their community or their country."[74] Ten years later, in 2001, Bauer reiterated this point. "What is amazing in this story is that the underground leadership of a remnant of a Jewish community in a satellite state should have tried to rescue not just itself but all the Jews in Nazi-occupied Europe in a daring plan of ransom negotiations with the murderers," through a Jewish organization led by a female activist and her principal confederate, an ultraorthodox Talmudic-trained rabbi.[75]

The Hungarian Phase

With the Germans in full control of Hungary, following their invasion of that country on March 19, 1944, they planned to facilitate the quickest roundup of the 800,000 Jews in that country before the arrival of the Red Army. Thus the importance of calming the fears of the Jews in order to avoid what the Germans feared: a repetition of a Warsaw ghetto uprising. With that in mind, ss officer Dieter Wisliceny had Weissmandl prepare a letter of recommendation addressed to Philip-Fülöp (Pinchas) de Freudiger, head of the Orthodox community in Budapest, with the soothing words that Wisliceny was a trustworthy person whose word could be relied on in possible negotiations. However, never the fool, Weissmandl then dictated a second and secret letter to Freudiger, delivered by special courier, in which he warned him that if the Germans began by concentrating the Jews into ghettos, it could only lead to one thing—deportation to Auschwitz. If such were the case, the Jews should refuse to go, refuse to board trains, "for the start of murder starts with entering the ghetto," but instead try to escape from the ghettos, even if half of them were to be killed in the attempt; but the other half would survive. It was better than boarding the trains—where no one would survive.[76] However, the advice was disregarded, for reasons still debated by historians.[77]

Back in Slovakia, Weissmandl was obsessed with one goal: mapping the route where the trains from Hungary were passing on their way to Auschwitz and giving the information to the Allies, coupled with a request to bomb the railway tracks and thereby paralyze the movement of victims to the gas chambers. He pinpointed the exact train route: the border crossing between Kassa-Košice and Prešov, and the tunnel through which the trains were bound to pass. At first Weissmandl thought of having some of his yeshiva lads engaged in these acts of sabotage, but he was persuaded that the Germans and their Slovak lackeys would surely retaliate against the remaining Slovak Jews, who were momentarily safe and sound.

On May 16, 1944, one day after the actual start of the large-scale deportations of Hungarian Jewry, Weissmandl drafted one of his most impassioned appeals for help.[78] He gave a mathematical computation of the number of trains scheduled to pass daily on their way to Auschwitz, as well as the estimated number of persons in each train and in each boxcar. He detailed the route as originating in Csap (near Ungvár-Uzhhorod) and continuing through Kassa and Prešov to the Polish frontier. Also included was information on Auschwitz, with sketches and maps of the gas chambers and guard towers as they would appear to pilots flying overhead.[79] One is amazed at the precise information that he had carefully assessed and now divulged to outside sources. He specified that "starting from yesterday, 12,000 Jewish souls—will be taken daily to be choked, to be burned, and to be manure for the fields." Then addressing his fellow Jews and non-Jews living in peace and security, he charged,

And you, brother Jews! And you, ministers of state in all countries! How can you keep quiet at this murder in which up till now some six million Jews [actually somewhat less] have already been murdered and even now tens of thousands more are being killed every day?! . . . The murdered Jews cry out to you: "You are cruel! You are murderers, because of your cruel silence and because you do nothing! Surely, you can do something to object and stop it—now!" Therefore, in the name of the blood of the millions and the tears of the millions, we beg you, we plead with you, we claim and demand of you: do something immediately![80]

Never in the annals of the Holocaust has a more impassioned plea been uttered by anyone.[81] What else, practically speaking, could be done to stop the trains from running? According to Weissmandl, there were several practical steps: first warn the Germans and Hungarians of retributions; continue by asking the pope to warn Hungary not to collaborate with the Germans in this fiendish act; alert the world press and radio services to publicize what is happening in the camps; ask the Red Cross to visit the extermination camps immediately, and if this is rejected, Germany must be expelled from that organization. Most important—and here's the punch line—bomb the gas chambers and furnaces in Auschwitz, bomb the roads and railway tracks leading to the extermination camps from Hungary to Poland and from Hungary to Germany, especially the routes from Csap, Kassa-Košice, Prešov, and Medzilaborce, and bomb the railway stations and bridges along the routes. These were also used for German troop transports between Poland and Romania, Weissmandl pointed out, should the Allies be hesitant to divert planes simply to save Jews (as indeed they were, it actually turned out).[82] He could not have spelled it out more clearly. He could not understand why his appeal was not accepted by the world at large. It seemed to him that neither the Jewish leaders nor the rest of the world really cared. As he exclaimed in a July 10, 1944, letter: "A sane man must go mad, and he who has not gone mad cannot be sane."[83]

Half a year later, when the Germans, now masters of Slovakia, renewed the deportations, Weissmandl reportedly went to see the Vatican nuncio Giuseppe Burzio to plead for his help to save the lives of the remaining Jews who were about to be transported to the death camps. Weissmandl wrote of the shocking response he received: "'First of all, today is Sunday, and on Sunday we do not deal with profane matters,' said the nuncio. I could not believe my ears. . . . Could it be possible that he doesn't know about Auschwitz? 'Your Eminence,' I said, 'we are all going to be slaughtered; is the blood of thousands of innocent children a 'profane matter'? . . . I cried before him. I cried very much."

According to Weissmandl, the nuncio said: "There is no such thing as blood of innocent Jewish children—all Jewish blood is guilty [for the sin of the Crucifixion, of deicide], and the Jews must die because that is their punishment for that sin. . . . As to you, I shall call the Gestapo immediately to arrest you." Weissmandl immediately turned and fled. This account is quite shocking and difficult to comprehend in light of Burzio's previous attempts to stem the deportations of Jews, in direct confrontation with Slovak leaders.[84]

Escaping and Hiding

In October 1944, while imprisoned in Sered camp, Weissmandl tried his hand again at negotiating with the rabidly antisemitic ss officer Alois Brunner for the release of Jewish internees, but the lengthy discussion led nowhere. He was then included in the transport to Auschwitz that left on October 10, 1944, together with his wife and five children. As the train sped to its gruesome destination, Weissmandl managed to loosen an iron bar with a small saw that he had carefully hidden inside a loaf of bread, and was able to cut open a little slit, space enough to squeeze through. When the train slowed down as it turned a curve, it was time to jump. According for Siegmund Forst, who talked with him after the war, Weissmandl begged his wife to jump with him with the children, but she was resigned to her fate and declined, so he jumped alone.

No one really knows for sure what prompted him to do so during that terrible ride. According to one account, it was at the urging of others on that wagon, so that he might still do some good for others not yet deported. He must have undergone a terribly painful ordeal, knowing the horrors of Auschwitz that his wife and children were about to face. After the war, he almost went insane with grief. He could not forgive himself, and the thought haunted him for the rest of his life, despite the fact that he later remarried and fathered more children.[85]

After jumping, Weissmandl wandered through the woods and entered a village where a compassionate woman offered him a piece of bread, which the starved rabbi gobbled down. One of the village girls took a message from him to a certain Natali, a printer by profession. Natali came to fetch him and took him to a bunker located in a storage room in the yard next to a home belonging to Janku Provaznik, who worked for the Railway Police in Bratislava and lived in a private home in a hilly suburb. Arriving there surreptitiously, he was introduced to seventeen other Jews in hiding, including the Hasidic rabbi Menachem Mendel Halberstam, known as the Rebbe of Stropkov. Due to the cramped conditions, people in the bunker had to remain in a sitting position, and Provaznik and his family supplied the group with milk and food. While in hiding, Weissmandl studied the Talmud from two volumes that he found there, which he intermingled with frequent pangs of depression for having failed to abort the deportation of Slovak Jews, including his own family.[86]

In a totally bizarre setting, Rudolf-Rezső Kasztner from Budapest visited the hiding group on several occasions in the company, on one such visit, of ss officer Max Grüson, to the consternation of the bunker's inhabitants. Kasztner's intention was meritorious: to explore the possibility of extricating the hidden group safely with the assistance of ss officers, at a time when these ss men were in desperate need of alibis to avert their condemnation for war crimes in postwar trials that loomed on the horizon.[87] Then came the final visit by Kasztner, in April 1945, in the closing days of the Third Reich, again accompanied by an ss officer, this time a man named Schmidt, and with a truck that was to take the whole group to safety across the Swiss border. In this surreal scene, the truck was driven by an ss officer and accompanied by a number of German soldiers.[88] Once on safe ground, Weissmandl suffered a massive heart attack, the beginning of a series of health problems.[89]

Postwar

Siegmund Forst, in his interview with Claude Lanzmann, related that when he met Weissmandl again after the war in New York, Weissmandl was a broken man. He was then staying in the Williamsburg section of Brooklyn in a small room in a friend's home. "He was lying in bed all day, and hammering with his fist on the wall. He was crying and screaming. . . . Like a man in a fever, not coherently, in a compulsion." Forst sat with him often, listening to the harrowing details of the Holocaust in Slovakia. Forst was taken aback as Weissmandl shouted at him: "What were you doing while we were there? . . . He was shaking his fist at me. . . . Very slowly he came to himself. He was not insane; he was emotionally deeply upset. He accused the whole world, me, and everybody" for not sending the money that he felt could have saved many more Jews.[90]

Then, in November 1946, together with his brother-in-law, Rabbi Shalom Moshe Ungar, Weissmandl reestablished the Nitra Yeshiva in Somerville, New Jersey, gathering surviving students from the original yeshiva. In 1949 he moved his yeshiva to Mount Kisco, 40 miles north of New York City, where he established a self-sustaining agricultural community known as the Yeshiva Farm Settlement. Weissmandl designed the community's yeshiva to conform with Talmudic descriptions of agricultural settlements, where a man would study Torah continuously until an age suitable for marriage (without any input of secular studies), whereupon he would farm during the day and study in the evenings.[91] While this novel approach was not fully realized, the yeshiva flourished and is still in existence.[92] He also married a rabbi's daughter, Leah Teitelbaum, who bore him six children. In 1957, stricken with a renewed outbreak of chronic heart disease, he was hospitalized and died at age fifty-four.[93]

In the words of David Kranzler, Weissmandl was the foremost Jewish proponent at the time to apply on a grand scale the age-old Jewish command of *pidyon shevuyim*, the ransoming of Jewish captives.[94] His first, and one may add only, priority was to save lives at any price and by whatever means, but particularly through ransom money, as it had often worked in the past. It was not that money possessed some mysterious intrinsic value; its importance was only as a tool to save lives.[95]

Gisi Fleischmann

> She headed the clandestine Working Group, organizing
> parcels, medicines, and money for Jewish deportees in
> Poland and securing money with which to bribe officials.

An equally important member of the Working Group was Gisi Fleischmann. Although of an Orthodox background and related to Rabbi Ungar of Nitra, Fleischmann, born in 1892, differed from the intense anti-Zionism of her Orthodox relatives. In fact, she was quite the opposite: she was intensely Zionist and affiliated with WIZO, the women's section of the Zionist movement. During the turbulent war period, Gisi assumed the leadership of the Slovak branch of the American-based Joint Distribution Committee.[96] As she was the funnel through which funds flowed from other organizations, such as the World Jewish Congress and the Zionist Jewish Agency, the other members were confident that their financial needs would be met. Money was transmitted through a bank in Switzerland in a special account and sent over by paid couriers.[97]

In 1938 and 1939 Fleischmann sent her daughters to Palestine. Caring for her own husband, Josef, as well as her ailing mother prevented Gisi from joining her daughters, no less than her sense of responsibility toward her fellow Jews as the dark clouds gathered over Slovakia. Her brother, Dr. Gustav Fischer, succumbed to injuries sustained after a brutal beating by a group of antisemites; his wife, Lilly, suffering the loss of her husband, committed suicide by jumping from her third floor window. Another brother, Dr. David Fischer, with his family survived the Holocaust, having been granted letters of protection with 300 other Jewish physicians by the Slovak Fascist regime under its policy of exempting from deportations persons highly valuable to the country's economy and welfare.[98]

On December 20, 1939, a group of refugees who had left Vienna on their way to Palestine via the Danube River and the Black Sea, organized by the Jewish Berthold Storfer with Nazi encouragement (under their still-operating policy of forced emigration), were held up in an abandoned munitions factory in Patrónka, on the outskirts of Bratislava, because they lacked river boats. Gisi Fleischmann was deeply involved in providing these stranded refugees with food and other vital necessities. Government officials had to be bribed to prolong the stay of these people, while the heads of the illegal immigration organization known as Aliyah Bet (later Mossad), planned the refugees' ongoing voyage.

The green light for the departure of a first group was finally given on September 4, 1940, aboard the *Uranus* and the *Helios*, to be followed several days later with two more steamers, the *Schoenbrunn* and the *Melk*, carrying the remainder of the original large contingent of 4,000 people.[99] When, on September 26, 1940, the UZ was created by government decree, Fleischmann assumed the post of head of the emigration department. A year later she was elected to head the separate and clandestine Working Group WG.[100]

Throughout her wartime activity, Fleischmann kept busy organizing parcels, medicines, and money, all dispatched with the help of paid emissaries to the deportees in Poland. She also kept her sources outside Slovakia fully informed of the fate of deportees in Poland. Especially gripping was her report of March 3, 1943, in which she wrote about the expulsions of Jews from Slovakia and elsewhere. She mentioned that "several hundred thousand of our people . . . have been transported to the region between Rawaruska and Przemysl. . . . Until now, we have had no reports from there, or rather, we have received such news from the villages in which people have remained that it is rather unlikely that those exposed to the repeated transports are still alive." She repeated her terrifying concern in another letter the following month, addressed to the Jewish Agency representative in Istanbul.[101]

She seemed to have known for sure about the genocide taking place in the main concentration camps in Poland, but believed it to be the result of the extremely hard labor imposed on the Jewish deportees. However, some six months later, she knew that the camps mentioned in her previous message were nothing less than killing centers. On September 5, 1943, she wrote: "We know today that Sobibór, Malkyne-Treblinki, Belżec, and Auschwitz are annihilation camps," but the precise details of the scope of killings in these camps, especially Auschwitz, were still unknown to her.[102]

Seeking additional funds, in December 1942 Fleischmann journeyed to Budapest to raise money in the Jewish community, but she returned empty-handed. At the time the Hungarian Jewish leaders insisted on a strict legality of financial transactions, and that of course was unacceptable to the WG, which needed some of the money for bribing people in top positions. She expressed her frustrations in a January 14, 1943, letter to Nathan Schwalb (representing the Zionist pioneering Hechalutz movement) in Geneva: "We have set up work camps, which stand at the point of collapse due to material needs. . . . Our plea goes out to you in these tragic hours that you may stir up the consciences of all the Jews living in security on the other side of the borders. . . . Our request is only for money, at any time a replaceable good, while human lives are irreplaceable."[103] Thanks to her efforts and her WG colleagues, 3,000 to 5,000 Jews found solace in the three main Slovak labor camps—Sered, Novaky, and Vhyne—for more than two years, until late summer 1944.[104]

Negotiations on the Europa Plan

During the negotiations on the Europa Plan she was perplexed by what seemed to her a lack of interest by her Swiss interlocutors. As she wrote to Saly Mayer on January 14, 1943: "You write to me that I should not lose faith, yet please understand that it exceeds the strength of a person, on the one hand, to see and experience so much sorrow and, on the other, to feel the lack of readiness to help. . . . Misfortune is hard to bear even when it comes from the hands of an enemy; still harder if one's own brothers desert one in the hour of need."[105]

Fleischmann's problems with Mayer were compounded by her uncertainty of SS officer Dieter Wisliceny's reassuring words. When Mayer and the Jewish Agency office in Istanbul informed her of the continued deportations, despite Wisliceny's assurances to the contrary, she at first doubted these reports. She wanted to continue to believe that, following the earlier halt of the deportations from Slovakia, Wisliceny, although representing a killing organization, was at least a man who kept his word. She believed that if his terms were met, many Jews of Europe would be saved. On May 11, 1943, she wrote of her meeting with Wisliceny:

On principle, they are prepared to stop the deportations entirely, but they are asking our friends there to make a definite proposal. I told him that in view of the difficulties of communicating we would need some time, and asked him to tell me the amount we would have to expect. To this he answered that it would have to be fairly large and that we ought to allow two or three million dollars. . . . I suggested the following to him: I shall pass the information on at once. Roughly between 1st and 10th June I will call on him and let him know whether our friends are in a position to enter into such large commitments. I would then make one thousand dollars available as a preliminary payment and in return be granted several weeks further extension during which the deportations [in other European countries] will be halted. Within this period an agreement would have to be reached and the planned installments be determined. On the whole, Willy [Wisliceny] has agreed to my suggestion, only he is asking for a preliminary payment of two thousand dollars, because below this sum he would not be able to negotiate for the moratorium. In any case, I have an assurance that there will be no deportations before 10 June 1943.[106]

Bribe Money

Failing to receive the money for the Europa Plan, she journeyed again to Budapest, but came back almost empty-handed, although Joel Brand (Kasztner's aide) claimed she was given $57,000 by his Zionist rescue committee. All Saly Mayer could offer was to set aside money in a special account that could only be touched after the conclusion of the war, something that no ss officer would accept. To this Fleischmann wrote back on July 17, 1943, that she could not fathom appearing before Wisliceny with such a proposal.

My dear Uncle Saly. Can you really believe that I will go to the German after a 10-weeks delay and . . . tell him all the conditions you are setting and, on the other hand, promise him that he will have the $200,000 advance payment in America after the war and that until then we cannot give anything? Do you not realize that he will believe we are mocking him? . . . By doing so I will not only put all the Jews in all the districts of evil into extreme danger, I will also be endangering the Jews here.[107]

Money did in fact come in from Mayer, but not the sums requested by Fleischmann for the success of the Europa Plan. During the second half of 1943, Mayer sent up to $68,000 for use as bribes, for support of the Jewish work camps, and for help to the "hikers"—the term used for Jews who had escaped from Poland and were temporarily staying in Slovakia before proceeding to Hungary. They needed to be fed and clothed, in her words, "before they will look like human beings again." She added that these people who have escaped from the Nazi inferno in Poland report that "indiscriminate extermination of men, women, and children in large numbers is an everyday occurrence. . . . Thousands of children have been collected from the camps and ghettos and wiped out with machine guns."[108] After the Europa Plan was finally abandoned, she again expressed frustration to Mayer (September 1943): "I must therefore understand that the will to help is not present. I am not stronger than iron. I have done everything humanly possible, yet my will is shattered on the rigidity of our comrades there."[109]

In the fall of 1943 Wisliceny suddenly came up with a new proposal: to send 10,000 children from Poland to safety in Palestine via the Romanian route.[110] It appeared that Eichmann had been told by Himmler to activate this idea as a trial balloon, and the children were then sent to Theresienstadt camp to await their departure. But, according to Wisliceny, the plan was derailed at the last moment due to the intervention of the Jerusalem mufti (Haj Amin al-Husseini), representing the Palestinian Arab cause, who was staying in Germany as Hitler's guest and aiding him in encouraging Muslims to help Germany win the war.[111] As the WG suspected that Dr. Isidor Koso, of the Slovak prime minister's office, had a hand in this, it was decided for Gisi Fleischmann to sound him out by contacting his wife, whom she had known before the war. Fleischmann took along a banknote of 50,000 Swiss francs and an expensive ring, and both were gratefully accepted by Mrs. Koso. Then the two women got involved in an intricate personal matter that unfortunately led to Fleischmann's arrest.[112] Released for a while, she was rearrested on January 9, 1944, and remained imprisoned for close to four months. She was finally released thanks to a ransom payment by her colleagues at the WG. She was then urged to flee the country and try to get to Palestine and rejoin her daughters there, but she declined. To the pleadings of her sister-in-law, Lilly Fischer, on this point, Gisi replied firmly: "My whole being is bound up with saving the Jews. I must do what my conscience tells me."[113] While others in her family went into hiding, Gisi Fleischmann refused to join them. "I have work to do," she told them."[114]

After the German takeover of Slovakia, in the fall of 1944 she turned down the invitation by ss officer Max Grüson to join him in Budapest, where she would be under his protection, and not to count on the good-will of ss officer Alois Brunner, known as a notorious Jew hunter, who was on his way to Bratislava to take control of the renewed deportation of the remaining Jews. She would stay put in Slovakia, she adamantly insisted, for as long as there were Jews there threatened with deportation. She also refused an invitation to join the partisans in their Tatra mountain retreat. "I shall stay at my post with my comrades."[115]

When Brunner arrived on the scene, Fleischmann and her colleague Dr. Tibor Kovăc went to see him with new negotiation ideas. Brunner, ever the sly practitioner, initially displayed a false interest and asked the two to see him the next morning for further discussions at Sered camp, presently turned into a concentration and transit camp. Instead, he had her arrested and brought before him for a brutal interrogation. He offered to spare her life if she would reveal the hiding places of her friends, which she categorically refused. Her fate was sealed. Brunner ordered her deported to Auschwitz, with a note to the camp commander that her return was not desired (Rückkehr unerwünscht), a code word for immediate elimination. She left on the convoy of October 17, 1944, and arrived in Auschwitz-Birkenau the following day, when she was led away straight to the gas chamber.[116]

Yehuda Bauer, while praising Gisi Fleischmann's personality and cour-age, is critical of the position taken by her and her colleagues in WG for their belief in the strength of bribery to stay the deportations, instead of urging the Jews to flee rather than rely on miracles. "But we were not in their place," Bauer adds, "and we don't know how we would have acted." His concluding evaluation of Fleischmann is that of "a brave woman, a brave leader," a person who "chose to stand at the head of a group that tried to save a community. I don't know of any other woman who did something similar during the Holocaust or, indeed, before it."[117]

Rabbi Abraham-Abba (Armin) Frieder

> He did what few other Jewish leaders were brave enough to do:
> he spoke out early and loudly, urging his hundreds of congregants
> to save themselves in any way they could from deportation.

Born in 1911, Rabbi Abraham-Abba (Armin) Frieder received an Orthodox Jewish education, studied in several yeshivot, and was ordained in 1922. Ideologically he was close to the religious Zionist Mizrahi movement that found itself in an ongoing debate with the ultraorthodox elements in the country, who opposed Zionism. During the early war years he served as rabbi in three Slovak cities, Nové Meste, Váhom, and Zvolen. He then became active in the efforts to save Slovak Jewry.[118] When new restrictions were imposed almost daily on the country's 90,000 Jews, Rabbi Frieder confided in his diary his hopes of emigrating to the land of Israel as soon as humanly possible. He wrote:

> I am determined to fulfill my Zionist aspirations and move to our ancestors' home and settle there. . . . We have to stop wandering from Diaspora to Diaspora, to end the period of exile and live as an independent people on our soil and in our promised land, so that we may no longer be the target of oppression and hatred. . . . Here, this is not the place for us, . . . but in our ancient homeland, in the land of the divine presence, the land of the prophets.[119]

On the night of February 25, 1942, Frieder was suddenly called to an urgent meeting of the Working Group (WG) in Bratislava. The meeting was to discuss the government's decision to deport all of Slovakia's Jews to Poland and into German hands. There were to be no exceptions. "We were in shock," Frieder wrote. "Fear and anxiety overtook us all." It was decided to immediately make appeals to all influential government agencies and church leaders in order to abort this decree. A special six-member committee was elected, including Frieder, who was to draft a memorandum to President Tiso in the name of all the rabbis.[120]

Two days later, Frieder met Jozef Sivák, the minister of education and culture, in his office. Sivák customarily passed on to the rabbi pertinent information about imminent government decisions concerning the Jews and planned restrictions. The rabbi, in turn, sent this information to the

WG. The two had known each other since Sivák had been a school inspector and Frieder a student in the same city.[121] On this occasion Frieder came straight to the point. The deportation decree was meant to destroy the Jewish people in Slovakia. It is surprising, the rabbi continued, that the Slovak people with its Christian tradition had decided to annihilate the Jews. When Sivák confirmed the dreaded news of the deportation decree, tears flowed from Frieder's eyes. "I could not hold back," the rabbi confided, but Sivák said that he could do nothing about it. Frieder did not relent: "I asked whether the government was aware that the transfer of 90,000 innocent people, in wartime, to a country occupied by an enemy power, means disappearance?"[122] After some reflection, Sivák suggested that Frieder contact a certain Mrs. Baleg, who operated a pharmacy in Bánovce, where President Tiso usually picked up his medications. Perhaps she could persuade him to accept the rabbi for a secret interview. Sivák also suggested that Frieder seek out the head of the Jesuit order, who also happened to be the confessor priest of Tiso, and speak to the Vatican nuncio.

Frieder immediately conveyed the gist of this conversion to his colleagues, and all were horrified. In their meeting with the Jesuits' head, Frieder and UZ head Sebestyen asked for his intervention with Tiso and the Vatican. Frieder told him to view the request from the perspective of a Catholic dignitary who was probably well aware of the impact of the Inquisition on his church's history and the many apologetic studies that were written to cleanse the church of this terrible stain. Here, now, in the twentieth century, we were witnessing a resurgence of the Inquisition by a nation identifying itself as a Catholic stalwart. How was this possible? The Jesuits superior promised to inform the Vatican nuncio as well as the Vatican directly, but this intervention proved of no consequence. Prime Minister Vojtech Tuka's answer was brief and uncompromising. He would not allow any interference in the internal affairs of Slovakia, and the deportation edict would not be reversed.[123]

The rabbis' letter to president and Catholic priest Jozef Tiso, on March 8, 1942, bearing Frieder's signature, also proved to be of no avail. It read:

> In desperation we call upon you, dear President, the supreme judge
> of the country, convinced that your Excellency also believes in the
> Supreme Judge above him, and as servants of the Supreme Being,

in our sorrow we ask with humility, listen to our plea and respond to us, for we find ourselves facing a great calamity. Are we not all created by the same God before whom we are fated to give an account? Have pity on us, on our families, our wives, men, children and elders, who with tears implore our Father in heaven for deliverance and mercy. We place our fate in your hands."

A few more pleading words followed, but it went unanswered.[124] Rabbi Frieder then decided that, contrary to the behavior of other Jewish leaders who counseled patience to their public and trust in their leadership, he would warn his congregants of the dire fate awaiting them. On Thursday, March 12, 1942, returning to Nové Mesto from Bratislava, he spoke in synagogue before hundreds of people. He urged the single people to marry, for the first deportees were rumored to be single women. The public notary had permitted him to issue marriage certificates. In the days that followed he married off forty-five couples. He also told them of an important sermon he was to deliver the coming Sabbath. As he wrote in his diary: "I felt that it was my moral obligation to counsel people how to act and what to do in the face of coming developments. I was fully aware of the likely consequences of my sermon, but decided nevertheless to take the risk and speak out, for the threat to life was imminent and the sacrifices which would be exacted from the public was great." On Saturday, during a break in the service, with the synagogue packed tight—more had come than on the usual crowded Yom Kippur Kol Nidrei service—"a rush of emotion seized me as I walked up to the pulpit, making it hard for me to begin my speech. This, I felt, was the last time I would address this large audience." Regaining his composure, he spoke out:

I have called you together in order to talk with you, with all the tribes of Israel. . . . We are all Jews, with one law and one decree threatening us all. It is this decree which I wish to talk about, this decree of the government to deport the Jews to Poland. Jewish leaders from all circles have tried to avert this evil decree, but to no avail. Since I see no chance of reversing the decision, we must know that we are facing one of the more difficult periods in our history, a new chapter in the annals of expulsions of the Jews. This time, however, we shall be expelled as slaves to a foreign land, and who knows if we shall return and see our loved ones again. To begin with, we shall lose our daughters, and after them, our sons. As families are broken apart, the rest—men, women, and children—will be deported as well. More than once have the nations of the world sought to destroy us, to annihilate us by expelling us from one exile to a more difficult exile, fraught with danger.

What did our forefathers do before they went into exile? . . . They tried to flee to neighboring countries where this danger did not threaten; they hid, they went underground and disappeared. They did not register in any census and did not report to any authorities. . . . They did all they could to transfer their wealth into lightweight, valuable, movable possessions to support them in their hour of need. [Frieder continued to drive home the urgency of the situation.] My dear ones! Perhaps you do not fathom my words; perhaps I have caused you heartbreak; perhaps your illusions have been dashed by the bleak picture which I have presented you. But this is how I perceive the situation and the hopelessness of our position. You might say: No law has been issued yet, no regulation or directive; it is inconceivable that this will happen to us. Would that I be mistaken, would that I be proven wrong. Act prudently and instead of criticizing, take action today and tomorrow! We are speaking of saving lives, saving human beings. He who saves one Jewish life is as if he had saved an entire world. Perhaps it is decreed from Heaven that it be impossible to save the whole community— therefore, save yourselves, each and every individual. 'I call heaven and earth to witness against you this day, that I have set before thee life and death, the blessing and the curse; therefore choose life, that thou should live, thou and thy seed' (Deuteronomy 30:19). [He ended with the benediction] May God bless you and keep you.[125]

Frieder wrote that many were offended by the severe words he had spoken and felt that the rabbi's duty was to calm the spirits and not disclose the bitter truth. But Frieder stood firm in his resolve to warn of the approaching calamity so that it might save some from a bitter fate. The next day he continued to perform marriages, including one for his wife's sister, Margareta Berl, and Rudolf Spielman. During the modest wedding feast that followed the ceremony, he was suddenly arrested (the first of several arrests to follow), imprisoned, and interrogated. The interrogator queried him, how was it that he knew so much about the deportations? Who told him, and what is the meaning of these sudden marriages? Why did he try to create panic among the people? Surely some authorities had been bribed. So who were they? Frieder responded calmly that he only did his duty as a rabbi to try to help his people as much as he could without any payment of bribery. On the contrary, if he were able to avert the terrible decree with bribery, he and the rest of the Jews would deliver to the authorities all of their property in a legal and proper manner. After an imprisonment of ten days, the rabbi was freed on March 25, a day ahead of the slated first deportation of close to 1,000 Jews.[126]

Within the WG, a small group was formed to try to prevent the deportations: Rabbis Frieder and Weissmandl, Gisi Fleischmann, Oskar Neuman, Tibor Kovăc, and Andrej Steiner. Kovăc had earlier studied law with Anton Vašek, now head of the dreaded Section 14 in the Interior Ministry, who was in charge of implementing all anti-Jewish measures, and later they worked together amicably in the legal department of the Bratislava municipality. Kovăc was able to exploit his friendship with the now-powerful Vašek, and this afforded an opening for Kovăc's WG colleague, Rabbi Frieder. Thanks to this, Frieder was able to procure from Vašek "protection papers" that ensured for their holders exemption from deportation and labor camps. In this way he was instrumental in saving many Jewish lives. Unauthorized entrance to Department 14 was strictly forbidden to any Jew, but Kovăc and Frieder visited that place regularly.

Vašek had some unsavory personality traits; he was addicted to drinking, womanizing, and gambling, three grievous sins for a Catholic, and this required more money than his official salary allowed him. To make up for his shortcomings he began to view himself as a serious scholar, and he wanted to write a scientific study of the so-called Jewish question, in the antisemitic spirit of those days.[127] For this purpose he approached Frieder, and dull-witted as Vašek was, he expected the rabbi to assist him in writing an anti-Jewish diatribe. Frieder, at first taken aback, decided to exploit this relationship in order to help his people without supplying Vašek with anything derogatory about Jews and perhaps even try to stop the deportations. The two met twice a week, and after giving him the material that he had prepared, Frieder followed up with special requests.

Frieder's manuscript for Vašek was less damaging in contents than the other items Vašek had read, such as the wildly antisemitic Nazi weekly tabloid *Der Stürmer*.

One of the positive results of Frieder's frequent visits was to destroy anonymous letters by informers and accusers and false claims against Jews from the pile of letters that landed on Vašek's desk and that only occasionally he bothered to look at. When on several occasions Frieder happened to be alone in Vašek's office, he read and tore up the dangerous material, or took them with him, and thus helped many people who did not and never were to know the nature of the charges against them. As for the "scientific work" on the Jewish question, Frieder suggested that Vašek first publish a compendium of all the laws recently enacted against the Jews. That, in the rabbi's mind, would serve after the war as an indictment against the Slovak regime and would by itself not cause any additional harm to the Jews. Vašek fell for this idea. Frieder wrote that he and his colleagues purchased many copies of the book and stored them away in the hopes of using the book in the postwar period before an international court of justice.[128]

The deportation convoy of July 31, 1942, was especially painful, since it targeted elderly people from nursing homes and hospitals, including Rabbi Frieder's Ohel David, an old-age home. There were 74 there on that day, and with great difficulty Frieder managed to save 45 of these elderly people. On September 22 Frieder was again arrested, this time on the charge of sending money to Jews in Poland. In his defense he stated that he acted in accordance with his obligation to help his brethren and this had nothing to do with illegal currency transactions. He was kept imprisoned for three days and released in return for a fine of 150,000 Slovak crowns.[129]

Deportations stopped in October 1942 and did not resume until two years later. But when, on June 14, 1944, it was decided that all remaining Jews should be concentrated in ghettos as the first stage for their deportation, Rabbi Frieder confronted Vašek and told him in no unclear terms:

Our brothers are killed in gas chambers and burned in crematoriums. . . . I will not obey these orders, even if you have me killed. I will only die once in this world, but will live in the next and true world (Olam Habah).[130] . . . You know as well as I do that expulsion to Poland means murder and extermination. Sir, there will be no deportations, for we shall resist to have us killed. Today, all Slovak Jews know about the gas chambers, the crematoria, and the extermination camps. We will use all means at our disposal to defend ourselves and even fight against the killers. If we are fated to die, we will die here, not in the gas chambers of Auschwitz-Birkenau and other extermination camps. If to die, we shall die here in our homes and our cities and be buried in Jewish cemeteries.

Vašek calmed Frieder and assured him that there would be no further deportations. Perhaps, Frieder noted in his diary, men like Vašek were more conciliatory than before, as they could foresee the end of the war with Fascist Slovakia on the losing side, and people in his position would be in dire need of some good standing, some reason to prevent their arrest and trial by the victors.[131]

But then, unforeseen, but due to the failed Slovak rebellion, German troops occupied Slovakia in September 1944. When German units showed up in Nové Mesto on September 2, Frieder decided to shave his beard. "It was a hard and depressing feeling," he confessed, "but I did it, since I wanted to continue my public career, and in Bratislava I could no longer be seen with a beard." He added, "I thought of the powerful Samson when his strength left him after they cut the seven plaits of his hair. My strength left me too as well as what influence I had when I was forced to shave my beard. We of the WG met for the last time."[132]

When he learned that on September 6 the German commandant asked the city authorities for a list of Jews in Nové Mesto, Rabbi Frieder assembled all the remaining Jews in the synagogue and urged them to leave the same day and hide in bunkers. He repeated these admonitions to the people in the Ohel David home for the aged, but for himself he decided to remain at his post for whatever assistance his community needed. His parents, brother, and sister with their families as well as most Jews of Nové Mesto left and sought hiding places in distant and isolated villages inside forests. Of preference were the small villages of fifteen to twenty houses inhabited by farmers of the evangelical community, who were opposed to the Catholic controlled regime. Some, in return for payment, afforded shelter to Jews, helped them build bunkers in the forest, and provided them with food and other necessities. Frieder decided to keep his wife and two children close to him.[133]

On September 7, 1944, Frieder was arrested and thrown into a cell in an army barracks. On the way to jail, Frieder managed to pass a message to his wife, urging her to seek help from the regional councilman and flee with the children.[134] Frieder was released after three weeks. In the meantime, he learned that Rakovski, the regional councilman, had proven his friendship and had moved Frieder's family in a Red Cross ambulance to a bunker in Hôrka and that they were now in Banovce, in a region controlled by the partisans, which they reached after walking for two days. The partisan commander then moved them to Banska-Bystrica, where they stayed for a while. As soon as he was released on September 28, he was arrested again with 1,960 other Jews with the help of the Slovak Hlinka Guards and taken to Sered camp. There were now 6,000 imprisoned Jews there.[135] On September 30, 1944, 1,860 men, women, and children were deported to Auschwitz.

As for Frieder, he was sheltered by a certain Josef Levinger, who as a carpenter in the camp was momentarily exempt from deportation and who took Frieder in with him, passing him off as a carpenter under the name of Abraham Kenig. In the camp hospital, he met Rabbi Weissmandl, pale and downcast, sitting and staring at a photograph of his family with many children. "I ran up to him, and he called on me: 'Dear rabbi! *Carmi sheli lo natarti*' (My own vineyard I did not guard)," a play on the words in the biblical Song of Songs 1:6. In other words, he was distraught with guilt for having neglected his family and not cared for their rescue.[136]

On October 14 Rabbi Frieder was shocked to run into his parents, Rabbi Pinchas and Sarah Frieder. They had been discovered in their hiding place and arrested. Three days later they were deported together with Gisi Fleischmann. Before their departure Abraham Frieder impulsively decided to join them, but they rejected his decision and adjured him to take an oath to do the utmost to be strong and save himself. Before the final parting, the parents placed their hands on Abraham's head and recited the traditional blessing: "May God bless you . . ." All then wept. It was to be their last blessing.[137] Another shock for Frieder was when he also beheld his sister Rosie-Rachel and her two sons arrive in Sered. Her husband, Meir-Max, had already been taken in 1942 to Treblinka. The same for his sister Leah-Malvin, husband Aryeh Jungleib, and their two children. They had been caught in hiding. On November 2, 1944, Rabbi Frieder's two sisters were deported with their families.[138]

With the Nazis frantically looking for him, Frieder continued to remain incognito in Sered as a carpenter, and on April 3, 1945, he escaped from the train that was transporting the last of Sered's inmates to Theresienstadt. He headed to his trusted friend Rakovski, who gave him valuable protective documents and a reference to the father superior of the Franciscan monastery in the village of Beckov. After a strenuous walk over a distance of 22 kilometers, he arrived in front of the cloister gates and was sheltered by the monastery head, Father Quardian. Frieder remained secluded in a cell until April 7, when the area was liberated by Romanian soldiers, who had the previous August switched sides and were now fighting alongside the Red Army.[139] He then went to fetch his son, hidden by a friendly farming family, and began to make plans. But he suddenly took gravely ill and died on June 6 at the prime age of thirty-five while undergoing surgery. Thus ended the career of one of the principal rescuer activists of Jews in Slovakia.[140]

Andrej Steiner

He participated in Europa Plan negotiations and forestalled the death of thousands of Jews by persuading authorities to employ them in labor camps.

Architect Andrej Steiner was also of the Working Group, and he replaced Karl Hochberg during the negotiations for the Europa Plan as an intermediary between the WG and SS officer Dieter Wisliceny. He fearlessly stood his ground in face-to-face encounters with the SS officer. Steiner tried to assure Wisliceny that substantial sums of money were available if deportations stopped forthwith. In one such discussion, furious at being lectured to by a Jew, Wisliceny lost his temper and shouted insults at Steiner. Unperturbed, Steiner said: "You believe that Germany will win the war, but we think it may lose it." But if Germany should win, Steiner calmly added, then Wisliceny would have profited from the money paid him, while if the Allies won, the Jews, in gratitude, would testify on his behalf and he would thus save himself. This line of argument seemed to assuage Wisliceny's nerves, as he invited Steiner to please take a seat: a rare invitation by an SS officer to a Jew of whatever rank and position. The conversations continued in a friendly tone that led Steiner to ask Wisliceny how he came to be in charge of the expulsion of Jews. To which

Wisliceny responded that, heaven forbid, he was not an antisemite, but the Germans and the Jews were at war, and as a German and a soldier he was doing his duty.[141]

Steiner also played a key role in overseeing the three principal labor camps of Sered, Novaky, and Vhyne, which were administered internally by Jews and produced useful products—furniture, textiles, and the like. There, thousands of Jews lived securely for the greater part of three years until the country's takeover by the Germans. In fact, these camps were to a large extent Steiner's brainchild. He had pointed out to Dr. Isidor Koso, of the prime minister's office, that the use of Jewish labor would go a long way toward offsetting the acute shortage of skilled craftsmen from which the country suffered. Koso had reluctantly sanctioned the establishment of these camps, clashing on this point with Interior Minister Alexander Mach.[142] Koso won this round.

Andrej Steiner survived the Holocaust and emigrated to the United States, where he resumed his career as an architect and worked as a planner for the city of Atlanta on housing projects as well as for Emory University.[143] In 2008 he celebrated his hundredth birthday and passed away peacefully the following year.

The final toll of Slovak Jewry losses was quite high: 57,837 were deported in 1942, of which only 282 survived; in 1944/45, 10,668 were deported, of which an unspecified majority number perished—for a total of 70,143 deported, of which 66,227 (94 percent) perished and 3,916 survived. To this must be added the several hundred Jews who died during the Slovak rebellion of September and October 1944, most of them fighting the Germans.[144]

As for the Working Group, through its efforts and especially by its three leading activists—Rabbi Michael Dov-Ber Weissmandl, Gisi Fleischmann, and Rabbi Abraham-Abba (Armin) Frieder—thousands of Jewish lives were saved. Initially the WG was instrumental in stopping the deportations in October 1942 and then by aiding Jews fleeing to Hungary, Romania, and other destinations. The two-year deportation hiatus in Slovakia gave several thousand Jews time to plan their escape by seeking hiding places with compassionate non-Jewish rescuers—558 of whom have been, as of January 1, 2016, awarded the Righteous title by Yad Vashem.

Fig. 1. Recha Freier, Berlin, 1938. Courtesy of the Zionist Archives, Jerusalem.

Fig. 2. Vladka Meed (then Feigele Peltel), Theater Square, Warsaw, 1944.
Courtesy of the United States Holocaust Memorial Museum.

Fig. 3. Cigarette sellers, Warsaw, wartime photo. Courtesy of
Yad Vashem Archives.

Fig. 4. (*top*) Miriam Peleg-Marianska, postwar photo. Courtesy of Avery Peleg.

Fig. 5. (*bottom*) Zerach Warhaftig and Japanese diplomat Chiune Sugihara, Israel, early 1960s. Courtesy of Yad Vashem Archives.

Fig. 6. (*top*) Tuvia Bielski and his wife, Lilke, New York, ca. 1950. Courtesy of United States Holocaust Memorial Museum.

Fig. 7. (*bottom*) Rabbi Michael Dov-Ber Weissmandl, ca. wartime photo. Courtesy of Yad Vashem Archives.

Fig. 8. (*above*) Rabbi Abba-Armin Frieder visiting Nováky labor camp, Slovakia, 1943. Courtesy of the United States Holocaust Memorial Museum.

Fig. 9. (*opposite top*) *Right to left*: Zvi Goldfarb, Ottó Komoly, Rezső Kasztner, Hansi Brand, and Peretz Revesz, members of the Relief and Rescue Committee (known as Va'adah) in Budapest. Courtesy of the Yad Vashem Archives.

Fig. 10. (*opposite bottom*) Josef Indig, in priest dress, Nonantola, Italy, September 1943.

MOUSSA ET Odette, à Nice, en 1947

Fig. 11. Moussa Abadi and his wife, Odette Rosenstock, Nice, 1947.

Fig. 12. Joseph Bass, Denise Siekerski (*right*), and Madeleine Rocca (*left*), Marseilles, 1943. Courtesy of Memorial de la Shoah.

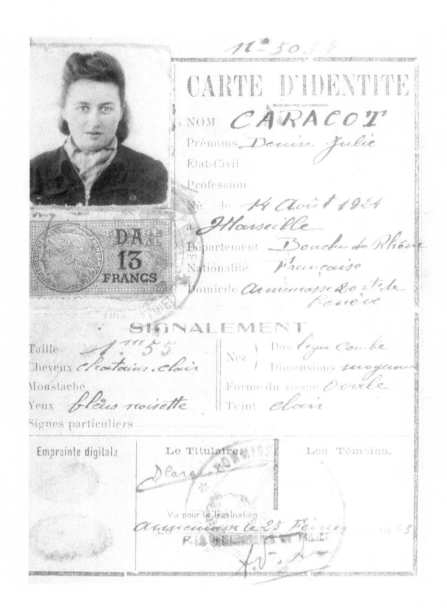

Fig. 13. Denise Siekierski, false ID photo, wartime photo.
Courtesy of Denise Siekierski.

Fig. 14. Marianne Cohn, wartime photo. Courtesy of Memorial de la Shoah.

Fig. 15. Robert Gamzon, wartime photo. Courtesy of Memorial de la Shoah.

5 Hungary

Zionist Diaspora Youth at Its Best,
Some Debatable Rescue Undertakings

It seems that there were ample warning signs coming from news of the mass extermination of Jewish communities across Hungary's borders of what the Jews in Hungary could face in the event of a German takeover. Yet, strangely, Jewish leaders prepared no contingency plans if the unexpected happened and were at a total loss to direct, advise, and act when the impossible turned suddenly into the inevitable. Historians have since debated the reasons for this paralysis of Jewish leadership. It certainly had something to do with the fact that, in spite of some antisemitic legislation, Hungary was a country where Jews felt secure; they were looking forward to a continued integration in the country's social, economic, and cultural life, and so they overlooked the dangers lurking from their country's alliance with Nazi Germany.[1]

Jews lived in what is today Hungary, when it was part of Dacia (also known as Pannonia, and which included some regions in today's Romania during the Roman Empire).[2] During the Middle Ages, Jews in Hungary underwent the same reign of sufferings, restrictive laws, fines, expulsions, and burning at the stake as their coreligionists elsewhere in Europe. Jews living in the parts of Hungary occupied by the Ottoman Empire in the sixteenth century were treated far better than those living under the Austrian Habsburgs. During the eighteenth century the whole of present-day Hungary returned to Austrian rule (the Habsburg monarchs), and in 1783 Emperor Joseph II issued a decree allowing Jews to engage in various industrial occupations and to be admitted into the guilds. All distinctive marks hitherto worn by the Jews were abolished. The process of assimilation took off at full speed: many Jews adopted Hungarian-sounding family names, and most used Hungarian as their primary language. In 1910 Budapest counted over 200,000 Jews, and they also populated other cities; such as 44 percent of the population in Munkács (Mukacheve), 37 percent in Máramarossziget (Sighetu Mar-maţiei), 31 percent in Ungvár (Uzhhorod), 21 percent in Szatmárnémeti (Satu Mare-Satmar), 20 percent in Miskolc, and 12 percent in Kolozsvár (Cluj-Napoca; Sanz-Klausenburg).[3]

At the end of World War I, Hungary's Jewish population shrank to 471,000 (representing 6 percent of the total) as a result of the country's loss of territories to other countries. The Jewish population was further reduced to 445,000 by 1930, as a result of emigration and conversions. Sixty-six percent of Jews belonged to Neolog communities (in today's terms positioned between U.S. Conservative and Reform denominations), 29 percent were Orthodox, and 5 percent called themselves Traditional-ists. Unfortunately for the Jews, they had now become the most visible minority in Hungary, as the other large "non-Hungarian" populations (the Slovaks, Slovenes, Croats, and Romanians, among others) had been cut off from Hungary by the territorial losses at the end of World War I.[4]

In March 1919 the Communists, led by a non-practicing Jew, Béla Kun, created a so-called Hungarian Soviet Republic that lasted less than five months. This was followed by the conservative government of Miklós Horthy, accompanied by a series of pogroms directed at Jews and some other elements, known as the White Terror. Horthy himself admitted to his antisemitism, arguing in a letter to one of his prime ministers, "I have considered it intolerable that here in Hungary everything, every factory, bank, large fortune, business, theater, press, commerce, etc., should be in Jewish hands and that the Jew should be the image reflected of Hun-gary, especially abroad."[5]

At the same time, most Jews continued to view themselves as an essen-tial part of the country, spoke its language, identified with its national aspi-rations, and continued to be well integrated into all facets of the country's economic, social, and cultural life. The figures speak for themselves. In 1920, 60 percent of Hungarian doctors, 51 percent of lawyers, 39 percent of all privately employed engineers and chemists, 34 percent of editors and journalists, and 29 percent of musicians identified themselves as Jews. Strikingly, more than half of Hungarian industry was owned or operated by a few closely related Jewish banking families. But danger lurked for the Jews: more and more anti-Jewish laws were imposed by Hungary's leaders, who were committed to regaining the lost territories of "Greater Hungary" and chose to align themselves with Hitler's Germany. The 1930s also saw the emergence of the deeply antisemitic Arrow Cross Party.[6]

During 1938–39, Hungary acquired land (Felvidék and Carpatho-Ruthenia) from dismembered Czechoslovakia and the newly created Nazi-inspired state of Slovakia. Northern Transylvania was annexed from Romania and in 1941 the city of Novi-Sad and environs was taken from dismembered Yugoslavia. Many Jews lived in these regions (especially the Orthodox in the newly acquired northeastern regions), causing the Jewish population to swell to 725,000 with 184,500 of them in Budapest. These numbers did not include the 80,000 Jews who converted to Christianity but were still considered Jewish by the country's antisemitic legislation modeled on the Nuremberg laws. Hungary's total population was some 14.5 million.[7]

On June 26, 1941, Hungary joined Germany in the war against the Soviet Union and declared war on the United States in December 1941. As a result of its alliance with Nazi Germany, Hungary enacted a series of antisemitic laws. The law of May 29, 1938, limited the number of Jews in financial, commercial, and industrial enterprises to 20 percent, and this affected some 15,000 families. A year later this percentage was reduced to 6 percent and caused the dismissal of Jews from virtually all the public services. It also introduced a religious and racial definition of who was a Jew. On August 2, 1941, another law was enacted that defined a Jew as Germany's 1935 Nuremberg laws did, prohibiting marriage and sexual relations between Jews and non-Jews.[8] At the same time, the Hungarian regime continued to turn a blind eye to the entry of some 15,000 to 35,000 Jewish refugees, illegal for the greater part, from Poland and Slovakia, fleeing to avoid deportation to the concentration camps.[9]

The other side of the coin is less pleasant, in light of some tens of thousands of casualties suffered by Jews as a result of actions initiated by the Hungarian regime without German pressure, such as the labor service system. Some 50,000 Jewish men were conscripted into battalions of army workers to build roads, construct rail lines, remove snow, clear minefields, and carry munitions. Over 40,000 died, emaciated by hunger or succumbed to disease, the harsh Russian cold winter, the risky removal of landmines, or the bad treatment by their non-Jewish Hungarian commanders.

In August 1941 the government expelled 16,000 Jews of dubious and non-Hungarian citizenship from the annexed Carpatho-Ruthenia region into German-controlled Ukrainian territory—to the embarrassment of the ss, who had their hands full with their own slaughter of Jews. The Hungarians refused to take them back, and so they were marched to a series of craters near Kamenets-Podolsk, and most were shot.[10] An additional 1,000 Jews were killed during a Hungarian raid against suspected anti-Hungarian elements in the southern Novi-Sad region. All these actions claimed some 59,000 Jewish lives in still fully independent Hungary. Inside Hungary proper, the central Jewish leadership, mostly represented by the assimilated elements, continued to delude itself to the very end. It refused to believe that what was happening in German-occupied Poland could possibly happen in the more civilized Hungary and hence failed to take any precautionary measures in the event that its assumption turned out to be wrong.[11]

The Zionist movement, headed by Ottó Komoly, represented only a fringe group of the Jewish community, and its impact was little felt. It counted barely 5,000 members, and in the words of historian Asher Cohen, it was regarded by the rest of the Jewish community with "open animosity." It consisted of various Zionist ideological groupings, such as the religious Mizrahi, the socialists Hashomer Hatzair, Ihud (Mapai), and middle of the road General Zionists.[12] A special clandestine section within the Zionist movement, known in short as the Vaadah (full title: Vaadat Haezrah Vehahatzalah—Aid and Rescue Committee), headed principally by Dr. Rudolf-Rezső Kasztner and Joel Brand, dealt in the rescue of Jews escaping from Poland and Slovakia.[13]

The Vaadah's activities were code-named *Tiyul* (hikes); in practice it meant helping persons in Poland and Slovakia arrive secretly and safely in Hungary, assisted by professional smugglers. It succeeded in bringing over between 2,000 and 3,000 persons.[14] The newcomers were then registered under false names as non-Jewish refugees and helped either to stay in Budapest or, after the German conquest, to cross clandestinely into Romania, where in 1943-44 the Fascist regime had greatly moderated its anti-Jewish measures and from where the fleeing Jews hoped to continue to Palestine.[15]

Separate but integral to the Zionist movement were the various Zionist youth movements (*Halutzim* in Hebrew), which rose to approximately

500 to 600 members at the time of the German invasion, most of whom had themselves originated in Poland or Slovakia and had come secretly to Hungary in the early 1940s. They included the Hashomer Hatzair (Socialist-Marxist), Maccabi Hatzair (originally a sports organization), Bnei Akiva (religious), Noar Tzioni (liberal), and Dror (left-wing). Saving Jewish lives ultimately became their prime objective, over their previous priorities of combat and resistance.[16]

The German Invasion

German forces struck without warning on March 19, 1944, in an apparent attempt to prevent Hungary from backing out of its alliance with Germany, and this spelled doom for Hungarian Jewry.[17] Hundreds of Gestapo and ss intelligence officers (SD) followed in the wake of the German army, as well as a Special Commando of 200 to 300 men headed by ss officer Adolf Eichmann, who had obtained from his superiors carte blanche to deal with the Jewish question.[18] Nazi ambassador Edmund Veesenmayer, appointed as Hitler's personal plenipotentiary, in practice held the reins of power over the ostensibly sovereign Hungarian regime, while the decision of Miklós Horthy to stay on as head of state practically legitimized the German occupation. This proved disastrous for the country's Jews, who relied on Horthy to stay Germany's hand on the Jewish question as he had done in the past.

The new prime minister and minister of foreign affairs, Döme Sztójay, and the minister of the interior, Andor Jaross, hitched their antisemitic wagon to Eichmann's in their zeal to rid the country of the Jews as fast as possible. Two senior government officials, László Endre and László Baky, both secretaries of state in the Ministry of the Interior and outspokenly antisemitic, colluded with Eichmann's team in drawing up detailed plans for the massive deportation of the country's Jews. The gendarmerie (sort of National Guard), numbering between 3,000 and 5,000 men and headed by Lieutenant Colonel László Ferenczy, was entrusted with carrying out the deportation program, which it did swiftly and brutally.[19] All central and local administrative and executive organs of the country collaborated in this effort, aided by most of the federal and local officials, civil servants, and law enforcement officers, including the mayors and police chiefs of the municipalities, as well as many of the social and religious organizations and institutions. This sudden outburst of an enthusiastic zeal in ridding itself of its Jewish population was shocking in a country not marked in its recent history by anti-Jewish outbursts.[20]

In light of the rapid advance of the Red Army in the east, it was essential for the Germans to lull the large Jewish community into a false sense of security in order to forestall a repetition of a Warsaw ghetto-type uprising and other acts of resistance.[21] Immediately after March 19, 1944, Jewish leaders in Budapest were consequently summoned by Eichmann's close aides Hermann Alois Krumey and Dieter Wisliceny for an urgent meeting. Jewish leaders were assured that no harmful action would be taken against their population; there would be only certain restrictions dictated by the war conditions. The Jewish delegation gullibly swallowed these assurances. At the same time, they were told that Jewish matters would henceforth be solely controlled by the Germans; that a Jewish Council (Judenrat) was to be constituted, and that all Jewish publications would be subject to censorship by the Gestapo. Nonetheless, on the very day of the German takeover, March 19, 1944, the ss and Gestapo arrested a large number of Jews who happened to be inside or near the railway stations, as well as 200 physicians and lawyers who were picked out at random from the telephone book on the basis of their Jewish-sounding names. Arrests continued, and several thousand were detained in the first three weeks of the German occupation.[22]

Hardly had the Nazi assurances been uttered than an avalanche of drastic anti-Jewish decrees by the Sztójay regime nullified these promises. All Jews were dismissed from the civil service, lawyers were barred from practicing, pharmacists were deprived of their licenses, and journalists and artists found themselves expelled from their professional associations. Jews were also obliged to declare the current value of all their assets, including objects of art, rugs, silverware, jewelry, gold, savings and checking accounts, and securities and were permitted to withdraw only a small amount from the banks, while their safe-deposit boxes were confiscated. Jewish commercial and industrial establishments were also taken over.[23] In addition, Jews were prohibited from owning telephones, forbidden to travel or change residence, and forbidden to own automobiles and radios. The compulsory wearing of the Yellow Star was introduced on March 31 for every Jew aged six and up. Jews were also prohibited from using public baths and swimming pools and forbidden to frequent public restaurants, pastry shops, bars, espresso stands, and cafes.[24] Within two months of the German occupation, the Jews had been reduced to a pariah status.

The Jewish leadership continued to delude itself that these were mainly temporary emergency measures and would soon be annulled in light of Germany's military debacles on all fronts. From Slovakia, Rabbi Michael Dov-Ber Weissmandl suggested to Philip-Fülöp (Pinchas) Freudiger, head of Hungary's Orthodox community, that he test a possible ransom arrangement with ss officer Dieter Wisliceny in return for the rescue of Hungarian Jewry, in the spirit of the scuttled Europa Plan. Wisliceny, indeed, claimed to be open to a deal by demanding $2 million, with a first installment of $200,000 within a short period, and this was delivered on time, largely through the intercession of Rudolf Kasztner and Samu Stern, head of the Gestapo-appointed Jewish Council.[25] However, all that Eichmann's underling Krumey was willing to concede was to confirm that the emigration of 600 people who held immigration certificates for Palestine, plus an additional 100, would be allowed to leave. Kasztner, together with fellow Zionists Zvi (Ernő) Szilágyi and Ottó Komoly, subsequently went ahead with preparing the list, which evolved into the famous Kasztner train.[26]

Deportation from Provinces

The Germans and their Hungarian collaborators lost no time in working out the massive deportation of Hungary's Jews. The country was divided into six operational zones, with Budapest and its environs left for the last. Four weeks after the German occupation, Jews everywhere, but not yet in Budapest, were herded into temporary ghettoes, usually abandoned quarries or non-operational brick factories, empty warehouses, Jewish community establishments and synagogues, or open fields—all with close access to adequate rail facilities—without sufficient food and elementary sanitary conditions.[27]

Carpatho-Ruthenia was the first region to be hit, on April 16, 1944, the first day of Passover, including the large Jewish community in Munkács. Northern Transylvania was next targeted, with its 160,000 Jews. Using deception, the Jews were reassured that they were simply taken for agricultural work to a fictitious place called Kenyérmező or another invented name, on Hungarian soil, or the equally nonexistent Waldsee, in Germany.[28] The deportations began as scheduled on May 15 with four daily departures.

Three thousand were crammed into each chained and padlocked train; with 70 to 90 per cattle wagon that also contained two buckets: one with water and the other for bodily wastes. Within a seven-week period, close to 434,500 Jews were deported, mainly to Auschwitz, where most were gassed upon arrival—a daily average of 12,056 people and 3,145 per train.[29]

News of the Holocaust and Response

The question still haunting historians is what Hungarian Jews knew was happening to their brethren across the country's borders, especially in Poland. Many of the thousands of Jewish refugees who had escaped into Hungary from Poland via Slovakia gave accounts of the mass murders taking place in Poland and western Ukraine, news that also reached Hungarian Jewish leaders through the Jewish Working Group in Slovakia. On May 9, 1943, for instance, Gisi Fleischmann of the Working Group (see chapter 4) brought news that even those selected for labor in Polish camps were murdered. On September 5, 1943, she stated in no uncertain terms: "We know today that Sobibór, Malkyne-Treblinki, Bełżec, and Auschwitz are annihilation camps."[30] It should also be noted in this regard that Oskar Schindler, who visited Budapest in 1943 and met there with Kasztner, confirmed and validated the mass extermination reports of Jews taking place in Poland. In addition, Hungarian soldiers fighting alongside the Germans in Russia certainly witnessed or heard of the massive killings of the ss Einsatzgruppen in their courtyard.[31]

In Ungvár (Uzhhorod, today Uzgorod), a letter from Rabbi Weissmandl, in Slovakia, to his Orthodox friends urged them to resist boarding the deportation trains and flee, but his alarming call went unheeded. People either did not believe or were resigned to their fate. This led historian Yehuda Bauer to speculate on the distinction between information and knowledge and the way people process threatening news. According to him, the news emanating from Poland was so horrific and unprecedented that it led to a certain psychological numbing and a paralysis of action. Randolph Braham, the foremost historian of the Holocaust in Hungary, has questioned Bauer's reasoning.[32]

Many in the Zionist Youth Movement held a different belief: they were convinced that Hungarian Jewry would suffer a catastrophe similar to their brethren elsewhere.[33] During the deportation phase, Moshe Weisskopf, for instance, arriving in Miskolc, went to the ghetto where Jews had been herded and encouraged them to flee, but no one listened. "I spoke to them in the very midst of this ghetto, told them what was happening in Budapest, and showed them the documents I had brought with me. They were not prepared to stir; they were terrified and confused. They believed that if they obeyed the law nothing could happen to them. . . . Nothing doing; they were convinced that all this would pass." David Grünwald, also of the Zionist Youth movement, reported: "I went to my parents (in Munkács), seeking to rescue them. There I witnessed something that was typical of Hungarian Jews. My parents were unwilling to do anything illegal, and were upset that the Polish refugees had led me astray. . . . A colleague brought documents to us in the ghetto, but even then my parents refused to use them, and my mother forbade me to take flight." He did not listen to this advice, left the ghetto, and survived.[34]

The most dramatic and direct evidence of what Auschwitz really meant came from two escapees, Rudolf Vrba (Walter Rosenberg) and Alfred Wetzler (Josef Lanik), who held camp positions that enabled them to collect detailed information on the transports, selections, and extermination of the victims. Successfully eluding their captors, on April 25, 1944, they arrived safely in Žilina, Slovakia, and told their story to Oskar Krasniansky of the Working Group, which included a detailed description of the camp facilities, the selection process, the tattooing, gassing, and cremation. This was further corroborated a few weeks later by two more escapees, Arnost Rosin and Czeslaw Mordowicz, who also told of witnessing the arrival of the first contingent of Hungarian deportees. Copies of the report were forwarded to various non-Jewish and Jewish organizations in Hungary (including Kasztner) and abroad, including to Giuseppe Burzio, the papal nuncio in Bratislava, and Angelo Rotta, the nuncio in Budapest, who transmitted the information to the Vatican.[35]

Tiyul and Re-Tiyul

While the deportations were taking place at breathless speed in the provinces, those Jews in Budapest who were not involved in clandestine activity built bunkers for illegal refugees who needed places to hide. Others were entrusted with the fabrication of false documents and organizing flights, mostly to Romania. The Zionist Betar movement (separate from the mainline Halutz movement) kept a bunker in the Budapest Polytechnical University, where large quantities of equipment and food were stored.[36]

In Hungary, everything happened at such breakneck speed that the only hope of survival was either flight into Romania (where the Holocaust had come to a standstill), Slovakia (where the deportations had been suspended), or to guerilla-controlled areas in Yugoslavia. For Halutz members, therefore, rescue, not resistance, became the watchword. Although there were endless discussions within the Zionist organization over the choice between rescue and revolt, the decision was in favor of rescue, not a Warsaw Ghetto suicidal-type rebellion.[37] Hungary presented a bizarre situation. Before the German arrival, many had fled there from Slovakia under the *Tiyul* (hikes) program. Now the course had been reversed, as many tried to flee back to Slovakia, an operation known as *Re-Tiyul* (re-hiking). Many of the leading Halutz operatives had indeed come to Hungary from Slovakia and now were organizing the flight of Jews back there.

Romania, however, seemed a more attractive option, since it lay on the road to Palestine via the Black Sea. The major points of departure for the crossing into Romania were Koloszvár-Cluj, Nagyvárad-Oradea, and Békéscsaba, with the shortest route leading from Koloszvár to Turda-Torda and Arad, in Romania. On one such group trip, led by Hana Ganz, on the way to the Oradea crossing point, the smugglers who were helping them deserted them and they had no choice but return to town, where they were arrested. In Turda, on the Romanian side, fellow Halutz member Aryeh Eldar-Hirsch, with local activists, joined hands to receive the fleeing Jews.[38]

Budapest remained the focal point of departure for the *tiyul* to the Romanian frontier. Every day between five and ten people were sent off, and only at the very last moment were they told the precise routes they would be traveling. Statistics vary on the number of people who crossed safely into Romania. According to Asher Cohen, between 5,000 and 7,000 crossed the border in the Transylvania region, with about 1,000 of these linked with the Zionist youth movements.[39] The *tiyul* period across the Romania border ended abruptly on August 23, 1944, when Romania switched sides and joined the Allies. Then the border between Hungary (held by the German army) and Romania became a battlefront.

Deportations Halt

With the provinces emptied of its Jews, attention turned to the Budapest Jews. At first it was decided to relocate them into specially designated buildings in each of the city's fourteen districts, which were to be identified as "yellow-star houses." No Jew was permitted to live anywhere except in a yellow-star house.[40] In addition, curfew time was extended to all hours of the day and night, with the exception of three hours, between 2:00 and 5:00 p.m.[41]

As the pressure by the outside world began to mount in late June, with President Roosevelt's blunt warning of dire consequences to the perpetrators of the deportations in postwar trials, reinforced on July 2, 1944, by an unusually heavy air raid on Budapest, Horthy ordered the halting of the deportations.[42] Furious at the sudden suspension of the deportations, on July 9 Eichmann used devious ways to entrap a few thousand more Jews, especially those already interned in camps near Budapest. Less than a week later, an additional 1,500 internees were suddenly deported by the ss and their Hungarian accomplices. The following month, Himmler had Eichmann and his ss team recalled from Budapest.[43] The Jews in Budapest breathed a sigh of relief. It seemed that, with the Red Army quickly advancing across the Romanian-Hungarian border, the worst was over, and they would be spared the fate of their fellow Jews in the provinces. Again, a twist of bitter fate evaporated these illusions.

The Arrow Cross Movement

As the Russian armies advanced to Hungary's eastern borders, Horthy decided to act, and on October 15, 1944, following Romania's example of seven weeks earlier, he announced a unilateral cease-fire. But no sooner was his proclamation read over the radio than that same afternoon the pro-Nazi and virulent antisemitic Arrow Cross movement (Nyilas, in Hungarian), with German support, staged a coup d'état and installed their party head, Ferenc Szálasi, as the country's new leader. Budapest Jews were about to enter one of the most horrible phases of anti-Jewish excesses.

Soon frenzied gangs of armed Nyilas youths, many of them in their teens, began a spree of murder and looting. During the first night of the coup, Nyilas gangs randomly accosted Jews on the streets, with many taken to the banks of the Danube and shot, their bodies falling into the river. Two days later, Eichmann reappeared on the scene and concluded an agreement with the new regime to dispatch on foot 50,000 Jews to Austria, with the remaining able-bodied Jews of Budapest (men and women) to be drafted into labor gangs to dig trenches and construct defense fortifications along the perimeters of the capital. Thousands of others were taken to the Óbuda brick yards and from there forced on a Death March by Hungarian gendarmes to Hegyeshalom, on the border with Austria, where they were turned over to German guards. The marches, begun on November 8, claimed many victims who were not able to keep up with walking in inclement weather, and the route became a veritable highway of death.[44]

In Budapest, gangs of armed Arrow Cross men continued roaming the streets, looting and killing defenseless Jews, especially those found hiding in shelters, but also Jewish inmates in hospitals, with many shot on the spot. As estimated total of 17,000 Jews became victims of these Arrow Cross excesses, including Zionist leader Ottó Komoly, murdered on December 31.[45] Anarchy reached its peak on Christmas Eve, when the Russian ring closed the city from all sides. The government was disintegrating.

Zionist Youth Organizations

> Brave Jewish youth rose up against the Arrow
> Cross and other anti-Jewish atrocities.

During this murderous period Zionist youth (Halutz) were at their most courageous best. They rescued Jews about to be shot by Arrow Cross thugs, freed others from prison in daring attacks, fabricated an astounding number of false papers (an estimated 100,000) that included diplomatically recognized protective letters, food coupons, false military papers, and work documents. They also organized children's homes with the help of the International Red Cross representative in Budapest, Friedrich Born.[46]

To keep fellow members from arrest, as well as other victimized Jews, some Halutz members donned Arrow Cross uniforms and went from house to house rescuing their people. Efra Teichmann (Agmon) and Moshe Alpan dressed in the uniforms of railway officials, enabling them to cross undisturbed from Buda to Pest over one of the bridges spanning the Danube River. When Efra was recognized by an Arrow Cross member, and he and Alpan were about to be led away for a torture session at Arrow Cross headquarters, two armed Arrow Cross men suddenly surged out from a corner and the two captured Jews were handed over into their custody. These two pro-Nazis were none other than Betzalel Adler and Willy Eisikovits, members of the Zionist youth Dror movement. Alpan and Teichmann were safely led away, ostensibly to be questioned by these supposedly masked Arrow Cross men.[47]

Others kept busy fabricating false credentials, such as David (Coca) Grünwald, of Hanoar Hatzioni youth movement, who found a printing press where the workmen agreed to print identification and birth certificates. Still others in the Zionist Halutz resistance found hiding places for their friends in the movement—in cellars, attics, and storerooms or in the business places of friends or gentile acquaintances.[48] One had also to be constantly on the lookout for informers. Disaster struck at one of the secret printing places, when the three Halutz members, Micky Langer, Avraham Feigenbaum (Feigi), and David Grósz (Gur), were denounced, arrested, and brutally interrogated. Langer died during questioning. On December 8, the police arrested a large group of Halutz youth, including Asher Arányi, and all were tortured. A bunker commanded by Eli Shlomovitz (Shalev) was uncovered a few days later.[49]

An interesting aspect of the Halutz activities was its association with a volunteer unit formed in November 1944 by the Arrow Cross for fighting in "dangerous" places and known by its initials as Kiska. Hundreds of Halutz operatives were able to infiltrate this poorly managed organization. They dressed in that organization's uniform and, armed with weapons, guarded a number of institutions and houses in which Jews were hidden, including the Home for Crippled Children, saving the children there from deportation. Kiska units were also used to guard the food shipments for Jews in the ghetto where all remaining Jews were relocated in November 1944 (other than the Jews hiding in the International ghetto, as explained later in this chapter).[50] As told by one Halutz operative with Kiska, unit No. 13/1:

I found several men from the Zionist movement in a platoon of about 40 to 50. . . . I was the commander of our platoon. . . . Legally we were soldiers. . . . At night we used to go around in groups of 40 to 50; our purpose was to get Jews out of the hands of the Arrow Cross people. . . . Everybody used to shoot in those days, and we would fire, too. . . . When we would see a group of Fascists with Jews, we would stop them. We were soldiers, and there were more of us. . . . We would ask to see their orders; who gave the order? What did the order say? We would simply tell them that this was not their function; or we would say that we already had a bunch of Jews, and we would do the whole thing in one fell swoop, with a submachine gun, or something. . . . It was not worth their while to start anything with us.[51]

However, one night the Arrow Cross, having learned of the true nature of this unit, arrested its members and demanded they hand over their weapons. They were taken to Arrow Cross headquarters, at 60 Andrássy Avenue, where they were made to swear allegiance to the Szálasi regime. The surprised Halutz men, in Kiska uniform, were given some cans of food and sent to fight the advancing Russian army that on January 12, 1945, had already made it to the city. The Kiska units, who often clashed with Arrow Cross members, even leading to pitched street battles, were eventually disbanded that month.[52]

Halutz members also helped Jews in the forced marches in November and December 1944, when tens of thousands of Jews were forced to walk from Budapest to the border town of Hegyeshalom (a distance of 200 kilometers), on the border with Austria, where they were handed over to the Germans as forced labor workers. The deportees had to cover the distance in seven to eight days, with meager supplies of food and water. Many, fully exhausted, fell on the wayside and were shot by Hungarian guards.[53] Rescue attempts by Halutz members began at the assembly points, as they arrived with trucks to distribute food, and on their return they sometimes succeeded in concealing a few people in the vehicles. Eliezer Kepes (Kadmon) explained that he was traveling in a Red Cross car, assuming the role of a representative of the International Red Cross. "I traveled the road from Budapest to the Austrian border three times. Each time I had to extricate some people from groups of 700–800. I don't know if I saved 100 or 200, but we did bring people back and settled them in [diplomatic guaranteed] protective houses or in the ghetto."[54]

Assistance by Diplomats of Neutral Countries

After the initial free-for-all killing spree in the fall of 1944, the Arrow Cross regime relented a bit by allowing those protected by neutral embassies (Switzerland, Sweden, Spain, Portugal, and the Vatican) to be relocated by November 15 into specially designated buildings, known as the International ghetto, and numbering up to 30,000 people.[55] On July 9, 1944,

Raoul Wallenberg arrived in Budapest as a Swedish diplomat on a special relief mission for the U.S. War Refugee Board. He headed a special department in the Swedish legation dealing with persons provided with either provisional passports or protective letters (*Schutzpässe*), and who were subsequently relocated in thirty-two Swedish protected houses in the International ghetto. Through these and other efforts, Wallenberg was instrumental in saving thousands of Jews.[56] Of equal importance, Switzerland, through its representative consul Charles Lutz, also saved thousands of Jews through the issuance of Swiss protective letters.[57]

Here, too, Halutz help came in handy by fabricating a large number of false protective letters, ostensibly issued by the aforementioned neutral diplomats, to many Jewish members of the labor battalions who deserted their units to save themselves from being turned over to the Germans.[58] David Gur in his testimony fixed the number of false protective passes as high as 120,000. Historian of the Holocaust in Hungary Jenő Lévai also calculated the number at "more than 100,000."[59] Whatever the actual figure, the amount is quite astounding and a sign of the commitment, good organization, and efficiency of all elements of the Zionist Youth Halutz movement. In the words of one of its activists, Efraim Agmon-Teichmann, "The aim was that anyone who asked for a pass would get one, and that's how it was in reality. We forged protection passes and supplied them to everyone. We received orders and supplied the 'goods.' We printed forms and set up a special office with a staff, typewriters, lists, announcers, and ushers."[60]

In the case of Swiss *Schutzpässe*, the necessary rubber certification stamp was kept in the office of Swiss diplomat Charles Lutz. The daily procedure was for one of the clerks, usually accompanied by Arthur Weiss or Mihály Salamon, to take all the forms requiring authentication from the Glass House (see below) to Lutz's office, and the stamped forms were usually returned the following day.[61] This was not without any risks. As related by Moshe Weisskopf, Sanyi Grossman gave him a package of passes for a forced labor unit that was located on the other side of town:

We were supposed to give the documents to the commander, so that he would release the men. . . . He said that anything to do with the Jews was a matter for the Arrow Cross, and he asked one of the soldiers to phone them to come over. . . . When the Arrow Cross people came and saw us drinking coffee, they asked for our papers and inquired why we were engaged in saving Jews. We replied that the Red Cross was also saving Hungarian soldiers who had been captured by the Russians. We asked them to deliver the *Schutzpässe* to the men, but they didn't want to. . . . We finally agreed that the commander who had received us would see to their delivery. The following day we learned that they were indeed handed over.[62]

This episode could have ended tragically if the Halutz members had been arrested by the gun-toting Arrow Cross men.

The Glass House

Miklós (Moshe) Krausz, of the religious Zionist movement Mizrahi, headed the Palestine office, which was responsible for issuing British-approved travel certificates to people for travel to Palestine. When the Germans entered Hungary, Krausz fled and hid in the Swiss consulate, where Charles Lutz represented the interests of the Allied countries at war with Germany. With Lutz's consent, an additional wing of the consulate was opened in the Glass House, located at 29 Vadász Street, that bore the sign "Swiss Consulate, Representing Foreign Interests, Emigration Department," and Krausz installed himself there.[63] The Glass House became the hub of a massive network of underground activities headed by the Zionist Halutz movement.[64]

During the Arrow Cross period, Krausz's staff issued Swiss protective passes to this large group. It was at this stage that the Glass House began to assume major importance. In this building, covered by diplomatic immunity, one could receive people, unafraid of being watched or overheard. It was also an ideal spot to plan clandestine activities from one of its many rooms in the building's many floors. The basement was occupied by the Hashomer Hatzair, Dror, and Maccabi Hatzair Zionist youth movements, the attic by the Hanoar Hatzioni, and part of the cellar by an Orthodox group.[65]

After October 15, many residents frantically trying to escape the murderous rampage of the Arrow Cross thugs stormed the entrance of the Glass House. In the evening, the office rooms became dormitories where people stayed overnight. Within a week or two the building was full, and by the beginning of November there were close to 2,000 residents. While hundreds of Jews managed to squeeze into the building, thousands waited outside. Toward the end of November and early December 1944 there were over 3,000 people in the Glass House.[66]

Aid to the Ghetto

As the Arrow Cross regime in Budapest was reeling from the effects of bombardments and the approaching Russian steamroller, already on Hungarian soil, the estimated 70,000 Jews still living openly in the city (not counting those in hiding and apart from the 30,000 others ensconced in the diplomatic International ghetto) were hustled into a ghetto of 162 buildings, which was fenced off with wooden boards and where conditions were horrible even by minimal standards.[67] At this critical juncture for Budapest Jews, the Zionist youth Halutz underground tried to feed the starving ghetto people. This included items secretly funneled into the ghetto, taken from various storerooms, between November 28 and December 23, 1944, such as flour, coffee substitute, beans, noodles, pumpkin for baking, barley flakes, cheese, dried peas, tomatoes, corn flour, eggs, squash, dehydrated vegetables, and salt, as well as straw mattresses, coal, and cleaning utensils.

In his postwar account, Efraim Agmon-Teichmann noted with satisfaction that when the Russians entered the city, "we still had stocks" of these hard-to-get items. How was this managed and paid for? Money came from a secret Joint Distribution Committee fund. As for the purchases: "About 20 wholesalers did the buying for us; they were the ruling 'big sharks' of the food market in Budapest. . . . We had a big sugar storeroom near the Western railway station. [In this surreal nightmarish situation] a German sergeant who stood two meters tall enlisted the help of a German soldier and together they deterred robbers. This happened three days before the ghetto was liberated."[68]

Homes for Children

By far, the most impressive heroic achievement of the Zionist youth Halutz movement during the harrowing Arrow Cross period was the rescue of thousands of Jewish children, achieved under the most trying circumstances and without anything comparable in other countries under German domination. This happened when in November 1944 many persons of working age were rounded up and taken away, leaving behind the aged, the sick, pregnant women, and children without parents or guardians. Halutz youth in Arrow Cross uniforms collected the children and brought them to the safety of their newly created children homes.

The operation was led by Ottó Komoly, whose working office was located in the main office of the International Red Cross Committee (IRCC), headed by Friedrich Born. An engineer by profession, Komoly had been the official head of the Hungarian Zionist Association. Primarily concerned with saving Jewish children, with the permission of Friedrich Born, Komoly established a special unit (Department A) within the International Red Cross for this purpose. A number of buildings were either bought or rented to house thousands of children and store supplies and to serve as bases of clandestine operations by Zionist youth organizations. At one time, according to Randolph Braham, Department A was in charge of thirty-five buildings, 550 employees, and up to 6,000 children.[69] Efraim Agmon-Teichmann, who was responsible for the food allocations in the children's homes, organized the administrative branches of Department A, with the principal responsibilities handled by him and several other Halutz members.[70]

The Jewish (and non-Halutz member) László Szamosi also helped out. In one of these homes, housing 50 to 60 children, Szamosi supplied various necessities such as dishes, pots, eating utensils, cleaning implements, kerosene, and even anti-lice material. Yitshak Junger, director of one of the children's homes, stated that the apartment of Géza Lakatos, a former Hungarian prime minister, was one of the places designated for a children's home, including 71 babies brought over by Pastor Gábor Sztehló, who also sheltered children elsewhere as part of Born's Department B. People used to bring him abandoned Jewish children and babies, and Sztehló would transfer them to the Halutz members, who would distribute them among the various homes according to age and room space. At the end of the occupation there were 314 children and 71 infants in Lakatos's residence, which officially was designated as a shelter for children of Hungarian soldiers, under the auspices of the Red Cross.[71]

Another children's home was located in a most elegant quarter, remote from any Jewish homes, and was therefore considered a bit safer. Sajó (Yeshayahu) Rosenbaum related that he was told by Dajnus (Adoniyahu) Billitzer to go to a house that an aristocrat had given away and hang up a sign with the symbol of the Red Cross, since a children's home was to be opened there. While there, two military vehicles suddenly stopped. One of the men was Eliezer Kepes (Kadmon) in a Kiska uniform, who brought between 80 and 100 children with him. Two more trucks came the next day, bearing food, blankets, more children, and also adult caretakers. "At the end, we had close to 300 souls."[72]

But the children's homes were not the safe havens Komoly and the others had hoped they would be. Many were visited by the police or by Arrow Cross men seeking to transfer the children to the ghetto. Most such efforts were foiled at the last moment, but on December 24, 1944, orphans were forcibly taken out of two large homes. Protests by the Red Cross and the Swedish legation were of no avail. In one house, during the evacuation of the building three children and three adults were shot. The fate of another such home was no less appalling. The children in the second house never reached the barracks; two were shot and the rest began to march in the direction of the Danube River. On the way, about thirty children managed to escape. At the Danube, two children and a teacher were killed, and finally the rest were allowed to return to the children's home.[73]

According to historian Asher Cohen, when the Soviet army liberated the Pest part of the city, where all the children's homes were located, on January 17, 1945, there were about thirty children's homes, with 3,000 to 4,000 children and some 1,500 to 2,000 adults. Another estimate, as told, places the number of children saved at 6,000.[74] There is nothing comparable to this in the annals of the rescue of children during the Holocaust. A large group of dedicated Zionist youth saved them amid the chaos in Hungary in late 1944 and early 1945, with its frenzied killing of Jews by a hate-filled regime, with the support of their German overlords.

Jewish Losses

During the last days of December 1944, Komoly scattered his staff and took up residence at the Hotel Ritz, where he was arrested, and he disappeared—probably shot by the Arrow Cross. The Russians liberated the ghetto on January 17, 1945, and the rest of Pest the next day; Buda, on the other bank of the Danube, fell on February 13, 1945. By that time, 40,000 Jews had been deported from the city in the forced marches, and between 10,000 and 20,000 had been killed.[75]

As for the overall tally of Jewish losses in Hungary prior to the German occupation of March 19, 1944, 59,000 Jews were lost: about 42,000 as forced labor servicemen; over 16,000 who were deported as "aliens" in July and August 1941 and mostly massacred by the ss near Kamenets-Podolsk, and 1,000 were killed in former Yugoslav territory. During the German occupation, the Jewish community suffered 501,500 casualties; this figure includes fatalities of the 435,000 deported from the provinces and the rest as a result of other depredations, such as the Arrow Cross killings and death marches. The overall losses of Hungarian Jewry during World War II is hence tallied variously as between 560,000 and 565,000. Survivors included close to 120,000 in Budapest itself: 95,000 in the general ghetto and the International ghetto, and a further 25,000 who were in hiding or on the run. Some 5,000 were liberated from the labor service, and 20,000 were survivors of the camps. For the remaining few thousand, no credible information is available.[76]

Principal Zionist Youth Activists

Having recounted the context in which the Zionist youth operated, I feel it necessary to highlight the individual acts of heroism and bravery of some of the more significant members from among the hundreds of Zionist youth involved in rescue activities. Prominent among them were those associated with the leftist Hashomer Hatzair and the centrist Dror movements, most of whom fled to Hungary from Poland and Slovakia.[77] It is important to note, as pointed out by Randolph Braham, that the several hundred members of the Zionist pioneers decided to concentrate on rescue rather than full-fledged open combat, unlike Jewish partisans in the Russian zone. There were good reasons for this. First, the Zionist youth did not possess the kind of power and organization needed for active combat. And second, the Hungarian terrain, with few uninhabited and deep forests, did not lend itself to partisan activity. But the main reason was to concentrate on saving as many Jewish lives as possible rather than fighting, in light of the huge losses of Jewish lives already sustained in other parts of Europe.[78]

Significantly, at the time of the liberation, the Zionist Halutz movement was the only organized rescue force in the Hungarian Jewish community. In the words of Yehuda Bauer, the Zionist Halutz youth in Hungary are "Righteous Jews," although sadly forgotten in Jewish postwar annals of heroes—an unforgivable omission that hopefully will soon be rectified.[79]

Following are individual accounts of some of the more prominent rescuers; in some cases, they are referred to by both their current Hebrew names and their wartime names.

Rafi Benshalom (Richárd Friedl)

He forged documents to help Jews circulate
in the open and avoid arrest.

Rafi Benshalom was one of the principal leaders of the Zionist youth Halutz movement. Born in Cluj-Kolozsvár in 1920 (then part of Romania), his family first moved to Germany in 1931, then to Bratislava, Slovakia, in 1933. There Rafi joined the Zionist socialist Hashomer Hatzair in Slovakia and also enlisted in the Slovak army, where he served as a photographer. Living underground during the Fascist rule in Slovakia, in January 1944 he secretly arrived in Hungary, months before the German takeover, sent there by his movement together with Moshe Alpan and Aaron Rosenfeld.

Rafi spoke good Hungarian and German, and his deep blue eyes and blond hair gave him an alluring Aryan countenance. Budapest was totally different from what he had experienced in Slovakia. A colleague had alerted him to the unbelievable news that in Budapest Jews could visit the cinema, theater, and opera, whereas in most other European countries Jews were being deported in cattle cars to the death camps. In the evening Rafi was taken to a club, where people gathered for a party and sang Hebrew songs with tremendous gusto. "For me, in Europe of 1944, this seemed like a fantasy," Rafi recalled. "I tried to express my shock. . . . We seemed to be the only ones refusing to be swept away by this. We were afraid, were cautious. We warned, and we went on warning."[80]

For the most part, the Jewish population was overconfident, or at least they forced themselves to believe that nothing bad would happen to them this late in the war, with Germany's defeat just around the corner. No wonder that in Rafi's words, "No one in Budapest was willing to stand by us. Thus we were obliged to rely on our own resources and befriend members of the underworld. . . . We purchased our first documents at a high price from cunning forgers, many of them members of the underworld. . . . We found a sympathetic ear with the KEOKH— the foreigners' police—and arranged a kind of legal status for a certain sum of money."[81] Rafi Benshalom and his comrades debated about what should be the proper Halutz response in the event that a calamity were to befall Hungarian Jewry. Should it be one of defense, in the form of armed combat, or rescue, to save lives? Some were in favor of armed combat, on the model of the Warsaw ghetto uprising. "I for one felt that a suitable rescue system would enable us to save lives," and of "the importance of saving each and every individual, if we wanted to maintain the existence of our nation." No final decision was reached, Rafi Benshalom wrote, but future events would dictate that they focus on rescue.[82]

While Germans had not yet crossed into Hungary, Rafi and his fellow illegal refugees and Slovak colleagues had to be cautious, since they were in the country illegally. In his words,

> We thus had to teach the people how to be "street wise," to pay attention to the buildings' doormen, learn the rudiments of the "ration card" and how the "tenants' roster" was managed. Everyone had to invent a "life history" and learn it by heart. . . . I continued to live outside in a small room in the back yard of a beer factory. It had no window and was bitterly cold. But there was one enormous advantage: the house had no concierge. The gate was open day and night. I could come and go at will. The landlady was not too concerned about me. [Then came the unpredictable German invasion of Hungary.] We all learned anew the meaning of fear. We were gripped by terror. The mere thought that we were destined to perish was unbearable to us. We had only just survived the deportations from Slovakia. The terror dissipated gradually. We had simply become accustomed to the constant tension.[83]

Benshalom then goes on to describe the massive false document fabrication process: "We were able to produce any kind of rubber stamp for any purpose. . . . We had blank Slovak passports, Swiss protection passes, various Wehrmacht and ss forms, and all the forms issued by the Arrow Cross. . . . We began producing forged letters of protection, issued by the Swiss, under the nose of the Swiss consul. Every day, . . . more and more people were seeking asylum in this exterritorial haven [the Glass House, where Rafi was one of those in charge of operations]." The working personnel there almost suffocated under the pressure of the crowds. He also related the fate of his colleagues arrested due to betrayal and those released in return for ransom: "Miky was not among them. He had been beaten to death. Marek, too, was missing. He had disappeared without a trace, forever. . . . Miky lost his life in the party offices of the Arrow Cross."[84]

Rafi luckily survived that harrowing period, having also acted under several false names, such as Dr. Rafay and Janos Sámpias. In 1947 he left for Palestine and then served as a diplomat for Israel in Prague and other stations. A member of kibbutz Haogen, he passed away in 1996.[85]

Moshe Alpan (Márton Eléfant)

One of the most prominent figures in the Zionist youth movement, he arranged and accompanied Jews fleeing across the border into Romania.

Born in Bazin-Pezinok, Slovakia, in 1918, Moshe Alpan (Márton Elefánt, "Pil") was one of the most prominent figures in the Zionist youth movement. He studied law and philosophy at the University of Prague and then joined the Hashomer Hatzair movement. He served in a forced labor unit in Slovakia while his parents, older sister, and her husband were deported to Auschwitz, where only his sister survived. In 1942 he went underground, obtained forged documents, and organized illegal activities. Since he spoke Hungarian fluently, on January 19, 1944, his movement decided to send him to Budapest. There he used the name of Michael Solsky, a Polish refugee, and later János Szabó and Mihály Rajec. He mainly provided assistance to refugees from Slovakia and Poland. After the German occupation of Hungary, he dealt with the *Re-Tiyul* (re-hiking) to Slovakia, often traveling to the border himself.

Alpan made the first trip to Vagyvárad, on the Romanian border, with a large group of fleeing Jews. Some of them were arrested en route; others, fearing failure, returned at once to Budapest. Alpan remained there and finally succeeded in reestablishing the crossing network. This route later became the most important. The other crossing point in Oradea was particularly risky, since most Jews there had already been assembled in a makeshift ghetto in preparation for their deportation. As told by Alpan:

> On my arrival at Oradea, . . . I was traveling with Hava in a carriage to meet a smuggler. Arriving at a farmhouse, we found an old woman. She burst out into tears and told me that the Gestapo had arrested

her son that same day. Unfortunately, several more Jews were found hiding in her house. It was clear that the house was under constant surveillance. . . . We decided to stay in a hotel. I returned to Budapest and learned that a group of our people was arrested. . . . Jews were falling like flies into the hands of the Gestapo in Oradea.[86]

The border smugglers could not be trusted, since most were motivated purely by greed and were prepared to desert their wards right there on the border at the first sign of trouble. Many even robbed the confused refugees and left them to their own devices.[87] Each time Alpan arrived in Oradea, he tried to make contact with the town's remaining Jews still outside the ghetto. There were only a handful of Jewish doctors temporarily left behind, and they were gripped by fear and would not cooperate. The non-Jewish population was also not helpful; many, indeed, enjoyed watching the brutalities inflicted on the Jews, as related by Alpan:

Once I rode the train to Oradea. I witnessed the arrest of a man in my compartment. I barely managed to contain myself at the terrible sight. They tied the fellow's hands to the luggage rack and beat him mercilessly, until he admitted that he had indeed been born Jewish. My blood boiled to see the other passengers and their evil pleasure at seeing the young man punished so. The gendarmes' cruelty and the sound of the terrible jeer "Zsidó [Jew]," with all the other passengers joining in unison.[88]

After the antisemitic Arrow Cross's assumption of power, Alpan was mainly engaged in helping out people serving in forced labor units and Budapest Jews. He also took part in the establishment of children's houses. In December 1944 he was the principal planner and organizer of the liberation of Zionist youth members held in the central military prison on Margit Boulevard. After the war, he was also active in organizing illegal emigration to Palestine, via the Aliyah Bet effort. He left for Palestine in 1946 and joined some of his wartime colleagues at Kibbutz Haogen. He died in 2006.[89]

David Gur (Endre Grósz)

He was adept at manufacturing thousands of false credentials.

David Endre Grósz was born in 1926 in Okány, Hungary, into an assimilated Jewish family. In 1943, at age seventeen, he left for Budapest where he worked as an apprentice for a Jewish building contractor. That same year he joined the Zionist Hashomer Hatzair movement and, thanks to his drafting skills, became a member of the forged documents workshop. There he made a name for himself, for under his guidance the production of forged documents assumed gargantuan proportions, as documents were made not only for all Zionist youth groups requiring them but also for non-Jewish resistance groups. His operation was in fact the largest in terms of size and variety in occupied Europe. David Grósz (later in Israel, and henceforth here, Gur) recalled detailed information on the fabrication of false credentials:

> The main methods of operations were: (a) Drawing. Some stamps were hand drawn directly onto the documents with black ink or stamp pad ink. (b) Copying the stamp. Chemical ink on transparent drawing paper allowed us to produce twenty to twenty-five stamps in twenty-four hours. (c) Montage. (d) Authentic original documents and forms. A certain type of document was on the open market, because the non-Jewish population also needed forms. We bought vast quantities of these from various sales counters. (e) Altering original documents. In certain cases, we washed original documents in chemicals, partly or wholly erasing what was written, replacing it with different data or style. When we didn't have a place for the workshop, Hansi Brand [wife of Zionist activity Joel Brand] offered her apartment. . . . A Protestant priest gave us a considerable number of forms and birth, marriage, and baptismal certificates—most of which had original stamps.[90]

The documents included Swiss, Swedish, and Vatican diplomatic protective papers for groups such as the Van der Vaals group, which included British and Dutch officers who had escaped from German POW camps. Gur: "I supplied them with Swiss birth certificates." Or the Communist Pál Demény group: "We supplied them with documents and they [in turn] made hiding places available to us in a factory."[91] When the secret workshop had to move again, the Communist underground helped by arranging a safe place in a building owned by the Fascist students' organization on the premises of the Academy of Science—of all places! Here the Halutz people posed as an auxiliary security unit and dressed accordingly.

According to Gur, during a nine-month period, up to December 21, 1944, his documents department produced a stupendous amount—thousands of false credentials, including 10,000 birth certificates, 8,000 marriage certificates, 10,000 personal ID cards, 4,330 baptism certificates (Catholic, Protestant, Unitarian), 2,550 religious marriage certificates of all denominations, 830 Polish, Slovak, Swiss, and Hungarian birth certificates, 200 Slovak residential identifications, 80 death certificates, 25 school grades booklets (by subject and index), 9 matriculation certificates, and 30 university student ID cards. Also manufactured were military exemption cards stating that the bearer was exempt from serving and/or labor in Germany, 1,500 certificates testifying that the person worked for the Hungarian Steel Company, and 600 certificates of work in other industrial establishments. Also fabricated were ID cards from the Ministry of Foreign Affairs, the embassies of El Salvador, Paraguay, Switzerland, and Switzerland, Vatican protective letters, and Slovakian citizenship certificates; various KEOKH (foreigners police), Gestapo, and Arrow Cross certificates, military ID cards, military pay books, and travel passes. This is quite an astounding achievement by any account.[92]

This immense secretive undertaking, fraught with so many dangers, almost cost David Gur his life. In December 1944 he was caught inside the forgery workshop with the whole staff and all the equipment. He admitted that this arrest "was the result of our own negligence and stupidity. We had left our revolvers in our jackets in the hall." Sensing danger, Gur and a fellow worker frantically began to unpack one of the suitcases, feverishly looking for the revolvers, but the police caught them before that. When they opened the suitcases, only then did they realize what a big catch they had made. The six suitcases contained documents for the whole of Europe. "They began to beat us and ask questions. They took us to the party headquarters." An hour before arriving there, the Arrow Cross men took fourteen or fifteen people to the Danube River to be shot.

They then looked at us indicating that the same fate awaited us the following day. . . . We used the time to destroy the documents we still had in our pockets; we chewed and swallowed them. As a result, they didn't discover where we were living. At midnight, they began to beat us. They broke a rubber truncheon on Miky Langer. I was beaten. They ordered us to remove the things from the suitcases. . . . From midnight until five o'clock, we were beaten without a break. They stripped us to our underpants, with blows on sensitive parts of our bodies. The 14 to 15 year old boys [from among the Arrow Cross] were the cruelest. Ambitious to prove themselves to their elders, they intensified their blows. Not one of us broke or handed over any kind of information—neither names nor addresses. Miky collapsed and died in our arms. The beating ended, and it was time for the verdict.[93]

Fortunately for that group, on December 24, 1944, the Russians began their assault on Budapest, and this caused the senior staff at the prison to flee, leaving behind the low-ranking jailers. This proved a propitious moment to negotiate with them. "We offered them money—millions. But they wanted guarantees, documents of protection from the allies' delegation." Suddenly they began to read out names, one of which being Tibor Rapos Farkas. But this was David Gur's previous assumed name, and Moshe Alpan was the only person who knew it.

I understood at once that [Moshe Alpan] Pil had a hand in this. I identified myself as Tibor Rapos and stepped forward. The others, seeing what I did, followed suit. . . . We marched through the empty streets of Buda escorted by soldiers armed with submachine guns. When we crossed the Lánc Bridge over the Danube, I turned, at the head of the 17 of our people, and without a word, headed for the central [Zionist] party headquarters on 17, Wekerle Sandor Street (one of the houses under the protection of the Swiss legation). I saw my friends waiting for us at the entrance to the building. I was happy to have been rescued by my friends. The ruse was repeated the next morning, with a new list that we helped to complete.[94]

In 1949 David Gur left for Israel and joined kibbutz Gaaton. He is one of the initiators and founders of the Society for Research of the History of the Zionist Youth Movements in Hungary, which brings to the Jewish public a greater awareness of the central role of the Zionist youth Halutz movement in Hungary in the rescue of thousands of Jews.[95]

Efraim Agmon (Ernö Teichman, Efra)

He dressed in enemy uniform to save Jews facing execution.

Born in 1922 in Kisvárda, Efraim Agmon was drafted into the forced labor battalion in 1943, but managed to evade and participate in underground activities in Budapest as a member with Hashomer Hatzair. Starting in mid-March 1944, he was sent to secretly make contact with Jewish communities in the provinces in order to assist them and warn them not to board deportation trains. In his words: "I was sent to Munkács, where I stayed from March 15 to April 15. . . . There were some 20,000 Jews in the town and surrounding areas at the time. . . . The Jews believed that 'Here, it couldn't happen!' . . . They believed that the assimilated Jews—always loyal sons of the Hungarian nation, who fought with them in World War I—would never be treated in this way." He also took part in the illegal immigration (*Tiyul*) activities and distributed forged documents. He was one of the founders of the children's houses under the auspices of the International Red Cross, and he supplied food and necessities to them as well as to the central ghetto and the Glass House in Vadász Street.

On his many missions, he traveled under an assumed name. As related by him: "We obtained leave permits and became 'soldiers' ourselves. I had obtained two railways documents. We pasted our photographs on the documents, sewed uniforms, and I traveled under the name of Imre Benkő, an officer of the Hungarian Railways."[96] During the Arrow Cross period, he undertook even more dangerous missions. Together with fellow Josef Meir,

We obtained Arrow Cross uniforms, armbands, and arms. Also documents, which included "execution orders." We managed more than once to rescue Jews who were really being led to execution by rioters. Joshka (Josef Megyezi) wore the uniform and leather coat of a Hungarian-Fascist army officer, and I wore the uniform of a railway officer. . . . Gangs were breaking into houses, indiscriminately dragging people out, mercilessly beating them, and shooting them on the spot. The street was running wild and filling with dead and wounded. We joined those units that were leading Jews. We were now an "Execution Squad" and people were handed over to us without difficulty. We went into one house by ourselves because we had been informed that one of our comrades—Yehuda Alpár—was supposed to be there. We appeared without loaded weapons. Yehuda was not among them, but his mother fell at our feet. She didn't recognize us in those clothes, and we could not reveal our identity.

When we left the house, as I was walking with Joshka, a boy of about 14 popped up. "Look," he yelled, "that's a Jew! That one in uniform's a Jew!" He was the son of Gentile neighbors of ours in my hometown and he recognized me. Curious onlookers rapidly clustered around us. There was no possibility of withdrawal. I fell on him with threats and shouts, but he persisted. The crowd insisted that the matter be cleared up at the police station and were closing in on us. At that moment, two fellows in Arrow Cross uniform appeared and on hearing what was going on, drew their revolvers, held them to our backs, and ordered us to move on. They shoved us along until we reached a quiet street. There we fell on their necks. They were two brave members of Dror [Zionist youth organization], on patrol like us, who had come to our rescue at the last moment.[97]

Other Important Young Activists

They freed Jews from Arrow Cross gangs, distributed false credentials, and smuggled people across borders with some donning enemy uniforms.

Josef (Joshka) Megyeri (later, Meir)

He was one of the most adventurous and most risk-taking members of the Halutz underground, making the most of his non-Jewish appearance and his proficiency with the Hungarian street-style slang language. Dressed in a look-alike Arrow Cross uniform, sporting a submachine gun and grenades tied on his belt, he would reconnoiter the streets to try to save Jews being led away to be killed. It all began when the Germans marched in on March 19, 1944. Josef Meir was in one of the forced labor units, as a political prisoner, and being interrogated on his connections with the Communist underground. Making his escape, he arrived in Budapest a few days before the Arrow Cross takeover on October 15, 1944. That same evening, he renewed his contact with a former Arrow Cross activist, a retired army colonel named Kálmán Rátz, from whom he received some Arrow Cross party service-unit armbands, a few badges, and caps. Together with Efraim Teichmann, they managed to elude an Arrow Cross team that suspected them to be Jewish, only to be rescued by another group of Zionist youth dressed in Arrow Cross uniforms.[98]

Meir also worked to find secure hiding places for his underground colleagues. He wrote: "We preferred to house our members temporarily in various industrial plants. Nobody was ever caught in these places. We even had a hiding place equipped with electric light and a supply of food in a spacious paper warehouse in the center of the city. We also had a few bunkers in the suburbs."[99] During the siege of Budapest by the Russians, he organized armed patrols composed of young people. In his words, "We extricated Jews from the Arrow Cross mobs and the militia on the excuse that killing them was our job. When conditions were appropriate, we shot as many Arrow Cross men as possible."[100]

Yitzhak (Imre) Herbst ("Mimish")

Born in 1916 in Eperjes-Prešov, Slovakia, Yitzhak Herbst was with the Zionist socialist Hashomer Hatzair movement. In 1942 he escaped to Hungary, where a year later he was caught, arrested, and brutally tortured, but luckily released. In June 1944, together with his wife, Judith, he was about to cross the border into Romania within the framework of the *Tiyul* operation when he was apprehended by the Hungarian gendarmerie and taken to Szeged prison. He managed to escape, but Judith remained in the custody of the Gestapo and was cruelly tortured. "Mimish" succeeded in liberating her in a daring operation with the help of Tzipora Schechter (Agmon) and the Serbian non-Jewish Milan Gligor-ijevic. Herbst continued his underground activities until the end of the war. In 1948 he left for Israel and joined kibbutz Haogen, where he stayed for two years. He died in 1948, due to severe health problems resulting from the torture undergone in Hungary.[101]

Asher (István) Arányi

Born in 1924 in Újpest, Asher Arányi trained members of the Halutz underground in the use of weapons. Evading conscription into forced labor, he also helped others escape from forced labor camps. In addition, he traveled to the border zone in the Carpathian Mountains with a bag full of forged documents to give to Jews to avoid being deported. Sadly, most people refused to flee, falsely believing they were only being sent to some labor camps. Asher Arányi also smuggled Jews into Romania and often accompanied them to the crossing point. Arrested on one such mission in Nagyvárad-Oradea by the Gestapo, he was interrogated for eight days, but released. Arrested again on December 8, 1944, by Hungarian policemen for possessing a gun, he was interrogated for three days, but did not reveal his real identity. Again, luck was with him, and he survived this ordeal. Moving to Palestine after the war, he was arrested, this time by the British for entering the country illegally and taken to Cyprus for detention for ten months. Freed in September 1947, he returned to Palestine and joined kibbutz Maagan.[102]

Tzvi (Cvi) Goldfarb

Born in 1921 in Biała Podlaska, Poland, into an ultraorthodox family, he received a religious education, but later opted for the secular Dror Habonim Zionist youth movement. He was sent in 1942 to Slovakia to report what was happening to Jews in Poland and warn of similar consequences for Jews in Slovakia. He continued to Hungary in 1943, where he operated under various fictitious names, including that of an Italian tourist. He eventually assumed the leadership of the Dror movement there and was active in smuggling Jews across the Romanian border. He was one of those arrested by the Arrow Cross and brutally tortured, but liberated in a daring operation by fellow Halutz members, as described in the stories of Efraim Teichmann and Josef Megyeri-Meir elsewhere in this chapter. After the war, he moved to Israel in 1949, where he died in 1977.[103]

Peretz (László) Révész and Others

Born in 1916 in Holics-Holič, Slovakia, as a member of Maccabi Hatzair, he was one of the prominent figures of the Zionist underground. In 1942, together with his wife, Noemi-Nonika, he slipped across the border into Hungary, and in 1943 he became a member of the illegal immigration *Tiyul* committee. In 1949 he settled in kibbutz Kfar Hamaccabi, Israel.[104]

In this context it is well to underline that many women were part of the Zionist youth movements, and they participated in various rescue operations, such as Hedva Szántó (Hedvig Müller). Arriving in Budapest in 1939 from her hometown of Visk (Viskove), the sixteen-year-old Hedva joined the Dror youth movement. She and friends assisted refugees fleeing from Poland and Slovakia. After the German invasion of Hungary on March 19, 1944, Hedva kept busy distributing false forged documents. With the Arrow Cross in power, in October 1944 she helped Jews escape from the Budapest-installed ghetto and the Yellow Star Houses. She also traveled to the Mohács labor camp and smuggled documents to her comrades there, as well as clothing and money. Working as a dental assistant in one of the city's hospitals, she stole medicines and various medical supplies for her comrades. Arrested, she was brutally interrogated and tortured but was released with others during a daring operation of the Zionist underground.

Also worth mentioning are Tzipora Agmon (Franciska Schechter). Born in 1920, after the German takeover of Hungary, she was active in finding apartments suitable for hiding, and she distributed forged documents and money to people in need. She also participated in a daring raid to liberate a member of her movement. After the liberation, she collected Jewish children and supervised the children's homes where they had been placed. Married to Efraim Agmon, the two moved to Israel, where she died of heart disease at age forty-six.

The following is a comprehensive list of leading Zionist youth activists (out of a total of close to 420 members) that David Gur, the former Zionist youth activist in Hungary, has prepared at my request. He is the founder in Israel of the Association for Research of the Zionist Youth Movements of Hungary. The list is arranged alphabetically by postwar last names and, in parentheses, wartime names. Betzalel Adler, Efraim Agmon (Ernö Teichmann), Tzipora Arieli (Ágnes Wertheimer), David Asael (Dezsö Auslander), Alice Balázs (Edinger), Rafi Benshalom (Richárd Friedl), Tamar Benshalom (Kató Brunner), Moshe (Oszkár) Biedermann, Adonyahu (Dezsö) Billitzer, Yaakov (Jenö) Diósi, Zeev (Wilhelm) Eisikovics, Baruh (Ferenc) Eisinger, Andrej Fábry (Endre Feigenbaum), Avigdor (András) Freimann, David (Dezsö) Friedmann, Joseph (József) Gárdos, Neshka Goldfarb (Ágnes Szandel), Tzvi (Cvi) Goldfarb, Alexander (Sándor) Grossmann, Hanna Grünfeld (Anikó Ganz), David Gur (Endre Grósz), Yitzhak (Imre) Herbst, Uri (Endre) Hermann, Simha (Sándor) Hunwald, Manahem-Tzvi Kadari (Ernö Schwarcz), Eliezer Kadmon (László Keper), Anna Klein (Csech), Menaham (Elemér) Klein, Sarah Kohavi (Zsuzsa Miklós), Miklós Langer, Arie Levi (László Löwy),

Shmuel (Sándor) Löwenheim, Joseph Meir (József Mayer), Ephraim Nadav (Ferenc Löwinger), Róbert Offner, Ernest Paul (Ernö Pál), Tzvi (Herman) Prizant, Peretz (László) Révész, Pinhas (Tibor) Rosenbaum, Yeshayahu (Sándor) Rosenblum, Stephan (Zsigmond) Roth, Eli (Péter) Sajó, Dov Shimoni (Erwin Schwartz), Hedva Szántó (Hedvig Müller), Shmuel (Andor-Miklós) Szántó, Esther Vardi (Edit Schächter), Mordehai (György) Weisz, Vera Weisz (Lefkovics), Moshe (Ernö) Weiszkopf, Menahem Yakovi (Emil Jakubovics), and Dan (György) Zimmermann. The Halutz members did most, if not all, of their rescue work clandestinely and employed various unorthodox and illegal methods to achieve their principal aim—to help and save as many Jews as possible. Side by side with them were a few others, also affiliated with the Zionists, but separate from the Halutz youth movements. Some of their methods have aroused controversies among historians and bitter recriminations among survivors.

Miklós (Moshe) Krausz

He managed to distribute thousands of protective letters for would-be immigrants to Palestine.

Krausz was born in Mezőladány, Hungary, in 1908. In 1932 he headed the Mizrahi religious Zionist movement in Hungary, and two years later he was appointed secretary of the Jewish Agency Palestine office; from 1938 to 1946 he was its manager. He was thus in control of emigration to Palestine based on British-approved immigration certificates. In June 1944 Krausz was able to obtain an abbreviated version of the Vrba-Wetzler Auschwitz Report and secretly forward it to Jewish activist George Mandel-Mantello in Switzerland. Months earlier, when the Germans invaded, the Palestine office was closed, and Krausz took up residence and refuge in the Swiss consulate. A close relationship then developed between Krausz and the Swiss consul Charles Lutz, who allowed Krausz to work out of his office.[105]

When, on June 26, 1944, the Horthy regime announced its approval of the emigration of 7,800 Palestine certificate holder Jews, Krausz interpreted the 7,800 figure to stand not only for family heads but also their families (wives and children), thus in effect bringing the number of would-be emigrants up as high as 40,000 people. To handle the paperwork for such a large group, Krausz persuaded Lutz to acquire the Glass

House and rename it as the Swiss Legation Representation of Foreign Interests: Department of Emigration and consequently acquire exterritorial status. He staffed his department with many Halutz underground members, who as "Swiss employees" were exempt from some restrictions applied to other Jews. Soon a collective Swiss passport was issued for this large group of 40,000 people, specifying what the bearer's name was until his/her departure to Palestine under the protection of the Swiss legation, and including a Hungarian exit and a Romanian transit visa.

This protective letter scheme became the springboard for a more extensive use by Swedish diplomat Raoul Wallenberg and was also used by diplomats representing neutral countries. Unbeknownst to Krausz and his fellow workers, however, Hitler had consented to the emigration of only 7,800 Jews, and these only if Horthy agreed to deport the remaining Jews of Budapest, while the Hungarian leader had by then decided to hold up their deportations. In addition, British and American spokesmen showed no particular enthusiasm for this plan, and discussions dragged on until it was finally abandoned, when Romania switched sides on August 23, 1944, and joined the Allies, thereby transforming the Hungarian-Romanian border into a military front, and travel by Jews to Romania was no longer an option.[106]

In the Glass House, the personal relations between most of the Halutz activists and Moshe Krausz, tense as they had been in the past, due to Krausz's disapproval of the Halutz use of excessive quantities of fabricated documents (that in his opinion could have compromised the whole undertaking), turned sour as the Halutz activists transformed the Glass House into their main base of operations for various sorts of illegal acts, including the printing of false documents.[107]

There can, however, be no question of Krausz's dedication to the rescue of Jews in Hungary through the use of emigration certificates to Palestine, which he claimed, justifiably or in a tongue-in-cheek assertion, were sanctioned by the British government. As testified by Halutz operative Moshe Weisskopf: "At the request of Moshe Krausz I was to take a bundle of fifty *Schutzpässe* to Lutz in the Swiss legation for stamping. I was approached by three movements, each with about twenty additional documents, and was asked to try to get them stamped also. Krausz sent me instead of fifty more than a hundred. . . . The Consul did not count them, but instructed the clerk to be sure to stamp them all. . . . I pulled this trick many times."[108] After the war, Moshe Krausz left for Israel, where he was the manager of an emigration center in Jerusalem and worked for the Ministry of Social Welfare. He died in 1985.[109]

Joel (Jenő) Brand

> He went on a mission to save Jews on a
> fantastic plan concocted by the Nazis.

Born in 1906 in Naszód (Năsăud), Transylvania (then inside Hungary, today part of Romania), Joel Brand was educated in Erfurt, Germany, where he joined the Communist Party. Arrested when the Nazis came to power, he was released in 1934 probably because of his foreign citizenship, and he settled in Budapest, where his father was the founder of the telephone company. There he became a Zionist, joining the moderate Socialist Zionist youth movement in Budapest, Ihud (linked to the Mapai Party in Palestine). As a member of the separate Relief and Rescue Committee (Vaadah), together with Kasztner, and with the assistance of his wife, Hansi,[110] he was instrumental in aiding refugees who arrived from other German-occupied countries, and as such was in contact with the Yishuv (Palestinian Jewish community) representatives in Istanbul. Then, to his total surprise, he was launched into a rescue undertaking, for which he was totally unprepared and, according to some, also not the best qualified for such a fantastic undertaking.

The Nazis' Trucks for Lives Proposal

It all began when ss colonel Adolf Eichmann summoned Brand and in two meetings in April and May 1944 proposed a "trucks for blood" deal. In return for 10,000 military trucks, plus a certain amount of commodities, such as tea, coffee, and soap, Eichmann offered the lives of a million Jews—to be taken out of Nazi-controlled Europe via Spain or other neutral country. Brand flew aboard a German aircraft to Istanbul to meet with his Zionist counterparts to discuss this arrangement and was to be accompanied by a certain Bandi Grosz, a half-Jew in the service of the German intelligence.

According to Yehuda Bauer, the Brand-Grosz mission was engineered by the ss mainly to establish contact with the Americans via Grosz who, as a previous German military (*Abwehr*) agent, had already been in touch with Allied intelligence people. Behind the Brand mission was the fantastic notion by Himmler that the Jews, who according to him were behind all of Germany's woes, might in return for Jewish lives engineer an exit of the United States and Britain from the war and thus break up the alliance with the Soviet Union. Why did Eichmann choose Brand over the more politically suave Kasztner? Perhaps it was due to Brand's more passive personality and his perfect spoken German; we don't know for sure.[111]

From Brand's account, at the second meeting with Eichmann, German ambassador Edmund Veesenmayer and SS commander in Hungary Otto Winkelmann were present. That gave the meeting an unusually extraordinary importance. Eichmann offered to "blow" up Auschwitz and free the first "ten, twenty, fifty thousand Jews." After the war, Eichmann said to Dutch journalist Willem Sassen in his Argentine hideout that the "basic objective of Reichsführer Himmler [was] to arrange if possible for a million Jews to go free in exchange for 10,000 winterized trucks, with trailers, for use against the Russians on the Eastern Front. . . . I said at the time, 'When the winterized trucks with trailers are here, the liquidation machine in Auschwitz will be stopped.'" At Brand's last meeting with the Nazi overlords of Hungary on May 16, Winkelmann and Veesenmayer were again present.[112]

As for Brand's companion, Bandi Grosz, he was told by SS intelligence officer Gerhard Clages to arrange a meeting in any neutral country between two or three senior German security officers and two or three American officers of equal rank, or as a last resort British officers, in order to negotiate a separate peace between the SS and the Western Allies. Grosz later claimed that he was told that his mission was the central one, Brand's the subsidiary one. At the 1961 Eichmann trial in Jerusalem, Brand stated that Eichmann made it clear to him that the deal originated with SS head Heinrich Himmler.[113] The clumsiness of the approach has amazed many observers. On the very day Brand left for Istanbul, Eichmann traveled to Auschwitz to make sure that Auschwitz commander Rudolf Höss would be ready to receive the first shipments of Hungarian Jews, starting May 15. The crucial question remains, according to Bauer, whether the intensely antisemitic Himmler would indeed have let a million Jews go free? Perhaps not that much, but still a lot.[114]

Obstacles and Misunderstandings

On May 17, 1944, Joel Brand and Bandi Grosz left Budapest in an SS car for Vienna. Brand had with him recommendations from the Budapest

Jewish Council and from the Vaadah legitimating him as the representative of Hungarian Jewry. His passport was in the name of Eugen Band, but he had no Turkish visa (Grosz had one). Brand cabled to Istanbul that he was coming to meet the central figures of the Zionist movement. The answer was that "Chaim" would be waiting. Brand assumed that this meant Chaim Weizmann, head of the World Zionist Organization. It turned out to be Chaim Barlas, the Jewish Agency representative in Turkey. "What about Chaim Weizmann?" Joel Brand asked when he got off the German plane in Istanbul. "What about our visas and permission to stay in Turkey until we finish negotiations?" Brand could not understand that the Mossad (Zionist intelligence) and Jewish Agency people were in Turkey on sufferance and were closely watched by Turkish and British intelligence agents.[115] In the meantime, Grosz was whisked away by the Turkish police, while Brand was threatened with arrest and deportation but allowed to stay for a brief time.

In a follow-up tense meeting at the Pera Palas Hotel, Brand related Eichmann's proposal. His Palestinian Jewish listeners were stunned, rather shocked, and at a loss for words. Venya Pomeranz (later, Zeev Hadari) and Menachem Bader, both representatives of kibbutz movements, immediately cabled to Jerusalem that Pomeranz would be flying to Palestine to report, and on May 24 Pomeranz met Moshe Shertok of the Jewish Agency (later, Sharet and Israeli foreign minister). The two went to David Ben Gurion's house with a message from the two kibbutz emissaries: "We are waiting in desperation for your decision, upon which depend perhaps tens of thousands of lives." Ben Gurion, head of the Jewish Agency and the most important Zionist political figure in Palestine, decided to summon a meeting of the Jewish Agency Executive, where he rejected the idea of negotiations with the Germans without the knowledge of the Allies; the British had to be informed officially, he stated, and the sooner the better, before they got wind of Brand's mission through their own intelligence network.

On May 26 Ben Gurion and Shertok went to see the British high commissioner, Sir Harold MacMichael, no great friend of the Jews and Zionists, who asked whether this was not a Nazi ploy to split the Allied alliance—which, indeed, it was—on the eve of the Allied Normandy landing in France. Was it not unthinkable to even consider giving the Nazis trucks in the middle of the war? MacMichael argued. Ben Gurion countered that no goods were to be shipped to the Nazis, but negotiations had to be undertaken because lives might be saved. It was agreed that Shertok should fly to Istanbul and meet with Brand.[116]

Back in Istanbul, Brand and Grosz were given three days to leave Turkey or be expelled. Grosz immediately chose to give himself up to the Allies and never return to Hungary. At the same time, Shertok received word that the Turkish consul in Jerusalem refused to issue Brand a visitor's visa to Turkey.[117] At this point, everything looked quite dismal. Brand protested that he could not return to Budapest empty-handed without his escort, Grosz. This would be tantamount to his mission's failure. In desperation, he wrote out his last will.[118]

Finally Bader suggested an official-looking document in legalistic language be drawn up that would be termed an "interim agreement" and immediately dispatched to Budapest for Eichmann's eyes—a fictitious document stating that the Jews accepted the Eichmann offer in general terms, provided the deportations were discontinued. The Germans were promised a ransom of $400,000 for each 1,000 Jewish emigrants to Palestine and 1 million Swiss francs for each 1,000 Jewish emigrants to Spain. In addition, in return for permitting the Allies or World Jewry to supply the Jews in the camps, the Germans would receive equivalent supplies for themselves.[119] In the meantime, the British suggested that Brand proceed to Jerusalem via Syria and meet Shertok and his colleagues there. Brand left immediately in the company of Mossad operative Ehud Avriel.[120]

Quashing the Plan

However, instead of stopping on the Turkish side of the border, as originally planned, the train crossed into Syria, then under British control, and stopped in Aleppo. There Brand was detained by the British and was whisked away under detention to distant Cairo.[121] The Brand mission had failed, but not fully. On July 9, 1944, when deportations from Hungary had momentarily ceased, Menachem Bader received a cable from Kasztner in Budapest asking him to proceed to Hungary for urgent negotiations, and the German Foreign Office was instructed to prepare a flight to Vienna for Bader. The plane would be at his disposal at the Istanbul airport. Bader was all ready to go, but his orders from the Jewish Agency were strict: he was not to go, since he was a citizen of an Allied nation at war with Germany.

As British Foreign Minister Anthony Eden made clear to Shertok, when the two met in London: "The proposal you defend is not meant to save Jews. It is intended to sow distrust between us Western Allies and our Russian friends. But assume for a moment—just for the sake of argument—that you are right and I am wrong. Where, Mr. Shertok, shall we put these Jews if Eichmann keeps his word and sends them to the border?"[122] Evidently, from the outset, the British made sure of the Brand mission's failure, so as to avoid the possibility of a stampede of Jews heading toward Palestine.[123]

Meanwhile, in Cairo, Brand was held there against his will. He went on two hunger strikes and threatened at times both a breakout and suicide. On October 5, 1944, he was finally released, a bitter man. The Brand mission had received its coup de grace earlier, on July 20, 1944, when, with government sanction, it was disclosed in the British press and denounced as a diabolical Nazi attempt at blackmail.

The Brand mission remains a mystery, mainly from the Nazi perspective (what were their real intentions?), and it has continued to baffle historians. As for Joel Brand, settling in Israel, he testified at the Eichmann trial in Jerusalem in 1961. He died in 1964 in Frankfurt, Germany, from a heart attack while there to testify against Nazi criminals on trial.[124]

Rudolf-Rezső (Israel) Kasztner

> He used his cunning to make controversial deals
> with Adolf Eichmann and other high-ranking Nazis to
> save numerous Jews from the gas chambers.

No other Jewish person, deeply involved in rescue operations during the Holocaust, has stirred so much passionate emotions and controversy as Kasztner. Lauded and hailed by some while castigated and damned by others, equally by survivors and historians, he inspires continuing debate.

Known in Hungary by his first names, Rudolf or Rezső, and later by his Hebrew name, Israel, Kasztner was born in 1906 in Kolozsvár, then part of Hungary, and after World War I was known as Cluj, as part of Romania. The city again reverted to Hungary in 1940 under German pressure to solidify its alliance with Hungary. Jewish people also referred to it by its German name, Klausenburg.

At age fifteen, Kasztner became a Zionist in a city that was still part of

Romania, and later joined the Ihud youth movement, which was affiliated with Mapai, the leading Socialist Zionist party in Palestine. An elder brother, Gyula, had already emigrated to Palestine in 1924 to work on a kibbutz, while Rezső wrote articles in *Új Kelet*, a local Jewish newspaper. He also became an assistant to Dr. József Fischer, a lawyer, member of Parliament, and president of the Jewish Community, whose daughter Elizabeth he married in 1934. As a committed Zionist, he aided Jewish refugees who arrived in Cluj fleeing from Nazi Germany.

In 1941 Kasztner, then thirty-six years old, decided to move to Budapest to look for a job. There he met Ottó Komoly, an engineer and president of the Hungarian Zionist movement, as well as Samuel Springmann and Joel Brand, and the three then set up the Relief and Rescue Committee (Vaadat Haezrah Vehahatzalah), known as Vaadah. They operated along unconventional lines, for the most part illegally, to help Halutz refugees fleeing the Holocaust infernos in Poland and Slovakia to escape to Hungary and continue to Palestine via Romania.[125]

In a meeting on March 24, 1944, with ss officer Dieter Wisliceny and a German intelligence officer, Kasztner (falsely representing himself as a Joint representative) and Brand offered $2 million, similar to the Europa Plan of Rabbi Weissmandl, with $200,000 as a down payment, to prevent any harm to Hungarian Jewry. This was supposed to have been paid by April 9, but only $92,000 was forthcoming, and it was turned over to Wisliceny's two ss confederates, Otto Hunsche and Hermann Krumey. On April 21, another $77,000 was paid. At that meeting, Kasztner and Brand were told that deportations were unavoidable, and apparently the money paid had been a waste.

Still hoping for a positive outcome of the Brand mission, Kasztner did not give up on the German negotiation line. However, the Hungarian authorities became suspicious of the comings and goings of Kasztner with ss officers. He was arrested on May 10, released and rearrested (this time, together with Joel Brand's wife, Hansi), and surprisingly freed by ss interventions. In the words of Yehuda Bauer, the Germans had no wish to let the Hungarians in on their Brand mission secret. When Kasztner finally received on July 10 the so-called interim agreement between Brand and Bader of May 29, he rushed it off to Adolf Eichmann and ss officer Kurt Becher, who were impressed by its contents, but it did not lead to a letup in the deportations from the provinces.[126]

In his meeting with ss officer Krumey, Kasztner learned that while the deportation of Hungarian Jewry could not be avoided, the Germans would allow 600 holders of Palestine immigration certificates to leave. They could not go to Palestine because of a German commitment to the mufti, Haj Amin al-Husseini, to prevent Jews access there, but they could go to any other country. Krumey then allowed an additional 100 Jews to be added against an additional substantial payment. The number steadily rose—to 1,000, then to 1,300, and finally to 1,685. Kasztner divided the passengers into several categories: Zionists, prominent personalities (including 388 from Kolozsvár), rabbis (some of whom were rabid anti-Zionists), writers, journalists, professors, and intellectuals in various fields. Finally he included passengers who bought their places by making large payments and therefore made it possible to add persons of other categories who could not afford to pay.[127]

Some historians have questioned whether the large contingent from Kolozsvár, Kasztner's hometown, including many of his friends, was perhaps a bait for Kasztner not to arouse panic among the Jewish population there about what was really destined for them.[128] An even greater mystery is what Kasztner told the people in Kolozsvár when he visited them on the eve of their deportation in order to gather up his select group. In 1948 Kasztner admitted: "We had, as early as 1942, a complete picture of what had happened in the East to the Jews deported to Auschwitz and the other extermination camps." In 1954 in Israel he added: "Toward the end of April 1944, the German military agents informed me that they had finally decided on the total deportation of Hungarian Jews. . . . I also received information from Auschwitz that they were preparing there to receive the Hungarian Jews. . . . A few days later [in early May 1944] I visited Wisliceny at his home in Budapest. He told me that it had finally been decided—total deportation."[129]

In other words, when he visited Kolozsvár, he knew precisely what was in store for the 18,000 Jews already enclosed in a makeshift ghetto. Did he relay this news to them? This visit by Kasztner to Kolozsvár in May 1944 has emerged as one of the great controversies on the response of the Jewish leaders during the Holocaust. Kasztner's closest friends denied having been told anything about Auschwitz.[130] The evidence on this point is not conclusive.[131]

Eventually a group of 388 out of the 18,000 Jews in the ghetto of

Kolozsvár were whisked off to Budapest in a special train on June 10 and placed in a barracks on Kolombusz-Columbus Street. They were guarded by ss troops, thus guaranteeing their safety. In the end, 1,684 persons took the freedom train. A small committee headed by Komoly and including Kasztner, Hansi Brand, and Zsigmond Leb (of an Orthodox group) put the stamp on the final list, with Kasztner undoubtedly the central figure.[132] Eichmann had originally demanded $200 per head, then upped it to $500. Kurt Becher, the senior ss officer sent by Himmler to seize for the ss whatever economic utilities he could lay his hands on, demanded $2,000 and ultimately settled for $1,000. It was to be paid in a mixture of foreign and Hungarian currency and in gold and jewels.

On June 20 Hansi Brand and Andreas Biss, also of the Vaadah, handed over three suitcases with the money, jewels, gold, shares of stock, and watches to ss officer Gerhard Clages to give to Becher. The train was then allowed to leave Budapest on June 30. It included nationally known Jewish figures, Zionist operatives, and Rabbi Joel Teitelbaum, head of the strongly anti-Zionist Szatmár Hasidic sect, with his family. But instead of heading directly to Switzerland as promised, Eichmann had the train diverted to Bergen-Belsen camp, where the passengers were forced to stay for a number of months before they were allowed to continue to Switzerland, as part of negotiations taking place there between the ss and Saly Mayer of the JDC, with the participation of Rudolf Kasztner.[133]

What was then the purpose of the train in Kasztner's own mind? In Bauer's estimation, Kasztner was hoping that the first train would be followed by a second and a third; once a pattern was established, perhaps an attempt could be made to stop the murder machine altogether. It could, however, be another Nazi trick, and the passengers would wind up in Auschwitz. The gamble was a tremendous one, and to convince others that it was worth the try, Kasztner put his own family on the train, with him staying behind. Kasztner's detractors accused him on two main points: first, of having pushed the idea of the train instead of warning people of deportations; second, of saving his own family and friends; that is, subjectively assuming the role of the one to decide who were the few to be spared.[134]

Strasshof Convoy

On June 14, 1944, while the deportations were proceeding from the provinces at full speed, Eichmann unexpectedly told Kasztner that he was willing to allow 20,000 Hungarian Jews to be "laid on ice" in Austria as a demonstration of his goodwill and in return for an immediate payment of 5 million Swiss francs. As it turned out, Eichmann had been instructed by his ss chief, Ernst Kaltenbrunner, to meet the demands by many Austrian war industry owners and government officials to provide them with desperately needed slave labor to offset the workers drafted in the German army. Arriving in Strasshof, Austria, in early July 1944, between 15,000 and 20,000 Jews were distributed for labor among various industrial and agricultural enterprises in eastern Austria. Many were lucky to be treated humanely, and about 75 percent of them survived the war.

According to Randolph Braham, this was in fact a monstrous extortion scheme exploited by Eichmann to ease the labor shortages. With the endorsement of the Jewish Council leaders, Kasztner first offered Eichmann 5 million Swiss francs in jewelry, Hungarian *pengös*, and foreign exchange. Kasztner's critics point out that he had been duped into this large payment for no reason, as the ss high command had ordered this group of Jews to be transferred irrespective of whatever corollary arrangements were made. At the same time, Kasztner cannot be accused of not being privy to the secret instructions of the ss leadership, and he acted sincerely when he acceded to the payment demand after being told that this would save the lives of up to 20,000 Jews.[135]

Palestinian Parachutists

In a plan worked out by the Palestine Jewish Agency and British military authorities, it was decided to send a group of Palestinian Jews to several countries under German occupation in order to stir the local Jewish population to acts of resistance. Three Palestinian parachutists sent from Palestine were destined for Hungary: Joel Nussbacher (Palgi), Peretz (Franz) Goldstein, and Hanna Szenes. Palgi and Goldstein managed somehow to elude the Germans as they crossed into Hungary from their drop-off point in Yugoslavia, and they went directly to Kasztner, whose address they were given before leaving on their mission.

It was June 19 when the two showed up at his home, at a time when Kasztner was deeply immersed in making the final arrangements for his rescue train, which was to leave a week later. Fully surprised by their appearance, Kasztner did not know what to do with them. Fearing that their presence and mission would jeopardize his train rescue venture, he at first suggested that they might give themselves up. Then, recalling that ss colonel Kurt Becher had suggested bringing a JDC emissary from Palestine to Hungary, since Joel Brand had not returned, in order to seal the deal with him, and realizing that Brand's mission had failed, Kasztner came up with the staggering idea that Joel Palgi should present himself to Eichmann as a representative of the Jewish Agency, supposedly dispatched from Palestine to carry on the negotiations with Eichmann. As if taken from a Hollywood movie script, Palgi met with the ss and emerged unscathed. It was only several days later that he was arrested, not by the Germans but by the Hungarians and held in various prisons until November. Palgi managed to jump from the train that deported him, probably to Mauthausen. He did not return to Kasztner, but was aided by the Zionist Halutz underground to hide. As for Peretz Goldstein, he decided to turn himself in. His parents were part of the group from Kolozsvár kept at the Columbus Street house, and they left Hungary on the Kasztner train. Peretz Goldstein perished, probably in Mauthausen camp.[136]

The parachutists' venture was a complete failure. As for Kasztner's role in this affair, there are many questions but few answers. Did he tell the Germans that the two Palestinians had contacted him before they gave themselves up? If not, should he have hidden them while negotiating with the ss? How could he knowingly tell these two young emissaries from Palestine to give themselves up? Kasztner was also accused of doing nothing to rescue Hanna Szenes, who was captured on the point of crossing into Hungary, imprisoned, and later executed. Quite possibly Kasztner was so engrossed in the train venture that he would allow nothing to jeopardize this escape route, meticulously worked out in difficult negotiations with the ss and at a high monetary price. The three Palestinian parachutists, whose mission he felt was a terrible miscalculation on the part of his Palestinian colleagues, was an annoying distraction from what was more important—the rescue of over 1,600 Jews.[137]

Mayer-Becher Negotiations

On August 1, 1944, still hoping for a breakthrough in continued negotiations with the ss that would save the remnants of Hungary Jewry and perhaps others as well in the Nazi world, Kasztner suggested that the talks between the ss and Jewish representatives should take place in neutral Switzerland with the participation of Joseph Schwartz of the Joint Distribution Committee (the organization that in Nazi eyes was part of that mysterious secret world Jewish government that was really making the decisions for the Allies at war with Germany) and the JDC representative in Switzerland, Saly Mayer. Four meetings actually took place between Kasztner, Mayer, and senior SS officers, including Kurt Becher (see chapter 14 for a fuller discussion of these negotiations, chaired by Mayer).

Bauer believes that these drawn-out negotiations did at least lead to the decision to spare the remnants of Budapest Jews, and that thanks to his participation in the negotiations with Becher, Kasztner is to be credited for this, although as pointed out by Randolph Braham, Kurt Becher during his postwar interrogation had difficulty remembering any role in the Budapest matter and had to be reminded by Kasztner, who was present, that he indeed played a role—quite a strange scene![138] This leads to another bizarre development in the relationship between Kasztner and Becher. In the words of Bauer, "Kasztner had become a kind of walking life insurance for the Nazis, who must have seen the end approaching, and Becher had become Kasztner's only remaining contact." A more serious and damaging development for Kasztner's reputation was his role after the war helping, in Bauer's words, "his good friend Kurt A. Becher" to avoid condemnation by an Allied trial when he testified for the defense on his behalf.[139]

According to Bauer, Becher's previous duties in Poland involved robbing and stealing wherever he could, and he was also investigated by his own SS on charges of corruption and sexual cohabitation with non-Aryans. In August 1941 he was an SS platoon commander involved in killing many Jews.[140] Yehuda Bauer surmises that there must have been some kind of an understanding between Becher and Kasztner: Becher would save Kasztner's life, still under control of the Nazis, in return for Kasztner's defense of Becher after the war.[141] Braham also reminds us that Kasztner intervened not only on behalf of Becher but also for several other top SS officers on trial, some of them avowed criminals, including Hermann Krumey and Dieter Wisliceny, two leading members of Eichmann's infamous Sondereinsatzkommando.[142] What on earth could have led Kasztner to be an advocate in the defense of these criminals?

After he was cleared of all charges at Nuremberg, Becher returned to Hamburg, where he lived a very prosperous life until his death in 1995.[143] As for Kasztner, sadly, after the revelation of his defense of Becher and his ss cronies, an admission that he earlier denied, in 1957 he was gunned down in front of his Tel Aviv apartment by persons who considered him a Nazi collaborator—which he certainly was not.

Whatever his attributed character flaws and some questionable tactics in his dealings with the Nazis, Kasztner tried in his own way to save as many Jews as possible. This took place against the desolate landscape of a total paralysis of the Jewish leadership within Hungary and very much so elsewhere. He had to act without guidance by others, and he had to rely on his own cunning and the use of stratagems. If he sometimes overstepped moral boundaries at a time when morality had been relegated to a backseat and placed on hold, it was not done on purpose but in a frantic effort to save his brethren. And save he did, and that stands to his credit.[144]

6 Croatia and Italy

Children on the Run

Croatia was created in April 1941 as an independent state, but in reality it was a satellite of Nazi Germany, upon the dismemberment of Yugoslavia by the German invasion, and it included the regions of Bosnia and Herzegovina. Ante Pavelić, leader of the ruling Ustaša movement, headed a Fascist-type regime. His regime enacted anti-Jewish legislation, modeled after the German Nuremberg Laws, which first stripped Jews of their civil rights and later murdered them. Croatia's population of 6.3 million consisted of 3.3 million Catholics, with the rest divided between Serbs, Muslims, Germans, Hungarians, and 40,000 Jews, of which 11,000 lived in Zagreb, the capital city. Soon after its formation, the Ustaša regime embarked on a large-scale purge of the large Greek Orthodox Serbian minority (1.9 million), with more than 500,000 Serbs killed and others expelled or forced to convert to Catholicism.[1]

Jews were also not spared persecution. Various anti-Jewish measures included the confiscation of Jewish businesses, factories, and enterprises. Jewish civil servants, lawyers, doctors, veterinarians, and other professionals were dismissed and prohibited from dealing with non-Jewish clients and were required to wear the Yellow Star on their outer garments. This went hand in hand with the arrest of Jews, who were sent to Jasenovac, one of the most atrocious camps in Europe, on Croatian soil. By the end of 1941, two-thirds of Croatian Jews were to be found in Croatian concentration camps, where most were killed upon arrival or soon afterward. The surviving Jewish internees were eventually deported to German concentration camps, where most died. It is estimated that 30,000 Jews were murdered in Croatia—80 percent of its Jewish population. Most Jews who survived owed their lives to fleeing to the Italian zone on Croatia's Dalmatian coast.[2]

Italy was a Fascist country allied to Nazi Germany, and its army occupied certain regions of Croatia. But many Italian officials were outraged by the unspeakable atrocities committed against Jews and other minorities in Croatia and other regions held by the Germans. They persuaded their superiors in the Foreign Ministry and the General Staff in Rome to protect Jews from extermination, regardless of their nationality, if they were seeking asylum in the Italian zones of occupation. As a result, a genuine rescue operation was launched in areas under the supervision of the Italian army, including Dalmatia-Croatia, where 5,000 Jews found refuge. The situation for Jews under Italian control changed drastically and for the worse when Italy capitulated to the Allies on September 8, 1943, and all former areas held by the Italians came under direct Nazi German control.[3]

Josef (Joshko) Indig

He led close to 100 Jews, mainly children, through continuous dangers for more than two years, finally crossing safely into Switzerland.

This is the story of Josef (Joshko) Indig (later in Israel, Itai), who rescued a large group of Jewish children who arrived in Croatia before the German invasion of April 1941, when Croatia was still part of Yugoslavia. One of the Austrians in this group, Robert R. Weiss, wrote an account of the rescue in 1998. *Joshko's Children* follows the group's travails in Fascist-rule Croatia, their move to the Italian zone in that country, their transfer to the Italian mainland, and their surreptitious escape into Switzerland.

In May 1940 Recha Freier, the founder of Youth Aliyah, escaped from Germany and arrived in Zagreb, then still part of Yugoslavia, with a number of her young charges. She stayed there until she received certificates for ninety children to head to Palestine in March 1941. On the eve of the German invasion of Yugoslavia, thirty-two children remained in Zagreb under the charge of Josef Indig, Freier's Youth Aliyah co-worker. Eighteen Jewish girls who had crossed illegally from Austria to Maribor, in Slovenia province, joined them.[4] They were there when the Germans struck on April 6, 1941, and soon thereafter the country was dissected into several parts, under the authority of Italy, Hungary, Bulgaria, German-occupied, or the newly independent Fascist state of Croatia, led by Ante Pavelić, and closely allied to the country's main benefactor, Nazi Germany. Croatia's regime immediately began a severe persecution of Jews.[5] It was time to get out, but where to go?

Help came from a source in nearby Slovenia, then under Italian control, stating that a refuge for Indig's children could be had in the Novo Mesto region. "Joshko," as Indig was lovingly known, thought, "Something has to be done. Should I travel to the Italian zone alone and prepare the children's trip from there?" What if he were arrested by the fiercely antisemitic Ustaša militia when he attempted to cross over to the Italian-controlled area? Who would look after the children left behind? The police denied him a travel permit when they found out he was a Jew, but he decided go anyway, for he felt that the children were at a greater risk staying in Zagreb than his risk in traveling without a permit.

Indig put on his nicest suit and at night headed to the railroad station. There he boarded a first class passenger car. Making himself comfortable, he could not conceal his anguish at the thought of his arrest. As the train approached the demarcation line between the two Fascist-controlled regions, an Ustaša guard entered the cabin. Indig: "I am taking the cigarette out of my mouth. I show him my [old Yugoslav ID] paper, keeping all the time my eyes on the Ustaša newspaper that I am holding," and the policeman, evidentally impressed by the newspaper in Joshko's hands, left for the next compartment. Crossing over to the Italian side, the Italian guards there did not even check identification.[6]

From Croatia to Slovenia's Italian Zone

With the help of a colleague, Indig combed the Novo Mesto area for a suitable place for his youths but did not find anything. So they headed to the nearest big city, Ljubljana. "What a difference between Zagreb and Ljubljana," Indig noted. "There, murder and sadism; here, in the Occupied Territory, we have radio and you may read newspapers of neutral countries. You can even go to the opera, and nobody will consider it a shame that you are a Jew."[7] From Ljubljana, Indig telegrammed to the Joint and HICEM offices in Lisbon about his predicament. He was even able to telephone his Zionist Halutz colleague in Switzerland, Nathan Schwalb. "What can they do?" Indig wondered. "Intervene? With whom? Send money? How much?" Whatever, the children had to be gotten out of Croatia and brought to the Italian zone in Slovenia.

Turning for assistance to Eugenio Bolaffio, the local representative of

Delasem (Delegazione per l'Assistanza degli Emigranti Ebrei), the principal Italian Jewish assistance agency, Indig was told to keep the children in Zagreb, since Delasem could not take on new financial responsibilities. Eugenio's brother, Carlo, then suggested a refuge not far from Ljubljana in an old manor on top of a hill.

The problem now was how to have the children cross the border between the Croat and Italian held zones undisturbed. To clear any hurdles with the Italians, Indig relied on Eugenio Bolaffio, who promised to explain to them that the group had a final destination inside Slovenia— Grad Lesno Brdo, near the town of Horjul, a distance of 16 kilometers from Ljubljana. The main worry was the attitude of the Croat border guards. One advantage was that the children had not yet registered with the Zagreb authorities as all Jews were required to do, so they would not appear on any list and would not arouse suspicion by not wearing the Yellow Star. For added security, Indig secured an Ustaša document, signed by some official, agreeing to the group's departure. Would it work?

Friday, July 4, 1941, was set for the children's departure. A few more children were added whose names were not included on the original list, such as Robert Weiss. In Austria he had experienced what a Nazi labor camp meant. "I shall not go again!" Weiss asserted in his memoir.[8] Standing before Weiss, who was anxious to find out whether he could join him, Indig told the seventeen-year-old, "All right, let's hope you'll be a good *haver* (Zionist companion)."

At dawn on Friday, July 4, 1941, forty youngsters rose very early to hurry to the railroad station. On the train, they noticed that the Croat guards were not thorough in their inspections of passengers and their belongings. Crossing into the Italian zone, the inspection and search were lackadaisical as well. The cabin with the youth was swept with joy as everyone embraced.[9] What would happen now?

They were supposed to continue, first to Ljubljana and then straight to Grad Lesno Brdo. Suddenly the train stopped at a small station. An Italian officer stared at the many curious faces staring out of the windows, and he shouted, "*Che belli bambini!!*" How strange to be complimented by an officer in an army allied to the Germans. "Do you need anything?" he asked. With hardly a word, cigarettes and candies flew into the car. They found friendly Italian officers at every stop. In one place, an officer commanded: "Quick, bring water for the children," then asked, "Why are you being persecuted? You are human, too! But now you'll be all right." Indig noted in his diary, "These soldiers were human indeed," as chocolate, candies, and cookies kept being distributed to the children.[10]

At one of the train stations, Bolaffio appeared, accompanied by an Italian general and a nurse from the Ljubljana Red Cross. The Italian officer began to organize food for the hungry children, and while they were eating, the Italian general reappeared and told Indig reassuringly, "I gave the necessary orders. You shall get a separate car. The train for Lesno Brdo leaves at two p.m. . . . I wish all the best to the children. . . . Tell them to be of good cheer. . . . They're still very young. . . . Everything will be all right." And with that, the general left.[11] Indig thought of the difference from the attitude of the Fascist officers in nearby Croatia.

A Temporary Respite from Fleeing

The building at Grad Lesno Brdo where Indig's children settled down was a small two-story house with thick walls, built in the style of a fourteenth-century castle. Luscious green vegetation, trees, and flowers covered the veranda. The owner, Malvina Golub, and her sister-in-law, Mitzi Golub, occupied two rooms. A lake could be seen below. The building still lacked electricity, and candles provided light.[12] When the water level in the cistern dropped to zero, the children would fetch water from a spring. On such days, some of the boys went there three or four times and brought back pails of water. It was heavy and tiring work. In the summer, as the prospect of rain was practically nil, the laundry was washed near a little ravine. Lighting, too, was a problem, as not always were there sufficient candles, with sixteen people sleeping in one room.

But the place's main advantage was the security it offered to its inhabitants, as it was far removed from any danger, at least for the time being. This was where Indig hoped his wards could live peacefully until a chance break, making possible the emigration to Palestine. An officer in the Italian Carabiniere (police) assured them that no harm would befall them. They all felt that they could live there in peace. Still, the children were concerned about the welfare of their parents, as letters received from relatives in Germany told, in coded words, of the ongoing deportations.[13]

With the coming of winter 1941/42, electricity was fully installed, but the lack of heating, in the sometimes freezing cold, was difficult to bear.

Distraction came in several forms. One day Italian officers stationed in the village came up to the house and brought along a radio because they wanted to dance with the older girls. "What could we do?" Indig, in his memoirs, belatedly bewailed. "Explain to them that we did not know how to dance? After all, they had seen us dance the Hora!"[14]

The biggest problem was the lack of sufficient food, due to the war conditions. The children stole from the surrounding maize fields, and this was highly risky, as the farmers guarded their crops with rifles. The group also lacked proper shoes and warm clothes. Robert Weiss's mother, who was eventually allowed to join them, helped out by taking charge of the sewing and knitting needs of the children, with the aid of a sewing machine that was brought in by a certain Marco Rossner.[15]

The Partisan-Italian Conflict Threat

The year 1942 brought with it another problem and new difficulties—the increase in resistance activity by local partisans against the Italian occupation. As their attacks mounted, the partisans began to burn the village homes of those suspected of collaborating with the Italians or not willing to contribute animals and food to the fighting partisans. The Italians, in retaliation, were punishing those suspected of aiding the partisans—burning houses and slaying farm animals so as to keep them out of the hands of the partisans. Indig's inhabitants of Grad Lesno Brdo could clearly see the fire and smoke of the nearby village of Korene rising toward the sky.[16]

On one occasion, during a large-scale sweep of partisans in the area, Italian soldiers with guns ready to fire invaded the youth house and were about to expel the inhabitants, but finally relented. The Italian commanding officer had only one question: why wasn't Indig's group not afraid to stay put in an area infested with partisans? Taking the officer's warning at his word, Indig offered to evacuate, but surprisingly the officer changed his tune. "Are you out of your mind? . . . I can't allow you to hike back unprotected. Nobody walks here alone. Until the partisans up here have been liquidated, you must stay with us. We will protect you."[17]

What, Indig feared, would be the response of the partisans to this friendly Italian gesture? Would they view him as collaborating with the Fascists and a traitor to the cause of Slovenia's liberation from a foreign occupier? For the moment, he could not think of any other viable alternative. It was clear that staying in this war zone was becoming riskier, as he tried to maneuver between the Italian hosts and protectors of his children and the partisans, whose suspicions of the group's true sympathies kept mounting.

As noted by Indig in his diary on May 11, 1942, "Almost every evening we can see burning houses in the mountains around us. . . . Not always are the Italians to blame for those atrocities. Often the partisans are also burning the houses of the collaborators. . . . It seems you cannot win in this war." That same day, a partisan detachment passed by the house. After they departed, a group of Italian soldiers showed up, staying for a few hours. Then again the partisans; this time their intentions were not clear. "We have to calm their doubts about us. . . . They wanted to know what we were doing here." Indig assured them of his group's neutral stance with regard to the political situation in Slovenia, and the partisan unit departed. But with the continuous fighting between the Italians and the partisans, it was clear to Indig that his group could not remain in Grad Lesno Brdo. Luckily for him, he then learned from Bolaffio that the Italian Interior Ministry had consented to the group's relocation to the interior of Italy, and Delasem was searching for a proper location.[18] No departure date had yet been set.

In the meantime, the fighting around Indig's house continued, with the partisans executing anyone suspected of collaborating with the Germans, and gradually the partisans gained a greater control of the area. The Italians, too, began to look askance at the presence of Indig's group in the fighting zone. They came to install machine guns around the house, and they searched the premises for hidden weapons, as Indig hurriedly hid some of the anti-Fascist literature that the children had brought with them. An Italian officer told Indig: "A group of children dwelling in the middle of the battle zone. This is not the way to conduct the war! No, you must leave the house," though not immediately. "Well, for the time being you're OK!"[19]

Then, unpredictably, Joshko sustained a slippery fall, breaking his hand, and had to be removed to a hospital in Ljubljana. While he was away, the partisans occupied the Grad Lesno Brdo house in full force— about seventy-five fighters. "They sang and danced in our courtyard. We showed them how to dance the Hora. . . . They taught us many partisan songs," Weiss recalled.[20] At the news that the Italians were in the vicinity, the partisans quickly left and retreated into the forest, throwing hand grenades to distract and slow down the Italian advance. Fighting soon broke out, and everyone scurried into the cellar, which had been fortified with sandbags for protection against stray bullets. The Italians burst into the house and thoroughly searched it, almost hurling a hand grenade in the direction of the basement. At the last moment, they stopped when told that small children were there, seeking shelter from the fighting above and around them. The Italians then retreated to their base in nearby Horjul.

Safe Passage to Italy

Soon word came that the children could head to a small town called Nonantola—a name they had never heard before—situated some 11 kilometers from Modena in central Italy. To speed up the departure, Indig left the hospital with his arm still in a cast and returned to his children's home. There he had a face-to-face encounter with Josip Cerni, the local strong-armed partisan leader (known as the "black one"). The departure could not be delayed, as a major Italian offensive against the partisan strongholds was in the offing.

"Come, fight with us as volunteers!" Josip Cerni screamed. He was especially interested in the older boys, but Indig explained that his children would soon be leaving the battle-infested region. He added, as an afterthought, that the boys spoke only German; anyone encountering them (peasants or partisans alike) could kill them by mistake. "Another thing, Cerni," Indig quickly added, capitalizing on Cerni's change of mind. "Tomorrow morning we have to leave here. Can you give us a note that enables us to remove the barricades? I can't see how we can take out our belongings otherwise."

"Of course I can do that!' Cerni answered. He immediately dictated an order to his confederates. "To all it may concern!!! Death to the Fascists!!! From the Brigade of the red flag . . . permits [given for the] removal of barricades on the road between Grad Lesno Brdo and the railroad station . . . that they shall be put back in place after the carts with the belongings of the children have passed through. Farmers of Grad Lesno Brdo shall supply wagons and horses required for transportation and all the manpower required." Then, with a shout and a Marxist raised fist, they left the house, with all the children returning their salute. "Thus ended our last encounter with the partisans of Slovenia," Indig noted with relief.[21]

Arriving in Ljubljana, a pleasant surprise awaited them. They were going to have their own private railroad car in a train heading to Trieste. While en route, they learned that the German Railway Command had tried to divert the railroad car to Treviso and the Austrian border, but the Italian authorities had refused. Arriving in Trieste, the group went sightseeing. While there, they passed under the control of the Italian national police, the Carabinieri, and its commanding general, Giuseppe Pieche, who proved to be friendly to Indig's group. It was he who turned down the German demand to transfer the children and divert the train to the Austrian border, a country then part of Nazi Germany. He insisted that the group's itinerary not be altered in the direction of Nonantola. After the war, General Pieche was honored by the Jewish community in Italy.[22]

Safety inside Fascist Italy

Although Fascist, Italy did not physically abuse or kill Jews—at least not until the Germans took control of Italy.

The Jewish community in Italy counted among the oldest continuous Jewish settlement in Europe—more than 2,000 years. In 1870, when Italy achieved full unification, Jews were fully emancipated. In 1922 the Fascists came to power, headed by Benito Mussolini. In the first decade of Fascist rule, government officials repeatedly assured the Jewish community, some of whom were even members in good standing of the Fascist Party, that there was nothing to be concerned about, since Fascism was entirely free of antisemitic tendencies. Mussolini publicly condemned racism and antisemitism and had cordial talks with Zionist leaders, even going so far as to call for the establishment of a Jewish state in Palestine.[23] But this was before Italy's rapprochement with Nazi Germany.

In the fall of 1936, Mussolini launched an antisemitic press campaign, and this culminated in the racial laws two years later. The civil rights of Jews were restricted; marriages between Jews and non-Jews were abolished, their books were banned, and Jews were dismissed from public office and higher education. Jews were also banned from positions in banking, government, and education, and their properties were confiscated. At the same time, it is well to remember, Fascist antisemitism was not a logical development of the Italian Fascist creed, as was the case with Nazi antisemitism, but the consequence of Mussolini's alliance with Hitler.

The result was a watered-down version of Hitler's Nuremberg Laws; there was also no comparison between the internment camps in Italy and the concentration camps set up by the Nazis in Germany and in the countries they occupied. In the Italian camps, families lived together; there were schools for the children and a broad program of social welfare and cultural activities. The work imposed on the prisoners involved only services required for the camp itself.[24] Some of the camps were situated in the southern districts, which were the first to be set free when the Allies landed there in the fall of 1943.

When Italy surrendered to the Allies on September 8, 1943, the Germans immediately swept in and occupied the central and northern parts of the still unliberated country, including Rome. Tragically, these two regions were where most of the country's Jews lived. At the time of the Italian armistice there were some 44,500 Jews in Italy and Rhodes Island (held by Italy), 12,500 of them foreigners. By the end of the war at least 7,682 of these had perished in the Holocaust, most of them deported to Auschwitz.[25] On October 16, 1943, the Germans arrested more than 1,000 Jews in Rome. Arrests also took place in Trieste, Genoa, Florence, Milan, and Ferrara.

Jews were first imprisoned in camps on Italian soil, such as Fossoli di Carpi, Bolzano, and La Risiera di San Sabba before being deported to Auschwitz.[26] Italy had its share of collaborators with the Germans, such as the men of the Fascist Black Brigades and the volunteers of the Italian ss. There were also informers among the Italians, from ideological reasons or mostly civilians who were motivated by greed. Most Italians, however, including a substantial part of the Italian clergy, gave aid to the Jews in hiding and crossing into Switzerland, thus saving the greater part of the Jewish population in Italy.[27]

Settling in a Village Mansion

Returning to our story, en route to Modena the children were welcomed at the train station by the sexton of the local Jewish community. Here, too, they took off to visit the city's sights, including the still functioning synagogue. The rabbi held a short thanksgiving service, and then the ladies of the small Jewish community fed them. "What change!" Indig wondered. "In the heart of Fascism. No fighting or curfew here! Life goes on practically undisturbed." After a short rest, the group proceeded to nearby

Nonantola. It was the afternoon of July 17, 1942, when they descended the train and headed on foot to Villa Emma.[28] The building with its forty rooms was largely unoccupied, with the exception of a small number of Jews from Benghazi, Libya, then an Italian-held colony.

The boys in the group struck up a friendship with the local youngsters who belonged to Ballila, the Fascist Youth Organization, which was supposed to be similar to its counterpart in Germany, the Hitler Youth. They wore black shirts, short pants, and black caps. Yet their behavior toward the Jewish boys was a world apart from any other Fascist youth organization in the Axis camp. The Ballila boys showed them how to get on the train for a visit to nearby Modena without having to pay and lent them their bicycles.[29] For his part, Indig established friendly ties with Gino Friedman, founder of a local factory and head of the Jewish community of Modena. Friedman arranged for older boys to work in the factory and local cannery. Some of the older girls also found work making baskets and shopping bags. All this added to the common fund benefiting the entire group.[30]

For its part, Delasem appointed Dr. Umberto Jacchia as its representative at Villa Emma. Due to the frequent air raids on Genoa, Delasem transferred its offices and the central storage and clothing depot to Villa Emma, where two rooms on the ground floor were set aside for the new offices carrying the sign Delasem Ufficio Assistenca. Some more Jewish refugee children were added to Indig's group, ages six to ten, some of whom were recent arrivals from former Yugoslavia.[31] Medical care for the children was provided by the local doctor, Giuseppe Moreali, who did not hide his strong anti-Fascist conviction. Friendly relations also prevailed with Father Arrigo Beccari of the Catholic abbey of Nonantola.[32]

Sanctuary by the Local Catholic Clergy

The long period of tranquility, lasting twelve months, changed and became worrisome, then alarming, when Mussolini was removed from power by his own Fascist Party on July 25, 1943, and some German troops began making their appearance in the country, still allied to Germany.

Then on September 8, Italy capitulated to the Allies, and that was followed by an immediate German military takeover. At first, moments before the German full-fledged invasion, Indig was elated, as he happily told his group: "*Haverim* [comrades, or friends], the war is over! We have a truce."[33] The following day, a sizable German troop force arrived in Nonantola and was quartered in the school across from Villa Emma. Indig's group was now in peril, bearing in mind that camp Fossoli di Carpi, the soon-to-be main concentration camps for Jews in Italy, was only a short distance from Nonantola. As rumors circulated that the German military intended to requisition Villa Emma for its own use, Indig decided to move out his now larger group of eighty children and have them relocated until a plan could be devised to spirit them out of the town to safer locations.[34]

Indig turned to the town's leading Catholic prelate, Monsignor Otaviano Pelati. Indig told him in no uncertain terms: "The children are in danger. We are leaving Villa Emma. I should like to ask you to take at least the younger ones into the seminary for a number of days. . . . Here they will be safe." Pelati agreed. Indig continued: "What about the girls? They like to live, too!" Here the Monsignor hesitated. "That is more difficult, as you know; in the last thousand years, not a single woman has crossed the threshold of the building." But then he said, "Well, in God's name," and making the sign of the cross, he whispered a prayer. Finally, "Bring them . . . but everybody together" and secretly.[35]

That night, forty boys and girls moved into the monastery, getting there by furtively passing through the narrow streets of Nonantola, uncomfortably close to the ss quarters. They entered through a side door, where they were met by elderly nuns who prayed and crossed themselves. The girls were placed on the ground floor in the nuns' quarters, and the boys, up on the second floor, next to young seminarians training for the priesthood. For beds, the boys slept on classroom benches. Some of the older boys had left for the village to watch after some of the valuables left behind, and they found shelter among the farmers, including some with Dr. Moreali.[36]

Back in the seminary, at midnight the children heard the bells chime—it was prayer time for the seminarians upstairs and the nuns downstairs. Indig reflected: "From now on, they will pray every day for the rescue and the deliverance of the children, and we are forgetting the differences between them and us that were allowed to develop over the centuries. They are not trying to convert anyone."[37] Listening to the BBC radio, Indig learned that on September 14, 1943, British forces had liberated the large refugee camp of Ferramonte di Tarsia in southern Italy and freed its 2,000 Jewish internees. But in the seminary, the pressure of the archbishop on Pelati to remove the children was beginning to show troubling telltale signs. "You know, our archbishop is very old and like all the old gentlemen he is afraid," Pelati confided one day to Indig. He, too, was worried about the seminary's safety. "I would not want the monastery to be endangered."[38] It was clear to Indig that the stay in the seminary could not be prolonged, and another solution had to be found.

During this early period of the German occupation, before he could figure out what to do next, Indig walked around disguised in a priestly cassock as protection against the watchful eyes of the Germans.[39] Some adults in the group found refuge as sharecroppers on a small farm near Villa Emma and slept in a partly open air hayloft. Nine boys and one girl decided to go south, in the direction of the fast advancing Allied armies, and succeeded in reaching safe haven.

Crossing into Switzerland

Indig decided that the best alternative for his children's rescue was, in spite of the dangers, in attempting to cross into Switzerland. He had been told that the least risky point on the border was near Ponte Tresa. One evening, dressed in a cleric's cassock, he met with the cleric Don Arrigo Beccari and Godredo Pacifici (also known as Cicibu), and considered the news brought to them by Robert Weiss, one of the boys staying with the group. Weiss had told them that he and his companion Arnold had already arranged to meet a man in Cernobbio, near Como, who had promised to help them cross the frontier into Switzerland. If the two succeeded, they would then try to get some money sent back to Indig and prepare a way for all the children to follow. After a lengthy debate, Josef Indig and Cicibu agreed to this course of action, which seemed the only way out of the children's predicament.[40] Pacifici cautioned them about the large amount of money needed to bribe the smugglers. That night Weiss and Arnold were joined by several others.

On September 26, 1943, Weiss and his six companions rode the train from Nonantola to Modena and then to Regio Emilia, where Italian Fascist guards boarded it in search of deserters from the Italian army. An ss man stopped Weiss and asked for his *Ausweiss*, his ID card. Weiss (originally from Austria) responded in perfect German that he had left it with another inspector on the train. The ss man saluted and continued on his inspection tour.[41] Arriving in Milan late in the evening, Weiss's group could not leave the station because the curfew had already set in, and nobody was allowed on the blacked-out streets, so they had no choice but to pass the night in the darkened main hall of the train station.

Early next morning, the group continued to Como on a small local train. As they boarded, they could not help but notice the posters at the station, signed by the German command, warning the population not to hide or aid refugees. Alighting in Como, they proceeded by bus to Cernobbio, the last village before the border. There, they met their prearranged contact person in a little restaurant. One of Robert Weiss's companions, who spoke Italian with a Modenese dialect, led the conversation, as many German ss men were sitting in the main room gulping down beer and singing German songs. The group was taken to a home where they bedded down in one of the spare rooms to wait for the night.

Their companions were apparently accomplished smugglers, who were adept at crossing the border frequently, exchanging Italian cigarettes and tobacco in return for Swiss-made saccharin and other scarce items in Italy. After midnight, two sinister looking characters with masked faces appeared and told Weiss's group to walk in total silence toward the fence separating Italy from Switzerland. At a certain spot, one of them whistled and sure enough someone from the other side crawled to the fence and lifted it from the bottom with the help of a wooden board. As the two smugglers exchanged their sacks of goods, Weiss and his companions crawled under the fence as fast as possible. They were now safely on the Swiss side, but had to elude arrest by the Swiss border guards.[42]

They walked in the dead of the night to a little barn in a nearby village. There, they boarded a train heading from Lugano to Zürich that was jammed with Swiss students returning from an outing. Arriving safely, very early Friday morning, October 1, in Zürich, they dodged the many Swiss men in uniform in the station. Once out on the street, Weiss approached an old woman walking slowly with a cane and a big shopping bag and asked her where the Jewish community center was. She stared back and said sarcastically, "*Du chaible auslanders*" (you dumb foreigners), but motioned to follow her. She even accompanied them on the streetcar and paid the fare for them. She then motioned to them to get off and pointed out the Jewish building. There they met

Saly Mayer, the JDC representative and head of the Swiss Jewish community, and they also spoke on the phone with Nathan Schwalb, the Hechalutz delegate in Switzerland, to whom they passed on Indig's urgent request for help. It was immediately decided to send money to the border point and alert the people helping in the crossing to expect a large group of children.[43]

Back in Nonantola, Indig agonized over the plan to spirit his eighty children across the Swiss border. He wanted first to check out the route himself. He and Alfredo Pacifici headed to Regio Emilia, safely passing several inspections on the train ride, and an Allied air raid, which made the passengers scurry for safety. Arriving in the middle of the night at Ponte Tresa, a man who appeared drunk led them to a location near the border and agreed to facilitate the children's escape across the river that separated Italy from Switzerland. The next morning Indig and Pacifici headed back to Nonantola, with Indig wondering where was he going to find the 1,000 lire per child that the border smugglers requested.

Passing through Como, they met Pacifici's brother, who reassured Indig that the money would be available from Nathan Schwalb in Switzerland, who had already been alerted of the children's coming by Weiss. The man continued: "You will cross at Ponte Tresa and the Swiss government will [in this instance] advise the border guards to permit your entry. Give them the name of the official in the Yugoslav embassy in Bern as a password. Here is pocket money for the children that they have entrusted to me."[44]

Returning to Nonantola, Indig was now prepared for the long trip to cross the Swiss border, in an area swarming with German and pro-Nazi Italian troops. Indig was counseled to leave quietly. "Don't wake the monks." Don Beccari added: "Indig, don't forget us!" At dawn, one of the old nuns came into the kitchen where some of the women were preparing food packages for the children, and said: "Signora, may God bless you and the children. . . . We prayed all night. Why are they persecuting you? After all, you are good people." At noon Indig's first group of forty children (the others were to follow a bit later) slipped away quietly, but it was not a secret to the villagers, who knew the reason for their departure and wished them well as they watched from their shuttered windows. Upon reaching the railroad station, they met the two Jewish refugee families from Benghazi who were determined not to be left behind. They included a seventy-year-old deaf and half-blind man and two obviously retarded women with whom it was difficult to communicate. "We are coming with you!" they insisted. "You don't like it? We'll scream! We are Jews, and so are you."[45]

As the train reached Regio Emilia, the children took out their papers and held them open before the passing ss officer who threw a glance at them and then left. Arriving in Milan, Indig searched frantically for Pacifici, who was to guide them on their onward journey toward the Swiss border, but did not see him. Had he been arrested, Joshko wondered? Then they noticed a man sleeping on a chair near the station restaurant. It was Pacifici. Awakened by Indig, he exclaimed: "Madonna mia, did I fall asleep? I waited a long time for you. . . . Come, in half an hour our train will depart for Varese." But that train was not scheduled to leave until the following morning. What was one to do with forty children? After spending a few hours on the streets of the city, Pacifici succeeded in bribing the guards of a building belonging to the city, and everyone crowded into its rooms and halls for a night's stay.

Late the following morning, the group reached the small town of Varese and noticed a large detachment of ss troops near the station. Indig and the children quickly left on a streetcar for Ponte Tresa, filled with Italian soldiers of the reconstituted Italian neo-Fascist army. It was raining. Posters on street walls warned the population against aiding the partisans who were known to be active in the region.[46]

The sun came out as the tramway, ever climbing uphill, reached Ponte Tresa. A border smuggler named Pietro was waiting for the group. The children were told to walk in a long line as though out on a hike, with Pietro steadily whistling up in front. They stopped at an old house nestled amid hilly rocks and surrounded by brooks dashing down the mountainside. There Pacifici-Cicibu left them. "I still have to bring a number of Jews to safety," he excused himself. "It is my duty! . . . *Che sera sera.* I shall go to Venice to take my wife to safety. Then to the mountains . . . I must kill a few of them." He was eventually captured and deported to Auschwitz, where he died in December 1943.[47]

When evening settled in, the children left the house and proceeded on a trail, including the odd Benghazi people. It was to be a three-hour walk to the border point, with Pietro leading the way. The night was stiff dark, and the people figured that there were probably many others, Jews,

Italians, British prisoners of war, trying to flee to freedom. The group settled on top of a ridge until a German border patrol had passed and returned to its station.

It was October 8, the night of Yom Kippur, the Jewish most holy festival, when Indig and his forty children crossed into Switzerland. Joshko found this highly symbolic, thinking to himself as he and his wards got their feet and more of their bodies wet in the rushing Tresa River that precisely on the Day of Reckoning they were crossing into freedom. The noise of the river drowned out any sound the group may have made. An Italian soldier, who was paid 5,000 lire, opened the border fence for them. For an additional 550 lire he opened up an additional gate through which one could crawl without activating the little bells. Soon everyone waded through the river, up to their knees. They had to be careful because the current was strong. When one of the girls fell, she was pulled up by her hair.[48] The river carried away many of the group's bundles of clothing. At the nearby Swiss police station, the group was allowed to dry themselves. It was now up to the commanding officer at this station to decide whether to let them in or order them back into German-held Italy. They were taken to a nearby camp to await his verdict.

When a lady from the Red Cross showed up, Joshko implored her to inform Nathan Schwalb of the group's arrival and that another children group would be coming the following night, but the Red Cross lady refused to be of any assistance. As evening fell, the group organized the traditional Ne'ilah prayer, ending the Yom Kippur holiday. Another day of uncertainty passed without any news. When the Swiss officer entered, everyone listened tensely. He stated in a rather somber tone, "In consideration of the preceding days and based on the discussions that took place in the last few days, the government of the Swiss confederation has decided that you may remain on Swiss soil." An explosion of uncontrollable joy enveloped everyone. They were now safe.[49]

Eventually Saly Mayer and the Jewish organizations were able to find the group an empty hotel in the little village of Bex-le-Bains located on the Rhone River. Not far from them was an Orthodox Jewish children's camp, headed by a certain Maurice Ascher (where I, Mordecai Paldiel, and my sister Annie also stayed at about the same time, having crossed with my parents and siblings from France into Switzerland, on September 8, 1943), and from time to time the two groups joined in the festive

Oneg Sabbath get-together. The Villa Emma group was later joined by a children's group from Hungary, who also converted part of the Bex-les-Bains home to accommodate part of the Kasztner train from the Bergen-Belsen concentration camp.[50]

On to Palestine

After the war, Indig and his children left for Barcelona on their way to Haifa, in what was then still Palestine, where they arrived on June 20, 1945. There they were reunited with the "mother of the children," Recha Freier. In 1965 Don Arrigo Beccari and Dr. Giuseppe Moreali were awarded the prestigious title of Righteous Among the Nations by the Yad Vashem Holocaust Memorial in Jerusalem, for their help to the children during their long stay in Nonantola.[51]

In summary, of those youth who reached Yugoslavia before the German invasion, only ninety had succeeded, leaving for Palestine with the Youth Aliyah in March 1941. As for the Grad Lesno Brdo group, headed by Josef Indig, it originally consisted of forty-seven children and ten adults. During the Nonantola period, an additional thirty-four children from Split (in Croatia, but at that time under Italian rule) were added, sent there by Delasem, and eight adults. In Bex-les-Bains, an additional thirty children and eight adults from the Bergen-Belsen concentration camp joined them.[52]

And so a group of Jewish children fled from Germany and Austria to Yugoslavia-Croatia, continued to Italian-held Slovenia, and proceeded to Italy proper, then crossed secretly into Switzerland, where they were finally safe from harm. Josef Indig, the man mostly responsible for the rescue of these many children, later known by his Hebrew family name of Itai, retired to kibbutz Gat, Israel, where he lived a long life, dying in 1998 at eighty-one years of age.

7 France

The Many Who Helped Save Most of the Country's Jews

Jews lived in France since Roman days, when the country was known as Gaul. During the early Middle Ages, it was a center of rabbinics, with such notables as the famed biblical and Talmudic commentator Rashi (Solomon son of Yitzhak), who lived in Troyes, but Jewish life was also dotted with long periods of persecution and expulsions. Later France changed course in its policy toward Jews as it became the first European country to grant them full emancipation in 1791, during the French Revolution.[1] After World War I, tens of thousands of Jewish immigrants from Eastern Europe entered France, to be supplemented with thousands of Jewish refugees from Germany in the 1930s, after the Nazi assumption of power, and more so from Austria, after that country's absorption by Germany in March 1938. Of the approximately 325,000 Jews to be found on the eve of World War II, most lived in Paris and environs, with more than half of all Jews not having yet obtained French citizenship.

Paris also remained the center of Jewish life in France, where Julien Weill held the post of chief rabbi.[2] The majority of foreign Jews read Yiddish newspapers, with many of them active in various leftist organizations, such as the Bund, as well as Socialist-Zionists, and the Communist-inspired Immigrant Manual Labor, known by its French initials as MOI (*Main-d'oeuvre immigrée*). The immigrant Jews were generally not well accepted by their more assimilated co-religionists of French origin, who dominated the Jewish leadership. Thus, on the eve of the war, the Jews of France were to a large degree a fragmented community.[3]

Victorious in World War I but having paid a stiff price in losses and wounded soldiers and much destruction in the northern part of the country, France followed a liberal immigration policy in the postwar period. Foreigners, numbering 3 million, made up 7 percent of the population.[4] A 1938 law was passed making it an offense to publish material that incited racial hatred. At the same time, there was a rise in xenophobic outbursts, spiced with large doses of antisemitism, directed against the many foreigners who had entered France to seek refuge from persecution and bad economic conditions. This led to a government decision in November 1938 to confine certain foreigners in special detention camps, a measure that in the words of historians Michael Marrus and Robert Paxton represented the "founding of concentration camps in France."[5]

War and Defeat

With the start of World War II, some 15,000 German and Austrian political and racial refugees, mostly Jews, were confined in the camps of Gurs, Le Vernet, and Saint-Cyprien. While almost half were freed within three months, they were arrested again when Germany invaded France in May 1940. No one could fail to notice that of the 40,000 civilians then detained in camps, 70 percent were Jews. After France's traumatic defeat in June, the Jews became largely the scapegoats responsible for the country's humiliation, not even sparing the tens of thousands who had fought in French uniforms and were presently detained and stigmatized as "unworthy of our hospitality."[6] Defeated France was divided into two: an occupied zone (approximately two-thirds of the country, including Paris) and an unoccupied (so-called Free) zone, in the south and southeast, where a satellite government was allowed to operate from the city of Vichy (hence, Vichy France).

The following year, a nationwide census by the Vichy regime counted 340,000 Jews, including refugees from Belgium and thousands of German Jews dumped by the Germans in French camps, while 10,000 had already emigrated. Included were 12,000 as prisoners of war in Germany and 35,000 held in French camps and labor facilities.[7] Very few people realized that the legal step of requiring Jews to register with the police later facilitated their roundup and deportation to the death camps, especially the foreign-born Jews.[8] The region of Paris alone had some 150,000 Jews, now under the watchful eyes of the German occupiers. In the unoccupied zone, some 150,000 Jews flocked to the major cities: Lyon, Marseilles, and Toulouse.[9]

Vichy, France, and the Jews

Under the Vichy regime, whose laws were to apply equally in the occupied zone, the republican emblem of "liberty, equality, and fraternity" (*liberté, égalité, fraternité*) was replaced with "work, family, and homeland" (*travail, famille, patrie*), what has been referred to by critics as the "anti-France" period.[10] The head of state was the aged World War I hero Marshal Philippe Pétain. His prime minister, Pierre Laval (especially as of April 1942), worked diligently for a closer collaboration between France and Germany, even if it meant sacrificing the Jews to the Germans and sending French non-Jewish laborers to Germany.[11] On November 11, 1942, days after the landing of U.S. forces in French-held Morocco and Algeria, the Germans also occupied the Vichy zone, and Fascist Italy was granted direct control of eight southern regions east of the Rhône river, including the city of Nice. Italian control lasted until September 8, 1943, when Italy surrendered to the Allies, and the Germans occupied these regions as well.

In contrast to other countries dominated by Nazi Germany, the Vichy regime was afforded a considerable degree of autonomy, including its self-controlled police, headed by René Bousquet. Thus it was quite surprising that without even German prodding, the Vichy government initiated a series of antisemitic laws, starting with the Jewish Statute (Statut des Juifs) of October 3, 1940, which was amended by a new law on June 2, 1941, and meant to apply to all Jews living in France in both zones. These laws defined a Jew as a person with three grandparents "of the Jewish race," or with two Jewish grandparents if the spouse was also Jewish. It drastically reduced the role of Jews in French society, excluding them from top positions in the French civil service and the professions that had a public bearing, such as teaching, the press, radio, film, and theater.[12]

On October 4, 1940, another law granted the prefects (heads of provinces—*départements)* the power to intern at their discretion foreign and non-naturalized Jews. Three days later, the Jews of Algeria, who in 1870 had been granted French citizenship, were deprived of their nationality and subjected to a system of exclusion. In addition, an October 18 directive dealt with Jewish-held economic enterprises (such as banks, insurance companies, law firms, and real estate offices), involving some 42,000 Jewish businesses that were to be nationalized and to have government-appointed trustees provisionally assigned over them.[13] Another Vichy law required the stamping of *Juif* on identity cards and ration books of any Jewish person ages six and above. Finally, to enforce these restrictive laws, on March 29, 1941, the Vichy government established a special ministry, General Office for Jewish Affairs—Commissariat Général aux Questions Juives (CGQJ), headed at first by Xavier Vallat, a known antisemite, who was soon replaced by a more virulent antisemite, Louis Darquier de Pellepoix.[14]

Jewish leaders failed to see that the Vichy leadership was pursuing its own French traditional and pre-Revolution version of antisemitism and not necessarily at the prodding of the Germans, as Jews mistakenly believed.[15] In the occupied zone, the Germans were busy enforcing anti-Jewish measures of their own, such as the placement of a yellow sign on Jewish-owned stores, with the words *Affaire Juive* (Jewish business). In the occupied zone Jews were allowed to use only the last car in the metro (subway) trains, and all public places were forbidden to them. On June 7, 1942, the Germans imposed the wearing of the Yellow Star in their zone.[16] This was their final act before the start of massive deportations.

Detention Camps

The Vichy regime called the concentration camps of Gurs, Rivesaltes, Les Milles, and other places of detention for non-naturalized French Jews "lodging centers" (*centres d'hébergement*); this, in spite of the high rate of mortality there—1,000 in Gurs alone. Some 40,000 foreign-born and stateless Jews were to be incarcerated in these camps. They lacked proper hygienic facilities and nourishment, leading to the death of the first victims of the Holocaust in France in these camps—about 3,000. At the same time, Vichy authorities permitted senior female social workers, Jewish and non-Jewish, to enter and remain there as "voluntary detainees" to ease conditions of the hapless detainees.[17] Until July 1942, camp directors gave detainees furloughs and permitted the sick to be treated in the nearest city hospital. Some took advantage of these liberties to flee. One estimate places the number of detainees released from Gurs camp between November 1940 and July 1942 at 2,000, while there were about

1,000 who managed to escape.[18] No one could imagine then that these camps would soon serve as way stations to the death camps in Poland.

Deportations 1942–1944

The Germans had acquiesced to French demands to delegate the arrest of Jews to the French police. The first arrests were made in Paris in May and August 1941, when nearly 4,000 Jews were apprehended and interned in the Pithiviers and Beaune-la-Rolande camps, then moved to the Drancy transit camp, north of Paris, before being deported further to concentration camps in Germany or Poland. Sporadic arrests of Jews continued in Paris, and on December 12, 1941,more than 1,000 doctors, lawyers, and literary figures were arrested in their homes and deported to Auschwitz on March 27, 1942.[19] This was only the first signal of more massive arrests soon to follow.

July 16, 1942, was chosen as the date to begin the massive arrest of 22,000 foreign Jews of both sexes in the Greater Paris region. The raid by the French police that lasted two days netted 12,884 Jews of all ages including 4,051 children—to the disappointment of the German over-lords who had anticipated a much larger number. The winter sports stadium (Vélodrome d'Hiver, in short, Vel d'Hiv) in Paris was chosen as their temporary internment place before being moved to Drancy, for deportation to Auschwitz. In the southern Vichy zone mass arrests of foreign Jews began on August 26, 1942, and by October 22 Vichy had delivered 11,005 foreign Jews to Drancy.[20] Deportations continued into 1943 and 1944, but at a slower pace, due in part to logistical difficulties of transportation to Poland.

The arrests and detentions of Jews by the thousands, including infants and children of all ages, caught the Jewish organizations entirely unprepared and sent thousands of Jews into a frenzy. Many sought hiding places in dozens of French villages and rural communities, while others attempted to cross the border to Switzerland. The deportations of the summer and fall of 1942 also stirred the first serious opposition to Vichy, with highly placed Catholic clergy now making their first open protest against the anti-Jewish measures of the Vichy regime.[21] The deportations continued, with the last convoys leaving France in the summer of 1944, as the country was being progressively liberated by the advancing Allied armies.[22]

Jewish Children

During the first two years of the occupation, Jewish schoolchildren were allowed to attend public schools without any outward discrimination. Some children were also allowed to make their way out of the country. However, everything changed on July 16, 1942, when thousands of Jewish children were arrested with their parents by armed policemen in their homes in Paris.[23] In the detention camps, screening commissions sorted out adults for deportation, while allowing their children to be whisked away and placed with child care organizations.[24] In his diary Raymond-Raoul Lambert of the UGIF (Jewish Judenrat-type organization) described the drama accompanying the separation of parents from their children in the Les Milles camp: "Buses taking seventy children [ages two to fifteen] away from parents who are going to leave this evening. . . . The fathers and mothers must be restrained when the buses leave the courtyard. . . . Mothers scream in despair, and no one can keep back his tears. . . . I hide to weep."[25] Some 400 children abandoned during the days following the July roundups found shelter in UGIF homes, while others managed to escape arrest.

A particularly harrowing experience was the rescue of children incarcerated with their parents in a camp in the Vénissieux suburb, outside Lyon. The 1,100 arrested persons were subjected to a screening committee, on August 26, 1942, to determine who was to be exempt from deportation.[26] After three days of determined effort, 108 children and adolescents and about 500 adults were either exempted and released or made their escape when released for medical reasons; the rest were deported. As told by Dr. Joseph Weill, of the OSE:

> We feverishly notified the parents and obtained, after much persuasion, the authorization to take over the care of the children . . . about a hundred of them. . . . Almost all of them [parents] informed us of their last wishes, handed their jewels and clothes over to their children. . . . Many of them blessed their children with a biblical phrase. They asked them to be courageous, worthy of their Jewishness, and not to forget them. And with an abrupt gesture, they turned around to hide their emotion. . . . We then collected the children in the dining hall to feed them and to distract them while their parents were being sacrificed. We got the promise from the bus

drivers to drive their vehicles past the illuminated windows of the dining hall so that the parents could leave feeling reassured. No one will ever forget those tearful looks, those silent glances straining for a last look at their children. Toward seven o'clock in the morning, we had the children get into the bus, while we hid the bigger ones underneath the seats.[27]

The lesson of the night of Vénissieux was clear: all Jewish children were at risk. The Jewish children's homes, until now safe from harm, had to be dissolved and the children dispersed.[28] Continuing into 1942 and in the following two years, Jewish children were targeted for deportation, such as the Gestapo raid on April 3, 1944, of the Izieu children's home outside Lyon, which netted forty-four children as well as the staff. There was a sole survivor—a staff worker.[29]

The Italian Zone

In late 1942 the Italians were assigned by the Germans areas in southeastern France extending mostly east of the Rhône River and covering six whole provincial regions. Though allied to the Germans and having instituted anti-Jewish racial laws in November 1938, the Italians were opposed to the brutal manner and the extreme racial underpinnings of the Nazi Final Solution and the collaboration of the Vichy regime in that heinous undertaking. It is also possible that foreseeing the downfall of the Axis cause, the Italian government reasoned that it must not be compromised by the stain of racial persecutions, and appropriate instructions were related to its officers in the Italian zone of France.[30] The Italians entered Nice on November 11, 1942, and Jews began to flee there from other areas in France, and the Nice region soon became home to over 25,000 Jews. The Italians went so far that when the French gendarmerie in Annecy interned a group of Jews, Italian troops surrounded the barracks of the French gendarmerie and insisted that the imprisoned Jews be released, and the French police were forced to submit.[31]

Italy came under intense German pressure to "rectify" the situation regarding Jews in their zone, and on February 20, 1943, the Italians assigned Guido Lospinoso as a special racial expert to coordinate with the Germans and the French the application of anti-Jewish measures in the Italian zone. But he acted in opposition to this.[32] Lospinoso enabled Jews to live undisturbed in a sort of assigned residence in the Italian zone, and for that purpose, the Italian army requisitioned hotels under their control where, in collusion with a Jewish refugees committee, on rue Dubouchage in Nice (hence its name as the Dubouchage Committee), some 4,000 who were sent under terms of forced residence, for all practical purposes remained under the sole control of Jewish relief organizations.[33]

Teams of doctors visited the sick, and makeshift pharmacies were opened. Schools, kindergartens, and children's homes were also opened, including a religious one in Saint-Étienne-de-Crossey in the Isère Department, operated by Rabbi Zalman Schneerson of the Lubavitch Hasidic movement. In the city of Grenoble, also inside the Italian zone, the first center to record events affecting Jews under German domination was created in April 1943, headed by Isaac Schneerson, and later renamed Centre de Documentation Juive Contemporaine.[34]

This tranquil situation for Jews in that part of France began to falter when Benito Mussolini fell from power on July 25, 1943, followed with the surrender of Italy to the Allies on September 8, 1943. This led to an immediate occupation of the Italian zone in France by the Germans, trapping the Jews there. Between 1,000 and 1,500 Jews did manage to flee and cross the Italian border, but there, too, they faced arrest by the Germans who also occupied Italy proper. The ss launched an unprecedented manhunt of Jews, aided by the French Milice (a paramilitary force collaborating with the Germans) and informers, and raiding the city's 170 hotels and boardinghouses, where it was suspected that many Jews were staying. Despite these frantic efforts, by the time of the liberation in August 1944, only 1,819 Jews had been netted, by one account, as most Jews sought refuge among the local population.[35]

Statistics

All told, between 77,000 and 80,000 Jews from France died, mostly deported to concentration camps in Poland, including up to 3,000 dying while in detention on French soil. Seventy-five percent of the Jews in the country on the eve of the German invasion somehow survived—some thousands having left in time or fled to other destinations; other thousands in hiding, and many more simply overlooked and not betrayed by local inhabitants. Of the estimated 84,000 Jewish children in France under the age of sixteen, some 72,400 survived the war, of which 10,000 children were helped by Jewish organizations, while about 11,600 died in deportation.[36]

Jewish Assistance Organizations

The hard-working Jewish self-help groups that
staved off detentions and deportations.

UGIF

Before the war, various immigrant societies and welfare and assistance organizations existed, but the most important Jewish organization was the Central Consistory of the Jews of France (Consistoire Central des Israélites de France), a religious organization under the authority of the chief rabbinate. Philanthropic in nature, it was considered the official representative of native French Jewry.[37]

Then, intent on copying in France the system of Judenrats, as in other German-occupied countries, the Germans as well as the Vichy regime enforced the creation of an all-embracing Jewish umbrella organization that they hoped to control more effectively.[38] Thus was born the General Union of Jews in France (Union Général des Israélites en France), better known by its acrostic, UGIF. Created on November 29, 1941, it was to be the sole representative body of French Jewry in both French zones. All Jews living in France were automatically affiliated with the UGIF, and all Jewish associations, charities, and organizations were dissolved and their assets transferred to the UGIF, with the exception of religious associations (still controlled by the Consistory), which were authorized to retain their private status.

UGIF was to be administered by a team of eighteen members and was under the authority of Vichy's CGQJ and responsible to it. It included Albert Lévy as its head and André Baur and Raymond-Raoul Lambert—the latter was eventually to represent UGIF in the Vichy zone. To finance its activities, funds were drawn from confiscated Jewish businesses.[39] UGIF was mainly involved in relief work, which represented half of its budget, and worked to release Jews from detention (it succeeded for 817, including 192 children under sixteen). During 1942–43, Section 5 of the UGIF, dealing with children and headed by Juliette Stern, also took charge of some 1,500 children, of which 1,100 were turned over to foster families or non-Jewish institutions, while the rest were kept in the seven children's centers operated by UGIF.[40] All this, strangely, while other Jewish children were randomly being picked up and deported to concentration and death camps in Poland.

UGIF files were neatly arranged according to category: "French Jews," "Foreign-born Jews," "Jewish Institutions," "Homes for Children." This made them easy prey to the Germans when they decided to raid UGIF premises. Thus some Jewish clandestine units felt it was of the greatest importance to destroy these files. Maurice Hausner related one such operation in which he participated: "We entered the UGIF's headquarters and told all employees to line up against the wall; we told them they were doing nefarious traitors' work in keeping their official files; . . . by having records of names and addresses, deportations would be greatly facilitated for the Germans. We then removed as many files as we could, and later destroyed them; but the headquarters housed thousands, and many still remained."[41]

The official status of UGIF hindered it from a too open collaboration with Jewish resistance operatives, though it surreptitiously maintained contacts with various Jewish associations that slipped into more clandestine activity and at times looked the other way as some private organizations took children from UGIF establishments and placed them with foster families. One exception to this were the children classified as "blocked" (bloqués), who were separated from their parents in Drancy camp, temporarily released, and therefore on the Gestapo lists. In order not to openly implicate the UGIF in illegal operations and yet help these "blocked" children, some were allowed to be kidnapped by Jewish secret operatives, in silent complicity with Juliette Stern of the UGIF.[42] This, however, did not prevent the UGIF from being severely criticized by rescue organizations for what they considered the UGIF's too close adherence to legal procedure. Children in UGIF homes were at risk of sudden capture, such as occurred as late as July 22, 1944, when 250 children were apprehended by the Gestapo, a month before the liberation of Paris, and deported, because the UGIF leadership failed to disperse the children in time.[43] A year earlier, in February 1943, the Jewish Communist-oriented Solidarité decided to take matters into its own hands and carried out the "kidnapping" of 163 children who were forcefully taken from UGIF homes, an act copied by other organizations in similar "kidnapping" fashions.[44]

Gilbert Weissberg of MOI (Jewish communists) described one such operation: "Our boys, weapons in hand, rang the bell, entered, and knocked out the guards. They ran off with six of the children. We had some women disguised in nurses' uniforms waiting outside to take charge of them. We were able to find shelter for them with families living on the outskirts of town."[45]

The personnel of the UGIF believed themselves safe from roundups, but this proved an illusion, as they were all arrested in stages.[46] As for UGIF head Albert Lévy, to avoid capture he secretly made his way to Switzerland toward the end of December 1943, but his UGIF colleague André Baur was arrested on June 21, 1943, and deported. The same fate awaited Raymond-Raoul Lambert, the UGIF head in the south, who was arrested together with his wife, four children, and relatives on August 21. Consistory president Jacques Helbronner was arrested on October 23. None survived. Finally, in May 1944, the UGIF closed its southern offices, though still continuing to operate out of its Paris location, but clandestinely, even providing provisions to Drancy camp internees.[47]

Amelot

On June 15, 1940, as France was going down in defeat, thirteen Jewish aid activists met under the leadership of Marc Jarblum in the Paris apartment of Léo Glaeser and decided to create a day camp (Colonie Scolaire), to include a dispensary and soup kitchen, with David Rapoport (who belonged to the Socialist-Zionist Poalei Zion movement) appointed its secretary-general. It was to be located at the dispensary, called Mother and Child (La Mère et l'Enfant), at 36 rue Amelot—hence the Amelot Street committee (Le Comité de la Rue Amelot) was born, some seventeen months before the official creation of UGIF.[48] Amelot's attempt to involve native French Jews in the relief and assistance enterprise failed to materialize, but the charity work continued, with support from the U.S.-based Joint Distribution Committee and the U.S. Quakers (food, clothing, and medicine). The Amelot Committee did not comply with the German decree on August 28, 1940, requiring all associations to have German approval to operate, and it continued its clandestine work of relief and rescue throughout the northern zone until the country's liberation in 1944. In 1941, about 100 children, wards of Rue Amelot, were dispersed in the countryside, and after David Rapoport's arrest on June 1, 1943, the soup kitchen and dispensaries of Rue Amelot continued to be administered by UGIF.[49]

OSE

The Oeuvre de Secours aux Enfants, or Children's Rescue Program (OSE), was created in Russia in 1912 by a group of Jewish doctors to help those with medical needs. Later, when it moved to France, it turned to strictly aiding children in need.[50] Before the war, it was active in establishing children's homes and vacation colonies, mainly for refugee children from Germany and Austria, such as Montmorency in the Paris region. When the Germans invaded, the OSE leadership moved its base to Montpellier in the Vichy zone, where approximately 2,000 Jewish children were living in some thirty OSE shelters. OSE-south eventually moved to Chambéry (Savoy province), before going fully underground in late 1943.[51]

Originally the Vichy regime allowed foreign or stateless children in detention camps to be released and admitted to a children's home, but only if their guardians could produce a certificate of domicile delivered by the prefect of the *Département* where the shelter was situated. This made it possible for the OSE to receive and place the liberated children and disperse them in various locations, such as in Masgelier, one of the largest OSE homes, located in an old chateau with amenities. A school was installed there with lodgings for the teachers, and in 1942 it had 122 children. The list of the released children and their addresses were kept by the police.[52] OSE reports written after the war estimate that the organization freed up to 1,300 children from detention prior to July 1942. To make room for children in the OSE homes, an estimated 527 other children were placed in foster homes.[53]

Until mid-1942, Jewish organizations innocently believed that whatever fate befell the parents, no harm would come to the children—this in spite of the constant urgings of OSE medical head Dr. Joseph Weill to close the homes and disperse the children. He was one of the few who feared the worse for the children. He was proved right when, in mid-1942, Vichy reversed its policy on the children and ordered their return to their parents in the camps, under the deceptive-sounding policy of "family reunion" (*regroupement familial*)—in truth so that both parents and children could be deported.[54] Yet it still took more than a year for the directorate of the OSE to become fully convinced that its homes had become death traps. Some homes had already been closed, and soon the rest were hastily closed and the children dispersed, with the OSE continuing to operate clandestinely and continuing to care for some 6,000 children, all of whom were in hiding.[55]

As early as April 1943, the OSE began to smuggle its wards into Switzerland, and this was accelerated toward the end of the year, especially from its main base in Chambéry, then in the Italian zone, where organized children convoys left for the Swiss border. As the Swiss police did not turn back parents with very small children, pseudo-families of unmarried couples and babies were organized. But on most occasions, children were smuggled across the border alone without any accompanying fictitious parents, and great care and much work were consequently invested to prepare the children on their routes across the border. This included sewing a record of the real civil status of each child into its clothing, arranging rest stops and provisions, escorting, exploring, inventing new ways to cross the border—all this under the greatest secrecy. Between January 1 and June 7, 1944, 569 Jewish children crossed into Switzerland illegally without their parents. According to another estimate, some 1,069 children made the illegal crossing into Switzerland, between autumn 1943 and July 1944, with the help of the OSE and several other clandestine Jewish organizations. In addition, an underground OSE team led by Andrée Salomon charted escape routes across the Pyrenees into Spain.[56]

For children placed with non-Jewish foster homes, the OSE helped them to maintain awareness of their Jewishness. This occurred via monthly visits, which were necessary to pay allowances to the host families and inquire into the child's welfare. These occasions were an opportune moment for discrete conversations with the hidden children and a reminder of their families and Jewish heritage. In the words of Pierre Vidal-Naquet: "We wanted to save . . . not only children but Jewish children, destined to remain so."[57]

Jewish Scouts Movement (*Eclaireurs Israélites de France*, EIF)

Created in 1923 by Robert Gamzon (nicknamed Castor), the EIF integrated within its ranks both native and foreign Jewish youth, from affluent and poor families, observant and secular. It had its own centers, lectures, library, musical choir, kitchen, workshops, and a farm in Saumur. Gamzon introduced the idea of vocational training and manual labor as part of membership in the movement. By the time of the war, it counted 4,000 young activists, half of whom were in metropolitan France; the others were in French-controlled North Africa.[58] Upon France's defeat in June 1940, Gamzon decided to take the scout movement in a new direction, farming (surprisingly, with Vichy approval), and he assigned fellow scout leaders to find suitable farming locations in the Vichy zone.[59]

But first there were more immediate needs, as the EIF helped in the placing of children of families without means in four evacuation centers and instilling in them a Jewish education with special emphasis on productive work. For this purpose it recruited young teachers and officials who found themselves without jobs following the anti-Jewish laws of the Vichy regime. EIF's network of rural training camps, all in the Vichy zone, included three properties in Lautrec and four others, including Taluyers and Moissac. Lautrec became the EIF's main center, including several contiguous farms. Most trainees were students who had never touched a spade or shovel in their lives.[60] In May 1941 the Vichy Ministry of Agriculture entitled the EIF centers to a monthly grant per pupil of French nationality and three salaries for the staff of each center. Keeping in step with formality, officially the EIF worked as a branch of the UGIF for mainly tactical reasons. Under the UGIF umbrella the EIF's work would be freer also to undertake illegal work when the time came for this.[61]

On the Taluyers farm, the Sabbath was observed in the effort of returning to Jewish roots of so many of the assimilated, practically nonobservant Jewish youth, although nothing was done to enforce a strict religious observance. In the words of Isaac Pougatch, an EIF leader: "We wanted to practice a living Judaism . . . to restore the Sabbath as a day of joy . . . to show them that, on the contrary, Judaism was essentially a religion of joyous optimism."[62] In Lautrec, a more intensive religious life was practiced, including daily religious services and a stricter observance of kosher food.

Then, when in the summer months of 1942 the Vichy government began to arrest foreign Jews, many of whose youth constituted the farming communities of the EIF, it was time to disperse and flee. The EIF in Moissac had already been warned by the commissioner of police: "I have to tell you, I am an anti-Semite. . . . When I receive orders to proceed against you, I will carry them out. And when the day arrives, I must arrest you."[63] Presently Gamzon decided to disperse his youth in stages, and by late 1943 all the farms had been closed.

Jewish Clandestine and Resistance Organizations

When conditions deteriorated, Jewish organizations turned to clandestine work and some even to combat.

Historian and Holocaust resistant Léon Poliakov wrote that during that period the Jew "found himself enrolled almost automatically in underground life, because to flout the laws, to enter the area of illegality, was the best way of surviving."[64] Indeed, many Jews chose resistance as a way to combat the enemy rather than the rescue of their brethren. As pointed out by historian Henri Michel: "The participation of Jews in the Resistance was the highest, proportional to the population of Jewish religion or origin." In Algeria a great number of Jews facilitated through various military operations the American landing of troops on November 8, 1942.[65]

French Holocaust survivor and historian Georges Wellers claimed that a strictly authentic Jewish resistance was limited not to those who joined the general resistance but to those who helped Jews by either finding them a secure hiding place, forging various counterfeit credentials for them, or affording them safe passage over the Swiss or Spanish borders or across the demarcation line separating the two parts of France—or, again, by killing informers and "Jew-hunters." They also served by helping and instigating the escape of Jewish detainees and by composing, printing, and circulating news meant to give the persecuted people moral support and arouse sympathy for them among the non-Jewish population.[66] The following are examples of such resistance groups.

Sixth (Sixième)

On January 5, 1943, the Vichy governmental General Office for Jewish Affairs (CGQJ) decreed the immediate dissolution of the Youth Department within the UGIF—the EIF (Jewish Scouts). At about the same time, the EIF decided to call itself the Sixth and continued to operate, this time as a clandestine organization.[67] Regional meetings were held to plan the hiding of young adults (while the OSE dealt with children), fabricate false identities, and assist in spiriting people across the border into Switzerland or Spain. One of the more bizarre hiding places was a leper clinic at Pont-Saint-Esprit, near Valence. Or, in another place, such as told by EIF activist Henri Wahl, "in Grenoble we hid some youngsters in Notre Dame de Zion [convent]. We did this almost against our own will, the ultimate goal of that order being to convert Jews! . . . One of the Sisters . . . she, and all the others, carried cards bearing the Jewish stamp! All of them were converts from Judaism. . . . The Sisters gave me their word they would not try to convert them."[68]

Sixth activists branched out across many regions, traveling individually or in small groups of two or three, at times knocking on the doors of convents: "Mother Superior, we are seeking hiding places for young girls whom the Germans want to deport." "My poor children," often came the reply, "I have no room here. . . . But I will pray for them." But at other times: "But of course, come in, bring them, and God keep you!" Or Nicole Bloch (later, Renée Klein) and Lucien Fayman were fabricating false credentials in the home of Abbé Albert Gau, in Carcassonne, who himself was hiding British aviators in the attic. Or in private homes, as also noted by the Sixth activist Fichtenberg, who wrote that on March 17, 1943, a large meeting in the home of Dr. Sigismond Hirsch planned and arranged the placing of about 100 children on neighboring farms. Moissac remained the focal point of the Sixth, where false papers were also produced. When this place proved too dangerous, the Sixth leadership moved its operational center to the large city of Lyon. In late 1943, the Sixth moved again, this time to Grenoble, under the security afforded by the Italian presence there. A more dangerous period arose when the Germans took over the Italian zone and arrested several Sixth leaders. Sadly, of the eighty-eight young people in the permanent ranks of the Sixth (several hundred were part-time members), four were shot and twenty-six were arrested and deported.[69]

Jewish Army (Armée Juive)

This unique organization, with its military-sounding name (but not really an army in the conventional meaning of the term) was born out of a preceding equally military-sounding grouping calling itself "Strong Hand" (Main Forte), founded by David Knout, wife Ariane, and Paul Roitmann in Toulouse. Then, under the leadership of Alexandre (Abraham) and

Eugénie Polonski, both adherents to Vladimir Jabotinsky's more militant Zionist Revisionist movement, it renamed itself the Jewish Army (henceforth AJ), dedicated to fight the Germans and help Jews to survive, and by 1943 it had branches in Toulouse, Nice, Grenoble, and Lyon. Upon induction into AJ, people had to take an irreversible oath, such as "I swear allegiance to the Jewish Army and obedience to its leaders. Let my people live again! Let Eretz Israel be born again! Liberty or death!" During its four-year activity span, the AJ was able to recruit close to 2,000 members, all willing and ready to fight.[70]

In early 1944, the AJ's activity became more aggressive as its units broke into UGIF offices in Lyon and Marseille and destroyed files and lists. In March and April the AJ Nice group succeeded in tracking down some of the most redoubtable so-called physiognomists, mostly Russian émigrés but also local informers, in the pay of the Gestapo, who assisted them in hunting down Jews circulating freely and passing as non-Jews. They, in turn, were presently tracked down and assassinated. This was the fate of a notorious Russian-born denouncer in Nice, Serge Mojaroff, as well as his successor, Georges Karakaïeff. Likewise in Paris, a concierge who denounced four Jewish families was executed on July 1, 1944. A month earlier, another informer, called Daniel, well known to Jews in Nice, was discovered in Paris and was duly executed on June 23, 1944.[71] The AJ was also active in organizing crossings into Spain and later was incorporated in the general resistance movement when it took part in military operations against the German occupation.[72]

United Zionist Youth Movement (Mouvement de Jeunesse Sioniste)

On May 10, 1942, in a hastily gathered conference in Montpellier, Vichy zone, after a spirited discussion it was decided to unite all Zionist youth movements of various ideological factions into one functioning clandestine organization, the United Zionist Youth Movement (henceforth MJS). It was headed by Jules-Dika Jefroykin and Simon Lévitte, with Otto (Toto) Giniewski (later in Israel, Ginat) as secretary-general and Rabbi René Kapel as spiritual guide. The emphasis was on educational, physical, and vocational retraining. Coincidentally, many of its 2,000 members also joined the AJ, and it eventually synchronized its activities with the Sixth.[73] The MJS was active in posting anti-Nazi posters on walls and distributing thousands of false identities, ration cards, and other credentials that were fabricated in a small hamlet in Seyssins, near Grenoble. From that place, MJS operatives specialized in escorting children to Switzerland.[74] In Nice, the MJS affiliate headed by Jacques Weintraub operated from within the synagogue on Dubouchage Street. By a bitter twist, Weintraub ended tragically. One day after the German occupation of Nice, the Gestapo took Weintraub in for questioning and then released him. Stepping out, he suddenly remembered that he had left behind his briefcase, filled with money and false papers. He returned and was promptly arrested, sent to Drancy, and deported. In a dispatch from Marseilles to Paris on November 19, 1943, the Gestapo stated: "Weintraub had already sent three convoys of twenty-five children each to Switzerland, but we were able to arrest him half an hour before the next group's departure." He did not survive deportation.[75]

Document Falsifiers

French Holocaust historian Lucien Lazare has pointed out that in the Vichy zone, a Frenchman normally carried a half dozen identity documents: an identity card, a military booklet, a certificate of demobilization, ration cards for food, textiles, and tobacco, to which a work certificate was added a little later. Thus Jews living underground and appearing under different names, addresses, and occupations needed a host of false documents in order to pass as non-Jews. Hence the importance of Jewish underground document falsifiers who used several methods to manufacture documents. A more sophisticated method was to "wash" off names listed on identity and ration cards with available solvents, such as hydrogen peroxide or bleach, and then inscribe non-Jewish first and last names as well as other details.[76]

Document falsifiers also learned to manufacture seals themselves or gained possession of original seals, either with the collaboration of friendly mayoral offices or police station workers, or by swiping a seal from an official's desk while his attention was turned elsewhere. It then became possible to fabricate new identity papers, code-named "bifs" for some reason. At the same time, a bif could prove dangerous, as a telephone check to the mayoral office or police headquarters by a slightly skeptical official could give away the forgery.

Activist Gilbert Leidervarger was especially adept in the art of forgery. Starting in Moissac, he would carve into a piece of rubber eraser to produce a seal. Moving to Lyon he began a systematic manufacture of forgeries for the Sixth as well as the MJS.[77] As for Ninon Haït, she used another method. For instance, she knew that the archives at Fourmies, in the north, had been destroyed during a bombing raid; so she sent a letter saying she was born in that town, and would they please send her a copy of her birth certificate? The municipality of Fourmies, of course, replied that they were sorry but they could not. And now Ninon had a letter with the town's stamp on it! All that needed to be done was to copy it.

Another method was to obtain from friendly officials in a town hall—an assistant mayor or a secretary—the birth certificate and identity card of someone deceased or a prisoner of war. Sometimes non-Jewish Frenchmen permitted their own civil status to be copied by a Jew, who was thus "Aryanized."[78] As the EIF activist Charlotte (Shatta) Simon recalled: "There wasn't a single document which the Moissac town hall and the prefecture of Montauban would not give us. Mr. Darac, secretary to the mayor of Moissac, had me come at night to get the first false papers stamped. Then he said: 'You take the stamp home, and bring it back tomorrow.'"[79] Of course, not all municipality workers were that friendly. It could have landed them in deep trouble.

Ninon Hait recalled visiting Bishop Pierre-Marie Théas in Montauban to bring him blank forms and stamps for the benefit of the Jewish protégés who were placed under his care. "I'd start making the false I.D.'s with the Sixth's equipment. . . . Later, as these trips became more difficult, I could come as often with my 'gifts'; the bishop cried: 'If you can't come regularly, what will we do?' Then he added: 'Show me—maybe I can do it myself.' I did and left the materials with him. I would return each month to replenish his supplies. But he was manufacturing all the false documents himself."[80] A Jewish underground workshop in Nice, headed by Maurice Loebenberg (Cachoud), achieved the most astonishing performance in this regard and supplied false credentials not only to Jewish operatives but also to the French resistance. Loebenberg's expertise was of such a high standard that he was sent to Paris by his Jewish confederates, where he was put in charge of the false paper section of the resistance National Liberation Movement (MLN).[81]

MOI—Jewish Communists

There had always been a strong presence of Jews in the French Communist Party, leading some to create a special Jewish section, known as

Immigrant Labor (Main-d'Oeuvre Immigrée), henceforth MOI, within the Communist-oriented General Labor Federation (CGT). In September 1940 MOI decided to create a clandestine movement composed of neighborhood committees, by the name of Solidarité, for the purpose of distributing material assistance to the needy among Jewish workers and making available false credentials; there was also a public soup kitchen and dispensary. The prewar daily Yiddish newspaper *Die Naye Presse* now reappeared as an underground paper, *Unzer Wort*. This Jewish-Communist publication and other leaflets were the first and almost the only ones in France that, thanks to leaks from the French police to Communist operatives, circulated substantial information about the mass arrest in Paris in July 1942, the extermination camps in Poland, and the Warsaw ghetto uprising.[82] More significantly, Solidarité militants did their best to distribute warnings, such as the flier in Yiddish:

Do not wait passively in your apartments for the arrival of the bandits. . . . If they come to arrest you, resist the police by every means. . . . Call for help, fight, do everything possible to escape. . . . Hide, and above all, hide your children with the help of the non-Jewish population.[83]

The Jewish communists constantly demanded that the German-prompted UGIF dissolve itself, since it saw it as an unwitting tool of the enemy. MOI also established the first units of freelance guerilla insurgents who placed time bombs and struck at German soldiers and French police agents in Paris.[84] These units took part in raids against Jewish factories and workshops that were producing equipment for the German army under pressure; they also urged their workers to sabotage these products.[85] As a strongly ideological organization, subservient mostly to the Communist Party, military action in the eyes of MOI took precedence over any other clandestine operations, especially those that served Jewish interests solely. In the postwar regretful words of Maurice Kriegel, who fought in the ranks of the MOI militants: "I would have wished so much to have contributed to the saving of Jewish children rather than trying inconsequentially to kill a few more German soldiers."[86] In all fairness, one must credit the Jewish Communists for being the only Jewish group that publicly warned Jews to resist deportation by whatever means, after warning them of the bitter fate that was in store for those who allowed themselves to be deported.

Attempts at Escape

Rescuers were active in organizing emigration and border crossings to save Jews from capture and deportation.

HICEM, a subsidiary of the U.S.-based HIAS immigration organization, was permitted to open emigration offices in each of the detention camps. The most prominent was in Camp des Milles, north of Marseilles, where detainees destined for emigration were kept. Between the armistice in June 1940 and the end of 1942, when the Germans overran Vichy France, HICEM was able to help 6,449 Jews to reach freedom outside of France. These were legally sanctioned departures.[87]

Crossing the Border

One significant area of Jewish assistance to fellow Jews was the organization of secret convoys across the Swiss border, which rose in number over the occupation years, despite the increasing surveillance of the border. Attempts were also undertaken to cross into Spain via the Pyrenees, whose heights and unpredictable weather presented a serious challenge. The intention was not to remain in Spain but to proceed either to Lisbon, Portugal, and on a boat away from Europe or to a seashore harbor and catch a boat heading for Palestine. The first escapes of young Jews to Spain were arranged by the Sixth, headed by Robert Donoff, on December 17, 1942. After braving the formidable Pyrenees in deep snow, the group reached Spain, only to find themselves arrested in Pampelune, where they were kept confined for two and a half months, followed by seven months of forced residence in a Spanish village, before being allowed to leave the country on October 23, 1943. Another convoy spearheaded by the Sixth left on January 1, 1943, and others were to follow.[88]

The AJ (Jewish Army) also organized convoys on a large scale for its men, who hoped to rejoin the Allied forces. On May 3, 1944, Jules-Dika Jefroykin took charge of a convoy of fifty-nine people, representing several clandestine groups, across the Pyrenees. This turned into a seven-day nightmare after the border smugglers left them stranded. One young man lost his footing and fell down a steep precipice to his death. Jefroykin's father-in-law also died on that difficult crossing. Finally, reaching Spain the entire party found itself arrested and interned. Jefroykin was set free through the intervention of the Red Cross, and he obtained the release of the others held in the internment camp of Miranda. The next convoy, similar in composition, left on May 17, 1944. Before the departure from Toulouse, the Gestapo was tipped off and arrested the convoy organizer, Jacques Roitman, on the station platform together with five of the escapees. The forty others escaped but were forced to return to their departure base due to other hindrances related to this trek. Léo Cohen was at the head of another convoy, leaving Toulouse on May 26, 1944. Just when he was about to board the train, the Gestapo stopped him. He managed to chew and swallow the papers containing the names of the young adults he was escorting to Spain. The group succeeded in getting across, but Léo Cohen died in deportation.[89]

Children were also among those who attempted the difficult crossing into Spain. Gisèle Roman of the AJ related how she was entrusted by Abraham Polonski with escorting such a group of children. Most, ranging in age between seven and twelve, were brought to the departure point by Andrée Salomon, a major OSE activist. Another of Gisèle Roman's groups, composed of adults and children, had a narrow escape that ended on an amusing note. In her words: "Around 3:00 a.m. I was standing at the railroad station with the children and several young women. . . . We were waiting because the train was late. Finally it pulled in. I had a suitcase with two Tommy guns inside. As we were about to board, I put the valise down for a moment; just then two men appeared—obviously police, despite their civilian dress. What to do? Let the train leave . . . without the suitcase. . . . I turned right around with the children and left." Gisèle later learned that the police had asked whose suitcase it was, and a woman who had witnessed Gisèle's leaving behind that handsome-looking case had claimed it as her own. When the police opened the suitcase and saw the contents, that woman was immediately arrested. Her dishonesty had cost her dearly. "I got eighty-seven children across—excluding the older ones," Gisèle recounted. "All this happened more than 25 years ago, and believe me, I haven't slept well since that time. I still have nightmares: I see German soldiers about to drag my children off!"[90]

During the 1944 summer months, six convoys of escapees, each carrying twenty-five to forty-five people, arrived safe and sound in Spain, with most of them taking a route that passed through the principality of Andorra. In total, an estimated 600 people were able to make their escape via the Spanish route, with many allowed to continue to other destinations.[91] The Swiss border presented a safer route, due mainly to its more favorable topography (flat terrain) and political feasibility during the Italian administration of the Franco-Swiss border. More on these crossings will follow in the stories of Georges Loinger, Denise Siekierski, Mila Racine, and Marianne Cohn.

Lucien Lazare, in his study of the Jewish resistance in France, estimated that 72,400 children below the age of sixteen escaped extermination. Of these, 62,000 remained with their parents or were directly placed by them with non-Jewish institutions or families. The various Jewish organizations mentioned above were thus responsible for the rescue of slightly over 10,000 children. Of these, between 1,500 and 2,000 were spirited across the Swiss border, 6,000 to 7,500 were placed with non-Jews, 88 to132 crossed into Spain, and 311 emigrated legally. This totals 9,943 children, plus some more unaccounted for, for a grand total of slightly over 10,000.[92]

Drancy

There was at least one serious attempt at a mass escape from the main French transit camp of Drancy that almost succeeded. A tunnel 35 meters long, dug at a depth of 1.5 meters, ended less than 2 meters away from a trench situated outside the camp—before it was discovered. It was part of a most ambitious plot hatched by a group of detainees who were planning a mass escape. Designed by two inmates, Major Georges Kohn and Colonel Robert Blum, digging began on September 15, 1943. The workers cut an opening 1.30 meters high and .80 meters wide that was lit by electricity and entirely timbered. The plan envisaged the escape of all the inmates of Drancy. Less than two months after the beginning of the work, when only 1.5 meters was left to dig through, the ss made a systematic search of all the cellars and the tunnel was discovered. Under torture, the ss identified fourteen of the seventy plotters. Deported on November 20, 1943, ten of them jumped from the train and were able to avoid recapture.[93]

Guerrilla Activity

The EIF (Jewish Scouts) also participated in the liberation of France following the Allied landing on the Normandy beaches. With the advance of the Allies under way, on August 8, 1944, the Marc Haguenau company (named after the late EIF activist) under the command of Robert Gamzon, who appeared under the pseudonym of Lieutenant Lagnès, engaged the Germans. When later that month German forces in the southwest began a quick retreat, the Marc Haguenau unit engaged them again and forced the surrender of a large German force on August 21, counting 4,000 soldiers in Castres, to men who proudly stated before them, "*Ich bin Jude.*"[94] Other mostly Jewish units also took part in guerrilla operations, especially the Communist-led OS (*Organisation Spéciale*), where one of its four units was entirely Jewish.[95]

Unfortunately, no similar Jewish combativeness took place to attempt to free inmates in detention camps, such as Drancy, or derail trains inside France taking these unfortunate men, women, and children to the German border and to a destination that everyone knew did not bode well. For whatever reason, sabotaging military convoys and waylaying German personnel remained of preeminent importance.

Now to the stories of some of the legendary Jewish rescue activists, whose individual accounts need to be told in greater detail.

Joseph Bass

He created his own private rescue network and combined this with training a select group of Jewish men to fight the Germans.

Joseph Bass was one of the most unlikely men to get involved in the rescue business, and his contribution was enormous. Born in Grodno, Belarus, in 1908, he arrived in Paris alone at the age of sixteen. While supporting himself as a stevedore at the Halles open-air market and working in a factory, he studied for his baccalaureate and thereafter took up studies in engineering and law. He then dealt as a legal counsel in cases arising out of industrial holdings. On the eve of the war in 1939, he prudently had his business office registered under the name of his non-Jewish partner, Madeleine Rocca (Mickey). Interned by the Vichy authorities as a foreigner Jew (he was still officially a Soviet citizen) in Argèles, then Vernet camp, he made his escape and arrived in Marseilles, where Rabbi Zalman Schneerson engaged him as a teacher in industrial drawing in his Jewish religious school.[96]

After the massive roundup of Jews by the French police in August 1942, Bass decided to dedicate himself to assisting fellow Jews threatened with deportation. At first he worked as part of a larger nondescript group, but after a short spell, he decided to create his own network, since he felt that the focus should not be merely helping Jewish refugees with financial assistance, or even only with false credentials, but fanning out the refugees among the population with the help of Christian clergy and equipping them with false identities. He gave his network the flamboyant title of Action Group Against Deportation (Groupe d'Action Contre la Déportation), but it was better known by the code word Service André, and he was nicknamed Monsieur André.[97]

Bass sought out various clergymen for their help in either finding hiding places in France, such as in the Protestant enclave of Le Chambon, or spiriting Jews across the border into Switzerland. His approach to these clergymen was direct and not always courteous, such as his talk with Father de Parceval of the Dominican Order. As related by Bass:

> I had never met him before, and I said: "I am a Jew with illegal status—but that isn't the issue. I'm not asking for help for myself. . . . I only want to know whether you are just going to make a lot of speeches and sermons, or whether—in thinking back to your patron Saint Dominique, who did so much to harm the Jews—you are prepared to do something to make amends. . . . What will you do for us?" He was flabbergasted, but finally asked: "But what is it you want of me?" I said: "Whatever you wish to give—nothing or everything." Whereupon he asked me to return the next day. I did, and he said: "All right. I am at your disposal." [De Parceval's Dominican convent became central to Bass's operation.] "I could spend the night, hold meetings [there]. . . . Father de Parceval, and other priests, too, even more friars, belonged to our group and devoted themselves almost entirely to our cause. Several times I had to disguise myself as a Dominican, Jesuit, or Capuchin monk. I wanted to act as gatekeeper, so I could pick up messages. I was called Brother André.[98]

Protestant pastors referred him to their colleague André Trocmé in Le Chambon-sur-Lignon, who agreed to open his Protestant enclave in the hilly region of Haute-Loire as a refuge for thousands of Jews. The Protestant community there took the Bible literally and considered the Jewish people God's own chosen, to be protected from the Nazis.[99]

Bass hardly slept at night; two to three hours was enough for him. He traveled by train, first class, where his companions were Gestapo men and underworld people (who were mostly collaborators), sporting a leather coat similar to a Gestapo agent. This, coupled with his large and heavy physique, his deep voice, the furtive look in his eyes, and the prominent leather briefcase (which was incidentally filled with forgeries), his ventures into the lion's den were to fool passers-by and onlookers into believing he was either a Gestapo agent, a top French collaborator with the Germans, or a Mafia boss of the notorious Marseilles underworld.[100] He miraculously succeeded in avoiding arrest, sole for the one exception that almost proved fatal. On a visit to Marseilles from his base in Saint-Etienne, not far from the Le Chambon area, on March 8, 1944, he was dining in a restaurant when German police stormed in and went directly to Bass's table. He related what followed.

> The police had me—one struck me on the head with his pistol, and the blood began to flow. I was thrown into a car and ordered to give my address; I had many and gave one, a maid's room nearby. I was handcuffed and locked in the room, with a Gestapo agent remaining to begin the interrogation. It extended over several hours, he repeatedly asking if I were Jewish, and I steadfastly denying it. . . . About three or four in the morning, the fellow dozed off.[101] I took a chance and stealthily approached him and struck out with the handcuffs hitting him over the head. He was out. I went to the door . . . the key was on the inside. I quickly left, locking my jailor within, and rushed down the stairway and out a back door. . . . The streets . . . were deserted; curfew hours. . . . I safely reached the house of a friend of the family and was taken in—with handcuffs on my wrists and my head bleeding. . . . He got me into a furniture van, and that's how I made it to Aix-en-Provence, hidden in a wardrobe.

He eventually made it to Chambon-sur-Lignon. It was a lucky break, and it did not deter him from pursuing risky ventures if it meant helping fellow Jews to avoid capture.[102]

It was in the hilly St. Etienne–Le Chambon region, inhabited by many of France's minority Protestant community, that Joseph Bass made his greatest mark as both a Jewish rescuer of Jews and a military combatant against the Germans. In early 1943 he established his main operating base in the home of Simone Mairesse, in Mazet-Saint-Voy, near Chambon-sur-Lignon. She was enlisted in the arduous task of scouring the immediate Le Chambon countryside to find shelter for Jews.[103] But Bass was not satisfied with merely rescuing Jews. Like his unknown counterparts in the depths of the Belarus forests, the Bielski brothers, he felt that Jews must also show a willingness to combat. Assembling a small contingent of Jewish partisans, he saw to it that they received proper military training and were armed with appropriate weapons received from other partisans units.

From a secondary base in the house of Oswaldo Bardonne, in La Ricamarie, a miners suburb of Saint-Etienne, Bass planned the military aspect of his clandestine activity. Bass proved so renowned that the so-called Jewish Army decided to send some of its young people to Bass's operation to receive military training for a period of several weeks. The trained Jewish insurgents were later incorporated into the FFI, the central French underground movement, with Bass officially nominated as commander of this group. They saw action during the fighting with regular German troops, following the Normandy invasion of France in June 1944, with Bass by now an officer in the French resistance.[104] With the war over, Joseph Bass returned to his work as legal counselor in Paris, and seeking neither accolades nor honors for his vast rescue work, he kept to himself. He died in 1970.

Denise Siekierski-Caraco

Hardly out of high school, she was active in manifold
rescue undertakings before becoming Bass's
principal aide, helping many Jews on the run.

Denise Caraco received a strict secular upbringing, far removed from any Jewish practices and solely faithful to France and its republican ideals. As she stated, "My family's religion was France."[105] As a teenager, Denise joined the Unionistes, a Protestant scout movement. The war, followed by the anti-Jewish legislations of the Vichy regime, sensitized her to her Jewish identity. Denise dreamed of a journalism career in the French colonies, but the anti-Jewish laws of the government (*numerus clausus)* excluded her acceptance into the university. Then, in September 1941, meeting Robert Gamzon, she decided to switch to his scout movement to better her Jewish commitment.[106] Sent to the EIF training school in Lautrec, near Toulouse, she became a *cheftaine* (scout leader).

In late August 1942 Denise and others were sent to scour the countryside, to explore possible sheltering places for foreign-born teenagers who were in danger of arrest and internment. Returning to Marseilles in mid-September, she joined the EIF for the Marseilles region, helping foreign Jews, who numbered in their thousands, avoid arrest and deportation by the Vichy authorities.[107]

Denise (code-named Colibri, hummingbird) and her colleagues also fabricated false identities, especially from inside a "laboratory" set up in Adrien Benveniste's home. Denise's activity became diversified, working for both the OSE and the EIF. It included monthly visits to people in their hiding places to make sure they were well treated and distributing money and ration cards. Denise's ploy was to stuff these incriminating items in her knapsack and cover it with spoiled food. The unpalatable smell emitting from the suddenly opened baggage was enough to discourage any inspectors from proceeding further. Help was also extended to persons held captive at the Camp des Milles, who were sometimes given a one-day pass (and left their credentials behind) to ostensibly visit the OSE dispensary in Marseilles, since medical facilities were lacking in the camp. Once at the OSE dispensary, if they were prepared for a life on the run, they were instructed to return in the evening, after the offices had formally closed, when they would be helped to flee by Denise and her coworkers, on behalf of the OSE or the other rescuer groups. At times, she accompanied Jews on train rides to Annemasse on the Swiss border, where they would attempt to cross the border illegally.[108]

Returning to Marseilles after a stay in Grenoble in June 1943 for a quick check on her family, she was happy to learn they were temporarily safe in several locations. Not knowing exactly what to do next, she took a stroll on the Canebire, the city's main promenade boulevard, and ran straight into Joseph Bass.

"Isn't it Colibiri?" he asked her. "What may I ask are you're doing here?" Denise related her visit to relatives in Vaucluse, as well as her grandmother in a Marseilles clinic.

"This is not what I had in mind," he quickly retorted, hinting that he had alluded to her clandestine work.

"Nothing, Mr. André; I've resigned from the Sixth" [due to an altercation over a policy matter].

"So you're doing nothing? And for how long?"

"Just three days."

"This is three days too much," Bass replied. "Since you're doing nothing, you're going to work for me."

"Doing what?"

Bass assumed an angry tone. "I beg of you, don't act like a choir girl. You know exactly what I am involved in."

Denise: "I need to think it over."

Bass: "Fine, let's have a drink."

After a short stop in a coffee store, Bass again confronted her: "It's been half an hour that we've been here. Have you thought about it?" Denise heard herself saying: "Well, it's yes."

"Good," Bass quickly responded. "Meet me tomorrow morning, 8 a.m., under the staircase of the train station. We're leaving for Nice."

"This is how I joined the Service André," Denise later wrote in her testimony. It was July 1943, and Denise was merely nineteen years old.[109]

In Nice, Joseph Bass was busy evacuating people to the Le Chambon region, for which he had established excellent contacts with Pastor André Trocmé. Denise would often journey there to defray costs of families hosting Jewish fugitives. In fact, she had so much work in Le Chambon that she rented a room near Hotel May and took all her meals at the hotel. Together with Bass, she was continuously on the road, helping hundreds. A bit further north, in the Haute Loire region, she also helped out with moving hidden weapons from one place to another for distribution to Bass's Jewish *maquis* (general French term for resistance fighters), who were training to fight the Germans.

After the war, Denise Caraco underwent another experience, similar to what happened to other survivors—the memory blocking of the traumatic events of the war. "I just knew, but I didn't remember." She further elaborated, "It was a much too difficult period, too painful, and if after the war we had continued talking about it, I would not have been capable of going on with life, or have the will to build something, to do something . . . if I would have continued to think about this all the time."[110] In the meantime, burying the memories of the war, she married a man named Siekierski, bore two children, joined a newly established kibbutz, moved to Brazil, then returned to Israel in 1978. It all began to unravel in 1984, some forty years after France's liberation, when she realized "that really, one ought to talk, so that something remains for the memory of my dead comrades, who were not able to talk; that if I'm still here, . . . if I had things to tell, I had to tell them. Not for me, but that something remains of everything we did together, my departed comrades and myself." Slowly she began to recover tidbits from her blocked-out war memories and was able to reconstruct events, give interviews, and even write her memoirs. Still, she believed that she had not fully retrieved everything of importance that happened to her during that horrific period. She lived to a ripe old age of eighty-nine, dying in Jerusalem in 2013. We give the final word to historian Léon Poliakov, who worked closely with her during the war and described her in flowing terms.

Colibri, the 19-year-old scout—always on the move; her blue eyes seeming to look at the world with wonder. However, make no mistake, this young maiden meant business. Colibri slept in trains, took her meals in train stations and breakfast in post offices; her co-workers numbered in the dozens, spread over the whole of southeast France—maintaining contact with various leaders. . . . Colibri acted as a fish in water. She began her clandestine work straight out of her high-school bench. . . . Little Colibri was André's principal assistant. Everything passed through her hands; nothing was done without her [knowledge].[111]

Georges Garel

The Circuit Garel became legendary for saving some 1,600 children—more than any other rescue network.

Georges Garel was born Grigori Garfinkel in Vilna in 1909, which was then part of the Russian Empire. His family moved to Kiev, then Berlin, finally arriving in France in 1926, where he finished his engineering studies. In the French army with the rank of artillery lieutenant, he was demobilized in 1940 and became active in the OSE in 1941. In 1942 he happened to be in Lyon when he was invited to be part of the screening committee in the Vénissieux camp. That was a turning point in Georges

Garel's life, because he realized that all Jewish children were now in danger of deportations, not just their parents and other adults. Dr. Joseph Weill, head physician of the OSE, proposed that Garel create a special rescue section within the OSE for the purpose of saving children. Garel was a perfect candidate for this undertaking for, unlike the other activists associated with the UGIF, Garel was not too well known to them or to the police. He could therefore operate without the authorities knowing who was in charge of the operation.[112]

Referred to Archbishop Jules-Géraud Saliège in Toulouse, Garel received his undivided support, as Saliège placed the facilities of the Church at the disposal of Garel's illegal organization. Armed with a reference letter by the archbishop, Garel was able to create a network of safe havens for children in the south of France in Catholic, Protestant, and secular institutions. Hidden children were equipped with false papers by the OSE and then transferred to the Garel network (known as Circuit Garel), which then took full responsibility for them.[113] The activities of the Garel network grew to such dimensions that Garel was forced to subdivide it into several geographical regions—center-east, southeast, center, and southwest—with Garel directing operations from a secret location in Lyon.

As the number of children to be hidden rose, especially when all OSE children's homes were closed in October 1943, Garel made sure to compartmentalize his operation so that if some of his activists were apprehended, they would know nothing of the activities of the others. Lists were kept in three sets in different secret locations. The real name of the child and the location of his parents would appear on the first list. The second list contained the child's true and false names, and the third list would carry only the child's assumed name and place of residence. At the same time, the OSE secretly transferred to Geneva the information on each of the hidden children, in the event that all the lists kept by the Garel network would fall into enemy hands or were lost due to mishandling.

The Circuit Garel became legendary among children's rescue organizations for the scope of its activity and the numbers rescued.[114] Danger lurked everywhere, and of the original thirty-three members of the Garel network when liberation came, only four remained, for dozens in the whole network were arrested and deported. At the same time, the network succeeded in saving some 1,600 children, a feat unmatched by any other rescue network.[115] After the war, Garel returned to his profession of engineer with the Companie Electro-Mécanique de Paris. From 1951 to 1978, he was president of the OSE. He died in Paris in 1979.[116]

Moussa Abadi and Odette Rosenstock

This courageous couple initiated a large-scale rescue operation that saved 527 Jewish children.

Born in Damascus, Syria, in 1910 into a religious Jewish family, Moussa Abadi headed to Paris in 1920 to continue his studies at the Sorbonne University. Drawn to the theater, he joined a professional acting team (Compagnie des Quatre Saisons) that performed in local theaters. With the onset of the war, Moussa fled to Nice, in the Vichy zone, where he performed medieval religious plays and taught grammar to young Catholic religious seminarians.[117]

Odette Rosenstock, Moussa's wartime companion and future wife, was born in Paris in 1912 to nonreligious Jewish parents. She graduated in medicine in December 1939 and landed a job at a medical school. Dismissed by Vichy's anti-Jewish laws, she headed to Nice, where she joined Moussa Abadi, whom she had met earlier in Paris, and found work as a doctor and social worker in the OSE dispensary of the city.[118]

Sometime after arriving in Nice, Abadi experienced two shocking events that left him spellbound as to what would happen in the event of a German takeover. The first one was when he witnessed the brutal beating of a woman on the streets of Nice by a French Milice man. Then, during the Italian period, a chaplain in the Italian army, Dom Giulio Penitenti, who just returned from Russia on leave, urgently called upon Abadi. Meeting him in a hotel room, Abadi listened quietly to the cleric's words. "Sir, what I am about to tell you will not believe, but I insist on telling it because I will return to the Russian front where I will certainly die, and I wanted someone to know. . . . What I saw, I want to tell it to a Jew." He then detailed witnessing the large-scale killing of Jewish children. At first Abadi doubted these accounts. Penitenti then unbuttoned his priestly shirt, and placed his hand on a large crucifix, and swore on the blood of Christ that what he had just told him was the truth. Before leaving, the priest added, "When the Germans will be here, your children will suffer greatly; I have warned you." It is then that Abadi decided that in the event of a German takeover he would forswear armed resistance against the enemy (a thought he had considered previously), but instead dedicate himself to the rescue of children. But how was he going to go about it?[119]

Scheming with the Bishop

Shocked by the Italian chaplain's revelation, Abadi asked for an audience with Bishop Paul Rémond. In one account of the words exchanged by the two, Abadi told Rémond: "Monsignor, I am a Jew. . . . I have come to ask you for a risky undertaking. . . . You can throw me out; you can evict me, but without you I will not be able to save children." The Monsignor responded: "But doing what?" Abadi repeated, "Only to save children." "But how do you propose to save them?" "One must remove them from the reach of the Gestapo," Abadi replied. Rémond tremblingly said, "What you ask me is indeed very serious. . . . Can you imagine . . . that the Nazis could raid this place, have me arrested, as well as my secretary, Abbé Rostand? To which Abadi responded resolutely, "Exactly, exactly." The bishop then asked for time to think this over, and seeing Abadi to the door, he said that in the event of his consent, no arms were to be involved, to which Abadi said, "Never." When Abadi returned two days later, Rémond said, "You are still decided to undertake this action. You have considered all the risks?" "Yes, and it is now up to you to say if it is acceptable to you."[120]

Having said that, Abadi thought to himself: "It's a fiasco; he will give me his blessing, wish me good luck, and that's it." But Rémond surprisingly told Abadi, "I've thought it over, and well, we will try to do something together." Abadi: "But, Monsignor, doing things together means doing something here, at your place, for we don't have locations; we have nothing."

The bishop responded by telling Abadi that he could consider the prelate's home as his home as well and by assigning him an office on the ground floor (so that in case of an alarm of a police raid, he would have sufficient time to escape). There Abadi was to quietly manufacture falsified credentials, except false baptismals, an undertaking that the bishop reserved strictly to himself. Abadi thanked him and suggested that henceforth he was to be known as Mr. Marcel. To Holocaust narrator Anny Latour, Abadi related, "That's how I came to have an office in the bishop's home in Nice. . . . I was given access to all rooms, for hiding places for my false papers. And we hid them everywhere—in the mattress, the Monsignor's private desk. . . . Everywhere!"[121]

Rémond began by drawing up a list of religious institutions in his diocese capable of sheltering children under fake names, similar to Monsignor Saliège's help to the Garel network, and arming Abadi with appropriate letters of recommendation with the bishop's signature and seal, with which Abadi could circulate freely. Rémond also introduced Abadi to several of his religious colleagues, who were sworn to secrecy.[122] Rémond facilitated Abadi's preparatory work by nominating him, under the name of Mr. Marcel, as "Private School Inspector for the Nice Diocese." The document, under Rémond's signature, added: "We ask the institution heads to accord him the best cooperation during the execution of his functions," which led these people to assume that Abadi was a priest in civil garb. As for Odette, she received the nomination of a social worker, under the name of Sylvie Delattre, for the ostensible evacuation of children in the event of air bombardments, and this afforded her to travel everywhere.[123]

Christian Safe Havens

From a downstairs room in the bishop's office, Abadi would check out Catholic institutions, and Odette would investigate Protestant pastors and private homes in the Nice region. Moussa Abadi was not sure how things would turn out. "We did not know how we were going to proceed, for one was not absolutely certain that the Germans would occupy Nice," a city still under Italian control.[124] Then, on September 8, 1943, it happened, and without warning, and "we were there, with Odette, to pick up the children who came from everywhere, from the concierges who sent them to us; the parents who came with them; they dropped them off and left. We started to place them a bit everywhere; in religious institutions, in convents, a little everywhere."[125] One had to hurry, even placing them in temporary shelters for one or two nights until one could figure out a more permanent place for these children. Ages varied from three months to seventeen years, the youngest being Marlenne Weiss, born that same year.[126] In placing these children, Moussa made the runs between mostly religious institutions on his bicycle. Abadi estimated that of a total 527 children, approximately 300 were admitted into Catholic institutions of the Cannes diocese.[127]

There were, of course, many children who were sent to live with families. The most difficult aspect of child rescue was the initial stage of reprogramming them into different child-bearing names and personal histories. As remarked by Moussa Abadi, "We had become identity robbers."[128] "Your name is no longer Epelbaum, your name is Rocher," Abadi recalled one such session. "Repeat! What's your name? Rocher. And starting again." For places of birth, some were told to present themselves as born in places where records no longer existed due to bombardments, or born in North African countries belonging to France, or on the French-held island of Corsica, both of which had already been liberated by the Allies. This would also necessitate providing them with false papers and ration cards under their new names. "I personally delivered more than a thousand false identity papers," not only to hidden children but also to non-Jewish evaders for forced labor in Germany," Abadi recalled.[129] When dealing with children of a very religious background, one could foresee insurmountable difficulties in their adopting a different lifestyle, and the solution for them was to turn them over to the Sixth or the OSE and spirit them into Switzerland.[130]

Rosenstock took it upon herself to visit the hidden children on a regular basis, traveling long distances in all kinds of weather to see how they were treated, as well to as pay the monthly pension to the host families and bring along additional clothing, toys, and even hard-to-get delicacies, such as chocolate—let alone words of comfort and love. Some visits were hard to bear. When on one occasion she was told by certain girls, sheltered in an institution, that instead of singing, some intoned instead the Jewish credo "Shema Israel" (Hear, O Israel . . .), she was quite mad at the girls, as she tried to caution them not to repeat such otherwise meritorious intonations.[131]

"Some say that it was a time of courage," Abadi recollected. "No," he corrected himself, "it was a time of fear. It would only take one link of the chain to snap for the whole thing to crash. Every morning, we started by asking whether we'd be there that evening, and who would then take care of the children?"[132] Odette Rosenstock was eventually denounced under her assumed name of Sylvie Delattre in April 1944 in her apartment by the Milice. Under intense and torturous interrogation, she admitted involved assisting children. They kept asking her "Where is Marcel (Abadi's false name)? Where are the children?" "I did not talk," she recounted. "They acted as though they were going to shoot me." Taken to Drancy on May 2, 1944, and deported three weeks later to Auschwitz and then to Bergen-Belsen, she miraculously survived.[133] Left alone, and not knowing what information the Gestapo managed to extract from Odette, Abadi dared not return to his hotel room or to the bishop's office. The headmistress of a girls' school, instead, allowed him to pass the nights in one of the empty classrooms, sleeping on a thin carpet, on the condition that he evacuate the premises early in the mornings before the arrival of the cleaning women.

Postwar Work and Acknowledgment

Luckily for him, liberation was only three months away (August 28, 1944), and he avoided arrest.[134] Then came the equally difficult task of fetching the children and returning them, either to their families or to Jewish organizations, such as the OSE. Abadi shared with the OSE this arduous work, meeting with surviving parents, frantic to be reunited with their children. Of the 527 saved children, more than half were now orphaned. Some, whose parents did not survive, had relatives overseas, and the child was sent to start a new life in another country.[135]

After learning of Odette's survival, and after the two married, Abadi gave one newspaper interview in 1948, then he and Odette slipped into near-obscurity, as both returned to their prewar professions. Abadi's spectacular rescue operation had been all but forgotten for some fifty-odd years when his name cropped up again in stories of French non-Jewish rescuers who acted in collaboration with Abadi and were awarded the Yad Vashem Righteous title. In 1994, bowing to the pressure of former hidden children, Moussa and Odette allowed themselves to be celebrated by those whom they had saved five decades earlier. The following year, during a gathering with a group of his former wards, in self-effacing words Moussa Abadi minimized his personal role in their rescue. "We were simply there at the right time and the right place." He died in 1997, followed by Odette in 1999.[136]

Angelo Donati

Using his special connections, he planned a vast escape of thousands of Jews in the Italian occupation zone.

Born in Modena, Italy, in 1885, Angelo (Mordechai) Donati came from one of the most prominent Jewish families dating back to the sixteenth century. He studied law, practiced banking in Milan and Turin, and served as an infantry captain in the Italian army during World War I. He then settled in Paris, where he dealt in various financial and banking undertakings and was president of the Franco-Italian Chamber of Commerce. He also was the consul-general of the microstate San Marino Republic. In June 1940 Donati left Paris ahead of the German army and eventually moved to Nice. While there, he operated the Franco-Italian Bank.[137]

With the arrival of the Italian troops in Nice on November 18, 1942, Donati, taking advantage of his good relations with the Italian military and diplomatic personnel, committed himself to the welfare of the Jews under Italian control, especially in coordination with the local French Jewish Committee for help to the refugees (known as the Comité Dubouchage). As reported by Ignace Fink of the Dubouchage committee: "Donati, to the Jews of that region, was like a god."[138] They asked for his intercession with the Italian authorities for the safety and protection of the Jews, especially the stateless ones, from deportation by the French Vichy authorities.

Safety in the Italian Zone

Quite significantly, when the Vichy government ordered the prefect of Nice, Marcel Ribière, to arrest all foreign Jews who had recently arrived in the Côte d'Azur, Donati immediately alerted Alberto Calisse, the Italian consul-general, and the Italian military commander countermanded this decision on the grounds that it was up to the Italian military occupation authorities to have the final word. The Italians even placed Carabinieri gendarmes in front of a Nice synagogue to protect it from threats of attack emanating from the French Milice. Donati's idea that the newly arrived Jews be moved under a mild supervision to the more interior and hilly parts of the Italian zone, such as Saint-Martin-Vésubie, some distance from Nice, under a "forced residency" policy was also adopted. Calisse also followed Donati's advice in refusing to affix the mention of *Juif* on identity and ration cards held by Jews, as required by Vichy laws.[139]

The Germans obviously were furious at being unable to place their hands on the Jews in the Italian zone, and they blamed Angelo Donati. This led to increased protests by the Germans and to Mussolini's assignment of Guido Lospinoso, of the Italian police, to deal with the Jewish question in the Italian zone in France, in collaboration with the Germans. Here, too, disappointment awaited the Germans, as after meeting Donati (and his close collaborator, the Capuchin monk Marie-Benoît), Lospinoso was persuaded to put brakes to any attempts to harm the Jews. In the words of Marianne Spier-Donati, the adoptive daughter of Angelo Donati, her father "had become the Grey Eminence of inspector Guido Lospinoso, that some said that he did nothing without seeking his [Donati's] advice."[140]

To North African Havens

When, on July 25, 1943, Mussolini fell from power, Donati was optimistic. From an initial plan to transfer all the Jews in the Italian zone to Italy proper, he now envisaged things on an even larger scale: from Italy the refugees would proceed to Tunisia, Morocco, and Algeria, in North Africa, recently liberated by the Allies.[141] As he recalled after the war: "At the start of August 1943, I undertook negotiations with the English-American governments, for support of sending between 20,000 and 30,000 Jews to North Africa. These negotiations took place in the Vatican, to where I was secretly introduced by Father Marie-Benoît to Sir [Francis D'Arcy] Osborne, the British minister, and Mr. [Harold] Tittman, the American minister." The Italian government had at the start given its consent to admit to Italy, as a first stop, the number of Jews that could practically be evacuated to North Africa, and the two Anglo-Saxon ministers had advised their respective governments of this. According to this plan, once in Italy, thousands of Jews were to be taken in shifts by four specific boats (*Duilio, Giulio Cesare, Saturnia*, and *Vulcania*), in the second half of September, to North Africa havens, with funding subsidized by the U.S.-based Joint Distribution Committee (JDC).

"I was not the principal artisan and even less the author of this transference plan of Jews to Italy, then to Africa," Father Marie-Benoît admitted. (He separately also rescued many Jews.) "The initiative and merit go to the very dear Angelo Donati who went to Rome on many occasions . . . to discuss it with the Badoglio government [which replaced Mussolini]. . . . I asked the pope for his intervention with the Italian government in support of the Donati project."[142] With approval from all relevant parties, Donati felt confident of the evacuation plan's success. Then, suddenly, while dining with his family in Florence on September 8, 1943, he was shocked to hear the radio announcement of the Italian armistice. In the words of his niece: "It had the effect of a bomb on my uncle. General Eisenhower had betrayed his solemn promise to keep secret the agreement that he had achieved with Marshal Badoglio and prematurely announced the signing of the armistice of September 3 between the Americans and Italy. . . . A gigantic chaos overtook Italy."[143] The Germans immediately swept in.

With the Germans in control of the Italian zone in France, Donati went into hiding in Italy, after he learned that the Gestapo had him on their wanted list, before taking refuge in Switzerland on October 14.[144] As the German records that came to light after the war demonstrate, they had correctly singled out Donati as the principal author of the special beneficial treatment of thousands of Jews in the Italian occupation zone. Therefore, a Gestapo report continued, "the arrest of Donati is of the highest importance, for he was the active brain in favor of the Jews in the Italian zone." Failing to arrest him, the Gestapo instead detained his secretary, Germaine Meyer, and she died in deportation.[145] With the war over in 1945, Donati returned to Paris and reportedly adopted two Jewish children who were hidden in Italy during the German occupation. Angelo Donati died in 1960.[146]

Andrée Salomon

Dedicated to helping Jewish children, she also smuggled them across the Swiss and Spanish borders.

Born in 1908 in Grusssenheim (Alsace), then part of Germany, at age sixteen Solomon moved to Strasbourg (France), where she worked in a law firm and became a leader in EIF, the Jewish scouting movement and was also a staunch Zionist. Immediately after Kristallnacht in Germany, Salomon learned that the director of the Jewish orphanage in Frankfurt-am-Main wanted desperately to transfer to France the Jewish children in his care. She was successful in getting a collective visa for the children and persuading the Jewish aid organizations in Strasbourg to cover the expense of helping them.[147] Crossing over to the German side, on December 6, 1938, in Kehl, she took charge of a group of fifty-two children aged eleven to fourteen. She was told by the headmistress, "As of today these children have no parents, and we entrust them to you. . . . There is no other solution for them."[148] She crossed with them into France and referred them to foster families in and near Strasbourg. On April 24, 1939, an additional group from Karlsruhe was taken in. Some of these children had been turned over without any identity papers. This, then, was the starting point of a life's work dedicated to rescuing Jewish children.

When the Germans invaded France, Salomon and her husband fled to Clermont-Ferrand in the south, but not before arranging refuges for every one of the children rescued from Germany, with whom Andrée continued to be in touch. As part of the OSE, she was principally involved in organizing volunteers to penetrate the French internment camps, such as Gurs, Rivesaltes, and Les Milles.[149] Her main concern was to make life a bit easier for the thousands of Jews interned there by the Vichy regime. To facilitate her work, she was permitted to take up residence, with four assistants, in Rivesaltes camp. She also visited various prefects (*département* heads) to obtain exit permits for those who could show proof of self-support, as well as obtain the release of children below the age of sixteen for a temporary stay in children's homes. She also sought to find legal ways to liberate as many adults and children as possible, in accordance with prevailing laws or in illegal ways, such as payoffs to some of the camp guards to look the other way as Andrée and her assistants walked out with some children.[150]

Resisting "Family Reunions"

The rescue of children took on a most dramatic twist when the Vichy authorities tried to implement what they called "family regrouping," which really meant returning the children, previously liberated, to the camps so that they could be added with their parents for deportation by the Germans. Salomon instructed her assistants to warn parents in the camps not to divulge the addresses of their children. Tragically, some mothers, believing in the sincerity of the "reunions," did give away the information, with tragic consequences for them and their children.[151] Andrée left us with a stirring account of how she and her trusted confederates tried to prevent these "reunions" during the summer months of 1942.

> This so-called reunion, which meant deportation and undoubtedly death, had to be prevented at all costs. . . . Suddenly, without even knowing how it had happened, about a hundred children found

themselves one morning concentrated in Block K, destined for the next deportation. . . . All our intercessions with the [screening] commission led nowhere. The order was precise: the children had to leave. . . . It was then that our secretary-general joined us from Montpellier and went with us to Perpignan to try out on the prefect our last approach for liberating that group of children (those under the age of sixteen; as for the others, they unfortunately had no chance at all). . . . As we showed him what a monstrous idea it was for a hundred children from the Unoccupied Zone to be given over for extermination. . . . All that we were able to extract from him were so-called deficient children. . . . It was appalling, for we had to make a choice. We had to choose those ten children (who in reality became twenty in number) that we would thus restore life, deliberately letting others go to their death. . . . This deep injustice obsessed us for months and still weighs on our conscience today. . . . Twenty children were thus saved while eighty-two were deported from Rivesaltes. But we continued to do our best to try to liberate other children. . . . [Later,] the prefecture of Perpignan assumed the responsibility to liberate children under sixteen years of age in the *département* of Pyrénées-Orientales, as long as we submitted their files to the officials. . . . Four hundred and twenty-seven children had been saved from deportation.[152]

Smuggling Children to Safety

As the deportation of Jews from the Vichy kept rising, Andrée Salomon turned her attention to planning the escape of children, either by hiding them inside France or spiriting them across the Swiss and Spanish borders. She often stayed in the town of Annemassse on the French-Swiss border for emergency arrangements for children who missed crossing into Switzerland.[153] Border smugglers had to be paid. One had to prepare their false identities, and one had to "indoctrinate," that is, instruct the children in what false information they were to say of themselves if stopped. In this new mission of hers, Salomon had gone underground and was to be found everywhere: Lyon, Marseilles, Toulouse, Montpellier, and Limoges.

While on train rides, she made notes on her manual typewriter before falling asleep. She wore a red ribbon in her hair as a recognizable sign to her friends.[154] In her words, "I have acquired the habit, from these many kilometers across France, to sleep at the start of a vehicle's movement, the only means to recover from the fatigue." This habit apparently stuck with her in the postwar years, for it is said that, when visiting the cinema, she would fall asleep during the whole screening and awake when the movie flashed the sign "The End," and would then exclaim, "What a beautiful film."[155]

Andrée Salomon also turned her attention to the Spanish border, which was in close proximity to the Gurs camp, and for this purpose she was especially interested in children who had relatives in Palestine. The plan was to smuggle them over the Pyrenees, via the small principality of Andorra and further into Spain, then proceed to one of the sea harbors and hope to board one of the boats heading to the Promised Land. Beginning in March 1944, Salomon arranged for between 85 and 134 children to take the Spanish route. Seventy-nine of them were then able to board a boat in October 1944 and sail to Palestine.[156] Financial payments for her large-scale activities were covered by the JDC.[157] At times money was sought from private individuals and organizations, such as from a banker in Grenoble.[158]

After the war, Andrée Salomon was for a time active in the OSE and Israeli-related causes. She strenuously refused any honors for her wartime work, including the French Legion of Honor. As reported by Georges Weill, "She tore up under my eyes a request form that was proposed by Julien Samuel, one of her wartime collaborators."[159] Salomon, her husband, and son settled in Omer, near Beersheba and later moved to Jerusalem, where she died in 1985.[160]

Vivette Samuel

A principal OSE worker, she helped liberate children
from the Rivesaltes internment camp and later
helped them cross into Switzerland

Born in Paris in 1919, Vivette Hermann Samuel joined an organization to collect milk for Spanish children during the Spanish Civil War in 1936. Soon after the fall of France, Vivette moved to Marseilles, where she received a telephone call asking her to meet Andrée Salomon at the Marseilles OSE office. Taking her from there to a nearby synagogue,

Salomon began to question her about her studies and her family. "She spoke very rapidly to me—in German—of the camp of Rivesaltes" and the children kept there. Children in camps? That's impossible, Vivette thought. "Pétain would not allow it."

But he did. Still incredulous at what she had learned, she was told that in October 1940 entire families had been rounded up in several German provinces bordering France and dumped in French internment camps, including Rivesaltes. Andrée described the activities of the OSE in the camp, including the presence of a resident physician, Dr. Isia Malkin. Quakers, Cimade, Swiss Aid, and the Unitarians were also part of the welfare organizations present there, and Andrée Salomon told Vivette that her assignment was to arrange the liberation of Jewish children, and this required her to live inside the camp. The meeting with Salomon was a turning point in Vivette's life "She seemed self-assured. . . . Faced with her determination, I was ready to go to the ends of the earth."[161]

On November 3, 1941, Vivette took a taxicab and entered Rivesaltes camp. Once inside, the children flocked to her. It was a horrific experience. In her words, they were, "dirty and in rags . . . wrapped in gray blankets. They carried rusty cans—they were going over to the Swiss Aid [office] to get a warm drink. This was the reality of the camp. . . . What a contrast, from the very beginning, between the places I came from and the destitution of the camp. It was dark, cold, and humid: there was no heating system. An acrid smell of human sweat floated in this never-ventilated lair."[162] The supply of water was inadequate, and there was no central sewer for drainage. The smell of human decay pervaded everything. Rodents circulated freely, and malaria was endemic.

Andrée Salomon was there to help Vivette settle down. "I was to occupy a small room that was sparsely furnished but that had electricity and could be heated. . . . A second bed was set aside for Andrée, who came to the camp about every ten days."[163] At the time, the camp held 20,000 people, including 5,000 children ages four to fifteen. The OSE made possible the purchase of nonrationed goods from wholesalers in the Marseilles and Toulouse regions, and the Swiss Aid organization served rice and milk to children in the morning and milk for the afternoon snack five times a week.

A week after her arrival, Vivette opened her room for office visits. Soon a mother rushed over and implored Vivette in German, "*Nehmen Sie mein Kind weg*" (take my child away). Vivette obtained permission to free ten little girls (of whom six were ill with lice and scabies), and ten places were found for them in a home in a nearby town.[164] There were a few uplifting moments, such as when in December 1941 Hanukkah was celebrated, "a feeling of communion never before felt took hold of us." Vivette jotted down in her notebook, "With a shaky hand, one of the veterans lights the first small flame of the gigantic menorah that had been made by the internees. And the traditional canticle, sung by hundreds of voices, rises as the night descends upon the camp. For the moment, suffering has given way, and I too am seized by this immense hope."[165]

In the meantime the OSE had succeeded in getting a handful of the children out of the country, mainly to the United States. In May 1942 Vivette arranged for parents to leave the camp so as to bid their children good-bye as they embarked on a boat in Marseilles. Of the ten mothers on the quay, nine were eventually deported to the death camps in Poland. When only five children remained in Rivesaltes, whose parents refused to be separated from them, Vivette considered her mission there accomplished, and she left for Lyon. From there, she circulated among the different OSE centers and with her confederates, helping Jews flee to Switzerland. In Marseilles she met the OSE head there, Julien Samuel, whom she married on October 6, 1942.

Vivette and Julien survived a near arrest when the Gestapo visited them on one morning of April 1944 and explained that they had arrested someone at the Swiss frontier who had a notebook that carried the address of the Samuels. Julien explained the mistake, that they had not been living here for a long time and that the listing had to refer to other tenants who had previously lived there. As the Gestapo undertook a thorough search of the apartment, Vivette, under the pretext of heating up a bottle for the baby, went to the kitchen and burned the compromising papers she had in a wood stove. The Gestapo left without returning.[166] A little while later Julien was arrested and placed on a train for deportation. But he managed to jump off and be reunited with Vivette, and both remained in hiding until the country's liberation in August 1944.[167] Julien died in 1981 and Vivette in 2006.

Madeleine Dreyfus

As a principal fieldworker in the OSE-Garel network, she moved children to safe locations and took care of their needs.

Born Madeleine Kahn in 1909 to nonpracticing Jewish parents, and mingling in the Parisian surrealist milieu, Madeleine Dreyfus rubbed shoulders with Jean Cocteau and André Breton and corresponded with famed public figures—Pierre Mendes-France, Roger Martin du Gard, Robert Aron, and Claude Lévi-Strauss—while working as an English-French bilingual secretary in an import-export firm. After the French defeat in 1940, Madeleine's family moved to Lyon, in the Vichy zone, where as a psychologist she was invited by Elisabeth "Böszi" Hirsch to help out at the medical-social center of the OSE. She began by dispersing children into various parts outside the city, as well as distributing false identity and ration cards. She was especially adept in canvassing religious and lay institutions in the Lyon area, and she assumed responsibility for the Lyon/Le Chambon link in the Garel network. Several times a month, she would take the train from Lyon to Saint-Etienne with a group of children, while counseling those who had only recently arrived in the county not to speak any other language save French, if they knew it, while on the train ride.[168]

Madeleine Dreyfus's trips benefited over 100 children, whom she often visited in their new sheltered homes, bringing them much-needed clothing, medicine, food tickets, and letters from their loved ones.[169] She recalled one such search for a sheltering place:

> I remember one day when there remained for me to find a place for two fourteen-year-old boys—a very difficult business. I went from place to place through the area around Chambon. . . . Nobody wanted the two boys. I came up to a rather old couple, the Courtials, and told them my "fable": city children who are hungry and need the fresh air of Le Chambon. . . . The Courtials' answer was friendly but firm: it was not possible for them to take them in. They themselves were too old, and these boys were too big. Having thrown out a feeler, I decided to disclose the secret: "The truth is that these are two young Jewish boys whose parents have been arrested and whom the Germans are looking for everywhere to imprison with their parents." No more hesitation. "But you should have said that before! Of course, bring them, your two boys."[170]

Tragedy struck when on November 23, 1943, she received a phone call from the father of a child she had hidden in a deaf-mute institute in

Villeurbanne. The father was alarmed, since he was informed of a soon-to-be Gestapo raid on that home. Then came a woman's voice: "You must come very quickly," as she was being held at gunpoint. Madeleine suspecting the worse, decided on the spot to go there, and was immediately arrested. She asked to be able to phone her home and ask that her baby daughter be bottle-fed; in actuality it was meant to be a warning to her colleagues to be on the watch. With the Gestapo's consent, she dialed a certain colleague and said: "This is Madeleine Dreyfus; please warn my family that I am under arrest by the Gestapo and I will not be home to feed my daughter." The Gestapo agent grabbed the receiver from her hand. She pleaded again to be allowed to go home to feed her daughter, and this was now granted her with a Gestapo agent at her side.[171]

She was kept imprisoned for two months in Fort Monluc, Lyon, and in Drancy for four months. From there, she managed to get a letter out to her mother with a coded message to urge her husband to have their sons, Michel and Jacques, taken to Switzerland. The message read, "The boys must stop eating ham." In French, the word for ham, *jambon*, sounds like *Chambon* (where the boys were in hiding), and the family understood. Raymond immediately arranged to have the two boys smuggled into Switzerland. Deported to Bergen-Belsen in May 1944, Dreyfus survived for eleven months the sufferings of the camp and lived through liberation. Returning to France on May 18, 1945, she eventually resumed her work with the OSE. She died in 1987.[172]

Elisabeth "Böszi" Hirsch

As one of the leading OSE and Garel network operatives,
she, along with her teammates, spirited hundreds of
children and adolescents out of the camps.

Born in 1913 in Sighișoara, Romania (Segesvár, when it was part of Hungary), she came to France in 1930. In 1940 she was asked by Andrée Salomon of the OSE to join her team of voluntary resident social workers in Gurs camp to help out with the internees there. She eventually became one of the great activists in the OSE and the Garel network. Together with her teammates, including Ninon Weyl-Haït and Ruth Lambert, they succeeded in spiriting out of the camps legally or otherwise hundreds of children and adolescents.[173] Later, in August 1942, she participated in the rescue operation of the 108 children in Vénissieux camp. Moving to Grenoble, with her sister Charlotte "Shatta" Simon, they organized children convoys traversing illegally to Switzerland and later across the Spanish border.[174] In April 1944 she decided to escort a group of 12 children, ages eight to fourteen, through the high Pyrenees Mountains. Candidates for this dangerous trek were youngsters chosen to continue to a Spanish or Portuguese seashore and board a ship heading to Palestine.

> We changed in Perpignan about 20 miles from the Spanish border, from where the railcar took us in the evening to the little village of Quillan. One of the frontier runners was waiting for us. . . . We were twelve children and five adults, plus six runners. . . . Next morning . . . after having consumed warm drinks offered by the maquisards [French underground], we resumed our march and sang, "*Ce n'est qu'un au revoir, mes frères . . .*" [Auld Lang Syne]. At noon we lunched on the bank of a lake. An hour of obligatory siesta was announced. Then the march resumed until the evening, with a stop for the four o'clock *gouter* [snack] . . . a short halt to pass out a piece of sugar soaked in cognac or lemon juice. The night had fallen, and we had settled down; the runners had made a fire that they kept going until five in the morning. . . . Our climbing continued the next day. . . . We crossed the valley and tackled the mountain; night had fallen, and we were in a thick fog. . . . The runners noticed that they had taken the wrong path. This was the most serious moment of our trip, for everyone was exhausted. . . . We finally found the right road.[175]

In Barcelona the children, all of whom made it through safely, were welcomed by a JDC (Joint) representative and placed in a villa outside the city. They continued on to Lisbon and boarded a boat that arrived safely in Palestine on October 26, 1944.[176]

Marianne Cohn

> She snuck more than 200 children in small groups across the Swiss border, then she was murdered by her German captors.

Marianne Cohn was born in 1922 in Mannheim, Germany, and then with her family moved first to Barcelona and then to Paris. During the war years, her parents were incarcerated in Gurs camp, and Marianne and her sister Lisette were sent to the Jewish Scout Movement-EIF Moissac camp. There Marianne assisted Simon Lévitte in the development of a documentation center, which was really an intelligence gathering center, for information on the hidden children, including their true identities, their origins, the places where they were hidden, and an index of possible hiding places.[177] When Lévitte moved the center to Grenoble, in the Italian zone, in 1943, Marianne followed him there.

Border Tactics

Carrying identity papers that listed her name as Colin instead of Cohn, she smuggled groups of children across the Swiss border from January through May 1944.[178] As recalled in 1994 by Emile Barras, one of the border smugglers living in a village close to the border, on May 20 he was told by grocer Joseph Fournier that a group of thirty-four children would be arriving at the Viry train station, led by Marianne Cohn. Luckily for them, the German guards at the station had already departed for their lunch break. The group proceeded by truck, driven by Fournier, along the railway tracks leading to St. Julien-en-Genevois. Then, to avoid a bridge that would have been visible from a German position, they sidetracked by foot through the fields of Viry village, approaching the Swiss border near Rougemont. Guided by Emile Barras, they arrived on the border point, and Marianne Cohn then pulled apart the parallel barbed wires to allow the children to get through. Having herself also crossed over, Marianne then told a Swiss custom official what number to phone in Geneva to come and fetch the children. She then returned to the French side. The crossing had taken place at high noon and was over by 2 p.m.

On May 31 Marianne Cohn went to the town of Annecy to meet another group of twenty-eight children ranging in age from four to sixteen, who had just arrived from Lyon. That night they traveled by truck, again driven by Joseph Fournier, along the road west of Saint-Julien-en Genevois, parallel to the Swiss border. At about 8 p.m., Fournier stopped the truck near several huge stalks of hay that served as good concealment and told the children to get off and head toward the border, about 200 meters away. But suddenly a German patrol car appeared on the scene and stopped the group and began questioning Fournier and Marianne.

As related in 1995 by Marcel Katz, one of the children, when the truck stopped in the middle of the road, "I heard voices, 'go on, jump, hurry,' and the canvas sheet was removed to let us out. Since I was all the way in the back, I was one of the first to get off. I took a little boy that was near me by the hand and began running . . . pulling along that little one who had a hard time following me. . . . After a small distance, suddenly several shots were fired very close to us, followed with strong shouting. . . . We were surrounded by barking dogs, [and they were about] to launch themselves on us. The Germans came up and grabbed me for not having obeyed their orders. . . . I was taken back to the truck."[179]

Back on the road, Marianne Cohn (presenting herself as Colin) told the Germans that these were children of railway workers on vacation (they carried with them false identities with French-sounding names), and were heading to the children's home of Pas de l'Echelle, in the nearby village of Etrembieres. Why had they stopped at night in the middle of a country road? Simply to relieve themselves, Fournier answered with a smile. The Germans followed the truck with the children to that home. When they arrived, the house matron confirmed that she was indeed expecting a group of children but that these were not them. So they were all taken to Annemasse city and to Hotel Pax, which had been converted into a prison. At Pax, Joseph Fournier was brutally interrogated, and then he was surprisingly released.[180]

Imprisonment

As for Marianne Cohn, she underwent severe interrogations every morning, accompanied by brutal beatings, to make her reveal her associates in the children's escape operation. She would respond: "Yes, I have saved the lives of more than 200 children, and if I were freed now, I would continue. Nothing could keep me back," and she continued to maintain her silence. In her cell she scribbled the following moving poem, which she then gave to one of the children.

Tomorrow I will betray, not today. Tear out my nails. I will not betray. You don't know how long I can hold out. But I know. You are five rough hands, with rings—You have hob-nailed boots on your feet.

Tomorrow I will betray, not today. Tomorrow. I need the night to decide. I need at least one night, to renounce, to abjure, to betray. To betray my friends, to forswear bread and wine, to betray life, to die. Tomorrow I will betray, not today. . . . Today I have nothing to say. Tomorrow I will betray."[181]

Jean Deffaugt, mayor of Annemasse, who was allowed to visit the prisoners, succeeded in getting seventeen of the children released to him with the understanding that he would return them upon request. He placed them in safe locations. Marianne and the remaining eleven children were assigned kitchen duties for the German military. They would leave the prison each morning, accompanied by guards, and work in the German kitchen in the Hotel de France. Deffaugt and Jewish resistance activist Emmanuel Racine decided on a plan to rescue Marianne. In Deffaugt's words: "There was only one possible time—when she and the children are en route to the hotel. If a car were standing at the corner, Marianne could be thrown inside and rushed off." When apprised of this plan, Marianne flatly refused. "It's out of the question. These children were entrusted to me. I have no right abandoning them. . . . The Germans would only take revenge on them. No, I must fulfill my duty to the end."

In the meantime, with the approach of the Allied armies, following the invasion of Normandy, starting on June 6, 1944, the commanding officer at the Pax prison threatened to have the remaining children shot. "Herr Mayer," Deffaugt pleaded with him, "you cannot do that. They are children. They are not responsible. You are a father yourself. These children won't prevent you from winning the war." To which Mayer shot back: "All I know is that I must get rid of them. What would you do with them?" "I'll take care of it," Deffaugt heard himself saying. "I'll find places for them." Mayer went on. "They'll spit in your face—you don't know Jews!" Deffaugt kept insisting, and Mayer conceded after forcing the mayor to sign the following statement: "I, the undersigned, Jean Deffaugt, mayor of Annemasse, acknowledge receiving from Mr. Mayer, chief of Security Services, eleven children of Jewish faith, whom I pledge to return at the first order." The released children were first placed in a summer camp and later they were led safely across the Swiss border into Geneva.[182]

As for Marianne Cohn, several weeks before the release of the children, on the night of July 7–8, 1944, she was taken out of prison, tortured, and killed. In 1982 French president François Mitterand, during his official visit to Israel, dedicated a garden at Yad Vashem to the memory of Marianne Cohn. Two schools bear her name, one in Annemasse and the other in the Tempelhof section of Berlin.[183]

Robert Gamzon

> As founder of the Jewish Scouts movement (EIF), he was active in various rescue activities and also commanded a Jewish unit that captured many German soldiers.

Born in 1905 in Lyon into a well-integrated Jewish family, Robert Gamzon is best known for his creation of the Jewish Scouts movement, Éclaireurs Israélites de France (EIF), in 1923, giving the movement a pluralistic definition by welcoming people of various religious and social shades. Gamzon was a charismatic figure, and those who followed him looked up to him with admiration and claimed that his teaching had transformed their lives and given a deeper meaning to their Judaism.[184] The motto of the EIF was "*Simcha va-Avoda*"—joy and work; in other words, the union of the spiritual and the manual types of activity, including traditional Jewish ritual practices, such as kosher food and observance of the Sabbath and holidays. Following this principle, Gamzon created workshops to train Jewish scouts in productive work, combined with lectures and lessons in Judaism.[185]

On July 19, 1940, in Clermont-Ferrand, together with EIF colleague Fréderic Hammel, the two decided to activate agricultural communities for the EIF youth. Inspired by Gamzon's call, the first group led by Isaac Pougatch ("Poug") and his wife, Juliette Pary, headed to Charry; others established a farming community in Lautrec including workshops, where Gamzon (code-named "Castor") also established his base. The Lautrec center counted three adjoining farms, managed by Gamzon's wife, Denise, and with Léo Cohn as religious instructor in Judaica.[186] After heated discussions, it was decided to integrate the movement under the auspices of the UGIF. The consideration was that being part of the UGIF, the EIF could act more freely and with less suspicion when deciding on clandestine action. When, in 1942, the Vichy regime disbanded the EIF, it converted under the code name of the Sixth to a fully clandestine organization, acting to produce forged identity papers, finding asylum for children and teenagers in non-Jewish private homes and institutions, and smuggling Jews of all ages across the borders into Spain and Switzerland.[187]

In 1944 Gamzon took up the military struggle, and as Lieutenant Lagnès, he formed a Jewish partisan unit, counting 120 men in the Tarn district of southwest France, which was affiliated with the French underground forces (Forces Françaises de l'Intérieur). On August 19, 1944, the Jewish Marc Haguenau unit (named after a martyred EIF leader), under Gamzon's command, seized a powerful German armored train, and on August 21 it participated in the liberation of two cities, Castres and Mazamet, capturing many German soldiers. In 1949 Robert and Denise Gamzon moved with their three children to Israel, where he died in 1961.[188]

Georges Loinger

He found ingenious ways to move hundreds of Jewish children to safety across the Swiss border.

One of the most audacious smugglers of children across the Swiss border, Georges Loinger was born in Strasbourg in 1910. After escaping from a German prisoner of war camp in 1940, he joined the OSE-Garel network, where he served as traveling inspector of the children's homes, including organizing physical education programs for the youngsters.[189] He also participated in finding sheltering places for children.[190] Loinger, however, is better known for organizing and leading Jewish children across the Swiss border, all of them successfully, in spite of the attending risks.

Starting in late 1942, convoys of twelve to twenty-five children would leave Lyon two or three times a week to Annemasse, on the Swiss border, where the mayor, Jean Deffaugt, whom Loinger knew well, was particularly helpful in accommodating the fugitives in an absorption center. Loinger then guided them across the border into Switzerland and also paid the professional guides to do the job. It was quite a big undertaking, with the participation of Emmanuel Racine, Jacques Salon, Germaine Masour, and other Jewish activists, stretching over a long period between May 1943 and June 1944, that helped smuggle hundreds of Jewish children into Switzerland. Some of these passages transpired in several places, such as a cemetery near Annemasse whose walls abutted the French side, where people would arrive wearing black veils and carrying the wreaths of deep mourning, praying and weeping. Then, with the help of a gravedigger's ladder, the "mourners" would climb over a wall and find themselves within feet of the Swiss border.[191]

Another tactic used by Loinger was to lead the children onto a football field situated about 50 meters from the Swiss border. Loinger relayed: "With the children lined up in two orderly rows, we would proceed, quite 'officially', singing all the while. I organized some really terrific football games. And while the game was in progress, some of the kids would cross the barbed wire—there were always fewer kids in our returning group, but no one noticed. This would continue for several days, until all those who were supposed to cross had crossed. Since I was operating at full steam, my activities were eventually noticed, and then, by the end of 1943, I discovered the Gestapo was looking for me."[192] Danger was never far away, as in the following story recounted by Loinger:

> I was taking some children by train from Aix-les-Bains to Annemasse, when suddenly I saw a group of fifty to sixty German soldiers, all somewhat older men, on their way to sentinel duty on the frontier. I had about fifty children with me who had just learned their new names, and kids being kids, they were running all over the train. . . . I find a big group of them—but in the German soldiers' car! The soldiers had them on their laps, were feeding them candy and chocolates. "Who are these poor little things?" they asked. I had my story all ready and replied that they were from Marseilles, where certain sections of the old city had been hard hit. "The children have been through a lot, and are now on their way to a camp for health reasons." The Germans pitied them and came to visit the children's compartments with all kinds of little gifts. Meanwhile, I was in a cold sweat; if just one youngster mispronounced his new name or spoke or showed he understood German . . .
>
> We had almost reached the Annemasse station. The big problem would be getting the children past the police patrols. We had been using a plan involving *cheminots* [railroad workers] who cooperated by affixing a sign on the doors of the station reading, "This Exit for Campers." We would head straight for that particular exit where the *cheminots* would be waiting to hurry us through. . . . The Germans were still playing with the children. And then one said: "Come, we'll

all go together!" The leader of the detachment, an older noncommissioned officer, asked me where I was taking the youngsters, and I replied: "To the SNCF Center (national state-owned railway)." He said, 'Listen, these kids are tired. Let us hasten the exit procedure. I'll tell the police you're with us." Then followed an extraordinary sight: fifty German soldiers, singing, en route through the city of Annemasse, with fifty Jewish children and me marching in step behind! Once we reached the reception center, the convoy came to a halt. The German saluted me, and the children and I went in— seen to the door under official German protection.[193]

It could have ended disastrously if someone other than the cool-headed and good-humored Georges Loinger had been in charge. In other instances, the crossing was done by trusted border smugglers for a rather large sum of money. As for the children, they had documents with their real names sewn into their clothing underneath the armpit, which was to prove useful once they arrived in Switzerland. After a compulsory stay in a reception camp, they were taken in charge by the OSE affiliate in Geneva and placed in Swiss children's homes. In order to keep his family out of danger, Georges Loinger sent his wife and two children—the youngest of whom was just a few months old—to Switzerland. It is said that he actually hoisted them over the barbed wire with the agreement of the Swiss soldiers. With his family out of the danger zone, he continued his rescue work until the Liberation, managing to elude capture. After the war, he became director of the Israeli shipping company Shoham Zim in Paris and vice president of the Association of Former Jewish Resistants of France.[194] In July 2016 Georges Loinger celebrated his 105th birthday!

Rabbi Zalman Schneerson

This charismatic Hasidic rabbi moved his young wards from chateau to chateau, staying one step ahead of the Germans.

Rabbi Zalman Schneerson, scion of the Lubavitcher rabbis, was born in 1898 in Gomel, present-day Belarus, and during the communist period of the Soviet Union he underwent severe persecution at the hands of the regime for his continuous spreading of religious teachings. The authorities had him arrested several times, but he found a way to talk himself free. In April 1935 he was allowed to leave the Soviet Union after his emigration requests were rebuffed sixteen times. His extensive persecution at the hands of the Communists left him with a bitterness toward that regime that he later equated with Nazi Germany.[195]

Rabbi Schneerson first went to Palestine and then was in France throughout the war. During the German invasion in May 1940, he moved to Vichy, then continued to Marseilles in October. There he established two institutions: one for adult Jews in need, and the other for children needing care and protection. He opened his adult center at 33, rue de Silvabelle, a narrow street in the heart of the city. This became his base, and he sent kosher food parcels to religious observant Jews in French internment camps as well as extending aid to all needy people knocking at his door. This house contained a yeshiva; a section where women were taught knitting, sewing, and dressmaking; a section for the teaching of radio technology to young men; and a kosher kitchen for feeding the rabbi's family. It also housed youthful vocational trainees, as well as those who succeeded in dodging the internment camps and were sought by the police and came furtively late at night for a quick hot meal and a slight rest before disappearing at dawn.[196]

Rabbi Schneerson also took care to create a cordial relationship with the police chief in charge of foreigners (Service des Etrangers) in Marseilles, a man by the name of Roux, who took a liking to this rabbi, his charm, and his exotic clothing. A radio technology course was opened by Schneerson in order to prevent young adult foreign Jews, ages eighteen to twenty-five years, from being drafted into French labor groups, as decreed by the Vichy regime. With the help of Mr. Roux, Schneerson's radio technology school was registered as a regime-sanctioned "labor group."[197] Léon Poliakov, the later Holocaust historian, who for a time worked as Schneerson's personal secretary, admitted having come under the spell of this Hasidic rabbi and wrote of the man's charisma, adding, "Talented with a prodigious vitality, he knew how to enrapture people, not excluding the bureaucrats or the Vichy policemen."[198]

Schneerson rented a beautiful château, la Maison d'Enfants, Château de la Vieille Chapelle, 8 kilometers from Marseilles, where a children's home was organized on a hilltop overlooking the Mediterranean Sea. It operated from October 1940 until the German takeover of the Vichy zone in November 1942. The home could accommodate up to sixty children, and Schneerson developed a curriculum of both secular and religious subjects. During the big raid on foreign Jews in summer 1942, many found temporary shelter in that home or under the stars in a nearby grove. Unfortunately, four children were taken by the police to be reunited with their interned parents and deported under the deceitful policy of "family reunions."[199]

To Dému, St. Etienne-du-Crossey, Nice, and Elsewhere

Days after the German takeover of the Vichy zone in November 1942, and assuming that the presence of his young wards would be less noticeable in the countryside interior of France, Schneerson moved his children's home to a farmhouse (Château de Seignebon) near the city of Dému. The police issued a safe-conduct pass to Schneerson and the children under his care, altogether close to eighty people, in two railroad cars with all their belongings. The Dému site was well chosen, hidden inside a forest some 400 meters from any road. The old building, however, lacked running water, heating, and electricity, and some of the windows were broken. The local Red Cross brought many blankets, sleeping bags, and other needful items as the winter months settled in, while warm clothing and shoes were received from the Quakers. The inhabitants of Dému village were surprised to see Jewish yeshiva students tilling the soil, plowing with acquired oxen, and chopping wood—and not least of all, Rabbi Schneerson in his black caftan and hat and his reddish beard. Daily activities were as previously in Marseilles: courses in French, arithmetic, and religious studies for children speaking a babel of languages, Yiddish, Polish, Russian, German, Hungarian, and Romanian. Bread was baked on site.[200]

When the gendarmes appeared for routine inspections, the older students, who feared being drafted into labor groups, fled to the nearby forest, returning when the gendarmes left. However, due to the increasing danger, Schneerson decided in March 1943 to move to the safety of the Italian zone of occupation. The decision to leave was quickly taken, and Schneerson evacuated the entire home surreptitiously, with the children divided into small groups and taken to Grenoble. There the rabbi was helped to find a new home, known as Château du Manoir, in the village of Saint-Etienne-de-Crossey, where he settled his charges. It was an old three-story house surrounded by a large garden. Financial assistance came surreptitiously via lawyer Mathieu-Meir Muller, head of Agudath Israel of France, who had fled to Switzerland, as well as from the UGIF. Some children were also taken back by their parents, while others were spirited into Switzerland.

After the fall of Mussolini on July 25, 1943, followed by the gradual withdrawal of Italian troops to the Nice enclave, Rabbi Schneerson decided to move his wards to Nice, so that they could continue to be under the protection of the Italians. The move took place on September 6, 1943, which unfortunately was only two days before the German occupation of Nice itself, when Italy switched sides and joined the Allied camp. Nice, to which thousands of Jews had moved, now became a trap: the Germans immediately began a systematic manhunt for all Jews. It was now imperative to get out of Nice and find a way to return to the relative safety of the Château du Manoir.[201] Until a way could be found to extricate oneself from a city filled with ss, Gestapo, French Milice, and local collaborators, one had to remain in hiding. His former Marseilles secretarial aide and future Holocaust historian, Léon Poliakov, took it upon himself to help Schneerson's young wards, who remained out of sight, dispersed in several of Nice's many hotels—with the ss raiding hotels every night.

It took two weeks to smuggle everyone out of the hotels, with the rabbi leaving last, hidden under empty cardboard boxes on grocery trucks that took them out of the city back to Voiron. Once out of Nice, the children posed as vacationers hiking in the countryside. For added security, the youngsters had to dress accordingly, and so those who had beards or sidelocks (*payot*) cut them off.[202] Back in St. Etienne-du-Crossey, the children were divided into groups and lodged in hamlets specially rented to accommodate them, with Fanny Vinograde-Orlowski, the rabbi's secretary, shuttling from one place to another to provide them with nourishment. As for Hadassa, the rabbi's sixteen-year-old daughter, she rode her bicycle throughout the Voiron countryside to deliver messages back and forth among the other hiding places and to obtain medicine for those who became ill.[203]

The French Milice struck on March 23, 1944, raiding several of the homes where children were suspected to be in La Manche and La Martellière. In the La Martellière home the Milice nabbed eighteen youngsters, who were taken to Drancy and then deported to Auschwitz; only one survived.[204] The rabbi, who was lame in one leg, and his remaining several dozen wards lived out the months of the occupation in hiding until France's liberation in August 1944.

Liberation

After the war Rabbi Schneerson returned to Paris before leaving for the United States in 1947. Responding to a call from French Jews, he returned to Paris, where he stayed for several years, returning to New York in 1953 to be close to his two children, who had recently married.[205] In New York he founded the Shevet Yehudah yeshiva, which combined Talmudic studies with an Institute of Technology where courses were given in electronic technology and computer science for both men and women. It is rumored that he had hoped to be in the line of succession after the passing of the Lubavitch rebbe Josef Yitzhak, but instead his distant cousin, Menachem Mendel, was chosen.[206] When he died in 1979, his life-saving record in France was largely unknown; in fact, it was totally forgotten until recent years. Before passing, he deposited the papers and documents of his wartime Association des Israélites Pratiquants at the YIVO institute, New York, where they are currently stored.

Rescuers Also Meriting Special Mention

Space does not permit the stories of many more who participated in rescue activities, so there is only brief mention here of the principal activists.

Marc Jarblum, president of the prewar Jewish social organization Fédération des Sociétés Juives, refused a leading position in the UGIF as he feared that it might eventually become an instrument for harming Jews—by the Vichy authorities or the Germans. Sought by the Nazis, he fled to Switzerland in April 1943, and he worked with Saly Mayer, representing the JDC, to support Jewish clandestine activity in France and obtained assurances that convoys of children under age sixteen that entered Switzerland would not be sent back.[207] David Rapoport headed the Rue Amelot Committee in Paris, but gradually turned to more clandestine activity, including finding hiding places for children, while turning over the Rue Amelot committee work to his friend Henri Bulawko. On June 1, 1943, David Rapoport was arrested, with his wife a day later; they were never to return from the camps.[208] Rapoport's associate at the Rue Amelot center, Henri Bulawko, had been arrested in November 1942 and deported to Auschwitz. He, too, did not survive.[209]

Dr. Joseph Weill, who during the war headed the medical section of the OSE for the whole Vichy zone, was one of the earliest to warn that Jewish children kept in the OSE homes were not safe, and it was better to have them dispersed as soon as possible. It was the Vénissieux incident, in which he and other Jewish activists participated, that finally convinced all Jewish organizations of the need to save the children from deportation, and Dr. Weill persuaded Georges Garel to launch a vast operation of children rescue. Sought by the Gestapo, he fled to Switzerland in May 1943. From there he organized the reception of children who were spirited out of France by his OSE affiliates.[210] Together with E. Walk, Dr. Eugène Minkowski (a psychiatrist, he wrote a major work on schizophrenia) assumed responsibility for the OSE section in the northern zone. Work included placing children with foster parents living in the countryside. In an interview with Anny Latour, he stated: "We succeeded in saving eight hundred children. I am coming to the end of my life; but I can say, with no false modesty, that in my life, this was one of the most beautiful pages."[211]

Albert D. Akerberg of the Sixth participated in the daring "kidnapping" of children from UGIF homes. He stated: "We arranged with UGIF aides to take a few children to the doctor or dentist. At a rendezvous point, one of our assistants . . . would take the child . . . they were told they were going to the country. . . . Not one of the children sent out there was ever caught."[212] Jacques Salon organized many of the children's convoys, on behalf of the OSE, bound for Spain. Arrested on a tramway in Lyon, he was tortured but escaped and remained in hiding.[213] His wife, Nicole Weil-Salon, was active with the OSE in Marseilles and Chambéry, where she and Huguette Wahl organized and accompanied numerous convoys of children to the Swiss border. In September 1943 both were assigned by Georges Garel to help Moussa Abadi in his rescue operation in Nice. Nicole was arrested on October 24, 1943, and Huguette several days later. They were both deported to Auschwitz and did not survive.[214]

EIF (Jewish Scouts) activists include Frédéric Shimon Hammel ("Chameau"), who together with Robert Gamzon decided to create a farming network for the training and rescue of Jewish youth. Hammel and his wife, Jeanne ("Fourmi"), were active in organizing the smuggling of children into Spain and Switzerland. He wrote the book *Souviens-toi d'Amalek* on the Jewish resistance in France.[215] Jacques and Monique Pulver were active in the EIF. Inspired by Gamzon, the two left for Moissac to head an agricultural school for foreign Jews. For the next two years, they carried out various missions for the EIF, including aiding fleeing Jews. When Jacques's sister Edith Pulver was arrested in February 1944 (she died in Auschwitz), Jacques (then appearing under the name of Pierre Couvret) and Monique fled to Switzerland with their twin daughters.[216] Edouard ("Bouli") and Charlotte ("Shatta") Simon headed the EIF Moissac home in the southern Tarn-and-Garonne department, where Jewish youth, ages six to sixteen, were sheltered after their parents had been interned in French camps. When these children were targeted by the Vichy regime, the Simons helped to disperse them in various locations. A square in Moissac, erected in 2004, is dedicated to the memory of Bouli and Shatta Simon. Léo Cohn was a member of the orthodox Ezra youth movement and was the Judaica educator in the EIF Lautrec camp. Arrested while boarding a train with a convoy of children bound for Spain, he was sent to Drancy, then deported; he did not survive.[217]

Moving on to the Sixth, an offshoot of the EIF, we note the following activists. Anny Latour, author of the book *The Jewish Resistance in France*, one of the pioneering studies on this subject, worked for the Sixth adult department in Lyon, with Roger Appel as assistant, who was later arrested and deported. She escaped a denouncement and went on to move her protégés to safety in the Toulouse region with the assistance a Red Cross worker. The Jesuit Father Roger Braun ("that exceptional human being") put her in touch with a farmer in Condom, who found her sheltering places for Jews on the run in his region. "I was placing people anywhere I could, even in the Condom hospital." With Anny Latour's help, the farmer referred to her by Braun claimed to have aided over 100 persons.[218] Henri Wahl, a leader in the Sixth, was involved in the fabrication of untold numbers of false credentials: identification cards, marriage certificates, ration cards, and driving licenses. He estimated that this undertaking saved the lives of more than 1,000 Jews.[219]

Marc Haguenau, a leader in the Sixth and the son of a rabbi, was deeply involved in various clandestine assignments, such as finding hiding places for EIF youth in danger of arrest. Arrested by the Gestapo in Grenoble, together with his assistant, Edith Pulver, on February 13, 1944, he reportedly died while trying to escape by jumping from a window. Another source claims he was murdered by the Gestapo. The Jewish Maquis unit that fought for the liberation of Castres in August 1944 was named after him.[220]

For those within the Zionist Youth Movement (MJS), we have Otto ("Toto") Giniewski (later, Ginat in Israel). He was in charge of the movement's branch in Grenoble, where from a small room in nearby Seyssins he organized his clandestine work with the help of young women emissaries. Neighbors were made to believe that Otto, often away from home, was an incorrigible womanizer. He stated, "When at 8 a.m. one morning my young wife left to bring me an urgent message, the neighbors murmured, 'Poor thing! They've been married only a few days, and already she's running out, first thing in the morning, looking for him!'" Professionally a chemist, he continued his studies at the Grenoble University, and false credentials were produced in great numbers in his laboratory.[221]

Simon Lévitte was a leading figure in the Zionist youth movement, and when all Zionist youth movements were integrated into one movement (MJS), Lévitte was appointed its secretary-general. Under his charge the MJS center fabricated many false credentials, participated in the rescue of Jews, and arranged their flight to Switzerland.[222]

Mila Racine, also a member of the MJS, was arrested on October 21, 1943, on her way to a Swiss border crossing point with a group of children and some adults. While in prison, she wrote on her cell door: "For a friend who passes, and one day occupies this cell, remember: always keep your faith and smile, whatever happens—do it for France." Annemasse mayor Jean Deffaugt related: "What courage that young girl had! When she knew they were coming to take her, she asked me, 'Monsieur le Maire, I'd like to look my best when I leave.... Can you get me some lipstick and powder? I won't cry. I promise you—when I get onto the van, I won't cry, but I'd like to be beautiful.'" Deported, Mila died during a bombing raid near Ravensbrück camp, where she had been interned. Others placed her death in a field outside Mauthausen camp.[223]

Jeanne Latchiver at first shared a room with Otto Giniewski and his wife in Seyssins village, where she lived with her two children and where the local MJS team also slept. There the typewriters kept rattling away late at night with secret messages, causing the neighboring farmers to inquire, "What on earth are you up to all night making so much noise?" When equipping Jewish children on the way to the Swiss border, Latchiver wrote: "We had to unravel all the linings of the clothing and conceal papers inside with the children's real names: we worked all night." A Swiss restriction allowed only children under age sixteen ingress into the country. "So we practiced trickery, using false cards to 'rejuvenate' the older of the children."[224]

As for the Jewish Army, there is David Knout, one of the founders of the first Jewish clandestine combat organizations that emphasized armed struggle, known as the Strong Hand, which later integrated into the Jewish Army. His Russian-born wife, Ariadna (Ariane) Scriabine, had converted to Judaism and was equally fiery in her conviction of the need of armed struggle against the Germans. Sought by the Gestapo, David managed to flee to Switzerland. Ariadna was murdered by the French Milice in Toulouse in July 1944.[225]

Henry Pohorylès was active in both the Zionist youth movement and the Jewish Army, first in Nice, then in Paris, where he was arrested on July 17, 1944. Placed aboard a deportation train in the last convoy leaving France for Auschwitz, he succeeded with others in making their escape on the night of August 20–21, 1944.[226] On one mission he went to see the Mother Superior of Moissac's Carmelite convent and told her: "We are persecuted Jews, and we appeal to you, out of your love of your fellow man. We have twenty or twenty-five girls we would like to hide here, in your convent, for a little while, a few days." As he was speaking, the Mother Superior kept staring at him until she said: "So, gentlemen, you truly are descendants of the Hebrews, who crossed the Red Sea without ever wetting their feet?" "Yes, Mother," Pohorylès quickly responded, catching his breath. "We are descendants of those Hebrews for whom God wrought a miracle. And I hope he creates further miracles for our generations." She replied: "Have no fear of it—God will help you. He has helped you already. And the doors of my convent are open to you."[227]

During the war years, Abraham Polonski was one of the founders of the Jewish Army and remained active throughout the occupation period.[228] Jules-Dika Jefroykin was also active in the Jewish Army, as well as the MJS, and represented the JDC (Joint) in southern France.[229] Jefroykin wrote: "Up until January 1944 . . . the American government had forbidden any funds being sent to Europe, no matter what they were meant for . . . [even for] saving Jewish victims. . . . Authorization to send the money was withheld." So the money had to be brought in secretly or raised on the spot. In a report in August 1944, Jefroykin claimed that $360,000 had been spent on illegal work, presumably including the Spanish and Swiss border crossings. He himself crossed into Spain and reached Barcelona on May 8, 1944, where he set up an organization that provided a hotel and guides in Andorra, the tiny principality between France and Spain.[230]

Some other noteworthy Jewish resistants include André Chouraqui. Originally a rabbinical student from Algeria, he was in charge of Le Chambon for the Garel network, where he dispersed people sent to him from the Lyon center. "I traveled hundreds of kilometers by bicycle," he recalled, identifying willing host families with the help of the local clergy.[231] Maurice Loebenberg ("Cachoud") was an expert in devising false credentials, even for the French resistance movement. He was active in Nice and Paris, where he was arrested on July 18, 1944, and tortured to death.[232] Emmanuel Racine responded to the appeal of Robert Gamzon, Simon Lévitte, and Georges Loinger to help with the passage of children and adults across the Swiss border, emanating from the regions of Lyon, Chambéry, and Aix-les-Bains, which he carried out with the help of his sister, the aforementioned Mila Racine.[233] Léon Poliakov, aide to Rabbi Zalman Schneerson and active in the French resistance, was one of the principals of the Paris Centre de Documentation Juive Contemporaine after the war and the author of many studies on the Holocaust and antisemitism. Finally, Rabbi René Samuel Kapel, a military chaplain, was active in internment camps and resistance work.[234]

We end with the story of Rabbi Elie Bloch. During the German invasion Bloch fled to Poitiers, where his home served as a synagogue and he cared for the Jewish internees in the nearby Route de Limoges camp. With the help of Father Jean Fleury (the "Gypsy Priest") and a small group of Jewish aides—Rivka-Régine Breidick (later Dimant), Mr. Friedman, and a Miss Rosenbaum—Bloch arranged for the children in the camp to be released and placed with Jewish families that were not yet in danger of arrest.[235] In January 1943 his wife, Georgette Bloch, was arrested and held in the Limoges camp. He intervened with his relatives in Paris to have her released, but it was in vain, so he decided to turn himself in. On December 17, 1943, the Blochs and their six-year-old daughter, Myriam, were deported to Auschwitz, never to be seen alive again.[236]

In closing, the work of Jewish rescuers would not have succeeded without the assistance of thousands of non-Jewish rescuers, some mentioned here, who in different ways aided in saving Jews from arrest. Among them may be counted peasants, clergy, entrepreneurs, blue-collar laborers, teachers, policemen, medical doctors, housewives, concierges, artisans, and railroad workers. As of January 1, 2016, 3,925 such men and women have been awarded the Righteous title by Yad Vashem. Working in tandem with Jewish workers, who also merit being known and still await being honored, they saved close to three-quarters of all the Jews in France.

8 Belgium

Organized Self-Help, Stopping a Deportation Train

Persecuted and evicted during the Middle Ages, Jews began to return to Belgium in the sixteenth century from Portugal in the form of *marranos* (Jews who had been forced to conceal their Judaism). During the eighteenth century, some northern European Jews also settled in Belgium. In 1830, when Belgium became an independent country, there were a little over 1,000 Jews there. The Jewish population kept growing, and on the eve of the German invasion on May 10, 1940, there were 66,000 Jews concentrated in four cities: Brussels, Antwerp, Liège, and Charleroi, but principally in the first two.[1]

During the German occupation of 1940–44, the country was mostly under a military-type rule, with the officials in the various ministries, led by ministry heads known as secretary-generals, remaining at their post, while the government itself fled to England to create a government-in-exile. On January 10, 1941, it issued a statement that declared all the decrees of the German administration null and void and warned of punishing Belgians collaborating with the Germans.[2] Most of the population remained hostile to the German occupation (the second such occupation in two decades), with the exception of two collaborating organizations: the Vlaams Nationaal Verbond-VNV (National Flemish Movement), headed by Staf de Clerk, and the French-speaking Rexist movement, led by Léon Degrelle. On April 14, 1941, Flemish antisemites vandalized two Antwerp synagogues and the home of Rabbi Marcus Rottenberg. There were, however, no serious antisemitic outbreaks in the rest of the country.[3]

On the Jewish front, Nazi German anti-Jewish laws followed in quick succession, with the aim of eliminating Jews from all positions of influence, depriving them of their possessions and livelihood, and eventually deporting them to their death. The anti-Jewish measures began with the prohibition of ritual slaughter of animals, on the excuse of cruelty to animals, followed by defining who was Jewish, and then many new directives: requiring all Jews to draw up a list of all their property, eliminating Jews from publishing businesses, administration, the legal and teaching professions, and the media; requiring them to display signs over Jewish enterprises, restricting withdrawals from bank accounts, permitting Jews to reside only in four cities—Antwerp, Brussels, Liège, and Charleroi; a nightly curfew from 8:00 p.m. to 7:00 a.m., severe restrictions on the practice of medicine, and Germans' plunder of Jewish art work and Jewish religious and folklore objects.[4] As of January 17, 1942, Jews were forbidden to leave the country and required to perform special forced labor, such as building the Atlantic Wall in northern France (which involved some 2,200 Jews). Finally, the creation of a Judenrat, the Association des Juifs en Belgique (Association of Jews in Belgium, AJB), headed by Rabbi Salomon Ullmann, which required a listing of all Jews in Belgium. When, however, on May 27, 1942, the Germans issued the Yellow Badge decree, the Greater Brussels city council stood out among Belgian cities by refusing to distribute the badge; other municipalities obliged, especially in Antwerp.[5] Deportation began on August 4, 1942, and lasted well into the last days of the German occupation. Roundup of Jews was done mainly by the German field police, as Belgian policemen, with the exception of those in Antwerp, refused to participate.[6] There were an estimated 29,000 losses of the Jewish community to the Germans due to the deportations.[7] Transports left from the Dossin camp in Mechelen (Malines), halfway between Brussels and Antwerp. Some 25,000 Jews were concealed from the Germans, mostly in hiding inside Belgium.[8] When, at the start of the deportations, Belgium's Queen Mother Elisabeth intervened on behalf of the Jews of Belgian nationality, the Germans obliged, since it cleared the way to deport the rest of the Jews, 90 percent of whom were not naturalized.[9] Several thousand others had fled to France during the German invasion of Belgium and either went into hiding or found a way to leave the country across the seas via Spain and Portugal or into Switzerland.

Jewish Defense Committee

The single largest Jewish clandestine organization in Europe, with 768 activists, saved more than 3,000 Jewish children and thousands of adults.

As the deportation of Jews got under way in September 1942, a clandestine Jewish rescue organization was secretly created, the Jewish Defense Committee (Comité de Défense des Juifs, CDJ), for the purpose of trying to save as many Jews as possible. Ghert Jospa, active in the Belgian underground Front d'Indépendence (FI) was the principal initiator.[10] The story told is that sometime in the summer of 1942, Ghert Jospa approached Professor Chaim Perelman, who taught philosophy at Brussels University, to discuss the creation of a separate clandestine Jewish organization to help Jewish adults and especially children to evade deportation through various illegal methods. The meeting in Perelman's home, also attended by his wife, Fela, included six people other than Jospa, representing five Jewish organizations and one non-Jewish one. Six of the founding members were eventually arrested and deported, and only two of them survived.[11]

The CDJ's main purpose was to find hiding places and provide false credentials (identification and ration cards) for those in hiding or living secretly in the open.[12] Its children's section, in cooperation with the nondenominational National Children's Committee (Oeuvre Nationale de l'Enfance), headed by Yvonne Nèvejean, succeeded in hiding more than 3,000 children.[13] Other than its main base in Brussels, it opened branches in Antwerp, Liège, and Charleroi/Namur. The CDJ maintained contact with Belgian officials who were open to the idea of helping Jews and to cooperating with members of the AJB, the so-called Belgian Judenrat, whose activities were controlled by the German authorities.[14]

The CDJ created two main departments, one for adults, headed by Chaim Perelman, and one for children, headed by Maurice Heiber, and four subsidiary departments—administration, finance, false credentials, and food ration cards, as well as a clandestine press and propaganda section.[15] The finance department was first headed by Benjamin Nykerk; later, by David Ferdman ("Alfred Feremans"). Abusz Werber and Chaim Perelman were responsible for press and propaganda, in the form of publications that appeared in both spoken languages of the country, Flemish and French (such as *De Vrije Gedachte* and *Le Flambeau*) and Yiddish (*Unser Wort, Unser Kampf*).[16] Articles dealt with the deportation trains and news of the destination and fate of those deported, urgent appeals to avoid boarding the trains; and news on the fate of Jews in other countries under German rule.[17] A special section within the CDJ dealt with traitors and informers. It was headed by Albert Domb, and it used the services of the non-Jewish Jeanne Daman in tracking down persons who collaborated with the Gestapo in denouncing CDJ activists.[18]

Ghert Jospa, of the CDJ, maintained a direct link with the mainline underground Front d'Indépendence, together with his wife, Yvonne, and Maurice Bolle. Financial support came from several sources, such as the Banque de Bruxelles and the Société Belge de Banque, which advanced substantial amounts to the CDJ and its helpers through intermediaries, such as Jules Dubois-Pélerin, against written notes of repayment by the Joint Distribution Committee after the war.[19] Benjamin Nykerk, in charge of finances, traveled to Switzerland twice to acquire funds from the JDC and certain Swiss banks. Belgian banks also contributed, against assurance of reimbursement after the war. Nykerk was arrested while on a third mission in Paris and did not return from deportation.[20] The Secours d'Hiver, a self-help welfare organization created with encouragement of the occupiers on the model of the Winterhilfswerk in Germany, also provided assistance in the form of provisions and food stamps to the CDJ through its contact representative Roger van Praag.[21]

The CDJ eschewed armed resistance in favor of rescue, but it did not prevent CDJ associates who acted on their own or in cooperation with the Belgian resistance from such activity. On two occasions, in the summer of 1942, Jewish activists targeted the AJB, trying to seize the card index that the AJB maintained in its office.[22] The single most significant resistance operation carried out by the Jewish underground was the attack on a deportation train, on the night of April 19–20, 1942, containing a transport of Jews from the Mechelen camp (transport No. 20) headed for Auschwitz; 231 Jews escaped, of whom 23 were shot to death by the train guards. It is the only recorded instance of an armed attack in Europe on a deportation train carrying Jews to their death.[23]

The Rescue of Children

The CDJ dedicated itself especially to the rescue of Jewish children, ages up to sixteen years, and a large team of personnel was assigned to this sensitive task. Administration and planning was mostly in the hands of Jewish workers (such as Maurice and Esta Heiber, Yvonne Jospa, and Sophie Werber), whereas conveying the children to their new homes and keeping tabs on how they were cared for, an undertaking that necessitated much travel—this was the province of non-Jewish women workers (such as Andrée Geulen and Suzanne Moons), who fetched the children from their distraught parents and turned them over to new hands.[24] How were the children found? Persons assigned by the CDJ first located parents who, panicked by the ongoing roundup of Jews, had appealed for help to various Jewish and non-Jewish children and welfare organizations, such as the ONE, the Red Cross, and Secours d'Hiver.

First the CDJ agents, without identifying themselves, approached the anguished mothers with a friendly conversation that led to the suggestion of placing the children with non-Jewish host families. The CDJ delegate began by telling the mother: "I was told . . ." The parent would interrupt to ask: "By whom?" Answer: "A secret organization." The tactic was to make the mother have full confidence in the undertaking and that she understood that this was being done in order to save her children and ease her burden. The names of the children, ages, and gender were noted down, and this information was then submitted to the placement section in the CDJ so that it could find suitable places for the individual children.[25]

The mothers were then approached again, this time by one of the trained child conveyors with the delicate job of persuading the mothers to let go of their children. The conveyors told of the shock by the parents who were asked to surrender their children to strangers, mostly non-Jewish young women who presented themselves as social workers, who matter-of-fact stated that they had come to fetch the child without giving any indication of where they were to be taken and how contact was to be maintained between both sides. The conveyors were instructed not to divulge any such information, not even allowing the parents to correspond with their children. In the words of Maurice Heiber: "Here, one of the greatest heroic acts took place, when the mother agreed to confide her child to a stranger, to a strange organization. . . . She might have to separate herself [from her child] forever."[26] In some select cases, it was felt safe to arrange afterwards one or two meetings between parents and their children, but this would take place in a neutral location, not in the home where the child was staying. In some extreme cases, parents had to satisfy themselves by observing their children only from a distant hidden location—and avoid a close and intimate meeting for fear of a sudden uncontrollable emotional reaction on the part of the parents that could jeopardize the child's safety.[27] In general, it was preferable that contact between parents and their children be done only through third parties, mostly representatives of the CDJ.

Finding safe sheltering places was a superhuman effort, involving traveling over long distances by train, bus, and bicycle. Places surveyed included religious institutions, children's homes, and private families. Before the actual placement, children were given a preliminary medical examination, such as at the tuberculosis sanatorium of Dr. Christine Hendrickx-Duchaine, in the Brussels region.[28] This was followed by the escort, usually a woman, being provided with the child's new false identity, false food ration cards, the destination of the child's sheltering, passwords, and code names of other persons the conveyor would have to meet while on the road with the child. Also, the escorts, known as *marraines,* made occasional visits with the hosts to check on the child's treatment, and when necessary, make payments to the hosting family or institution. The *marraines* were also responsible for providing clothing and other necessities for the children. In some cases, parents who could afford it shared in their children's upkeep. This would last until the parents themselves had to go into hiding or were picked up and taken away for deportation. All future financial arrangements were then placed solely on the shoulders of the CDJ.[29]

It should be noted that the Nazis, in their tactic of deception to facilitate the deportation process by falsely claiming that the parents were simply being taken to perform some temporary work assignment in Germany, allowed the Jewish community to maintain several homes for children, under Gestapo supervision, whose parents had been deported, in the expectation of picking up these children later. One was the Wezembeek-Oppem home near Brussels. But one could never rely on German assurances. When, on October 32, 1942, for instance, the Gestapo suddenly raided the Wezembeek-Oppem home and took the children to the Mechelen/Malines detention camp, the AJB, CDJ, ONE, and even Queen Mother Elisabeth interceded with the German authorities to have the children released and returned to the children's home.[30]

Statistically speaking, according to one source, about 3,000 to 3,500 Jewish children out of an estimated total of slightly over 8,000 under the age of fifteen were not deported—of which 3,000 at least were under the patronage of the CDJ.[31] In one of his publications, historian Lucien Steinberg speculated that the number of Jewish children saved directly by the CDJ could even be higher, closer to 4,000, while as many as 10,000 adults were also saved through the help of the CDJ.[32]

This remarkable achievement was mostly thanks to the initiative and the vigorous and risky work of the CDJ, the single largest Jewish clandestine organization in Europe, specifically created in 1942 for the sole purpose of helping Jews avoid deportation with the help of a wide range of non-Jewish rescuers—many of them honored by Yad Vashem with the Righteous title. Thousands of Jews owe their lives to the CDJ, whose many members await proper recognition by the Jewish public at large.

Ghert (also Hertz and Joseph) Jospa

He was one of the principal founders of the CDJ,
which brought together many Jewish organizations
with the sole purpose of rescuing Jews.

Born in 1905 in Resina, Bessarabia, then part of Russia, Jospa left for Belgium in 1921. He was active in leftist political movements, such as the Belgian anti-Fascist committee and the League against Racism and Antisemitism. Then came the war. Initially drafted in the Belgian army, he was demobilized with Belgium's defeat in May 1940, and he returned to his home in Brussels.[33] Convinced that the Jews in Belgium faced an existential threat, Jospa at first joined the all-Belgian clandestine FI organization, but soon decided to create a special affiliate devoted exclusively to the assistance of Jews. Thus two years into the German occupation, the Jewish Defense Committee (Comité de Défense des Juifs—CDJ) was born out of an amalgam of several Jewish organizations, Leftist, Zionist, non-Zionist, and other ideological tendencies—not as a combat group but limited solely to rescue.[34]

Ghert Jospa was married to Yvonne ("Jaspar"), born Hava Groisman, in 1910 in Popouti, Bessarabia (today in Moldova). In the CDJ, she was especially active in the rescue of children and in locating places of refuge for them through contacts with various children's organizations (such as ONE, the Catholic JOC, Aide Paysanne aux Enfants de Villes, Foyer Léopold II), and with preferably farming families.[35]

Ghert Jospa was arrested on June 21, 1943, in Brussels when he had arranged to meet a certain woman confederate to turn over to her a package of false identification. In his words:

We were to meet on a bench on De Fray Avenue, near a park. As we met, suddenly a Gestapo car stopped, and out stepped Jacques [surnamed "Fat Jacques," whose family name was apparently Goglowski, and who was infamously known as a Jewish informer for the Gestapo]. We both had false non-Jewish ID cards. But Sarah's looks were somewhat Semitic. Jacques looked at her and shouted: 'False card,' and she was taken to the car. Then came my turn. Ordered to open my briefcase, and there was the package with a host of IDs. I was immediately carted off to the car.[36]

At the Gestapo office, Jospa was continuously beaten during interrogation for refusing to disclose information. Three persons struck him simultaneously—one with an iron chain, another with a stick, the third with a whip.[37] When Jospa passed out, he was revived with a pail of water, and the interrogation continued. "I was then convinced that everything was finished with me."[38] Jospa decided to commit suicide but could not get hold of a razor blade. A friendly German soldier who brought him bread and water encouraged him to keep hoping. The soldier was sent to beat him, but instead only pretended to hit him, while Jospa was told to scream every time he heard a beating sound.[39]

After eight days, with two signs attached to his clothes—a yellow one for Jewish and a red triangle for communist—he was taken by car to Breendonck camp, where mostly political prisoners were held. His whole body was covered with cuts and scars, some of them reaching his bones. He was also almost blinded. In Breendock, he was assigned the most disgusting job, of cleaning the toilets, from which he suffered eight or nine boils on his body. He was also constantly beaten while undergoing additional interrogations.[40] A bit later he was able to receive a letter from wife Yvonne and a package containing butter and various creams. "That night, I could not close my eyes."[41] He was then placed on a transport and sent to in Buchenwald camp. There he joined the clandestine organization set up by other political prisoners (German communists), and without the others at first realizing that Jospa was Jewish, he was admitted into the political section of the camp underground.[42] Luckily for him, he survived the tribulations of that camp and saw liberation in April 1945.

Chaim and Fela Perelman

They were key CDJ members and turned their home into
a temporary hiding place for Jews on the run.

Born in 1912 in Warsaw, Chaim Perelman moved to Belgium in 1925. In
September 1942 he agreed to Ghert Jospa's call for the creation of the
CDJ, which was to be launched in Perelman's house. He prevailed upon
Jospa that the new organization be all-inclusive, representing all shades
of political opinions in the Jewish community and not necessarily be
limited to left-wing Socialist and Communist tendencies.[43]

Perelman immediately volunteered to head the adult department of
the CDJ, a position that he kept until the eve of the country's liberation
in September 1944. He also was involved, together with Abusz Werber,
in the publication of the CDJ's clandestine publication, *Le Flambeau*.
According to historian Lucien Steinberg, Perelman also appealed to
Yvonne Jospa to take the lead in managing the child placement section, and this led to Jospa's recruitment of Ida Sterno to help out in this
important work.[44] In addition, Maurice Heiber, then working within
the AJB (the so-called Belgian Judenrat), was also contacted by Perelman inviting him to join the CDJ. Heiber agreed, while still retaining his
position at the AJB, as urged of him by his CDJ colleagues. When Heiber
was arrested in May 1943, Chaim Perelman replaced him as a listening
agent within the AJB.[45]

Also to be noted is Chaim Perelman's work with friendly non-Jewish
civic organizations and individuals. Uccle (a Brussels suburb) mayor
Jean Hérinckx's brazen letter to the German authorities in the name
of mayors of the Brussels metropolitan region, and signed by Brussels
mayor Jules Coelst, denouncing the anti-Jewish measures, such as the
wearing of the Yellow Star (according to Lucien Steinberg) was composed, or at least inspired, by Perelman, after a meeting between Perelman and Hérinckx.[46] Perelman also contacted in September 1943 Major
Caelb, the responsible official in the Ministry of Provisions, asking that
foodstuff be made available in the Dossin barracks in Mechelen/Malines
camp for Jews interned there, awaiting deportation. He succeeded in
soliciting food for Jews in hiding from the Wijgaerts family, who operated a big food chain in Brussels.[47] Furthermore, the printing firm of

A. Wolf in Liège provided Perelman with numerous false ration card stamps. In the Antwerp municipality, Alphonse Goethals, in charge of provisions, also responded to Perelman's appeal for ration card stamps, in the amount of 1,500 stamp pages per month, out of the 8,000 pages that he produced.[48]

His wife, Fela Perelman, was born in 1909 as Fajga Estera in Łódź, Poland. Moving to Belgium, she earned a PhD in history from Brussels Free University; there she met Chaim and married him in 1935.[49] When the Germans forbade Jewish children from attending public schools, Fela Perelman appealed to Hérinckx, as well as other officials in the Brussels municipality, to make possible the creation of a special school for Jewish children, under the name of Nos Petits, a request that was granted. Hérinckx also arranged for a special tramway to take the children to and from school in broad daylight. Fela (under the pseudonym of Denise Dumont) interviewed candidate teachers willing to serve in the Nos Petits school, and especially the non-Jewish teacher Jeanne Daman, who became the school principal and Fela's right-hand person.[50] When the Germans closed the Nos Petits school after only a few months of operation, Fela and Jeanne helped find safe sheltering places for the children with help from ONE. This occurred before even the creation of the CDJ.[51] Later Fela helped additional women as escorts for the hidden children, providing their hosts with payment and food ration cards when necessary.[52]

With the formation of the CDJ, Fela Perelman also helped out by placing Jewish women as live-in maids in non-Jewish homes.[53] As for the Perelmans' daughter, Noemi, born in 1936, she too was placed in foster homes in 1941, a year ahead of the deportations.[54] The Perelman home served as temporary hiding places for Jews on the run, while fleeing from their home country in Holland, via Belgium and then France, where they hoped to cross into Switzerland or Spain.[55]

After the war, Fela was instrumental in starting four orphanages for children whose parents had not survived. She was also active in various Israel-oriented charitable foundations until her death in 1991. As for her husband, Chaim, he pursued his philosophical studies, publishing his theories on what he termed "regressive philosophy" and "new rhetoric," and was highly renowned among academic circles in Belgium. He died in 1984.[56]

Maurice Heiber

He headed the CDJ's children's section, which arranged hiding places for children.

Maurice Heiber ("Hache"), who joined the FI in the summer of 1942, was persuaded by Eugène Hellendael (later, of the CDJ) to join the Judenrat-type AJB (Association of Belgian Jews) where he was active in the children's section. Upon his later recruitment into the CDJ, he was assigned to head its children's section.[57] The following is from Heiber's postwar account of rescue activities that he undertook.

In a Brussels suburb, where many Jewish children had been placed by the CDJ, the Gestapo had already raided several homes due to denunciations of persons sheltering children. "We learned that that same evening a large-scale and methodical search was to be undertaken in that whole neighborhood. Young women from our various teams who were available were immediately dispatched there to quickly remove the children, with the Gestapo on their heels. Truly, like in the movies or fictional adventure stories."[58]

In another story, fifteen girls, ages between twelve and fifteen, had been placed in a convent near Ghent. One day Heiber was informed by telegram that these girls were to arrive in Brussels in less than an hour's time and they needed safe lodgings. It turned out that the reason for this sudden trip was a letter by one of the girls to her mother, telling her the convent where she was staying, and the mother decided to visit her daughter. To pay for her trip, she exchanged some leather goods, made by her husband before his deportation, in a store when she arrived in Ghent. During the price negotiation with the storekeeper, she inadvertently revealed the reason for this business exchange and the name of the convent. For fear of denunciation, the children had to be quickly removed.[59]

We follow with a particular moving story: One day, during an inspection tour by one of the CDJ *marraines* in a home where a five-year-old boy was sheltered, she was told what had just taken place there. The family's own daughter of around eight years had received a Christmas gift in the form of a manger with the baby Jesus surrounded by saintly figures, and had kept this treasure next to her bed. One evening, before going to sleep she was shocked to reveal that the baby toy and the saints were missing. None other than the boy could have taken it. After a lengthy questioning, he admitted to the offense, but excused himself: "I did not steal them." "But didn't you take them?" "No, I did not take them. I hid them." But why? After a long silence, the boy explained in tears. "Mademoiselle, the small Jesus and the saintly virgin are Jews, so I hid them. The Gestapo will not have them." He then could not control his tears.[60]

In yet another gripping story involving a hidden child, one couple came to ask for a girl in the hope of adopting her, having lost their own daughter. They could not decide between the two girls presented to them: a dark-haired girl to remind them of their lost Carmencita or a blonde girl to help them overcome their grief. The man then decided for the darker girl. Reason: "She looks more sad," implying that she was in greater need of help.[61]

Heiber was arrested in May 1943, in retaliation by the Germans for the rescue of a group of children from a Brussels convent and was imprisoned for eight months in the Mechelen-Malines transit camp. He was then released due to the intervention of higher-ups in the Belgian civilian administration.[62]

Ida Sterno

She worked in the children's section of the CDJ, placing children with families for safekeeping, sometimes many times for the same child.

Born in Bucharest, Romania, in 1902, Ida Sterno ("Jeanne") left for Belgium in 1914, where she worked as a social worker, helping refugee children of the Spanish Civil War. During the German occupation, she was initially hired as a social worker in the Charleroi region for a gas and electricity firm; she was then fired because she was Jewish. She stated that in solidarity with her fellow Jews, she registered as Jewish, as required by the Germans, although she could have avoided this, taking advantage of the marriage of her brothers to non-Jewish spouses. She then met Yvonne Jospa and accepted her offer to work in the rescue of Jewish children, under the direction of Maurice Heiber, head of CDJ's children's section.[63]

As part of her work, she arranged for children to be placed with families for safekeeping. Records of all these hidden children were kept in two locations in Brussels. She recollected: "I hid the list of the sheltered children, with the names of their hosts, under a rug in my apartment, rue de Belle Vue—an illegal residence that I shared with Andrée [Geulen]. A copy of this list was kept with Mrs. Nèvejean, director of the ONE, on Rue du Trone."[64] Then there were separate notebooks with valuable information, each with a different indication of a child's data. One would bear the child's true name, plus a code letter; another would have the child's borrowed name; then another notebook with the previous address; finally one with the new sheltering address. Also noted were payments that had to be made and anything of particular concerning each child.[65]

Often it was necessary to transfer the children to new locations for various reasons such as danger of denunciation, the host not deemed appropriate to keep the child, better conditions for the child in another location, or the child having advanced to the age where he needed to frequent a school.[66] Ida Sterno wrote: "One day, for instance, I was informed that two small children of three and four years, placed in an orphanage at Huy for approximately a year, were taken back by their parents. They were covered with scabs, infected, lice-ridden, and clearly feeble. That is why we struggled to arrange a system of inspections, since similar cases were possible."[67] When absolutely necessary, parents or relatives were allowed to see their hidden children, but only from a distance. "Such as when one day, we showed, between two trains, a child and its grandmother. . . . The old woman was overwhelmed with joy. She had seen again her grandson, the only child that was left her of a large family."[68]

Ida Sterno was arrested on May 31, 1944, and confined in the Mechelen/Malines transit camp. Luckily for her, her arrest was just months before Belgium's liberation in early September 1944. Her arrest came as a result of her meeting with a certain lady at the café Beau Séjour in Brussels in broad daylight. They took precautions by choosing to sit not inside but on the terrace, where they could observe the comings and goings on the outside street. Ida carried in her bag compromising documents, including the names of a dozen children needing to be placed. The two women failed to notice the appearance of the infamous Jewish informer "Fat Jacques," who was the terror of any Jew circulating on the streets. Presently he appeared in the company of a Gestapo agent and immediately began to interrogate Ida's lady companion.[69] However, since she had an official AJB employee card and was thus exempt from deportation, she was let go.

During that tense interval, Ida had silently removed the documents from her bag and slipped them on the next chair whose seat was covered by the tablecloth and, consequently, it remained unseen. Then came Ida Sterno's turn to be interrogated. "I explained that in my capacity of social worker, I dealt with Jewish children, like the Spanish children that I dealt with previously."[70] But she adamantly refused to give any information on the Jewish children in her care. Fat Jacques promised that no harm would befall the children, since they would be placed in the Wezembeek-Oppem children's home. "If I did not speak, it would be Breendonck [a notorious camp for political prisoners] . . . [Jacques] pushed me to a corner and pointed a revolver at my chest."[71] She stood her ground and was taken away—not to Breendonck, with its torture chambers, but the relatively less harsh internment and transit camp of Mechelen/Malines. All this time, she had only one thing on her mind—the incriminating papers left on the chair in the cafeteria. She was relieved to learn later that her lady companion had noticed them and taken them to a safe location. The lists of the hidden children were later recovered from Sterno's home by Andrée Geulen with the help of a trustworthy colleague.

Ida was placed in a cell with twelve to fifteen others. She later learned that persons in the CDJ had intervened in her favor, even appealing to the Queen Mother Elisabeth, which may have helped to preclude her deportation. During her incarceration, she met many parents for whose children she had arranged sheltering places, but since they had known her under her codename of Jeanne, she preferred not to disclose her true identity.[72] On the morrow of September 4, 1944, the Germans having left, due to the approach of Allied armies, Ida Sterno walked out of the Mechelen/Malines camp. Soon Maurice Heiber and Andrée Geulen arrived and took over the administration of the camp.[73] After the war, Ida Sterno went back to her social work, aiding Jewish survivors, until her death in 1964 at the age of 62.

Other Active CDJ Members

Many other men and women were active in this extensive clandestine organization; here are some of them.

Benjamin-Benno Nykerk ("Nestor"), a Dutch Jewish businessman, served as the CDJ treasurer until December 1943, and for a short time he was also the head of the children's section. As treasurer he ensured the receipt

of money from the Joint Distribution Committee (JDC), for which purpose he traveled to Geneva for discussions with the JDC head there, Saly
Mayer. In late 1943, he also was involved with the "Dutch-Paris" clandestine group run by John Weidner, who operated out of France to help
people (mostly Jews) cross into Switzerland. Returning to France from
one of his missions to Switzerland in March 1944, Nykerk was arrested
in Paris under his false name of Bernard Smits and deported to Neuengamme camp near Hamburg, where he died. He was thirty-eight years
old.[74] David Ferdman ("Alfred Feremans") took over as CDJ treasurer from
Nykerk. As "banker" of the CDJ, he created a financial committee to assist
him in raising funds from various financial sources and individuals.[75]

In Antwerp the CDJ operative was Abraham Monastir ("Peeters").
Arrested on August 2, 1944, he was imprisoned in Mechelen/Malines until
Belgium's liberation.[76] Marianne Strelitzky-Judels ("Marie") headed the
children's section in Antwerp. She too was arrested, in September 1943,
and imprisoned in Mechelen/Malines. Her fate is not known, but considering her age, then sixty-four, it is unlikely that she survived.[77] Earlier
Chaim Perelman had sought contacts with Antwerp militants, one of
whose principal leaders was Joseph Sterngold, who worked closely with
Alphonse Goethals in the provisions section of the Antwerp municipality,
from whose hands Sterngold received food ration cards given to Jews in
hiding. Earlier, in spring of 1942, Sterngold was conscripted for forced
labor to build fortifications of the Atlantic Wall in France, from which
he escaped.[78] In Charleroi, the CDJ was represented by Sem Makowski,
Max Katz, and Pierre Broder, who also belonged to leftist organizations.
They enlisted the help of Abbé Joseph André, in Namur, who arranged
hiding places for many Jewish children. Max Katz was arrested in 1944
and deported to Buchenwald. He did not survive.[79]

Roger Van Praag ("Delvaux") headed the children's section after
Heiber's arrest. He also was active in fetching false credentials from a
printer in Liège. When his partner, Arnold Perlgericht, was arrested,
the Gestapo failed to notice the suitcase in the room that contained
the incriminating material. Later Van Praag surreptitiously entered the
room, after breaking the Gestapo seals on the door lock, and took the
suitcase to a colleague, Vera Larsen, who was unaware of its contents.
But she had the foresight to alert Fela Perelman about the suitcase, and
she immediately suspected what it contained. Fela hurried over with

Abusz Werber and recovered the documents, which helped many Jews living under assumed names.[80] Roger Van Praag's luck eventually ran out; he was arrested in 1944 and deported to Buchenwald camp, but luckily survived.[81] Finally, Maurice Bolle ("Albert"), originally from the Netherlands, represented the Belgian underground in the CDJ. Denounced and arrested in July 1943, he was incarcerated in Breendonck camp for many months before being deported in May 1944 to Buchenwald camp in Germany; he too survived.[82]

A few more notable CDJ activists merit mention, such as Eugène Hellendael, who came from an assimilated Jewish family and maintained contact with Queen Mother Elisabeth and King Leopold. He proposed to intervene with the queen in order to obtain from Hitler, via Leopold, that Belgian naturalized Jews (representing less than 10 percent only of all local Jews) not be deported. The CDJ was opposed to this approach, since it was felt to be ethically wrong, for it underscored giving a carte blanche for the deportation of the vast majority of the other Jews. The CDJ also felt it would place Hellendael at risk of arrest. But he insisted and went to see the queen, and she promised to help out. Upon his return, Ghert Jospa urged him to go into hiding immediately. That very same day the Gestapo arrested Hellendael and his family, and they were all deported; he did not survive.[83] Eugène Rotkel represented the observant orthodox Jewish community in the CDJ. He was eventually arrested and deported. He did not survive.[84] A final word—some Jewish self-help organizations that joined the CDJ included the Secours Mutuel Juif, through its representative Sophie-Shifra Werber ("Micheline"), and Pauline Trocki, who were also active in the Zionist Poalei Zion–Left movement. They brought to Yvonne Jospa lists of children needing to be sheltered, especially those that the Secours Mutuel Juif did not succeed in hiding.[85]

Historian Lucien Steinberg also mentions the puzzling case of one Isaac Szatan, who in mid-1943 wished to contact the Jewish Agency representatives in Geneva to suggest a plan to issue fictitious British Palestine immigration certificates that would then qualify certificate holders as British nationals. The idea behind this subterfuge was that the recipients of these prized documents would not be able to travel to Palestine, due to the war, and hence the British in Palestine would not be in a position to void these immigration certificates. But, in the meantime, the holders would be exempt from deportation, since the Germans were interested in releasing British nationals in exchange for German nationals held by the British, and such exchanges did indeed happen.

It was David Ferdman who brought this idea before the Jewish Agency men in Geneva, where Dr. Chaim Pozner decided to give it a try. He raised this point with the International Red Cross, who in turn referred it to the German authorities. The Germans unexpectedly fell for this ploy, and those holding these fictitious certificates were not harmed. Some were even freed from wearing the Yellow Star, and those already held in Mechelen/Malines were released. CDJ affiliate Abusz Werber himself was a recipient of one of these documents, and it once saved him from arrest. Not all in the CDJ approved of this ploy, due to the risks to the organization in the event the true nature of this scheme would be discovered by the Germans. At the same time, it saved some lives.[86]

Non-Jewish Helpers

The work of the CDJ would not have been possible without the assistance of many non-Jewish individuals and organizations within the Belgian population. First and foremost—Yvonne Nèvejean, head of the country's national children's welfare organization (Oeuvre Nationale de l'Enfance-ONE), who was of immense help in admitting Jewish children into her organization's homes that were to be found along the length and breadth of the country. Her organization also served as a conduit for money relayed by the Belgian government-in-exile in London for the benefit of the CDJ.[87] Also, already mentioned is the legendary Andrée Geulen, who acted as courier and kept tabs on some 300 Jewish hidden children. After the war she (as well as Nèvejean) were awarded the Righteous title by the Yad Vashem Holocaust memorial as well as the Israel Honorary Citizenship.[88]

CDJ Significance

A total of 25,437 Jews were deported, of which only 1,207 survived. A slightly higher number than 25,000 Jews survived by mostly going into hiding inside Belgium. There are no definitive statistics on the actual number of Jews saved through the work of the CDJ, through its various operations. Some place it as high as 12,000, including between 3,000 and 4,000 children. What's important to remember is the role of the CDJ as the nexus of an organized Jewish large-scale rescue operation in a country occupied by the Germans who were determined to carry out the systematic destruction of the Jewish community. After the war, 768 associates of the CDJ were formally recognized as civil resistants by the Belgian government. Lucien Steinberg holds that this does not fully represent all those involved in one way or another in the CDJ's widespread rescue activities, carried out right under the nose of the Germans.[89]

The Dramatic Rescue of Children at the Très-Saint-Sauveur Convent

This largely self-initiated rescue operation by four Jewish men—Paul Halter, Toby Cymberknopf, Bernard Fenerberg, and Jankiel Parancevitch—foiled the Gestapo's plans.

On May 20, 1943, just before 10:00 p.m., the doorbell of the Très-Saint-Sauveur convent rang in the Anderlecht section of Brussels—70, Avenue Clemenceau. Several armed men and women stormed the convent, cut the phone lines, and ordered all the nuns to assemble in the Mother Superior's office. The nuns were told to prepare the fifteen Jewish girls hidden with them, since they were about to be taken away. Most children had been ensconced safely in the convent for the past eight months. The fearful nuns obeyed, and after delivering the children, the abductors locked the nuns up in the office, separate from the Mother Superior, Sister Marie Amélie (Eugénie Leloup), who was placed in an upstairs room. To still the fears of the frightened Jewish children, one of the abductors whispered a few words in Yiddish: "*Kinder, mir zenen Yidden, mir kumen aich befreien*" (Children, we are Jews; we've come to free you).[90] Who were these people appearing late in the evening to take the children away to an undisclosed location?

In a postwar statement, one of the nuns, Sister Claire d'Assise (Yvonne Vernant), related that the fifteen Jewish girls had been brought there by the CDJ for hiding. Then, on May 20, 1943, the Gestapo raided the place, accompanied by the traitorous Jew, Fat Jacques, and told the Mother Superior to have the girls dressed and ready for departure the following morning. "This is not to kill them," the head Gestapo agent sarcastically reassured the worried Mother Superior, "but only to unite them with their families."[91]

After the war, the convent's Mother Superior, Sister Marie Amélie, stated that after the Gestapo left, she phoned Father Jan Bruylandts, who went to see Cardinal Jozef-Ernest Van Roey, Prince Primate of the country's Catholic Church. Receiving no satisfaction there, Bruylandts hurried to the palace of the Queen Mother Elisabeth. She was unable to see him, but left a message promising to try to do something.[92] When Ida Sterno of the CDJ, who often visited the convent bringing money and food stamps for the hidden children, received a phone call from a certain priest warning her not to show up at the convent, it was obvious to her that something was amiss. According to Sterno, the Gestapo had come to round up the children, when they learned that only thirteen of the fifteen girls (ages two to nineteen) were present; the two others were schooling but in a different location.[93] Then, still according to Ida Sterno, the Mother Superior persuaded the Gestapo (together with Jacques) to return the following morning, when she would have all the children present and ready for departure. This delay gave her time to alert her clergy colleagues. She may also have contacted Ida Sterno, under her pseudonym "Jeanne," and this led to Maurice Heiber's organized kidnapping raid that same evening.[94]

A slightly different version appeared in the accounts of three of the four Jewish men who raided the convent: Paul Halter, Bernard Fenerberg, and Toby Cymberknopf. Fenerberg, who was in hiding, but occasionally took meals in the home of Father Bruylandts, happened to be dining there when the maid came with the alarming news of the Gestapo visit: finding some of the children missing, the Gestapo promised to return the following morning.[95] Fenerberg immediately went to see Cymberknopf with the terrible news, and the two headed to see Paul Halter, an officer in the Belgian resistance. In Halter's words, "We realized that we only had a few hours at our disposal . . . and thus decided to take it upon ourselves to rescue the children."[96] The three decided on an armed break-in into the convent to snatch the children before the Gestapo could lay their hands on them, and they enlisted another Jewish man in the operation, Jankiel Parancevitch, as well as two underground non-Jewish young women, Andrée Ermel and Floris Desmedt—altogether six rescuers.

They waited for darkness to descend, knowing that the operation had to take place before the 10:00 p.m. curfew time. Halter reported, "We then forced our way in at gunpoint. We locked up the Mother Superior, ripped out the phone line, and tied the nuns to chairs in the convent's office."[97] Paul Halter is the one who rang the bell of the convent with a gun in his hand. Andrée Ermel then told the Mother Superior the purpose of their visit. "I had to calm the nuns who were afraid about the reactions of the Gestapo," she related later. According to Fenerberg, the nuns demanded that they be tied up so that nobody would incriminate them in the abduction raid. Half an hour after the kidnappers left, one of the nuns managed to reach a window and alert a passer-by who called the Belgian police. The police took their time to carry out their investigation, until the dawn of next morning, before alerting the Gestapo, thus affording the kidnappers time to escape with the children.[98] When the Gestapo appeared at the prearranged 11:00 a.m. to collect the children, they were dumbfounded to learn that they had been duped by a Jewish-led group the previous evening and could do nothing to the frightened nuns, who claimed they were unaware of the plot.

In the meantime, the children had all been transferred to safe locations with the help of the CDJ. In retaliation, the Gestapo arrested Maurice Heiber, accusing him of having planned the kidnapping.[99] Paul Halter was later arrested for altogether different activities, and in September 1943 he was deported to Auschwitz, which he luckily survived. Bernard Fenerberg: "It still gives me the shivers to think of what could have happened to the children if I had not gone to Father Bruylandts for lunch. If I had learned only in the evening what had happened, it would have been too late to intervene."[100] In 1991, as a participant in the first Hidden Children reunion in New York, he was reunited with several of the girls he had saved.[101]

The Liberation of Train Convoy 20

This was the only known deportation train stoppage throughout German-occupied Europe, organized by CDJ operatives and carried out by Jewish activist Georges "Youra" Livchitz.

On April 19, 1943, deportation train number 20 left from the Dossin detention camp in Mechelen/Malines, on its way to Auschwitz, with 1,631 people aboard. While still well inside Belgian territory, near Tirlemont, it was stopped, and 231 men jumped off. Those that escaped were each given 50 Belgian Francs and told to flee. An estimated 115 were able to evade capture (the youngest, Simon Gronowski, was only eleven years old), while 75 were recaptured and the Germans shot 23 who tried to escape. Other sources give slightly different figures.[102]

In Ghert Jospa's account, there were 1,586 persons, including children on that convoy. Jospa claims to have initiated the attack plan, together with fellow CDJ colleagues Maurice Bolle, Maurice Heiber, and Benjamin Nykerk. The train was believed to make several stops, or slow down, on its route from Brussels to Tirlemont, and the plan was to stop the train a little after Louvain. After agreement was reached on the plan's execution, Jospa asked a member of a Belgian partisan organization to help out, but was turned down on the claim that it was too risky.[103] According to a slightly different account, the planning was done by CDJ affiliated persons, in the home of Professor Chaim Perelman, and included Ghert Jospa, Maurice Bolle, Abusz Werber, Benjamin Nykerk, and Maurice Heiber. The group decided that the train had to be stopped while still on Belgian soil. Physician Georges Livchitz, known as "Youra" in the resistance, was appointed to lead the action with several of his underground companions. He chose for this operation two non-Jewish resistance colleagues, Jean Franklemon and Robert Maistriau.

Armed with a pistol, Livshitz positioned himself on the tracks between the municipalities of Boortmeerbeek and Haacht, in the Tirlemont region, and waving a lantern with a red paper used by train workers, signaled for the train to stop, which it did. Livshitz's two companions then swung the cattle wagons doors open and while handing out nearly a total of 20,000 francs, at the rate of 50 francs each, the passengers were urged to flee. The three led the first group of escapees to a nearby field and returned to persuade the others to flee as well. All this, while under fire from the German guards.[104]

Several hundred jumped off the train, and many made good their escape (the numbers vary according to the different eyewitness accounts).[105] Simon Gronowski, born in 1931, testified in 1993 that he was on that convoy with his mother and told the following:

We were about fifty people in a cattle wagon. Suddenly the train stopped, in Boortmeerbeek. I heard shouting in German and gunfire. . . . I also jumped. . . . I fled into the forest and stayed there throughout the night. The following morning I knocked at the door of a nearby village home and was taken to the village policeman. He told me: "I know everything. You were in the train of Jews. You need not have fear. We are good Belgians. I will not turn you in." A little later, he took me to the train station and bought me a ticket for a trip to Brussels. After meeting my father at his hiding place, I was hidden in another place until the country's liberation. I never met again my mother and sister.[106]

Some of the fugitives were wounded, captured, and taken to the Mechelen/Malines camp. Eight were hospitalized in Tirlemont, and it was decided to try to free them, but the attempt failed because of the betrayal by someone involved in the operation, and this also led to Livshitz's arrest.[107] Then, in a scene like out of a movie script, Jospa learned from Father Bruno Reynders, at Mont César, near Louvain, that Lifshitz was hiding in the home of a niece of a certain Father Augustin in Brussels, after making good his escape. Jospa went to see him with a colleague, and Livshitz told them that with the help of a pin, he was able to spring open his handcuffs, and when one of the guards came to his cell with food, he jumped on him, grabbed the guard's revolver, and shot him. Livshitz exchanged clothes with this ss guard and walked out of the compound, then hid among friends. Finally Father Bruno hid him, and Father Augustin arranged for Livshitz to hide with his niece in Brussels.[108]

Overcome with rage at having been betrayed during the Tirlemont hospital raid, "Youra" Livshitz swore to avenge himself at all cost. "My life is no longer of any importance," he said. "It will no longer have any meaning if I cannot avenge myself." Jospa tried to dissuade him, but Livshitz categorically refused. He wanted to continue to fight and left for France with the intention of reaching England. But the car in which he was traveling was apprehended, and he was imprisoned in Breendonck camp. Livshitz was shot on February 15, 1944.[109]

The convoy number 20 liberation remains the only recorded deportation train stoppage throughout German-occupied Europe, organized by CDJ operatives and carried out by a Jewish resistant, Georges "Youra" Livchitz.[110] On May 16, 1993, to celebrate the fiftieth anniversary of the stoppage of convoy 20, a statue was placed near the train station of Boortmeerbeek—also in remembrance of the thousands of Jews and the Roma Gypsies who were deported over that railway track to the concentration camps.

It is to be hoped that the Jewish rescue activists mentioned here will soon also be celebrated under a program honoring Jews who risked their lives to save their own brethren and succeeded in saving thousands.

9 The Netherlands

Pulling the Wool over the ss's Eyes,
Hiding and a Run across Borders

The few Jews living in what is today the Netherlands during the Middle Ages were expelled but then allowed to return starting in the late sixteenth century. The first who came were fleeing religious persecution in Spain and Portugal, and they were followed a century later by northern and eastern European Jews, seeking to escape persecution there. In 1795 Jews were emancipated, and no further antisemitic violence is recorded. On the eve of the German invasion on May 10, 1940, there were 140,000 Jews in the Netherlands (including refugees from Nazi Germany), representing 1.6 percent of the population, with some 75,000 Jews residing in Amsterdam alone.[1]

Germany treated the Netherlands differently and more severely than other western European countries, as it considered the Dutch a lost Germanic tribe that would soon be incorporated in the German homeland, as was Austria. Hence a civil administration was installed with one of the top Austrian Nazis, Arthur Seyss-Inquart, as Reich commissioner, directly responsible to Hitler. Seyss-Inquart had five commissioners-general serving under him, including Hanns Albin Rauter of the ss, who was also in charge of the Dutch police and directly involved in the roundup of Jews when deportations began in the summer of 1942. A Dutch administration, headed by secretaries-general under German overall control, was allowed to function, although Queen Wilhelmina and the Dutch government had fled to England and set up a government-in-exile.[2]

As in other countries under German occupation, Jews were soon subjected to discriminatory measures. This started with the dismissing of Jews from the civil administration, such as Lodewijk Ernst Visser, the president of the Dutch Supreme Court, and Jewish university professors. Academic circles reacted strongly, and students of the Leiden and Delft Universities went on strike in protest. The German response was to shut down these universities. All Jews and anyone with a Jewish grandfather or grandmother had to report for registration. A total of 159,806 registered, of which 140,245 were Jews and 19,561 were the offspring of mixed marriages. Under the Aryanization program, 20,690 Jewish business enterprises were registered.[3]

This was followed by the confiscation of Jewish property, affecting close to 10,000 enterprises, the appointment of trustees (*Treuhänder)* in their stead, and the sale of the remaining properties. All Jews had to deposit in one Jewish bank (Lippmann, Rosenthal and Company) all the cash and checks in their possession worth more than 1,000 gulden, including their stocks, bonds, and saving accounts, and they could no longer draw freely on their accounts. Jewelry, paintings, and even stamp collections were taken away.[4] Jews were barred from museums, libraries, public markets, the stock exchange, and other public places. A night curfew went into effect for Jews from 8 p.m. to 6 a.m., and shopping was restricted between 3 and 5 p.m. The use of public transportation required a special permit, and then only if space was available, and all Jewish students were removed from public schools.[5]

Then, as a result of an incident on February 19, 1941, in which a German policeman was injured in a confrontation with Jews in a Jewish coffee shop, the Germans reacted by randomly arresting 389 men and deporting them to Buchenwald and Mauthausen camps, where they all perished. This led Communist activists in the transportation system to call for a general strike that soon encompassed all business sectors and caused a standstill of the entire transportation system, the large factories, and the public services. The Germans responded by suppressing it. A Judenrat-style Jewish central council, known as Joodse Raad, was ordered installed in February 1941, with Abraham Asscher and David Cohen as its most prominent members.[6] The Yellow Star badge was introduced on May 3, 1942, for every Jew over the age of five.[7] The stage was now set for the deportation of all Jews.

Dutch Jews were deported to two main concentration camps in Poland: Auschwitz and Sobibór, where most were gassed on arrival. Trains left at regular intervals from the Westerbork internment and transit camp, located in northeast Holland, at the rate of up to 7,500 per month.[8] Oddly enough, the transportation workers who a year earlier had gone on strike against the first anti-Jewish measures now complied with the deportation of Jews, and the municipalities and the Dutch police also lent a hand. The last Amsterdam Jews were rounded up on the eve of Rosh Hashanah, the Jewish New Year, September 29, 1943, and with that, the Joodse Raad ceased to exist.[9] The death toll of Dutch Jewry was quite high: 101,800 victims, or 73 percent of the original Jewish population of 140,000, the highest percentage of murdered Jews of any western European country.[10]

Roughly 25,000 Jews went into hiding (of whom about a third were discovered and deported, including the family of Anne Frank), and thousands of their rescuers were honored by Yad Vashem with the Righteous title.[11] Four groups of Dutch students were credited with saving 1,000 children.[12] Some of the children were whisked away from the Crèche (a prewar day care), located opposite the Dutch Theater, which served as the main assembly point for Amsterdam Jews before their transfer to Westerbork camp. Some Jews, such as those affiliated with the Zionist Hechalutz movement, managed to flee to Spain via Belgium and France and from there continued to Palestine. A handful of Jewish activists saw the handwriting on the wall and sought ways to abort Nazi deportation designs, such as Walter Süskind, one of the great Jewish rescuers of the Holocaust.

Walter Süskind

He said, "I am a Hun myself, thus I know exactly how to handle the Huns." And because he did—with bribes, liquor, and the doctoring the lists of internees in the Dutch Theater—1,000 Jews survived deportation.

He was born in 1906 in Luedenscheid, Germany, to Hermann and Frieda (Kessler) Süskind. After Walter's eight years of schooling, his parents, lacking sufficient funds for their son's continued education, sent him to a grain dealer firm as an apprentice. In 1928 he found work with Boelk and Company, one of the largest margarine producers in Germany and part of the Unilever concern, and he was kept busy delivering cheese, sausages, and margarine on house calls.[13] In 1929 Walter married Johanna Natt. Soon after his father's death in 1931, Süskind moved to Cologne. During the early Nazi period, he took lessons in the Dutch language in preparation for his eventual move to the Netherlands.

In March 1938 Boelk bowed to Nazi pressures and fired Walter. So he moved to Holland, where he easily found employment with the Unilever Company. He had by then mastered the Dutch language.[14] At the same time, he inquired about the Unilever branches in the United States, in the event that circumstances in Holland would force him to leave for America. After much bureaucratic hassle, he was informed in June 1941 (Germany and the United States were not yet at war, but Holland was already under German occupation) that the immigration papers were in order. But Süskind's joy was short-lived; the following month, the Germans clamped down on the emigration of Jews from Holland.[15]

The Dutch Theater Prison

On June 26, 1942, ss Hauptsturmführer (Captain) Aus der Fünten informed the Joodse Raad (henceforth JR) of the start of mass deportations, purportedly for work assignments in Germany. The JR was asked to send out the summons to the people already registered with it. Certain groups of Jews were exempted from deportations, such as members of the JR and their families, spouses in mixed marriages, diamond workers, and those employed by the German military in Holland.[16] The Germans converted a theater in the heart of Amsterdam, known as the Dutch Theater (Hollandse Schouwburg), to serve as a makeshift prison for thousands of Jews who were gradually moved to the large Westerbork transit camp in the northeastern part of the country, where trains left at regular intervals for the death camps in Poland.[17] As reported by Lisette Lamon, one of the theater's internees, people spent days crowded in the auditorium, where no daylight penetrated. Hygienic conditions were sorely lacking. When used as a theater before the war, it had 789 seats on the orchestra floor and the two balconies. Presently, up to 1,600 people were packed in the Schouwburg during any one time, until their departure to Westerbork camp.[18]

In the theater, Dr. Edwin Sluzker and Walter Süskind were nominated by the Joodse Raad to represent the Expositur, a subunit of the JR, to deal directly with their German overlords, since the ss eschewed any direct contact with Jews.[19] Süskind was charged with supervision of the Jewish personnel and responsibility for the daily affairs there. It is not clear from the records why Süskind was selected for this role and who had decided it. Probably his origin in Germany and his knowledge of both German and Dutch played an important role. They may have had the impression that he was a good administrator. As for his colleague Sluzker, he was an Austrian Jewish lawyer who had fled to Holland in 1938.[20] ss officer Ferdinand Aus der Fünten was in charge at the Dutch Theater, as well as responsible for the roundup of Jews in Amsterdam, Rotterdam, and The Hague, and the liquidation of various Jewish institutions.

Families at the theater initially stayed together, but soon to reduce the crowded conditions children up to ten years of age were lodged in the day care, known as the Créche, across the street. The theater ceased to function on September 29, 1943, when the Germans cheerfully declared Amsterdam "surgically clean" of Jews.[21]

Walter Süskind was responsible for keeping tabs on the registration of the incoming persons and those slated for transport to Westerbork camp. He and Sluzker, working as a team, negotiated with Aus der Fünten or other ss men to allow some of the interned Jews to be temporarily released to their homes. Sometimes forty people were released; at other times, twenty, and sometimes not even one. It was touch and go with Aus der Fünten.[22] Some claim that Süskind's success with that ss officer stemmed from the fact that they knew each other from before the war, but there is no proof of this. At the same time, Süskind prided himself on being able to deal with the Germans. On one occasion he facetiously told one of his aides, "I am a Hun myself, thus I know exactly how to handle the Huns."[23]

Doctoring Lists

Süskind went even further and contrived to have Jews leave the theater illegally by doctoring the list of internees and deleting the names of those slated to go to Westerbork. To this day, no one is quite sure how Süskind managed to do this without the ss noticing something was afoul with the lists. Those fortunate enough to have their names removed were then picked by Süskind for escape and were slipped out of the theater's windows or back entrance, at times in connivance with one or several ss guards who were bribed to help. As the man responsible for the administrative side of the operation, Süskind made sure that the paperwork was kept in a disorderly condition, the better to be able to tamper with the names when the time seemed ripe. While more than 100 Jewish personnel were employed in the theater at one time or another or in different work shifts, Süskind was dedicated to saving as many Jews as possible.[24]

While his colleague Suzkever tried to do everything by the book, Süskind handled the illegal side, pulling the wool over the eyes of ss guards
and bribing some of them.[25]

At the theater, the chairs in the main gallery had been removed to
make more room for the internees, and the floor was covered with straw
mattresses and blankets. Süskind and a team of trusted aides were there,
registering the newcomers. They took down personal data and special
details under the watchful eye of a German guard. Whenever the guard
dozed off, the staff took advantage of the situation to alter registration
information. Under Süskind's supervision, the lists of incoming Jews
were later typed up, and the names of people whom Süskind or others
wanted to spare would be secretly erased. The lists were transcribed on
cards that were then stored on the building's second floor, and only Süskind and three other trusted co-workers had access to them. Cards of
people who were to be rescued were subsequently removed by Süskind,
and when not observed, he tore them up and discarded them. Then
there were the lists of those who had the possibility of being exempted
and even released, for whom Sluzker or Süskind negotiated with Aus
der Fünten or his underlings. Most of the incoming Jews, of course, mistakenly believed that they were only being sent to a labor camp. Those
who suspected something worse had already gone into hiding and had
not shown up.[26]

In the evening, some of those working with Süskind would meet in his
room to plan how to liberate people. As related by Grete Weil:

> Every one of us had wishes: members of family, friends, acquain-
> tances, protégés, that one could not overlook. Yes—this one was
> possible; no—this one cannot be arranged, too old; not reliable;
> too prominent; too outspoken by his behavior; not skillful enough
> and would probably be brought back not later than three days. . . .
> Süskind, of small physique, robust, with blond stubble hair and
> large blue eyes, was crafty as Odysseus and eloquent as Achilles;
> Süskind, the rescuer, the hero, the gambler. He says yes; says no;
> selects, and decides on life and death. He is the man responsible,
> makes the Germans drunk, falsifies lists, knows every trick, con-
> siders the situation anew, knows on which nights it is possible, and
> he always succeeds.[27]

According to Dutch historian Johannes ten Cate, Süskind may simply have thrown away the cards from the file cabinet of those for whom he arranged an escape.[28] It is worth noting that it was of great importance that the card index at all times matched the actual number of Jews who were (officially) present there and in the Crèche, the children's day care center across the street.[29]

Even at the very last moment, the day of the transport to Westerbork, Süskind and Raphaël (Felix) Halverstad were able to spirit people out of the theater with the help of his rescue confederates. Süskind, of course, bore ultimate responsibility if something went wrong. Transports to Westerbork camp usually took place twice a week. When people learned that they were slated for transport, many turned to Süskind for his help to get a postponement. Queuing up in a long row, they assembled in front of the table where Süskind sat, and he patiently listened to everybody. He promised nothing in advance, but many people were nevertheless helped. Those lucky enough to be chosen were carefully instructed on certain precautions so as not to endanger themselves and Süskind and his fellow rescue conspirators.[30] Some were sent by Süskind to his colleague, Bernard de Vries Robles, in the hospital room, who then declared that they were too ill to be transported to Westerbork camp, and sometimes they were taken by ambulance to a hospital. At first, the German physician on site did not object to the decisions by de Vries Robles.[31]

More Trickery with Armbands, Numbers, and Alcohol

Sluzker, the formal head of the JR affiliate at the theater, and Süskind, the man with the most influence, were able to free some of the arrivals by the use of another deception—by having them don an armband with the letters JR in black, an armband worn by all JR (Joodse Raad) employees. The two, together with their two trusted aides, Jack van de Kar and Sam de Hond, regularly gave an armband to one of the young men they could trust, and these youngsters then told the guards that they had a message for the JR main office (which, of course, was not true). On at least two occasions, Walter Süskind—his pockets stuffed with JR armbands— mounted the trams that brought people directly to the central train station for embarkation and distributed them, telling the conductor that these people were to be released because they worked for the JR.

This scheme became risky when the Germans arrested a man with such an armband who they discovered was not a JR worker. Jewish personnel at the JR managed to talk themselves free from suspicion by claiming that the man had found the armband which had accidentally been dropped on the street, but after that Süskind discontinued this ploy.[32] While some who worked for the JR were not prepared to endanger their special status by risky ventures entailing help to others, this was not the case with Walter Süskind.[33] His main motive for joining the JR was to try to help others rather than himself.

Only when people had a place to hide would Süskind agree to arrange their escape. Then he went into action. The guards had to be distracted, and Erich Süssenwein, who worked for the JR as a doorkeeper in the theater, distracted them with jokes so that people could make their escape. Sometimes the guards were given drinks to get them inebriated, a job executed by two trusted confederates.[34] When he could not effect a release, Süskind tried to get a postponement of the person's transport to Westerbork. This succeeded with some but failed with others.

Another of Süskind's schemes was to miscount people slated for deportation to Westerbork camp. When their names were announced by loudspeaker, people had to go outside through a corridor and stand in rows. There Halverstad at Süskind's signal counted the people incorrectly while Süskind distracted the attention of the guards. The counting may have proceeded as follows: "85, 86, 87, 99, 100." In this way eleven fewer people were put on a transport.[35] This led to some people, who "mistakenly" were in excess of the allotted quota, to be led out of the assembled rows by Süskind's helpers and secluded in the theater by Van de Kar; then they were whisked away in a car that had come to transport the luggage of the deported people. With the assistance of outside clandestine rescuers, the escapees were then taken to prearranged sheltering places.[36]

Another of Süskind's antics involved the release of those already sitting on trains, ready to be taken to Westerbork. His network had discovered that the keys of the lockers in an Amsterdam bathhouse fitted the locks on some transport rail cars used in deporting Jews. Sam de Hond, one of Süskind's secret operatives, remembered many Jews being freed with the help of these keys, after Süskind made sure that their names had been removed from the official register.[37]

A master performer since his youthful days, Süskind knew how and when to distract Aus der Fünten (who was always present and watchful at the theater) when he learned of that man's weakness for liquor. It is told that Aus der Fünten was in the habit of always appearing a bit tipsy or in the company of a prostitute. He and Süskind would be seen bantering about the good old days in Germany, with drinks and cigars, to the consternation of other Jews who suspected that their supposed helper was in fact a Nazi stooge. Very few could know that the same man was risking his life in his various rescue antics, tampering with files and removing index cards of those whose escape had been arranged by his accomplices. But one had to be on one's guard, for sometimes, even while inebriated, Aus der Fünten would appear in the company of Willy Lages, the feared Gestapo chief in Amsterdam, who always stayed sober and alert.[38] As for Süskind, displaying to the full his cherubic and smiling face, he was able to fool those he had to fear the most and keep hidden from them his real activity—that of a full-time rescuer of imprisoned Jews.

Operation Kidnap and the Crèche

Frederika Elburg was pregnant when she arrived with her family (husband and three-year-old son) at the Schouwburg Theater on August 2, 1943, and they remained there for three weeks. She had arrived just in time for the baby's delivery. It was decided to keep her in the dispensary for a longer period, and Süskind arranged for her to be exempted from each of the next transports. When she asked him when she would be freed, he told her that for the moment it was still impossible. "He had to act in a very quiet way. Besides, the Huns were sitting there in front." He then assured her that he was working on her escape, but would give no further details.[39]

Then, on August 24, 1943, one day before the next transport, he told her, "I can no longer keep you behind. Aus der Fünten said, 'That woman, who daily walks over to the crèche, is always about to give birth when there is a transport. Let her give birth at Westerbork.' . . . Now, I said to myself, only the good God can help. Let the child come now!" That night, about 3 a.m., she began to feel the birth pangs. She asked the attending doctor to take her elsewhere for the birth, not at the theater. After some head scratching, it was decided to take her to the only Jewish institution still open, the Joodsche Invalide, an institution that cared for the elderly, the physically disabled, blind, deaf, and mute Jewish people, and they had not yet been taken away. So, at 4 a.m. she was carried there on a stretcher while her husband remained behind.[40]

The following morning her husband, Karel, was waiting with a ruck-sack on his back to leave with the next transport. Suddenly he was called to see Süskind, who told him: "Congratulations, you have a little daugh-ter, and you certainly want to see her. Stay here until I call you again." A little while later, he was taken to the Joodsche Invalide to see the baby. He stayed there for a few days. Suddenly the building was surrounded by Germans who had decided to liquidate the institution's inhabitants. When Mrs. Elburg ran upstairs to the baby's room, she was told that the previous night the underground had come and spirited the child away. In fact, the baby had been taken to the crèche, which is where Mrs. Elburg found her. She was then smuggled out of the building together with a group of thirty to thirty-five children to a hiding place in Limburg province with the help of Joop Woortman of the Dutch underground.[41]

The Crèche was a day care before the war that served mostly Jewish mothers. In the summer of 1942, the Crèche became an annex of the the-ater, transformed into a holding place for children whose parents were brought into the theater or children who had been caught in their hid-ing places. Some of the children joined their parents when they left on deportation. Others were smuggled out and went into hiding. Although Henriette Pimentel was in charge of the Crèche, the ultimate responsibil-ity remained with Walter Süskind. When children arrived, Süskind took advantage of the occasional split-second moments when the guards did not pay attention to registering children. For those already registered, it was still possible to erase their names from the lists that every evening were retyped under his supervision. Then the cards of the children whose names had been left off the list were secretly taken out and discarded. From the administration's point of view, the children were not there; in reality, they were being cared for in the crèche. These "illegal" children were then taken by different resistance groups to sheltering homes.[42]

It is well to point out that on top of saving adults in the theater, Süs-kind's greatest effort was rather expended in what he considered his major undertaking—saving the children at the Crèche who had been separated from their parents on arrival at the theater and were slated to rejoin their parents when they were sent off to Westerbork camp. Whenever parents could supply a safe address for their child, Süskind's accomplices on the outside would verify if the people were indeed ready to conceal a Jew-ish child. It is well to remember that parents, when they arrived at the theater, had no inkling of what stood in store for them or their children. The crèche personnel went over to the theater to talk to the parents about placing their trust in Süskind's ability to take their children to safety with foster parents, "until you will be united with them later on." Those who agreed had their children's names stealthily removed from registration lists. The "illegal" children then had to be hidden from sudden German visits of the Crèche.[43]

Once or twice a week, early morning meetings took place in the house of a trusted colleague, not far from the theater, and where Süskind and Halverstad informed the leaders of some resistance groups of the number of "illegal children" staying in the Crèche, including their age, sex, hair color, and other details. The underground members then indicated which of the children they could accommodate. The "illegals" were distributed as follows: the less fair-skinned children went to Limburg province in the south, where more people have an olive skin tan; the blond went to northern Friesland region.[44] For escapes to be successful, precise plans had to be made with the several resistance groups with whom Süskind was secretly in touch.[45] Coded messages were used: "Ersatz tea" meant a blond Jewish child who could be taken to Friesland to mix with other light-skinned children. "Ersatz coffee" implied a darker child who was sent to the Limburg region in the south, where many inhabitants were of a similar facial complexion.[46]

In the words of an eyewitness, Lisette Lamon: "Walter [Süskind]—the heart and soul of Operation Kidnap—would only allow a child to be smuggled out if it had a verified home."[47] When a rescuer family had been located for a child, one of the nurses informed the parents. "I was then 19 years," nurse Sieny Kattenburg related. "When I approached the parents, I could not guarantee them anything. If they asked how and where, I had no answer. I did not know where the children would be taken; this was my supervisor's worry; it was not our business." After getting the parents' consent, Sieny gave the parents a small blanket wrapped around a doll and dressed in rags. "The parents were frightened when I placed this package in their arms, for it weighed almost nothing." When all parents were lined up for deportation, they held these bundles close to their chest, pretending to rock their sleeping child. "We brought a doll or a piece of cloth or a blanket . . . or a dressed-up pillow in our arms across the street." The parents had to play their role to the end. They had to show happiness at being reunited with their "baby." With the dressed-up pillow, they went on a transport. In the meantime, children were smuggled out of the nursery in rucksacks, laundry bags, crates, breadbaskets, burlap bags, or under a coat. One infant passed through a cordon of ss men in a cake box. Occasionally they were given tranquilizers or sleeping pills to minimize their chance of detection.[48]

Süskind's nephew, Hans, remembered his uncle (who was allowed to stay outside the theater) once appearing in the home of his nephew's family (momentarily exempt from deportation), trembling, sweating profusely, and wet as though he had just taken a shower. He had smuggled a child from the Crèche, rolled up in a blanket on the back of his bicycle, when as he was leaving, Aus der Fünten suddenly appeared and stopped him for a chat. "Hot day," Aus der Fünten remarked. "Hot, indeed," Süskind responded, perhaps wondering when the blanket was going to start twitching. The two men exchanged light talk until Süskind felt he could nonchalantly excuse himself. Luckily for Süskind, no suspicion crossed the ss officer's mind on the bundle on the bike. Süskind bicycled around the corner, delivered the child to a Resistance member, then cycled fifteen blocks to the home of Hans to calm his nerves. But it was a close call.[49]

In principle, only children whose parents had given permission for their removal were saved. Otherwise, it would have caused terrible scenes on the evenings of transport, with uninformed parents screaming for their lost children, and this would have scuttled the whole rescue operation. Süskind also wanted to avoid parents surviving the war without their children, and so he gave preferential rescue consideration to those children who were caught in hiding while their parents were safe in separate hiding places.[50]

One escape route from the Crèche was from behind the building that bordered the playground of a religious school, the three-story Reformed Church teaching college. To make this possible, the children would be lifted over a low hedge to descend into the school courtyard.[51] When Süskind was tipped off that the Germans were about to clear the Crèche on September 29, 1943, one day before Rosh Hashanah, he and his non-Jewish clandestine comrades made a final attempt to get as many children as possible out of there. They succeeded in getting fourteen children out in one swoop.[52]

There are no exact figures on how many Jews were saved through the efforts of Walter Süskind and his staff. Some place it as high as 1,100, from among the tens of thousands who passed through the theater and crèche. This included between 385 and 600 children saved; some claim closer to 1,000.⁵³ Whatever the true number, Süskind's achievement is nothing short of phenomenal.

Saving Others, but Not Himself

Tragically, the end for Walter Süskind and his family was anything but phenomenal. At first, as a member of the Joodse Raad, Walter, Hanna, and little daughter Yvonne were temporarily exempt from deportation and allowed to stay outside of the theater. Nevertheless, taking no chances, for added security Walter sheltered Yvonne with his brother Karl, who, due to his marriage to a non-Jewish woman, was for the time being also exempt from deportation. As for himself, he could easily have arranged his own escape had he so elected. As early as mid-1942, Piet Bosboom from the Dutch underground had given Süskind a secret phone number to call him to immediately come and lead Süskind to a hiding place. Süskind, however, would not consider leaving his family behind, and besides, he was deeply immersed in the rescue work in the theater and would not discharge himself of this responsibility.⁵⁴ Süskind was arrested once, perhaps twice, but talked his way out without his operation ever being uncovered.

After his second release from jail in September 1943, he placed his daughter in hiding, while his wife, mother, and mother-in-law continued to live five blocks from the theater. After a while it was decided to reunite Yvonne with her mother—a fatal decision, for they were soon all picked up and sent to Westerbork camp. Süskind was able to convince Westerbork commander Hermann Gemmeker that as a supposedly wealthy man, he needed to return to Amsterdam to settle his affairs. Gemmeker agreed, but retained Süskind's family in the camp as hostages. By then, the theater/crèche had already been closed.⁵⁵

When he was summoned back to Westerbork, his underground friends tried to talk him into not going. But he dismissed these pleadings. He had to be with his family. It is told that Süskind urged the camp's internal Jewish leadership to explore escape possibilities, but they declined, fearing repercussions.⁵⁶ On October 4, 1944, he was deported with his family, first to Theresienstadt camp, then to Auschwitz. Before departing Westerbork, he reportedly had obtained a written declaration by Aus der

Fünten praising his merits and work in the interest of the Third Reich that he hoped would save him and his family, but it proved of no use. Clare Ebrecht, a Jewish internee in Auschwitz, caught her last glimpse of him when they were prisoners at Birkenau, in late January 1945, on the eve of the Auschwitz death march. She recalled seeing him without a coat. He was gaunt, his head shaved, his feet sockless, in wooden shoes. He died somewhere during the forced evacuation march from Auschwitz in late January or February 1945.[57]

Boston Globe columnist David Arnold summed up Walter Süskind as follows: "He was a master performer. Amsterdam was Süskind's stage; the Nazis were his actors. The script he wrote saved perhaps thousands of lives, although it couldn't save him or his family." Lisette Lamon, one of his associates and a courier in the Dutch resistance who was herself eventually deported to Bergen-Belsen but survived—stated that Süskind never asked for or accepted any reward. While he was unable to save himself or his family, "well over a thousand are living today because of him and those who were his accomplices." In 1972 a bridge in Amsterdam was named after Walter Süskind. The Jewish community at large has yet to commemorate his memory.[58]

The Hechalutz Underground

Menachem Pinkhof, Mirjam Waterman, Joachim Simon, and their colleagues saved hundreds of Zionist youth pioneers, some by hiding, and others by smuggling them over dangerous terrain to Spain and on to Palestine.

With 800 members, the Dutch Zionist Hechalutz was the only Jewish group in the Netherlands to establish an underground operation. Many of its young members had fled from central European countries and were preparing for a pioneering life in Palestine. For this purpose they underwent training (*hachshara* in Hebrew) to become farmers in the Land of Israel, to become vanguards in the creation of a new and better society based on labor, equality, and social justice. Hundreds of these youths lived and apprenticed with Dutch farmers. The girls worked mostly in Jewish public institutions, such as hospitals, orphanages, old-age homes, restaurants, and private households. To be eligible for immigration to Palestine one had to complete at least two years in farming and vocational training. Then they might wait five or six years for an available certificate, due to British immigration restrictions for Palestine.[59]

An offshoot Hechalutz religious pioneer group, under the patronage of the Mizrahi religious Zionists, took care of its fifty-six members, enabling them to observe Jewish dietary laws and the Sabbath and Jewish holidays, as they ate and lived with Jewish families. A first center was established in Almelo in 1930, and a second in Ommen in 1933. The even more religiously observant organization Agudath Israel opened a pioneering center in Enschede in 1933, which eventually counted seventy members, mostly from Germany and Poland. Another center, the Werkdorp, was modeled after a kibbutz and opened in 1934 in the north. It was designed to admit hundreds of Jewish refugees from Germany, Zionists and non-Zionists alike.[60]

In August 1939 a new location was opened by the Hechalutz in Loosdrecht, near Hilversum. The Dutch government required that these youths leave the country upon completion of their training. Since the British granted very few Palestine immigration certificates, some tried to run the British blockade. There was the boat, the *Dora*, which sailed in July 1939 with 300 pioneers and landed safely on the shores of Palestine. But with the start of the war, no more ships could then sail out of Dutch ports.[61]

After the German invasion of Holland in May 1940, the members of the Werkdorp were evacuated to Amsterdam, where the Germans obtained their names and addresses from the Joodse Raad. The Germans then arrested 65 youths, among them 57 from the former Werkdorp, and they were all deported to concentration camps, where they almost all perished. For the other pioneers, the critical moment arrived when, in July 1942, the full deportations of the country's Jews began. Not sure if the local population would lend a helping hand, many Jewish youth were reluctant to go underground. The results were tragic; of the 716 pioneers in the training camps, about half lost their lives mostly in deportations. Of the 387 who chose to go underground, 80 percent of them survived. The Loosdrecht Hechalutz training center leaders had from the start decided to defy the German orders to report and instead go into hiding, which all but one did; 33 of the 50 survived. Many of the youths were smuggled from Holland over to France via Belgium. From there, they were led to the Spanish border, helped by Johannes (Joop) Westerweel, a non-Jewish educator. The group formed under his guidance—Jews and non-Jews—is commonly known as the Westerweel group.[62]

The Loosdrecht Group and Joop Westerweel

Officially the Pavilion Loosdrechtse Rade, the Loosdrecht Hechalutz group was led by the Dutch-born Menachem Pinkhof and German-born Joachim Simon. Nicknamed Shushu back in Germany, the 1919-born Simon joined a Zionist youth movement linked to the Labor movement in Palestine. Arrested during Kristallnacht in November 1938, he spent a full month in the Buchenwald concentration camp. Released, he left for Holland, where he soon joined the Loosdrecht group as a Hebrew teacher. As for Menachem Pinkhof, born in 1920 in Amsterdam, he belonged to the Mizrahi religious Zionist youth movement. He finished his studies at a technical institute and was then asked to serve as a youth leader in the Loosdrecht home. Through Menachem's girlfriend, Mirjam Waterman, a connection was made with the Dutch educator Joop Westerweel and his wife, Wilhelmina.

Born in Holland in 1916, Mirjam grew up in an assimilated Jewish home knowing little about Judaism. Her mother, born Lopes Cardozo, was of Portuguese Jewish descent. With her four siblings, Mirjam moved from Amsterdam to Loosdrecht. There she learned of a special school in nearby Bilthoven, called the Children's Community Workshop (Werkplaats Kinder Gemeenschap). A nondenominational educational institution, it formed a closely knit community and inculcated to the students a high level of moral values and idealism. Mirjam taught there, too. When Jewish youth began arriving from Nazi Germany and were admitted in the Werkplaats, Johannes (Joop) Westerweel, one of the school's most charismatic teachers, asked Mirjam to teach this particular group because of her Jewish origin.

In fall of 1941, bowing to German pressure, the school dismissed Mirjam Waterman, and she returned to her parents' home in Loosdrecht, where she opened a school for the local Jewish children who could no longer attend public schools. Six students came to her house every day for lessons. She also became acquainted with the Loosdrecht Hechalutz center. She had never given much thought to Zionism before the war, Mirjam admitted, "but when Hitler invaded Poland in 1939, I began to think about it. When the Germans occupied Holland in 1940, I became a Zionist. It was only then that suddenly something inside told me I belonged to the Jewish people. . . . I joined the Zionist youth movement. Like most people starting something new, I entered it with a great deal of enthusiasm."

Closing ranks with the Loosdrecht center, she met Joachim (Shushu) Simon, who had already experienced a German concentration camp, and Menachem Pinkhof, her future husband. Pinkhof persuaded Simon that one must prepare to find safe hiding places for the fifty-one youth in the camp in the event of an emergency. Joachim was at first a bit hesitant, but he soon changed his mind when Mirjam enlisted the help of Westerweel. "From the moment Joop Westerweel came to help us, everything changed," Mirjam underlined. "We set up a small group—most of them were gentiles . . . [and] included Jews like myself, Menachem, and Shushu." They prepared a list of all the children and the people willing to hide them. "We searched all over Holland." When Erica Bluth, a worker at the JR in Amsterdam, secretly informed the group on August 15, 1942, of an upcoming German raid on the Loosdrecht center, they had already devised plans for escape, so when the Germans appeared on August 18, 1942, the Loosdrecht home was empty except for two stray dogs.[63]

As some of the host families refused to make long-term commitments, alternative solutions had to be found. An escape attempt was made on September l, 1942, by a group of eight youths who followed a track set out by Westerweel and Pinkhof, but they were betrayed by border guards and landed in the hands of the Gestapo, who deported them to Auschwitz. Only one survived. Joachim (Shushu) Simon was now chosen to find a safer passage into France through connections with underground Jewish and Zionist movements in Belgium and France. Equipped with forged Dutch passports, Shushu and his wife, Adina, set out on October 3, 1942, to make the initial connections. Safely reaching Paris, Joachim contacted the Jewish clandestine organization, known as the Amelot Committee. Then he returned to Holland to start the escape line. He left again for France on November 22, 1942, to explore alternative escape routes.

In the meantime Adina made it into Switzerland, but the Swiss policy of sometimes forcing Jews back into German-held territory forced Shushu to seek an escape route for the Loosdrecht people into Spain. For this purpose, he made contact with the Armée Juive, the so-called Jewish Army clandestine Jewish organization, whose center of operation was in southern France, not far from the Spanish border. After formalizing with that organization an escape route, he returned to Holland on January 13, 1943, but was arrested on January 26, when he crossed into Holland and was imprisoned in Breda. There, fearing he would not withstand the expected torture, he committed suicide. A second group of four already in Belgium crossed into Spain on February 9, 1943, the first Hechalutz group to successfully cross over.[64]

Safely to Spain, Thanks to Forged Work Papers and Vouchers

In June 1943, when another group of thirteen pioneers waiting to cross the border into France from Antwerp were in a quandary and did not know what to do, Hechalutz activist Ernst (Willy) Hirsch found an alternative method to illegal crossings: the use of German documents meant for Dutch workers of the German Todt organization, which was building fortifications along the Atlantic coast.[65] The forms were then filled in with the assumed names of the Hechalutz pioneers and duly stamped with Nazi seals, and this allowed those holding them to travel freely and legally from Holland to France. It turned out that inspections were less thorough and painstaking in German-occupied France than in Holland and Belgium. The German Todt organization and its French subcontractors were always short of men, and if any reported for work, they did not look too closely at the papers brought with them. The pioneers hiding in Antwerp thus became the second group to cross the border into France under the noses of the Germans.

They were able to move south to the Spanish border, taking the night train from Paris to Bordeaux, where a contact person gave them jobs and a document (*recépisse*) entitling its holder not only to food coupons and unhindered travel within France but also to the status of privileged "helpers in the German war effort." This included hard-to-get perks for being a laborer in the German war effort, such as the right to use the German army canteen and a travel voucher, known as *Marschbefehle*, or marching orders, that requested the German military to "extend all possible help and protection" to the voucher holder. In practical terms, it meant getting free tickets on trains, obtaining food including butter, meat, and cigarettes as well as free tickets to performances reserved for German army personnel. Hechalutz members made use of these highly prized German documents to ease their way from Holland to the French-Spanish border.[66]

Hans (Chanan) Flörsheim was one of the lucky Hechalutz youth that made it to Spain. He was born in 1923 in Rotenburg an der Fulda, Germany. At the age of fourteen, he was sent to relatives in Amsterdam. (His sister, Edith, two years younger, left for England on a Kindertransport.) At first Hans joined the Werkdorp in northern Holland, where several hundred boys and girls of about his age learned farming, horticulture, and other trades, with the objective to emigrate later to Palestine. When the Werkdorp group closed, Hans moved to Amsterdam and later Rotterdam, where he met Menachem Pinkhof, who arranged his crossing into Belgium with a friend. The two then hopped a train to Brussels, and with documents stating they were workers for a German company, they continued by train to Lille, where they found accommodations at the expense, amazingly, of the German armed forces. As told by Hans, "We were able to go to the army canteen where we ate a wonderfully thick soup and drank coffee surrounded by German soldiers. All of it for free, of course. . . . We were allowed to board an almost empty car reserved for members of the German army. . . . Our trip to Paris did not cost us one centime." They continued toward the Spanish border.[67] Hans Flörsheim eventually joined a group that crossed into Spain on April 16, 1944, and in October he boarded a boat that left Cadiz for Palestine.

Hard Times for Those in Hiding

Back in Holland, Mirjam Waterman and Menachem Pinkhof were busy fetching food, ration cards, money, and books for the youth still in hiding, including making frequent visits to keep up their morale, and delivering letters from their friends and relatives, as well as finding alternate hiding places when the host families declined to keep the Jewish youth any longer, usually for fear of denouncement. In Mirjam's words, "The most difficult was finding hiding places. When I came to a house, I never knew if I could trust the people or not. The only way to figure it out was to have a talk with them. I always looked them straight in the eye and asked myself, can I trust you?"

Sophie Yaarie was one of those aided by Pinkhof, Simon, and Waterman. As she related in an interview in her home in Beer Tuvia, Israel, in 1988, she was born Sophie Nussbaum in 1925 in Emden, Germany. As her family had relatives in Holland, Sophie and her ten-year-old sister, Ruth, were allowed to leave for there in January 1939. "I never saw my parents again." The two girls eventually were admitted into the Loos-drecht center. She recalled Menachem Pinkhof being "crazy about classical music—especially Bach—and he taught us to love music."[68] Then, on the evening of August 13, 1942, Menachem addressed the children:

Pioneers, we have received notice that we are to report to the train station in Amsterdam. We have decided not to go. We have found many good Christian friends who will help you for the duration of the war. How long it will be, nobody knows. You must do what these people ask of you, even if it is not always pleasant. There may not always be enough to eat, but they are helping you and saving your lives. Be good.[69]

Menachem was followed by Simon (Shushu), who told them that in barely half an hour, people would be coming to take some of them away, but not everyone, since places had not yet been found for all. He added: "Some of you may be at your first addresses only temporarily until a better place is found. We won't forget you. We will be working for you." That same evening Shushu took Sophie and her sister and a boy, Paul Zonderman, by train to Amsterdam.

He took us up three or four flights to the attic in one of these houses. There were two very dirty rooms, and no toilet or shower. We were told to use a flower vase for a toilet, and empty it out of the window on to the roof—there was no other way. The other rooms in the house were rented to students, two or three to a room. We were in the flat of a writer who was away on a two-week holiday. We could stay until he came back, but the woman who owned the house was not supposed to know we were there.[70]

Shushu stayed with them that first night, since it was already past curfew. After about nine days Paul went downstairs and was seen by someone who asked the landlady about him. That same evening, she came up and told the children: "I'm very sorry, but you will have to leave this house immediately. If you don't, I will phone the police. This is a war, after all." They picked up their rucksacks and left the house. Not knowing where to head, Sophie volunteered to seek help from a ship captain in the harbor, but was turned down. At that point, Paul took off on his own, leaving Sophie and Ruth to their own devices. That night, they slept under a bridge.

The next morning the girls decided to find Hanna, one of the Loosdrecht leaders, and were admitted by a tearful Hanna, who told them, "You can't stay here. Yesterday they took my brothers, and my father has had a heart attack. He must not know that you are here, even for a few hours." Her husband took them to another address. From that day in August 1942 until the end of the war, the two sisters were hidden in eighteen homes in Amsterdam, Rotterdam, Doorn, and other towns and villages in Holland. Throughout that time they were cared for by the so-called Westerweel group—a combined Jewish and non-Jewish clandestine group. At Doorn, for instance, Mirjam Waterman sometimes came to visit. "She brought us life and hope. . . . She wanted to know how the people were treating us. . . . I'll never forget it. Mirjam was blonde and didn't look Jewish. She had so many non-Jewish friends, she could have easily left and made a life for herself. But she didn't do that. . . . She worked with the non-Jewish organizers as if she were not a Jew—with false papers. It greatly endangered her life."[71]

Southern Holland, where Sophie was staying, was liberated on November 23, 1944. It was not until the following May that Sophie was reunited with Ruth, who had been hiding in a different and not-yet liberated part of the country. As for Mirjam Waterman, in March 1943 her parents were picked up, as well as her younger sister and brother, and dispatched to the Westerbork transit camp in northeast Holland. Mirjam was able to bribe the Gestapo to release her relatives, and she found a hiding place, where they stayed safely until the end of the war. One hundred and fifty other youths were spirited into France, and seventy crossed safely into Spain and were even able to make it to Palestine during the war.

During that phase of her clandestine life, Mirjam Waterman slept every night in a different place. Then tragedy struck when Joop Westerweel, returning from a trip to France, was arrested by the Germans and imprisoned in Rotterdam. Mirjam and Menachem made plans for his escape, but they were betrayed and arrested, and in April 1944 they were deported to Bergen-Belsen camp, where they stayed for a year until the camp's liberation. After the war, Mirjam and Menachem Pinkhof married and moved to Israel.[72] Menachem died in 1969; Mirjam, in 2011.

Max Windmüller also merits mention in this context. Born in Emden, Germany, in 1920, he arrived in Holland in 1933 and worked for the Hechalutz organization. During the war, under the code name "Cor," he was active in Paris, helping many Dutch Jewish youths obtain false German documents testifying to them being Dutch workers for the German Todt organization. This allowed them free travel almost everywhere in France, as well as meals and accommodations similar to German soldiers. He was eventually betrayed and arrested on July 18, 1944, and deported to Buchenwald camp, and reportedly died while on a death march toward Dachau on April 21, 1945, some two weeks before the end of the war.[73]

Paula Kaufmann is also worthy of special praise. While working closely with Max Windmüller, she was somehow able to obtain, in January 1944, a position as secretary in the office of a Gestapo-related department. Born in Drabowa, Poland, in 1920, Kaufmann lived in Vienna with her parents, so German was her mother tongue. Moving to Holland, she worked as a nanny with a Dutch family, then escaped to Paris, where she reportedly obtained (heaven knows how!) a job as a shorthand typist in the Gestapo office, and from that strategic location was able to smuggle out the documents that later served Windmüller in distributing them to the Hechalutz youth who traveled through France in the guise of valuable workers for the German Todt organization.

Max Leons

He and his rescue partner, the non-Jewish Arnold Douwes, saved hundreds of Jews by hiding them in the Dutch countryside.

Born in Rotterdam in 1921 into an assimilated Jewish family, Max ("Nico") Leons and his family moved to Voorburg in 1926. Although his father once emphatically stated to him, "We are 100 percent Jewish and that's it," it did not mean practicing any of the time-honored Jewish religious rituals. On May 15, 1940, when the Netherlands capitulated to the Germans, Max's parents and siblings left for Scheveningen Harbor, hoping to flee by boat to England. Max declined to join them. A few hours later, they returned, since the harbor was already in German hands. During the first year of the occupation, the nineteen-year-old worked in a factory manufacturing spare parts for bicycles.[74] He urged his parents to switch to a non-Jewish name and move elsewhere. In his words, "I had the premonition that we could expect anything except something good." His parents disagreed; they felt that no evil would befall them.

In the meantime, local antisemites also jumped on the bandwagon. One night someone wrote the word *Jew* on their home in big letters, followed with another slur, when someone scribbled the words *Dirty Jew* on another wall. Friends of the family came over to help clean up the graffiti and offered flowers to the distraught family. Fearing a physical attack, the Leons family decided not to spend nights in their home. At the time, 1941, Max Leons responded to the call of a friend to secretly help distribute stenciled news items culled from the British BBC radio. This was Max's first act of resistance, as listening or transcribing news from that London station was strictly forbidden by the German authorities.[75]

With the surge of anti-Jewish measures, Max's father sought a way to fend off danger to his family. In early 1942, he urged Max to try getting a job with the Joodse Raad, the German-appointed and controlled Jewish Council. He felt that since that organ was an instrument of German rule, being employed there would secure the person's family from harm and deportation, at least for a while. But Max was skeptical, as he was convinced of the Nazi resolve to destroy the Jews in the country. At the same time, he decided to follow his father's advice and see the person in the Jewish Council office in The Hague, to whom he was referred.[76] The man told him that his job was to escort old people that were to be deported to the railway station, help them with the luggage, and soothe their fears. Max Leons felt repelled by this idea and left abruptly, to the displeasure of his family. He took on another job, installing drilling machines in garages.

When his father got the dreaded summons to report for deportation, he was helped by a doctor with a false medical report of a supposed bad case of ligament rupture that necessitated his admittance into a hospital, and consequently he could not report. When Max's other relatives received in their turn the deportation summons, they hurried to the hospital, and Max's father got up and left quickly. The family had already made plans to go into hiding and had solicited new identity cards without the telltale *J*. Max's parents and his sister went their separate ways, while Max and his brother stuck together. They removed the Yellow Star from their garments. "Our life as *onderduikers* [Dutch term for persons in hiding] had begun."[77]

Safe Cover and Aid for Those on the Run

In the spring of 1943 the Leons brothers parted ways. Fred went to Amsterdam, and Max found his way to the tiny village of Nieuwlande. There Max's fortunes took a dramatic turn when he met Arnold Douwes, who was already deeply involved in the rescue of Jews. Douwes and Leons became close friends, and their friendship and their work lasted into the postwar period. Their activities consisted of finding hiding places for Jews on the run, providing ration cards for them, delivering letters from their loved ones, distributing illegal readings, supplying false identity cards, and aiding downed Allied pilots. The two never carried weapons with them—on principle. Arnold Douwes was the son of a Dutch Reformed minister. Max was to present himself as a Christian and one belonging to the more fundamentalist Calvinist-Protestant Gereformeerde Church.[78]

All Jews needing to be hidden were divided by Douwes and Leons into four categories and three subdivisions for each. AI stood for a typical Jewish-looking man who must never appear in public, even if armed with the best of papers. AII for such a person who could step out after sunset, AIII could circulate in the open equipped with authentic-appearing papers. Similar restrictions for B, standing for boys; C, for women, and D for girls. Messages over the phone always spoke of pieces or goods, type A, B, C, or D. "Goods" were usually deposited at the train station in nearby Hoogeveen and sometimes at Dedemsvaart or Nieuw Amsterdam. Jews seeking shelter arrived mostly accompanied by a girl courier. Either Max, Arnold, or both would be there to fetch them. When the situation required it, they would head to Amsterdam to pick up the fugitive Jews and lead them to their village hideouts.

The new anxious arrivals would first be calmed and put at ease, offered coffee and cake, and then taken after dark to their prearranged destinations. When small children were involved, Max and Arnold would sometimes take them on their bikes, one in the back carrier and the other on the handle or cross bars. Extra bikes were on hand for adults. Children were taught to learn by heart their new personal story, such as "I came from Rotterdam [which had been bombed during the German invasion and suffered many casualties]; my name is so-and-so, my home at so-and-so street has been destroyed." These youngsters were later referred to as "little Rotterdammers." They could step out in the open and attend school if they did not look too Jewish. Children, type BI and II and DI and II, could not go to school and remained out of sight. The youngest charge cared for by Leons and Douwes was only two weeks old.[79] Those needing to stay indoors constantly bore the heaviest discomforts. They could not be seen during daylight hours, not on the street or in public places. Fresh air was out of bounds for them. When indoors, they had to keep silent, not open the water faucet or flush the toilet when no one else was at home. Persons caught hiding Jews were, as a rule, sent to a camp, and some never made it back home.

What tactics and ruses were employed to solicit hiding places for Jews? After some polite preliminary greetings, the person solicited would be asked if he/she were willing to take in a fleeing Jew, with ration and if necessary money provided. An "of course, I will" response was a rarity. Usually all sorts of excuses were proffered: an NSB (pro-Nazi movement) person lived nearby; children at home might inadvertently give away the secret; no suitable hiding place; not enough room; it's too dangerous; suspecting neighbors might talk, and more. In Max's words, "We fell back on our last line. 'Try it please for one week. No? One day, two days? A fortnight?' Or 'Please, it's raining; they will get pneumonia if you force them to stay outside. We promise to find another place, and we'll come back soon,' promises that were often not kept. We gave people the choice: a man, a woman, a married couple, children, one child. We sometimes even lied to the fugitive Jews, because many people did not see the danger and would not come with us or send their children with us unless we told them a pack of lies. So we went through life lying right and left. It brought us the enmity of everybody, but *it worked*. . . . Many people eventually got a hiding place."[80]

Leons and Douwes were resolved to a single course of action, namely, every fugitive crossing their path must be aided. "We never said no," Leons underlined. "Any address was welcome." In their rescue work, they were assisted by several couriers, Jews as well as non-Jews, such as Nel Asscher, Hennie Winkel, Lenie Visser, and Piet Byleveld. They brought to Leons and Douwes anyone needing to be hidden, as well as clothes and letters from relatives. Also Peter (Ish Davids) and Herman (Lou Gans) were of help; they were especially handy in the falsification of all sorts of documents and in drawing all sorts of politically slanted caricatures.[81]

Leons further detailed the day-to-day activities of their secretive rescue work. "We were busy from early morning until late at night. . . . We never slept two nights in a row in the same place. We never slept in the same place together. . . . We used to sleep in haystacks a lot." Max arranged two emergency underground hiding places for himself in the wooded parts of Nieuwlande, deep enough to stand up inside with bended head. He and Douwes did not go into hotels, cafes, or restaurants, so as to avoid unnecessary risks. "We kept going under all weather conditions: rain, wind, snow, frost. . . . It has happened more than once that we were soaked wet, in spite of raincoat and galligaskins." No time to wait until the rain had passed, "because we had no time for that. Perhaps because we had to be at a railway station or some other place at a certain time or there was something else. . . . We were always very short of time."

Once a month all hidden persons had to be resupplied with ration cards, and one always needed to inquire after their well-being and smooth out tensions and upsetting situations affecting them. After all, they were thrown amid total strangers, often people with a different mentality, different outlook on life, and different habits. Leons added that what impressed him deeply among these Calvinist rescuers was that in their prayer at the dinner table, when Leons and Douwes were their guests, they thanked the Lord that the two were in good health and that they had met them. "When the Lord brings such a person onto my path, who am I to refuse?" one such friendly host innocently explained.[82]

Persuasion, Disguise, and a Bizarre Taxi Ride

Leons mentioned a few events and incidents that stood out in his mind. One time he was urgently asked by Douwes to find a place for a married Jewish couple. Stopping over at the Nienhuis house in the company of Douwes, Leons reminded them that they once promised to shelter a fugitive Jew. But the man of the house had gotten cold feet. "Yes, Nico [Max's code name], I do, but my wife—" Interrupting him, Leons admonished him: "Nienhuis, remember your duty as a Christian to help your neighbor." The man agreed. "Okay, Nienhuis," Leons continued, "I have a surprise for you. I have not one but two fugitives for you. A married couple, nice people. They are waiting outside."

At this Nienhuis stomped his feet. "Oh, no! We only have one bed!" "No problem," Leons cut him off. "But we have no room," the man continued, and the tête-a-tête continued, airing all the excuses, dilemmas, and predicaments that Leons was accustomed to hearing. Leons then said,

"Nienhuis, thanks very much, that's agreed. Fellows, come inside." Before the man and his wife knew what was happening, "our couple was inside, we were outside, on our bikes and vanished in the darkness. Another of our problems had been 'solved,' momentarily."[83]

In another story, one of Max's courier girls handed him a list of Gestapo agents, complete with photos. There was nothing unusual about this except that one of these agents was a Jew who lived in disguise, together with eleven other Jews. The courier then mentioned two of the other authentic hiding Jews as the Leons from Voorburg. Max Leons blurted out, "These people are my parents." Max and Arnold headed to that place to check the authenticity of the report. After several adventurous escapades with the police, they finally reached their destination—a certain upstairs apartment. Max's reunion with his parents, whom he had not seen for eighteen months, was a stormy one.

When his father saw him, he exploded. He had completely lost his usual calm composure when he realized that his son, who had a Jewish face, recognizable even from a distance, had not stayed in hiding. This was also confirmed by Arnold Douwes, who wrote: "Nico himself is an AI type,' a very pronounced Jewish appearance, who should never be seen, not even with the best of documents. . . . Talk about irony! When I met Nico for the first time I saw, still 50 meters away, that he was a Jew, plain as day." Max's father screamed at him: "So you travel around these days. . . . They think you are St. Francis or something? . . . You, the invisible man! Good heavens! Never before have I seen such stupidity." He continued to rave on for quite some time, disappointed as he was in always thinking that his son was tucked away somewhere in a foolproof hiding place.[84]

When he finally calmed down, Max explained the real purpose of his visit—about the Gestapo agent in their midst who pretended to be a victim himself. His parents discounted this rumor and assured Max that the information was mistaken. But the information was correct; less than two weeks later, Jews on that street were rounded up, with the traitorous Jew showing the way to the Germans. Luckily for Max's parents and the others in hiding, they were able to make their escape in the nick of time.[85]

Finally, under the heading of "A Very Special Taxi," in his memoirs Max Leons related when he and Arnold were asked to find a hiding place for a Jewish girl, Mirjam, about eighteen years old, as they all three rode in a cab. Suddenly the cab was stopped by three men: one wore the uniform of the dreaded German Green Police; the second was one of the most notorious Gestapo agents in the country. Leons recognized him immediately, as he was the number three man on his list of traitors who specialized in Jew baiting. He presently was dressed in a black ss uniform. The third person was a little boy in the uniform of the Hitler Youth. It was obvious from their appearance, all spruced and polished, that they were on their way to a party or celebration.[86] They were not interested in the three passengers; they simply wanted to hitch a ride to Wageningen. But there was a problem: there was not enough room in the cab for all of them.

Then, with the sweetest voice she could muster, Mirjam invited the boy to sit on her lap. This friendly overture was graciously accepted by the boy's fellow Nazis. In Max's words, "The boy in the Hitler Youth uniform took his place on the very Jewish lap of Mirjam. He was flanked on the right by someone whose picture had appeared in the official Police Gazette as being wanted by the Gestapo [Arnold Douwes] and on his left was someone, too, . . . being wanted as a Jew [Max Leons]." The three got off ahead of Max, Arnold, and Mirjam. "This was by far the most remarkable taxi ride I ever had," Max concluded.[87]

Close Calls

Max Leons had a few lucky breaks. But not so his main confederates. This was especially so in the year 1944. As Leons explained, the more obvious it became that the Nazis were losing the war, the more furious the Dutch traitors became and all the more energy they spent hunting down the innocents. Johannes Post, the overall regional underground leader wanted by the authorities, for instance, was arrested in July 1944 while trying to liberate a friend from a jail in the center of Amsterdam, and he was executed that same month, before his underground colleagues had formalized plans for his rescue.[88] Arnold Douwes, Max's closest rescue partner, had become well known by friend and foe, and there was a price on his head—as well as on Max's. "The Gestapo knew about us and they were furious and out to get us. So I became a real *onderduiker* [a person in hiding] myself once more . . . hiding with the Nieuwboer sisters in Nieuwlande."

Then, on October 19, 1944, Douwes was caught while sleeping in a bed at the home of a friendly family (instead of a shed or a barn as he and Leons usually did). There were seven Jews there hiding under the floor of the living room, but they were not found. Douwes tried to escape from jail but failed, and he was put in a straitjacket and taken to Assen, the capital of Drenthe province. Luckily for him, on December 11, 1944, he was freed from prison by a surprise attack by a regional underground unit, including thirty other prisoners. Douwes was one of seventeen men scheduled to be shot that day. His liberation came at the eleventh hour, and he went into hiding.[89]

Leons and Douwes met again in early April 1945. Leons learned that his family was safe.[90] His ordeal was finally over. As for Douwes, in 1965 he was honored by the Yad Vashem Holocaust Memorial in Jerusalem.[91] Not so Max Leons, since no analogous citation exists for Jewish rescuers of Jews.

Two More Jewish Rescuers

Saving Jews under different circumstances, they also merit mention.

Sig Menko was head of the Jewish Council of Enschede. Disregarding the advice of the Joodse Rad in Amsterdam to obey the German summons for "labor in the East," he counseled the Jews in his community to go into hiding. As an entrepreneur, he had access to money to assist Reverend Leendert Overduin, a prominent Protestant minister, to head a clandestine organization that found hiding places for Jews. As a result, in Enschede 500 out of the 1,300 Jews there were saved. Menko himself was eventually deported to Theresienstadt camp, but he survived.[92]

Samuel Schrijver was a Jewish prisoner in the Westerbork transit camp who, on April 11, 1945, managed to slip out and meet a unit of advancing Canadian soldiers who were preparing to bomb the camp; they assumed it was an enemy military depot. Schrijver persuaded them otherwise, because he knew there were 875 innocent Jewish prisoners still there. The Canadians at first demurred, but finally agreed to stealthily approach the camp for a closer inspection instead of shelling it from a distance. When they discovered that the ss guards had already left, the bombing was cancelled. The imprisoned Jews inside were spared a bombardment and a probable loss of lives, thanks to the courageous initiative of Samuel Schrijver.[93]

10 Toward Palestine, the Land of Israel

Boat People on the Danube with the
Connivance of the Nazis

Up until the first two years of World War II, Nazi Germany dealt with "the Jewish question" through forced migration—either leave areas under German control voluntarily or be pressured to do so. Up until November 1941 the question of where the Jews should go did not concern the Nazis as long as they left. The Germans were not beyond aiding Jewish organizers of illegal immigration, although it was to be done covertly, so as not to embarrass countries with which it still maintained diplomatic relations.[1] Adolf Eichmann, who started his career in the ss as an emigration expert, was prepared to facilitate procedures so that shipping and travel agents could procure entry permits for emigrants, even if it involved surreptitiously paying large bribes to consular officials. He also was able to release Jews arrested in Vienna who could produce destination documents to other countries. This led Eichmann to set up, first in annexed Austria in August 1938, a Central Office for Jewish Emigration to simplify the complex bureaucracy surrounding emigration. In January 1939 a similar agency was established in Berlin, at which time Reinhard Heydrich (Eichmann's superior) declared:

> We should continue to promote emigration by all available means. . . . First the Jews themselves should be approached. On the basis of their international connections they are in the best position to find opportunities for entry into other countries and to obtain the necessary foreign exchange. . . . In the case of Palestine it is undeniable that groups are making their way there from many countries in Europe. . . . Germany should also, at least unofficially, take advantage of the opportunity.[2]

Fig. 16. Georges Garel, postwar photo. Courtesy of
Memorial de la Shoah/Garel Collection.

Fig. 17. Andrée Salomon with a group of Jewish children about to leave for
the United States, Marseilles, 1941. Courtesy of the United States Holocaust
Memorial Museum.

Fig. 18. Rabbi Zalman Schneerson, Paris, postwar photo. Courtesy of the United States Holocaust Memorial Museum.

Fig. 19. (*right*) Chaim Perelman and his wife, Fela, Brussels, postwar photo. Courtesy of the United States Holocaust Memorial Museum.

Fig. 20. (*above*) Maurice Heiber (*second left*) and Ida Sterno (*in black dress*) with some of the children they saved in Belgium, late 1944. (Andree Geulen, in the white dress between Heiber and Sterno, is a non-Jewish rescuer, awarded the Righteous title.) Courtesy of the United States Holocaust Memorial Museum.

Fig. 21. Walter Süskind with his daughter in Amsterdam, 1941.
Collection Jewish Historical Museum, Amsterdam.

Fig. 22. Max Leons, self-portrait, wartime. Courtesy of Mordecai Paldiel.

Fig. 23. (*above*) *Left to right:* Max Leons, Mordecai Paldiel, and Arnold Douwes, early 1990s. Courtesy of Mordecai Paldiel.

Fig. 24. (*left*) George Mandel-Mantello, Geneva, wartime photo. Courtesy of the United States Holocaust Memorial Museum.

Fig. 25. Recha Sternbuch, her husband, Yikzhak Sternbuch (*first left with hat*), and Isaac Lewin (*behind him*) opening a children's home in France, 1945. Courtesy of Netty Segal, daughter of Recha Sternbuch.

Fig. 26. Aleksander Pechersky (*left*) with Aleksei Weizen, a fellow Sobibor
survivor, Russia, postwar photo. Courtesy of Yad Vashem Photo Archive.

Fig. 27. Hadassah Rosensaft (née Bimko) (*second left*),
British officer Captain Winterbottom, and Dr. Ruth
Gutman, Bergen-Belsen camp, Germany 1945. Courtesy
of the United States Holocaust Memorial Museum.

Fig. 28. Ben Hecht (*left*) and Peter Bergson

Fig. 29. Rabbis' March on Washington DC, October 6, 1943. Rabbi Eliezer Silver (*first row holding paper*), and Rabbi Abraham Kalmanowitz (*behind Silver with long beard*), United States, wartime photo. Courtesy of the David S. Wyman Institute for Holocaust Studies.

Fig. 30. Joseph Schwartz (*speaking*), JDC European head, in Paris
with Rabbi Zalman Schneerson (*sitting to his left*). Courtesy of
the United States Holocaust Memorial Museum.

Side by Side with the Revisionists and Mossad

The two major Zionist organizations involved in illegal immigration to Palestine were the Revisionist (a.k.a. New Zionist Organization) movement, through its youth movement Betar, and the Labor Zionist Hechalutz youth pioneer movement, via its Mossad Le-Aliyah Bet, a secretive branch of the Hagannah, the underground military force of the Jewish community in Palestine.[3] Both organizations worked out of several stations in Europe, as the changing political situation warranted. They organized and selected those ready to emigrate, prepared the needed documents (exit permits and transit visas), and supplied the trains, boats, crews, and food for the voyage. Working with these two major organizations were individuals who were motivated by the possibility of economic gain and others who were ideologically committed to Jewish solidarity. These private organizers are credited with arranging the escape of up to 10,000 people.[4]

Nazi collusion in the illegal migration of Jews went so far that when Pino Ginsburg, an emissary of the Zionist Hechalutz movement and the Mossad, and his colleague Max Zimmels came to Germany in January 1939 to plan the flight of Jews, they were granted extended visas by the Gestapo in Berlin to facilitate their work. They were even contacted by an ss middleman, Alexander von Hoepfner, who offered to assist them and suggest travel companies with which they could work, such as the Hamburg Line.[5]

German Push for Emigration: British Resistance

In the summer months of 1938, Vienna and Prague were the centers of illegal immigrations, with persons heading by train to Greek ports, where they embarked on boats. Later, the main route was switched to sailing down the Danube River to Black Sea ports in Romania and Bulgaria and continuing past the Turkish Dardanelles waterway into the Mediterranean Sea. Insofar as Palestine was concerned, the major obstacle was not the Nazis but the British, who since 1937 had applied a restricted Jewish immigration quota to Palestine. Its May 1939 White Paper further limited Jewish immigration to 75,000 for the next five years, and none thereafter, unless the Arabs agreed to it. Immigrants caught trying to furtively land in Palestine were placed under arrest and their numbers were deducted from that year's immigration quota. Britain also exerted strong diplomatic pressures on countries with Black Sea and Mediterranean ports to prevent the passage of immigrants to Palestine or providing them with supplies.

When war broke out in September 1939, the difficulties of organizing illegal immigration increased. Shipping costs soared as available vessels became scarce, and countries anxious to use vessels in their own war effort prohibited the transfer of ships' ownership to foreign citizens. At the same time, the Germans kept the pressure on for emigration, legal or otherwise, no matter the ultimate destination—the United States, Shanghai, or Palestine.[6] In the German embassy in Rome, for instance, Von Hoepfner tried to obtain Italian transit visas for Jews lacking entry permits to a final destination. Kurt Lischka, deputy to Gestapo chief Heinrich Müller, wrote, "It is of utmost importance to explain to the Italians that passage through their country is the only way for German Jews to immigrate, and since it is in the German interest, they should do everything to facilitate it—even for those who do not have certificates to Palestine." The Italians were not eager to allow illegal immigration activities to be conducted in their country after the outbreak of war. In the Nazi *Zentralstelle* (emigration office for Jews) in Berlin, the obstacles placed by their Italian allies were viewed with grave concern.[7]

The Germans did not waver in their support of illegal emigration. The Mediterranean Sea was still open to the sailing of boats (at least until Italy's entry in the war in June 1940) and the Balkan States, mainly Romania, allowed illegal immigrants passage through their ports. German pressure on the Jews to leave kept mounting as the war extended into the Low Countries and France. On July 1, 1940, in a meeting with Eichmann and Lischka, representatives of the Reichsvereinigung (sole Jewish recognized organization) and Jewish communal representatives from Austria and Prague were ordered to present within twenty-four hours a draft plan for the mass removal of all Jews from the expanded Reich. Eichmann stressed that what was envisioned was total emigration—in line with the Nazi policy of mass extermination adopted a year later.

While it wished to increase Jewish immigration to Palestine, the Zionist leadership had mixed feelings concerning illegal immigration, since its official policy was to align itself with England in the war against Nazi Germany, and any attempt at undermining coordination with the British was considered undesirable. This ambivalent Zionist policy hampered the activities of the Mossad while it was in the process of organizing the exit of some 10,000 Jews from Germany in collaboration with the German Hapag travel company and groups of Hechalutz pioneers in Bratislava and Vienna.[8]

Before the start of the war, in the late 1930s, Zionist leaders such as David Ben Gurion and Moshe Shertok had been halfheartedly in favor of illegal immigration. Ben Gurion at first thought of organizing dozens of boats to arrive in broad daylight and thus force the British to appear before the world in a bad light. In this sense, his approach was similar to Vladimir Jabotinsky's of the Zionist Revisionists, as both considered illegal immigration a provocative weapon in the struggle against Britain that was constantly adding immigration restrictions to Palestine. Then, in January 1939, the opponents to illegal immigration gained the upper hand, and with the outbreak of war that same year, the Mossad's operations were suspended.[9]

Ben Gurion once upbraided Mossad activist Zeev Shind on the Mossad operations and was furious at the self-appointed decision by the Mossad on illegal immigration. "Where shall we get to if a bunch of self-appointed saviors make decisions of their own volition and then inform the responsible leadership it is too late to undo the consequences of their acts?" Ben Gurion shouted at Shind? Then suddenly changing his tune, he added that when the boat arrives, "I shall go down to the shore, take off my shoes, wade into the water, and help the boys disembark the newcomers and bring them to shore on my own back. But then I shall go directly to a meeting to have you all disciplined for your utter irresponsibility."[10] Hence the paradoxical situation of the Germans firmly supporting illegal immigration, the British seeking ways to stop it, and the Zionists (with one exception) not sure whether illegal immigration was good or bad.

That one exception was the Zionist Revisionists. Its leader, Vladimir Jabotinsky, unequivocally supported illegal immigration. He also urged the Romanian and Polish governments, who were interested in reducing the number of Jews in their countries, to assist in illegal refugee efforts.[11] The route often used was down the Danube River to the Black Sea, since as an international waterway the Danube eliminated the need for transit visas. The Revisionists also promoted illegal passages on land routes, via French-controlled Beirut and Damascus, and sea voyages to Palestine.[12]

When the war broke out in September 1939, the Revisionists had a group of 400 in Prague waiting to leave, but the German invasion delayed its departure. After the cancellation of a voyage by boat, the group, reduced to 350, made its way to Romania in early November 1939, and there they waited several months for the arrival of a seaworthy boat for the Black Sea voyage. A few months earlier, two boats, the *Parita* and *Naomi Julia*, had been chartered, and they landed their passengers in Palestine in August and September 1939, but were seized by the British. Another group, led by Yehoshua Citron (Halevi), leader of Betar (Revisionist youth) in Slovakia, was awaiting departure in Bratislava.[13] Joining the Citron group were about 100 freed Buchenwald inmates who had been released through the efforts of Recha Freier, founder of Youth Aliyah.

The *Pencho*, a Bulgarian registered ship, took on this group in March 1940. After leaving Bratislava, the ship was driven from port to port, as the Romanians refused to allow the *Pencho* to transit through its territory, and the boat drifted on the Danube River between Bulgaria and Romania, unable to put into port. Only on September 11, 1940, five months after leaving Bratislava, was the boat allowed by the Romanians to take on fuel and continue its route to the Black Sea exit. But after having sailed past Varna, Bulgaria, the engines malfunctioned and the sailing came to a standstill. After some repairs, the *Pencho* continued on its haphazard route, but it then struck a reef and sank off an Aegean island on the eve of Yom Kippur 1940. The passengers and crew were rescued by the Italian navy and transported, first to Rhodes island and later to southern Italy, where they remained interned, though not harmed, until liberated by Allied forces in September 1943.[14]

Berthold Storfer

> With Gestapo assistance he helped 3,500 Jews to
> exit from the German-occupied lands.[15]

Born in 1882 in Czernowitz, then part of the Austro-Hungarian Empire, Berthold Storfer was for many years in the timber trade, and during World War I he was engaged in transporting supplies to the Austrian Army on the Russo-Romanian front, where he was decorated twice. After the war he moved to Vienna, served as a financial advisor to the Czech and Austrian governments, and also worked for large commercial firms. He was not a central figure in the Jewish community until July 1938, when he appeared as an observer at the U.S.-sponsored Jewish refugees conference in Evian, France. This evidently spurred him to become increasingly involved in the illegal immigration of Jews to Palestine, especially since March 1939 when he headed Zentrum (probably with German prodding), one of the major travel agencies engaged in Jewish emigration by legal or devious ways. The Germans did not mind, as long as Jews were leaving, and the more the better. It is assumed that Eichmann trusted Storfer to be able to carry out the forced emigration of Austrian Jews.[16]

Close ties with the Gestapo

With the coming of war in September 1939, Storfer's stature and importance grew. It seems that Eichmann was impressed with Storfer's work and appointed him as the emigration czar. From August 1939 onwards, Storfer was to give his stamp of approval to emigration plans initiated by other organizations. He was empowered to cancel plans or halt groups of emigrants either before their departure or en route, and by March 1940 he was in sole charge of organizing emigration from all parts of the Reich and supervising the emigration plans of other Jewish organizations, all with Eichmann's approval.[17]

One of Storfer's tasks was to weed out the corrupted elements dealing in emigration who swindled people out of their monies, then left them stranded. In this undertaking he worked closely with Dr. Josef Löwenherz, the formal and Gestapo approved head of the Jewish community in Vienna, who also kept tabs on Jews anxious to emigrate, especially after the Kristallnacht event of November 1938. To streamline Storfer's operation, the Germans forbade Jewish organizations to collect funds for emigration purposes unless done through Storfer's office, and this made Löwenherz totally dependent on Storfer's help on matters of emigration. At the same time, persons applying for emigration had to forego practically all of their valuables, as odiously practiced by Eichmann's Zentralstelle emigration office, and leave with hardly pocket money.[18]

In all his activities Storfer employed a Greek shipping agent, Sokrates Avgerinos, who made contacts with other travel and shipping firms on Storfer's behalf. Several of Storfer's family members represented him in the Balkan countries. His brother Joseph was sent to Bucharest, and his brother-in-law Goldner served as a roving agent in Slovakia, Hungary, and elsewhere. He also established contact with Robert Mendler (who worked with Wilhelm Perl, to be told later), and Baruch Confino in Bulgaria. Storfer made numerous trips to Greece, Romania, Slovakia, and Hungary to secure bank guarantees and short-term loans, and he personally conducted negotiations with the national Danube shipping companies. He became the main link in the transit route from the Danube to the river's seaport outlets in Romania.[19] Again, with the Holocaust in hindsight, it boggles the imagination to remember that Storfer's activities were possible only because the ss was steadily pressuring the Jewish leadership to speed up emigration, whatever the obstacles.

Eichmann would sometimes summon the heads of the Jewish community organizations and berate them for what he considered the slow pace of emigration. He insisted that all Jews be out of Vienna by February 1940, which proved impossible. Storfer was also told to work solely with national river companies and with the German Hapag Line when organizing the flight of Jews on the Danube River, and these shipping companies were told to offer affordable prices.[20] As Storfer was required to synchronize his activity with the Gestapo, they were not beyond dropping in unannounced on sudden visits to his office to examine the correspondence with foreign countries and private individuals. Eichmann once bluntly told Storfer: "Either you disappear across the Danube or into the Danube." All this must have made it quite clear to Storfer that his freedom was on the line, and he was always on guard not to compromise his special status by an inadvertent mistake.[21]

Jewish community leaders in Vienna knew of Storfer's links with the Gestapo, but were not necessarily hostile to him. Historian Dalia Ofer wrote of the many letters of thanks to Storfer, praising his efforts and accomplishments in the emigration cause.[22] But the Aliyah (migration to Palestine-Israel) organizers of the Hechalutz and Revisionist movements were appalled by Storfer's close ties with the Gestapo and suspected him of totally subjecting himself to the demands of his Nazi overlords. How, they additionally argued, could one be sure that he would not use funds entrusted to him for personal gain or that he would not subject his passengers to inflated travel costs?[23] Emigrants who reached Palestine on board Storfer's ships claimed that some people paid him hundreds of dollars, which he pocketed, but the evidence is not clear. His critics overlooked the fact that anyone responsible for emigration from the

Reich had to work closely with the German authorities and sometimes pay bribes or accomplish nothing.

Boat Problems

In December 1939 Storfer organized a group of some 600 refugees in Bratislava to sail on the Astria, but the boat sank in a storm and the refugees were stranded. Storfer then began to plan a spring departure on a ship large enough to hold over 1,000 passengers. By February 1940 he was considering two ships, the *Sirus* and *Popi*, to carry 1,400 to 1,600 people, and he asked the Joint Distribution Committee (JDC) to pay for it, but the money never came. It appears that the JDC held up the $55,000 due to the intervention of Dr. Chaim Weizmann, worldwide head of the Zionist movement, and the Mossad, who urged the JDC to withhold support of Storfer unless a way was found to exercise a greater control over his operations and his funds. Such control, they felt, would ensure that the Germans would not be able to use emigration as a cover for espionage activities, as the British erroneously claimed. Storfer refused to agree to this demand, and this added to the distrust of Storfer by the Mossad's lead man, Zvi Yehieli.[24]

On February 25, 1940, Yehieli and Storfer met in Bucharest, Romania, to try to sort things out, but the meeting did not go well. Storfer tried to convince Yehieli that collaboration with him would be to the Mossad's advantage, proposing that he, Storfer, continue organizing the groups of emigrants in accordance with German directives but at the same time consider the Mossad's interests and requests in selecting candidates for emigration. Yehieli, however, did not agree to this arrangement, which was a blow to Storfer, as he needed the Mossad's collaboration to bolster his status with the still-existing Jewish communities in Berlin, Vienna, and Prague, as well as in everything related to sailing the Mediterranean and clandestine landings on Palestinian shores.[25]

At a second meeting between the two, Storfer disclosed to Yehieli his plan to take 3,500 Jews out of Germany using three boats. The plan called for Storfer to assume responsibility for the sea voyage through the Black Sea and the Mediterranean, with the Mossad arranging transit documents through Romania and the secret disembarkation on the Palestinian coast. The Mossad would also be responsible for getting the JDC to provide funding. They argued over Storfer's refugee lists, which Yehieli contended did not include 1,000 Prague Zionist pioneers to whom the Mossad had promised passage, nor did it include another group, stranded in Kladovo, Yugoslavia. Storfer countered that future lists would include the Prague group and that he would try to help the Kladovo people if he could.

From Yehieli's viewpoint, this amounted to a rejection, and the Mossad practically gave up on efforts to emigrate people from Germany proper, as it sought to distance itself from Storfer.[26] This was an error, for a unique chance was lost for the possibility of a larger immigration at a time when Germany was still committed to a forced emigration policy. The aforementioned Prague group that failed to leave in time was first deported to Theresienstadt and then to Auschwitz.[27] The Kladovo episode also ended tragically partly through the failed efforts at cooperation between the Mossad and Storfer.

With the help of JDC funds, Storfer succeeded in sending the largest-ever group of refugees to Palestine aboard the three ships: *Milos, Pacific,* and *Atlantic.* According to Storfer's plan, the *Atlantic* was to carry some 1,800 passengers, the *Pacific* about 1,000, and the *Milos* about 700, bringing the total to approximately 3,500. Another ship, the *Rosita,* was to carry a separate group of 1,200. The ships were first to head from Piraeus, Greece, to Tulcea, Romania, at the mouth of the Danube, to pick up the refugees due to arrive via German Danube Line riverboats. The refugees, originating in Vienna, were to sail down the Danube on September 2 and 4, 1940, and stop in Bratislava to pick up more passengers. Storfer—with Eichmann's help—reached an agreement with the German Danube Line on the fees to be paid. The German Foreign Office had instructed its commercial attaché in Bucharest to assist Storfer with the foreign-currency transactions. Panamanian registry for the boats was obtained with the help of a bribe to the Spanish and Panamanian representatives in Bucharest.[28]

In spite of difficulties and frequent delays, the Jewish refugees reached the port of Tulcea in August and September 1940, where Storfer's ships were waiting. In the meantime, the British consulate in Bucharest was instructed from London to take whatever measures needed to scuttle the departure of the boats, and it successfully exerted pressure on crewmembers not to sail, causing a delay until new crews were recruited. The three overcrowded boats carrying over 3,000 passengers included a number of freed inmates from the Buchenwald and Dachau concentration camps, as well as 100 children.[29] Storfer assured the JDC that the vessels were seaworthy, but in reality they were ill-equipped freighters and were operated by disorganized crews.

Sailing on October 7, 1940, the *Atlantic* docked in Istanbul, where provisions were brought on board, and the ship proceeded to Crete, where it loaded coal. British intelligence knew of the boat's sailing, and as it approached Cyprus, the British navy seized the *Atlantic*. In the meantime, on October 29, 1940, Italy declared war on Greece, and this turned the eastern Mediterranean Sea into a war zone, as the *Atlantic* with its 1,061 passengers was escorted to Haifa, where it arrived on November 15. There, the British decided on a stiffer penalty; they would no longer temporarily confine the passengers and, and, and deduct their numbers from that year's immigrants quota. Instead, the new arrivals were to be transferred to another boat and taken to the distant Indian Sea island of Mauritius, where they were to be interned for the duration of the war.

As the passengers of the *Pacific* and *Milos* (seized earlier) were being transferred aboard the *Patria*, a French cargo vessel held by the British, the Palestine-Jewish Hagannah underground decided to disable that boat so as to prevent it from sailing to Mauritius. But the quantity of explosives required was overestimated, and the explosion on November 24, 1940, caused the boat to sink rapidly, drowning 202 people (other sources cite 254 or 267 victims). In a rare and unusual charitable step, the British government allowed the survivors to remain ashore in Palestine, but the *Atlantic* passengers, who had not yet boarded the *Patria*, were deported to Mauritius.[30] These three ships constituted the last organized transport out of Germany to Palestine with Nazi approval.[31]

In March 1941 Storfer tried organizing travel on the *Rosita*, but it came to naught. By then, the Nazis had lost faith in a plan for mass Jewish emigration. As the Nazi war of expansion continued, the number of Jews under German rule increased, and the proportionate impact of forced emigration seemed insignificant in their eyes. At that point the Nazis turned to extermination, known as the Final Solution, and ruled out emigration of Jews to Palestine.[32]

Controversial to the End

To summarize, Berthold Storfer clearly did save 3,500 Jews from the Nazis. "Such a feat, given wartime conditions, was extraordinary," wrote historian Dalia Ofer.[33] And he did not sacrifice any other group of would-be immigrants in order to rescue them. It is also worth noting that Storfer made no distinction between young or old, healthy or ill emigrants, and he did give special consideration to those freed from concentration camps following Kristallnacht. (They were freed on the condition that they leave the country in the shortest time possible or face reimprisonment.) In contrast, the Zionist Mossad and Betar organizations were mainly interested in emigrating younger people, those capable of adding their youthful energy and stamina to the building of a future Jewish state. Yet Storfer remains a controversial figure and the object of harsh and unfair criticism.[34] The claim that he abused his authority for personal gain was never proven, and it is possible that he had a personal commitment to save fellow Jews.[35] Precisely when and why Storfer's activities ceased is also unclear.[36]

In the fall of 1943, Storfer was reportedly given leave to go to Switzerland, but the offer was then withdrawn. He went into hiding with his brother, but he was apprehended and deported to Auschwitz. When Eichmann was captured in 1960, he told Israeli police officer Avner Less of his meeting with Storfer in Auschwitz camp, where Eichmann told him: "My dear Storfer, what bad luck we've had! Look, I really can't help you. On orders of Himmler, no one can get you out. I can't get you out. . . . I heard that you've done a stupid thing here, that you hid out or wanted to flee, which really wasn't necessary."[37] Eichmann then claimed that he asked Auschwitz camp commander Höss to exempt Storfer from hard labor, and this was granted him, but only for a short time. It was reported that in October or November 1944, Storfer was shot in Auschwitz.

The Mossad: Ehud Avriel and Moshe Agami

They used subterfuge in order to do everything possible to get the Jews to leave Europe, in spite of the many risks and obstacles.

Born as Georg Überall in Vienna in 1917, the later-known Ehud Avriel joined the Zionist youth organization Blau-Weiss (Tchelet-Lavan), which was linked to the Socialist Zionist movement and affiliated with the Hechalutz. As he stated, "I prepared myself for pioneering in Palestine, and trained as an apprentice in a carpentry shop."[38] Avriel's colleague Moshe Agami represented the Zionist pioneering Hechalutz organization in Austria and was the Zionist youth organization's leader in Vienna when the Germans marched in on March 12, 1938. The Gestapo office was located directly across the street from where Agami and Avriel operated, and their agents knew exactly where the Zionist operatives were and what they were doing, but they caused no problem, since the Nazis were themselves at the time interested in getting as many Jews out of the country as possible.

The illegality began only at the shores of Palestine with the British blockade. For one, illegal immigration to Palestine was sometimes organized by what Avriel terms "highway robbers," who would collect the money and then disappear. Fleeing refugees were, moreover, placed on completely unseaworthy ships that tossed about the seas. In 1937, a year before the German takeover of Austria, Avriel's co-worker Yehuda (Yulik) Braginsky took off to Greece to find a small craft that could successfully slip through British seashore patrols. "What the hell," he would say. "Columbus discovered America in a 49-ton barge."[39]

Pressure to Accelerate Immigration

In summer 1938 the green light was given for intensifying illegal immigration. Hagannah had established the Mossad for this purpose, and Shaul Avigur was appointed as its head.[40] At this point, in a dramatic and paradoxical twist, Rudolf Loehner, a high-ranking Austrian Nazi, became a loyal friend of Agami and his team. Through him, Agami's men met Gerta Haas, the Jewish wife of a Hungarian nobleman, and Giuseppe Matossiani, an Italian playboy who had connections with Wolfgang Karthaus, a high-ranking Nazi (one of the founding members of Austrian Nazism) who, in a surprise move, decided to lend a hand in facilitating the emigration of Jews. In return for 1,000 Marks, Matossiani promised to submit a list of Jews who were in Dachau camp, to affect their release, and to transfer them to one of Agami's farms in Austria that was training Zionist pioneers for agricultural work in Palestine. As for Karthaus's willingness to assist, apparently he had come to detest the vulgar, indiscriminate antisemitism of the Nazis, or so he claimed, and as a form of penance he was going to help Jews get out of the country.[41] This was an important break, since Karthaus was a close friend of the Gauleiter, the Nazi governor of Vienna.

Agami felt he could have some of the refugees infiltrate into Yugoslavia in the guise of German workers and then continue to a waiting ship on a faraway shore. Matossiani accompanied Agami to his first meeting with Karthaus, which began in a coffee shop that bore the sign "Jews not wanted here." The Nazi Karthaus took a liking to the Jewish Agami and promised to obtain for him regular transit visas through Yugoslavia, provided of course that there was a boat waiting when they arrived in port. In this endeavor, he would clear it with his friend, the Gauleiter, for approval by the highest Gestapo authorities.[42] In Avriel's words, "We could hardly grasp the ease with which Karthaus disposed of difficulties that appeared insurmountable to us." He indeed made available about 20,000 Yugoslav transit visas within a few days, bearing the seal of the Yugoslav Consulate General in Vienna.[43]

The *Attrato* was the first ship, meant for a large-scale illegal transport, arranged by Agami's group. It was scheduled to sail from Piraeus, Greece. But as a result of British pressure on the Greek government, the ship was diverted to Italy. Under a Panama registration, the ship docked in Bari, southern Italy, where the refugees embarked, and made it safely and undetected to Palestine with its 386 passengers, and the ship returned for a second voyage.[44] Agami alerted the fourteen training farms in Austria where over 1,000 Zionist youths were waiting anxiously to leave at a moment's notice.[45] At the same time, Agami's colleague, Zvi Yehieli, had acquired another boat, the slow-moving *Colorado*, since the *Attrato* would not hold more than 400 passengers and they expected 680. All safely arrived in Palestine, undetected, in January 1939.[46] When the British learned of the *Colorado*'s departure from Yugoslav soil, it forwarded a sharp protest and asked the Yugoslav government to stop the passage of refugee traffic through its territory.

Attempts to Avoid British Detection

Back in Vienna, Agami was summoned to appear before Karthaus and Dr. Lange, head of the Jewish Department in the Gestapo. Lange contended that other destinations needed to be taken into consideration, to which Agami suggested Mexico. Lange: "All right, so it is Mexico."[47] Lange then handed Agami a fake statement to sign that read: "I, the undersigned, a citizen of Palestine engaged in organizing the emigration of Jews from the Greater German Reich to the Western Hemisphere, affirm that the destination of the convoys at the present time is Mexico."[48] Giuseppe Matossiani had also arranged for the consul of Mexico to issue a collective passport for fleeing Jews, in return for payment to Matossiani, that stated, "The holders of the attached collective visa are entitled to immigrate to

Mexico." These people did not really head to Mexico, so the document was meant to avoid incriminating the consul in this risky paid arrangement. The people would, of course, head to Palestine.[49] But, at this time, the Germans did not mind either way, as long as this led to more Jews leaving Greater Germany, which included Austria. This prompted Agami to start using the Black Sea route via the Danube River.

Agami then learned that in order to expedite the emigration of Jews by whatever means, Eichmann had decided to establish a central office for illegal convoys to Palestine under the leadership of Berthold Storfer, the man who alone would determine who was to leave and who was to stay. "We resented Storfer, Eichmann's unscrupulous pro-consul," Avriel wrote, "who had no regard for our selective process . . . and for the difficult landing off the shores of Palestine." But Karthaus indicated to Agami that his work would still go on, independent of Storfer. It proved otherwise when Agami was peremptorily summoned before Eichmann, who told him, "Either you disappear or I shall make you disappear!"[50] That same afternoon Agami left by plane for Geneva, where he joined Zvi Yehieli.

Shortly after Agami's departure, Avriel was told to attend a meeting at Storfer's office. The discussion centered on how to land the refugees in Palestine without British detection. Storfer appeared too dictatorial in Avriel's eyes, and Agami by phone from Geneva suggested that he persuade Storfer to come see him in Zurich. Agami: "I want to impress on him as strongly as I can who is really in charge among the Jews."[51] In the meantime, the Mossad had transferred the *Colorado* and *Attrato* to the Danube outlet in the Black Sea. The two ships were filled in Constanța, Romania, with refugees from Germany and Poland. A few Romanian Jews were added, and this was to be the *Attrato*'s seventh and last trip to Palestine. Before leaving, an additional 100 passengers, newly arrived from Austria, were added to the overcrowded boat. Approaching the shores of Palestine, this time a British cruiser blocked the ship's approach to the beach and rammed the little ship, pushing her in the direction of the Haifa port. The *Colorado* was also intercepted by a British warship on its fifth trip to Palestine on July 28, 1939, with 377 passengers on board.[52]

To facilitate arrangements for sailing on the Danube, the Slovak consul in Vienna allowed Avriel the use of his diplomatic telephone (in return for payment) for important phone messages. For each call, Avriel had to transfer a certain amount to a bank account in Zürich. In Avriel's words,

"I had taken over the switchboard of the young sovereign State of Slovakia's Consulate General in Vienna."[53]

Eichmann Raises the Pressure for Jews to Leave

As Avriel's team arranged voyages on the Danube River, he was suddenly ordered to present himself before Eichmann at his office in the sequestered Rothschild Palace. As Avriel entered Eichmann's spacious office, the latter with a whip in hand shouted: "Three steps away!" and the whip cut the air with a vicious whistling sound. "Progress is too slow!" Eichmann shouted. "We did not work quickly enough." He added, "Why did we get so few people down the Danube to the Black Sea and through Yugoslavia to the Adriatic and from there to Palestine? And why did we not push more people into England and America?" It was time to make the place *judenrein*—and soon.

"We do all we can," Avriel responded and explained the obstacles faced in the work of illegal voyages.[54] "Mere excuses!" Eichmann shouted back. We moved so slowly because the Zionists insisted on young people only. "He had no time to lose while we were indulging our caprices. I insisted that the only reason for our selectivity was the hardship of the trip. The passengers had to be able to jump into the sea near the shore to escape the British. Eichmann shrieked back: 'Let the old and the sick jump into the water, too! From now on you will have to take them!' He ordered me to contact his handyman Storfer, who would coordinate the work and speed up emigration."[55]

After this meeting, when Avriel's team applied for 1,000 passports at Eichmann's Central Office, they were surprisingly treated like "preferred customers; even invited by the ss corporal to take a seat!" And to save work and time for everybody, Eichmann's office proposed issuing a collective passport. There would be a list of 1,000 names with particulars and photographs attached—just one passport that would be valid for the entire group for sailing down the Danube River. The transport was subdivided into groups of 20, each with a leader. Fifty such group leaders were selected.[56]

First Departure for Slovakia

Everything was ready for the first such voyage when the Danube Steamboat Company suddenly changed its mind after they found out that there would be no seagoing ship to receive the passengers to be discharged in Romania. At this crucial juncture, another Austrian Nazi stepped in to help out. He was Ferdinand Ceipek, who was beginning to have second thoughts about the regime and wanted to help Jews—so he stated. He told Avriel, "I want to make up, in a small way, for having helped to bring this about."[57] He saved the day by taking the collective passport to the Slovak consul and obtaining regular Slovak entry visas for the 1,000 persons on the list. The persons would consequently be able to stay in Slovakia until a ship was on hand in Romania.

The group left for Slovakia without any word about a ship waiting for them in Romania. Avriel decided to go to Bratislava to check on the conditions of the Jewish refugees stranded there. Leaving Vienna in the company of Ferdinand Ceipek, Ehud Avriel was dressed in the uniform of a military officer (so as to avoid using his German passport, since in that case, as a Jew, he might not be allowed to return to Vienna). His cover was that of a high-ranking Luftwaffe (German air force) officer on a secret mission to Bratislava. Visiting the refugees transit camp, he saw people sleeping on mattresses on the floor in a huge hall of an abandoned factory. They had received an ultimatum: either leave for Yugoslavia or return to Austria within ten days.

With Ceipek's help, Avriel visited the office of Colonel Houssek, a high-ranking Slovak police officer, and paid him a handsome bribe. Going a step further, at Ceipek's urging, Avriel added that he was also ready to do something for the Slovak Police Pension Fund, and "imperceptibly I pushed the briefcase [filled with money] so that it just touched Colonel Houssek's foot. For the briefest second a warm glimmer appeared in his eye. He would do what he could, he said. He would give them another three months."[58] The two then returned to Vienna. In December 1939, with Europe at war, Avriel, as a British national, returned to Palestine and stayed there until he was reassigned to Istanbul, Turkey.[59]

Baruch Confino

Through his efforts, along with that of private boat organizers and the Mossad, over 3,000 reached Palestine on eight separate transports.

Dr. Baruch Confino and a group of private boat organizers, with some connected to one or other factions within the Zionist movement, played an important role in promoting the movement of several thousand illegal immigrants about to sail to the shores of Palestine. Dr. Confino, an ophthalmologist in Sofia, Bulgaria, and a prominent Zionist, had been involved in the early 1930s in helping German Jews who had reached Bulgaria to leave Europe in cooperation with Recha Freier from Berlin. Through his efforts, 3,683 people reached Palestine on eight separate transports, some with help from the Mossad. He explored alternative routes to Palestine, such as first going to Libya, whence they would proceed to Palestine overland or by boat. He also aided Storfer in organizing his three ships—*Pacific*, *Milos*, and *Atlantic*. A dark cloud shadowed Confino's work from the summer of 1940 on, starting with the British capture of the *Libertad* passengers in July 1940 and the sinking of the *Salvador* in December 1940—a voyage he had organized, and these disasters ultimately ruined Confino's reputation.[60]

Confino had planned for 700–800 passengers to fill the *Libertad*. As it sailed from Bulgaria before it had been fully refitted, due to Bulgarian pressure, the voyage was plagued by misfortune, and passengers suffered from hunger and dehydration. It reached Palestine in July 1940 with an escort of British vessels, and the ship was confiscated. As for the *Salvador*, it was a very old sailboat and lacked an engine. It was also quite small and weighing but 100 tons. It was in poor condition and needed extensive repairs and refitting. No more than 250 people were to go aboard, but it actually sailed with 350 people. The boat left Varna, Bulgaria, on December 3, 1940, and reached Istanbul under sail, where Bulgarian Jews and Confino's agents provided the passengers with food and water. It then left Istanbul on December 11, and in the Sea of Marmara it hit a storm, split in two, and sank. Most of those on board drowned. Confino was held responsible for sending the ship out in such poor condition, and as a result the Bulgarian authorities ordered Confino out of Sofia until further notice. In his defense he claimed that it was necessary to go with illegal *Aliyah* and grit one's teeth at losses sustained. The sea would always claim its victims, but this alone was not reason enough to cease operations. In the estimate of Dalia Ofer, Confino willingly risked his own reputation and his position in the community for the sake of trying to help Jewish refugees reach safe havens.[61]

Wilhelm Perl

He organized his own independent *Aliyah* operation of close to 4,000 Jews desperate to leave war-torn Europe.

Wilhelm (Willi) Perl, born in 1906 in Prague, was a Vienna lawyer and former Revisionist Betar activist. Independently from Storfer and the Mossad, he planned the voyages of two ships that reached Palestine in October and December 1938, respectively. In fact, Perl's *Draga II* was the first vessel to sail down the Danube. Perl and two co-workers arranged several other boat voyages in the following months, with a total of 3,758 passengers.[62] After the war began, Perl hired a German riverboat, the *Saturnus*, to take 200 Jews from Vienna and 600 from Prague to Sulina, Romania. There, they hired the Turkish boat *Sakariya* on December 10. But when the ship's Turkish owners and crew learned that the ship that regularly carried coal was now to carry fleeing refugees, they canceled their contract, and a new agreement had to be concluded. It was now December 25, 1939, when Perl's group totaling 1,350 passengers boarded the *Sakariya*. Later more passengers were added, some by the Romanian authorities, and the boat now counted 2,200 passengers. On February 1, 1940, the *Sakariya* finally sailed off the Romanian coast, but was stopped and boarded by a British naval vessel as it exited the Dardanelles and then escorted to Palestine. The crew members were freed and the ship was released, while the passengers were interned, then released after their number was deducted from the quota of admissible immigrants.[63]

The British, the Balkans, and the Kladovo Group

The Aliyah organizers were caught between pressure from the Germans to leave and obstacles from the British not to let that happen, which at times ended in tragedy.

One of the tragedies of the Holocaust that could have been prevented was that, up to October 1941, the Nazis were assisting Jewish organizations to speed up the emigration of Jews to Palestine or elsewhere while the British were doing their utmost to stop the flow of Jewish emigrants. Seizing ships in international waters was not condoned by international laws, but the British disregarded this prohibition, arguing that the Germans would surely infiltrate Nazi spies on Jewish refugee boats or use Jewish emigrants as fifth column agents by holding their families hostage in Germany.[64] The extent of German involvement in organizing Jewish emigration seemed to offer no other explanation to the British.

The British were quite aware of the efforts made by the various refugee organizers to move refugees on the Danube River toward the Black Sea outlets and thence via Turkey to Palestine. Consequently extensive diplomatic action was taken to forestall any such development. The British asked the countries of the Danube basin—Romania, Bulgaria, Hungary, and Yugoslavia—to bar Jewish refugee transports from entering their territorial waterways. At one point, the British requested that the Yugoslav authorities check the passports of Jewish refugees from the Reich to see that they were properly stamped with the letter *J* (for *Jude*), and therefore forbid their passage. The Yugoslav authorities (up to the German conquest in April 1941), beholden to the British, obliged.[65]

Romania, although an ally of Nazi Germany since mid-1941 and participating in horrific acts against Jews in territories conquered by its armed forces, such as in Bukovina and Transnistria, followed a kind of permissive policy toward Jewish emigrants passing through its territory.[66] Before the war, Revisionist leader Vladimir Jabotinsky was received by the Romanian king on two occasions. In these meetings, an agreement was reached regarding transit visas and assistance for Jews en route to Palestine.[67] Romania instructed its diplomats in Eastern and Central Europe to issue the necessary transit visas without unnecessary red tape. In January 1939 Wilhelm Perl in Vienna obtained transit documents for groups of up to 400 and 600 people from the Romanian consuls in Austria and Czechoslovakia, and the refugees were able to travel directly to Constanţa and embark on their sea voyage. The government also agreed to permit local Jewish aid organizations to help the refugees purchase provisions for the trip to Palestine (some of it with the help of bribery), much to the dismay of the British government. Illegal immigration (*Aliyah Bet*) in Romania was organized by two Mossad emissaries, Yosef Barpel and Ruth Klueger-Aliav.[68] The Romanian support of Jewish emigration produced a steady stream of refugees heading for Turkey before and during the war.

One ruse the Aliyah organizers employed to evade the Greek governmental ban on the use of Greek boats for illegal immigration was to transfer the boats to Panamanian, Uruguayan, and other such registries. The British countered by eliciting a promise from Balkan countries to forbid the use of a Panamanian flag. The British also asked Liberia and Paraguay to take disciplinary measures against certain of their diplomatic consuls who made a practice of issuing fictitious visas for Jewish refugees.[69] Aliyah Bet organizers were resigned to the expectation that the refugees and their boats would fall into British hands, but they were determined to continue sending Jewish refugees to Palestine.[70]

In the meantime more illegal boats were cruising the Mediterranean Sea trying to find a secret location on the Palestinian coast to discharge their human cargo without British detection. The *Hilda* began its voyage in October 1939, arrived in January 1940, and was seized by British warships off the coast of Istanbul and escorted to Haifa.[71] The Revisionists too were sending refugees on rickety boats. On the day the war broke out, they dispatched a number of ships from Romania. The *Tiger-Hill* arrived off the Tel Aviv shore with 1,400 Polish refugees. It was first held up in Romania under British pressure, but Ruth Klueger-Aliav succeeded in persuading the Romanian royalty to countermand the strict orders of the government and allow the boat to leave. The shots fired by the British at this boat as it approached Tel Aviv were the first shots fired by the British in the war. Three women and one man were killed. Other boats kept arriving, such as the *Zakaria*, whose passengers were detected and imprisoned in a detention camp in Palestine. Earlier, on November 20, 1940, to discourage refugees from trying to flee to Palestine, the British announced a new policy: from now on all who attempted to enter illegally would be deported to a British colony. But Jewish refugees disregarded this threat. There was nothing waiting for them in Nazi-occupied Europe except death. At least the British did not kill indiscriminately.[72]

With the German attack in the Balkans in April 1941, one British Foreign Ministry official sarcastically noted: "Now that the Germans are everywhere, the problem is solved by itself."[73] But the Germans still allowed Jews to leave if, of course, they had a place to go. It was only on October 23, 1941, that ss head Himmler made it official that Jewish emigration from all countries controlled by Germany was henceforth forbidden. The Nazis had switched to full extermination of the Jewish people throughout Europe, a campaign already begun in the east, on June 22, 1941, with the invasion of the Soviet Union. The German navy in the Black Sea was now ordered to prevent ships bearing Jews from heading to Turkey.[74]

The Struma *Tragedy*

This indirectly resulted in the *Struma* tragedy. It was a very old ship, under Greek ownership, and flying the Panamanian flag, and it originally served as a cattle barge on the Danube River. The engine failed as the boat limped toward the Turkish coast, and it was towed by a Turkish vessel to Istanbul and anchored in quarantine. Not one of the 781 passengers was allowed to go ashore. Repeated offers of bribe money failed to move the Turkish authorities. Sanitary conditions grew worse, and the ship's twenty doctors were busy round the clock. Moshe Shertok of the Jewish Agency and the Palestinian chief rabbis pleaded with the British to allow the passengers to proceed to Palestine and deduct their number from the immigration quota—but to no avail.

At the end of ten weeks, at dawn on February 23, 1942, the boat was towed from the harbor even though it had no provisions for a trip of any kind: no water, no food, no fuel, and no motor oil. There was suddenly a loud explosion and the boat sank 10 kilometers from shore—mistakenly sunk by a Soviet submarine. David Stoliar (later Ben-Yaakov) was the only passenger to survive.[75] As a result of the *Struma* sinking, on July 2, 1943, the British switched to a new policy: any Jewish refugee who reached a neutral country in transit would receive clearance for Palestine. In practice, by late 1943, the British reverted to the restrictions prescribed by the 1939 White Paper.[76]

The *Struma* disaster did not deter Jews from trying to leave via Romania, as long as the Romanians placed no obstacles, and the refugees were aided by various officials and bureaucrats, at times in return for payment. A small but steady trickle of Jewish refugees left on yachts and small vessels throughout 1942 without assistance from Jewish organizations. The boats evaded German naval patrols active off the Romanian and Bulgarian coasts.[77] Between March and August 1942 seven small boats left Romania carrying some 200 refugees. Exit permission was granted despite German opposition. But only two of the boats, *Mirchea* and *Michai*, survived the journey, as most were wrecked off the Turkish coast.[78] The British had all their passengers interned in Atlit, near Haifa.[79]

The Kladovo Incident

Another tragedy, different from that of the *Struma* but no less calamitous, that also could have been averted is known as the Kladovo incident. In November 1939, two months into the war, Mossad agent Ehud Avriel had organized a group of 1,000 Hechalutz members (mostly from Austria) and approximately 200 others from Germany. The plan was for them to travel by train to Bratislava, Slovakia, then head down the Danube River to the Black Sea and sail to Palestine. Avriel had obtained temporary visas for Slovakia with the aid of Storfer (and bribes paid to the Slovak consul in Vienna). The group stayed at a hotel awaiting word on the arrival of their ship in Sulina, Romania. Finally, Sime Spitzer of the Jewish Federation in Yugoslavia helped with getting three Yugoslavia riverboats to take the group to Sulina. But by the time these boats arrived to fetch the people, the Danube had frozen and the group was held up in the small Yugoslavian port of Kladovo.

Winter passed, then spring, and in early June 1940 a boat for them had been found. But on June 10, 1940, Italy entered the war, and this delayed their trip. Then another boat, the *Darien*, was placed at the disposal of the Mossad, and plans to bring out the Kladovo refugees went into high gear. However, members of the Palestinian Jewish Agency Political Department intervened, and in a heated debate with Aliyah activists Ruth Klueger-Aliav and Yehuda Braginsky, the Agency forced them to agree to sell the *Darien* to the British for a naval operation. When the *Darien* was again available and reappeared in Sulina, Romania, six months later, the Danube had again frozen, and the Kladovo people could not be moved. The *Darien*, instead, took on another group of refugees and departed. The Kladovo refugees were crushed, as they had to wait for spring 1941 to come. However, on April 6, 1941, the Germans invaded Yugoslavia, and the following month, the Kladovo group was interned.

A bit earlier, in March 1941, 111 children and 96 adults from the Kladovo group were allowed to proceed to Palestine under the Youth Aliyah framework. They traveled via Bulgaria, Turkey, and Syria. They were the sole survivors of the Kladovo group. They had left just in time, barely a month before the German onslaught on Yugoslavia that doomed the rest of the Kladovo group—over 900 victims. In October the men were all murdered by the Germans, and the women and children were gassed the next May. As for the *Darien*, it arrived in Istanbul harbor on March 2, 1941, with a different load of 789 refugees. On March 19 the ship was intercepted and captured by the British. The passengers were interned at Atlit for a year and a half before being released into Palestine.[80]

Late-War Illegal Ship Travel Attempts

In April 1943 Romania signaled that it would permit the remaining orphans from the occupied Transnistria region to leave. British Colonial

Secretary Oliver Stanley grew increasingly concerned at this and also at Bulgaria's readiness to release some Jewish children, and on April 14, 1943, he wrote to Foreign Secretary Anthony Eden and asked for his support to prevent the transfer of children from Bulgaria to Palestine. Eden assured Stanley that his ministry also expressed reservations about the Bulgarian offer.[81] Ultimately the British government succeeded in preventing any child from leaving.[82] That same year, the Romanians proposed that for a price they would permit the emigration of 70,000 Jews from the occupied Transnistria province. The refugees were to embark from the port of Constanța and head to Palestine. This naturally alarmed the British government, which scurried for ways to scuttle the idea. This time German pressure caused the plan's failure, as the German ambassador in Bucharest reminded the Romanians that emigration ran counter to the Nazi principle of a "comprehensive European solution of the Jewish problem"—in other words, extermination.[83]

Then, in mid-1944, Hungarian leader and Nazi ally Miklós Horthy announced that Jews with Palestine immigration certificates would be permitted to emigrate there or to other destinations. The British were alarmed about this because these would-be immigrants held immigration certificates for Palestine recognized by British authorities. Colonial Secretary Stanley painted before the British government a daunting picture of an inflated number of 800,000 to 1 million refugees clamoring to enter Palestine. How, he asked, could Britain expect to cope with that? (Stanley did not mention to his colleagues that by December 1942, about half of the Palestine immigration certificates allotted to Jews under the White Paper of 1939 had not yet been utilized; some 34,000 were still waiting to be filled.) But this time as on previous occasions, Germany, which controlled all geographical exits from Hungary, unwittingly came to Britain's assistance and vetoed the plan.[84]

Turkey: Chaim Barlas, Mossad, and Ira Hirschmann

This was a frustrating struggle to overcome both Turkey's ambivalent policy toward Jewish refugees and British pressure to keep this escape route closed.

Jewish communities have existed in modern Turkey since at least the fifth century BCE, as we know from the accounts of Flavius Josephus, the Jewish historian of the first CE century. The New Testament mentions Jewish synagogues in Anatolia, such as Iconium (today, Konya) and Ephesus. There was also a sizable synagogue in Sardis. The Byzantine Empire, which ruled from Constantinople (today, Istanbul), continued to tolerate the Jewish presence under certain restrictions, and Emperor Justinian's attempt to forcibly convert the Jews to Christianity met with no success. During the long period of the Turkish-Ottoman Empire that succeeded the Byzantines, the Turkish Empire seemed paradise to Jews compared with the persecutions in Christian Europe. In 1933, with Turkey transformed into a modern and secular state since the demise of the Ottoman Empire in 1918, its minister of education allowed for thirty-four Jewish scientists expelled from German academic institutions to be admitted into Turkish universities. That said, Turkey took an ambivalent and often negative position concerning Jewish refugees seeking safe passage through its territory.[85]

During the war, especially the period of 1943–44, Istanbul was a listening post and the information center concerning the fate of Jews under Nazi dominance. It was also chosen by Jewish rescue activists for a few reasons: Turkey's neutrality, its proximity to the Balkans, and the presence of envoys from European governments-in-exile and the Allies. All these contributed to Turkey as the ideal target for Aliyah Bet activities. At the same time, Turkey's self-declared neutrality in the war, which at times veered toward the German side and at other times submitted to pressure from the Allies, and its own harsh conditions for refugee passage through its territory complicated matters for the Zionist rescue agencies operating there, acting relentlessly to bring as many Jewish refugees to Palestine as possible.

In December 1942 Chaim Barlas represented the Jewish Agency in Istanbul. Also present in Istanbul were Venya Pomerantz-Hadari and Menachem Bader, both representing separate Kibbutz movements, while Zeev Shind represented the Mossad. Future Jerusalem mayor Teddy Kollek was there on behalf of the political department of the Jewish Agency. Also present were Joseph Klarman and Aryeh Altman for the Revisionists, David Zimend of the General Zionists, Akiva Levinsky of Youth Aliyah, and Jakob Griffel on behalf of the non-Zionist Agudath Israel. The different agendas of all these people complicated the work of rescue operations at times. Insofar as Turkey was concerned, only Barlas had the official standing as a Jewish Agency representative. All the others were there under the guise of private businessmen, merchandise purveyors, or newspapermen.[86]

Transport without Permits

In 1943 Mossad operative Zeev Shind and his colleagues decided to arrange a transport without official permits. Searching for an available older vessel, he located the *Maritsa*, a Turkish freighter that could be refitted to carry about 250 people, and in April 1944 it set sail from Bulgaria to Turkey. Shind followed this up with other boats, such as the *Milca*, *Bela-Chita*, *Salah-a-Din*, and *Taurus*. That year other Mossad-acquired small vessels brought refugees to Turkish shores. This led the British in December 1944 to inform the Turkish government that it was no longer prepared to guarantee entry to Palestine to every refugee coming there via Turkey—a reversal from a previous position following the *Struma* disaster.[87]

On the night of August 3, 1944, three Turkish ships, *Bulbul*, *Morina*, and *Mefkura*, departed from the Romanian port of Constanța. Organized by Mossad agents in Turkey in conjunction with the Zionist organization in Romania, the vessels were carrying about 1,000 Jews destined for Palestine. The *Mefkura* was fired upon by either a Soviet or German submarine, and most of the passengers drowned; only 5 of the 320 victims were rescued by the *Bulbul*. The *Bulbul* and *Morina* passengers then were allowed by the British to enter Palestine, where they arrived by overland routes via Turkey and Syria.[88]

British Change of Policy

After leaving Vienna, Ehud Avriel became a Mossad agent in Istanbul under the cover of a newspaper correspondent. Arriving in August 1943, he headed straight to a flat that was shared by Zeev Shind and Teddy Kollek.[89] Kollek and Shind worked closely with Major Arthur Whittal of the British Secret Service. Whittal, against the policy of his superiors, proved to be very helpful to the Mossad. As mentioned above, following the *Struma* disaster, the British advised its embassy in Ankara that henceforth all Jews who reached the Turkish shores under their own steam (not via organizations such as the Mossad) were to be issued a visa to Palestine, but news of this was to be kept confidential in order to prevent a stampede of refugees. Whittal, in a private conversation with Avriel and Shind, disclosed to them the good news; in his words, "I have here the second Balfour declaration that could perhaps save the lives of several people," adding that his superiors "will no doubt kill me if they know that I have communicated this to you." His motivation? "Because first of all I am a Christian, and as a Christian I am interested in doing something to save people. Then I am a British spy, and I believe that it is a formidable mistake on the part of my political colleagues to prevent the emigration. . . . Instead of preventing them, I want you to let them leave and come to Turkey. You deliver them to me, I examine them, I ask them questions about the moral, political, and military situation in the Nazi-occupied countries, and then they can according to this secret directive be able to leave for Palestine."[90] It goes without saying that to cover his tracks, Major Whittal asked for full discretion on the Mossad's part.

Moshe Agami, also in Istanbul, left the same evening for Izmir, also in Turkey, to speak with Mossad friends from the Greek underground and to encourage them to send the people from the occupied Greek mainland to Turkey. Publicity had to be avoided, and it was feared that the Turks had not yet been told of the British change of policy. Large groups of Jews from Athens and southern Greece began arriving secretly in very small fishing boats in cooperation with the Greek underground.[91] Rafael Baki, head of the Jewish community in Izmir, secretly provided the refugees with medicine, and with the assistance of his brother in Athens, cabs were hired to transport small groups from Athens to the coast of Euboea, from where they were taken to Turkey and then Palestine.[92] At first the Turkish foreign minister objected, but later changed his mind, and allowed the new arrivals to disembark, but on condition that they proceed immediately by train to Syria on their way to Palestine.[93]

Ira Hirschmann

> Through his negotiating skills he coaxed Turkey to stop
> hindering emigration passage and got Romania and Bulgaria
> to ease the flight of Jews out of their countries

Ira Hirschmann arrived in Turkey on February 14, 1944, as a special envoy of the War Refugee Board, created by President Roosevelt in response to intensive public pressure by various political figures and especially by the Bergson-Hecht group (see chapter 14). The Board's purpose was to help Jews escape the Nazis' dragnet with the assistances of U.S. diplomats and representatives of neutral countries. A former businessman and currently a Bloomingdale department store executive, Hirschmann had attended the dismal Evian conference in July 1938 as part of the U.S. team, and he was later active in the Bergson-Hecht group. His stay in Turkey was initially for six weeks—from February 26 to April 8, 1944—and then from June to September.[94]

As the U.S. government-approved War Refugee Board representative, Hirschmann enjoyed diplomatic status and was authorized to meet with diplomatic counterparts of enemy countries. He met with Alexander Cretzianu, the Romanian envoy to Turkey, on March 11, 1944, and again a week later. Hirschmann told him that he would not get involved in political matters with a country still allied to Nazi Germany, as per instructions by the State Department, only in matters concerning Jewish refugees. This was especially true in matters concerning the 5,000 orphans and other survivors from Transnistria (the area inside Ukraine that had been annexed by Romania but was in the process of being liberated by the Red Army), who had already been transferred back to Romania proper. Cretzianu read Hirschmann a cable sent by Romanian dictator Marshal Ion Antonescu, in which he promised to release the Jews in Transnistria and transfer them to Constanța, in groups arranged per Hirschmann's stipulations. Hirschmann was overjoyed, as some 48,000 persons had already been moved out of Transnistria back into Romania.[95] The Bulgarian envoy, A. Balabanov, representing another Axis country, was also interested in extricating his country from the German embrace. Here, too, Hirschmann made it clear that Bulgaria had to guarantee the safety of its Jewish population.

Hirschmann also succeeded in persuading U.S. ambassador to Turkey Laurence Steinhardt (a Jew) to change his opposition to illegal immigration by way of Turkey, and they both began to intervene with the Turkish government to permit the refugees to land even without valid documents since, as they argued, it was unthinkable that they should be forced back to Nazi-held territory after having escaped from there.[96] Hirschmann felt that Turkish delaying tactics to granting transit visas had played a significant role in halting the emigration of Jews to Palestine. In his eyes, it was intolerable that processing a transit visa took fourteen to seventeen weeks, during which time the applicants often lost the chance to emigrate, despite having valid immigration certificates for Palestine. And then there was the Turkish policy of allowing only nine Jewish families per week to pass through the country to Palestine, and newcomers had to be out of Turkish territory within twenty-four hours.[97]

From Jewish Agency representative Chaim Barlas, Ira Hirschmann learned that a number of Turkish boats might be suitable for refugee travel, but only with the approval of the Turkish government. He decided to take up the challenge of persuading the Turks to change their position—through Steinhardt. Turkey's foreign minister rejected the request for a group of three boats, instead offering a better passenger vessel, the *Tari*, with conditions: A safe-conduct guarantee had to be obtained from Germany, and the United States had to give its commitment to replace the *Tari* with a ship of similar specification should the *Tari* come to any harm. Both the U.S. and British navies objected to the replacement guarantee. A lengthy and heated correspondence evolved between Hirschmann, Steinhardt, and the War Refugee Board heads, on the one hand, and the Joint Distribution Committee and the Anglo-American naval command in the Mediterranean, on the other.

After long weeks of negotiations, an agreement was finally reached. The Red Cross and Jewish organizations in Romania were to prepare groups of refugees for the trip. In late March and early April 1944 it appeared that the voyage would take place within a few days, but the Germans refused to give a safe-conduct guarantee, and that eventually scuttled the whole deal. When the German consent failed to arrive, Hirschmann turned to Monsignor Angelo Roncalli, the Vatican's apostolic delegate in Turkey, to intercede, but despite his good intentions, he too was stymied.[98] In spite of this failure, Dalia Ofer summarizes Hirschmann's first six-week stint in Turkey as "dynamic, possessed of momentum, and crowned with [some!] success."[99]

Hirschmann returned to Istanbul in mid-June after a two-month hiatus in the United States. He succeeded in removing the Bulgarian ban on transport of refugees aboard boats flying the Bulgarian flag.[100] Romania's surrender to the Soviets in August 23, 1944, and the entry of Soviet forces into Bulgaria the next month altered the Jewish situation. The peril hanging over the Jewish communities in these two former German-allied countries had finally been removed.

In closing, refugee figures of those who either made it or attempted to make their voyage to Palestine are not precise, and historians differ on the numbers. But it is assumed that from 1938 until the end of the war, over 40,000 Jews reached Palestine and 17,240 of these were illegals. Those who immigrated legally still had to brave difficulties and risky voyages, and here too, help from Jewish rescue emissaries proved crucial. The Revisionists and private individuals were responsible for the transport of some 12,000 illegals, and Hechalutz and the Mossad for some 5,500. To these must be added an untold number of illegal refugees that reached Palestine in an earlier period—from the start of the Nazi takeover in 1933 until 1938.[101] German and Austrian Jews constituted more than 70 percent of all illegal immigrants.[102]

The rescue of these thousands of Jews would not have been possible without the direct assistance of Jewish rescuers such as Berthold Storfer, Ehud Avriel, Wilhelm Perl, and Baruch Confino, who at times had to brave dangers to themselves in their negotiations with Nazi authorities and collaborating governments. They also had to fend off attempts by the British to close escape routes and the capture and internment of those who succeeded in reaching safe haven. Initially (up to the first two years of the war) the Nazis—the villains in this story—were eager to let the Jews go, and they collaborated with various Jewish escape agencies to make this possible, while the British—the good guys—begrudged any attempts in that direction and took steps to keep the escape routes closed, even as Jews frantically sought to escape as the Nazis switched to a policy of mass extermination. Jewish rescue activists had to brave these difficulties in this unbelievable situation, and with a combination of courage, guts, determination, and self-acquired negotiating skills, they succeeded in saving thousands of fleeing Jews.

11 Switzerland

Outstretched Hands from Nearby

Jews settled in Switzerland during the Middle Ages, but in small numbers. Before the modern period, the small population suffered various discriminations in the Swiss cantons, such as the call of the mayor of Zürich in 1634 "to drive the useless, godless swarm of Jews out of the city and its territory with hue and cry." They were not admitted into guilds, and they were excluded from all artisan occupations. Even as late as 1787, the mayor of Bern issued a strict prohibition against trade by Jews.[1] It was not until 1866 that Jews received full political rights. On the eve of World War II, the Jewish population numbered only 18,000 (0.4 percent of a population of 4 million) and were organized in the Federation of Swiss Jewish Communities (Schweizerischer Israelitischer Gemeindebund, SIG), headed by Saly Mayer, who also represented the Jewish Joint Distribution Committee (JDC-Joint).[2] Since the end of the Napoleonic Wars in 1815, Switzerland was recognized as being permanently neutral in future conflicts, and it avoided being involved in any confrontation with other countries.

Historically Switzerland has a long record of affording hospitality to people fleeing persecution, but it was different when it came to Jews fleeing persecution by the Nazis, especially after Austria's annexation to Germany. No entry was allowed to them on the excuse that they were persecuted not because of their beliefs (such as political or religious), for which asylum was permitted, but because of their race as defined by the Nazi regime—not recognizable by the Swiss as justification for admittance. Of the 300,000 foreigners who passed through Switzerland during the Nazi period (1933–45), only 30,000 were Jews. To endear itself to Nazi Germany, Switzerland refused to host the conference that President Roosevelt called in the summer of 1938 to deal with Jewish refugees; it was moved to Evian-les-Bains in France.

To add insult to injury, the chief of the Swiss Alien Police, Heinrich Rothmund, acquiesced to the German proposal that Jewish passports be marked with a special sign so that they could not enter the country as tourists (who did not require a visa). This came into force on October 5, 1938, with all Jews having a capital *J* stamped in red on their passports. Antisemitism in the country did make a certain comeback during the triumphant days of Nazi Germany. In 1942 arriving refugees were sent to labor camps in Switzerland, while the entry of refugees from France was banned altogether, and those trying to sneak in were expelled on the spot, known by the malicious term of *refoulement,* except for unaccompanied children under sixteen, pregnant women, the ill, and people over sixty-five.[3] Still, several thousand did succeed in making it in, especially in 1943. In September of that year, with Italy's capitulation to the Allies, some 20,000 Italians who crossed the Swiss border (10,000 of them partisans) included several thousand Jews. In 1944, 1,684 Hungarian Jews arrived from Bergen-Belsen, and in 1945, 1,200 Jews came from Theresienstadt, as a result of negotiations with ss head Heinrich Himmler. The JDC looked after incoming Jewish refugees by giving them room and board.

Despite its harsh anti-Jewish refugee policy, Switzerland allowed Zionist organizations to operate from its soil. Some acted as listening posts to gather information on the fate of the Jews in German-dominated countries. Gerhart Riegner of the World Jewish Congress stunned leaders in the United States in August 1942 with his secret message, based on a reliable German source, that the German government intended to exterminate all of Europe's Jews as quickly as possible with the use of prussic acid.[4]

George Mandel-Mantello

Through his friendship with the consul-general of El
Salvador in Switzerland, he was able to give false Salvadoran
citizenship papers to Hungarian Jews who had never
set foot in that country, saving thousands of lives.

George Mandel-Mantello was born György Mandl in 1901 into a Jewish Orthodox family in Lekence, Transylvania, then part of the Austro-

Hungarian Empire.[5] On the eve of World War II, George and his brother, Josef, owned a prosperous textile manufacturing business in partnership with several highly placed non-Jewish Romanian army officers.[6] It was a stroke of good luck that in 1939 he befriended Colonel José Arturo Castellanos, the consul-general of El Salvador in Switzerland, whom Mandl had helped with some business transactions. In return, Castellanos appointed Mandl as El Salvador's honorary consul for Hungary, Romania, and Czechoslovakia, which included Salvadoran citizenship and reportedly a Salvadoran diplomatic passport.[7] It was at that time that he changed his name from Mandl to Mandel-Mantello and he usually went by Mantello, which was more fitting for a Latin American representative. Mantello, however, was an unusual Salvadoran, as he spoke no Spanish.[8]

When the United States entered the war in December 1941, and a month later the Central American and South American countries broke diplomatic relations with Romania, Mantello and other diplomats were forced to leave the country. Mantello left for Portugal, but when passing through Croatia, he was removed from the train by the Gestapo and arrested. With the help of the Swiss consulate, he was released and left on a plane headed for Bucharest, passing as the plane's co-pilot. From there he continued to Geneva, wearing the uniform of a Romanian army officer named Captain Vasilescu. At the time, Switzerland had taken over the protection of most Latin American consuls in Axis lands, including El Salvador, and Mantello as a Salvadoran citizen therefore came under Swiss protection.[9] Castellanos appointed Mantello first secretary of the El Salvador consulate in Geneva. Now he was a fully accredited diplomat.[10]

From 1932 to 1944 El Salvador was ruled by a military president/dictator, General Maximiliano Hernández Martínez, a man with clear Fascist sympathies who maintained cordial relations with the Axis powers.[11] At the same time, Martínez could not disregard the leverage of the United States, and shortly after the Japanese attack on Pearl Harbor, he broke relations with the Axis powers, which included Romania, Mantello's home country.[12]

Failed Scheme to Protect Jews' Property

Soon after his arrival in Geneva, George Mandel-Mantello organized the Association of Swiss Rabbis (Schweizer Rabbinerverband) as a lobbying organization, headed by Rabbi Dr. Zvi Taubes.[13] Mantello presented before them the idea of rescuing the property held by Jews under German occupation by forming a trust association, whereby Jews everywhere in Europe could guarantee their property by transferring it to this trust fund, located in Switzerland.[14] Mantello offered 500,000 Swiss francs as a down payment to initiate the fund, an amount that would only be paid back to him one year after the end of the war. He stated he wished to have no controlling position in that proposed trust fund. He followed this up by inviting leading Jewish circles to a meeting on May 18, 1943, in Bern. But other Jewish organizations in Switzerland opposed this trust fund because they viewed Mantello as an upstart and a Johnny-come-lately in rescue affairs.[15]

Switzerland, a Hub of Major Jewish Organizations

Zionist and non-Zionist alike had representatives there, with many of them working at cross purposes.[16] Some placed the emphasis on finding ways for Jews to reach Palestine, in spite of British obstructions. Others were active in trying to help Jews in ghettos and concentration camps with food parcels. All served as listening posts for news on the fate of their brethren across the border. The Zionists were represented by the Palestine Certificate Office, called Palestina Amt; also active there was the Jewish Agency and the youth pioneering Hechalutz movement. The non-Zionists had the World Jewish Congress and the Joint Distribution Committee (JDC).[17] The JDC was the most influential because of its financial support, and it was mistakenly viewed by the Nazis as the center of the world Jewish financial power. There was also the Jewish Labor Committee (Dr. Emanuel Sherer), which maintained strong connections with the Jewish Bund in Poland,[18] the religious Agudath Israel, the U.S.-based Vaad Hatzalah, and the HIJEFS relief agency, caring for religious Jews stranded in Shanghai and headed by Recha and Yitzhak Sternbuch and his brother, Elias Sternbuch.[19]

These organizations did not always work in unison. They were beset by deep-seated ideological and internecine rivalries that divided them into antagonistic camps.[20] Mantello was viewed as an unrecognizable newcomer and a "lone ranger" type, not part of the mainline organizations. He was an antiestablishment Jew, accused of the grave "affront" of solely representing himself and with the audacity of his own novel ideas on how to promote more effective rescue efforts of Jews in German-dominated

Europe.[21] Yet he maintained his independent course as long as he felt he could contribute to the rescue of fellow Jews.

Some of these representatives dealt in Latin American diplomatic papers, distributed in return for stiff payments. In fact, a thriving black market had developed among some Latin American diplomats who sought to cash in on the misery of the Jews. The Germans were not opposed to this, for they considered it a possible basis for the exchange of German nationals in certain South American countries, such as Paraguay.[22] The Paraguay consul in Switzerland was the first to sell passports, and hundreds of Jews in occupied Poland held such passports.[23] Once the Germans learned of Paraguay's refusal to recognize them, it withdrew its recognition of these papers, with tragic consequences for a large group of Jews (mostly from Poland) interned by the Germans in the Vittel camp in France.[24]

Citizen Papers Became Lifesavers

Mantello then came up with a different and, in his view, a better way to save endangered Jews in large numbers: not diplomatic passports but citizenship papers issued by the Salvadoran government. His diplomatic superior, José Castellanos, and the former (and future) World Court president, Dr. José Gustavo Guerrero, then residing in Switzerland, both supported the idea, and it was later approved by the Salvadoran government.[25] In 1943 Mantello opened at his own expense a special office dedicated to this job, and it produced several thousand sets of Salvadoran citizenship papers, which were smuggled to their destinations. These papers turned European Jews into Salvadoran citizens. The papers were literally lifesavers, since they were honored by the German authorities due to a generally held assumption that it would constitute a basis for exacting a future exchange of German citizens living in Latin America. There are not even approximate estimates, but it is generally assumed that these 10,000 documents saved between 20,000 and 30,000 Jews.[26]

The efficacy of the papers varied greatly; in some countries, particularly Belgium, Hungary, and the Netherlands, the certificates saved significant numbers. Tragically, in other countries, such as Poland and Lithuania, the Germans ignored them and treated the bearers as they did all other Jews. Most recipients had no idea who Mantello was and never contacted him directly; they believed that the certificate had been obtained through the efforts of relatives and friends in Latin America.[27] To help him with this onerous work, Mantello hired Mathieu-Meir Muller, a French Jewish lawyer, and a small group of college students.[28] The Salvadoran government only belatedly, on September 12, 1943, gave its approval to this vast rescue project initiated by Mantello and approved by ambassador Castellanos.[29]

The Salvadoran citizenship papers were sent by couriers to various countries under German occupation.[30] Unfortunately, some of the intended recipients had already been murdered, as was the case of Rabbi Abraham Bloch, one of the administrators of the Telz rabbinic yeshiva, whose Salvadoran certificate was dated December 16, 1943, but who was shot by Lithuanian collaborators on July 15, 1941.[31] As for Belgium, of the 137 Jews who received certificates, only 12 were deported.[32] Jonas Tiefenbrunner, one of those Belgian beneficiaries, wrote after the war: "These papers were very useful because the holders of these papers were covered and could not officially be deported. If they were taken in a roundup while holding Salvadoran papers, they could only be interned as enemy aliens. . . . Anyone who was still in Belgium when they received the papers was saved."[33] Several certificate recipients had already been interned in the Bergen-Belsen camp, such as Julius and Felicia Joseph and their two sons, who were released by the Germans on January 19, 1945, and allowed to proceed to Switzerland.[34]

But it was in Hungary, especially in Budapest, that the Salvadoran certificates saved the greatest number of people. As soon as he learned of the German occupation of Hungary in March 1944, Mantello created the Swiss Assistance Committee for Hungarian Jewry, headed by Mihály Bányai and other public figures.[35] This committee held meetings on March 27 and 28, with the participation of representatives of several other Jewish organizations, where it was decided to address a request to the Vatican nuncio, Monsignor Phillipe Bernardini, to alert the pope of the situation in Hungary. The sympathetic nuncio promised indeed to relay the information to the Vatican.[36] Mantello then issued thousands of Salvadoran citizenship papers for the benefit of Jews in that country. An average of 250 to 300 signed Salvadoran papers were dispatched weekly to Budapest by several trustworthy couriers, including diplomatic attachés from Turkey and Portugal, the Czech diplomatic representative in Switzerland, and Bernardini, and soon some 10,000 Salvadoran citizenship papers were in the hands of Hungarian Jews.[37]

Paradoxically, there was not a single "real" Salvadoran citizen in Budapest.[38] Zionist activist Joel Brand in Hungary recalled: "We sent a courier [in 1943] to see Mantello, and he declared himself ready to give us hundreds of passports [really, citizenship papers], all duly stamped and signed. We only had to supply him with the names. . . . Salvador's colony of nationals in Budapest increased enormously at this time [in 1944]—its numbers exceeded those of all foreign groups put together."[39] Paradoxically, since Salvadoran citizens were considered enemy aliens who were not allowed to leave Hungary, they also could not be deported and could obtain Swiss protection for enemy aliens, in contrast to other Jews whose Hungarian citizenship exposed them to deportation to the death camps by the Hungarian authorities, who worked in collusion with Eichmann's ss team.[40]

Swiss government recognition of Mantello's irregular documents was essential in order for the Swiss officials in Budapest to protect their holders, but at first Swiss officials demurred. They objected to the fact that thousands of what they considered illegal papers had been issued earlier by Mantello, before their approval, and the notion of granting them retroactive recognition went against their legalistic grain.[41] It is reported that soon after arriving in Budapest on July 8, 1944, Swedish diplomat Raoul Wallenberg received a phone call from Mantello, who asked him to assume the protection of holders of the Salvadoran papers temporarily, as negotiations with the Swiss government had not yet borne fruit. Wallenberg quickly accepted this additional charge, relinquishing it only after the Swiss finally took over.[42] By September 25, 1944, Swiss diplomat in Budapest Charles Lutz confirmed to Mantello that his government had formally approved recognition of the Salvadoran papers, yet official recognition would not be forthcoming for more than two months, by which time the recipients of the Salvadoran documents would receive an additional document stating that the bearer was a bona fide Salvadoran citizen subject to Swiss protection.[43]

In a long letter by Lutz to Mantello on October 28, 1944, he wrote:

The San [really, El] Salvador certificates have already saved thousands of lives. . . . In the [Obuda] tile factory . . . we always came across S[alvador] certificate holders, for whom we were able to obtain freedom because of these papers. . . . You can take satisfaction in the fact that . . . it was your management of San Salvadoran interests which has enabled us to create a humanitarian work that will bring you the thanks of thousands of rescue people . . . of thousands of human beings whose lives you saved. . . . It must be clearly established that San Salvador is the only state to overcome any hesitancy and to undertake an active rescue operation.[44]

Exposing Auschwitz: Hungary's Complicity

Lutz's help also came in handy in another context, and it has to do with the role of Dr. Florian Manoliu, who led Mantello to launch a widespread publicity campaign in order to force the Hungarian regime to stop delivering Jews to the Auschwitz gas chambers. Months earlier, before the German invasion of Hungary, Mantello had provided his wife with a regular Salvador passport that had since expired, and Mantello now wanted to bring her an updated one.[45] It was also crucial to get Salvadoran papers to Mantello's parents, living in Beszterce (Bistriţa), Transylvania, to prevent their deportation. For this mission Mantello chose Manoliu, the commercial attaché at the Romanian consulate in Bern (who strongly disagreed with his government's alliance with Nazi Germany) and a former business partner of Mantello's brother, Josef Mandl.[46] Mantello armed Manoliu with 1,000 stamped Salvadoran citizenship papers with names to be inserted later (so as to avoid losing precious time by asking for photos and filling in the information, then sending the documents back to Hungary), for delivery to Swiss envoy Charles Lutz in Budapest. Mantello also gave him an undisclosed sum of money and a supply of medication for his parents and other Jews, for whom he prepared 100 Salvadoran protective papers.[47] On or about June 3, Manoliu arrived in Bucharest. Crossing into Hungarian territory he headed to Beszterce to contact Mantello's parents, only to discover that the town's Jews had all been deported four days earlier.[48]

Manoliu continued to Budapest, where he turned over most of the Salvadoran papers to Lutz. Lutz took Manoliu to Miklosz-Moshe Krausz, who dealt with persons holding or being given Palestine immigration certificates.[49] Manoliu suggested that Krausz write a summary of a report that detailed the ghettoization and deportation of Hungarian Jews, town by town, to Auschwitz.[50] Krausz's June 19 report was addressed to Dr. Chaim Pozner, the Jewish Agency representative stationed in Geneva, and it read in part:

335,000 Jews have been deported up to June 7. . . . In the provinces, there are only four towns left that still have Jews. . . . It will soon be Budapest's turn. . . . There is no possibility of hiding. . . . We do not even have the chance of escaping to a neighboring country.. . . . There are only two possibilities left to us: suicide or the acceptance of our fate. . . . I don't know if I shall have the occasion to write to you again. But I will be satisfied when you now or later make public my words and report so that the world will be made aware of these 20th-century horrors. . . . We are sure that the Americans and the English will help. Help! Help! Help![51]

That very night of Manoliu's return, on June 21, 1944, Mantello and his brother set to work on a campaign to force the world to listen. Hungarian university students were hired to prepare translations and multiple copies of the reports of Auschwitz camp and events emanating from Hungary. That evening George Mantello also summoned the members of the Association of Swiss Rabbis and the Banyai Committee for an emergency meeting the next morning, at which he presented the summarized Auschwitz Protocol and the accompanying Krausz letter.[52] On June 22 Mantello met with Commodore Freddie West, a military attaché and high-ranking member of British intelligence, who agreed to urge Walter Garrett, director of the British Exchange Telegraph, to prepare a press release.[53] Together with West, Mantello went to see the oss (Office of Strategic Services, forerunner of the cia) chief, Allen Dulles. Dulles immediately sent to U.S. Secretary of State Cordell Hull four long cables in which Garrett condensed the reports from Auschwitz and Hungary.[54]

Next came a meeting with Mantello's friend Pastor Paul Vogt of Zürich, head of the Fluchtlingshilfe (assistance to refugees reaching Switzerland), and Pastor Hans Schaffert, secretary of the Swiss Protestant Council. Vogt came to the forefront of the campaign within the influential Swiss Protestant Church to awaken not only the Swiss but also the free world to the plight of the Jews.[55]

The press campaign, launched by Mantello, was carried by more than 180 Swiss newspapers. It also spanned the full political spectrum, from the Socialist left to the ultraconservative, usually Catholic right. In more than 470 articles, the Swiss press attacked the Third Reich, its brutal policies toward Jews, the monstrosities of Auschwitz, and the complicity of the Hungarians. Hundreds of articles appeared throughout late June and the whole month of July. Many of these were front-page articles, revealing the gruesome facts of Auschwitz.[56] On June 16, 1944, the Hungarian chargé d'affaires in Bern, Imre Tahy, in a cable to the Hungarian head of state, Horthy, wrote: "These reports have caused a great sensation and great scandal within [Protestant] relief organizations in Switzerland. According to press reports, the Hungarian authorities are responsible for the atrocities committed. It is feared that anti-Hungarian feelings will develop in neutral countries."[57]

The first reaction from the publicity of the Auschwitz protocols was an open letter by Pope Pius XII to Horthy on June 25, asking for a moderation of the anti-Jewish measures. This was followed the next day by a strongly worded warning to Horthy by Franklin D. Roosevelt, threatening dire consequences for Hungary after the war if the deportations were not stopped. A week later, on July 2, 1944, Budapest was subjected to a heavy American air raid, which Horthy interpreted as a result of American displeasure. Sweden's King Gustav V also sent an appeal to Horthy, followed by the dispatch of Raoul Wallenberg on June 30 to Budapest. All this pressure led Horthy to inform his ministers that he had decided to stop any further deportations, which in the meantime had gobbled up most of Hungarian Jewry except for those in the Budapest region.[58]

Historian David Kranzler is convinced that Mantello's press campaign was a catalyst for pushing Hungary to decide on July 7, 1944, to halt the deportation process, which momentarily saved the Budapest Jews.[59] After the war Swiss diplomat Lutz recalled the consternation caused by the Swiss press campaign: "I myself have seen the red-lines articles from the Swiss press in the German embassy. . . . As a matter of fact, under the pressure of this campaign, the deportations were really stopped. Roosevelt's note [to Horthy] was also inspired by this press campaign. It was a combination of the Swiss press campaign and Roosevelt's note that caused things to change in Budapest."[60] Earlier, on July 20, 1944, Lutz wrote to Mantello:

You stand out as the "spiritus rectus" behind the press campaign in Switzerland, which has brought to the public at large information concerning . . . [the] distress of the Jewish population of Budapest. . . . The reaction, as expected, was very strong. . . . The immediate effect has been the suspension of the deportations. . . . It can be said that thanks to your campaign, the imminent catastrophe was greatly reduced."[61]

Accusations and Vindications

A serious distraction to George Mandel-Mantello's rescue concerns of fellow Jews were the accusations, nasty swipes, and false rumors spread by some Jewish organizations who in their jealousy of Mantello's efforts urged the Swiss authorities to closely supervise Mantello's issuing of documents in such great numbers on supposedly false premises. Ambassador Castellanos was called in for a discussion in Bern on the delivery of fictitious Salvadoran documents to people who in truth were citizens of other countries. Some Jewish community activists denounced Mantello to the Swiss government, charging him with profiteering from the "sale" of Salvadoran papers, as a result of which the Swiss detained him for sixteen days in May 1944.[62] Heinrich Rothmund, head of the Swiss Alien Police, sought to annul Mantello's diplomatic credentials even after the official Swiss recognition of the Salvadoran papers.[63]

These accusations continued to haunt Mantello even after the end of the war. He was also accused of bringing his son Enrico illegally from Budapest into Switzerland without a Swiss entry visa. This led Mantello, on September 25, 1945, to send a letter to the Federation of Swiss Jewish Communities (SIG) requesting a panel of judges to oversee a public inquiry, so as to clear his name once and for all. SIG complied and appointed three highly qualified Swiss Jewish personalities to serve on the panel.[64]

The panel concluded its hearings on June 27, 1946. It not only cleared Mantello completely of even the slightest wrongdoing but it even complimented him on his work. It stated that when Mantello learned that Jews in German-occupied countries had to pay anywhere from 500 to 3,000 Swiss francs for a Latin American visa,

he successfully persuaded the Consul General of the El Salvador Consulate . . . [to issue] Salvador citizenship papers . . . sent to Holland, Belgium, France, Poland, and Czechoslovakia, even to some in Germany, [that] averaged about fifty a month, [that] rapidly increased to hundreds, and eventually even more. [In Hungary,] holders [who] were Salvadoran citizens . . . were under the protection of the Swiss embassy. . . . By August 1944, the local representative was instructed to give protection to 5,000 holders of these papers. . . . In Hungary, a vast number were rescued, thanks to these citizenship papers . . . solely for the purpose of assisting his endangered coreligionists in a totally selfless manner.[65]

World Jewish Congress representative Gerhart Riegner also admitted to his colleague Leon Kubowitzky: "There is no doubt that he [Mantello] has sent several thousand nationality papers and that he has saved many Jews in doing so. . . . It also seems to be a fact that Mantello sacrificed much money of his own for this purpose."[66] Many letters of thanks and appreciation by community leaders and private individuals landed on Mantello's desk, such as the letter by M. C. Levy-Walich and Germaine Grumsinger on October 16, 1945, on behalf of the Jewish Community of Geneva:

Now that all of the refugees who had been in our country are going back to their own homelands, we are eager to express in this letter our deep appreciation of the great kindness and the spirit of humanity that you have shown to thousands of human beings. . . . Indeed, our unfortunate coreligionists who owe their lives to you number in the thousands. Appeals came to you from every country, . . . and to each and every one you responded by sending Salvadoran citizenship papers, using the Jewish organizations and the Swiss Federal Political Department as intermediaries. Thanks to these citizenship papers, thousands of men, women, and children . . . of all nationalities escaped a horrible death in the Nazi extermination camps. . . . We can, however, bear witness to the fact that your help was entirely without personal motive. Not only have you declined to accept any reimbursement for the innumerable papers you sent to us, but, in your lifesaving mission, you have also spent considerable sums of your own money. [Signed] On behalf of the Jewish Community of Geneva.[67]

Sadly Rothmund of the Swiss Alien Police continued to hound George Mandel-Mantello, even after his name had been cleared and to harass him for several more years—to the point when Switzerland was even ready for a time to deprive him of his right of residence and to expel him from the country.[68] Finally, in 1948, Rothmund gave up his pursuit of Mantello.[69] In 1950, Mantello went into partnership with the Israeli government in establishing the Swiss-Israel Bank. He also sent provisions to Israel worth $1 million and financed 500 apartments in Hadar Joseph for the housing of disabled persons. In 1956 Mantello moved to Rome and passed away there in 1992.[70]

Recha and Yitzhak Sternbuch

Feisty and determined, the Sternbuchs worked tirelessly to save over 1,000 Jews in various ways and at some risk to their freedom and safety.

Recha Rottenberg was born in 1905 in Antwerp, Belgium, the fifth of Chief Rabbi Mordechai Rottenberg's nine children. After marrying Yitzhak Sternbuch, Recha lived in Switzerland, first in St. Gallen and later in Montreux.[71] Yitzhak's father, Naftali Sternbuch, was the scion of the Chortkower Hasidic sect in Czernowitz, Bukovina, and had settled in Basel, Switzerland.

Recha's rescue work began with Austrian Jews who were summarily expelled from the Burgenland province of Austria (known as the Seven Communities—Sheva Kehillos), soon after Austria's takeover by Germany in March 1938.[72] Many tried to cross into Switzerland, which at that time still had open borders with Germany. Via Recha's contacts in Vienna, she gave them instructions on which routes to take, and she established links with farmers, truckers, taxi drivers, and policemen who would bring the refugees across certain designated places along the border and across into the St. Gallen sector of the Swiss-Austrian border. Once across, the refugees were hidden in camouflaged vehicles, taken to the Sternbuch house, afforded a change of clothing, and with the help of the friendly regional police chief Paul Grüninger, they received legal refugee status. Herself very religious, Recha helped every Jew, observant or not, as she believed that the religious obligation of saving a life (*Pikuach nefesh*) overrode all other considerations.[73]

Saving Jews at Gunpoint

One quiet winter night, the telephone rang. It was Recha's contact man, informing her that a group of Jews had tried to enter Switzerland but were about to be sent back to Germany by the Swiss Gendarmerie, and they were now in the hands of the Gestapo. Recha rushed to the Swiss-German border by motorcycle. There she heard warning shots. She had gone too far—into no-man's-land, and she was blinded by dazzling light. A German uniformed man appeared, accompanied by barking dogs. Not dismayed, Recha told him: "I want to talk to your chief. I have an important matter. Please announce me." They led her to the border house where the hapless Jews were being held.[74] She was asked: "What do you want?" She responded: "I am Swiss. These Jews came upon my initiative. I am responsible for them. I would like to ask you to turn them over to me. I am taking them into Switzerland."

The officer's eyes reddened with fury as he shouted back: "I'll send you away with these dirty Jews! You cursed Jewish woman! I'll rip up your Swiss passport if you don't disappear from here this minute!" Recha stood her ground, and there was a fearful silence. Then: "Take your twelve Jews and be gone immediately," he shouted; "but at once! Otherwise, I'll change my mind." Undauntingly, she had saved twelve Jews literally at gunpoint, for whom she later arranged a temporary stay in Switzerland.[75]

In another story, in their Montreux home, it was a Saturday morning, and the Sternbuchs' son was about to celebrate his bar mitzvah when suddenly the police swept into the nearby Etz Chaim yeshiva to arrest three young men who had entered the country illegally. Recha's husband, Yitzchak, dropped everything and went to police headquarters while Recha began making telephone calls. The young men had been taken to a military base in Martiny on the border point. Dr. Julius-Yechiel Kühl, a Jew in Bern who served as the assistant for Jewish affairs to the Polish ambassador, Alexander Lados, intervened by calling the police and guaranteeing Polish protection to the men. He also called the papal nuncio, Monsignor Phillippe Bernardini. All these intercessions proved successful, and the young men were set free.[76] Recha was largely aided by the aforementioned police captain, Paul Grüninger, who in 1938 helped her smuggle hundreds of refugees into Switzerland. Someone informed on them, and as a result Grüninger lost his job and pension, and Recha was arrested and jailed.[77]

Defiant in Court

In the spring of 1939, Recha Sternbuch was charged with violating the regulations of the Alien Police, which required refugees to have a visa, as per the government decree of March 28, 1938. She was also charged with complicity, acts of bribery in building an entire refugees network, and illegally harboring illegal refugees in her own home.[78] She was indicted for bribing a diplomatic consul in order to obtain Cuban end-visas. To the surprise of everyone, on the witness stand, in May 1941, she frankly admitted using third parties, "who in any way or manner were helping me with the illegal entry of immigrants into Switzerland." She admitted that in August 1938, some fifteen to twenty immigrants had stayed in her home; that in September 1938, she furnished the Waldau Heim in St. Gallen West, where she moved the refugees who had been staying in her home and where they remained under the care of refugee organizations.

She added: "I have financed these immigration transports out of my own means; when these refugees didn't have the money, I paid their debts to chauffeurs and others." Questioned by the district attorney: "Are you ready to divulge the names of the chauffeurs, be they taxi drivers or the drivers of private cars?" Recha replied: "It is quite impossible for me to permit myself to be used as an informer, and I think it grossly unfair to expect such a thing of me."[79] District attorney: "On December 31, 1938, you had a taxi driver take you to St. Margarethen where you picked up a family. . . . We wish to learn from you the names of all your middlemen of whose services you have availed yourself in order to bring immigrants illegally and unobserved over the Swiss border." Recha: "I will not answer that."[80]

Earlier, on May 10, 1939, in a letter written from prison to the district attorney, Recha stated:

> I always believed that when innocent persecuted people ask me for help and nobody suffers a loss through me, that only I will be punished—I will gladly choose to be punished, because if one has seen the mental and physical exhaustion of these people when they come from the border, one would prefer, with satisfaction, to endure punishment rather than to send them back. . . . I don't want anyone to cover up my actions or to try to cast them in such a light that I would escape punishment. I want the law to clearly judge my transgression. And if I deserve punishment, I want to bear it, because I have respect for the law and I do not fear it. . . .
>
> You demand, however, . . . that I should denounce human beings that haven't harmed anyone, and for the most part are poor, decent

workers who could not bear to suffer a punishment, be it financial
or a loss of their employment for a few months, bringing extreme
hardship to their wives and children, this I cannot do! . . . Mr. District Attorney! Totally impossible! I will not permit anyone to rob
me of the things that make a person's life pleasant and worthwhile.
I want you to know that I refuse unconditionally to give any information about third parties and that I also refuse to respond to any
further challenges of this sort.[81]

In May 1942, about three years after her arrest, her lawyer moved
that the case against her be dismissed, and the Swiss judge dismissed
the charges due to "lack of evidence." All costs were borne by the court.
The prosecutor himself, in a reportedly unthinkable and anticlimactic
move, presented her with 100 Swiss francs as his contribution toward
her rescue efforts.[82]

Recha Sternbuch had to contend with the opposition of local Jewish
leaders, who feared the rise of antisemitism due to the influx of Jewish
refugees. In one confrontation with JDC head Saly Mayer, he reprimanded
her for helping two fleeing refugee brothers named Blum. "Frau Sternbuch, if you were a good Swiss citizen you would consider it your duty
to take the two men who had crossed illegally by the collar and hand
them over to the police. You know the Jewish rule of *dina demalchusa
dina*—the rule of the land has *halachic* (Jewish religious law) validity."
She responded, "Herr Mayer, you obviously don't know me. I am a Jewish
mother, and I don't know what the law says. I only know that we have
to save these people. If you refuse to be of any help, I will have nothing
further to do with you."[83]

Aiding Stranded Jews in China, the Soviet Union, and Elsewhere

The Sternbuchs officially represented the U.S.-based religious rescue
organization Vaad Hatzalah, headed by Rabbi Eliezer Silver (who also
seconded as president of the Union of Orthodox Rabbis of the United
States and Canada, and of Agudath Israel of America) and Rabbi Abraham Kalmanowitz, for assistance to rabbinical heads and yeshiva students
who were stranded in various parts of the world. Messages between the
two sides were sent through the Polish embassy in Bern (with the help
of Jewish affairs assistant, Dr. Julius Kühl) to the Polish consulate in

New York, with whom Dr. Isaac Lewin, a leader of the Agudath Israel, maintained contact.[84]

For those stranded in Shanghai, the Sternbuchs created a special fund known by its initials as HIJEFS (Hilfsverein fur Judische Fluchtlinge in Shanghai—Relief Association for Jewish Refugees in Shanghai).[85] Help with money and kosher food was also sent to Jewish rabbinical students and their rabbis who, having fled from Lithuania, were stranded in the Asian interior of the Soviet Union. The HIJEFS office in Montreux was run by a minute staff under the de facto leadership of only Recha and Yitzhak Sternbuch, with the assistance of a number of rabbis and businessmen.[86] The fund's secretary was Herman Landau. Dr. Reuben Hecht, of Jabotinsky's Zionist-Revisionist movement and the only non-Orthodox member, was also a key figure aiding the Sternbuchs.[87] He became a sort of "foreign secretary" of HIJEFS as well as its director of public relations. He had excellent connections with government circles in Switzerland and with many of the foreign missions in Bern.[88] HIJEFS also supplied aid to JUS (Judische Unterstutzungsstelle), the Jewish self-help organization in Poland with headquarters in Kraków, headed by the controversial Dr. Michael Weichert, which operated with the permission of the German authorities (more on him in chapter 14).[89]

Phony Passports

When the Sternbuchs learned that a Jew in Warsaw with a foreign passport had been permitted to remain outside the ghetto without having to wear the Yellow Star, they began to purchase Paraguayan and other Latin American passports, of dubious legality, in return for stiff payments. At first the Germans chose to recognize them, hoping to exchange the holders of these documents with thousands of German nationals living in Latin American countries.[90] Holders of these documents were kept in a special camp for citizens of foreign countries, such as Vittel in France and Bergen-Belsen in Germany, and were not deported—for the time being. However, in April 1944 the Germans began questioning the legitimacy of these passports, and after Paraguay denied their validity, the Germans decided to treat the holders like all other Jews and annihilate them. That same month, Jewish holders of the Latin American passports held in Vittel camp, with a few exceptions, were deported to Auschwitz, including Recha Sternbuch's parents, in spite of the frantic appeals to the U.S. government via

Rabbi Kalmanowitz of the Vaad Hatzalah. Under U.S. pressure, Paraguay decided to honor the questionable passports, but it came too late to save the Vittel internees, who were deported to perish in the gas chambers.[91]

Cries for Help to the United States

Earlier, together with the well-known Riegner cable on the planned extermination of the Jewish people, the Sternbuchs communicated alarming news on the widespread killings of Jews, especially those taking place in Poland. In a cable sent on September 3, 1942, to Jacob Rosenheim at the Agudath Israel office in New York, via the Polish embassy in Bern, they described the murder of Jews from the Warsaw Ghetto. In contrast to the somewhat wavering stance of the Riegner cable, this one was unequivocal, and it differed radically in its conclusion. It read:

> The German authorities have evacuated the last ghetto in Warsaw. Bestially murdering about one hundred thousand Jews. Mass murders continue. . . . The deportees from other occupied countries will meet the same fate. . . . Do whatever you can to cause an American reaction to halt these persecutions. . . . Inform [Stephen] Wise, [Abba Hillel] Silver, [Jacob] Klatzkin, [Nahum] Goldman, Thomas Mann, and others.[92]

The next day, Jacob Rosenheim and Rabbi Abraham Kalmanowitz took the lead and arranged a preliminary meeting in the office of the Union of Orthodox Rabbis. They invited several prominent Jewish leaders, including Dr. Stephen Wise, Dr. Arye Tartakower, and Dr. Leon Aryeh Kubowitzky, and read the Sternbuch message to them, urging them to take immediate steps. This led to an emergency meeting of leaders of thirty-four major Jewish organizations, which unfortunately did not produce results, due to differences and recriminations between the various organizations.[93]

Reaching Out to Papal and Swiss Authorities

Dr. Julius Kühl, the Jewish diplomatic aide in the Polish embassy in Bern, also arranged for Recha Sternbuch to meet and develop a good working relationship with the papal envoy in Switzerland, Monsignor Phillippe Bernardini, dean of the Swiss diplomatic community. He gave her access to Vatican couriers for sending money and messages to Jewish and resistance organizations in Nazi-occupied Europe. It is told that, at their first meeting, when Bernardini asked her what she wanted of him, she replied, "A letter of recommendation." Bernardini: "Please tell me what to say, since I don't know the precise wording you need." Recha: "But you don't even know me." Bernardini: "I immediately recognized you by the way you came in and the way you sat down. Your demeanor gave you away." He was impressed and quite overwhelmed by Recha Sternbuch's selflessness and self-sacrifice and told her that his door was always open for her, and she could call him at any time, day or night.[94]

The Sternbuchs wrote that they visited Monsignor Bernardini two or three times a week: "At any time we choose. . . . He influenced the Vatican to intervene with the South American governments to recognize the [Latin American] passports." After the war, when Recha Sternbuch undertook her journey to France in July 1945 to remove Jewish children from non-Jewish homes, Bernardini gave her a warm letter of recommendation to present to the French church leaders. She befriended the priest Pierre Chaillet, and he was helpful in the release of many children from Christian institutions.[95]

In 1944, she asked that the War Refugee Board representative in Switzerland, Roswell McClelland, use his powerful office to urge the Swiss authorities to rescind the harsh laws of forcing fleeing Jews back across the border, pointing to the example of Sweden, which permitted the entry of Jewish refugees, such as the more than 7,000 Danish Jews admitted in the fall of 1943. Recha added, "It was six years ago [1938] that I learned to appreciate the refugee problem—as a result of a St. Gallen jail experience, after we brought hundreds of people across the borders from the Nazi territories."[96] To this McClelland reportedly wondered "why she chose to live in Switzerland when Sweden was far more friendly to refugees." She responded, "I do not believe that I should have to leave my mother country of the past thirty-five years and move to Sweden just because I disagree with some things, such as the laws of *refoulement*. . . . I consider it my duty to remain here, where I can contribute to an improvement, however modest."[97]

Collaborating with a Pro-Nazi Politician to Ransom Jews

Toward the end of the war, in her unending efforts to save as many Jews as possible from the Nazi inferno, Recha Sternbuch became involved in an operation that loomed as potentially one of the most successful rescue operations in the making. It began when, through Monsignor Bernardini, she befriended an influential Catholic woman, Mrs. Bolomey, the wife of a prominent colonel in the Swiss army, who in turn acquainted her with the former president of the Switzerland, Jean-Marie Musy.[98] Musy was known as an archconservative, the publisher of the pro-Nazi newspaper *La Jeune*, who viewed Nazism and Fascism as a bulwark against Soviet Communism and had a long-standing personal friendship with ss chief Heinrich Himmler. In September 1944 Recha learned from Mrs. Bolomey that in return for 10,000 Swiss francs, Musy had been able to free a Jewish couple from a concentration camp.

She contacted Musy with a fantastic proposal: the Germans might agree to the release of all remaining Jews under Nazi control (estimated as between 500,000 and 800,000) against the payment of a substantial negotiated sum.[99] Musy, who as a believing Catholic wished to do something to save innocent lives and to amend his previous pro-Nazi leanings, wrote to Himmler asking for an urgent meeting, and this was granted to him.

In late October 1944 the seventy-five-year-old Musy was driven to Berlin, with his son Benoît, a Swiss Air Force officer, at the wheel of the new Mercedes bought for them by the Sternbuchs and a large Red Cross sign painted on the car's rooftop, so as to prevent it being strafed by an Allied plane.[100] Believing he was indirectly dealing with a conspiratorial Jewish government that through its financial power controlled the affairs of the U.S. government and would be able to cause the United States to withdraw from the war against Germany, Himmler was willing to release Jews then in concentration camps in return for money, trucks, and other goods. Himmler's main incentive, though, at this late hour for Nazi Germany, was neither money nor goods but to create a climate of goodwill that would result in political benefits for Germany.[101]

At this point, a stumbling block appeared when both Roswell McClelland, of the U.S. War Refugee Board, and Saly Mayer, of the JDC, were dubious of Musy and were staunchly opposed to any form of ransom. McClelland favored Mayer's plan to keep the Jews interned in Germany, but under International Red Cross supervision, rather than bring them in great numbers into Switzerland, out of fear of increased antisemitism.[102] After a second meeting with Musy on January 15, 1945, Himmler decided as a sign of good faith to send a trainload of roughly 1,200 Jews from Theresienstadt. They arrived safely in Switzerland on February 7.[103]

Musy made a third trip to Germany on February 19, and the ss had already prepared a second convoy of 2,000 Jews—another 1,200 from Theresienstadt plus 800 from Bergen-Belsen. But then a monkey wrench was thrown in the form of ss General Ernst Kaltenbrunner, in conflict with Himmler's plan, who presented Hitler with a collection of critical articles from the Swiss press on the Himmler-Musy negotiations and the rumors that the deal involved Swiss asylum for 250 Nazis. Hitler, fuming with rage, ordered that "not a single Jew should be allowed to leave Germany," and any ss officer involved in this arrangement is to be shot without a trial.[104] Taking fright, Himmler washed his hands clean of any further arrangements with the Musy-Sternbuch team.[105] Although disappointed at the end of a six-month negotiating effort, Recha Sternbuch could take satisfaction that her Musy initiative had led to the liberation of 1,200 Jews.

Reuniting Jewish Children with Their Families

With the war over, Recha Sternbuch did not rest on her laurels, but now undertook a no less challenging undertaking: the liberation of Jewish children who were saved, indeed, but were held in non-Jewish homes, and they needed to be reunited with their families and the Jewish people. She established her base in Zakopane, a Polish resort town where over 100 Jewish children were kept in an orphanage under the management of pro-communist Jews. She managed to have the children released to her care.[106] Rabbi Samuel Orenstein reported:

> When Chief Rabbi Herzog visited Poland, he succeeded in taking out a large transport of Jewish children with him, with the permission of the government. Mrs. Sternbuch utilized the opportunity to send along with this same transport a substantial group of children from a children's home in Poland, which she had previously helped to establish. I suggested that she travel along with the transport. "Otherwise, Rabbi Herzog will get all the credit, while nobody will even remember how much effort you exerted to save these children," I told her. She would not—even for a moment—hear my arguments. "I'm not at all interested in who will get credit for saving the chil-

dren. I have to do my duty, and I still have to remain here. There are still so many Jews to be saved," she insisted.[107]

Also, as told by Israel Yitzhak Cohn:

My sister had been killed by some Polish bandits not long after the liberation. . . . I joined a kibbutz of [the religious] Poalei Agudath Israel. . . . One day, Mrs. Sternbuch appeared at our kibbutz [and informed us] that we would leave that night. We were given some documents, and that evening we indeed boarded a train to Kato-wice . . . but a hitch developed. Some police officers came . . . and started questioning our papers. A decision was made not to pro-ceed but to stay in Katowice. Mrs. Sternbuch went to Warsaw. . . . A few days later, Mrs. Sternbuch reappeared. She had worked out a "perfect" plan in Warsaw. Our group of about fifty Jewish youth was to join a big transport of Greek repatriates from Poland to Athens, supplied with some Greek documents which she brought with her from Warsaw. . . . We knew that these papers were fictitious. None of us knew a word of Greek. We were all frightened, but Recha Ster-nbuch told us that she was going along and that the border police had already been bribed. We were still not sure. . . .

At the border we were kept for a long time. . . . She was confer-ring with the new officer in charge. There were telephone calls to Warsaw, to the consulate of Greece. Finally the officer came out with Mrs. Sternbuch, smiling, and he waved the conductor to move on. A few minutes later we were in Czechoslovakia and on our way to Prague. . . . It was now close to Sabbath. . . . She went over to speak to the station manager. Our wagon was detached from the train and put on a sidetrack. We stayed there over Shabbos, and on *Motzaei Shabbos* (Saturday night) a special locomotive took our wagon to Prague. In Prague . . . we all had French visas. . . . Suddenly Recha Sternbuch appeared. . . . She was going to accompany us to France . . . to Aix-les-Bains.[108]

Many of Recha's children transferred from Poland to Prague on their way to other destinations, with Recha bribing border guards to facilitate the passage between Poland and Czechoslovakia.[109]

France became for Recha an important base of operation, also due to the importance of retrieving many Jewish children in non-Jewish religious institutions in that country. Going to France in May 1945, she began knocking on many doors. She went from one children's home to another and received the same answer: these children were given to us, put into our custody; we cannot release them to anyone but their parents, not to a "strange intruder" who asked for the children to whom she was not even related. Pierre Chaillet, a kind-hearted Catholic priest who was involved in the rescue of Jewish children during the German occupation, listened to Mrs. Sternbuch's plea after she handed him a warm letter of recommendation from the Swiss papal nuncio Phillipe Bernardini, and he lent a helping hand.[110]

A yeshiva was opened in Aix-les-Bains to reacquaint Jewish children (numbering about 250) with Jewish religious practices. As reported by Dr. Isaac Lewin in the New York *Jewish Morning Journal* on August 28, 1945: "Aix-les-Bains . . . near the Swiss Alps . . . I sat with Mr. and Mrs. Sternbuch. . . . Many of these children saying their Hebrew prayers had already been baptized and converted. Legally they are still Christian. . . . They once again belong to their own people. . . . By now many boys from Buchenwald and Dachau are registered."[111]

The physical and mental exhaustive efforts of the war and postwar years, however, took a toll on Recha's health. Suddenly, somewhere on the road, while on her way to another place, she died in 1971 at the age of sixty-five. As underlined by authors Friedenson and Kranzler, her entire life had been a response of *Hineni*–"I am ready." The charismatic Recha Sternbuch rarely wore jewelry and never any cosmetics; she dressed simply but well, her hair covered at all times, in a ubiquitous turban, part of a stylish outfit. She was buried in Zürich next to her husband, Yitzhak, who had died in 1968 at the age of seventy-five. They were survived by two daughters and a son.[112]

Chaim Israel Eiss

He was one of the first to use false Latin American
passports as a means of saving Jews.

The final story takes us to Chaim Israel Eiss, who was born in 1876 in Ustrzyki Dolne (Istrik in Yiddish), Poland. Family tradition has it that he was the only one of ten children to survive an epidemic of diphtheria, an illness for which there was no treatment at the time. After receiving the blessing of the Sadigora Rebbe, the additional esoteric and mystic "Chaim" (life) was added to his name. Later in life he moved to Zürich in Switzerland and became a successful businessman.[113] He also was among the founders of the Agudath Israel movement in 1912 and its emissary in Switzerland. Eiss belonged to the more radical anti-Zionist wing inside Agudath Israel, and he was critical of the religious Zionist Mizrahi's close association with secular Zionist movements.[114] But when it came to aiding fellow Jews, all ideological differences were put aside.

As he wrote to his Agudah counterpart in Turkey, Jakob Griffel, on August 19, 1943: "Even though I am considered one of the more radical/ extreme Agudath Israel members, that is only regarding matters pertaining to ideology . . . but *chas v'shalom* [heaven forbid] when it comes to saving Jews from physical danger, I decry any discrimination among the children of Abraham, Isaac, and Jacob."[115] Earlier, during World War I, Eiss was involved in setting up a large aid system that located refugees, found out what they most needed, and raised the required funds.[116]

In the early years of World War II Eiss dealt mainly with sending packages to Jews in the ghettos and assisting refugees. When he heard of the hunger and deprivation suffered by inhabitants of the ghettos, he immediately dispatched money to a Lisbon business associate. This associate used the money to buy cocoa, coffee, sugar, tea, and sardines, items that were scarce at that time, and sent them to the starving Jews. The recipients were able to exchange them for large quantities of flour and potatoes. Eiss often financed these purchases out of his own pocket. He also had a good relationship with the chairman of the Red Cross in Geneva and used the services of the organization to transfer parcels to Poland.[117] Eiss's four accomplices included Rabbi Dr. Shaul Weingort, the nephew of Yitzhak Sternbuch, and Mathieu-Meir Müller.[118]

Eiss's greatest contribution was using Latin American passports to save Jews. As confirmed by historian Dina Porat, Eiss was evidently one of the first who devised this rescue device and was one of the key operatives in this enterprise from early 1942 until his death at the end of 1943.[119] For Eiss, sending money and food parcels was not enough; what was really essential was to help Jews escape the clutches of the Nazis. With this in mind, Eiss contacted the Paraguayan consul, Rudolf Hügli, from whom he purchased Paraguayan identity papers and passports at great expense. Eiss had these documents copied and notarized and then sent off to Poland via special couriers.[120] It is estimated that several hundred such passports were dispatched; some claim as many as 3,000 passports.[121] Some Latin American consuls began hiking up the price of the passports, and in early 1943 the Swiss police initiated an investigation into Hügli's dealings and other Jewish rescue operatives, especially that of George Mandel-Mantello.[122] Eiss was permitted to continue with his work, but the police confiscated many lists and pictures of Jews from the Nazi occupation zones that were found in his apartment.

For a time the Germans were willing to recognize these passports if only because there were Germans who lived in the same countries represented by these documents and the Reich wanted to exchange them for Jews who held these passports.[123] As a result, about 3,000 passport holders were detained in Bergen-Belsen, but by October 1943, 800 of them had been deported to Auschwitz. About 250 passport holders were sent to Vittel, and in April and May 1944, most of them were also deported to Auschwitz.[124] In January 1945, with defeat staring them in the eyes, the Germans allowed an estimated 301 bearers of South American passports to head from Bergen-Belsen to Switzerland. As for Chaim Israel Eiss, he suddenly died in November 1943, still believing that the Latin American passport holders incarcerated in Vittel camp were safe and sound, not knowing that most would be deported to Auschwitz.[125]

One cannot write about prominent Jewish Swiss aid personalities without mentioning Saly Mayer, once head of the Federation of Swiss Jewish Communities (SIG), but better known as representing the U.S.-based Joint Distribution Committee during the war years, through which hundreds of thousands of JDC dollars were disbursed to various Jewish rescue causes across European countries. Controversies surrounding his mode of operation have already been alluded to in this and previous chapters and will be mentioned again in chapter 14.

12 Concentration Camps

*Flight and Rescue from Hell on Earth
and Challenging Himmler*

The extensive Nazi camps system included labor camps, transit camps, concentration camps, and extermination camps—the latter two being the most radical and horrific symbols of the Nazi system of oppression. Imprisoned in all these camps were political adversaries and people considered socially or racially undesirable, as well as tramps and beggars, dubbed "asocial elements," and "habitual criminals," gypsies, homosexuals, and convicted prostitutes.[1] Beginning in the summer of 1938, and reaching a peak in the wake of the Kristallnacht pogrom in November, Jews were interned in the camps solely because they were Jews. By the start of World War II, the prominent camps included Dachau, Oranienburg, Sachsenhausen, Buchenwald, Mauthausen, Flossenbürg, Ravensbrück (for women), Natzweiller, Neuengamme, Gross-Rosen, and Stutthof. In late 1941 Chełmno, in occupied Poland, was the first site to begin operating as an extermination camp. In spring of 1942 there were additional extermination camps: Auschwitz-Birkenau, Majdanek, Treblinka, Sobibór, and Bełżec. There, most of Europe's millions of Jews were brought to be killed—by gassing, shooting, or death due to the inhumane conditions there.[2] Auschwitz was the largest killing center on European soil, and it has become an iconic symbol of the horrific inhumanities of the Holocaust.

Forced labor in the camps was a method of punishment and persecution intended to humiliate the prisoners and lead to their early death through overwork, starvation, lack of sanitation, and constant beatings. Living conditions varied greatly, with the mortality constantly rising for those selected for hard labor. Prisoners were categorized by the ss according to their national origin, and the criteria applied by the ss to the different categories were determined by its racist ideology, with the Jews at the lowest scale. This classification certainly affected the chances of survival. Prisoners were identified by the color of the badges worn on their clothes (political, criminal, and asocial); Jews wore a yellow sign. From the very beginning, the treatment meted out to Jews was worse than that given to other prisoners. The humiliation, loss of personal identity, absence of the most elementary sanitary conditions and of any privacy, and the brutality of those in charge led to a high rate of collapse and death during the first weeks of internees' arrival. Some prisoners were put at the disposal of state-owned and private companies that needed manpower for arms production. In the fall of 1944, as the war fronts were drawing near, camps were gradually closed and the prisoners were sent on long death marches to other camps still in existence.[3]

Sobibór

In the eighteen months that it was in operation, this extermination camp slaughtered 250,000 people.

Sobibór, an extermination camp in the Lublin district, was built in March 1942 in a wooded, sparsely populated area. The camp staff included twenty to thirty German ss men, most of whom had previously taken part in the euthanasia program in Germany. In addition, 90 to 120 Ukrainians served in the camp; most were former Soviet prisoners of war, and some were Volksdeutsche, Russian nationals of German origin. The German staff filled most of the command and administrative positions, while the Ukrainian unit acted as guards and security personnel, their function being, among other things, to quell any possible resistance by the Jews who were brought to the camp and to prevent their escape.[4] The camp was surrounded by a barbed-wire fence with tree branches intertwined in it to conceal the interior. Most of the camp circumference was planted with mines to discourage escapes.

The reception area included the train platform, with space for twenty railway cars to be stationed, as well as living quarters for the German and Ukrainian staff. Nearby was the housing for the hundreds of Jewish prisoners and the workshops in which some of them were employed. When a train arrived, the passengers were told that they had come to a transit camp from which they would be sent to labor camps. They were to take showers, and at the same time their clothes would be disinfected. They then removed their clothes, women's hair was shorn, and all their possessions and valuables were confiscated. A path led from the reception area to the extermination area; on either side was a barbed-wire fence, and here too branches were intertwined to conceal the path from view. It was along this path that the victims were herded, naked, toward the gas chambers from the shed where they had undressed. The burial trenches were nearby. The gas chambers were inside a brick building. Each chamber had a capacity of 160 to 180 people. But some 450 to 550 persons were crowded in at a time.[5]

Everything was done on the run, accompanied by shouts, beatings, and warning shots. The victims were in a state of shock and did not grasp what was happening to them. The gas was carbon monoxide, produced by a 200-horsepower engine in a nearby shed, from which it was piped into the gas chambers. Within twenty to thirty minutes, everyone inside was dead. Gold teeth were wrenched from their mouths by "dentists," then the bodies were removed.[6] The whole procedure, from the arrival of the train to the burial of the victims, took two to three hours. In the meantime the railway cars that had brought the victims were cleaned up, the train departed, and another twenty cars, with their human load destined for extermination, entered the camp.

A select group of 600 able-bodied Jews (including 120 women) were chosen from among the first few transports to form work teams—as tailors, cobblers, carpenters, and the like. One such team was assigned to the reception area to handle the clothing and luggage left there by the victims on their way to the gas chambers—to sort out the clothing and prepare it to be sent to a destination outside the camp and to search for money and other valuables. The barbers, from among the Jewish laborers, had to cut off the women's hair, package it, and prepare it for dispatch. In the extermination area, 200 to 300 Jewish prisoners were assigned to remove the bodies of the murdered victims from the gas chambers, take them to the burial ground, and then clear up the chambers for the next consignment of victims. There were constant selections among the Jewish prisoners, with the weak and the sick slated for the gas chambers; new arrivals took their places.

Trains brought victims from Poland, the Czech provinces, Germany, Austria, Slovakia, France, the Netherlands, and various parts of Eastern

Europe. To keep pace with the thousands of arrivals and avoid a bottle-neck in the extermination process, the Germans found it necessary to add three more gas chambers.[7] The new killing capacity was consequently raised to 1,200 persons each turn, and the rate of extermination was doubled. By late summer 1942 the burial trenches were opened and the process of burning the victims' bodies began. The corpses were put into huge piles and set on fire. Subsequent transports were instead cremated immediately after gassing.[8] It is estimated that Sobibór camp murdered up to 250,000 Jews between April 1942 and October 14, 1943.[9]

Aleksander Pechersky

He planned and led one of the most dramatic uprisings and mass escapes of Jews from a Nazi camp—the Sobibór extermination camp.[10]

Born in 1909 in Kremenchung, Ukraine, Aleksander Pechersky (also known as Sasha) and his family settled in Rostov-on-Don. He was a lieu-tenant in the Soviet army when in October 1941 his unit was surrounded and captured in Viazma, not far from Moscow.[11] In May 1942 he escaped along with four other prisoners of war, but they were immediately recap-tured and sent to a penal camp in Borisov, Belarus, and then to a labor camp in Minsk. In Borisov, during a mandatory medical examination, his circumcision was discovered, and he admitted to being Jewish. On September 18, 1943, together with other Jewish prisoners, he was trans-ferred to the Sobibór extermination camp. Upon arrival, eighty prisoners, most of the Russian prisoners of war including Pechersky, were selected for work, The remaining 1,900 Jews were committed to the gas cham-bers.[12] Pechersky soon learned the true nature of this camp. In his words:

I was sitting outside on a pile of logs in the evening with Solo-mon Leitman, who subsequently became my top commander in the uprising. I asked him about the huge, strange fire burning 500 meters away from us behind some trees and about the unpleasant smell throughout the camp. He warned me that the guards forbade looking there and told me that they are burning the corpses of my murdered comrades who arrived with me that day. I did not believe him, but he continued. He told me that the camp existed for more than a year and that almost every day a train came with two thousand new victims who are all murdered within a few hours. He said around 500 Jewish prisoners—Polish, French, German, Dutch, and Czechoslovak—work here and that my transport was the first one to bring Russian Jews. He said that on this tiny plot of land, no more than 10 hectares (24.7 acres or 1 square kilometer), hundreds of thousands of Jewish women, children, and men were murdered. I thought about the future. Should I try to escape alone or with a small group? Should I let the rest of the prisoners be tortured and murdered? I rejected this thought.[13]

Five days after arriving in Sobibór, Solomon Leitman introduced Pechersky to Leon Feldhendler, the leader of the camp's Polish Jews. On this occasion Pechersky told him about the Red Army victory in the Battle of Stalingrad and large-scale partisan gains.[14] Also, the appearance of Soviet prisoners of war produced an enormous impression on the Sobibór Jewish prisoners. They had never seen men who had actually fought in the war and could handle arms. They began to think how to get out of that hell by force.[15] Already earlier, a bit before Pechersky's arrival, the inmates felt that the end was near, as only a limited number of transports were arriving. It looked like the Germans had decided that the camp had almost accomplished its task of murdering Jews, so the liquidation of the Jewish prisoners, the principal eyewitnesses, was surely approaching.[16]

Feldhendler lacked leadership ability and military training, qualities needed to inspire the prisoners and lead them through a complicated and risky breakout of the camp.[17] The fact that Sobibór was practically surrounded by a minefield necessitated a studious military plan to overcome this obstacle if a mass breakout was to succeed.[18] In the meantime, on September 26, Pechersky watched as twenty-five prisoners were whipped, and a young Dutchman tall and lean, who was chopping wood not fast enough, was hit on the head by an ss guard. Pechersky related what happened.

We were chopping wood. . . . "*Schnell, schnell*" [fast, fast]. . . . One of the Dutch Jews . . . Frenzel let him have one with his whip. . . . Frenzel noticed that I had stopped chopping. He called out to come: "*Komm*. . . . Russian soldier, you don't like the way I punish this fool? I give you exactly five minutes to split this stump. If you make it, you get a pack of cigarettes. If you miss by as much as one second, you get twenty-five lashes." . . . Frenzel handed me a pack of cigarettes. 'Four and a half minutes,' I heard him say. . . . But I literally could not take the gift from the scoundrel's hand. "Thanks, I don't smoke."

Pechersky's proud, bold behavior spread quickly among the prisoners.[19] He had made his mark on them and impressed the others that the chances for an escape attempt would be better under Pechersky's leadership.

Solomon Leitman and Boris Tsibulski turned to Pechersky and urged him, "Sasha, let us escape. We are only 200 meters from the forest. We can cut the barbed wire with our axes and run," said Tsibulski. Leitman excitedly continued, "Sasha, there are not many guards. We'll kill them and escape into the forest." "That is easier said than done," Pechersky told them. "While you are taking care of one guard, another will open fire on you with his submachine gun. . . . What are you going to do about our comrades who will be left behind? Do we have the right to forget all about them? They will all be finished immediately. If the plan is to run away, then we must all run together. Escape if you wish. I won't stand in your way; as for me, I won't go." That impromptu escape plan was dropped. For Pechersky, the thought of escape was bound up with the idea not of an escape by a few individuals but of setting the entire camp free and seeking out the partisans, and this had to be carefully planned.[20]

Aborted Escape Plans

Some of the prisoners had already thought of several escape plans before Pechersky's arrival. They thought about poisoning the ss men and staging a mass escape from the camp with the help of outside partisans. The poisoning was to be carried out by two Jewish boys who worked in the German kitchen, with the poison taking effect six hours after consumption. The partisans would then arrive that evening and liberate the men. But the plan had to be discarded when the German decided to dispense with Jews working in the German kitchen.[21] Another failed plan was to have the ss men killed while they were sleeping by the youngsters, the so-called *putzers,* who worked daily, from the early hours, in the ss living quarters. There were, however, serious doubts as to whether the boys, between the ages of fourteen and sixteen, would be able to kill a dozen or so ss men. The other drawback was that the killing could be carried out only in the early morning hours, with the escape from the camp soon after. This would give the pursuing forces the entire day to chase after the escapees.[22]

Perchersky's Plan

On September 29 Leon Feldhendler told Pechersky, "It is not the first time that we have planned to finish with Sobibór, but very few of us know how to use arms. Lead us, and we shall follow you." And so an underground committee came into being, with Perchersky as leader and Feldhendler as his deputy.[23] After attempts at digging tunnels failed, Pechersky came up with another plan: eliminate the ss men in the camp by force, one by one, all at about the same time, and then carry out a massive escape.[24] For this, one first had to map out the exact layout of the camp and the daily routine of the prisoners and the commanding ss officers. Pechersky began to learn the topography of Sobibór and its three main subdivisions: Camp 1, where the Jewish maintenance detainees lived, including workshops and kitchens; Camp 2, the reception center of the new arrivals, which also contained a storage holding the belongings stolen from the prisoners; and Camp 3 and its gas chambers.

Pechersky carefully studied the camp's daily routine of activities and decided that his plan could only be successfully carried out using arms stolen from the ss. For this, the prisoners would have to form combat groups armed with knives, axes, and shovels, and someone would have to break into the gun storage. Once out of the camp perimeter, they would run into the nearby forest and join up with one of the partisan units there.[25]

Pechersky noted that before the ss staff left on vacation, they usually visited the workshops of the tailors, shoemakers, and goldsmiths to have the Jewish prisoners there prepare special clothing and other presents for them to take to their families. Knowing this, Pechersky planned to have them lured into the workshops under some pretext and kill them. With the small ss contingent eliminated, the auxiliary Ukrainian guards would be leaderless and confused, giving prisoners an opportunity to obtain weapons, eliminate the remaining camp guards, and escape. The elimination of the ss was to start at 4 p.m. and the breakout one hour later. This would make it difficult for the ss, after they recovered and brought in reinforcement, to pursue the escapees in the dark of night. Having decided on this scheme, Pechersky asked Feldhendler to prepare in the workshops about seventy sharp knives.[26]

Meeting at night in the carpenters' workshop, Pechersky and his men carefully went over the details of their plan. The ss officers would be invited, one by one, into the workshops where two men would execute them. The liquidation of the ss men had to be accomplished instantly without the slightest sound. The task of killing would be assigned to the Russian prisoners of war. At 5p.m., this part of the plan should be over. While the ss men were being killed, another team would cut the telephone wires from Camp 2 to the guards' quarters. Soon afterwards, *kapos* (supervisors of group and work internees) Brzecki and Geniek would assemble the prisoners for the usual evening roll call. Standing in front would be the Russian prisoners, who were to take over the arsenal. Once the arsenal had been breached, armed men would lead the group and kill the guards at the gate. Stones were to be thrown over the fence in order to explode the mines. Such was the plan. Would it work?[27]

The conspirators went over the details meticulously. The exact timetable was set for the first ss liquidation stage to start between 2:30 and 4:30. The ss men would be invited to the workshops or warehouses for clothing or shoe measurements or other work-related excuses, and they would be dealt with by a special team of men armed with knives and axes in total silence. The camp's trucks were simultaneously to be sabotaged by the prisoners working in the garage. Stanislaw (Shlomo) Szmajzner, who was in charge of repairing the stoves in the Ukrainian barracks, was to smuggle out some rifles from there and bring them to the men who would lead the rebellion. Weapons would also be taken from the slain ss men—about a dozen revolvers. The next stage was set when the breakout from the camp was to take place between 4:30 and 5:30, as close as possible to nightfall.

Close to that stage, all 600 prisoners in the camp were to be assembled for roll call in an organized way. Sadly, the plan could not include the prisoners in Camp 3, the area separated from others, where over 100 men were assigned with the most miserable task of work in the gas chambers and the burning of the bodies. During that daily evening roll call, those prisoners who were still unaware of what was happening would be informed about the action soon to take place. Then the entire prisoner body would march to the camp's gate—the only exit that was free of the explosive mines.[28]

To keep his meetings and plans secret, Pechersky acted as though he had a romantic fling with a certain eighteen-year-old internee, known as

Lyuka (whose real name may have been Gertrude Poppert-Schonborn) so that he could surreptitiously discuss plans with Feldhendler. When others passed by, Pechersky would pretend a special affection to Lyuka, although the relationship remained strictly platonic. There was no choice but for her to listen to the conversation between the two men. On the eve of the breakout, she gave him a good luck shirt. After the breakout, the two never met again.[29]

Two days before the planned escape, scheduled for October 14, Leitman reported to Pechersky the final elimination arrangements. "At four o'clock Untersturmführer Ernst Berg will be invited to the tailor shop to be fitted for a coat. At four-fifteen Oberscharführer Gettsinger (the chief of the gas chambers section) will arrive there. Unterscharführer Emil Schumacher is supposed to be at the shoe shop at four o'clock. I'll attend to Unterscharführer Friedrich Gaulstick personally."

"Good," Pechersky responded. "Send me each of the friends whom you've selected to kill the Germans."[30] Pechersky was to remain in the carpentry workshop where, from the window, he could observe what was happening. Many of the others in the camp, not in on the secret, nevertheless felt a vague sense of anxiety, suspecting that something serious was afoot. Yom Kippur had passed two days earlier.

That same October 12, Camp Commander Reichleitner, his aide, Sergeant-Major Gustav Wagner, as well as some other ss men had left for vacation in Germany. This considerably weakened the German staff, and especially important was the absence of the shrewd and dreaded Wagner, who kept the strictest supervision over the prisoners. The uprising and escape would have to be carried out before these men returned. The following day, October 13, in the evening, the knives and hatchets were distributed to those who were assigned to use them on the ss personnel. That night, many did not sleep. Some of the older people, sensing a dramatic event to take place the next day, murmured prayers. They also removed money and valuables from their hiding places in the hope that this would increase their chances for survival once they were outside the camp.[31]

Escape Day

October 14, 1943, was a clear, sunny day. Pechersky held a last-minute briefing with commanders of the battle teams, one by one. The first phase started around 3:30, when ss officers were killed one after another as they were lured into the workshops. Other ss men were asked to come to the workshops at intervals of fifteen to thirty minutes later. Up until now, the uprising went according to plan. Most of the ss men had been liquidated, among them three key officers, and the prisoners had armed themselves with pistols and rifles. There remained four ss men; one was wounded, and three others were not to be found. The telephone wires had also been cut.[32]

At precisely 4:45, Pozycka, the *Kapo* who was in on the secret, blew a sharp whistle for prisoners to line up for roll call, and they came running from all directions. Some seventy men, nearly all of them Russians, had been selected to attack the armory, and they had been placed in the forefront of the column. When all reached the main gate, a German squad commander shouted at them to get in line, three in a row, and he was immediately killed.[33] At this point, several women, shaken by the unexpected scene, began to scream. A prisoner began to run blindly, without any direction, and it proved impossible to line up the people in an orderly column.

Then the sound of the gunfire prompted Pechersky to begin the revolt earlier than planned. He shouted: "Comrades, forward!" As he recounted later, "Six hundred pain-wracked, tormented people surged forward with a wild 'hurrah' to life and freedom." But they had to forego the attack on the armory because of a barrage of automatic fire. At that point, "all hell broke loose" as automatic fire from a watchtower and some other directions was opened on the prisoners running toward the camp's main gate. ss officer Frenzel joined in the fray, as he came out of a barrack close to the main gate, and some Ukrainian guards opened automatic fire, making it impossible to escape from the main gate. The prisoners had no other option but to run toward the fences and minefields.[34]

In the meantime, Perchersky's men silenced the guards at two watchtowers. But at this point, Pechersky and the other leaders lost control over things as people ran toward the fences, and disorganized groups of prisoners ran in every direction, rushing through the doors of the workshops, some shooting with rifles and cutting the barbed wire with pliers. As they stepped outside and ran into the field, mines started to explode. According to the original plan, stones and planks had to be thrown on the mines to explode them, but in the confusion nobody did it. Many found their death there, but they paved the way to freedom for those who followed them. Pechersky and the prisoners with him were able to leave from the field behind the commander's house, which they had correctly assumed was not mined, and they safely reached the forest.[35]

Those who reached the outer perimeter of Sobibór camp, beyond the minefield, were not familiar with the surrounding area nor did they know in which direction to run. Some began to run in circles and found themselves still very close to the camp. Pechersky's own group of fifty-seven avoided a passing train and some Polish railway workers and scattered in the bushes when they heard the sound of an airplane circling overhead. In Pechersky's words, "I proposed that we continue going all through the night, and that we should go in a single file, one behind the other. . . . No smoking; no talking; no falling behind; no running ahead. If the man in front lies down, all would do the same. If a rocket flared up, all would lie down at once. There must be no panic no matter what happened." They found wooden stumps lying by the shore of a canal and used them to cross the waterway.

At dawn Pechersky decided that it made no sense to continue together in so large a group. They were in danger of being uncovered, and all would be shot. So they split up into groups of nine, each going separate ways. Pechersky's group headed east, deep into the woods, walking at night, with the polar stars as their compass. They somehow obtained food from willing local farmers, from whom they learned that the Germans were combing the entire region in search of the escapees.[36]

Reaching the village of Stawki, a short distance from the Bug River, three of his men entered a hut. "Could you tell us where to cross the Bug?" The frightened farmer claimed ignorance. The men persisted: "You must know. You have been living here long enough. We know that there are places where the water is low and the crossing easy." The man changed his mind and said, "I will show you the direction, but I won't go to the river. Find it yourselves. Be careful. It is guarded everywhere." As they were leaving they heard a woman's voice. "Wait," she said. "Take some bread for the way." The same night, October 19, they crossed the Bug River, and three days later they ran into a unit of Soviet partisans in the Brest-Litovsk region and joined them, with Pechersky assigned as a demolition expert. Other escapees made contact with Jewish partisans, known as Yehiel's group (under Yehiel Grynszpan), in the Parczew region, northwest of Sobibór. They were active in sabotaging railway lines, cutting telephone wires, and hit-and-run attacks on German army units.[37]

The End of Sobibór

Following the death of eleven German ss personnel and an unknown number of Ukrainian guards, the ss executed the remaining 150 Jewish prisoners in the camp, men isolated in the gas chambers area who had known nothing about the uprising until the shooting broke out. With the exception of Pechersky's five-men unit, most of the others, especially the Polish Jews, headed in the opposite direction, toward the Polish-inhabited farming area.[38]

The escapees could not assume that peasants could be trusted, knowing from previous incidents that the Germans informed the peasants that anyone they captured and turned in and anyone who gave information as to their whereabouts would be compensated with vodka and sugar.[39] The escapees also had to contend with the antisemitic feelings that had deep roots in Poland. "There were also a few good Poles and Ukrainians," wrote escapee Dov Freiberg. "These people helped us and risked their lives because they had to fear every neighbor, every passer-by, every child who might inform on them."[40]

In summary, of the 300 Jews who escaped from Sobibór, about a third were caught and shot during the first four days. According to historian Yitzhak Arad, all the others survived the pursuit action. Ilya Ehrenburg and Vasily Grossman claim that no more than 50 escapees survived.[41] On the German side, the killing of eleven ss men and some Ukrainians guards, in addition to the wounded, produced turmoil among the German authorities and was reported to the highest authorities in Berlin. In the words of Arad, it was a rare—and perhaps the only—case where prisoners, Jews or non-Jews, revolted and succeeded in liquidating such a large number of ss men in a single event.[42] Within days after the escape, ss chief Himmler ordered the camp burned down. The ground was plowed and planted with cabbages and potatoes.[43]

Pechersky's Enforced Silence

As for Pechersky, as a partisan fighter, he was promoted to the rank of captain and received a medal for bravery. A Soviet commission took evidence from him, and his report was included in the *Black Book,* by Grossman and Ehrenburg. However, the book was forbidden by Soviet censorship in 1947.[44] The International Tribunal at Nuremberg wanted to call Pechersky as a witness, but the Soviet government did not allow him to travel to Germany to testify. In 1948, during the Soviet anti-Jewish drive, accused of leading "rootless cosmopolitans," Pechersky was fired from his job and imprisoned along with his brother. They were freed only after Stalin's death in 1953. The Soviet government also prevented Pechersky from testifying at the Eichmann trial in Israel in 1961, allowing him only a short deposition in Moscow that was censored by the KGB. He was denied permission to leave the country and testify in a 1987 trial in Poland, and according to his daughter, this refusal "just crippled my father. He almost stopped getting out of bed and instantly aged." He died on January 19, 1990. A decade later a small plaque was erected on the side of the apartment complex where he lived in Rostov-on-Don to commemorate his deeds at Sobibór. A street is also named in his honor in Safed, Israel.[45]

Auschwitz

It was both the most extensive of all German concentration and forced-labor camps and the largest camp at which Jews were exterminated.

Auschwitz was the largest Nazi concentration and extermination camp, located 37 miles (60 kilometers) west of Kraków. It lay in a region that had been annexed to Nazi Germany and was very close to the town of Oświęcim, after which it bore its Germanized name. The entrance to the camp was festooned with a grossly deceptive sign, "Arbeit macht frei" (Work liberates or Work makes one free). During the first period of its existence, most of the inmates were Polish political prisoners. Block 11 contained a special bunker for the most severe punishments, and in front of that building stood the "Black Wall," where regular execution of prisoners took place. The first groups of women to be imprisoned in this section, known as Auschwitz I, were 999 Germans from the Ravensbrück camp and an equal number of Jewish women from Poprad, Slovakia. A small gas chamber was installed, and on September 3, 1941, experiments with Zyklon B gas were carried out in it. Some 600 Soviet prisoners of war and 250 other prisoners were killed during the course of these experiments.[46]

But this presaged a much larger and expanded camp specifically meant to deal with the extermination of huge numbers of Jews. As told by Auschwitz camp commander Rudolf Höss in his memoirs, which he wrote while awaiting execution after the war: "In the summer of 1941, I cannot remember the exact date, I was suddenly summoned to the Reichsführer ss Himmler [who told him]: 'The Führer has ordered that the Jewish question be solved once and for all and that we, the ss, are to implement that order."[47] Actually, already a bit earlier, in March 1941, Himmler had ordered the erection of a second, much larger section of the camp, which was located at a distance of 3 kilometers from the original camp and known as Auschwitz II, or Birkenau. The gas chambers and the crematoria of the Auschwitz killing center were operated there.[48] The firm J. A. Topf and Sons in Germany won the contract bid to build much larger, permanent gas chambers. Altogether four such installations—II, III, IV, and V—were built in Birkenau.[49]

Most of the Jews deported to Auschwitz were killed on arrival, especially children, women, the old, and the weak. Usually ss officers conducted a quick selection process, with the majority sent directly to the gas chambers, gassed that same day, and their corpses burned in the crematoria.[50] Those selected for forced labor were tattooed with a number on their left arm, had their hair shorn—men and women alike—and were given striped prisoners' garb.[51] A much smaller group was selected for pseudo-medical experiments, and they underwent unbelievable suffering and torture, including sterilization experiments by the physician Carl Clauberg, who had the rank of ss-Brigadeführer. Groups of twins were selected, as well as dwarfs, and used in experiments by Josef Mengele, "the Angel of Death."[52]

Violations of orders in the camp were severely punished by flogging, solitary confinement, withholding food rations, and so forth. This led many to lose hope and await their demise. Termed *Muselmann,* such a person was so emaciated and weak that he could hardly move or react to his surroundings and would soon be consigned to the gas chamber. *Kapos* (prisoner orderlies), *Blockälteste* (block elders), and *Vorarbeiter* (foremen) were part of a group of privileged prisoners who received better food and conditions and more chances to survive, provided they helped to enforce the terror regime on their fellow prisoners.[53]

Trains with victims arrived in Auschwitz-Birkenau from all parts of Europe: Poland, Germany, France, the Netherlands, Belgium, Greece, Slovakia, and the Czech provinces. One select group from the Theresienstadt ghetto was interned in a section of Birkenau that came to be known as the Theresienstadt family camp. After a stay of six months they were killed in the gas chambers. On May 2, 1944, the first transport of Jews from German-invaded Hungary arrived, part of much larger waves that began arriving on May 16 and lasted until mid-July. Some 20,000 gypsies were also deported to Auschwitz-Birkenau and killed in the gas chambers.[54] Prisoners forced to work in the gas chamber area were dubbed *Sonderkommando*. They had to urge the victims to enter the gas chambers silently, and afterwards they burned the corpses in the crematorium ovens.

The Jewish prisoners there organized an uprising on October 7, 1944, that destroyed at least one of the gas chambers, but they all fell in battle or were executed later, with the exception of a handful.[55] Gunpowder used in the uprising had been smuggled in by a group of Jewish women who worked in a nearby facility known simply as Auschwitz III.[56] It was located in nearby Monowitz (Polish, Monowice), where a third camp was built, sometimes referred as Buna-Monowitz—the name Buna deriving from the Buna synthetic-rubber works in that place. In the course of time, another forty-five subcamps were built. The inmates, chiefly Jews, were worked to the point of total exhaustion producing synthetic gas by German oil firms, including the conglomerate giant I.G. Farben.[57]

The whole Auschwitz complex was guarded by 2,500 to 6,000 ss men, depending on the various periods.[58] Jewish prisoners Rudolf Vrba and Alfred Wetzler escaped on April 7, 1944, and wrote a detailed report on Auschwitz, known as the Auschwitz Protocols (see chapter 6).[59] In mid-January 1945, fearing the arrival of the approaching Soviet army, the ss forced some 58,000 prisoners, most of them Jews, on death marches, in freezing weather; most of them died on these marches.[60] On January 27, 1945, Soviet troops soldiers liberated Auschwitz.[61]

Auschwitz was the largest graveyard in human history. Various estimates exist for the number of Jews murdered in that horrific place—of up to 1.5 million. Auschwitz has passed into international usage as the iconic word for all that is the most bestial in human behavior—and for the Jewish people, the most devastating destruction of lives in its long history.

Alfred (Fredy) Hirsch

During the first six months of the family camp's existence, he made great efforts to give the children there a semblance of care, compassion, and hope amid the horrific conditions surrounding them—for as long as the youngsters were allowed to live.

Born in 1916 in Aachen, Germany, Alfred (Fredy) Hirsch was active in the German Jewish scouting movement. His brother, mother, and stepfather left for Bolivia, but Hirsch, an ardent Zionist, remained in Germany while planning to move to Palestine. In 1935 he left Nazi Germany for Prague, where he was active in sports training and preparing *halutzim* (pioneers) for life in Palestine and organizing summer scout camps. After the Germans took over in March 1939, he continued to organize sports contests and competitions of Jewish youth, as well as planning theater productions.[62]

On December 4, 1941, Alfred Hirsch was deported to Theresienstadt camp. There, too, he took an interest in the welfare of Jewish youth. Together with two others, he was in charge of the Jewish children, who were housed separately. He took care of their athletic training and day-to-day attention to their personal hygiene, to prop up their self-assurance and hope for a better day. One day he disobeyed orders not to wander into a special section of children who had arrived at Theresienstadt from Poland, and as punishment he was sent with 5,000 other Czech Jewish prisoners to Auschwitz, where he arrived in September 1943.[63]

Auschwitz's Family Camp

Surprisingly, to say the least, for an inhumane place like that—the children and their parents from among this group were incarcerated, not like other arrivals who either were straightforward committed to the gas chambers or selected for work, but were taken to a special section, known as B2b—a family camp, that was totally different in composition and activity than anything else in Auschwitz-Birkenau. The inhabitants of the family camp were spared the customary selection process and the subsequent extermination of those "unfit for work." Instead, in their special family camp, located not far from the main entrance gate, they were allowed to keep their civilian clothes, their hair was not cut, and women, men, and children were allowed to remain together as family units.[64] This episode has continued to puzzle historians of that horrific concentration camp.

Rudolf Vrba, one of the Jewish Auschwitz prisoners, watched the arrival of this group and was stunned. "Never before had families been kept together in Auschwitz, except in the gas chambers. Never before had they been allowed to retain their clothes and their luggage. It was a puzzle, a mystery and, we older prisoners felt quite sure, a trick of some sort . . . [for] getting V.I.P. treatment. The ss men treated them with consideration, joking with them, playing with the children."[65] The sight of children with unshaven heads who wore civilian clothes was practically unprecedented in Auschwitz.[66]

At the same time, during their registration at the ss office, where Vrba also worked, he noted that each of them, even the youngest children, who were about two years of age, had been tattooed with a special number that bore no relation to Auschwitz, and each had a card on which was added SB6, which Vrba correctly interpreted as SB: Sonderbehandlung = special treatment, then death. In other words, "six months quarantine; then special treatment."[67] After six months they were to be killed, so Vrba concluded, and he was presciently right. Then in December 1943 another transport of 5,000 Jews arrived from Theresienstadt—they too received the special family camp treatment. No one knew why these prisoners were accorded such privileges and assigned separately from other camp inmates. Would their fate be different than the other prisoners? Most hoped that this would indeed be so, or else why this preferential treatment in this hell on earth?[68]

Together with the December arrivals, the children now counted around 500, and Alfred Hirsch managed to obtain a special building for them. There were practically no other living Jewish children in Birkenau except those selected by Josef Mengele for his medical experiments or those who had lied about their age.[69] Although the *kapo*, or "camp elder," of the family camp was a German criminal prisoner, all other official duties remained in the hands of Jewish prisoners. Living conditions were not as bad as in others, but still many died the first six months of their incarceration, due mostly to starvation, and the mortality rate felled some of the adult prisoners in the family camp as well. But, in general, the children enjoyed better conditions. During the day, the 500 children left their parents, with whom they had spent the night, and headed to block 31, where cultural activities were organized for their benefit.[70]

Making Conditions Livable for the Children

Hirsch created a staff whose single purpose was to hide from their charges the reality of Auschwitz-Birkenau. The children's block was located close to the main entrance, a distance from the gas chambers and ovens. However, the smoke and the stench of burning bodies could not be concealed.[71] "I saw them set aside a barracks for the children," Vrba wrote after the war; "a nursery, no less, in the shadow of the crematorium. I saw a blond, athletic man of about thirty [probably Hirsch], organizing games, then lessons and somehow the sight of it was good for my morale, even though I had a nasty suspicion that those children were going to die."[72]

Fredy Hirsch was the leading spirit and organizer in making conditions livable for the children in the worst possible place on earth for any sort of human living. At first he served as sort of a *kapo* and afterward as the block senior, and in that capacity he managed to reserve one of the wooden buildings in the family camp for the children's block. The Germans agreed to Hirsch's request to have the children's roll call inside the hut, instead of outside in the cold weather, as well as to obtain better food for them, even milk and eggs—in Auschwitz-Birkenau, of all places![73] To the amazement of all, for some unexplainable reason, the Germans were keenly interested in meeting Hirsch halfway. He was an incredibly charismatic figure, as well as athletically built, a sportsman, a good-looking man who did everything he could for the children. "I don't know how he got the privilege," one of the surviving children reported. "We were able to spend the day in relative warmth. . . . We had educators there. We even tried to perform theater. We rehearsed various pantomimes and poems."[74]

In Block 31 Hirsch sought to create for the children an environment of a social-educational-treatment facility modeled after the "children's house" in Theresienstadt. The children were divided into small groups, mostly by age; sections in the block doubled as classrooms, and lessons were improvised. Each group with its teachers and guardians moved to a designated area of the block to spend three hours studying, with each group sitting on wooden bunks arranged in a circle around the teacher, and next to it sat another group. In the afternoon, three more hours were devoted to sports activities and games until roll call. Studies had to be done without the aid of books or notebooks, all based on memory, imagination, and the ability to tell stories. Lessons were in geography, history, and astronomy. Eight books found their way to the children's block, including H. G. Wells's *Brief History of the World,* a Russian-language textbook, and an analytical geometry text.[75] Then came supper. Afterward they were allowed to visit their parents and remain with them for the rest of the night.

Theatrical rehearsals were staged, and it included performances of a production of *Snow White and the Seven Dwarfs*. It was attended by SS men, including the dreaded Dr. Josef Mengele. He applauded the children enthusiastically, had them sit on his lap, and asked them to call him Uncle.[76] The children also staged a play entitled *Five Minutes in Robinson's Kingdom*, a local paraphrase of the story of Robinson Crusoe, a play written by Jirzi Frenkel—all this while thousands of others, in a most surreal setting, were making their way to the gas chambers. One girl was a gifted painter and drew on the walls of the block daisies and bellflowers, as well as motifs from children's tales, including Snow White. The walls turned into windows onto another world. Other activities included games and singing of German songs—sometimes so loudly as to attract the attention of SS guards, who came to check and be impressed by the singers, applauding along with the others.[77]

The children's daily schedule began early in the morning when they arrived at block 31. Their breakfast was brought by other children carrying pots and crates of food. They would start by washing themselves and performing morning calisthenics. Even here, in Auschwitz, Hirsch insisted on the children's hygiene and held physical activities in high regard as he organized gymnastics, games, and even soccer and handball competitions. He also tried to obtain clothes for the children that would lend a semblance of normality to their life. Strange as it may sound, the same SS officers who brutally led others into the gas chambers took steps in the family camp to improve conditions, going so far as bettering their diet, including meat, white bread, sugar, and milk.[78] Josef Mengele also used to visit the children's block, and he was always very kind to the children and asked them if they were happy with their educators and if they needed anything. In the words of one of the youngsters, Toman Brod, "He behaved more like an uncle, like a good guardian of the order and welfare of the children. He was particularly interested in twins. In my eyes, Mengele at that time did not represent the terrible murderer that he in fact was."[79]

Inevitably, as some including perhaps Hirsch himself suspected, this charade would one day come to an abrupt end. In late February 1944, the September 1943 transport neared the end of its six-month quarantine period. Hirsch was told that preparations were in place to move the children with their parents to a so-called nonexistent Heidelbreck camp. But he was secretly informed by the Auschwitz resistance movement that this was a hoax and that they would be taken directly to the gas chambers The underground urged Hirsch to head an uprising of the family camp, as this could produce a slim chance of escape for a handful of prisoners, although certain death for the great majority of prisoners in the family camp and certain death for all the children. On the morning of March 8, 1944, Alfred Hirsch discussed his options with Rudolf Vrba, who reaffirmed to him that the whole transport would surely head for the gas chambers. As recorded by Vrba,

I gazed across the room at this strong young German, at his open, enquiring face and I knew that here was a man who would follow his conscience, even if it meant death. "Fredy, you're the only man who can do it. The only man they'll follow." "But, Rudi," he said in something like a whisper, "what about the children?" This was the moment I had feared. I knew how much he loved those kids, how much they loved him. He was their second father, the axis on which their young lives turned. "Fredy," I said, "the children are going to die. That you must believe. But tens of thousands of children have died here before and now we have a chance to put a stop to it. To smash the camp so that no other kids will ever be gassed here. Think of it that way. . . . A few hundred die today because nobody can save them. But tens of thousands of other youngsters will live."

His face was pale and tense; his hand shook as he lit a cigarette. "How can I leave them, Rudi?" he said. "How can I march off to fight for my own skin and leave them to be butchered? Don't you see they trust me? They need me!" "They're doomed, Fredy. You can't save them. Think of others. Think of all the thousands of kids all over Europe. Kids who are at home with their parents but who'll burn in Auschwitz if we don't act now." . . . "Give me an hour, Rudi," he said. "Give me an hour to think it over." It was about eleven o'clock. The gassings I reckoned were unlikely to start before late afternoon. I said to Fredy: "Right, but remember . . . there's only one way you can help anybody."[80]

When Vrba returned, Alfred-Fredy Hirsch was lying on the bed unconscious but still alive. His heavy breath was growling in his throat. His face was bluish grey. Flecks of froth hung on his lips. It was clear that he had swallowed some poison or an overdose of tranquilizers. Vrba dashed from the barracks and searched frantically for one of the prisoner doctors. When they came, they had merely to confirm his death.[81] His body was taken to the crematorium for burning. It was later learned that before his suicide he had appointed several people as his successors to deal with the other children who had arrived in December 1943 and whose six-month grace period had not yet arrived.[82]

After Hirsch

As for the family camp inmates, shortly before their gassing, they were told to send postcards to relatives who had stayed behind in Theresienstadt and in other places; the postcards were postdated March 25, that is, two weeks after their senders were no longer among the living, and filled with false encouraging words.[83] As recorded by Filip Müller, one of the surviving Sonderkommando personnel, the family camp elders went into the gas chambers loudly singing the Czechoslovak national anthem ,"Where Is My Home," followed by "Hatikvah," the Zionist national anthem.[84]

Alfred's successors attempted to restore a semblance of routine to the life of the remaining children, those that had arrived in the second transport—studies, games, singing, and spectacles. Conditions in the family camp, strangely, improved; a Passover Seder was even organized in block 31, in April 1944.[85] An improvised children's choir sang from Beethoven's Ninth Symphony. Over 300 children and adults sang together "All men are brothers."[86]

In May 1944 another transport from Theresienstadt arrived at Birkenau and joined the surviving remnants of earlier transports. Hundreds of new children joined the block. By that time children no longer lived with their parents. They had a special block that served as living quarters.[87] As earlier, all prisoners were annotated on their registration card with the symbol SB6–"special treatment after six months."[88] The final curtain for the family camp came down in July 1944. The six months allotted to the December transport were almost up. On July 1, 1944, Mengele appeared in the camp, and the selection of men, women, and children commenced. All were told to get undressed, covering only the lower part of their bodies with their clothes, and pass by him one by one. Those selected to live were taken past the gypsy camp to the sauna, that is, the bath. The rest went to the gas chambers. The entire children's block was liquidated.[89] It had lasted ten months.

The whole existence of the family camp remains a mystery, confounding those trying to make sense of it. What was the purpose behind the camp's existence? Some reject the explanation that it was meant to be a show camp for a visit by a foreign delegation, since it was questionable whether the Germans would allow any outside visitors inside Birkenau, a few dozen meters from the gas chambers and crematoria. Historian Nili Keren thinks otherwise, that it was meant to refute reports of mass extermination of Jews by offering "proof" to the contrary, and that the Jewish inmates of B2b were held as living proof that reports about Auschwitz had been without foundation. She adds that the Red Cross delegation that visited Theresienstadt on June 23, 1944, was scheduled to continue to Auschwitz, but then they canceled. When that happened, the Nazis no longer needed the subterfuge of a family camp.[90]

For the six months they were allowed to live, thanks to Fredy Hirsch, the doomed hundreds of children enjoyed a semblance of life in a place otherwise associated with despair and death, and he is to be appreciated for his sacrificial self-effort in that regard. Then, when he could no longer save them, he saw no further purpose in his own life. In that sense, he too is to be counted among the Jewish heroes of the Holocaust.

Hadassah Rosensaft

> She was extraordinarily courageous in giving medical assistance to Jews in the Auschwitz and Bergen-Belsen camps, and after liberation she helped save survivors who were near death.

Born in 1912 in Sosnowiec, Poland, Hadassah and her parents lived a rather comfortable life. Father was a follower of the Hasidic Gur dynasty (so-called after the town of Góra Kalwaria, where that Hasidic movement was born). Hadassah wished to pursue a medical career, but as she had little chance of being accepted by a medical faculty in Poland because of anti-Jewish restrictions in institutions of higher learning, she left for France in October 1930 to study dentistry.[91]

Returning to Sosnowiec in 1935 as an accredited dental surgeon, she found work in a dental clinic and remained at her post until the start of the war. By then she was married to Josef Preserowicz, and in

December 1937 she gave birth to a son, Benjamin (Beni). Then came the German invasion of September 1939. Soon after the German takeover, Hadassah opened a dental practice in her parents' home, in the Sosnowiec ghetto, and also worked in the hospital.[92] She and her husband and son were deported on August 4, 1943, and arrived in Auschwitz-Birkenau camp. Father and son were sent to the gas chambers, while Hadassah and several hundred other women were spared and selected for work. She was taken to Camp A, where she slept with ten women on a bed, packed like sardines. Daily food consisted of a bowl of some kind of herbal tea, and for lunch they were served a so-called soup, made of water with turnip leaves. In the evenings they ate only black bread. Once a week, a very small piece of margarine was added, and a small piece of spreadable cheese. Once in a while also a little jam or marmalade was provided.[93]

Hadassah endured occasional physical abuse by the ss guards. On one occasion a female guard struck her with a club in the back of her head, in a spot called the "yellow point," where the visual nerves meet. As Hadassah recalled: "I fell on the stone floor and lost my sight. I was totally blind! I was thinking of how I could get some cyanide so I wouldn't have to go to the gas chamber. Little by little my vision started to return." She also fell ill with malaria, then hepatitis and a liver infection, but was able to get back on her feet in a short time[94]

Doctoring at Birkenau

She also met the notorious Dr. Josef Mengele, who called for all imprisoned medical personnel to report for work in the Jewish infirmary, also called the Jewish *Ambulanz*. Although she had been trained as a dentist, Mengele decided that as there were already two dentists, she would have to work as a doctor. Women came to the infirmary with abscesses, furuncles, and wounds inflicted by the dogs and whips of the ss guards.[95] The infirmary was short on supplies; they had only some paper bandages, which looked like rolls of toilet paper, and very few pills, mainly aspirin, and a little bit of ointment that resembled petroleum jelly.[96] Hadassah and her fellow workers tried various ways to prevent the sick internees from being sent to the gas chambers. They would dress the inmates in heavy clothes and send them out to work with a labor commando. When Mengele came to inspect, he was told there were no sick women and that they had all left for work. "To our great relief, he believed us, and we were able to save all our patients."[97]

A Hospital, an Infirmary, and the Children's Block at Bergen-Belsen

On November 14, 1944, after a year and three months stay in Birkenau, Hadassah and eight others were sent to Bergen-Belsen. Originally conceived as a place to hold people slated for exchange against German nationals residing in foreign countries, by September and October 1944 it had become inundated with transports of thousands of Jewish prisoners from evacuated Polish camps and death marches. As more such arrivals poured in, total chaos reigned inside the camp, with a typhus epidemic at its height. Between January and mid-April 1945, 35,000 perished.[98]

The ss camp doctor, Dr. Schnabel, an old man, ordered the Jewish medical women's team to start preparations for a Jewish hospital, and Hadassah was appointed to organize and supervise it. Tragically, there was no medication for the sick and very few beds, while epidemics raged, and hundreds of people were dying daily.[99] One December evening, a huge truck full of crying children from Holland arrived: forty-nine boys and girls between eight months and fifteen years.[100] A few weeks later, more Jewish children arrived: twenty-one boys from Buchenwald and some others from Theresienstadt. Also children in the camp whose mothers had died of typhus were taken in, and Hadassah's team ended up with 150 Jewish orphans, whom she and her helpers tried desperately to keep alive.[101] Anne Frank and her sister, Margot, arrived there from Auschwitz in March 1945; both girls succumbed to the typhus epidemic that was then raging in the camp.

In two of the barracks that once held Russian prisoners of war, Hadassah and her colleagues established a hospital and an infirmary; a third block was set aside for the children. They had their own beds, and Hadassah's group lived with them and attended to their needs day and night. "We talked to them, played with them, tried to make them laugh, listened to them, comforted them when they cried and had nightmares. When they were sick with typhus, we sat beside them telling fairy tales. I sang songs to them in Polish, Yiddish, and Hebrew—whatever I remembered—just to calm them until they fell asleep."[102] The biggest problem remained the shortage of food for these children. Some Jewish men who worked in the ss food depot risked their lives daily to steal food and pass it over to Hadassah's team under the barbed wire. The Jews working in the ss pharmacies did the same. "They gave us all the medication we needed, and not one of the children succumbed to the raging typhus and other epidemics, although they all went through them."[103]

The winter of 1944–45 was cruel, and the children desperately needed warm clothes, but where was one to get them? Clothes taken from the arriving inmates were kept in a storage room in the camp. Hadassah: "I went there with two of the nurses. To my surprise I was greeted and hugged by the two Polish women whom I had helped and protected from heavy work in the scabies block in Birkenau. They gave us all the clothes we wanted."[104] In early January 1945, Hadassah came into the infirmary and saw a young Jewish woman lying on the operating table, crying. The woman had a severely infected abscess on her foot and had been sent for surgery by the ss doctor, and she told Hadassah that she was afraid to be operated on without an anesthetic. "I calmed her down, then ran to the pharmacy under the pretext of fetching paper bandages and stole a bottle of ether. The woman was operated on and recuperated."[105]

When Bergen-Belsen was liberated by the British army on April 14, 1945, there were some 60,000 prisoners in the camp, most of them in critical condition. Thousands of unburied bodies were strewn all over the campground. In the first five days following liberation, 14,000 died; another 14,000 succumbed in the following weeks. Years later, Hadassah recalled the grim reality of her first days of freedom. "For the greater part of the liberated Jews of Bergen-Belsen," she said, "there was no ecstasy, no joy at our liberation. We had lost our families, our homes. We had no place to go, nobody to hug. Nobody was waiting for us anywhere. We had been liberated from the fear of death, but we were not free from the fear of life"[106]

After Liberation

Hadassah was asked by British officers Glyn Hughes and Colonel James Johnston to organize and head a medical team from among the survivors. Eight doctors and 620 still-convalescent men and women answered Hadassah's appeal for help. Only a few were certified nurses, but they all worked with great devotion together with the British army doctors, nurses, and other personnel under Colonel Johnston's leadership to save many of the debilitated inmates from dying.[107]

A month later, on July 23, Colonel Johnston appointed Hadassah as the senior internee doctor in Bergen-Belsen. Hadassah's group also transferred the surviving children, who were placed in two buildings with bright, spotlessly clean rooms, white sheets on the beds, good food, and constant medical attention.[108] She recalled: "I was busy from before six o'clock in the morning until after midnight, going from one barrack to another to see the patients, to talk with the doctors stationed there, to find out what was needed, how they felt. I supervised the doctors and volunteers from among the survivors who cared for 17,000 sick men and women."[109]

In 1947 Hadassah was elected vice chairman of the Central Committee's Council, representing the Jewish communities throughout the British zone. She was the only surviving Jewish woman in that senior leadership. Earlier, in September 1945, she testified for the prosecution at the first trial of Nazi war criminals before a British military tribunal held in Lüneburg, Germany.

After liberation, Bergen-Belsen became a displaced persons' camp, and it existed up until 1951 under the leadership of Josef Rosensaft, who managed to organize a lively social, cultural, and political life in the camp.[110] Earlier, on August 18, 1946, Josef and Hadassah married, while still in the Bergen-Belsen DP camp, and a son, Menachem, was born to them there on May 1, 1948. The newborn family remained in the DP camp until 1950. After living in Montreux, Switzerland, for eight years, they settled in New York in 1958. Hadassah Rosensaft was one of the founders and officers of the World Federation of Bergen-Belsen Association, serving as its honorary president after Josef Rosensaft's death in 1975. In 1978 and 1979 she was one of only three Holocaust survivors and four women to serve on President Jimmy Carter's Commission on the Holocaust, and she was influential in ensuring the integration of the survivors' perspective into the design and content of the U.S. Holocaust Memorial Museum in Washington DC. She died on October 3, 1997, of liver failure resulting from the malaria and hepatitis she had contracted in the Auschwitz-Birkenau camp.

Norbert Masur

One of the most incredible meetings was that between SS head Heinrich Himmler and Norbert Masur, a representative of the World Jewish Congress, that lead to the liberation of several thousand Jews.

Heinrich Himmler, the top commander of the ss (with the title Reichsführer ss), as well as the Gestapo and chief of thirty-five combat Waffen-ss divisions, was undoubtedly one of history's greatest killers of innocent lives, if not indeed the greatest. Next to Adolf Hitler, he was the most powerful man in Nazi Germany. The killing of the Jews represented for Himmler the means to achieve the racial supremacy of the Aryans and purify the world of contamination by "sub-humans." Toward the end of the war, however, aware of the inevitable German defeat, Himmler made a number of gestures, apparently hoping to ingratiate himself with the Allies. For this purpose, he tried to initiate peace negotiations with the Allies through Count Folke Bernadotte, head of the Swedish Red Cross, and ordered a cessation of the mass murder of Jews at this time. Hitler, infuriated by Himmler's attempt to negotiate with Eisenhower, in his last will and political testament stripped Himmler of all his positions. Captured by British troops, Heinrich Himmler committed suicide on May 23, 1945.[111]

On April 20, 1945, there took place one of the most incredible meetings on German soil between Himmler and Norbert Masur, a Jewish representative of the World Jewish Congress. Aware of Germany's desperate situation, as well as his own possible demise, Himmler decided on a last-minute gamble to negotiate with a representative of what he believed was the secretive world Jewish government, in order to forestall the utter collapse of Nazi Germany and perhaps also save his own life.[112]

According to his masseur, Felix Kersten, Himmler had told him: "I want to bury the hatchet between us and the Jews," adding that the Führer was a very sick man, and something needed to be done to save Germany, now being overrun by the hated Russian Communists.[113] He would, therefore, not be averse to meeting a high Jewish official, as proposed to him by Kersten, to see whether a deal could be struck. Himmler added a promise of a safe passage for the Jewish person who would agree to come for this incredible session. When word reached Hillel Storch of the World Jewish Congress (wjc) in Sweden, Storch feared for his life (after having already lost many relatives to the Nazis) and turned down the offer for him to fly to Germany to meet Himmler. Masur, also of the wjc, volunteered to go in his stead, hoping to negotiate a last-ditch effort to rescue the remaining Jews in ss concentration camps. But could anyone trust the wily ss head for the safety of a Jewish representative? Would he be allowed to return to Sweden, or be incarcerated instead? There was no such guarantee, but Masur felt he had to take the risk, Saving Jewish lives was uttermost in his mind.

Born in Friedrichstadt, Germany, in 1901, one of ten children, Norbert Masur fled to Stockholm during the Nazi period. There he worked for the World Jewish Congress, an organization founded in Geneva in 1936 to protect Jews against antisemitic onslaughts. On the morning of April 19, Masur was notified that ss chief Heinrich Himmler wanted to meet with him and Dr. Felix Kersten, Himmler's masseur. At 2 p.m. on April 19, the airplane, painted with the swastika emblem, left Stockholm for Berlin with Kersten and Masur as its only passengers. Masur reflected: "For me as a Jew, it was a deeply moving thought that, in a few hours, I would be face to face with the man who was primarily responsible for the destruction of several million Jewish people. . . . I finally would have the important opportunity to be of help to many of my tormented fellow Jews. . . . It was action at the front lines." As the plane approached Berlin, the signs of war from the plane's windows became more evident, with bombed-out houses and factories without roofs everywhere.

Masur did not have a visa, because only Himmler and his closest aides knew of his coming, and it was held in complete secrecy from all the other Nazi bosses. Bereft of such a visa, the Gestapo in Berlin simply ordered that the man in the company of Dr. Kersten be admitted without passport. They were quickly taken to an estate in Gut Hartzwalde, approximately 70 kilometers north of Berlin. The city had been under constant air bombing by Russian and British planes every evening and American planes during the day.

The meeting between Himmler and Masur in Gut Hartzwalde was not far from the Ravensbrück women's camp where the starving and mutilated inmates were unaware that these two men from diametrically opposing camps were meeting to decide their fate. Finally, close to midnight, the car arrived at its destination, the estate belonging to Kersten. Here they were told to await the arrival of Himmler. "That night I was not able to sleep," Masur recalled, "the tension at the thought of meeting with Himmler, the feeling that possibly the destiny of thousands of Jews were dependent on my words. . . . I was especially concerned about the prisoners in the Ravensbrück camp, which was only 30 kilometers from the estate." Early Friday morning, ss General Walter Schellenberg drove up and told Masur and Kersten that since it was April 20, the birthday of the Führer, Himmler was to participate at the birthday dinner that night and then would get to the estate as quickly as possible. "Hitler should only have known that Himmler, after the birthday party, would be negotiating with a Jew!" Masur reflected. "I was excited at the thought that in a few minutes I would be face to face with one of the greatest murderers of the Jewish people."

Face to Face with Himmler

At exactly 2:30 a.m., the noise of a car woke them up, and after a few minutes Himmler entered, followed by ss general Walter Schellenberg, Himmler adjutant Dr. Brandt, and Himmler's masseur, Felix Kersten. Himmler greeted Masur with "*Guten Tag*" and conveyed his satisfaction that Masur had come to see him. He then launched into a lengthy historical overview of the position of the Nazis vis-à-vis the Jews. "The Jews were a foreign element in our midst, which always evoked irritation. They were driven out of Germany several times, but they always returned. After coming into power, we wanted to settle this issue once and for all, and I was in favor of a humane solution through emigration. I conferred with American organizations to arrange for a quick emigration, but even countries who claimed to be friendly toward the Jews did not want to admit Jews"—an assertion that was not far from the truth.

Masur countered that perhaps it would have been more convenient for the German people not to have a minority in its midst. At the same time, it did not seem right to suddenly exile people whose ancestors had lived in a country for a long time. If Jews needed to depart as decreed by the Nazi regime, did this have to be done so quickly? Himmler disregarded this point and continued with his self-styled justification of the anti-Jewish measures. He accused the Jews of supporting Russian partisans and of being infected with many diseases, especially typhoid fever. "I lost thousands of my ss troops to these diseases," Himmler added defensively.

Himmler then got to the subject of the concentration camps. "The bad reputation of these camps was because of the unfortunate choice of names for them; that was a mistake, we should have called them 'educational camps.' . . . The treatment in the camps was severe, but just." Here Masur finally interjected, "But one cannot deny that many atrocities occurred in the camps," to which Himmler answered, with tongue in cheek: "I have to admit that this happened, but I then punished the guilty."

At this point Masur decided to steer the conversation to the purpose of his coming—saving the remaining Jews in German camps. "Too many things have occurred that cannot be changed or rectified anymore," Masur began. "But if in the future we need to build a bridge between our people, then at least the Jews that are still in the areas occupied by Germany should remain alive. Therefore we are asking that the Jews in the camps near the Swedish and Swiss borders be freed in order to evacuate them to these countries. Additionally we ask that the Jews in the other camps be treated well, be fed properly, that they get the proper medical care, and that the camps be surrendered to the Allies without resistance once the front lines get close."

Masur asked Himmler how many Jews were still alive in the camps, and Himmler listed the following figures: Theresienstadt 25,000, Ravensbrück 20,000, and Mauthausen 20,000 to 30,000, in addition to the smaller numbers in several other camps. Also he claimed, falsely, that in the camps captured by the Allies, many Jews were turned over unharmed, such as Auschwitz 150,000 (!), Bergen-Belsen 50,000, and Buchenwald 6,000. It was clear to Masur that the figure with respect to Auschwitz was a lie, but he decided that at this point it was best not to enter into a dispute over figures but to try to save those still alive.

In Hungary, Himmler continued, 450,000 Jews were left alive. "So what were the thanks for this?" he added sanctimoniously. "The Jews shot at our troops in Budapest." Masur objected. "If there were 450,000 Jews left of the original 860,000, it means that 400,000 Jews were deported to an unknown destiny." Annoyed at this rejoinder, Himmler nevertheless continued with his own version of events. "It was my intention to turn over the concentration camps without defending them, as I had promised. I turned over Bergen-Belsen and Buchenwald, but I got no thanks for this. . . . When I released 2,700 Jews into Switzerland last year, this also resulted in a press campaign against me personally. It was written that I only released these people in order to establish an alibi for myself. I do not need an alibi, as I only did what I thought was necessary for my people, and I will stand on that. I did not become a rich man. Nobody has been covered with dirt in the newspapers in the last twelve years as much as I have been." It was a surreal scene, with the history's greatest mass murderer of Jews trying to justify his nefarious behavior to a rather low-level Jewish organizational representative.

Masur thought to himself that, like other top Nazis, Himmler sincerely believed that the Jews really had the power to control the world press, as stated by the Nazi propaganda. "And maybe he thought that I, as a representative of the Jews, could influence the press of the Allied and neutral countries, even though he had been told that I had come as a private citizen." So Masur interrupted and called to Himmler's attention the freedom of the press concept in democratic countries and that a continuation of the policy to release prisoners was the only correct thing to do, regardless of what the press was writing, adding as a palliative, "Without a doubt the granting of our requests by you would make an excellent impression with the people and government of the Allies." Masur came back several times to the need to permit the evacuation of the Ravensbrück camp to Sweden.

Concessions from Himmler

Finally Himmler said that he wanted to discuss the matter with his adjutant, Dr. Brandt, in private. About twenty minutes later Himmler returned to the room and said:

> I am willing to free 1,000 Jewish women from the Ravensbrück concentration camp, and you can pick them up through the Red Cross. The freeing of a number of French women in accordance with the list of the Swedish Foreign Ministry is also approved. About 50 Norwegian Jews in camps will be freed and brought to the Swedish border. . . . A larger number of mostly Dutch prisoners who were listed by name in Theresienstadt will be freed, as long as the Red Cross can pick them up. The Jewish women in Ravensbrück, however, will be designated as Polish women rather than Jewish. It is very necessary that not only your visit here must remain secret [probably fearing Hitler's rage if this was revealed], but also the arrival of the Jews in Sweden must remain that way. With respect to stopping the forced evacuation and the surrendering to the camps to the Allies, I will endeavor to do my very best.

Masur felt much relieved at this unbelievable news. He thought that it was significant that even at this late hour for Nazi Germany, Himmler was afraid to designate the freed women as Jews. While Masur reflected on this point, Himmler suddenly said: "Hitler will be remembered in history as a great man, because he gave the world the National-Socialist solution, the only one which is able to stand up against Bolshevism." This was the only time during the entire conversation that he mentioned Hitler by name, and he continued, "We are asked to surrender unconditionally. That will never happen. I am not afraid to die."

Masur noted that Himmler did not ask for any concessions from him. For sure, Himmler did not think that he could buy his own life at this late hour. The talks had lasted exactly two and a half hours, and it was 5 a.m. when Himmler left by car. Masur had been alone with him for most of this time, in his words, "a free Jew face to face with the feared and unmerciful chief of the ss, who had 5 million Jews on his conscience." While Himmler spoke calmly most of the time, even when interrupted with some sharp challenges, Masur could sense the man's anxiety. As he bid good-bye to Kersten, Himmler said, "The best part of the German people will be destroyed with us; what happens to the rest of them is immaterial."

After Himmler's departure, Masur and Kersten tried to catch a few hours of sleep. It was now important to get to Berlin and then to Stockholm as quickly as possible in order to tell the Swedish Foreign Ministry and the Red Cross about the prisoner evacuations. The entourage left at 10 a.m. for Berlin. As they approached the city, the closeness of the front became evident. Artillery shootings were heard in the distance. Continuing to Gestapo headquarters, they learned that the evacuation of Scandinavian prisoners on the way to Denmark had begun. With Russian artillery beginning to pound Berlin, it was crucial to get out as fast as possible. Masur and Kersten left on an afternoon German military plane for Copenhagen. From there, they continued by car to Elsinore and crossed by boat to Sweden, arriving safely on Swedish soil at 9 p.m. April 20, 1945. The trip was over.

In the meantime, dozens of buses painted white and bearing the emblems of Sweden and the Red Cross left Ravensbrück for Denmark and eventually Sweden, carrying with them thousands of women, including many Jews. Eventually some 7,000 were released from Ravensbrück, of whom 3,000 were Jewish—more than the original number promised by Himmler, thanks to further negotiations between Bernadotte and Himmler. When the Russians liberated the camp on April 30, 1945, there were still 23,000 women and children in Ravensbrück from more than twenty countries. Of the 132,000 imprisoned there during the Nazi period, some 92,000 were murdered or died from exhaustion and illness.[114]

Norbert Masur eventually settled down in Tel Aviv, Israel, and led a modest life, asking for no praises and accolades for his risky tête-à-tête with Himmler that led to the saving of several thousand Jews. He died in 1971. He too belongs in the Jewish pantheon of Holocaust rescue heroes.

13 England

A Rabbi and the Religious Obligation to Save

Records show that Jews were settled in England as far back as 1070. But they were expelled in 1290 and only allowed to return in 1656. It was only much later, in 1829, that Jews were emancipated and in 1858 allowed to sit in Parliament. Due to the lack of anti-Jewish violence in Britain in the nineteenth century, the country acquired a reputation for religious tolerance, and it attracted a significant number of immigrants from Eastern Europe, especially those fleeing the Russian pogroms.

Britain again appeared as a place of refuge in 1933. There were an estimated 350,000 Jews there at the outbreak of World War II, including thousands of refugees and displaced persons. For many, Britain, with its liberal tradition of granting asylum to refugees, was the preferred country of immigration. Others sought temporary refuge there while awaiting transshipment overseas. Others considered Britain an entry point to elsewhere in the British Empire. The number of Jews seeking refuge in Britain rose considerably after Austria's annexation to Nazi Germany in March 1938, and it rose to a crescendo after that government-staged pogrom of Kristallnacht in November 1938.[1]

It should be mentioned that Britain's policy toward Germany in the second half of the 1930s was that of appeasement, championed by Prime Minister Neville Chamberlain. Inside the country, the British Union of Fascists (BUF), a small but vibrant and noisy antisemitic movement, was led by Sir Oswald Mosley.[2]

In Germany, Israel Wilfrid worked in tandem with British Jewish leaders to facilitate the exit of Jewish children to England, especially after Kristallnacht. But the process of admitting Jewish refugees from Germany to England had begun years earlier with the Nazis' rise to power. In March 1933 Otto Schiff established the Jewish Refugees Committee (JRC), the most important voluntary organization of its kind at that time in Britain. The JRC pledged that no refugee would become a public charge and that the Jewish community would ensure support of the refugees until they either had been integrated into British society or had emigrated to another country. The JRC looked after the needs of the refugees: their maintenance, education and training, and further emigration. It has been estimated that before the outbreak of the war, more than 80,000 Jewish refugees had come to Great Britain, and some 55,000 remained there.

In the wake of Kristallnacht, close to 10,000 refugee children, overwhelmingly Jewish, arrived on British shores. Several main organizations assisted them, including the B'nai B'rith, Youth Aliyah, and the Chief Rabbi's Religious Emergency Council, headed by Rabbi Solomon Schonfeld.[3] The children were divided into two categories: those guaranteed by private sponsors, and those guaranteed by the JRC. In February 1939 the government insisted that sponsors post £50 for each child to cover its eventual departure. Once in Britain, the children were housed in reception camps and later taken to foster homes or hostels. After heated discussion, it was decided to accept offers of hospitality in non-Jewish homes. The representatives of the Chief Rabbi's Religious Emergency Council, however, continued to warn against growing missionary attempts aimed at the children.

In 1939 the British government came under renewed pressure because of the acute political embarrassment caused by the May 1939 White Paper, in which the British limited Jewish immigration into Palestine, an attempt to win Arab support in the coming war against Germany.[4] But in September of that year, with the start of the war, all immigration into Britain and the British Empire from enemy or enemy-controlled territory came to a halt, and the treatment of refugees became worse. All Germans and Austrians in England were defined as "enemy aliens." They had to appear before special tribunals for examination, and some were interned.[5] The anxiety about the activities of a supposed "fifth column" caused mass hysteria and open hostility toward refugees. By early summer of 1940, about 30,000 were interned in camps, most of them Jewish refugees. Some were deported to Canada and Australia. The sinking of the ship *Arandora Star* carrying deportees by a German submarine with great loss of life led the government to change its policy, canceling the deportations and returning some of the deportees to its shores. Within a year almost all were released, and thousands of them joined the British army in the war against Germany.[6]

British and U.S. No-Negotiation Policy

The British and U.S. position during the war that there would be no negotiations with Hitler prevented any serious consideration of German proposals for the ransom of Jews. Added to this was another principle that the Allies would continue the war until the unconditional surrender of Germany. There would be no negotiations for a compromise peace that would lead to the war coming to an end earlier, as happened when World War I ended and Germany accepted the terms of President Wilson's proposals.[7] This meant that the Nazis would have a free hand in continuing to murder Jews until Germany's total defeat.

As for the British wartime leader, Winston Churchill, the debate is still on whether he could have done more to try to alleviate the plight of Jews fleeing from Nazi-held countries. He had often declared himself a supporter of the Zionist cause, and in 1939, from the floor of Parliament, he strongly condemned the 1939 White Paper, which slowed Jewish immigration to Palestine to a trickle. But strangely, from May 1940 until the end of the war, when he was prime minister, he upheld the provisions of the White Paper or took no action to overrule those in his cabinet and administration who staunchly defended that policy. While decrying what the Nazis were doing to the Jews, he rarely took an interest in their fate during the Holocaust and did nothing to foster active British support for programs of rescue, as strongly urged by Eleanor Rathbone, a lone voice among British parliamentarians. There was also no British equivalent to the U.S. government's War Refugee Board.

In July 1944 Churchill endorsed the appeals by the Zionist organization and other Jewish leaders that Auschwitz be bombed, but then allowed himself to be overruled by the lower-level bureaucracy. This is somewhat strange, coming from a man known for his strong personality, his stubbornness, and dominant leadership, especially his defiance of Hitler; of a man who on matters of importance to him did not allow lower-grade officials to waylay him. In this instance he acted contrary to his own professed declarations, fully aware of the desperate plight of millions of Jews under Nazi rule. It seems that Churchill supported the official British opinion that the rescue of European Jewry had to await the total victory and defeat of Nazi Germany. And so the doors of Palestine and other places of refuge were to remain closed for now.[8]

Kindertransport

In a 2013 article, Brana Gurewitsch wrote that the mechanism for sending German Jewish children to England without their parents was set into motion by Wilfrid Israel, head of the N. Israel department store, the largest in Berlin, who held both German and British passports.[9] According to Gurewitsch, after Kristallnacht, Zionist leader Chaim Weizmann and Chief Rabbi Joseph Herz appealed to Prime Minister Neville Chamberlain, as well as to the Quakers, for help regarding Jewish children in Germany. A delegation of British Quakers subsequently met with Wilfrid Israel in Berlin, and following his instructions, they made contact with the still existing Jewish communities throughout Germany. Upon their return to England on November 21, 1938, they reported to the British Home Secretary (i.e., Ministry of Interior) that German Jewish parents were ready to send their children to England. The Home Secretary gave its consent to this and facilitated procedures by waiving passport and visa requirements.

The government permitted unaccompanied Jewish children ages three to sixteen to be admitted on the condition that individuals or organizations guarantee their care.[10] The first transport of 200 children, mostly from a Berlin Jewish orphanage, arrived in England on December 2, followed by many more. Close to 10,000 Jewish children and close to 100 non-Jewish ones (and thousands more adult Jews under other immigration categories) were brought in before the outbreak of war.[11]

Applications for a place on what became known as the Kindertransports required parents to agree to have their child placed with any available family, even a nonreligious or a non-Jewish one, and this led many Orthodox families to have second thoughts. At this crucial juncture, Rabbi Solomon Schonfeld stepped in. Responding to appeals by Orthodox rabbinic leaders, Schonfeld decided to organize his own Kindertransport of hundreds of religious Jewish children, with or without the approval of the Jewish Refugee Committee, especially refugees from Vienna, then part of Nazi Germany.[12]

Solomon Schonfeld

> This determined rabbi arranged safe haven in
> England for several thousand Jews, including rabbis,
> teachers, cantors, and yeshiva students.

Solomon Schonfeld was born in London in 1912. His father, Victor (Avigdor) Schonfeld, led the small Orthodox congregation of Adas Yisroel in north London and was the founder of the British branch of Mizrahi, the religious Zionists.[13] Solomon was sent overseas to study at Rabbi Samuel David Ungar's yeshiva in Trnava, Slovakia, a bastion of Hungarian-style Orthodoxy, where he met and befriended Rabbi Michael Dov-Ber Weissmandl (richly described in chapter 4). He also did a stint in the famous Slabodka yeshiva in Lithuania where, in 1933, he earned rabbinical ordination while simultaneously earning a PhD degree from the nearby University of Königsberg.[14] Returning to London he succeeded his father (who died at age forty-nine) as rabbi of Adas Yisroel and was also principal of England's first Jewish Day School.[15] In 1940 he married Judith Hertz, the daughter of England's chief rabbi, Joseph H. Hertz. In personal appearance, Solomon Schonfeld was physically impressive: approximately six feet tall, broad-shouldered, walking erect, very handsome and charismatic, with friendly blue eyes and a red-blondish beard. He also impressed people with his quick mind, limitless energy, and great memory.[16]

Shelter for Orthodox Children

After Kristallnacht and British consent to the immigration of Jewish children, Rabbi Schonfeld began to plan the transport of children, especially those from religious homes, through the newly established Chief Rabbi's Religious Emergency Council (CRREC). While Rabbi Herz was its nominal head, Rabbi Schonfeld was its executive director and leading activist.[17] Soon a first batch of some 100 children under the age of sixteen arrived in London, sent over by Dr. Erich Klibanksy, director of the Yawne high school in Cologne.[18]

In December 1938, returning from a hurried trip to Vienna, Schonfeld met with an official from the British Home Office who wanted to see proof of temporary shelter in Britain for the 300 youngsters for whom Schonfeld requested entry visas. According to one witness, Schonfeld showed the official two empty schools—empty because the students had been dismissed for the Hanukkah festival. The desks and furniture had been cleared out from the classroom, and cots were set up. The official noted that the space, according to government regulations, could only hold 250 children.[19] "Where," he asked, "would the rest of the youngsters sleep?" Schonfeld took the official to the home he shared with his mother and youngest brother and showed him rooms filled with cots. "That's fine," said the official, "but where will you sleep?" Schonfeld took him up to the attic, where his own cot was located. That impressed the Home Office official, and permission was granted.[20] Schonfeld immediately prepared two Kindertransports, each of close to 300 Orthodox youngsters. He also doctored the records for some seventeen-year-olds who, due to their more advanced age, were not eligible for placement under the Kindertransport program.[21]

Rabbi Schonfeld brought the first transport of children from Austria in November 1938. His two schools were hurriedly equipped with beds, bedding, and bare necessities until the children could all be satisfactorily dispersed to families or hostels. With considerable risk to his own safety, Schonfeld traveled time and again to Europe to bring the children over, and he coaxed the hesitant youngsters into leaving their homes and following him, as though he were a religious Pied Piper.[22]

The children could not live in the school forever, and as Meir Eiseman, one of Schonfeld's aides, recalled:

> We young people walked the streets of N. 16 [London], going from house to house asking the people whether they would be willing to take a refugee boy or girl into their homes. These houses were mostly one-family homes, not small apartments. . . . It was hard work to persuade them to take in refugees. The British Jews in those days didn't quite believe what was going to happen. . . . Some of them said to us, "I have no room," when in fact they had five, six, seven and even eight rooms in their houses.[23]

Some of the children remember the painful experience of being separated from their parents and their arrival in a country whose language and customs they did not know. Thea Fingerhut (née Ginsburg), age seventeen in 1938, had arrived in England through the intervention of people she knew only slightly. She then wished to bring her family over as well. "Go to Dr. Schonfeld," she was told. "He will help." She told him about her three sisters and one brother who were still in Vienna. "What? Four children?" Dr. Schonfeld exclaimed. "This is not enough for a transport. We need more children! Get me more names of children in Vienna!" Thea wrote home, and her father promptly sent back a list of twenty-five names. Eventually all these children arrived in England. In her words,

> I myself saw Dr. Schonfeld send drivers to Oxford Street with hand-written instructions; they returned with truckloads of cots, beds, towels, blankets, and pillows. . . . We took over the elegant parlor in his mother's house at 35 Lordship Park. After storing the beautiful antique china and silver in a safe place, we set up two rows of beds . . . in front of the mantelpiece, and a row of cots on the opposite side for the younger children. Soon Mrs. Schonfeld's beautiful parlor looked like the dormitory of a camp. What a joy it was when my sisters arrived in London on December 22, 1938!

Her ten-year-old brother joined them on January 12, 1939.[24]

As for Leo Shick, he was one of the yeshiva students whose name was submitted by Rabbi Schonfeld to the Home Office. Just before the outbreak of World War II, Schonfeld had created a "paper yeshiva." When a rabbi wanted to come to England, Rabbi Schonfeld wrote to the Home Office informing them he was setting up a yeshiva in London and needed the man as a teacher there. But the yeshiva lacked students. So Rabbi Weissmandl (in Slovakia) submitted thirteen names of boys still in Vienna who would be the students, and Schonfeld promptly submitted them to the Home Office, adding that he would take personal responsibility for them. "I was one of them," Leo Shick stated. The visas were granted immediately.

In addition, Schonfeld brought over fifty older boys, also as yeshiva students. The later chief rabbi of England, Sir Immanuel Jakobovits, was one of the children whom Schonfeld brought over from Nazi Germany.[25] Another boy, later Rabbi Emanuel Fischer, a native of Vienna, told of the English lessons he took. "The first thing we learned in English was 'In the beginning God created the heaven and earth.' I'll never forget that."[26] Others recall Rabbi Schonfeld's first question upon meeting the arriving children: "*Hast du Taschengeld?*"(Have you got pocket money?)[27]

With the start of the war and then the fear of enemy air bombs, some 550 Orthodox children had to be evacuated from London immediately, together with thousands of other youngsters. They were brought to Shefford and several other villages in the London countryside. Many of the villagers in the towns surroundings London had never seen a Jew before, nor had they heard of Jewish dietary laws. To help the children avoid eating unkosher meat, Schonfeld asked them to tell their foster parents that they were "fish-eating vegetarians" until he could make arrangements to provide them with kosher food.[28]

Miriam Eiseman-Elias was staying with a non-Jewish family. "In accordance with Dr. Schonfeld's instructions, we informed the Taylors that we were fish-eating vegetarians and that therefore we could not eat any meat." But they were in for a surprise. "We came down to the dining room where the table had been set for lunch. And there, to our great shock, we saw prepared on each of our plates a huge red lobster! Jenny Wexner, our counselor, who was no more than sixteen or seventeen, had to explain to the Taylors that there were also certain fish that we couldn't eat. Our foster parents accepted her explanation."[29]

They were soon joined by two religious boys from Vienna, wearing *payot* (sideburns), who objected strongly in Yiddish to taking a bath with soap on the Sabbath. "We had to explain . . . that our religion forbade us to have a bath on our Sabbath day." The children took their meals in these non-Jewish foster homes until Schonfeld's school was able to set up a canteen for them.[30]

Children were not the only ones Rabbi Schonfeld helped. He obtained permits for his teachers through the Ministry of Labor and secured positions for them as functionaries in synagogues or as teachers in Jewish day schools and yeshivot. A week after Kristallnacht, Schonfeld brought over 45 rabbis of all denominations who had been inmates in concentration camps, along with their families. By the time war broke out, Schonfeld had brought 1,300 rabbis, teachers, and other religious functionaries and their families to England, according to historian David Kranzler.[31]

Schonfeld's Critics

As painful as it is to admit, Schonfeld's activities were not looked upon kindly by mainline Jewish organizations. The Board of Jewish Deputies, which represented the Anglo-Jewish establishment, viewed itself as the official organization to deal with the issues of Jewish refugees and resented Schonfeld's self-styled intrusion in this work.[32] Major Jewish relief organizations, such as the Central British Fund and the German Jewish Aid Committee, were created to specifically address the plight of German and Austrian refugees, and these "establishment" agencies kept their distance from Schonfeld, even trying to undermine and hamper his activity. They viewed him as a religious "separatist" and an interloper, a threat and a nuisance, a rule-breaker, and a competitor in fund-raising.[33]

While it is true that often he did not have accommodations and board ready for the children until after they arrived in England, in his view the most important thing was to save lives, no matter how or by what means, and as fast as possible before the doors of refuge slammed shut. He would worry about the refugees' accommodations and economic sustenance later, once they were out of the danger zone.[34]

Schonfeld suspected that much of the criticism was due to the fact that the Anglo Jewish leadership felt uncomfortable with the influx of Orthodox rabbis and students. In addition, Selig Brodetsky, a Board of Deputies member and an ardent Zionist, focused his endeavors on Palestine as the haven for refugees, while Schonfeld recognized that Palestine was a contentious issue for the British (due to the White Paper policy), and hence great efforts had to be made to find other safe havens.[35] In reality, the Board of Jewish Deputies was responsible for rescuing more children than Schonfeld. But Schonfeld worked alone and took a personal interest in his wards, visiting them and providing for their education, both secular and religious. To some, he became a substitute parent.

The biggest bone of contention between the establishment Jews and Schonfeld was the issue of placing refugees in non-Jewish homes. While appreciating the kindheartedness of the host families, Schonfeld was concerned with the consequences for the children's religious lives, and he aimed at keeping at least Orthodox youngsters together in Orthodox homes or in hostels that served kosher food.[36]

Internment Camps, Safe Havens Elsewhere

In May 1940, when fear of "fifth columnists," that is, persons spying for Germany, gripped the British public, coupled with fear of a German invasion, Jewish refugees from Germany and Austria had to suffer the shame and insults of being suspected of disloyalty toward England. The British government ordered the internment of some 30,000 Jewish German refugees over the age of sixteen as "enemy aliens," with many detained on the Isle of Man, between England and Ireland. Many of the internees were elderly and too sick to withstand the primitive conditions in the camps, and they began to die. Here, too, Rabbi Schonfeld took it upon himself to care for their physical, mental, and religious needs. Eventually he helped obtain the release from internment of about 1,000 people.[37]

With the war in full swing, Schonfeld worked to secure safe havens elsewhere in the British Empire for fleeing Jews. He was able to obtain 340 Mauritius end-visas for about 1,000 Jews.[38] He also lobbied the British Parliament, with the support of MP Eleanor Rathbone and the archbishop of Canterbury, to issue a proclamation to allow Jewish refugees access to British colonial territories. This motion was supported by 177 members of Parliament in March 1943, but the House of Lords shelved it.[39] In May 1943 Schonfeld met with the Ethiopian envoy in London, Ayala Gabra, to suggest opening Ethiopia as a place of refuge, but he was turned down.[40]

Young Survivors Back to Their Jewish Roots

Soon after the war ended, in May 1945 Rabbi Schonfeld once more implemented a new kind of Kindertransport. His immediate goal was to save the surviving children in Poland. Almost all of them were orphans, and many had been hidden with non-Jewish families. He wanted to find them and bring them back to the Jewish community and their Jewish heritage. He was able to arrange his first trip to Poland in November 1945. He found there a rampant antisemitism, coupled with many incidents of the murder of surviving Jews. On many occasions Schonfeld was forced to pay a ransom to regain a Jewish child from the family who had hidden it.

When visiting monasteries and convents, Schonfeld would recite the Jewish prayer Shema, familiar to even young Jewish children, and when voices joined his, he knew he had found them.[41] In his travels in Poland, Schonfeld dressed like a military man of top rank and acted like one. He wore a uniform he had designed himself. According to one observer, "People were not too sure about his rank, but he acted as if he were a high-ranking officer of the British General Imperial Staff. He gave orders right and left, set up soup kitchens, synagogues, and study rooms. Altogether he made five trips to Poland in 1945."[42]

While in Warsaw, Schonfeld discussed the problem of Jewish children with the first secretary of the British embassy, who agreed to issue British visas for the children based on Nansen passports (internationally recognized refugee travel documents for stateless persons, so named after Fridtjof Nansen, high commissioner for refugees for the League of Nations after World War I).[43] In 1946 Schonfeld chartered a boat in Gdansk and escorted 150 Jewish boys and girls to England. Between 1946 and 1947, Schonfeld organized several transports from Poland to London totaling hundreds of orphan children and youngsters.[44] After their arrival in London, he settled the newcomers with Orthodox Jewish families.

One of these was Henya Mintz: "I wanted to get out of Poland as quickly as possible, because the night before, rocks had been thrown at the building where we lived." She was told that Rabbi Schonfeld was staying in a certain hotel in Kraków. He met her there, wearing an army uniform and surrounded by youngsters anxious to leave Poland. He was not supposed to take anyone older than eighteen. "Since I was over eighteen, I had to make myself younger," and Schonfeld arranged that for her.[45] He said, "I'll send you a telegram to report to the British Consulate in Warsaw as soon as your visa is ready. We'll give you a sponsor."[46]

Schonfeld also visited the displaced persons camps in Germany and obtained ambulance-trucks that he transformed into "mobile synagogues" filled with kosher food, medical supplies, and religious articles—always while wearing his fake British uniform. In 1945 he succeeded in transporting Czech Jewish children to England just before the start of Passover.[47] In the spring of 1948, Schonfeld arrived in Prague to put together his last children's transport of some 150 youngsters ranging in age from six to seventeen. As he had done on the eve of the war, he temporarily cleared out his schools and used them as dormitories until all the refugee children were placed safe and sound.[48]

Altogether Rabbi Solomon Schonfeld is credited with having saved several thousand children and adults, both before and immediately after the war. Precise figures have to await fuller verification.[49] A modest and self-effacing person, he took no account of the statistics of his rescue efforts. Once when asked how many people he had saved, he replied, "How many *didn't* I save?"[50] In 1984 Solomon Schonfeld passed away at the age of seventy-two after a long illness.[51]

14 The United States

Organizational Assistance amid Conflicting Agendas

Any account of Jewish self-help during the Holocaust would not be complete without mentioning the role of certain Jewish organizations operating in the United States (who vied with each other, sometimes in bad taste) to save their Jewish brethren in Europe. These include the so-called Bergson Group, the Vaad Hatzala, the Jewish Labor Committee, and foremost, the Joint Distribution Committee. Their stories will presently be told at some length. But first a few words on the U.S. policy regarding refugees.

During the critical years between 1937 and 1941, just before the United States entered the war, the American economy had still not recovered from the Great Depression. There was fear that a steady stream of refugees would increase unemployment, and so policymakers continued to enforce the restrictive immigration laws that were legislated in the 1920s. There was also a strong isolationist sentiment, the aftereffects of the country's participation in World War I. Even after the U.S. entry into World War II, anti-refugee sentiments were still evident, buttressed by a new fear that Germany would infiltrate spies into the refugee stream.[1] Also not to be overlooked was the strident antisemitism of the 1930s, which was evident in many places and deeply concerned American Jews. In the view of historian Henry Feingold, this social antisemitism had a paralyzing effect on Jewish activism that even the visibility of Jews in high places in the Roosevelt administration could not allay.[2] Jewish leaders who urged a stronger U.S. intervention in European affairs, especially where it affected Jews, faced the staunch opposition of isolationist spokesmen like aviator Charles Lindbergh, who in a speech in Des Moines in September 1941 warned that Anglophiles and Jews were trying to bring the United States into the war, against its best interests.[3]

U.S. laws at the time limited immigration to only 2 percent of the number of each nationality present in the United States as of the 1890 census (before the start of the mass immigration of Jews from Europe), and this limited Jewish immigrants from Austria and Germany to 27,370 and from Poland to 6,542 per year. Even these quotas often went unfilled due to State Department pressure on U.S. consulates to place as many obstacles as possible in the path of refugees.[4] The State Department's attitude toward the refugees' plight hardened when, in January 1940, Breckinridge Long was appointed assistant secretary of state, with authority over the Visa Division and responsibility for formulating U.S. refugee policy. He further raised the barriers to European refugees.[5] Even after it became clear that Nazi Germany was exterminating Jews, the State Department attempted to prevent news of the Holocaust, transmitted through its channels, from reaching American Jewish leadership and the public at large.[6]

Resistance from FDR

President Franklin D. Roosevelt and his administration also failed to show much enthusiasm for helping Jews. In July 1938, when the United States invited thirty-two nations to meet at Evian-les-Bains, France, to discuss the plight of German Jewish refugees, it was obvious that little would be accomplished. The American delegation, headed by Myron Taylor, made it crystal clear that its restrictive immigration laws were sacrosanct and would not be liberalized. Feingold called this position the "politics of gestures."[7] In other words, they preferred issuing condemnatory statements to taking concrete action, such as the ineffective U.S.-British Bermuda conference in April 1943.[8] That conference was a particularly bitter experience for rescue advocates, as it came following the December 17, 1942, declaration by the United States, Britain, and the Soviet Union confirming the Nazi extermination of Jews.[9]

Earlier, in May 1939, the United States refused to accept some 960 Jewish refugees on the boat *St. Louis* boat (most were approved under the quota system, but they had to wait a long time before their turn came to enter the United States), after Cuba refused to allow the passengers (who held legal Cuban tourist visas) to disembark in Havana.[10] During the war, repeated requests were rejected for retributive bombing, negotiations, or ameliorating the situation, such as sending food packages to camps or changing the designation of their inmates to that of prisoners of war, on the claim it would interfere with the prosecution of the war.[11] And it was difficult to understand the decision to transport 335,000 German prisoners of war to the United States and shelter and feed them, while failing to do the same for their victims, the Jews.

Admitting Jews on a temporary basis as an act of compassion would have given the United States greater moral authority to ask neutral countries to do their share. But how could it persuade its allies and neutrals to liberalize its immigration policies when it refused to do so itself?[12] Bombing the concentration camps or at least the railways leading to them, at a time when the Allies had gained air supremacy over German-held areas, might have reduced the number of victims. But in both Britain and the United States, the governments accepted the military high commands' rejection of the bombing idea as needlessly interfering with the major "win-the-war" priority.[13]

Especially galling was Roosevelt's failure to take a more active stand on Jewish refugees. Jewish voters had supported Roosevelt enthusiastically; in the 1940 presidential election, nine out of ten Jews cast their ballots for him.[14] In the words of playwright and rescue activist Ben Hecht, if there was one thing of which the Jews were sure, it was that FDR was their friend.[15] Nearly all Jews worshipped Roosevelt, and their trust in him was strengthened by the fact that FDR surrounded himself by a coterie of Jewish advisors and political supporters. However, many of his Jewish advisors considered themselves Americans who just happened to be Jewish. In Feingold's estimation, they would not risk their careers to help foreign Jews and therefore refrained from putting any pressure on the Roosevelt administration.[16]

While the Nazis spoke endlessly of the demonic Jews and dubbed Roosevelt himself a Jew, the American government referred to Jews not by name but as "political refugees."[17] The large-scale murder of the Jews was not mentioned at any of the Allied war conferences (Casablanca, Tehran, Yalta). Rabbi Stephen Wise, the leading American Jewish spokesman of those days, was especially close to Roosevelt and went to great lengths to remove or trim to insignificance any criticism of Roosevelt's policy with regard to the unfolding Holocaust.[18]

American Jewry Divided and in Conflict

On the American Jewish front, things did not look bright either. During the 1930s, American Jewry lacked organizational cohesiveness and could not speak to power holders with one voice. And it remained divisive and leaderless throughout the Holocaust.[19] The two major constituent organizations were the American Jewish Committee (AJC) and the American Jewish Congress (AJCS). The AJC was composed of wealthy, assimilated German Jews who preferred quiet, behind-the-scenes diplomacy. Starting in 1940, it was headed by Judge Joseph M. Proskauer and followed a generally non-Zionist line. In contrast, the AJCS was made up of poor and middle-class, partly acculturated Eastern European Jews, and it was more outspoken.[20] The AJC opposed the anti-Nazi boycott rally sponsored by the AJCS in March 1933 and refrained from joining similar rallies afterward.[21]

The Joint Distribution Committee, established in 1914 to extend relief to Jewish communities abroad, was the third largest Jewish organization. It avoided political issues and worked through proxy agencies in Europe to help finance the rescue and sheltering of thousands of Jews.[22]

The Zionist Organization of America (ZOA) was another large Jewish organization with a well-defined pro-Jewish Palestine agenda. It was headed by prominent rabbis of the Reform movement, such as Stephen Wise (also head of the AJCS) and Abba Hillel Silver (who favored the Republican Party). Smaller organizations included the Jewish Labor Committee (JLC) and the Orthodox Vaad Hatzalah.

Then there was Peter Bergson and his group of supporters, newcomers to the fractious American Jewish scene and highly resented by all other major Jewish groups (except the Orthodox Agudath Israel movement) for meddling in the proper response to the Nazi threat. The Bergson group did not grow out of the American Jewish community but stemmed from Jewish Palestine, and it was linked to the breakaway Zionist Revisionist movement. It disagreed with the American Jewish establishment, Zionists and non-Zionists alike, over the traditional ways of intercession with the authorities (which they considered ineffective), and they stood for a public stand to save Europe's Jews.[23]

Peter Bergson and Ben Hecht

Together these two—an Irgun underground activist and a Hollywood writer—made the Nazi massacres headline news and a wake-up call for Americans.

Born Hillel Kook in Kriukai, in today's Lithuania, in 1915, Hillel Kook was the son of a rabbi and nephew of the famed Abraham Isaac Kook, chief rabbi of the Ashkenazic community in Palestine under the British. After studies at the Hebrew University in Jerusalem, he joined the Hagannah underground militia and then left it to help set up the more extreme Irgun underground. Kook left for Poland, where he was involved in fund-raising and establishing Irgun cells in Eastern Europe. In March 1940 Vladimir Jabotinsky, leader of the Revisionists, came to the United States to promote the creation of an independent Jewish army that would fight Germany alongside the British, similar to the military formations of Poles, Czechs, Dutch, and other countries occupied by the Germans. When Jabotinsky suddenly died in August 1940, Kook took over the leadership of the group, assuming for this purpose the alias of Peter H. Bergson, with Samuel Merlin as his right-hand man. On December 4, 1941, Bergson and a small group of confederates became the Committee for a Jewish Army of Stateless and Palestinian Jews.[24] It was about the same time that Bergson met Ben Hecht, the famed Hollywood journalist, playwright, and screenwriter, and a friendship was born.

As told by Hecht in his autobiographical *A Child of the Century* (1954), it was on an April day in 1941 that he agreed to meet Peter Bergson and two of his colleagues in Hecht's New York hotel room. Bergson began by praising Hecht for his column in the New York daily newspaper *PM* when he criticized the ambivalent attitude of American Jews toward Nazi Germany. "I had deplored," Hecht wrote, "Jews [who] were reluctant to speak out as Jews under attack and preferred to conduct themselves as neutral Americans." His agreement to meet with Bergson, this stranger from Palestine, "was the result of my having turned into a Jew in 1939. . . . In that year I became a Jew and looked on the world with Jewish eyes."[25] This was from a person dubbed the Hollywood screenwriter who "personified Hollywood itself," and who in the words of the *Dictionary of Literary Biography—American Screenwriters* was "one of the most successful screenwriters in the history of motion pictures."[26]

The Campaign for a Jewish Army

When he met Bergson, Ben Hecht was a man fuming at the lack of public response to the German brutal persecution of Jews. As he enlarged in a column called "My Tribe Is Called Israel," "I write of Jews today [1941], I who never knew himself as one before, because that part of me which is Jewish is under a violent and apelike attack. My way of defending myself is to answer as a Jew"[27] The meeting with the Bergson and his two aides turned on a switch in his heart. "I was to work intimately for seven years with these three young men.[28]

He later sharpened his critique of Jewish and general passivity as the killing of Jews was under way.

> There was no voice of importance anywhere, Jewish or non-Jewish, protesting this foulest of history's crimes. A people to whom I belonged, who had produced my mother, father, and all the relatives I had loved, was being turned into an exterminator's quarry, and there was no outcry against the deed. No statesmen of journalists spoke out. Art was also silent. . . . I felt the most deeply shamed by the silence of the American Jews. Around me the most potent and articulate Jews in the world kept their mouths fearfully closed. . . . The Americanized Jews who ran newspapers and movie studios, who wrote plays and novels, who were high in government and powerful in the financial, industrial, and even social life of the nation were silent.[29]

Returning to the April 1941 meeting, under Bergson's somewhat clumsy-sounding banner, the Committee for a Jewish Army of Stateless and Palestinian Jews, he and his companions had come to ask Hecht to bring such an army into existence. Bergson sent hundreds of letters to important Jews in New York inviting them to join Hecht in promoting the Jewish Army idea. "Imagine the kind of soldiers these Jews will make against the Germans!" Bergson said excitedly. "These 200,000 don't have to be shipped across oceans to join the battle. Most of them are in the Near East, only a bus ride from the front."[30]

Hecht immediately agreed and suggested a press campaign, followed by lobbying Washington senators and congressmen to make speeches in both houses, to force the British to accept the idea and put a Jewish army in the field. America was still not at war, and the Soviet Union and Nazi Germany were still "allies" under a treaty signed in August 1939.[31] The responses received from what Hecht terms "twenty Jewish moguls" were disheartening, though not surprising. In Hecht's words, "Jews fighting as

Jews! Was I crazy? If Jews wanted to fight, let them fight as Englishmen or Americans—or Chinese. I pointed out that they couldn't. The Americans weren't fighting. . . . A Jew, each explained in his own way, could do anything he wanted to as an American, but as a Jew he must be very careful of angering people and very careful not to assert himself in any unpopular way. As Americans they could boast and swagger, apparently, but as Jews they must be as invisible as possible." Hecht sadly noted, "They could not visualize Jews as heroes—only as victims."[32]

Hecht derisively noted that a Hollywood Jew "will support a synagogue with large gifts for thirty years without ever entering it."[33] But money pledges did pour in from lesser known persons—$130,000. Thus the first Bergson-Hecht Jewish propaganda undertaking was considered a fine success. "The Committee now had funds for an American office, a letterhead, and a mimeographing machine," Hecht somewhat sarcastically noted.[34]

Some Washington politicians came out in favor of a Jewish army, including many members of Congress.[35] Supreme Court Chief Justice Harlan Stone approved, but not the Jewish justice, Felix Frankfurter, who was against the Jewish army idea.[36]

When some of the earlier supporters of the Jewish army idea had a change of heart, Hecht discovered that it was due to the intervention of Rabbi Stephen Wise, who had come to Washington to scotch the Bergson-Hecht campaign, with Jewish congressman Sol Bloom spearheading the attack.[37] Bergson confidant Samuel Merlin wrote of his fellow Jewish opponent: "They fought the project not because they are against it, but because they are against us. Stephen Wise will not tolerate any other Jewish organization working for Palestine and stealing honors and publicity from him."[38] Earlier, when Jabotinsky launched a campaign in favor of the Jewish Army idea in March 1940, Wise issued a statement "disassociating themselves [himself and the British ambassador] from the plan of Vladimir Jabotinsky to create a Jewish Army as part of the Allied Forces."[39]

The Bergson group placed paid messages, usually in the form of full-page advertisements, in prominent daily newspapers and weekly magazines from coast to coast.[40] Some of the early advertisements were written by Pierre van Paassen, a Christian Zionist, but the best known of the ads were the work of Ben Hecht. Newspaper tycoon William Randolph Hearst was the only newspaper owner who supported the Bergson group without any reservations. In the words of Bergson's close aide, Samuel Merlin: "All his papers—he gave us pages after pages free. He gave us the whole editorial page—Hearst himself. He gave orders to print our material."[41] The famous artist Arthur Szyk created original illustrations to enhance a number of the ads. Then Bergson and Hecht turned to what seemed to them the more immediate need: the rescue of Jews.

An Ad Designed to Shock

On February 16, 1943, an advertisement spread across five full columns on page 11 of the *New York Times* read: "FOR SALE TO HUMANITY: 70,000 JEWS—Guaranteed Human Beings at $50 a Piece." The story was conceived by Ben Hecht, after it was learned that the pro-Axis Romanian government had offered to allow 70,000 Jews to leave the country in exchange for transportation costs, estimated at $50 per person. The ad continued: "Romania is tired of killing Jews. It has killed one hundred thousand of them in two years. Romania will now give Jews away practically for nothing. . . . This sum covers all transportation expenses. . . . Attention America!!! The Great Romanian bargain is for this month only! It is an unprecedented offer! Seventy thousand souls at $50 a piece! The doors of Romania are open! Act now!"[42] Not surprisingly, the ad set off a tremendous commotion in the Jewish establishment.

The Romanians were among the first to foresee Hitler's defeat, and the Romanian dictator Ion Antonescu sought ways to ingratiate himself with the expected victors, the Allies. Treasury Secretary Henry Morgenthau Jr. brought the Romanian offer to the attention of President Roosevelt, who directed him to Assistant Secretary of State Sumner Welles.[43] Cavendish Cannon of the State Department's European Division argued that to take up the Romanians' offer would create a dangerous precedent: other countries where Jews were being persecuted would make similar offers. It would mean inviting "new pressure for asylum in the Western Hemisphere. . . . So far as I know we are not ready to tackle the whole Jewish problem."[44] After much goings to and fro over an extended period of months, the Germans finally forced their Romanian ally to fully drop the idea.[45]

Hecht later recalled what drove him to write the ad. "Its object was to shock Jews, infuriate Jews, and set them to screaming. This they did, chiefly at me," Hecht wrote sarcastically. "Most people dismissed the offer, believing that if such an offer had been made, President Roosevelt would surely have snapped it up. No decent American could imagine that the American government could let seventy thousand Jews be butchered."[46]

The "We Will Never Die" Pageant

As more information on the extent of the Holocaust began to reach the United States, Kook and his fellow activists decided to press the Roosevelt administration to take concrete action to save the Jews of Europe by creating a new governmental agency specifically charged with the task.[47] Their plan was to stage a huge pageant that would arouse public opinion on the massacre of Jews in Nazi-occupied Europe. They reached out to representatives of thirty-four Jewish organizations, clubs, and fraternities to solicit their support and include their names in the pageant's advertised announcement. Hecht picked 100 students from the Yeshiva College and fifty cantors to recite Jewish religious prayers.[48] New York governor Thomas Dewey declared the day of the pageant an official day of mourning for the massacred Jews of Europe.[49]

The pageant, "We Will Never Die—A Memorial to the Two Million Jewish Dead of Europe" (a horrific number, which was disclosed and confirmed by the United States, Britain, and the Soviet Union on December 17, 1942), was staged on March 9, 1943, at Madison Square Garden, with the participation of actors Paul Muni, Edward G. Robinson, and Stella Adler.[50] That first night 40,000 people saw the pageant, with another 20,000 crowding the streets outside, and it went on to play in five other major cities including Washington DC, where First Lady Eleanor Roosevelt, six Supreme Court justices, and some 300 senators and congressmen attended.[51]

Major Jewish organizations had, however, sought to derail the pageant. Days before, according to Hecht, Rabbi Wise brought a delegation of twelve important Jews to Albany for an audience with Governor Dewey. He tried to induce the governor to cancel his "Day of Mourning" proclamation, threatening that Dewey was likely to lose most of his Jewish vote in New York City if he did not break with the "dangerous and irresponsible racketeers who are bringing terrible disgrace on our already harassed people." But the governor stood firm.[52] On a separate occasion, novelist Edna Ferber also raised her voice sharply. "Who is paying you to do this wretched propaganda," she demanded. "Mister Hitler? Or is it Mister Goebbels?"[53] Rabbi Wise telephoned Hecht and warned: "I have read your pageant script, and I disapprove of it [evidently someone in Bergson's office had spilled the news]. I must ask you to cancel this pageant and discontinue all your further activities in behalf of the Jews." At this point Hecht hung up.[54] According to Hecht, Bergson told him that Judge Proskauer, president of the American Jewish Committee, was concerned that such harsh criticism of the silence of the U.S. government "could well bring on Jewish pogroms" in the United States.[55]

The Emergency Committee

Following the pageant and the failed Bermuda conference on Jewish refugees a month later, the Bergson group decided to convene an emergency conference in the summer of 1943, where representatives of all strata of American society would be present, in order to put pressure on the administration to create a special agency to deal with the rescue of Jews. Those attending included former president Herbert Hoover; newspaper mogul William Randolph Hearst; Interior Secretary Harold L. Ickes, and labor leaders Philip Murray and William Green. Also in attendance were Senators Guy Gillette, Edwin Johnson, and Elbert Thomas and Bishop Henry St. George Tucker. The conference was held at the Commodore Hotel in Manhattan from July 20 to July 26, 1943, with more than 1,500 delegates attending. This was followed by full-page newspaper ads across the country and contacts with members of Congress, officials of the Roosevelt administration, and editors and reporters.[56] The conference decided to transform itself into the Emergency Committee to Save the Jewish People of Europe, with governors, admirals, generals, statesmen, philosophers, and even financiers, most of them non-Jews, on its letterhead.[57]

A delegation of the committee urged Secretary of State Cordell Hull to create a special governmental agency charged with the rescue of the Jews and to immediately establish temporary camps in Palestine, Turkey, Spain, Switzerland, Sweden, Portugal, and Morocco for Jews escaping from Nazi-dominated territory. Assistant Secretary of State Breckinridge Long, who took part in the meeting, claimed that there was no need to establish a new rescue agency, since the Intergovernmental Committee, created in 1938 following the failed Evian conference and supposedly revived at Bermuda in 1943, already existed, and one should have faith that it would do everything that was "practicable"—in other words, nothing.[58]

The Bergson group also wished to separate the demand for rescue from demands about the future status of Palestine, and this intensified the ire of the Zionist organizations against the Bergson group.[59] For the Emergency Committee, the issue was rescue first and Palestine second. As Bergson once explained to Wise in a private conversation, if the rabbi was trapped in a house that was on fire, his main concern would be how to get out alive, not how to get to the Waldorf Astoria.[60]

According to Bergson's close aide Samuel Merlin, what the Emergency Conference to Save Jewish People of Europe in July 1943 tried to impress were three imperatives: (1) That the disaster was of such magnitude that all the previous concepts of charity, of palliatives, were no longer valid; that the task at hand was no less than the rescue of all the people condemned to extermination. (2) Having stated the magnitude of the problem, the rescue was intended not for individuals or small groups of people but for larger groups of people, to be carried out on a mass scale. Therefore it could no longer be handled by private organizations regardless of how rich and powerful they are. (3) To divorce the imperative of rescue from ideological consideration, even the Zionist one to which the Bergson group adhered.

In Merlin's words, "To us what was more important than anything else was to save Jewish lives per se. We did not insist that they should go to Palestine; we made several alternative propositions—for example, establishing temporary camps wherever possible, in several countries, and to keep them there in safety until the end of the war."[61] However, much to the chagrin of the Bergson group and other Jewish organizations, "Rescue through victory" remained the Allies' stock answer—as if rescue before victory would undermine the chances for victory.[62]

Rabbis' March on Washington

One of the Bergson group's memorable orchestrated events was a large-scale protest known as the Rabbis' March on October 6, 1943, in Washington, DC, three days before Yom Kippur. Participants among more than 400 rabbis included Rabbi Moshe Feinstein, Rabbi Eliezer Silver, the Boyaner Rebbe of New York, Rabbi Avraham Kalmanowitz, Rabbi Naftali Carlebach (father of Shlomo Carlebach), Rabbi Arthur Hertzberg, and his father, Rabbi Tzvi Elimelech Hertzberg, all from the Orthodox branch of Judaism.[63] Starting from Union Station, they recited psalms as they marched to the Capitol. On the Capitol steps and in the presence of Vice President Henry Wallace, they read the petition in both Hebrew and English addressed to the president, which Wallace later read before the Senate. It began: "In the name of God, creator of the universe, blessed be He who voiced in our Holy Torah the commandment 'Thou shalt not stand idly by thy brother's blood,'" and continued on to the urgent need for a government rescue agency.[64]

The rabbis demanded that the U.S. government take immediate action to rescue Jews as well as open Palestine to Jewish immigration but not necessarily only there. Wallace responded by assuring the rabbis that all those present deeply felt the horrible Jewish tragedy, and he expressed how moved he was by the fact that the rabbis had come to Washington right before the holiest day of the Jewish calendar. At the same time, he added, it was important to remember that the tragedy of the Jews was part of a larger problem that would be solved only by an Allied victory.[65]

From the Capitol, the rabbis headed to the Lincoln Memorial, where prayers for the Jewish victims of the war were recited as well as a prayer for the United States and its leaders. The rabbis then proceeded on foot to the White House, where a delegation of rabbis escorted by Peter Bergson was received by Roosevelt's secretary, Marvin McIntyre, who apologized for the president's absence. In response, Rabbi Wolf Gold expressed the rabbis' deep disappointment in unequivocal terms and indicated that in view of the president's absence, there was no need for him to read the petition they had prepared. Actually, Roosevelt had a relatively light schedule that day and could easily have arranged a meeting with the rabbis, but he refused to do so. It was later learned that his absence had been orchestrated on the advice of his Jewish advisers, in particular Samuel Rosenman.[66] One Jewish newspaper commented, "Would a similar delegation of 500 Catholic priests have been thus treated?"[67] The march of the rabbis, nevertheless, had a tremendous impact on many congressmen. These rabbis with beards, black coats, tears streaming down their faces—some people said they looked like prophets of old—this was something new and moving to the legislators.[68]

Slinging Criticisms

Another of the sad symptoms of that period was publicly avoiding the mention of "Jew" or "Jews" when addressing a Jewish issue. Instead, the preferred code words were "unfortunate people," "persecuted people," "helpless people," "poor helpless people": in short, any sort of euphemisms as long as one disguised the religion of the victims.[69] The only people who were not inhibited in calling them Jews were the Nazis and Hitler himself in his public pronunciations and manifestos.[70] When, moreover, at the Tripartite Conference of the Allied foreign minister in Moscow, October 18–30, 1943, the Jews were omitted, either by word or by code word from among the victims of Nazism, who were listed as the "French, Dutch, Belgian, or Norwegian hostages, or of Cretan peasants," or "the people of Poland,"[71] Ben Hecht decided on a riposte, in a macabre parable of devastating sarcasm, published in the *New York Times* on November 5, 1943, under "My Uncle Abraham Reports." It read in part:

> I have an uncle who is a ghost. . . . He was elected last April by the two million Jews who have been murdered by the Germans to be their World Delegate. . . . That's how he happened to be in Moscow a few weeks ago. . . . Jews do not exist, even when they are dead. In the Kremlin in Moscow, in the White House in Washington, in the Downing Street Building in London where I have sat on the window sills, I have never heard our name. . . . Yesterday when we were killed we were changed from Nobodies to Nobodies. . . . My Uncle Abraham has gone to the White House in Washington. He is sitting on the window sill two feet away from Mr. Roosevelt. But he has left his notebook behind.[72]

It is reported that Roosevelt was angered by the ad and complained that this was "hitting below the belt."[73] Bernard Baruch, the venerable counselor of American presidents, telephoned Hecht two days after the ad appeared. "I was talking to Mr. Roosevelt," Hecht reported Baruch telling him, "and he was very upset about your Uncle Abraham ad. He told me he's going on an important trip soon, and that during this trip he will settle the Jewish problem in the Near East to my satisfaction— and yours. . . . I am taking the liberty of asking you to call off all further criticisms of President Roosevelt and his administration—until you hear from me again."[74] After Roosevelt informed Congress in March 1945 that in a conversation with King Ibn Saud of Saudi Arabia he had learned more about the Jewish issue in Palestine than anything else he had heard before (the monarch had suggested that all Jews be shipped off to somewhere in Africa), Baruch told Hecht in another telephone conversation, "I have had a two-hour talk with President Roosevelt about the Jews and the Jewish problem. I have spoken also to Governor Dewey on the same subject. I can only tell you as a result of these talks that, despite my having been a lifelong Democrat, I would rather trust my American Jewishness in Mr. Dewey's hands than in Mr. Roosevelt's."[75]

The anti-Bergson drive, spearheaded by large sections of the American Jewish leadership, went so far as to encourage the Internal Revenue Service to investigate the Bergson Group's finances in an attempt to discredit it, hoping to find funding misappropriations or at least careless bookkeeping. But the investigation led nowhere.[76] This did not curtail the harassment of Peter Bergson. Nahum Goldmann, of the World Jewish Congress, suggested that Bergson be deported or drafted into the army to silence him. Nothing came of this ploy either.[77] As for the British, they repeatedly pressed the United States to find a way to get rid of Bergson and his colleagues. The British ambassador in Washington reported to his foreign secretary, Anthony Eden, in 1944, "I have been pulling a few strings . . . either to get [Bergson] drafted or else to get the Department of Immigration to refuse a renewal of his visitor's visa."[78]

The War Refugee Board Is Born, a Bit Belatedly

At Bergson's Rescue Committee's initiative, a resolution was introduced in both houses of Congress on November 9, 1943, calling for "the immediate creation by the President of an agency to save the Jewish people of Europe . . . to be composed of military, economic, and diplomatic experts, and given full authority to determine and effectuate a realistic and stern policy of action to save the lives and preserve the dignity of the ancient Jewish people of Europe whom Nazi Germany has marked for extinction."[79]

As soon as the resolution was introduced, however, Representative Sol Bloom (Jewish), chairman for the House Foreign Affairs Committee and considered by many as beholden to the State Department, worked to delay it as long as possible before bringing it to the full House or perhaps better still to kill it in committee. His initial tactic was to question Peter Bergson's legal status and thereby cast aspersions on his integrity and character. In support of Sol Bloom, Rabbi Wise characterized the rescue resolution as "inadequate" because it did not call for the immediate lifting of all British restrictions on immigration to Palestine. Despite these attempted withholding tactics, on December 20, 1943, the Senate Foreign Relations Committee unanimously approved the resolution.[80]

Then, suddenly, after a small group of three high-ranking non-Jewish officials in the Treasury Department (Randolph Paul, Josiah E. DuBois Jr., and John Pehle), who worked under the Jewish Secretary Henry Morgenthau Jr., were convinced that the White House and State Department were following a deliberate policy of refraining from rescuing the Jews, Morgenthau asked his staff to prepare a report that would prove beyond a shadow of a doubt that the State Department had willfully sabotaged plans to rescue Jews.[81] A final report, written by DuBois, at Morgenthau's urging, was titled *Report to the Secretary on the Acquiescence of This Government in the Murder of the Jews.* The title was toned down to *Personal Report to the President.*[82] Accompanied by Pehle, Morgenthau met with Roosevelt on January 6, 1944, asking him to read the memorandum in their presence. The opening sentence went straight to the point. "One of the greatest crimes in history, the slaughter of the Jewish people of Europe, is continuing unabated." The document proceeded to demonstrate how, for years, the State Department not only willfully failed to act to rescue Jews but put up all kinds of obstacles of its own. Its procrastination had facilitated mass murder in Nazi Europe.[83]

Pehle then amplified the report by giving the president a draft of an executive order creating a governmental War Refugee Board, headed by the treasury secretary, the secretary of state, and the secretary of war.[84] On January 22, 1944, Roosevelt issued this executive order.[85] The WRB was given broad powers specifically to forestall "Nazi plans to exterminate all the Jews." The Departments of Treasury, State, and War were instructed to lend their facilities and channels of communication as well as some of their personnel abroad to assist in the tremendous tasks of the newly created agency. The Bureau of the Budget set aside $1 million for initial administrative expenses, but additional funds, which ultimately made up 90 percent of its budget, had to be provided by Jewish organizations.[86] Almost immediately, the WRB was faced with the crisis in Hungary, which the Germans occupied in March 1944. In Sweden, WRB agent Iver Olsen recruited Raoul Wallenberg, who went on to demonstrate what could be achieved on the rescue front when there was a will to save lives.[87]

Bergson's Emergency Committee was widely credited with having brought about the establishment of the War Refugee Board. In assessing the Board's record, one should take into consideration that by the time the WRB was created, it was too late for the millions already exterminated. Moreover, much of the work of the WRB was an exercise in futility so long as the Allies refused to take in the Jews. Without a decision to receive and shelter refugees even on a temporary basis, no agency or individual, regardless of their compassion or zeal, could accomplish anything on a significant scale.[88]

Temporary Haven for Refugees

In May 1944 Bergson's Emergency Committee launched a campaign in support of a free ports temporary havens idea. A free port is a place where merchandise traders can put things down for storage for a while without having to make a final decision about them. It was now proposed to do the same with regard to Jewish refugees needing a place to rest without deciding on their final destination. To deflect criticism, Roosevelt ordered that an unused army camp in the United States might be converted into a temporary haven for war refugees from abroad. The Oswego army camp in Fort Ontario, upstate New York, was designated for this. In the end, fewer than 1,000 Jewish refugees were allowed to benefit from this gesture.[89]

After the war, Peter Bergson, who took back his birth name of Hillel Kook, was involved in the struggle for Israel's independence and served for a time in the Knesset, Israel's parliament. When he died in 2001, he was still being maligned by historians and representatives of the mainline Jewish organizations that had ostracized him during the war. His close co-worker, Ben Hecht, returned to his playwright and screenwriting activity. He died in 1964.[90]

Vaad Hatzala (Rescue Committee) and Union of Orthodox Rabbis

The urgent need to rescue more than 1,000 East European rabbis, yeshiva students, scholars, and their families.

When it became clear that U.S. immigration regulations were detrimental to the efforts to rescue European Jews, a group of Orthodox rabbis gathered to create an organization that prioritized the care and welfare of rabbinic seminaries—known as yeshivot—and their students in war-torn

Europe. At an emergency conference of the Union of Orthodox Rabbis (Agudath ha-Rabbanim), in New York, on November 13–14, 1939, Rabbi Eliezer Silver of Cincinnati suggested sending an emissary to meet with the leading rabbis and yeshiva heads to ascertain the specific needs of the yeshivot. The rabbis established a special fund for this purpose and elected Rabbi Silver to head the new project.[91] The idea was to assist with provisions needed by the 4,000 Talmud students, mostly refugees from Poland, who had fled to Lithuania at the outset of the German invasion of Poland in September 1939. An office was opened in Manhattan, and the newborn committee was eventually to be known as the Vaad ha-Hatzala or Vaad Hatzala (hereafter Vaad or VH).[92]

The decision to found VH aroused considerable controversy in the Jewish community, stemming from the claim that it undermined the recently achieved unity in fund-raising efforts and was based on priorities that were not universally accepted by the Jewish community, in view of the existence of other and much larger Jewish aid organizations, such as the United Jewish Appeal (UJA) and the Joint Distribution Committee.[93] As the Orthodox Vaad rabbis were ideologically convinced that the entire future of the Jewish people was dependent on the continuation of the study of Torah, it was difficult for them to allow the JDC (headed mostly by non-Orthodox Jews) to decide on the distribution of funds to needy Jews, whatever their religious practices. Hence the decision to undertake a separate fund-raising campaign.[94]

In the attempt not to ruffle feathers with the other Jewish philanthropic organizations, the rabbis stressed the temporary nature of their work, "that this is a onetime campaign to meet an emergency situation," but this failed to pacify the others. A meeting on June 4, 1940, between Rabbi Avraham Kalmanowitz and JDC officials produced no results.[95] Rabbi Kalmanowitz had arrived in America in the winter of 1939–40, after fleeing from Poland to Vilna with the Mir Yeshiva, and devoted himself almost completely to the rescue of the refugee yeshivot, especially the Mir yeshiva. He was a physically impressive individual and also known for his ability to cry and faint at will to effectively drive home an important point.[96]

To the United States, the Far East, and Canada

On June 15, 1940, when Soviet tanks rumbled into Lithuania, the refugee rabbis there knew that the yeshivot could not exist for long under

Communist rule, and this forced them to seriously consider ways to flee Lithuania.[97] In an August meeting with the heads of major Jewish organizations, the Vaad rabbis presented their proposal to transplant to the United States the more than twenty Polish refugee yeshivot that had escaped to Lithuania, approximately 3,500 persons, including yeshiva heads, students, and their families. Reform Rabbi Stephen Wise led the opposition to this idea on behalf of the other organizations. He stated that the absorption in the United States of perhaps three to five yeshivot was sufficient for American Jewry, but the resettlement of a larger number was simply not feasible.[98]

In spite of this setback, the Vaad decided to send a delegation to Washington to meet with Assistant Secretary of State Breckinridge Long, a man not known for his eagerness to see more Jews admitted into the United States. To their surprise, Long responded by asking them to submit a list of rabbis whom they recommended for entry. The rabbis prepared two lists, one of 20 names and one of 100 names. At their next meeting, Long accepted the longer list and promised to cable the American consul in the Soviet Union (into which Lithuania had been absorbed) to ensure that the visas would be granted.[99]

By September 18, 1,200 had been granted U.S. visas including, in administrative terminology, 732 "alleged leaders of the intellectual thought of the Jewish religion and leading exponents of the Talmudic schools and colleges together with their families."[100] These were part of special emergency visas granted to European cultural, political, and intellectual leaders whose lives were in danger, under the terms of an arrangement worked out by the President's Advisory Committee on Political Refugees, headed by James McDonald.[101] Not only had the Vaad rabbis overcome the veto by the major Jewish aid organizations but with that success in their hands they had enlisted Rabbi Wise to their side. In mid-December Wise headed a delegation to Washington with Rabbi Aaron Teitelbaum of the Vaad that met with Long and asked that an additional 3,800 rabbis, yeshiva students, and the members of their families be approved for entry into the United States. But this time the effort failed. Long either had changed his policy or suspected that the rabbis were trying to take advantage of the department's earlier singular generosity. The request was denied.[102]

In spring 1941 several prominent Polish rabbis and yeshiva heads had emigrated from Lithuania via the Far East with the Vaad's help. Rabbi

Aron Kotler, head of the Etz Chaim yeshiva of Kletzk, even succeeded in making it to New York City, and he enlisted in the efforts to rescue Torah scholars.[103] On May 1 a boat arrived in Shanghai from Vladivostok, Russia, with fifty passengers, half of whom were rabbis and yeshiva students, members of their families, and other Orthodox Jews. The JDC later covered all the transportation costs of the boat voyage. In addition, a small fraction of the Torah scholars stranded in the Far East were brought to Canada that fall—29 rabbis and yeshiva students with the help of the Vaad.[104] According to the figures of the Vaad, it assisted 2,654 rabbis and their families in 1940–41, plus 1,400 non-Polish rabbis and students in the Lithuanian yeshivot, as well as 1,302 that had been resettled in other countries.[105]

First News of Horrific Mass Murders

On September 3, 1942, Sylwin Strakacz, the Polish consul general in New York, telephoned Agudah activist Dr. Isaac Lewin and informed that he had received an urgent cable for Jacob Rosenheim, the leader of world Agudath Yisrael. The cable was from Yitzhak Sternbuch in Montreux, Switzerland, who told of the murder of hundreds of thousands of Warsaw Jews. Together with the Riegner cable transmitted to Rabbi Wise via the World Jewish Congress representative in London, Sydney Silverman, these were the first confirmations received regarding the actual systematic annihilation of European Jews.[106] Rosenheim immediately cabled the contents of the cable to President Roosevelt and proposed that the United States initiate a joint intervention of all the neutral countries in Europe and the Americas to express their deep moral indignation. Rosenheim also asked Lewin, who served as the liaison between Orthodox circles and the Polish diplomats in the United States, to ask the embassy to arrange a meeting with Roosevelt via the State Department.[107]

On September 4, 1942, Rabbis Kalmanowitz, Silver, and Kotler joined with Rosenheim to meet with Stephen Wise, who was accompanied by Dr. Aryeh Tartakower and Dr. Leon Kubowitzky of the World Jewish Congress. The rabbis demanded that the information be fully publicized in order to mobilize the community for concerted action. However, after being urged by the State Department to withhold the information for the time being, Wise was much more cautious, claiming that they needed further confirmation before the details of the murders could be released to the media. What he apparently did not reveal to the rabbis was that Sternbuch's cable had been preceded by another telegram originally sent from Switzerland by Gerhart Riegner, which included a similar message regarding the planned extermination of all Jews by the Nazi regime.[108]

Stephen Wise and World Jewish Congress colleagues suggested that the response should be in the form of protest meetings and a march on Washington, but the Orthodox representatives were at this point adamantly opposed to such measures.[109] The Orthodox representatives believed that quiet lobbying (*shtadlanut*) would prove more effective than political protests. Ironically, within a year the tables would be turned, with the Orthodox organizations sponsoring a protest march by hundreds of rabbis in Washington and the U.S. leader of the World Jewish Congress working behind the scenes to mitigate its impact.[110]

Breaking the Silence

On September 6, 1942, heads of thirty-four leading American Jewish organizations met at the offices of the World Jewish Congress in New York to share the news from Europe. There are conflicting reports on whether Wise revealed the contents of Riegner's cable at the meeting, but Sternbuch's message was definitely presented. At this meeting a bitter argument erupted between the representatives of the Orthodox rabbis and the socialist-secular Jewish Labor Committee. An issue of contention was the advisability of threatening the Germans with reprisal attacks; the Orthodox representatives vehemently opposed such an approach, according to a report by one of the participants at the meeting.[111] It was decided not to publicize the terrible extermination news, and all agreed to this.

However, after two months, Agudah activist Dr. Isaac Lewin broke the silence. In the November 1942 issue of an Agudist Yiddish-language monthly, Lewin bitterly attacked the "silence" policy and called upon the Jewish organizations to publicize the news at least in the Jewish press and begin to take concrete action to save Jewish lives. However, Lewin's impassioned plea, published in a relatively obscure journal with an extremely limited circulation, had no immediate effect.[112] It was only after U.S. Undersecretary of State Sumner Welles summoned Wise to Washington on November 24 to confirm the horrible reports from Europe that the American Jewish leaders convened a press conference to reveal the information already in their possession: that 2 million Jews had already been murdered in a campaign to wipe out European Jewry. On December 2, 1942, Jews the world over observed a day of mourning and prayer.[113]

The activist leaders in the Union of Orthodox Rabbis viewed Peter Bergson's Emergency Committee to Save the Jewish People of Europe as more natural allies, especially in matters of rescue. That is why they agreed to participate in great numbers to Bergson's suggested Washington march on October 6, 1943.[114] In addition, the Vaad tried to save a group of more than 200 Jews who possessed Central and South American passports and were being held by the Germans in the Vittel internment camp in France. Several in that group were relatives of Recha Sternbuch.[115] Unfortunately, by the time the Latin American countries had validated, under U.S. pressure, the documents held by these persons, it was too late; they had already been deported to Auschwitz.

In summary, according to historian Efraim Zuroff, during World War II the Vaad Hatzala rescued 625 Polish rabbis and yeshiva students from Lithuania via the Far East. It also helped keep alive hundreds of refugee Torah scholars living under extremely harsh conditions in Central Asia and enabled approximately 500 rabbis and yeshiva students to survive.[116] To its credit, although originally created to help yeshiva heads and students, the Vaad made a serious attempt to save all Jews regardless of religiosity or affiliation. These efforts led to the release of 1,210 Jews from Theresienstadt, via the efforts of Yitzhak and Recha Sternbuch, and relief help to Slovak Jews through the Vaad's representative there, Rabbi Michael Dov-Ber Weissmandl.[117]

The Jewish Labor Committee

This secular Jewish organization acted with all the means at its disposal to help over 1,000 German, Austrian, and French Socialists, many of them Jews, to safety.

The Jewish Labor Committee (JLC) was founded in February 1934 by a number of Jewish trade unions in response to the rise of Nazism. It was headed by Baruch Charney Vladeck, and it maintained direct and personal ties with prominent Central European Social Democrats, many of them Jews. Known for the elegance of his Yiddish oratory, Vladeck had previously received his political apprenticeship in the Jewish Socialist Bund in Poland.[118] In 1935 Vladeck journeyed to Europe where he met with German and Austrian Social Democrats living in exile in Prague and Brünn (Brno), and they received substantial financial support from the JLC.[119]

In the wake of the German invasion on France in June 1940, an organized delegation made up of William Green, of the American Federation of Labor (AFL), David Dubinsky, of the International Ladies Garment Workers Union (elected treasurer of the JLC), Alexander Kahn, of the Yiddish daily *Forverts*, and Isaiah Minkoff met with Assistant Secretary of State Long and Secretary of State Hull and implored both to allow a group of "men and women prominent in the democratic and labor movements in Europe" to find immediate temporary haven in the United States. Hull agreed for such a limited number of prominent political refugees to be permitted to enter the United States on visitors' visas.[120] The JLC used most of the 400 emergency visitors' visas it ultimately succeeded in obtaining (each of which could also serve that individual's family) in order to aid its own. The lion's share of the emergency visas went to Socialist Jewish Bundists, Mensheviks (Communists opposed to the Stalinist line, many of them Jews), and Labor Zionists in danger of being arrested by either the Nazis or the Soviets.[121]

Dr. Frank Bohn, an American journalist, agreed to undertake a dangerous mission to get some of the endangered people out of France. He arrived in France in late July 1940 and presented himself as a representative of the AFL. He shuttled between Marseilles, Toulouse, and Vichy, helping people on his list leave the country, illegally if necessary. Bohn eventually acceded to pressures by the Vichy French and U.S. diplomats and left the country in 1941.[122] The JLC position, as described by Vladeck, was that "the Jewish question must be solved in the countries where the Jews live," and therefore together with Stephen Wise was originally opposed to any negotiations with Nazi Germany for the massive removal of Jews from there. Vladeck died in 1938 at the age of fifty-two and was succeeded by Joseph Held as JLC president. Well over 1,000 people, many of them Jews, were brought to safety by the JLC in 1940 and 1941.

The Joint Distribution Committee (JDC-Joint)

The largest and most effective Jewish aid organization, it provided millions of American dollars to aid European Jews, and cooperated with other aid organizations to facilitate the emigration of tens of thousands of European Jews.

The Joint Distribution Committee (JDC, or Joint), the largest Jewish aid society both before and during the war, made it possible for other organizations, legal and clandestine, to operate to save Jews from the Nazis. The accounts here are based on the two major groundbreaking studies of the JDC by historian Yehuda Bauer: *My Brother's Keeper*, for the period up to the start of the war, and *American Jewry and the Holocaust*, for the wartime period.[123]

The JDC was founded in November 1914, a few months after the start of World War I, and was led by the predominantly Americanized and liberal-minded German Jewish element. The JDC's policy was to extend philanthropic aid to Jews in other countries, principally Europe, so that they could achieve in their own countries what Jews had achieved in America, and not necessarily to encourage them to emigrate to the United States. In other words, it would help Jews help themselves in their own homelands.[124]

The major financial power in the circle of JDC's friends was Julius Rosenwald, an anti-Zionist Chicago millionaire who was the architect of the Sears Roebuck empire,[125] and its chairman was Felix M. Warburg, of German Jewish banking aristocrats. After Warburg's passing in 1937, he was replaced by Paul Baerwald, a banker also of German Jewish origin, associated with the Lazar Frères financial firm. In February 1941 Baerwald resigned, and Edward M. Warburg, son of Felix, who had joined the JDC in the late 1930s, became the formal head of JDC and the new predominant force among the laymen. Insofar as the war years are concerned, Joseph J. Schwartz was the principal JDC member responsible for the disbursement of funds to various Jewish communities in distress in Europe from his base in Lisbon.[126]

Born in Ukraine and raised in the United States, Schwartz was ordained an Orthodox rabbi in 1922. At Yale University he specialized in oriental studies, earning a PhD in 1927. After a stint at Cairo University in Egypt, he taught German at Long Island University and worked as a rabbi for a while, but then quit and spent ten years at the Brooklyn Federation of Jewish Charities before assuming the post of secretary of the JDC.[127] He emerged as the single most influential personality in JDC councils during the war. He was not beyond changing, ignoring, or reinterpreting directives from the New York head office consonant with European realities.[128] From his base in Lisbon, he became in name what he had already been in practice, JDC's chief overseas operative. In early 1942 he decided that the JDC would have to develop a second center in Europe outside Portugal and run by a citizen of a neutral country to serve as a conduit for funds. Switzerland was the obvious choice. Unlike Portugal, which had no common frontier with Nazi Europe, Switzerland was surrounded by Nazi-held territories, and its conservative regime was solidly democratic and basically though secretly pro-Allies.[129]

Over time JDC succeeded in building for itself a virtual monopoly in the field of overseas aid. Its official position was that Jews have a right to live in countries of their birth, or in a country of their adoption, and should not be encouraged to emigrate due to antisemitic pressures. This may account for their nonadherence to efforts by other groups in the United States to pressure the government to ease the immigration restrictions for Jews. There were, however, other voices in the JDC, such as Alexander Kahn, who argued that the JDC was also required to help refugees who landed on American shores. JDC eventually accepted the policy proposed by Kahn to support emigration of Jews as the occasion required.[130] It collaborated with HICEM, an organization that combined the Hebrew Sheltering and Immigrant Aid Society (HIAS) and the London-based Jewish Colonization Association (ICA), thus its title. Together they were involved in the emigration of some 440,000 Jews from Central Europe: 281,900 from Germany, 117,000 from Austria, 35,000 from the Czech lands, and 5,000 from Danzig—when emigration was still a possibility.[131] More were helped to leave during the wartime years, though in much fewer numbers.

When President Roosevelt declared U.S. neutrality in the war, James N. Rosenberg of JDC's Executive Committee held that JDC was to avoid engaging in any relief work that might infringe on U.S. laws. "Our rule must be 'When in doubt, ask the State Department.'"[132] But not all agreed to that stiff legalistic stand, as they noted that in spite of American neutrality, the United States was increasingly bending over backward to help Britain in its hour of distress as it stood alone facing Hitler's armies after the fall of France.[133] Morris Troper fought vigorously against the "neutrality" advocates. In an emotional appeal before the Board of Directors on September 9, 1940, Troper declared:

When I stand before you this morning, I am not here as Morris Troper alone; I am here as Hirsch of Berlin, Loewenherz of Vienna,

as Giterman, Guzik, and Neustadt of Poland, as Eppler of Budapest
and Friedmann of Prague, as Fueredi of Bratislava and Grodzensky
of Lithuania, as Van Tijn of Amsterdam and Ussoskin of Romania,
as Valobra of Italy and d'Esaguy of Lisbon. . . . They have nothing
to look forward to except starvation, disease and ultimate extinction. . . . Ours is the sacred task of keeping our brethren alive—if
not all, then at least some.[134]

Then, with America's entry into the war in December 1941, conditions
again changed regarding JDC's overseas work. As the agency of a bellig-
erent country, JDC could no longer send funds into enemy-occupied
Europe, and it was forced to follow U.S. government regulations forbid-
ding transfer of funds to, and human contacts with, anyone in Nazi-held
territories. But it still needed to find ways to aid such persons.[135] Two
years later, with the establishment of the War Refugee Board (WRB) in
January 1944, JDC became the main source of money for WRB operations. JDC and WRB cooperated not just on the financial level but in the
actual operations. These took place in Lisbon, where Schwartz was in
direct contact with WRB head John Pehle and the WRB representative
in Switzerland, Roswell McClelland, as well as the JDC representative,
Saly Mayer, in that country.[136] Space does not allow for a full account of
JDC assistance in various stations outside the United States. Following
is a brief recitation of some of the major JDC activities in various places,
regional and country by country.

Germany and Austria

As more Jews were evicted from their jobs under Nazi rule, JDC saw itself
forced to support an organized and orderly emigration.[137] Even though
this was its official position, some at JDC felt that emigration was a con-
cession to the Hitler theory that the country must rid itself of Jews. They
believed that Germany had been and should continue to be a center of
Jewish and world culture and that Palestine and emigration were not
the only answer.[138] In the meantime, the number of welfare recipients
prior to 1938 rose to about 20 percent of the Jewish population.[139] This
led the JDC to cover as much as 30 percent of the budget of the Central
Committee for Help and Reconstruction (Zentral-Ausschuss für Hilfe
und Aufbau—ZA), an umbrella organization that included welfare, edu-

cation, emigration, and vocational training organizations.[140] JDC also helped to finance the emigration of 4,000 German Jews to Latin American countries between April 1933 and October 1935 in collaboration with HICEM[141] and a smaller number who were allowed to enter the United States. These expenditures amounted to $237,180 in 1936 and climbed to $342,000 and $500,000 in the next two years.[142]

In January 1936 JDC, the U.S. Zionists, and a delegation of British Jewry (Herbert Samuel, Simon Marks, and Lord Bearsted) conceived a plan to help 168,000 adults and several thousand children leave Germany, but it came to nothing.[143] Another plan that failed was the so-called Rublee-Schacht plan, a complicated and convoluted idea conceived in a meeting between George Rublee of the Intergovernmental Committee on Refugees (IGCR) and Hjalmar Schacht, the Nazi head of the German Central Bank in 1939, that would have enabled, with German and World Jewry financing, several hundred thousand German Jews to leave the country. Negotiations dragged on until it ended abruptly with the outbreak of war.[144]

In March 1938, 185,246 Austrian Jews, the majority of them in Vienna, found themselves trapped as the country was absorbed into Nazi Germany, with a steady rise of people on relief.[145] By the end of 1938, JDC had spent $431,438 to help out destitute Jews in Austria, which was 10 percent of the total JDC spending for that year.[146] When SS officer Adolf Eichmann created the infamous Central Bureau for Jewish Emigration (Zentralstelle für jüdische Auswanderung) in Vienna to speed up Jewish emigration, but which deprived the departing Jews of all their possession, the JDC also stepped in to try to help out.[147]

Poland

Before the war, as close to one-third of the estimated 3.3 million Jews in Poland were living on subsistence level, and some 71 percent of the children were in various stages of undernourishment, the JDC expended a major part of its work in Poland.[148] This included support of vocational schools, children's homes, health centers, and summer camps.[149] During the so-called Zbąszyn incident, when on October 27, 1938, the Germans expelled some 17,000 Polish Jews in Germany to the Polish border, near the town of Zbąszyn, JDC contributed 20 percent of the money raised by Polish Jewry to assist them.[150]

After the German invasion in September 1939, JDC expenditures were funneled through a front organization created in Warsaw known as ŻETOS (Jewish Society for Social Help) and headed by the famous historian Emanuel Ringelblum. It spent $205,000 covering the costs for food, clothing, and health care as well as funds for vocational training, public kitchens, and support of children's homes and hospitals.[151] According to Yehuda Bauer, it is estimated that in 1940, 560,000 adults and 75,000 children received JDC foods as onetime gifts; also, 295,000 soup portions were distributed daily to some 260,000 people, including 42,000 children, throughout German-occupied Poland.[152]

JDC funds could be legally transferred into occupied Poland for as long as the United States maintained diplomatic relations with Germany, that is, until December 1941. Transfers of JDC funds into occupied Poland were done in several other ways, such as acted by JDC operative Leib Neustadt, in the form of loans from people who still had some wealth, promising repayment after the war. By February 1940, loans for $250,000 were contracted. Most of the people who received little slips of paper for the money they gave to JDC did not survive to collect.[153] With America's entry in the war in late 1941, the JDC Warsaw office was officially closed by the Germans, but JDC continued to operate underground. After that date, JDC operatives borrowed money against repayment after the war and controlled the operations of ŻETOS.[154]

After obtaining a license in December 1942 from the U.S. State Department, after a long delay JDC sent 12,559 food parcels between February and April 1943 from a fictitious address in Lisbon via the International Red Cross. Of these, only 925 were acknowledged; the other recipients were probably no longer alive. Later in 1943, 7,226 more parcels were sent, but only 42 receipts were received. Nevertheless, the sending of parcels continued. Substantial payments were also sent to Jewish underground groups in Poland throughout 1943 and 1944, with U.S. Treasury Department agreement, for a grand total of $650,000. Part of this amount also went to support Żegota, the Polish underground clandestine organization that helped Jews on the run and enabled a fairly large numbers of Jews to stay alive.[155] Money was also relayed directly to the Judenrat heads in the ghettos of Łódz (Chaim Rumkowski) and Zaglębie-Sosnowiec (Moshe Merin).[156]

A Jewish self-help association known as Jüdische Soziale Selbsthilfe (JSS) was recognized by the Nazis as the Jewish section of the only independent Polish welfare organization that was allowed to function, the Naczelna Rada Opiekuńcza (NRO). Michael Weichert, an actor and cultural worker, was nominated by the local JDC field workers to be the Jewish representative in NRO. By January 1940 JSS had been placed under civilian German control and was to play a controversial role during the Nazi occupation of Poland, as Weichert set about creating a network of local aid committees.[157] JDC was obliged to distribute money through JSS. Roughly half of the JSS budget came from JDC in cash, and the other rest was the money value of the NRO food allocations.[158] In the meantime, JDC in Warsaw lost control over the JSS in Kraków, where Weichert spent much of his time, and he was now free to continue his work with German permission. He operated solely as a receiving and distributing agent for medicines, foodstuffs, and clothes received from abroad that he supplied to Jewish slave laborers in Nazi camps, at least to those camps that the ss gave him access to.[159] He also got medical supplies from the Red Cross, supplemented by what he claimed were "thousands" of small parcels from Lisbon and Switzerland. He sold the contents of these, buying flour and medicines with the proceeds.[160]

Slowly the German authorities restricted his work to the Kraków area.[161] In March 1943 Weichert's organization was renamed the Jüdische Unterstützungstelle (JUS), but the Germans ordered it closed in August 1943 after only a few months of operation. Weichert was, nevertheless, still allowed to operate but with a skeleton staff. He apparently continued sending shipments to the camps until, strange as it may sound in light of the Holocaust in Poland, he was allowed to reopen his JUS office in February 1944; it continued to operate until July 1944, when the Russians were closing in on the Germans in Poland.[162] Weichert then slipped out of sight and went into hiding with the help of a German friend.

Throughout the whole period that JUS existed, Weichert's activities were looked upon with increasing distrust by the Jewish underground movement. Repeated appeals were sent by them and by the JDC in Poland to stop sending parcels and medicines to JUS from Jews outside Nazi Europe because, they asserted, Weichert was a German stooge and the materials would never reach the Jewish inmates of the camps. The JDC's Joseph Schwartz and Saly Mayer, however, took the line that if a reasonable proportion of the shipments reached Jews, they should be sent, even if the rest was confiscated by the SS.[163]

Michael Weichert survived the war and was tried and acquitted on charges of collaboration with the Germans. In his memoirs, published in Israel, Weichert argued that he and his organization were less dependent on Nazi authorities than the ghetto Judenrats because he had access to civilian German officials who were easier to deal with and that his interventions were often successful. Yehuda Bauer finds both of these claims difficult to accept.[164] In summary, Weichert's aid may have been a drop in the sea, but in Bauer's final judgment on the man and his activity, "Was not a drop in the sea infinitely better than nothing at all?"[165]

Lithuania

In this Baltic country, JDC was represented by Moses W. Beckelman, an American Jew who arrived there on October 11, 1939. The JDC spent some $717,000 there from September 1939 to December 1940.[166] During the German occupation of Lithuania, JDC found ways to help the illegal Jewish underground in Vilna, known as the Farainikte Partisaner Organizacje (FPO; United Partisans Organization), as evidenced by the memoirs of Haika Grossman, one of the leading clandestine operatives.[167]

Romania, Hungary, and Yugoslavia

A situation of Jewish distress, similar to Poland, prevailed in the prewar Romanian regions of Bessarabia, Bucovina, and parts of northern Transylvania. JDC ran summer camps, recreation and health centers for children, and vocational training.[168] Dr. Wilhelm Filderman, a lawyer and the head of the Romanian Jewish community, was JDC's most trusted contact in the country.[169] When Romania joined Germany in the invasion of Russia, it expelled from Bukovina and Bessarabia tens of thousands of Jews to the newly annexed territory between the Dniester and Bug Rivers, known as Transnistria, and conducted mass shootings and conditions that led to deprivations, starvation, and death.

Romanian dictator Ion Antonescu agreed to Filderman's request for permission to send help to the deportees in Transnistria, of which $35,000 originated indirectly with the JDC.[170] In New York, the JDC asked Washington for a license of $100,000 to ship food to Transnistrian deportees. The Treasury Department, stipulating that the shipments must be made through the International Red Cross, issued a license on November 1, 1943, and 10,000 food parcels were sent to Transnistria and Bucharest.[171]

In Hungary, when the Germans invaded in 1944, JDC sums rose to $884,786. Before the German takeover, the JDC put in place a clever way to transfer money from Switzerland to Hungary: Hungarian Jewish students from wealthy families were sent to study in Switzerland, their expenses paid by Saly Mayer, the JDC representative there, and in return the students' parents paid in Hungarian currency to Josef Blum, the JDC representative in Hungary.[172] Over 1 million Swiss francs, representing $227,000, was transferred by the JDC in cash to the Hungarian so-called Judenrat and Kasztner's Vaadah rescue committee, and according to Yehuda Bauer, Swiss diplomat Charles Lutz also received direct subsidies of about $18,000.[173]

During the chaotic period of the Russian siege of Budapest, starting in December 1944, JDC financed most of the rescue activities in the city—food, the upkeep of the children's homes, the protection papers, and even the youth movement's underground activities. Swedish diplomat Raoul Wallenberg was also the beneficiary of JDC aid in the amount of $100,000.[174]

Turning to Yugoslavia, before the German invasion of April 1941, the JDC sent small sums of money to support some 3,000 Jewish refugees who had been pushed over the border from Austria by the Gestapo, when Nazi Germany still practiced forced emigration.[175] Sime Spitzer, secretary of the Yugoslav Jewish community, was the main conduit of JDC's aid to Jewish refugees passing through the country, with a total expenditure in Yugoslavia of about $400,000 between 1933 and 1941.[176] JDC continued to support the Jews in Zagreb (capital of the newly created Croatia) via the International Red Cross. The small number of Jews still left at Zagreb, probably around 1,500, were literally kept alive by the JDC until their liberation in April 1945.[177]

Italy

Between September 1943 (when the Germans took over) and September 1944, Saly Mayer in Switzerland transmitted about $320,000 to Jews in northern Italy with the help of Vittorio Valobra, a leader of the Jewish community's Delasem organization. Valobra secretly crossed and recrossed the Swiss border and brought JDC money into Italy, where he distributed it to his agents, both Jews and others. On other occasions, Saly Mayer paid into a Swiss bank, and Valobra withdrew the money in Italian currency.[178]

France

Even before the war, as refugees from Nazi Germany began to stream into France, JDC was there to help out, and it spent $125,000 in 1933 alone. JDC continued to aid French organizations to an ever-increasing degree as more Jews fled to France from Germany, Austria, and even Poland and Romania, two countries that practiced a severe form of economic antisemitism. In 1939 JDC aid to French Jewish welfare organizations had risen to $589,000.[179] During the German occupation, with some 150,000 Jews living in Paris, JDC and the Quakers supplied half a million French francs to help out with four canteens and two dispensaries.[180]

In July 1941 Joseph Schwartz, in charge of the JDC European division, operating out of Lisbon, appointed Jules-Dika Jefroykin as the French representative of JDC.[181] Jefroykin, who was in leadership positions in both the MJS (Zionist Youth Movement) and the AJ (Jewish Army), was illegally financing the activities of these two organizations, probably with the silent knowledge of Schwartz, who gave Jefroykin a free hand to spend the money in the interest of saving as many people as possible.[182] It seemed that JDC in France was moving more and more into the shadow area of "gray" financing, supporting groups that tended toward illegal actions. One method used by Jefroykin and his assistant, Maurice Brener, was borrowing money from local institutions or individuals with a promise to reimburse the loans after the war without interest. The debts were honored in 1945 without contest.[183]

Schwartz himself was not beyond immersing himself in diplomatic activity when it came to helping Jews. On July 31, 1942, he met with S. Pinkney Tuck, the U.S. chargé d'affaires in Vichy, to urge stronger U.S. pressures on Vichy to scale down its anti-Jewish measures.[184] Schwartz's attempts failed, but as pointed out by Yehuda Bauer, the important thing is that he tried his best, even when acting without prior approval from his New York superiors.[185]

On September 16, 1942, JDC appropriated $400,000 toward an estimated cost of $950,000 for the transport of 1,000 children and their upkeep in the United States for their first year there. Two weeks later, Secretary of State Cordell Hull cabled S. Pinkney Tuck in Vichy that the visas were approved (for as many as 5,000 children, provided that the number was not made public), and for Tuck to try to get for them French exit visas—at the very time when the French were turning over thousands of Jews to the Germans for deportation. Very strong pressure by Tuck worked, and the Vichy government issued the first 500 permits. Things looked promising: on August 27, 1942, the Dominican government announced that it would accept 3,500 Jewish refugee children, followed by Canada's agreement to admit 500. JDC then pledged $400,000 for every 1,000 children, or $2 million for the whole 5,000. Canada then increased her offer to 1,000, and Argentina joined in with another 1,000.[186] Unfortunately, only a first group of 500 children left France for Lisbon on November 7, 1942. The following day American troops landed in French-held North Africa, and Vichy retaliated by severing diplomatic relations with the United States and canceling all further exit visas.[187]

Belgium and the Netherlands

JDC supplied tens of thousands of dollars to meet the rising costs of aiding the up to 10,000 Jewish refugees in Belgium during the German occupation. As a result JDC expenditure in that country rose from $106,000 in 1938 to $694,000 in 1939.[188] Further north, in the Netherlands, some 30,000 Jewish refugees entered the country from Germany between 1933 and 1940.[189] They were aided by a refugee committee led by David Cohen, a prominent classics scholar and a lifelong Zionist. He received considerable JDC support, probably through Gertrude van Tijn, a German Jewess. In April 1941, with Holland under German occupation, van Tijn was allowed to go to Lisbon, where she met Morris Troper of the JDC and made an arrangement under which JDC would leave funds in neutral countries for Jewish emigrants from Holland. When she returned, the Germans had changed their minds and no longer allowed large-scale emigration, although Jews were still allowed to leave in groups until that August and then occasionally as individuals in return for ransom.[190]

Switzerland

Swiss Jewry numbered about 18,000 in 1933 and was represented by the Swiss Jewish Federation (Schweizerischer Israelitischer Gemeindebund,

SIG). The flight of Jewish refugees rose significantly after Austria's annexation to Nazi Germany, and this placed a burden on the tiny Swiss Jewish community.[191] By the end of 1938, up to 12,000 Jewish refugees had failed to find another place to continue their sojourn and remained in Switzerland with JDC support.[192]

Until 1944 Saly Mayer was the central figure coordinating most of JDC's European work, in close contact with Joseph Schwartz in Lisbon. Born at Saint Gallen in 1882, Mayer made his living as a lace manufacturer. In the 1930s he sold his business and lived on the profits, but he was not an especially rich man. A religiously observant Jew, in 1936 he was elected to the presidency of SIG, representing the country's 18,000 Jews, and held on to this post until the end of 1942.[193] On May 30, 1940, on the eve of France's surrender to the Germans, Schwartz visited Mayer in Saint Gallen and asked him to accept the honorary post of JDC representative in Switzerland, to which Mayer agreed, although he never became a paid official; his work was all voluntary.[194]

Mayer's JDC role assumed greater significance when the United States entered the war. The U.S. Treasury Department forbade the transfer of funds to anyone if there was a chance that they might reach Nazi Europe, and so it was necessary for Schwartz to find other ways to pass on funds to Jews in German-occupied Europe. This is when Mayer came into the picture. He proposed that JDC double its allocation to Switzerland, thus paying a big share of the expenses of refugees there, and release the remaining funds, via Swiss currency, to pay for aid to Jews under Nazi rule. In other words, a larger JDC subvention to SIG would enable Swiss Jewry to extend relief to needy Jews who could not otherwise be helped directly by American welfare organizations.[195] Mayer received a grand total of $235,000 in 1942, and in 1943, $940,000, which was 10 to 11 percent of the entire JDC budget for that year. Another method, known as *après* ("after"), was to seek loans from local persons of means and financial institutions, with a commitment to be repaid by JDC after the war.[196]

Other aid organizations, made suspicious by Mayer's secretiveness and persuaded by the fable of the immensely rich "Joint," blamed Mayer for his miserliness and obsession regarding exact accounting when the lives of millions were at stake. As a result he soon ceased to have friends among the many organizations in Switzerland engaged in rescue work. He withdrew into a shell of increasing bitterness and loneliness.[197] Mayer continued to control most of the rescue funding operations in various European countries between 1941 and 1945, and he received substantial funds for this purpose, running into millions of U.S. dollars. And this brings us to his bitter conflict with Gisi Fleischmann and Rabbi M.D. Weissmandl over the disbursement of funds to Slovakia.[198]

Slovakia

Until the end of 1941, JDC was officially represented in Slovakia by Josef Blum and Bertrand S. Jacobson, who were responsible for the whole of southeastern Europe. With the U.S. entry into the war, Blum left for Buda-pest and did not return, and so in effect Gisi Fleischmann came to repre-sent JDC in Slovakia.[199] JDC appropriated $122,000 for Slovakia in 1940, most of which was spent feeding refugees arriving there from Poland, a number that kept increasing as the Holocaust spread inside Poland.[200] As deportations began in Slovakia in March 1942, large numbers of Jews fled to the relative safety of Hungary, and about 7,000 people managed to cross the border. There Blum and others rallied to facilitate the refu-gees' entry, with Blum receiving between $4,000 and $5,000 from Mayer for that purpose. The official Hungarian Jewish community, headed by Samu Stern, refused to extend help to people arriving in Hungary ille-gally.[201] Relations between Fleischmann and Mayer were exacerbated when on September 1, 1942, Fleischmann wrote to Mayer that she needed $100,000 for bribes, including a sum needed for a second installment for SS officer Dieter Wisliceny, as a condition for stopping the deporta-tion of Jews from Slovakia. Mayer decided to send $5,000 immediately and $5,000 in September, but he found it difficult to have that money transferred. JDC's reputation among Slovak Jewry suffered as a result of all this. According to Yehuda Bauer, Mayer could not respond because of the relatively small amount he held at the time that he had to disburse over vast European stations.[202]

A little later, under the so-called Europa Plan advanced by the Fleischmann-Weissmandl team, which required substantial payments to the SS, Fleischmann wrote harshly on January 14, 1943, on what she felt was Mayer's withholding of the money. Mayer at first procrastinated, but his JDC superiors announced on March 1, 1943, that they had rejected the whole idea, since they saw it as a deceptive ruse.[203] Mayer, nevertheless, decided to take some positive step, and on March 31, 1943, he wrote to

Fleischmann that he was trying to place $100,000 for ss officer Dieter Wisliceny in America, but to be drawn only after the war.[204] In early June 1943, Mayer was again pressed by Fleischmann for an answer regarding the Europa Plan.[205] Mayer refused to budge on the only-after-the-war stand, as Fleischmann and Weissmandl continued to press for cash now, not in the distant future.[206]

Mayer felt that Wisliceny's promises were not as serious as Fleischmann believed. The Nazis had promised to stop deportations while the negotiations were in progress, but deportations had continued from France. Nevertheless, despite his serious doubts, he sent 230,000 Swiss francs ($53,000) during August and September 1943. On September 3, 1943, Wisliceny finally announced that the Germans had withdrawn their offer under the Europa Plan, disappointing Fleischmann, who died in the Holocaust, and her rescue partner, Rabbi Michael Dov-Ber Weissmandl, who survived—though not his wife and children.[207]

Spain and Portugal

In Spain, of the refugees who successfully crossed the Pyrenees, some 3,500 were interned in the Miranda de Ebro camp, where the food was bad, the housing was worse, and mortality was high. Others were relatively lucky; they were placed in forced residence in Barcelona.[208] As the JDC was not permitted to operate on Spanish soil, it tried to help through various temporary arrangements. It transferred between $1,000 and $1,500 a month to Dorsey Stephens, wife of the American military attaché, and Virginia Chase Weddell, wife of the ambassador, who in turn tried their best to administer aid to refugees in Madrid and elsewhere. For refugee prisoners held in Barcelona, JDC used the good offices of Samuel Sequerra, who held a Portuguese passport and was permitted to enter Spain. Through him some 600 refugees received financial aid.[209]

In Lisbon, JDC and HICEM were able to move large numbers of refugees to the United States, Cuba, the West Indies, and other places. The refugees had to be maintained while waiting for ships, and it was JDC's task to do that. A camp was established at Caldas de Rainha for this purpose. At the end of 1940, there were 1,500 refugees (out of a total of 8,000 in Portugal) supported with JDC funds.[210] HIAS and JDC managed to get almost all of the refugees out of Portugal and Spain, so that at the beginning of 1942 there were only 1,000 left in each of the two countries.[211]

Japan and Shanghai

Jewish refugees waiting in Japan to continue to other destinations were also supported by JDC. A total of $350,000 was spent to support and feed them, over 75 percent of which came from JDC.[212] In Shanghai, after November 1938, refugees from Germany and Austria began streaming into the city, and 18,000 were there by the time war broke out in Europe. JDC increased its spending to $60,000 up to September 1939.[213] In 1940 and 1941 an estimated 4,000 to 6,000 Jews arrived. JDC sent a small initial sum of $3,500 for the Lithuania contingent, which included 1,000 Polish refugees, mostly rabbis and their students, among them the whole Mir yeshiva group of over 300.[214]

In March 1941 JDC decided to send an American representative to Shanghai, Laura L. Margolis, and she arrived on May 12. She was fully empowered by JDC–New York to do whatever she felt was right. Manuel Siegel was sent in November as her co-director. Throughout 1944 Saly Mayer transmitted about $517,000 there via the International Red Cross.[215]

Latin America

Since the start of the Nazi regime, refugees without visas attempted to reach safe haven in Latin America. JDC estimated that in March 1939, twenty-three boats with 1,740 refugees had sailed to Latin America without proper documents. But not all those ships managed to land their human cargo; some were forced to return to Europe.[216] Immediately upon American entry into the war, the ss *Cabo de Hornos*, carrying 107 refugees equipped with Brazilian visas, sailed for South America. While they were afloat, the Brazilians canceled the visas retroactively and only admitted the 20 Catholics among the boat's refugees when it arrived on December 1941. In the end, through JDC intervention, 86 Jewish passengers landed in Curaçao in the Dutch West Indies, where they were put up in a special camp at JDC expense.[217] Between January and July 1942, 4,058 Jewish refugees were transported to safety in eight JDC-organized sailings from the Iberian Peninsula.[218] Also, several hundred Jews who converted to Christianity in Italy escaped to South America, chiefly to Brazil, and their fares were paid by the Vatican out of JDC funds contributed for that purpose to Catholic aid organizations in America.[219]

Palestine—Land of Israel

The JDC policy concerning immigration to British-held Palestine was to participate only if the whole matter was open, public, and legal. Naturally this did not happen, as more illegal refugees squeezed into rickety boats on their way to the Promised Land, and JDC withheld help for them. This essentially remained JDC's policy right up to the outbreak of the war.[220] However, JDC's attitude toward illegal immigration was not that consistent. When shiploads of people were stranded in some Romanian harbor or on a Greek island, JDC did not approve, but it also did not decline help.[221] In November 1939 the Prague community, from which some of the illegal travelers originated, brought pressure to bear on Morris Troper of the JDC for financial aid. Seven to eight hundred illegal immigrants were on their way to Bratislava in Slovakia, from where they hoped to continue by riverboat on the Danube River. Troper was in favor of helping, feeling that the game of legality could no longer be played in the face of human suffering, and the New York office approved the necessary funds.[222]

At the end of 1939, three groups of refugees totaling over 2,000 people arrived at Sulina and Balchik, Romania, on the Black Sea. After most were taken aboard several ships, JDC paid $15,000 to transport those that remained behind after the Romanian Jewish community came up with $7,000.[223] In July 1940, when the *Pencho* was sailing on the Danube with illegal passengers, JDC found itself obligated to come up with $17,000 through the Yugoslav committee headed by Sime (Simon) Spitzer in order to support those aboard.[224] When another boat, the *Salvador*, sank in the Sea of Marmara off the Turkish coast in December 1940 and 126 Jewish refugees survived, the JDC responded to the appeal for assistance by Chaim Barlas of the Jewish Agency in Istanbul.[225] The JDC also sent money to Athens to help with some of the passengers of the *Pacific* who had stopped there on the way to Palestine, and to refugees stranded in Turkey.[226]

All these superhuman efforts by the JDC made it possible for many tens of thousands of Jews to obtain the basic necessities to make it possible for them to survive.

Saly Mayer and the SS

For the final episode in this section, we return to Saly Mayer and what to this day are still troublesome questions about the wisdom of trying to negotiate with the Nazis, as evidenced in the previously discussed

Europa Plan. On August 21, 1944, Mayer met with three SS officers and a Jew in the middle of the bridge spanning Switzerland and Austria in Saint Margarethen, because the Swiss authorities refused the Nazis' request to enter Switzerland. Mayer was supposedly representing not the JDC proper but its Swiss affiliate for the maintenance of Jewish refugees in Switzerland (Schweizerischer Unterstützungsfonds für Flüchtlinge). His partners in the conversation were senior SS officers Kurt A. Becher, Max Grüson, and Hermann Krumey, accompanied by the controversial Jewish rescuer Dr. Rezső Kasztner.

The SS proposed that in return for the Jews supplying 10,000 trucks and other machines for agricultural purposes, the Germans would in turn allow Jews to leave for the United States.[227] Mayer replied that he would not negotiate under pressure and would not do anything that was not consistent with moral principles. Becher shot back that there was nothing immoral in his suggestions. The first train from Bergen-Belsen with 318 people from Kasztner's group had come that very day to the Swiss border to show the seriousness of German intentions. Mayer asked for some time to consult his superiors.[228]

On November 1, 1944, the War Refugee Board representative in Switzerland, Roswell McClelland, informed Mayer that $2 million had been set aside in the United States for the purpose of the talks, but that any payment was preconditioned by WRB approval. Mayer, aware of the seriousness of this matter, wrote down what he told JDC-Lisbon on September 10: "Up to 800,000 Jews still in hands of 'Nasty' are in immediate danger of losing their lives. . . . I am by now well informed about 'don't' and 'noes.' But what about 'do it' and 'yes'? USA says no money for ransom and no goods for 'Nasty,' but do not let negotiations break down." There was no answer to this.[229]

Three more meetings were held between both parties in early November 1944. Becher, not satisfied with what was offered him, issued an ultimatum: if by December 2 there was no ransom money, the Jews would suffer, and the Budapest Jews would be the first to do so. Yet, surprisingly, on the night of December 6, the SS allowed the remaining 1,368 Jews of the Kasztner train in Bergen-Belsen to cross the Swiss border.[230]

In one of the earlier meetings, Mayer stated that he was in principle ready to open a bank account amounting to 5 million Swiss francs for the negotiations and would do his best to convince the Swiss government to permit the ss to buy goods in Switzerland, provided that the Jews under Nazi rule, including the Jews of Hungary, were kept safe. The goods, however, would not include war material. Grüson surprised everyone when he asked to negotiate with a political representative (in his words, someone with "full political powers"). Here, apparently ss chief Heinrich Himmler's real aim became clear. The Joel Brand–Bandi Grosz mission had failed (see chapter 5), but possibly the Swiss JDC-representative could lead Himmler's emissaries to the Americans and to a negotiated separate peace.[231]

On January 1945, more than a month after the Nazis' extended deadline, permission was received by the United States for the transfer of 20 million Swiss francs to Mayer by JDC, but none could be spent without prior governmental approval, and later Mayer was told that McClelland's approval was also needed. Mayer, according to Yehuda Bauer, believed that the money was to be used to pay the International Red Cross for keeping Jews alive in Nazi camps, which he felt was preferable to having the hundreds of thousands of Jews transferred to safer locations and out of Nazi hands.[232] Early in 1945 Mayer gave large sums to the International Red Cross to get parcels to Theresienstadt and Bergen-Belsen camps. On January 1 he sent 10,000 packages, and in March 1945 he gave money for ten trucks and a first convoy that left in March 1945, bound for Germany. In April another convoy went to Landsberg and Kauffering concentration camps, where 12,000 Jews were reputed to be interned. The 14,000 parcels sent there were largely used after liberation.[233]

In summary, nothing practical, favorable to the Jews, came out of the discussions between three senior ss officers, sent to negotiate by ss chief Himmler, and Saly Mayer, a rather low-level Jewish aid activist who had his hands tied by his superiors, including officials of the War Refugee Board—paradoxically, an organization created specifically for the purpose of rescuing Jews. Would a more prominent representation of Jewish leaders to negotiate with Himmler's aides have produced better results and saved more Jewish lives? We may never know. As for JDC representative Saly Mayer, he tried his best, under the financial and political constraints of his day, to help fellow Jews to the best of his capacity and his understanding of what needed to be done, and he is to be credited for this. He died in 1950.

Afterword

In evaluating the significance of the Jewish rescuers of Jews during the Holocaust, a few disturbing background factors need to be taken into consideration. First, there was the failure of Jewish leadership to properly assess the real nature of the Nazi onslaught on the Jewish people. Contrast this with the mostly unknown Jewish rescuers of the Holocaust period who were fully aware of the existential threat facing Jews and took action to try to stem this murderous avalanche. As stated by historian Yehuda Bauer, Jewish leaders did not grasp the full impact of what was happening to Europe's Jews. The Joint Distribution Committee, which otherwise performed very laudable work to ease the sufferings of Jews, also failed to grasp the full extent of the problem. In Bauer's words: "JDC leaders in the free world were acting out what may be called 'normal' reactions to 'normal' disasters." But what was needed was not normal responses but, wrote Bauer, "actions leading to the breaking of norms of ordinary warfare in the interest of Europe's Jews."[1]

Paralysis of Leadership

Jewish leaders could have done more, even in the weakened position they found themselves in during the war years by galvanizing their efforts instead of bickering among themselves for positions of prestige. While they were busy arguing and slandering each other (see the stories of Bergson group, George Mandel-Mantello, Rabbi Solomon Schonfeld, and others elsewhere in this book),[2] the Nazis and their collaborating countries were happily proceeding with the murder of the Jews in their midst. The Palestine Jewish community, known as the Yishuv, was overcome by a tragic sense of impotence, as it was utterly dependent on the goodwill of England, the major power that controlled Palestine, and that goodwill was lacking—not in words, but in deeds. The Jewish Agency in Palestine did form a rescue committee in March 1943, headed by veteran Zionist leaders

Yitzhak Gruenbaum and Eliyahu Dobkin, but that proved not up to the task. Geneva was the closest listening post to Nazi activities in German-occupied countries, and Jewish operations there, such as Zionist agencies represented by Nathan Schwalb, Richard Lichtheim, and Chaim Pozner and the Mossad in Geneva were more informed and frightfully conscious of what was happening to their brethren Jews.[3] Despite that, the Zionist movement failed to realize that the times called for a major realignment of priorities—with rescue at the top of the list.

Adding to the ineffectiveness of Jewish leadership was the disinclination to undermine the war effort of the British, who blocked Jewish refugees from reaching Palestine, but who also stood alone facing Hitler after the fall of France (and until the German attack on the Soviet Union in June 1941).[4]

Chaim Weizmann was considered Jewry's elder statesman and foremost leader. Through his astute negotiations with British leaders during World War I, he led them to identify with Zionist aspirations (a goal that eluded Theodor Herzl, who founded the Zionist movement) and to the issuance of the Balfour Declaration of November 1917. But twenty years later he failed to grasp the real nature of the Nazi phenomenon as it affected the Jewish people. This, even though he spoke of the precarious position of the 6 million Jews of Europe in dramatic words before the British Peel Commission in 1936, that for these Jews, "the world seemed to be divided into two parts—those places where the Jews could not live and those where they could not enter."

This somber analysis of the situation of European Jewry led Weizmann to favor a passive and limited rescue program when, at the 1937 World Zionist Congress in Zürich, he divided European Jewry into two categories: those that could be saved and those that, in his cynical words, would have to be left to await the arrival of the Messiah—in other words, to be abandoned to their fate. With a Jewish tragedy looming, his immediate goal was to get 2 million Jewish youth to Palestine to help rebuild a Jewish entity there. The rest, he likened to economic and moral dust, to be left on their own.[5]

Weizmann and his great Zionist rival, Vladimir Jabotinsky, were both aware of the volcano about to erupt, though not prescient of its horrific dimensions. But while Weizmann focused on saving a significant few, Jabotinsky urged listeners, especially in Poland in the late 1930s, to drop everything and start a march to Palestine without any planning. This, naturally, was anything but practical.[6]

In Weizmann's memoirs, *Trial and Error*, published a few years after the war, one searches frantically for actions and deeds by this tireless champion of Jewish causes, as the greatest tragedy in Jewish history was unfolding before his eyes. He mentions a letter received by fellow Zionist activist Richard Lichtheim informing him that if Hitler overran Europe, no Jews would be left alive, to which Weizmann added: "It was like a nightmare which was all the more oppressive because one had to maintain silence: to speak of such things in public was 'propaganda'!" The reader is left wondering what exactly he meant by these words.[7] While the Allies fighting Nazi Germany deliberately did not refer to the Jews as Nazi victims, Hitler always stated quite clearly in his public pronouncements (let alone in his writings, such as *Mein Kampf*) that the Jews were his main target and he was determined to rid Europe of them, one way or another—words which he constantly repeated during the war years.[8]

Dejected, disappointed, and feeling helpless to stem the Nazi extermination of Jews, Weizmann retreated to his laboratory, experimenting on improving the production of oil, or to discussions with world leaders on the future of the Zionist enterprise in Palestine. This was also evidenced during the Zionist Biltmore platform of May 1942, spearheaded by David Ben-Gurion, where the discussions mainly centered on the future of Jewish Palestine, coupled with a near-total disregard for the extermination of Jews on the European continent taking place at precisely the same time.[9]

Missed Opportunities?

Another troubling question: Did Jewish leaders miss a real opportunity to negotiate with the Nazi establishment for the release of Jews, at a time when the Nazi regime was still in favor of a Jewish mass evacuation instead of extermination? In the 1930s the Transfer Agreement between the Zionist movement and Nazi Germany gave German Jews the right to leave the country with a considerable part of their assets. An attempt at another such agreement was made on the eve of World War II, following the failed Evian Conference of July 1938. It involved negotiations between the Intergovernmental Committee on Refugees, created by the Evian conferees, and Nazi leaders (the Rublee-Schacht negotiations) for the emigration of hundreds of thousands of German Jews. The negotiations continued for months with only half-hearted Jewish support, until it ended abruptly with the outbreak of war on September 1, 1939. Yehuda Bauer surmised that "the Nazis took this plan seriously and were willing to consider it as a possible solution to the Jewish question."[10] Was an opportunity missed here?

Even as late as June 1944, with the Nazi killing machine in high gear (10,000 Hungarian Jews were murdered daily), the Germans were willing to discuss a deal with Jewish representatives and meet with either Menachem Bader (Zionist leader) or Joseph Schwartz (JDC) on neutral grounds.[11] But strong British opposition scuttled the plan. "Where, Mr. Shertok," Foreign Secretary Anthony Eden told the Jewish Agency's second most powerful man, "shall we put these Jews if Eichmann keeps his word and sends them to the border?"[12]

One also wonders why low-level Jewish delegates, hardly known except within their own immediate circles, were sent to negotiate with high-powered ss officials on the fate of millions of Jews. Critics have asked if a more significant Jewish personality than Chaim Barlas (representing the Jewish Agency in Turkey) would have been a better choice to negotiate with high-level Turkish officials as well as with papal envoy Angelo Roncalli on the rescue of Jews. Similarly, was Joel Brand (an activist of a low-level rescue organization in Hungary) the proper person to try to manage the Eichmann proposal (probably on Himmler's initiative) to liberate 1 million Jews in return for 10,000 military trucks?[13] Was Saly Mayer, the JDC representative in Switzerland, the right man to negotiate with high-level ss officers, one of whom (Kurt Becher) was very close to ss head Himmler, in an attempt to save the hundreds of thousands of Jews still under ss control? War Refugee Board representative Roswell McClelland, who worked closely with Mayer, once told a Jewish colleague, "Perhaps, had you picked more of a diplomat, a man with greater political background and savoir faire, more could possibly have been achieved."[14] Would anyone else, indeed, have done better, Bauer wondered.[15] Perhaps so. Someone with more political clout, such as Weizmann, a man who in an earlier period led the high-level negotiations that led to the Balfour Declaration. Furthermore, would a more prominent member of the Jewish leadership than the unknown Rabbi Weissmandl, who negotiated with Himmler's representative, have produced better results and saved more lives?

Again, Bauer: "The question must be posed whether a chance of negotiating the rescue of Jews was not missed in the failure of the Europa Plan
[proposed by Weissmandl]. No documentary proof can be offered, but
the circumstantial evidence provided by the story . . . points to the answer
that a chance was missed."[16] But there was no else around, as the Jewish
leadership was then in a state of near-paralysis or too much concerned
with the future of a Jewish Palestine as well as their own status vis-à-vis
competing organizations.

In a 1991 study, Yehuda Bauer stated that insofar as the Jews were concerned, Himmler might have been willing to sell, given certain conditions,
but "there were no buyers." In other words, there was no comparable and
matching response from the Jewish side.[17] Also, that "it is disturbing to
think that, with respect to the Madagascar plan proffered by the Germans
in 1940, more money might indeed have saved them."[18] To explain this
lack of foresight, Bauer surmised that "a specifically Jewish 'foreign policy'
simply had not yet emerged" among Jewish organizations that would have
placed the saving of Jews as a priority as Weissmandl urged, on the same
footing as winning the war.[19] These are harsh and condemnatory words
and not in substance greatly different from Weissmandl's own charges
voiced during and after the war. No wonder Jewish rescuer Zerach Warhaftig excruciatingly asked, "Could we have avoided the Holocaust, or
at least curbed it and limited its scope? Could we have saved more than
the pitiful few that were rescued, and could we have done more? Did we
let any chances slip by? Had we appraised the situation correctly? Had
we sounded the alarm with sufficient force and roused public opinion
that mankind might realize the great dangers inherent in the situation?
. . . Doubts gnawed at my heart."[20]

To Make Known the Heroic Efforts of Jewish Rescuers

Measured against the confusing, dilatory, and uncalibrated measures by
Jewish leaders of the stature of Chaim Weizmann, David Ben Gurion,
and Stephen Wise to come up with emergency measures in the face of
the decimation of entire Jewish populations across a continent, great and
small, the role of these lesser-known individuals like Basia Berman, the
Bielski brothers, Rabbi Michael Dov-Ber Weissmandl, Moussa Abadi,
Walter Süskind, and others mentioned in this study stand out more prom-
inently. They acted alone and in many cases with little if any backing by

others. It was for them a lonely and desperate undertaking, as they tried again and again—and succeeded—in saving thousands of Jewish lives, either themselves or with the help of non-Jewish rescuers. These Jewish rescuers still wait to be fully studied as well as acknowledged, praised, and honored, even posthumously. They represent a beacon of light capable of inspiring Jewish generations now and in the future. This is what I have attempted to do in this book.

Notes

Introduction

The proclamation by the Jewish Zionist Youth Group is found in Arad, Gutman, and Margaliot, *Documents*, 433, and the tract distributed by Solidarité is found in Poznanski, *Jews*, 260. Rabbi Frieder's sermon is found in Frieder, *To Deliver*, 71–72, and Feiner and Kirszenbaum's message to Karski is found in Karski, *Story*, 322–23, 328. Rabbi Weissmandl's letter is found in Fuchs, *Unheeded Cry*, 170, 185, and Dawidowicz, *Holocaust Reader*, 321–27.

1. She illustrated this by citing Oswald Rufeisen and the Bielski brothers, who acted in Byelorussia, a place of unspeakable horrors for Jews during the Holocaust. Tec, "Reflections on Rescuers," 657–58.
2. In 1951 Israeli prime minister David Ben Gurion, who was still opposed to the creation of the Yad Vashem Holocaust memorial, explained that the ethos of fighting was utterly foreign and unnatural for the Jews of Europe. A Jew coming to Eretz Israel undergoes a change of mentality, a kind of metamorphosis, in which he sheds his Diaspora mentality and acquires a new value system. From now on he relies on himself. Stauber, *Holocaust*, 53–54. Also see Shapira, *Old Jews*, 155–74.
3. Very little was made of the Zionist youth movements in Hungary that were responsible for saving thousands of lives. As they focused their efforts on rescue, rather than fighting the enemy, they too were lumped together with Diaspora Jews who in the Zionist historical reinterpretation failed, so to speak, to pull themselves up by their own bootstraps. David Gur, one of the still living former Zionist youth activists in Hungary living in Israel, is currently making great efforts to tell the story of his fellow rescuers and integrate their story in the Holocaust narrative of Israeli educational facilities.

1. Germany and Austria

1. Kulka, "Germany," 557–75.
2. In 1543 Martin Luther wrote a booklet under the scurrilous title "On the Jews and Their Lies," in which he called for the destruction of all Jewish synagogues and schools and for Jews to be required to perform forced labor or be expelled.

3. Kulka, "Germany," 558.

4. Fraenkel, "Germany," liii–lxiii.

5. Throughout the 1930s and up to 1942, there were up to fourteen Zionist agricultural training centers in which some 400 young adults, ages twenty-one to thirty, worked and studied, along with 400 youngsters under the Youth Aliyah program. In March 1943 the last 150 youth and 150 adults were deported to the east. Seligmann, "Illegal," 327–61, 335–36; Kulka, "Germany," 562, 566.

6. Under this law, it was sufficient for an employee to have only one Jewish grandparent to be ousted.

7. Kulka, "Germany," 562.

8. In 1939 the name changed to the Reich Association of Jews in Germany (Reichsvereinigung den Juden in Deutschland). Kulka, "Germany," 563, 569.

9. Kulka, "Germany," 566.

10. Kulka, "Germany," 567.

11. Kulka, "Germany," 568.

12. Kulka, "Germany," 571.

13. In late February 1943 the Nazis released Jewish men married to non-Jewish spouses, who had been arrested, after their wives protested vigorously on the streets of Berlin (known as the Rosenstrasse incident). Stoltzfus, *Resistance*; Kulka, "Germany," 574.

14. Seligmann, "Illegal," 335; USHMM, "German Jews." Ironically, no sooner was Germany declared *Judenrein* than Jews from the east began to be brought in as forced laborers and as participants in the infamous death marches that crisscrossed the German countryside in the final months of the war. Fraenkel, "Germany," lvii.

15. USHMM, "German Jews"; Seligmann, "Illegal," 337.

16. Fraenkel, "Germany," lviii; Seligmann, "Illegal," 347, 354, 360.

17. Seligmann, "Illegal," 328, 332, 340–41, 359. As of January 1, 2016, Yad Vashem had awarded the Righteous title to 587 non-Jewish Germans for helping Jews inside Germany or countries under German occupation.

18. Kulka, "Germany," 574. Survivors also included 3,000 to 5,000 who led a secret life in Germany, and up to 9,000 others who survived the depredations of concentration camps. There were also some 15,000 so-called *Mischlinge* who survived inside Germany. Kulka, "Germany," 574; USHMM, "German Jews."

19. Born in 1892 in Norden, Germany, to orthodox parents (Menashe and Bertha Schweitzer), Recha Freier showed an interest in music and poetry while studying philology at several universities and working as a teacher and pianist. In 1919 she married Rabbi Dr. Moritz Freier and moved with

him to Sofia, Bulgaria, where they remained until 1926. Then, as her husband was appointed rabbi at several synagogues in Berlin, the couple moved back to Germany. Their first son, Shalhevet, was born in 1920. In 1923 a second son, Ammud, was added, followed in 1926 by a third son, Zerem, and in 1929 a daughter, Maayan.

20. Freier, *Let*, 9.

21. Freier, *Let*, 9–10.

22. Freier, *Let*, 10.

23. Freier, *Let*, 11–12.

24. The treasurer of Ezra, Berthold Israel, was the father of Wilfrid Israel, owner of the largest department store in Berlin; Freier, *Let*, 12–13.

25. Freier, *Let*, 14.

26. The identity of the originator of the Youth Aliyah enterprise became a matter of a prolonged and bitter feud between Henrietta Szold and Recha Freier. Szold readily admitted that Freier was the first to initiate the separation of children from their families in Germany and their pioneering training in Palestine, but took on herself the credit of translating the idea into reality for many other children, as she assumed the leadership of Youth Aliyah out of her Jerusalem office. Gelber, "Origins," 147–71, 149. These two valiant women rarely met. Recha Freier was repeatedly rebuffed when she tried to speak with Henrietta Szold. Internet Jewish Women's Archive; jwa.org/encyclopedia/article/freier-recha.

27. Freier, *Let*, 15.

28. Freier, *Let*, 16.

29. Freier, *Let*, 17.

30. Gelber, "Origins," 148.

31. Freier, *Let*, 18.

32. Freier, *Let*, 19.

33. Freier, *Let*, 20–21.

34. Freier, *Let*, 27–28, 31, 37. As reported by Zionist activist Arthur Ruppin, before the Second Youth Aliyah World Congress in 1937. "In 1932 Mrs. Recha Freier came over as the pioneer of this idea in Palestine. . . . Mrs. Freier did succeed in putting her idea into practice in the same year by sending a group of 12 youth to Ben Shemen." The feud between Freier and Szold, both admirable women, did not diminish with passing time. On July 26, 1939, Szold wrote to Freier questioning her assertion of being the principal mover in launching the Youth Aliyah idea, but at the same time admitting that "our attitude in no way contradicts your claim to be the originator of the idea itself." Freier, *Let*, 86. She repeated this admission in her address before the 9th Zionist Congress in 1935. "On this occasion I

should like to express especial thanks to the originator of this movement, Mrs. Recha Freier. It was she who thought out this inspired idea and put it into practice in spite of the many difficulties and obstacles. We owe her our thanks for her selfless devotion to an idea which at first received so little encouragement and turned out so fertile." Freier, *Let,* 89.

35. Freier, *Let,* 34; Gelber, "Origins," 155, 157, 161, 163.
36. Freier, *Let,* 43, 50.
37. Freier, *Let,* 59, 61–62.
38. Freier, *Let,* 62–63.
39. Freier, *Let,* 66–67.
40. Freier, *Let,* 68.
41. Weiss, *Joshko's,* 8; Freier, *Let,* 68.
42. Freier, *Let,* 69.
43. Freier, *Let,* 70, 72; Weiss, *Joshko's,* 3.
44. Kalman Givon (Karl Kleinberger), "*Ich wurde von Recha Freier gerettet.*" Also, from the diary of Tilla Nagler: "All credit is due to Recha Freier, the woman with the heart of gold. . . . I was seventeen the oldest of the group. Our youngest was ten. For most of us, the separation from our mothers was to be a permanent one. . . . We went by train to Vienna and there, at the Palestine-Amt, we received final instructions. We reached the Yugoslav border; it was January 1941, very cold, snow everywhere. . . . Sunday morning in Zagreb. Sixteen girls are rushing from the railroad station to the cellar. . . . Recha is standing in the courtyard wearing that long black dress of hers and she is beaming. . . . Certificates, there weren't any and when we finally received ninety permits . . . no Turkish visas were on hand. . . . At last we urged Recha to leave by scaring her that her permit might be canceled. . . . We simply could not get used to the idea that Recha, whose papers were in order, should remain here. . . . She worried about the fate of the children and had dedicated her life to their Aliyah. The power of her vision was such that she saw herself welcoming them in Haifa!" Weiss, *Joshko's,* 34, 35.
45. Freier, *Let,* 73–74.
46. A square in the Jerusalem's Katamon neighborhood is named after her. As for her husband, Rabbi Moritz Freier, he had left for England in 1938, where he lived with the couple's three sons. In 1949 he returned to Berlin, where he took up a post as rabbi, and ultimately retired in Switzerland. In 1967 he moved to Israel, where he died two years later. Recha had been separated from her husband for a long time, and they never again lived together. Wikipedia, "Reicha Freier."
47. Shepherd, *Refuge,* 14, 17, 21. The House of Israel was started in 1815 by

Nathan Israel as a small secondhand store that soon developed into a world-renowned wholesale, retail, and export business. It was known for the high standard of its interiors as well as the highly trained staff. After Berthold Israel's death, the firm was owned by his two sons, Wilfrid and Herbert. Wikipedia, "Wilfrid B. Israel."

48. Shepherd, *Refuge*, 47, 69–70, 100.

49. Shepherd, *Refuge*, 72–74, 87, 98.

50. Shepherd, *Refuge*, 106.

51. Shepherd, *Refuge*, 90, 97, 116, 121. In 1999, the already departed Francis Foley was honored by Yad Vashem with the title of Righteous Among the Nations. Yad Vashem Archives (henceforth: YVA) M31.2/8378. Earlier his many benefactors planted a forest in his name in the Judean hills of Israel.

52. Shepherd, *Refuge*, 129–30, 131. Also, YVA 02/340 (Hubert Pollack: Captain Foley and Other Reports; turned over to Yad Vashem by the Wiener Library).

53. Shepherd, *Refuge*, 143, 145; Aderet, "Silent."

54. Shepherd, *Refuge*, 147.

55. Shepherd, *Refuge*, 146–48. If the British government waited for the United States to follow its example, it had hoped in vain. The Wagner-Rogers Bill for the admission of 20,000 children was defeated before it could reach the floor of Congress. Only 433 children who left without their families, many of whom had emigrated before the pogrom of November 1938, reached the United States under various voluntary schemes. Shepherd, *Refuge*, 149.

56. Shepherd, *Refuge*, 154, 158–60, 164.

57. Shepherd, *Refuge*, 228, 236, 239. The Wilfrid Israel Museum in Kibbutz Hazorea is an archaeology and art museum dedicated to his memory. Opened in 1951, it houses Wilfrid's unique collection and includes added items of art of India, China, Thailand, Cambodia, and the Near East, as well as local archaeology. Wikipedia, "Wilfrid B. Israel."

58. Shepherd, *Refuge*, 240–43.

59. Shepherd, *Refuge*, 244, 247–48.

60. Shepherd, *Refuge*, 249–50.

61. Aderet, "Silent."

62. Shepherd, *Refuge*, 114.

63. Glick's impression of Himmler was that of "an experienced title searcher in the office of the Recorder of Deeds of a county seat. . . . With the body of a tackle on a football team." Shepherd, *Refuge*, 115.

64. Glick, "Some Were Rescued."

65. Shepherd, *Refuge*, 115–16.

66. Attached to Glick's article is a copy of a May 19, 1937, letter by U.S. diplo-

mat Geist, in German, addressed to all U.S. consular officials in Germany, asking them to render assistance to Glick in his meetings with Jewish representatives on the matter of immigration. Geist added that Glick's presence and activity had the support of the Gestapo, a fact to which Geist himself was a witness. In German: "*Die Geheime Staaatspolizei unterstützt die Bestrebungen von Herrn Glick. Bei der diesbezüglichen Besprechung im Geheimen Staatspolizeiamt war der Unterzeichnete zugegen.*"

67. Corbach, *Jawne*, 265, 267–68, 271.

68. Corbach, *Jawne*, 281–82, 284–85, 287, 296–97.

69. Wikipedia, "History of the Jews in Austria."

70. Pauley, *From*, 275, 285, 300; Dwork and Van Pelt, *Holocaust*, 96, 280–82.

71. Pauley, *From*, 281–84, 287, 289–92; Yahil, "*Holocaust*," 107.

72. Borut, "Austria," xix–xxiii, xx, xxxii. In 1944 hundreds of mostly Hungarian Jews were brought in from Hungary and dispersed to work as forced laborers. Some were saved by their work supervisors or compassionate passers-by. Borut, "Austria," xxv; Dwork and Van Pelt, *Holocaust*, 98, 121; Pauley, *From*, 293–97. As of January 1, 2016, 107 Austrians had been honored with the Righteous title by Yad Vashem for helping Jews, some of them while serving in countries under German occupation.

73. Gordonia was founded in Poland in 1923; its members were inspired by the teachings of Aaron Gordon on the fulfillment of Zionism through labor, but were opposed to the Marxist indoctrination advocated by the leftist Poalei Zion and Hashomer Hatzair (Young Watchmen) Zionist youth movement. Central Committee of Jews from Austria in Israel, "Lehitraot," 10.

74. Weiss, *Joshko's*, 291.

75. Weiss, *Joshko's*, 23, 36–37, 258, 274–75.

76. Central, "Lehitraot," 30; Weiss, *Joshko's*, 24.

77. Central, "Lehitraot," 32; Weiss, *Joshko's*, 36–37.

2. Poland

1. Madajczyk, "Poland," 1143; Wikipedia, "The Holocaust in Poland."

2. Gutman, "Poland," xx–xlvii, xxi.

3. Gutman, "Jews," 1151–52.

4. Gutman, "Jews"; Wikipedia, "The Holocaust in Poland."

5. Gutman, "Jews," 1153–154; Gutman, "Poland," xxii– xxiii.

6. A Polish government-in-exile was set up in London, and its representatives on Polish soil within the Polish underground were known as the Delegatura. Madajczik, "Poland," 1145.

7. Gutman, "Jews," 1155–58.

8. Gutman, "Jews," 1156, 1159–161; Madajczyk, "Poland," 1147.

9. In August 1942 Hans Frank declared: "Nothing much has to be said about the fact that we are starving 1,200,000 Jews to death; that is self-evident, and if the Jews do not die from hunger, anti-Jewish decrees will have to be speeded up." Gutman, "Jews," 1162.

10. Gutman, "Jews," 1162, 1164. The planned death of Jews in the ghettos through starvation is dubbed by Israel Gutman "extermination without bloodshed." Gutman, "Poland," xxvi.

11. Gutman, "Jews," 1156–58, 1167; Wikipedia, "The Holocaust in Poland."

12. Gutman, "Poland," xxv–xxvi.

13. Gutman, "Poland," xxxi, xxxvi.

14. Gutman, "Poland," xxvi, xxviii.

15. Gutman, "Poland," xxxiii.

16. Gutman, "Poland," xxix, xxxiv.

17. Gutman, "Poland," xxx, xxxiv.

18. Gutman, "Poland," xl.

19. Gutman, "Jews," 1165, 1171; Wikipedia, "The Holocaust in Poland"; Kermish, "Activities," 367–98. According to Israel Gutman, hundreds of Poles paid with their lives for having rescued Jews. Gutman, "Poland," xlvii. As of January 1, 2016, 6,620 Polish rescuers of Jews have been awarded the Righteous title by Yad Vashem.

20. Gutman, "Jews," 1174–76; Gutman, "Poland," xx; Wikipedia, "The Holocaust in Poland."

21. As confirmed by Warsaw ghetto historian, Emanuel Ringelblum, writing in May 1942: "These heroic girls . . . In mortal danger every day. They rely entirely on their 'Aryan' faces and on the peasant kerchiefs that cover their heads. . . . They accept and carry out the most dangerous missions. . . . Nothing stands in their way. Nothing deters them. . . . .How many times have they looked death in the eyes?" Ringelblum, *Notes*, 273–74.

22. Ochayon, "Female."

23. Meed, *On Both Sides*, 257–60

24. Meed, *On Both Sides*, 261.

25. Meed, *On Both Sides*, 245–46.

26. Meed, *On Both Sides*, 269.

27. Meed, *On Both Sides*, 249–51.

28. Meed, *On Both Sides*, 265. In 1989 the rescuers within the Mieczyslaw Wolski family were awarded the Righteous title by Yad Vashem, YVA-M31.2/4252.

29. Meed, *On Both Sides*, 113, 115, 117–18, 214.

30. Meed, *On Both Sides*, 292, 293, 298.

31. Meed, *On Both Sides,* 299–303.
32. Temkin-Berman, *City,* 5.
33. Temkin-Berman, *City,* 1–14.
34. Temkin-Berman, *City,* 22.
35. Temkin-Berman, *City,* 58, 219.
36. Kermish, "Activities," 370–71; Tomaszewski and Werbowski, Żegota, 41; Berman, "Hayehudim," 691–92; Berman, *Mimei.*
37. Berman, "Hayehudim," 693–94, 696; Kermish, "Activities," 375, 377. Irena Sendlerowa is on Yad Vashem's list of Righteous Among the Nations. YVA-M31.2/153.
38. Temkin-Berman, *City,* 19.
39. Tomaszewski and Werbowski, Żegota, 75, 76; Berman, "Hayehudim," 693, 722; Kermish, "Activities," 370, 373, 376. Miriam Hochbeg-Marianska (later, Peleg), was one of its operatives there, and her Jewish identity was known only to a few persons in Żegota; her story appears later in this chapter.
40. Kermish, "Activities," 374, 394, 453.
41. Tomaszewski and Werbowski, Żegota, 44, 69; Temkin-Berman, *City,* 20. Others who helped included known Jewish underground operatives, such as Yitzhak Zuckerman and Stefan Grajek. Berman also kept in touch secretly with other Jewish escapees from the Warsaw ghetto, circulating secretly on the Aryan side, such as historian Emanuel Ringelblum and Zionist leader Menachem Kirszenbaum.
42. Tomaszewski and Werbowski, Żegota, 71. Berman, "Hayehudim," 711–12. Menachem Kirszenbaum, a public figure in the ghetto, fled to the Aryan side during the Warsaw ghetto uprising and succeeded in getting hold of citizenship papers for one of the South American countries. This did not save him, and he was reportedly shot in 1943. Berman, "Hayehudim," 108.
43. Tomaszewski and Werbowski, Żegota, 44; Berman, "Hayehudim," 691; Temkin-Berman, *City,* 18. Feiner was one of the two Jewish leaders who met secretly with Jan Karski to plead for help from the Allies to stop the Holocaust. Jan Karski, Story, 322–23, 328. Karski also took Feiner's report to Szmul Zygielbojm and Ignacy Schwarzbart, the two Jewish representatives in the Polish National Council of the Polish government-in-exile in London. The report described the murder of Jews by the Germans throughout Poland, the extermination camp at Chełmno (by the use of mobile gas vans) and gave the estimated number of murdered Jews as of May 1942 at 700,000. Feiner's instructions to Zygielbojm were to cease mere protests and organize retaliatory bombing, leafleting, and execution of Germans captured by the Allies in response to the Nazi Holocaust. Karski, *Story,* 321–38. The description of the condition of Jews in

German-occupied Poland and Feiner's instructions threw Zygielbojm into depression, since he knew that the Allies would be unwilling to help, and he eventually committed suicide in protest against the indifference of the Allied governments in the face of the Holocaust. Karski, *Story*, 338.

44. Berman, "Hayehudim," 694, 712–13; Kermish, "Activities," 373–75, 453. In January 1943 Emanuel Ringelblum, with wife and son Uri, aged twelve, escaped from the ghetto to the other side. Emanuel returned several times to salvage the storage of the archives. He was there during the ghetto uprising in April 1943 and was sent to a labor camp in Trawniki, near Lublin. A special unit of the Jewish underground succeeded in spiriting him out from there. He then spent months in a bunker until its discovery in March 1944, and he was shot together with his wife and son. Temkin-Berman, *City*, 29–30.

45. These included the architect and sculptor Richard Moskowski and wife, pianist Roza Atkin-Moskowski; historian Dr. Simon Zejczik and wife, Natalia; pedagogues Dr. Felicia Czerniakow (wife of Adam Czerniakow, who headed the Warsaw ghetto Judenrat), and Dr. Stefania Cigelstreich. Others named by Berman include Dr. Leon Handelsman, Batja Richter-Mamerman, and Stefan Szachor. Persons aiding resistance activist Yitzhak Zuckerman ("Antek") included Simcha Ratheiser-Rotem ("Każik"), Jadwiga Fulman, Ludzia Zilberstein, Irena Gelblum, Marisia Grasberg, Marisia Warman, and Esther Fiks. Other principal activists on the Aryan side named by Berman are David Guzik, of the General-Zionist faction and representing the Joint Distribution Committee; Anna Guttesman, Zofia Kimelman, Joanna Tikocinska, Natalia Mochorweska, Tauchner, and Lustig. Among the important Bund affiliates aiding Leon Feiner in his rescue operation were Vladka Peltel (later, Meed), Anna Margolies, Alla Morgulis, Dr. Inka Schweiger, Aniela Steinsberg, and Bronka ("Marisia") Feinmeser. Yiddish writer Rachela Auerbach, previously engaged with Ringelblum's secret Oneg Shabbat archives, may also be listed among those who worked with the Bermans, as well as Józef Zysman-Ziemian, whose story appears separately in this chapter. Berman, *Mimei*, 178–79; Temkin-Berman, *City*, 24.

46. Temkin-Berman, *City*, 41.

47. Marranos were Jews forced to convert to Christianity but who secretly continued practicing their Judaism despite the persecutions in Spain and Portugal in the late Middle Ages.

48. Temkin-Berman, *City*, 176, 263.

49. Zieman, *Cigarette Sellers*, 11–12.

50. Temkin-Berman, *City*, 141–44.

51. Temkin-Berman, *City*, 25, 49, 131.

52. Berman, "Hayehudim," 717, 720.

53. Temkin-Berman, *City*, 146–47; Berman "Hayehudim," 720, 723, 724.

54. Temkin-Berman, *City*, 163 164.

55. Temkin-Berman, *City*, 166.

56. Temkin-Berman, *City*, 23.

57. Temkin-Berman, *City*, 193, 195, 202. In 1965 Janina Bucholtz-Bukolska was awarded the Righteous title by Yad Vashem, YVA-M31.2/146. On the intricacies of residence registration for Jews hiding on the Aryan side, another dangerous undertaking by Basia Berman, see Temkin-Berman, *City*, 248–50.

58. Temkin-Berman, *City*, 68.

59. Temkin-Berman, *City*, 70.

60. Temkin-Berman, *City*, 71–75.

61. Temkin-Berman, *City*, 76–77.

62. Temkin-Berman, *City*, 79–80; also 251–53, on apartment registration and obtaining a food supply card.

63. Temkin-Berman, *City*, 286–87.

64. Temkin-Berman, *City*, 293.

65. Temkin-Berman, *City*, 279, 281, 285.

66. One of the victims was the Yiddish poet Yitzhak Katznelson, who wrote heart-searing poetry while incarcerated in Vittel camp. Berman, "Hayehudim," 721.

67. Temkin-Berman, *City*, 52.

68. Adolf's brother, Jakub Berman, headed the security services in the postwar Communist Poland, and reportedly remained an admirer and apologist for Stalin, even after his postmortem demotion by Soviet leader Nikita Krushchev. J. Berman's suppression of anti-Communist activities may have unwittingly contributed to the anti-Jewish feelings in Poland. Tomaszewski and Werbowski, *Żegota*, 98; Temkin-Berman, *City*, 31.

69. Temkin-Berman, *City*, 31, 42–43.

70. Tomaszewski and Werbowski, *Żegota*, 76.

71. Temkin-Berman, *City*, 124.

72. Ewa Brzóska, owner of a small vegetable store, about sixty-five years old, helped Jews in any way possible. Her store served as the meeting place for the Jewish underground.

73. Temkin-Berman, *City*, 268–69, 276.

74. Temkin-Berman, *City*, 272.

75. Temkin-Berman, *City*, 274.

76. Rada Glowna Opiekuncza—Official Polish Social Welfare Department.

77. Ziemian, Cigarette *Sellers*, 12–13. Basia Berman's account is a bit different, but was probably based on hearsay. According to her, the inciden-

tal meeting between Ziemian and the cigarette sellers took place when Ignaś ("Byczek"), one of the leaders of the children's group, approached Ziemian, as they passed each other. Ignaś, who looked after all the children, was at the time overcome by a terrible despair; the boys' money was barely enough to buy some bread; they wore tattered clothes, walked barefoot, and had no place to spend the night. So Ignaś decided to wait in the street and walk up to the first Jew he detected to ask for help, and that person turned out to be none other than Ziemian himself, who panicked, thinking it was a blackmailer. He took out a bill of 500 zlotys and wanted to give it to him, but Ignaś refused to take the money, but unfolded before him the story of a dozen Jewish children wandering the streets of Warsaw, selling mostly cigarettes, and other items as well, in order to survive. Temkin-Berman, *City*, 375–76.

78. Ziemian, *Cigarette Sellers*, 10, 13.
79. The Ostbahn was the German railway network in the occupied territories of Eastern Europe.
80. Ziemian, *Cigarette Sellers*, 13–14.
81. Ziemian, *Cigarette Sellers*, 15, 16, 19.
82. Ziemian, *Cigarette Sellers*, 17–19.
83. Ziemian, *Cigarette Sellers*, 22.
84. Zieman, *Cigarette Sellers*, 23–24.
85. Ziemian, *Cigarette Sellers*, 24.
86. Ziemian, *Cigarette Sellers*, 125.
87. Ziemian, *Cigarette Sellers*, 119.
88. Ziemian, *Cigarette Sellers*, 101; Temkin-Berman, *City*, 275.
89. Ziemian, *Cigarette Sellers*, 10, 126–30, 133–34. In Ziemian's book on the cigarette sellers, the full names of the children are not given, only their first and nicknames.
90. Peleg-Mariańska, *Witnesses*, 1, 7, 15.
91. Peleg-Mariańska, *Witnesses*, 13.
92. Peleg-Mariańska, *Witnesses*, 17.
93. Peleg-Mariańska, *Witnesses*, 4, 6–8, 15–16.
94. Peleg-Mariańska, *Witnesses*, 48–49.
95. Peleg-Mariańska, *Witnesses*, 51–52.
96. Peleg-Mariańska, *Witnesses*, 11, 18, 22, 32, 35–36. Miriam's Jewish companion, Mietek, also always carried a small tube with a cyanide crystal poison to avoid torture in the event of arrest.
97. Peleg-Mariańska, *Witnesses*, 11, 23–24, 52, 61.
98. Peleg-Mariańska, *Witnesses*, 61–63.
99. Peleg-Mariańska, *Witnesses*, 19–20.

100. Miriam Hochberg added in her book: "I thought . . . about all the Poles with whom we worked and who put their own lives in danger. Was it possible that these people belonged to the same nation; that they grew in the same land?" Peleg-Mariańska, *Witnesses*, 10–11.

101. Peleg-Mariańska, *Witnesses*, 80–81, 85.

102. Others in the Kraków branch of Żegota included the treasurer Anna Dobrowolska (no relation to Stanislaw), known as "Michalska," a teacher by profession, and Professor Tadeusz Seweryn ("Socha"), who seconded as a member of the Underground Court that handed out death sentences to collaborators and informers, as well as Wladyslaw Wójcik and Jerzy Matus. They represented various Polish political factions.

103. Peleg-Mariańska, *Witnesses*, 82–85. The following were awarded the Righteous title by Yad Vashem: Stanislaw Dobrowolski, YVA-M31.2/1681; Anna Dobrowolska-Michalska, YVA-M31.2/2909; Tadeusz Seweryn, YVA-M31.2/2230; Wladyslaw Wojcik, YVA-M31.2/1613; and Jerzy Matus, YVA-M31.2/2229.

104. Peleg-Mariańska, *Witnesses*, 152, 177–78.

105. Peleg-Mariańska, *Witnesses*, 91–93.

106. Peleg-Mariańska, *Witnesses*, 139, 158.

107. Peleg-Mariańska, *Witnesses*, 127.

108. Peleg-Mariańska, *Witnesses*, 149–50.

109. Peleg-Mariańska, *Witnesses*, 105–7.

110. Peleg-Mariańska, *Witnesses*, 111–12.

111. Peleg-Mariańska, *Witnesses*, 113–14.

112. Peleg-Mariańska, *Witnesses*, 133–34. Jadwiga Strzalecka was awarded the Righteous title by Yad Vashem; YVA-M31.2/810.

113. Peleg-Mariańska, *Witnesses*, 153–56.

114. Crowe, *Oskar Schindler*, 104–5, 114, 139.

115. Crowe, *Oskar Schindler* 102, 139.

116. Letter by Milson S. Hirschfeld, 2000, in author's possession.

117. Crowe, Oskar *Schindler*, 105.

118. Crowe, Oskar *Schindler*, 304.

119. As attested after the war, in a 1949 statement by Isaac Stern and Isaac Salpeter, in Miriam Kohn-Bankier file.

120. Bronia Gross-Guns, in the Miriam Kohn-Bankier file.

121. Solomon Urbach, in the Miriam Kohn-Bankier file.

122. Rena Fagen-Schontal, in the Miriam Kohn-Bankier file.

123. Crowe, Oskar *Schindler*, 363.

124. When part of Poland, the city was known as Drohobycz.

125. Miron and Shulhani, *Encyclopedia*, 173; Karpin, *Tightrope*, 247.

126. The Ukrainians falsely accused the Jews of having cooperated with the security apparatus of the Soviet regime, who before evacuating the city had shot Ukrainian political prisoners held by them, but also a few imprisoned Jews. That was their justification for the three-day pogrom. Miron and Shulhani, *Encyclopedia*, 173.

127. Thorne, *Out of the Ashes* 101–2; Miron and Shulhani, *Encyclopedia*, 174–75. Eyewitness Leon Thorne is very critical of the Drohobych Judenrat, calling them "wicked, corrupt men who took no cognizance of the bitter situation in which their fellow Jews lived. . . . If they did anything at all for their fellow Jews, it was not done out of the goodness of their hearts but because of self-interest." Thorne, *Out of the Ashes*, 108, 118–19.

128. Karpin, *Tightrope*, 201.

129. Karpin, *Tightrope*, 202–3.

130. Karpin, *Tightrope*, 247–48, 250–52.

131. Thorne, *Out of the Ashes*, 190; Schmalz-Jacobsen, *Zwei Bäume* 145. For the horse riding hall, Backenroth found a suitable spot, and a Jewish architect named Karol designed it with offices and rest rooms, all surrounded by gardens. The Jewish writer and artist Bruno Schulz, who enjoyed Landau's protection, was called in to decorate the walls with paintings of riders. When the riding hall was completed, one of Heinrich Himmler's personal representatives in Galicia was sent to inspect it and was quite impressed. Karpin, *Tightrope*, 274–75.

132. Karpin, *Tightrope*, 251–52.

133. Karpin, *Tightrope*, 257.

134. Karpin, *Tightrope*, 254.

135. Schmalz-Jacobsen, *Zwei Bäume*, 68, 71, 146; Karpin, Tightrope 254.

136. Karpin, *Tightrope*, 254–55.

137. Eberhard and Donata Helmrich were recognized by Yad Vashem as Righteous Among the Nations. YVA M31.2/154. It turned out that they had helped fellow Jews in Germany even before the start of the war. Eberhard explained his motive. "We were fully aware of the risks and the clash responsibilities, but we decided that it would be better for our children to have dead parents than cowards as parents. After that decision, it was comparatively easy." To which Donata added, "We figured that after we had saved two persons, we'd be even with Hitler if we were caught, and with every person saved beyond that, we were ahead." Karpin, *Tightrope*, 389–90.

138. Karpin, *Tightrope*, 272–73.

139. Thorne, *Tightrope*, 192–93.

140. Karpin, *Tightrope*, 270–71.

141. Karpin, *Tightrope*, 282.

142. Thorne, *Tightrope*, 190–91.

143. Karpin, *Tightrope*, 255. Tolle's subordinate, Felix Landau, could not control his murderous stream. On one occasion, he murdered a Jewish gardener working for him, since in Landau's estimation that man was too slow, so Landau killed him on the spot. When Backenroth, whom Landau respected, dared to protest this killing, Landau was baffled: "What are you complaining about? Others are killing all the time, and I killed one Jew." Karpin, *Tightrope*, 275. Landau was arrested by the Americans in Linz in 1946, but he was able to escape from the internment camp. He lived under a false name until 1958. Rearrested, he was finally sentenced to life imprisonment, but was pardoned in 1973. Schmalz-Jacobsen, *Zwei Bäume*, 144–45.

144. Karpin, *Tightrope*, 192, 276–77, 282; Schmalz-Jacobsen, *Zwei Bäume*, 142, 145.

145. Karpin, *Tightrope*, 301, 303; Schmalz-Jacobsen, *Zwei Bäume*, 146.

146. Karpin, *Tightrope*, 303–5.

147. Schmalz-Jacobsen, *Zwei Bäume*, 147–48; Karpin, Tightrope, 306–8. Michael Karpin underlines in his book that nothing in this story is exaggerated or fictitious. "Everything is true. I emphasize this because, upon reading the story of Naftali's change of identity, some readers may suspect that I have taken poetic license to exaggerate, add color, or touch up the facts, in order to create a new myth. Certainly not. Once again, I want to stress that all of the facts in Naftali's story have been checked and found true. He did not invent anything." Karpin, *Tightrope*, 393.

148. Karpin, *Tightrope*, 312, 314.

149. His son, Lucien Bronicki, a physicist, became an expert in constructing geothermal power plants to produce "green" electricity, and together with wife Yehudit (Ditta), he founded Ormat Industries Ltd., which constructs and maintains power plants in many world locations. Karpin, *Tightrope*, 351, 353, 399.

150. Karpin, *Tightrope*, 387.

151. The following is based on Drucker's lengthy testimony in Hebrew in 1968; YVA 03/3249.

152. The problem of the release of Jewish children into Jewish hands also existed in other countries, such as in the Netherlands, where the government tried to prevent it, claiming that it was better for the children's sake to keep them with their host families instead of returning them to their own Holocaust-traumatized loved ones. Fishman, "Jewish War Orphans," 31–36.

153. For a discussion of the Coordination, see Bogner, *Zionist Coordination*.

154. Rabbi Solomon Schonfeld (see chapter 13) arrived in Poland in November 1945 and returned twice. During these two visits he took with him some 200 children and youth with the aid of British visas that he obtained in the British embassy in Warsaw. Recha Sternbuch in Switzerland was also involved in the redemption of children in Poland. Her assistant in Poland, Sarah Lederman, opened a children's home in Bytom, Lower Silesia, for children that she collected from various places.

155. Some Jewish children were indeed saved by non-Jewish rescuers, but suffered bad treatment at their hands. Estimates of such cases are hard to come by, as most ransomed children's reminiscences are of the warm and good treatment during their stay at the home of total strangers, and their rescuers were justifiably awarded the Righteous honor by the Yad Vashem Holocaust memorial in Israel. There were also some cases of explicit sexual abuse of the hidden Jews, especially adolescent girls, as Drucker testified.

156. Abraham Foxman, until recently head of the Anti-Defamation League (ADL), was one the children whose Polish woman rescuer refused to return him to his parents, who had survived. The custody battle was decided in favor of the Foxman parents, but fearing her vengeance they quickly left the country with their boy. Gurewitsch, "Mothers," 33–46.

3. Lithuania and Belarus

1. Levin, "Lithuania Historical Introduction," lxi.
2. Wikipedia, "History of the Jews in Lithuania."
3. It is estimated that 83 percent of the commercial establishments and 57 percent of the factories that were nationalized by the Communists belonged to Jews. Levin, "Lithuania," 897.
4. Levin, "Lithuania: Historical Introduction," lxx.
5. Warhaftig, *Refugee*, 17, 22.
6. Warhaftig, *Refugee*, 25, 32–37, 40, 49.
7. Warhaftig, *Refugee*, 41–42, 134.
8. Warhaftig, *Refugee*, 52–53, 56–58.
9. Warhaftig, *Refugee*, 136–37.
10. Warhaftig, *Refugee*, 139–40.
11. Levin, Interview, 3.
12. Levin, Interview, 6.
13. Levin, Interview, 8–9.
14. Warhaftig, *Refugee*, 103–4.
15. Jan Zwartendijk, YVA-M31.2/7793; Chiune-Sempo Sugihara, YVA-

M31.2/2861. Years later when Warhaftig served as a minister in the Israel government, he was visited by the former Dutch governor of Curaçao. Warhaftig asked how he would have reacted had a ship actually arrived in Curaçao with hundreds of Jewish refugees aboard holding such visas? Would he have accorded them asylum? Nothing of the sort, was the curt response. He would have forced the ship back into mid-ocean, as had the American and Cuban authorities done in the case of the *St. Louis* boat in 1939. Warhaftig, *Refugee*, 104.

16. Warhaftig, *Refugee*, 61, 65.
17. Warhaftig, *Refugee*, 81, 89, 91.
18. Warhaftig, *Refugee*, 92–93.
19. Levin, Interview, 12–13.
20. Warhaftig, *Refugee*, 97.
21. Warhaftig, *Refugee*, 97; Levin, Interview, 15.
22. Warhaftig, *Refugee*, 98–99.
23. Warhaftig writes that Rabbi Grodzinski feared that once in Palestine, Talmudic students would be tempted away from a yeshiva lifestyle. "I showed him a newspaper clipping that reported that an agricultural yeshiva was being established at Kefar Haroeh in Eretz [Palestine] where young men could study both Talmud and farming. But my plan was rejected, and Rabbi Grodzinski demanded that I release the Baranovitz youngsters from the [agricultural training] seminar at once [in a location in Lithuania]. I followed his instructions promptly, though with great misgivings." Warhaftig, *Refugee*, 138.
24. Warhaftig, *Refugee*, 120–21.
25. Levin, Interview, 24.
26. Warhaftig, *Refugee*, 128, 144.
27. Warhaftig, *Refugee*, 145, 147–48, 152, 155.
28. Warhaftig, *Refugee*, 156–57.
29. Warhaftig, *Refugee*, 194, 196–98, 202–5.
30. Warhaftig, *Refugee*, 261–65, 331, 345–47. According to his estimates, a total of 2,500 children were fetched from Christian families and convents in Poland by the combined efforts of the Zionist Coordination Committee, Rabbi I. Herzog, emissaries of the Agudat Israel, such as Recha Sternbuch, and British rabbi Solomon Schonfeld. Warhaftig, *Refugee*, 332–33. Warhaftig had come to Poland armed with the names and sometimes even with the addresses of children who had been entrusted to the care of Christian families or convents, and due to his short stay in Poland, he transferred these lists to Drucker. Warhaftig, *Refugee*, 336.
31. Warhaftig, *Refugee*, 245, 385, 387.

32. Cholawski, "Belorussia," 169. Some 348 Belarusian villages were burned down in the Vitebsk region and 147 in the Mińsk region. More than 209 cities and towns (out of 270 in total) suffered immense damage and destruction. Wikipedia, "The Holocaust in Belarus."

33. Cholawski, "Belorussia," 170, 172–73; Wikipedia, "The Holocaust in Belarus."

34. Cholawski, "Belorussia," 173; Wikipedia, "The Holocaust in Belarus."

35. Arad, "Jewish," 333–35.

36. Arad, "Jewish," 338–41.

37. Arad, "Jewish," 346–50. One of the non-Jewish partisans, Nikolai Kiselev, led a group of 300 Jews and escaped Soviet POWs, starting in August 1942, over a several hundred kilometer trek from Ilja (Wilno District) to Velikiye Luki, beyond the front lines, a mission successfully accomplished in November 1942. He was awarded the Righteous honor by Yad Vashem; YVA M31.2/10672.

38. Arad, "Jewish," 170, 336; Wikipedia, "The Holocaust in Belarus."

39. Tec, *Defiance*, 1–2.

40. Judah Maccabi led the Maccabean rebellion against the Hellenic Seleucid-Syrians in the second century BCE. Tec, *Defiance*, 2.

41. Tec, *Defiance*, 3.

42. Tec, *Defiance*, 26, 28, 33, 34, 36–39, 43.

43. Tec, *Defiance*, 44–45, 47–48, 50, 52, 55.

44. Shor and Zakin, *Essie*, 38, 41.

45. Tec, *Defiance*, 43, 57–60.

46. Tec, *Defiance*, 85–88, 93

47. Shor and Zakin, *Essie*, 43.

48. Tec, *Defiance*, 102–3, 107–8.

49. Tec, *Defiance*, 61–62, 84, 112–13.

50. Arad, "Jewish," 348.

51. Tec, *Defiance*, 116–17.

52. Shor and Zakin, *Essie*, 53–54.

53. Tec, *Defiance*, 118, 134–35, 150.

54. Tec, *Defiance*, 124–27.

55. Tec, *Defiance*, 163.

56. Tec, *Defiance*, 164–66. Tuvia lost his wife Sonia to a German raid in a village where she was hiding. After a period of bereavement, he married again, to Lilka, a member of his partisan group.

57. Tec, *Defiance*, 263–65, 268–71.

58. Tec, *Defiance*, 180, 204–10.

59. Other than the common problem of warding off lice on the bodies and clothes, other health problems afflicted the Bielski members, such as blisters,

scabies, boils, and furuncles. The doctor and nurses had to cope in unconventional ways due to the shortage of medicine. One method was to extract the powder inside bullets, containing sulfur that, mixed with a creamy substance, could be used as a disinfectant to heal infections. Tec, *Defiance*, 243.

60. Tec, *Defiance*, 191–92, 197.

61. Tec, *Defiance*, 273–76.

62. Shor and Zakin, *Essie,* 54.

63. Tec, *Defiance*, 189, 194.

64. Tec, *Defiance*, 211; U.S. Holocaust Memorial Museum, "The Bielski Partisans."

65. Tec, *Defiance*, 248–50.

66. Tec, *Defiance*, 276, 278–80.

67. Tec, *Defiance*, 293.

68. Tec, *Defiance*, xix.

69. Tec, *Defiance*, 284–85. Tuvia's brother Asael was drafted into the Red Army and fell in battle inside Germany in the closing months of the war.

70. Tec, *Defiance*, 287; Bielski, YVA, 03/3607.

71. Smilovitsky, "Jewish Family Camps."

72. Wertheim, "Zorin," 392.

73. Cholawski, "Simcha Zorn"; Wertheim, "Zorin," 392; Wertheim, YVA 03/3861. Anatoly Wertheim was a section commander in the Zorin family camp, and the fourth in the line of command.

74. Twersky, "Strange."

75. Charchas, "Escape from the Ghetto."

76. Reuveni and Reznik, "Wondrous," 320.

77. Reuveni and Reznik, "Wondrous," 335.

78. Martin, "Resistance."

79. Goldman, "Meet Brother Daniel."

80. Twersky, "Strange."

4. Slovakia

1. Jelinek and Rozett, "Slovakia."

2. Campion, Lion's Mouth, 18.

3. Fatran, "The 'Working Group,'" 165. The Hlinka paramilitary Fascist militia was named after Andreas Hlinka, a politically active priest, who worked tirelessly for Slovakia's independence from Czechoslovakia. Antisemitism was a key weapon in the party's arsenal, although Hlinka once disclaimed antisemitic views. Campion, *Lion's Mouth*, 7.

4. Bauer, *Jews*, 63; Bauer, *American*, 357; Fatran, "Working Group," 165.

5. Bauer, *Jews*, 65; Fatran, "Working Group," 165.

6. Neumann, *Gisi Fleischmann* 15; Bauer, *Jews*, 64; Campion, *Lion's Mouth*, 50, 57.

7. Jelinek and Rozett, "Slovakia"; Rotkirchen, Destruction, xiv–xv, 196; Campion, Lion's Mouth, 59.

8. Frieder, *Lehatsil Nafsham*, 52; Jelinek and Rozett, "Slovakia," 1367.

9. Rotkirchen, *Destruction*, viii, xxxviii; Frieder, *Lehatsil Nafsham*, 47.

10. Bauer, American 358; Neumann, *Gisi Fleischmann*, 18. Some categories of Jews were also exempted from the Jewish Code, with the approval of President Tiso: mostly converts and a small fraction of people skilled in professions considered vital to the Slovak economy. Rotkirchen, "Europa Plan," appendix 4–7, 2.

11. Bauer, *Jews*, 66; Rotkirchen, *Destruction*, xxii; Bauer, *American*, 361.

12. Bauer, *Jews*, 66–67; Rotkirchen, *Destruction*, xxiv; Bauer, *Rethinking*, 177; Jelinek and Rozett, "Slovakia," 1367; Frieder, *Lehatsil Nafsham*, 86.

13. Bauer, *Jews*, 67, 71, 73; Bauer, *Rethinking*, 176.

14. Bauer, *American*, 357, 363.

15. Bauer, *Jews*, 68–69; Campion, *Lion's Mouth*, 56.

16. The WG included Rabbis Weissmandl and Frieder, Gisi Fleischmann, engineer Andrej Steiner, Oskar Neumann (former chairman of the Zionist Federation), Wilhelm Fürst, Tibor Kováč, Dr. Ernst Abeles, Aharon Grünhut, and Eugen Winterstein. The core members were Fleischmann, Weissmandl, Frieder, and Steiner.

17. Fatran, "Working Group," 194; Weissmandl, *Min Hametsar*, 18–20. *Min Hametsar* was published posthumously in 1960 by Rabbi Weissmandl's students, from a manuscript he prepared before his death in 1957. The title in Hebrew transliteration consists of the first two words of Psalm 118:5: "from the depths of despair."

18. Bauer, Rethinking, 173–74. Her distant cousin, Rabbi Weissmandl, favored Fleischmann's leadership for an additional psychological reason: he believed that a woman would not arouse the typical rancor and jealousy between competing persons likely to evolve in a male-dominated leadership. Fatran, "Working Group," 169–70; Bauer, *Rethinking*, 179.

19. Rotkirchen, "Europa Plan," 7. Dr. Imrich Karvas, governor of the Slovak National Bank, also helped the WG with valuable news and even support against the regime's repressive measures. Some others would help but only in return for bribery, such as Dr. Isidor Koso, director general of the prime minister's office. Campion, Lion's Mouth, 54. Monsignor Giuseppe Burzio, the Vatican representative in the country, was also sympathetic in conveying messages by the WG to his superiors. Campion, *Lion's Mouth*, 55.

20. Fatran, "Working Group," 182; Bauer, *Rethinking*, 180.

21. Couriers also told of extermination by "lethal fumes" in a place called Bełżec, one of the notorious death camps on Polish soil. During the summer of 1943, three survivors reported to the WG on the exterminations in Treblinka and Sobibor and mistakenly identified Birkenau as a heavily guarded labor camp, and this was passed on in detail to Jewish organizations abroad. Reports received by the WG in 1943 also told of the liquidation of the Warsaw ghetto. The WG helped refugees (estimated at 2,500) from Poland stranded in Slovakia, who awaited their continued flight to Hungary. Fatran, "Working Group," 181, 183–84, 311, 314, 316; Rotkirchen, *Destruction*, xxxix; Rotkirchen, "Europa Plan," 7.

22. The main proponent of the renewed deportations was the violently antisemitic interior minister, Alexander Mach, whom Weissmandl in his letters to Switzerland derisively dubbed *Mach Shemo*, a play on words, meaning "May his name be blotted out." But the decision went against Mach. Weissmandl, *Min Hametsar*, 152; Fuchs, *Unheeded Cry*, 143. As for Wisliceny, he falsely reported to Weissmandl that in Greece, too, negotiations were under way with Rabbi Koretz, in Thessaloniki, to avoid the deportation of Jews when, in practice, the Jewish population of over 50,000 had already been deported to Auschwitz within a matter of weeks. Fuchs, *Unheeded Cry*, 109. This led the WG to erroneously inform the Jewish Agency representative in Istanbul that the Jews in the German-held area of Greece (mainly Thessaloniki) would not be expelled, when actually they no longer were there. Weissmandl, *Min Hametsar,* 159–60; Fuchs, *Unheeded Cry*, 110.

23. Fatran, *Merkaz ha-Yehudim ha-uz* (Hebrew)—The Jewish Center Ustredna Zidov-uz, 325–27, 329–30, 334–35, 337. Burzio met with Prime Minister Vojtech Tuka on April 7, 1943, and expressed the Vatican's strong disapproval of the planned renewal of deportations. Tuka lashed back angrily, rejecting the Nuncio's demand, and accused the Vatican of having fallen under Jewish influence. Morley, *Vatican Diplomacy and the Jews*, 241–42; Fatran, Merkaz,

24. Fuchs, Unheeded Cry, 136–37. Kasztner thus knew the true nature of Auschwitz, either before or during the start of the deportations in Hungary. Fatran, *Merkaz*, 362.

25. Fatran, *Merkaz*, 361. In early June, two more escapees arrived in Slovakia: Arnost Rozin and Czeslaw Mordowicz. They could now report on witnessing the extermination of Hungarian Jews taking place in Auschwitz. They were referred to the Vatican nuncio, who interrogated them for six hours. Fatran, *Merkaz*, 363.

26. Campion, *Lion's Mouth*, 107.

27. According to estimates, between 1,500 and 2,000 Jews participated in the

Slovak rebellion of September and October 1944, with several hundred losing their lives.

28. Fatran, "Working Group," 189; Campion, *Lion's Mouth*, 115. For Andre Biss's account of these negotiations, see Biss, *Million Jews*, 112.

29. Fatran, "Working Group."

30. Rotkirchen, *Destruction*, xlvii.

31. Jelinek and Rozett, "Slovakia," 1370. In January 1993, with the dissolution of Czechoslovakia, Slovakia again became an independent country.

32. Fuchs, *Unheeded Cry*, 17–19, 21, 22–24; Lanzmann, "Siegmund Forst."

33. Kranzler, Holocaust Hero, 33–34.

34. Lanzmann, "Siegmund Forst." According to Kranzler, Weissmandl also urged Schonfeld to establish a yeshiva (the Ohr Yisroel) for Slovak students aged sixteen to eighteen who were ineligible for the kindertransports, so they could leave the country in time. He added jocularly, "Make sure they remain in yeshiva, rather than hanging around the markets of Whitechapel." Kranzler, *Holocaust Hero*, 35.

35. Weissmandl, *Min Hametsar*, 74, 79; Fuchs, Unheeded Cry, 131.

36. Fatran, "Working Group," 168.

37. Bauer, *American*, 365.

38. Fuchs, *Unheeded Cry*, 67, 262. Wisliceny added that the three large labor camps holding several thousand Jews, Sered, Novaky and Vyhne, and managed by the UZ in tandem with the Slovak authorities, should be enlarged to accommodate the remaining Jews in the country. Rotkirchen, "Europa Plan," 7.

39. Fatran, "Working Group," 170–71. The bribing of the Slovaks was left to Dr. Kovac, who lined the pockets of Anton Văsek, head of the dreaded Section 14 of the Interior Ministry. Architect Andrej Steiner, in turn, paid off Dr. Izidor Koso, director general of the prime minister's office. Fuchs, *Unheeded Cry*, 72–73; Fatran, "Working Group," 171; Bauer, *Jews*, 75.

40. Fuchs, *Unheeded Cry*, 79.

41. Bauer, *American*, 368. Bauer claims that the amount of JDC money allotted to Mayer's overall operations at the time did not allow him to grant the sums demanded by Fleischmann and Weissmandl. Bauer, *American*, 366.

42. Fuchs, *Unheeded Cry*, 79–81.

43. Fuchs, *Unheeded Cry*, 79–81; Bauer, *Jews*, 74–75.

44. Fuchs, *Unheeded Cry*, 82.

45. There are unsolved problems with the various accounts of the actual payments made. Was it actually $50,000 or $40,000? What were the dates of payment (in June and October) as well as their impact on the deportations? For instance, if the first payment was made in late June, why did five

transports leave in July? What about the transport that left on October 20, after the receipt of the second payment? Fatran, Merkaz, 264. Bauer goes so far as to speculate that perhaps Hochberg did not turn over the whole amount but pocketed about $30,000. Bauer, *Jews*, 98.

46. Bauer, *Jews*, 78; Bauer, American, 366; Fuchs, *Unheeded Cry*, 83.

47. Fuchs, *Unheeded Cry*, xiii; Kranzler, *Thy Brother's Blood*, 264.

48. Fatran, *Merkaz*, 272.

49. Bauer, *Jews*, 96; Bauer, *Rethinking*, 180–81. The Apostolic delegate in the country, Giuseppe Burzio, had firsthand information from Slovak soldiers who participated in the invasion of Russia what was truly happening to the Jews there, and he passed it on to his superiors in the Vatican. Rotkirchen, "Europa Plan, 9.

50. Fatran, "Working Group," 171–72; Bauer, American, 369; Fuchs, *Unheeded Cry*, 84, 90.

51. Bauer, American, 369. While imprisoned and awaiting trial after the war, Wisliceny wrote: "Hochberg slowly revealed to me in hints that the institution in whose name he was speaking was the Joint. . . . In my report [to Himmler] I recommended negotiations with a representative of the Joint. I pointed out the strong propaganda that would arise overseas when the Final Solution became known. . . . I received a promise from Eichmann that he would give me a free hand and that he agreed to stop the expulsions until the situation quieted down. . . . He also instructed me to listen to the Jewish representatives." Fuchs, Unheeded Cry, 86. Wisliceny's account is replete with many self-serving inaccuracies. Hochberg, who would have contradicted him, was no longer alive, having been eliminated by rebels during the Slovak rebellion. Fuchs, *Unheeded Cry*, 87.

52. Bauer, *Jews*, 79; Bauer, *American*, 370; Fuchs, *Unheeded Cry*, 97.

53. Fuchs, *Unheeded Cry*, 98–101; Bauer, *American*, 371.

54. Fuchs, *Unheeded Cry*, 102–4.

55. Fuchs, *Unheeded Cry*, 105.

56. Fuchs, *Unheeded Cry*, 105–6.

57. Fuchs, *Unheeded Cry*, 111–13. Lucy Dawidowicz dates this letter by Weissmandl to May 11, 1943, and in a different translation from the original rabbinic Hebrew, it partly reads: "The adviser [presumably Dieter Wisliceny] says that he is authorized by his superiors to grant what we ask: to suspend deportations throughout Europe for 2 to 3 thousand dollars [per person]. When he says 2 to 3, in my humble opinion, we should figure 3—a sum which is not subject to further negotiation, as it was arrived at after much discussion and approved by his superiors. He expects an advance payment

of $1,000, to be delivered between June 10 and 20. Deportations will then be cancelled for a period of about two months. . . . Stopping the deportations means an end to the massacre. . . . The deportations could, God forbid, involve more than a million in Europe—and the price is 2 or 3 bills to rescue a single Jewish soul after so many thousands and tens of thousands have already been massacred, many of whom could indeed have been saved with money." Dawidowicz, Holocaust Reader, 319. Weissmandl added this admonition: "If you are worthy, if you provide the money without discussion, without delay, even a moment's delay, then you will have atoned in some measure for the spilled blood. If, God forbid, you lose time in deliberation, talk, meetings, in doubts, negotiations, argument, consultations, and proposals, then there will be an unprecedented slaughter by Israel's own hand. We know these are harsh words. . . . Still, we must tell the truth as it is. For if, God help us . . . should we not have the money in our hand by mid-June, the thousand demanded as an advance . . . then our words will have been damaging. For, rather than canceling the evil decree, having failed to salvage the lives of the surviving remnant, we will have, God forbid, actually hastened their end, with the cruelty of a miser, sitting on his money. . . . Now the time has come—a singular opportunity for rescue. Please, I beg of you, do this deed immediately, without delay." Dawidowicz, Holocaust Reader, 320–21.

58. Bauer, Jews, 81, 87.

59. Bauer, American, 374.

60. Bauer, Jews, 375.

61. Bauer, American, 376.

62. Fuchs, Unheeded Cry, 114.

63. Weissmandl, Min Hametsar, 171; Fuchs, Unheeded Cry, 115–16. Siegmund Forst, who in the meantime had moved to New York, related in a postwar interview with filmmaker Claude Lanzmann that during the war years he heard of Weissmandl's frantic appeals, as part of them were read publicly in Forst's New York synagogue. "So we heard how he begged for money, and we collected money. . . . On the Sabbath, they interrupted the service and they read the letters of Weissmandl, and we organized actions to collect the money." He admits that the synagogue audience understood these letters "intellectually, but not with our heart. . . . We heard the words and we believed it, but with the intellect. We were born in Europe, in an orderly society, and the audience could not fathom such a barbaric regression of civilized life." Lanzmann, "Siegmund Forst."

64. Fuchs, Unheeded Cry, 89, 119; Bauer, Jews, 100. Wisliceny, in his 1946 testimony, while under arrest, stated that in August 1943 he was ordered, by

Himmler through Eichmann, to stop the negotiations and not to have any further contact with his Jewish partners or else he himself would land in a concentration camp. Bauer, *Jews*, 95.

65. Fatran, "Working Group," 175–76.

66. Campion, *Lion's Mouth*, 91.

67. Rotkirchen, "Europa Plan, 4, 5, 9, 18. Livia Rotkirchen ties the end of the Europa Plan negotiations to another main factor—the arrest of Carl Langbehn, a friend of Himmler, who was on a mission to explore the possibility of a separate peace with the Western Allies. This caused Himmler to cease negotiations with the WG, for fear of Hitler's ire. Fatran, *Merkaz*, 292.

68. Bauer, *Jews*, 90, 101.

69. Bauer, *Jews*, 103–7, 111–12, 117.

70. Rotkirchen, "Europa Plan," 4; Fatran, "Working Group," 174.

71. For more on Himmler's secret negotiations to open a link with the Western Allies, see Bauer, *Jews*, 102–44, and Rotkirchen, "Europa Plan," 9–14.

72. Dawidowciz, *Holocaust*, 325–26.

73. Weissmandl, *Min Hametsar*, 128; Bauer, *Jews*, 81.

74. Bauer, *Jews for Sale?*, 79.

75. Bauer, *Rethinking*, 181–82.

76. Weissmandl, *Min Hametsar*, 117; Fuchs, *Unheeded Cry*, 160–61; Fatran, "Working Group," 297, 304.

77. Freudiger, in his own attempt to measure up to Wisliceny's true intention, bribed him with gifts of valuable jewelry from his family's collection and with cash. Wisliceny later responded with a gesture of his own when he helped Freudiger and his family to escape to Romania, while other Jews were dispatched to the gas chambers without hindrance. Fuchs, *Unheeded Cry*, 162.

78. Weissmandl wrote this letter, supposedly "in a cave near Lemberg-Lvov" (to mislead possible denouncers), but most probably in Bratislava or Nitra.

79. Fuchs, Unheeded Cry, 168–69.

80. Weissmandl, *Min Hametsar*, 105; Fuchs, *Unheeded Cry*, 170.

81. Fatran, Merkaz, 359, 360, 364; Rotkirchen, *Destruction*, xli.

82. Fuchs, *Unheeded Cry*, 170–71; Weissmandl, *Min Hametsar*, 186–88.

83. Weissmandl, *Min Hametsar*, 218; Fuchs, *Unheeded Cry*, 207. Weissmandl also proposed an alternative plan to drop weapons into the POW compound in Auschwitz so that soldiers who happened to be imprisoned there could make use of them or in which commandos be parachuted into the camp to destroy the gas chambers; neither idea proved practical from a military standpoint. Fuchs, *Unheeded Cry*, 171.

84. Kranzler, *Thy Brother's Blood*, 279–80; Weissmandl, *Min Hametsar*, 25–27; Fuchs, *Unheeded Cry*, 147. Weissmandl also wrote of a similar response by Bishop Karol Kmetko to his father-in-law, Rabbi Samuel David Ungar, during an encounter between the two, as reported to him by Rabbi Ungar. Weissmandl, *Min Hametsar*, 23–24; Fuchs, *Unheeded Cry*, 145; Morley, *Diplomacy*, 79, 84.

85. Lanzmann, "Siegmund Forst"; Kranzler, *Thy Brother's Blood*, 280–81.

86. Fuchs, *Unheeded Cry*, 210–11, 213, 216.

87. Fuchs, *Unheeded Cry*, 214–15.

88. Fuchs, *Unheeded Cry*, 216–17, 219.

89. Fuchs, *Unheeded Cry*, 35.

90. Lanzmann, "Siegmund Forst."

91. Weissmandl based himself on a passage from the Talmudic tractate Eruvin (21b), where city dwellers are described as immersed in theft, immorality, and vain and false oaths, whereas those living apart from cities are freer to studying Torah. Rashi explains that large cities are rife with nonreligious enticements, with concomitant acts of immorality and dishonesty.

92. Fuchs, *Unheeded Cry*, 239.

93. Fuchs, *Unheeded Cry*, 39–40, 252.

94. Kranzler, *Thy Brother's Blood*, 264.

95. Lanzmann, "Siegmund Forst."

96. Campion, *Lion's Mouth*, 4–5, 9–10, 13, 19.

97. Fatran, "Working Group," 179.

98. Campion, *Lion's Mouth*, 23–25, 37–38; Neumann, *Gisi Fleischmann*, 16.

99. Campion, *Lion's Mouth*, pp.17, 26, 30–31. Bauer, *Rethinking*, 175.

100. Campion, *Lion's Mouth*, 42–43, 52; Neumann, *Gisi Fleischmann*, 17.

101. Campion, *Lion's Mouth*, 62–65; Neumann, *Gisi Fleischmann*, 19–20.

102. Campion, *Lion's Mouth*, 65–66.

103. Campion, *Lion's Mouth*, 75–77.

104. Campion, *Lion's Mouth*, 78. Throughout much of the war, Saly Mayer, of the Joint, Alfred Silberschein, representing the World Jewish Congress known as relico (Committee for Relief of the War-Stricken Jewish Population), and Nathan Schwalb of Hechalutz were Fleischmann's principal contacts in Switzerland. In Turkey she maintained contact with Chaim Barlas, of the Jewish Agency, and also kept in touch with other delegates of various Palestinian Zionist organizations, such as Venia Pomerantz (later Zeev Hadari), of the kibbutz movement.

105. Campion, *Lion's Mouth*, 83.

106. Neumann, *Gisi Fleischmann*, 25–26.

107. Fuchs, *Unheeded Cry*, 116, 118.

108. Campion, *Lion's Mouth*, 88; Neumann, *Gisi Fleischmann*, 29.

109. Campion, *Lion's Mouth*, 82, 89–90; Fuchs, *Unheeded Cry*, 111.

110. In her report of September 4, 1943, to Mayer, Fleischmann mentioned the figure of 5,000 children. Campion, *Lion's Mouth*, 100.

111. Wisliceny wrote after the war: "Then I was called to Berlin by Eichmann, who revealed to me that the Grand Mufti had gotten knowledge of the planned action through his news service in Palestine. He had lodged with Himmler the sharpest protest, on the grounds that these Jewish children would be grown in a few years and would add to the strength of the Jewish element in Palestine." Himmler therefore canceled the plan. Campion, *Lion's Mouth*, 101. According to Fuchs, the Nazis would allow 1,000 Jews to cross daily into Spain in return for the payment of $1,000 per family, but not to Palestine due to the promise by the Nazis to the Grand Mufti of Jerusalem that no Jews would be allowed to proceed to Palestine. According to Fuchs the reply received by Jewish sources in Switzerland was that Palestine was to be considered as the only acceptable destination, but Fuchs does not provide the source proof for this allegation. Fuchs, *Unheeded Cry*, 60, 62.

112. When the two women met, Koso asked Fleischman to help get her son admitted into a prestigious Swiss boarding school. Fleischmann reassured her that this could be arranged through her contacts in that country. In addition, as she knew no one in Switzerland, Koso asked for a letter of introduction to some of Fleischman's acquaintances there, a letter that would be sewed into the lining of her travel coat. Fleischmann also agreed to pay an additional sum and gave Koso a letter of introduction in her own handwriting. Unfortunately for both women, Koso's seamstress who sewed the letter into the lining of her employer's coat informed on her to the authorities, and this led to Koso's arrest. Fleischmann was implicated in the affair and was promptly arrested on the charge of illegal financial transaction and jailed. Campion, *Lion's Mouth*, 72–74.

113. Campion, *Lion's Mouth*, 102–4, 107, 110–11; Fatran, "Working Group," 177, 196.

114. Campion, *Lion's Mouth*, 114–15.

115. Campion, *Lion's Mouth*, 116; Neumann, *Gisi Fleischmann*, 33.

116. Campion, *Lion's Mouth*, 117, 119–20, 123; Neumann, *Gisi Fleischmann*, 35; Rotkirchen, *Destruction*, xxvi.

117. Bauer, *Rethinking*, 184.

118. Frieder, *Lehatsil Nafsham*, 3–8, 14, 16–17, 22, 49.

119. Frieder, *Lehatsil Nafsham*, 54.

120. Frieder, *Lehatsil Nafsham*, 58–59.

121. Frieder, *Lehatsil Nafsham*, iv; Campion, *Lion's Mouth*, 53.

122. Frieder, *Lehatsil Nafsham*, 60.

123. Frieder, *Lehatsil Nafsham*, 60–61.

124. Frieder, *Lehatsil Nafsham*, 63.

125. Frieder, *Lehatsil Nafsham*, 64–65; Frieder, *To Deliver*, 71–72.

126. Frieder, *Lehatsil Nafsham*, 66–67, 69.

127. Frieder, *Lehatsil Nafsham*, vi, 77–78.

128. Frieder, *Lehatsil Nafsham*, 79–80.

129. Frieder, *Lehatsil Nafsham*, 84, 93.

130. Frieder, *Lehatsil Nafsham*, 67.

131. Frieder, *Lehatsil Nafsham*, 169.

132. Frieder, *Lehatsil Nafsham*, 182–83.

133. Frieder, *Lehatsil Nafsham*, 183.

134. Frieder, *Lehatsil Nafsham*, 184. His wife, Ruzen, and daughter, Gitushka, were killed during the fighting between the partisans and the Germans. His son, Gideon, born in 1937, was saved and sheltered by the farming family Jozef and Paulina Strycharszyk in the village of Bully.

135. Frieder, *Lehatsil Nafsham*, 185, 189–90.

136. Frieder, *Lehatsil Nafsham*, 192.

137. Frieder, *Lehatsil Nafsham*, 193, 195–96.

138. Frieder, *Lehatsil Nafsham*, 197.

139. Frieder, *Lehatsil Nafsham*, 202–3.

140. Gideon Frieder later studied at the Technion University in Haifa, Israel, then became a professor of engineering and applied science at the George Washington University in Washington DC. Frieder, *Lehatsil Nafsham*, ix.

141. Fuchs, *Unheeded Cry*, 106–7.

142. Campion, *Lion's Mouth*, 68.

143. Fatran, "Working Group," 200–201.

144. Jelinek and Rozett, "Slovakia," 1370.

5. Hungary

1. Braham, "Hungary: Jews during the Holocaust," 2:698.

2. The first historical document relating to the Jews of Hungary is the letter written about 960 to King Joseph of the Khazars by Hasdai ibn Shaprut, the Jewish statesman of Córdoba, in which Jews living in "the country of Hungarian" are mentioned.

3. Wikipedia, "History of the Jews in Hungary."

4. Cohen, *Halutz Resistance*, 9.

5. Wikipedia, "History of the Jews in Hungary."

6. Wikipedia, "History of the Jews in Hungary."

7. At the time of the German occupation of March 19, 1944, according to one estimate, Hungary had 762,000 racially defined Jews, including converts, of whom 231,450 lived in Budapest. Braham, "Rescue Operations in Hungary"; Braham, *Politics of Genocide*, 21, 23, 29–30. The Orthodox were mostly to be found in the northeastern part of the country—about 29.2 percent. In 1930, 65.5 percent of Jews were affiliated with the Neolog (Conservative) Kehilla and its head, Samu Stern. Cohen, *Halutz Resistance*, 13.

8. Braham, *Politics*, 24–25. The law also distinguished those who had converted to Christianity before August 1, 1919, and were no longer to be considered Jewish, and those who had converted afterwards, and as many as up to 80,000 Christians now fell into the category of Jews. Cohen, *Halutz Resistance*, 11–12.

9. Braham, *Politics*, 25. By law, all refugees had to register with the National Central Alien Control Office (Keokh), a special department of the Hungarian police, though many skipped it by arming themselves with false credentials. Braham, *Politics*, 32. Illegal arrivals, when caught, were held in detention camps. Cohen, *Halutz Resistance*, 28, 42.

10. Braham, *Politics*, 27, 32–33, 37, 45. After the German takeover of Hungary in March 1944, an estimated 50,000 Jewish labor servicemen were handed over to the Germans, while others, stationed in various places, were simply massacred. Between 25,000 and 30,000 labor servicemen fell into Soviet captivity. Braham, *Politics*, 51. In addition, in January 1942 in the Bácska and Novi Sad regions of occupied Yugoslavia, the Hungarians shot some 700 Jews, together with a greater number of local Serbs. Braham, *Politics*, 34–36.

11. Braham, *Politics*, 13, 31, 77.

12. Benshalom, *We Struggled*, 22–23; Cohen, *Halutz Resistance*, 15, 20, 30. The Halutz leaders were in touch with their party affiliates from Palestine, stationed in Istanbul, Turkey, such as Venya Pomeranz (later, Zeev Hadari), Menachem Bader, Zeev Shind, and David Ziment. They were also in touch with Nathan Schwalb, the Zionist pioneer Hechalutz representative in Geneva. Cohen, *Halutz Resistance*, 252n2. Also Braham, in Cohen, *Halutz Resistance*, 6; Ofer, "Activities of the Jewish Agency Delegation."

13. Prominent among its members, other than Kasztner and Joel Brand, were Hansi Brand (wife of Joel), Samuel Springmann, Miklós-Moshe Krausz, Ottó Komoly, Eugen Frankel, and Ernst-Ernö (Zvi) Szilagyi. Bauer, *Jews*, 152.

14. Cohen, *Halutz Resistance*, 16, 22. It is estimated that as many as 10,000 to 15,000 Jews fled to Hungary, with or without organizational aid, up to the period of the German occupation; Cohen, *Halutz Resistance*, 35.

15. Cohen, *Halutz Resistance*, 24, 33, 62. The Zionist youth activist Hannah Ganz (Grünfeld), for instance, utilized the Budapest-Kolozsvár

route, escorting persons to the Romanian border. They would meet her in a Budapest street near the station and travel in separate railroad cars. Cohen, *Halutz Resistance*, 91.

16. Bauer, *Jews*, 158; Benshalom, *We Struggled*, 13, 26, 126; Cohen, *Halutz Resistance*, 35.

17. Braham, *Politics*, 13. In an earlier meeting with Hitler in April 1943, Hungarian leader Miklós Horthy was told that Hungary should follow the example of Poland, where "the Jews who did not want to work were simply shot." Foreign Minister Joachim von Ribbentrop added that the Jews "should either be killed or sent to concentration camps." Braham, *Politics*, 96.

18. Braham, *Politics*, 55, 65. Dieter Wisliceny and Hermann Krumey were the two leading figures of the Eichmann Sonderkommando. With such a relatively small ss team, Eichmann could operate only if it could rely to a large extent on the Hungarian state administrative machinery: the officialdom of the counties, the cities and the towns, as well as the police, the gendarmerie and the army. Cohen, *Halutz Resistance*, 54.

19. Braham, *Politics*, 56–57, 63, 66, 69–70; Cohen, *Halutz Resistance*, 54, 58. Péter Hain's police intelligence service assumed the role of the Hungarian counterpart of the Gestapo, responsible to László Baky, that prepared lists of Jewish journalists, lawyers, and other professionals who were subsequently arrested and mostly deported.

20. Braham, "Rescue Operations," 178; Braham, *Politics*, 71–72; Cohen, *Halutz Resistance*, 53–54.

21. Braham, *Politics*, 73n37. In retrospect it appears that the Nazis had nothing to fear, because the Halutz youth movements decided in January 1944— two months before the German invasion—not to organize any Warsaw-like uprising, believing it would fail and prove catastrophic. See also Bauer, *Jews*, 235.

22. Braham, *Politics*, 75, 80, 97, 100.

23. The Germans carefully maneuvered to take over the Jewish-owned Manfred Weiss Works, Hungary's largest industrial complex (armaments, machines, and many other products), headed by the family of Ferenc (Franz) Chorin and his brother-in-law, Moricz Kornfeld. Under the terms of the agreement signed on May 17, 1944, and engineered by ss colonel Kurt Becher, the ss acquired the controlling 51 percent of the shares owned by the non-Jewish (converted) members of the families. In return, a group of 32 persons (some place the figure at 45 to 48), including Chorin and most of the Kornfelds, left for Lisbon with passports and forged visas, where they arrived on June 26. The Hungarians were furious at this German takeover of this large Hungarian industrial complex. In the end, three

directors were Hungarians and five were ss officers. Bauer, *Jews*, 201–4; Braham, "Rescue Operations," 194–95.

24. Braham, *Politics*, 101–6. Those exempted from wearing the Yellow Star on their outer garments included decorated war veterans and their wives, baptized Jews who were married to Christians, and Jews of foreign nationality.

25. Braham, *Politics*, 203–5; Braham, "Rescue Operations," 188. On top of the $2 million, Wisliceny demanded an additional 10 percent as his commission for continuing the negotiations. This amount was raised. The first installment of 3 million Pengö (Hungarian currency) was delivered shortly thereafter to Hermann Krumey and Otto Hunsche, two leading figures of the Eichmann Sonderkommando. The second installment of 2.5 million Pengö was delivered to the same officers on April 21. Braham, "Rescue Operations," 189 and 201n41.

26. Wisliceny was also instrumental in helping Fülöp (Pinchas) Freudiger, a leading figure of the Central Jewish Council representing the Orthodox Jewish community, his family, and some of his friends to escape to Romania on August 9, 1944. His sudden departure was widely construed as a harbinger of imminent deportation for the Budapest Jews who until then had been spared. Previously, in return for a huge bribe paid to Wisliceny, Freudiger picked out some eighty Orthodox Jewish community leaders from various ghettos, including Debrecen, Nagyvárad, Pápa, Sopron, and Székesfehérvár, most of whom were subsequently included in the Kasztner transport. Braham, "Rescue Operations," 94.

27. Bauer, *Jews*, 156.

28. Braham, *Politics*, 117–21, 125–28, 202. Unlike Poland, in Hungary Jews lingered in ghettos for a short time. In the villages it lasted only a day or two. Budapest proved to be an exception, where the ghetto lasted for months. In Bözödujfalú a special group of converts to Judaism, known as Sabbatarians, were included among those deported. They were invited to renounce their Judaism and thereby avoid deportation, an offer that they declined. Braham, *Politics*, 133.

29. Braham, *Politics*, 110–12, 114, 136–37.

30. Braham, *Politics*, 90.

31. Elie Wiesel, in *Night*, wrote that up to the deportations in 1944, he knew nothing about Auschwitz. At the same time, he related the news on the Kamenets-Podolsk massacre from a survivor, a certain Moshe the beadle, but no one believed him. Wiesel, *Night*, 4–5.

32. Braham, "Rescue Operations," 482, 488; Bauer, *Jews*, 159.

33. See Moshe Alpan's statement in this regard. Cohen, *Halutz Resistance*, 47. They proved to be the exception.

34. Cohen, *Halutz Resistance*, 75–76. Dr. Alexander Nathan, read to his comrades in the labor battalion news of what Auschwitz was really like. "The reaction was awful. . . . [They called me] a defeatist, a traitor. . . . They threatened to turn me in. It was no joke. If not for a few Zionist friends they would have beaten me to the point of death. One of the young men fell upon me with a big iron bar which my friends took away from him. The entire company was convinced that I was a provocateur, and that's how they treated me." Cohen, *Halutz Resistance*, 130. Also, testimony of Dr. Alexander Nathan, YVA-1404/37-G, 10 in Cohen, *Halutz Resistance*, 266n2.

35. Braham, *Politics*, 92, 97; Bauer, *Jews*, 157.

36. Benshalom, *We Struggled*, 15, 29–31; Cohen, *Halutz Resistance*, 68, 70. In another bunker, during the later Arrow Cross period, in one of the city's suburbs, a fight ensued with the Arrow Cross, and all the Betar members there were apparently killed. Cohen, *Halutz Resistance*, 201.

37. Bauer, *Jews*, 161. Within the Zionist youth movements, Szilágyi was the foremost spokesman urging armed resistance, but he was overruled. At the same time, cases of grenades and dozens of new pistols, rifles, and submachine guns were acquired and secretly stored. Cohen, *Halutz Resistance*, 145–46. Within the Betar movement, Dr. Lajos Gottesman called upon Jews, especially the men in the labor service units, to rise up in armed opposition. Cohen, *Halutz Resistance*, 129, 145.

38. Benshalom, *We Struggled*, 32, 35, 37, 38; Bauer, *Jews*, 159.

39. Cohen, *Halutz Resistance*, 81, 83, 94, 97, 99. Yehuda Bauer advanced a lower figure of some 4,000–4,500 Jews. Bauer, *Jews*, 160; Benshalom, *We Struggled*, 51; Cohen, *Halutz Resistance*, 99, 244.

40. Braham, *Politics*, 158. The spreading out of the Jewish houses throughout the city was prompted by the consideration to prevent the bombing of the city by Allied planes that, in the mistaken estimation of the Hungarian leaders, would otherwise have spared a separately located Jewish ghetto.

41. Braham, *Politics*, 158.

42. Braham, *Politics*, 161–63.

43. Braham, *Politics*, 165–70; Braham, "Rescue Operations," 180.

44. Braham, *Politics*, 182–88.

45. Braham, *Politics*, 196–97, 289. Catholic priest András Kún, in his priestly robes and a pistol strapped to his side and carrying a submachine gun, led a group of marauding killers, shooting Jews whenever they accosted them. Cohen, *Halutz Resistance*, 237.

46. Bauer, *Jews*, 234.

47. Cohen, *Halutz Resistance*, 162; Benshalom, *We Struggled*, 81, 103.

48. Cohen, *Halutz Resistance*, 192, 202, 211. Notably among the clandestine groups was the Van der Waals unit that included Dutch and British officers who had escaped from POW camps in Germany. Also the Communist Pál Demény group. The beneficiaries also counted university students groups, personalities in literature, and trade unions. Cohen, *Halutz Resistance*, 212.

49. Cohen, *Halutz Resistance*, 232, 234. Rafi Benshalom related the unimaginable feat of a non-Jewish person, known as the Pole, who in return for 100 Napoleon gold coins for each prisoner, arranged the freeing of 100 prisoners, including 65 Halutz members—quite a feat. Cohen, *Halutz Resistance*, 235.

50. Cohen, *Halutz Resistance*, 213–14, 216, 218; Benshalom, *We Struggled*, 204n8.

51. Cohen, *Halutz Resistance*, 219–20.

52. Cohen, *Halutz Resistance*, 219–20.

53. Cohen, *Halutz Resistance*, 207.

54. Cohen, *Halutz Resistance*, 208–9.

55. The Arrow Cross was particularly interested in securing the diplomatic recognition of the neutral states. So the new government ratified all the privileges which the previous regime had granted to the neutral legations in Budapest. Cohen, *Halutz Resistance*, 160, 185; Braham, *Politics*, 190.

56. The exact number cannot be established with certainty. Braham, *Politics*, 236–37. Bauer estimates that Wallenberg directly saved 4,500 Jews. Bauer, *Jews*, 237. Valdemar Langlet, representing the Swedish Red Cross, also issued protective letters that did not confer Swedish nationality, only protection, but were honored by the Hungarians. He and wife, Nina, also occasionally concealed Jews in their home. Cohen, *Halutz Resistance*, 135.

57. Monsignor Angelo Rotta, the Vatican nuncio, likewise issued thousands of protective documents to persons who it falsely claimed were either baptized Jews or in the process of converting to the Catholic faith. He was posthumously awarded by Yad Vashem the Righteous title; YVA-M32.1/7690. Spanish diplomat Angel Sanz-Briz, the Italian Giorgio (Jorge) Perlasca, as well as the Portuguese minister Liz-Texeira Branquinho distributed thousands of Spanish protective passes to all Jews who could prove that they were of Spanish descent or had family in Portugal or Brazil but without this constituting a carte blanche for traveling to these countries. Braham, *Politics*, 97, 238–39, 241–43. Raoul Wallenberg was awarded the Righteous title by Yad Vashem (YVA-M31.2/31), as well as Carl-Charles Lutz (YVA-M31.2/46), Angel Sanz-Briz (YVA-M31.2/121), and Giorgio Perlasca (YVA-M31.2/3911).

58. Cohen, *Halutz Resistance*, 168, 190–91.

59. According to Cohen, *Halutz Resistance*, 273.

60. Benshalom, *We Struggled*, 131.

61. Cohen, *Halutz Resistance*, 189.

62. Cohen, *Halutz Resistance*, 205.

63. Owned by Arthur Weiss, the Glass House was so named for the glass that covered many of the building's walls and roof to advertise Weiss's glass products.

64. Benshalom, *We Struggled*, 196. When they became aware that the new regime was honoring the extraterritorial status of the Vadász office, the Halutz Resistance systematically began to bring their people there. Rafi Benshalom was the head of the youth movement office in the Glass House. Cohen, *Halutz Resistance*, 164.

65. Benshalom, *We Struggled*, 72–73; Cohen, *Halutz Resistance*, 163–66. Before the Arrow Cross coup of October 15, 1944, the Glass House was at times the scene of confrontations between the House management and some of the Halutz operatives. Rafi Benshalom recalled one such standoff, in the early hours of October 15, when Arthur Weiss in the presence of Krausz refused to hand the keys to one of the rooms to Rafi. Losing his temper, in Benshalom's words, "I picked up a chair and smashed in the glass door. Krausz asked us to calm down and discuss the matter quietly. Suddenly the door opened and somebody burst in with the news that Horthy had called for an armistice. It was October 15, 1944." Benshalom, *We Struggled*, 77–78. The new situation called for putting these altercations to rest or at least on hold. Arthur Weiss later lost his life at the hands of the Arrow Cross. The house was forcibly invaded on Sunday, December 31, and all the people were taken out onto the street, amidst blows and shots, as a result of which three people were killed. As the people were lined up to march away, orders from Arrow Cross higher-ups were received that prompted the attackers to return the people into the Glass House. Cohen, *Halutz Resistance*, 238.

66. Cohen, *Halutz Resistance*, 168, 186, 193. At the beginning of November, a third office of the Representation of Foreign Interests of the Swiss legation was opened at 17 Wekerle Sándor Street. Most of the Resistance workers and some of the original staff at the Glass House were then transferred to the new offices, where conditions were better, and the major work of the Resistance became centered there. Cohen, *Halutz Resistance*, 188.

67. When the ghetto was liberated by Russian forces on January 17, 1945, some 3,000 bodies were lying about awaiting burial. Braham, *Politics*, 191–92, 195; Cohen, *Halutz Resistance*, 188, 223. According to Yehuda Bauer, the unprotected Jews in the ghetto numbered 86,000. Bauer, *Jews*, 241.

68. Benshalom, *We Struggled*, 132–34.
69. Yehuda Bauer advances a lower figure of 1,500 children. Bauer, *Jews*, 235; Braham, *Politics*, 215. Friedrich Born established an additional children's section, known as Section B, and headed by Reverend Gábor Sztehló of the Protestant Good Shepherd Mission (Jó Pásztor Misszió), which had originally been established in 1942 to assist converts to Christianity, but was now involved in the rescue of Jewish children. Braham, *Politics*, 244–45, 293n44.
70. These included Peretz Révész, Zoltán Weiner, Hansi Brand, and Rafi Benshalom. The office staff consisted of twenty to twenty-five people, and about twenty buyers worked with Teichmann, most of them veteran food merchants and wholesalers. Zoltán Weiner dealt with the financial matters, and Dr. Moshe Osterweil (Kotarba) was in charge of the medical services for the children. Bauer, *Jews*, 236. Benshalom, *We Struggled*, 87, 131.
71. Cohen, *Halutz Resistance*, 172–73, 176–77. Gábor Sztehló was awarded the Righteous title by Yad Vashem; YVA-M31.2/722.
72. Cohen, *Halutz Resistance*, 178–79.
73. Cohen, *Halutz Resistance*, 221–23.
74. Cohen, *Halutz Resistance*, 170.
75. Cohen, *Halutz Resistance*, 203. Cohen puts the total Budapest casualty figure (including marchers) at 80,000. Cohen, *Halutz Resistance*, 204. See also Bauer, *Jews*, 240–41.
76. Braham, *Politics*, 251, 253; see also statistics breakdown of losses in Braham, "Rescue Operations," 174, and Bauer, *Jews*, 156. Some 837 non-Jewish rescuers from Hungary were awarded the Righteous title by Yad Vashem as of January 1, 2016.
77. Braham, *Politics*, 214, 217–18; Braham, "Rescue Operations," 184–85.
78. Braham disputes Bauer's claim, based on Josef Megyeri's account, of having sabotaged and derailed trains; Braham, "Rescue Operations," 185; Bauer, *Jews*, 235.
79. Bauer, *Jews*, 237; Cohen, *Halutz Resistance*, 248.
80. Benshalom, *We Struggled*, 7, 9, 11.
81. Benshalom, *We Struggled*, 10–11.
82. Benshalom, *We Struggled*, 14–15.
83. Benshalom, *We Struggled*, 14, 19, 27.
84. Benshalom, *We Struggled*, 82, 88, 105–7.
85. Benshalom, *We Struggled*, 5–7, 190; Gur, *Brothers*, 57.
86. Benshalom, *We Struggled*, 40–43.
87. Benshalom, *We Struggled*, 45.

88. Benshalom, *We Struggled*, 49. Some of the Halutz operatives caught while trying to traverse the border included Hannah Ganz. After undergoing torture, she was sent to Auschwitz but survived. Cohen, *Halutz Resistance*, 91–92. The Hashomer Hatzair faction within the Halutz underground were fortunate to be aided by a certain Serb, Milan Gligorijevic, who utilized various chicanery to free a group of Halutz people from jail, after they were caught on the way to the Romanian border. Gligorijevic, who risked his life in these endeavors, was honored by Yad Vashem as a Righteous Among the Nations (YVA-M31.2/1050). Cohen, *Halutz Resistance*, 100–11, 113; Benshalom, *We Struggled*, 37, 55–57.

89. Benshalom, *We Struggled*, 36–37.

90. Benshalom, *We Struggled*, 141–45. The two "necessities" most in demand during this period were, ironically enough, a baptismal certificate (on August 1, 1944, converts were granted release from planned deportations) or a permit to emigrate to Palestine. A gentile woman, widow of a Jew, who worked in the Bureau of Vital Statistics brought them genuine birth and marriage certificates; Cohen, *Halutz Resistance*, 138, 140.

91. Cohen, *Halutz Resistance*, 147.

92. Benshalom, *We Struggled*, 135, 149–53.

93. Benshalom, *We Struggled*, 154–55.

94. Benshalom, *We Struggled*, 155–58; Gur, *Brothers*, 121.

95. Gur, *Brothers*, 122.

96. Benshalom, *We Struggled*, 124–25, 128; Gur, *Brothers*, 34.

97. Benshalom, *We Struggled*, 129–31.

98. Benshalom, *We Struggled*, 115–17.

99. Benshalom, *We Struggled*, 117–18.

100. Cohen, *Halutz Resistance*, 218, 161. Zvi Reich (Nadivi) outfitted dozens of Resistance members with the Arrow Cross papers and uniforms. The party's symbolic green shirt could be purchased without great difficulty at Budapest's flea market in Teleki Square. Cohen, *Halutz Resistance*, 161–62. Mihály Salamon tells of two Bnai Akiva boys (religious Halutz youth) appearing at his home, in Arrow Cross uniforms, to take him and his family to the Glass House on Vadász Street, which enjoyed diplomatic protection. Cohen, *Halutz Resistance*, 166.

101. Gur, *Brothers*, 129–30.

102. Gur, *Brothers*, 41.

103. Gur, *Brothers*, 110–11.

104. Gur, *Brothers*, 193–94.

105. Cohen, *Halutz Resistance*, 30, 135. Benshalom, *We Struggled*, 26.

106. Braham, *Politics* 214, 230, 232, 234; Bauer, *Jews*, 232; Cohen, *Halutz Resistance*, 133, 136–37, 152; Gur, *Brothers*, 158. On July 17, 1944, in the sharpest language possible, Hitler, through his foreign minister, von Ribbentrop, threatened renewed intervention in Hungary as a result of Horthy's stopping the deportation of Jews from Budapest proper. Bauer, *Jews*, 213–14.

107. Cohen, *Halutz Resistance*, 164; Benshalom, *We Struggled*, 75. It should also be noted that Krausz also disapproved of Kasztner's negotiation tactics with the Germans, and according to Yehuda Bauer, Krausz even considered him a traitor. Bauer, *Jews*, 162.

108. Cohen, *Halutz Resistance*, 204.

109. Gur, *Brothers*, 158.

110. Hansi Brand, born Hartman in 1912 in Budapest, also assisted Jewish refugees who arrived from Germany, Austria, Poland, and Slovakia. The Brand house was open to all the refugees, and Hansi obtained and distributed forged documents and helped hide the forgery laboratory of the Halutz underground. On May 27, 1944, she was arrested by the Hungarian secret police, who wanted information on the laboratory and the documents and about her husband's mission to Istanbul. She withstood a brutal interrogation, but did not reveal anything, and was released due to the intervention of the Germans, who were still interested in the success of her husband's mission. Early in 1945, Hansi and her two sons went into hiding with a Christian family until liberation. Moving to Israel after the war, she died in 2000. Gur, *Brothers*, 67–69.

111. Bauer, *Jews*, 143–44, 163.

112. Bauer, *Jews*, 164–65.

113. Bauer, *Jews* 167; Avriel, *Open*, 175–77.

114. Bauer, *Jews*, 168–69.

115. Avriel, *Open*, 177–78.

116. Bauer, *Jews*, 173.

117. Avriel, *Open*, 181.

118. Bauer, *Jews*, 175.

119. Bauer, *Jews*, 176.

120. Avriel, *Open*, 182–83.

121. Avriel, *Open*, 184–85.

122. Avriel, *Open*, 187–88.

123. Informed of the Eichmann proposal, the Americans insisted on informing the Soviets, and on June 9 the State Department sent a cable to Moscow instructing the U.S. ambassador to fill in the Soviet leadership. On June 19 Andrei Vyshinski, the deputy foreign minister, announced his

government's opposition to any negotiations whatsoever with the Germans. Bauer, *Jews,* 177–78, 180.

124. Bauer, *Jews,* 194; Braham, *Politics,* 207–8; Gur, *Brothers,* 69.

125. Porter, *Kastner's Train,* 38; Bauer, *Jews,* 162; Cohen, *Halutz Resistance,* 30–31.

126. Bauer, *Jews,* 162–63, 187, 206.

127. Cohen, *Halutz Resistance,* 90, 101; Braham, "Rescue Operations," 189–90.

128. In Braham's estimation, the understandable eagerness with which Kasztner accepted the opportunity to save his family, friends, and some selected members of the Kolozsvár Jewish community raises the agonizing question of whether Eichmann's offer was one of the devices used to buy off or compensate Kasztner for his silence. Braham, *Politics,* 209.

129. Braham, *Politics,* 93–94.

130. Braham, *Politics,* 94. Of special interest is that Dr. József Fischer, Kasztner's father-in-law, was the head of the local council there. He and his family were among the 388 Jews who were moved to Budapest as part of the Kasztner "freedom train." Braham, *Politics,* 129.

131. Braham, "Rescue Operations," 192. In 1954 Kasztner admitted that he was aware of the warnings by Moshe Sharett and Izhak Ben Zvi, who respectively later became prime minister and president of Israel, urging the Jews to engage in rescue and resistance, a message he failed to communicate to his co-religionists in Kolozsvár; Braham, "Rescue Operations," 200. In the words of Justice Moshe Silber of the Israeli Supreme Court in 1958, in the decision to vindicate Kasztner of the charge of having collaborated with the Nazis, in his dissenting opinion, concluded that the Nazis' ability to carry out the deportation program in Hungary as easily and peacefully as they did was "the direct result of the concealment of the horrifying truth from the victims," to which Kaszter was willy-nilly a partner. Braham, "Rescue Operations," 192.

132. Braham, *Politics,* 209; Bauer, *Jews,* 187.

133. Bauer, *Jews,* 198; Braham, *Politics,* 210; Cohen, *Halutz Resistance,* 103. On the chaotic situation prevailing during the last days before the train's departure, with many people forcing themselves on the train, although not on the list, see Benshalom, *We Struggled,* 68–71. The camp on Columbus Street was an unusual phenomenon. Months after the Kasztner train departed, it was still fully occupied by about 3,000 people, all hoping to leave with a second Kasztner transport, which never did depart. It was then placed under the protection of the International Red Cross. Cohen, *Halutz Resistance,* 205.

134. Bauer, *Jews,* 198–99. During the Kasztner-Grunwald trial in 1954, Judge

Benjamin Halevi of the Jerusalem District Court ruled that "Kasztner sold his soul to the Devil" by sacrificing the interests of the Jews for the opportunity to save a "select few." Almost four years later, in January 1958, the Supreme Court overturned this defamatory condemnation of Kasztner as a collaborator. Unfortunately, he had been assassinated a year earlier, on March 15, 1957, by men who considered him guilty of collaborating with the enemy. Braham, *Politics*, 213.

135. Braham, *Politics*, 148–49; Bauer, *Jews*, 200; Braham, "Rescue Operations," 192–93.

136. Bauer, *Jews*, 215; Cohen, *Halutz Resistance*, 119–20; Benshalom, *We Struggled*, 97–101.

137. Bauer, *Jews*, 216; Cohen, *Halutz Resistance*, 118. Another subject worth further study was Kasztner's at times stormy relationship with the Halutz underground. He was not in full agreement with the Halutz illegal crossings into Romania that lasted until August 23, 1944, under the so-called *Tiyul* operation, while at the same time he included a large number of Halutz members on his rescue train. While agreeing with Kasztner's negotiating tactics with the Germans, the Halutz leadership kept a certain distance from him and did not divulge to him the ways and means of their clandestine operations. Benshalom, *We Struggled*, 35–36.

138. Bauer, *Jews* 221; Braham, "Rescue Operations," 199–200. During his debriefing by the FBI on May 17, 1945, Kasztner claimed that, through his dealings with Becher, he "saved the lives of hundreds of thousands of Jews." For source citation, see Braham, "Rescue Operations," 197n18.

139. Bauer, *Jews*, 228.

140. Bauer, *Jews*, 207–11; Braham, "Letters."

141. Bauer, *American* , 425.

142. Braham, *Yad Vashem*, 488.

143. Braham, "Rescue Operations," 182.

144. As told in the earlier chapter on Slovakia, Kasztner is also to be credited in arranging the rescue of Rabbi Weissmandl and a group of Jews hiding in the Bratislava region, and their secretive and safe conveyance from there Switzerland. Both the Zionist Kasztner and non-Zionist and ultraorthodox Weissmandl believed that there was room for negotiating with the top echelon Nazis in the rescue of many Jews.

6. Croatia and Italy

1. Shelah, "Croatia," 323.

2. Shelah, "Croatia," 324–25, 326–28. As of January 1, 2016, 115 Croatians were awarded the Righteous title by Yad Vashem for help to Jews.

3. Carpi, "Italy," 729–30. The Germans, in particular, brought tremendous pressure to bear upon Italy to hand the Jews over to them. Mussolini was ready to yield to the German pressure, but the high-ranking diplomats and officers in his entourage who would have had to implement this order refused to do so, and by various means they succeeded in thwarting this act. Outstanding in this effort was Guido Lospinoso, an Italian police inspector serving in southern France.

4. Uros Zun, a police commissioner in Maribor, ignored orders from superiors to close the border for all refugees from Germany. He was instrumental in obtaining the approval of a group of sixteen girls, who had crossed the border illegally, to stay on Yugoslav territory. In 1987 he was honored as a Righteous Among the Nations by Yad Vashem (YVA-M31.2/ file 3454).

5. Weiss, *Joshko's Children*, 41–42, 47, 316; Shelah, "Croatia," 323–29.

6. *Joshko's Children*, 56.

7. *Joshko's Children*, 58.

8. *Joshko's Children*, 61.

9. *Joshko's Children*, 62–64.

10. *Joshko's Children*, 65.

11. *Joshko's Children*, 66.

12. *Joshko's Children*, 71–74.

13. *Joshko's Children*, 92.

14. *Joshko's Children*, 114.

15. *Joshko's Children*, 110–11.

16. Lilly Newman, one of Indig's adult helpers, decided to join the ranks of the partisans. She participated in many acts of sabotage, and moving to Italy proper, she fell in battle in June 1933 in Istria. She was twenty-three years old. Weiss, *Joshko's Children*, 127–29.

17. *Joshko's Children*, 134.

18. *Joshko's Children*, 139–42.

19. *Joshko's Children*, 145.

20. *Joshko's Children*, 147.

21. *Joshko's Children*, 150–51.

22. *Joshko's Children*, 154–55.

23. Michaelis, "Italy," 721–23. Mussolini himself was not beyond at times uttering statements that could be construed as antisemitic, such as his repeatedly denouncing "Jewish" Bolshevism and "English" Zionism in his newspaper, *Il Popolo d'Italia*, between 1919 and 1922, adding that the "New Zion" of Italian Jewry should be not in Palestine but in Italy. Michaelis, "Italy," 722.

24. Carpi, "Italy," 726.

25. Michaelis, "Italy," 725. Carpi puts the figure of Jews in Italy in September 1943 at 37,000. Carpi, "Italy," 727.

26. Carpi, "Italy," 728.

27. Michaelis, "Italy," 726; Carpi, "Italy," 730. As of January 1, 2016, 641 Italians had been honored with the Righteous title by Yad Vashem, but this represents only a fraction of the Italians who aided thousands of Jews to avoid capture and deportation.

28. *Joshko's Children*, 156.

29. *Joshko's Children*, 166–68.

30. *Joshko's Children*, 174.

31. *Joshko's Children*, 179.

32. *Joshko's Children*, 162–63.

33. *Joshko's Children*, 188.

34. The work of Delasem, that presently went underground, was taken over by Don Francesco Repetto, in Genoa, who served as secretary of Cardinal Boetto. He appears on Yad Vashem's list of the Righteous (YVA-M31.2/1055). *Joshko's Children*, 189.

35. *Joshko's Children*, 190.

36. *Joshko's Children*, 191.

37. *Joshko's Children*, 191.

38. *Joshko's Children*, 193.

39. *Joshko's Children*, 196.

40. *Joshko's Children*, 199.

41. *Joshko's Children*, 201.

42. *Joshko's Children*, 202–3.

43. *Joshko's Children*, 203.

44. *Joshko's Children*, 206–7.

45. *Joshko's Children*, 208.

46. *Joshko's Children*, 209.

47. *Joshko's Children*, 292.

48. *Joshko's Children*, 211.

49. *Joshko's Children*, 213–14.

50. *Joshko's Children*, 219, 222, 226–28.

51. Aldo Beccari, YVA-M31.2/35; Giuseppe Moreali, YVA-M31.2/36.7.

52. *Joshko's Children*, 276, 280, 283, 285.

7. France

1. Cohen and Marrus "France," 509.

2. Cohen and Marrus "France," 509, 514; Lazare, *Rescue*, 8, 18; Wikipedia, "Union Générale des Israélites de France."

3. Lazare, *Rescue,* 12, 14, 17–18, 21.

4. Lazare, *Rescue,* 5, 7–8.

5. Lazare, *Rescue,* 5–7, 19.

6. Lazare, *Rescue,* 9–10.

7. Lazare, *Rescue,* 11–12. On the night of October 22–23, 1940, the Germans dumped more than 7,000 German Jews from the Baden and Palatinate provinces into France, in spite of French protests, and they were first detained in Gurs camp, then transferred to Rivesaltes camp. Latour, *Jewish,* 17; Lazare, *Rescue,* 37; Samuel, *Rescuing,* 32.

8. Lazare, *Rescue,* 37, 75, 86.

9. Before the war, barely 40,000 Jews lived in the southern zone. Lazare, *Rescue,* 20, 36, 37; Cohen and Marrus, "France," 513, 515.

10. Latour, *Jewish,* 30.

11. Cohen and Marrus, "France," 506, 508, 510.

12. Cohen and Marrus, "France," 509, 511; Marrus, "Statut des Juifs."

13. Samuel, *Rescuing,* 18; Marrus, "Statut des Juits"; Marrus "Commissariat," 306; Cohen and Marrus, "France," 510.

14. Lazare, *Rescue,* 218; Cohen and Marrus, "France," 510; Latour, *Jewish,* 19; Marrus, "Commissariat," 306. Darquier de Pellepoix was succeeded in February 1944 by Charles Mercier du Paty de Clam, who in May was replaced by Joseph Antignac, all known antisemites of various degrees. Marrus, "Commissariat," 307.

15. Cohen and Marrus, "France," 510, 515.

16. Lazare, *Rescue,* 36, 41, 144; Cohen and Marrus, "France," 510–11.

17. In the Milles camp, not far from Marseilles, famous artists such as Max Ernst, Gustav Herlich, and Hans Bellmer covered the walls of that former tile factory with impressive frescoes.

18. Lazare, *Rescue,* 63, 88, 93, 97, 121, 134; Cohen and Marrus, "France," 510. Originally these camps were set up by France to house the thousands of refugees from the Spanish Civil War.

19. Cohen and Marrus, "France," 512–13; Latour, *Jewish,* 49–50; Lazare, *Rescue,* 143. A fine of a billion francs was also imposed on the Jewish community for the crime committed by others in targeting German military personnel. Wikipedia, "Union Générale des Israélites de France," 5.

20. Lazare, *Rescue,* 69–70, 89, 145–46, 154, 218; Cohen and Marrus, "France," 511, 516.

21. Cohen and Marrus, "France," 511–12, 516; Lazare, *Rescue,* 130, 210.

22. Lazare, *Rescue,* 163, 208; Cohen and Marrus, "France," 512. Richard Cohen places the figure of Parisian Jews when liberated at 15,000. Cohen and Marrus, "France," 516–17.

23. Lazare, *Rescue*, 136, 140, 177.

24. Lazare, *Rescue*, 187.

25. Lazare, *Rescue*, 309.

26. The Jewish organizations, part of a screening committee approved by the authorities, were represented by Joseph Weill, Charles Lederman, and Georges Garel of the OSE and Claude Gutman of the EIF (Jewish Scouts). The non-Jewish members included Father Alexandre Glasberg of the Amitié Chrétienne and Gilbert Lesage of the Interior Ministry's Foreign Workers Service.

27. Samuel, *Rescuing*, 83. Twenty-eight parents attempted suicide during the night. Nodot, *Enfants*, 16; Perthuis, *Sauvetage*, 55, 57, 59, 67.

28. Samuel, *Rescuing*, 84; Lazare, *Rescue*, 189–90; Perthuis, *Sauvetage*, 58, 65. In Drancy camp a four-year-old boy was found hiding in a doghouse. "But what are you doing, my little man?" "I'm a dog. They don't deport dogs!" Lazare, *Rescue*, 134.

29. Lazare, *Rescue*, 172, 175, 185, 187, 195, 210.

30. Lazare, *Rescue*, 224; Knout, *Contribution*, 37–38; Latour, *Jewish*, 146.

31. Knout, *Contribution*, 39; Samuel, *Rescuing*, 88; Lazare, *Rescue*, 224, 225, 227, 230; Latour, *Jewish*, 146; Poznanski, *Juifs*, 465–66; Rein, *Rapport*, 10–12.

32. Lospinoso said, according to Ignace Fink: "I am of one of you—from way back," words that Fink and his colleagues interpreted as hinting of descent from a family of Marranos. Latour, *Jewish*, 148.

33. Lazare, *Rescue*, 228; Poznanski, *Juifs*, 464. Another source places the number of Jews in the Italian zone at 30,000. Cohen and Marrus, "France," 516.

34. Lazare, *Rescue*, 226–27; Poznanski, *Juifs*, 487; Knout, *Contribution*, 39–40; Rein, *Rapport*, 5, 7–9.

35. Lazare, *Rescue*, 230–32; Rein, *Rapport*, 13–14; Poznanski, *Juifs*, 466, 468; http://www.lamaisondesevre.org/cel/cel5.html, November 13, 2006; Marrot-Fellag, "Enfants," 9. Two thousand were caught, according to Poznanski, *Juifs*, 467. Lucien Lazare notes that the Gestapo considered their Jewish operation a failure for not having netted their goal of 25,000 Jews. Lazare, "Nice."

36. Lazare, "Nice"; Cohen and Marrus, "France," 512.

37. Wikipedia, "Union Générale des Israélites de France," 2–3; Lazare, *Rescue*, 18, 80; Cohen and Marrus, "France," 514.

38. Wikipedia, "Union Générale des Israélites de France," 2–3; Cohen and Marrus, "France," 514–15; Lazare, *Rescue*, 39.

39. Lazare, *Rescue*, 78, 80, 90, 117, 119; Cohen and Marrus, "France," 510, 514–15, 517; Wikipedia, "Union Générale des Israélites de France," 1, 4–5, 10–11.

40. Lazare, *Rescue*, 78, 176–77, 205; Wikipedia, "Union Générale des Israélites de France," 7–10.

41. Latour, *Jewish,* 23, 190.

42. In the south, on February 5, 1943, UGIF head Lambert nominated Jewish aid activists Jules-Dika Jefroykin and Maurice Brener as "social inspectors" of the UGIF. Lazare, *Rescue*, 177–78, 220; Hammel, *Souviens-toi*, 431. Wikipedia, "Union Générale des Israélites de France," 7.

43. Lazare, *Rescue*, 178, 204–5, 248; Wikipedia, "Union Générale des Israélites de France," 10. Similarly in the south a year earlier, on October 19, 1943, the UGIF office in Marseilles was informed that the Gestapo was preparing to raid the "blocked" children in the UGIF children's homes in Verdiere (Bouches-du-Rhone *département*). After considering several options, the UGIF management decided to stick to its legality stance, and this facilitated the Gestapo, who raided the home on October 20 and carried off the children. These arrests, which could have been preempted, led Serge Klarsfeld (otherwise favorable and indulgent toward the UGIF) to severely censure UGIF's behavior as a gross negligence, "forever" tarnishing it with an indelible stain. Wikipedia, "Union Générale des Israélites de France," 8, 10; Cohen and Marrus, "France."

44. Wikipedia, "Union Générale des Israélites de France," 8; Lazare, *Rescue*, 181, 205.

45. Latour, *Jewish,* 182.

46. Lazare, *Rescue*, 219; Wikipedia, "Union Générale des Israélites de France," 8.

47. Lazare, *Rescue*, 218, 222, 249; Wikipedia, "Union Générale des Israélites de France," 10; Latour, *Jewish,* 197. Some twenty rabbis were also arrested and deported, including René Hirschler, while others, such as Isaïe Schwartz, sought shelter with friendly non-Jewish persons. Lazare, *Rescue, 222.*
In 1944, close to liberation, the Representative Council of French Jewry (Conseil Représentatif des Juifs de France-CRIF), an umbrella organization, was founded to coordinate resistance activity among the Jewish groups while setting aside their ideological differences. It continued to speak for the Jewish population in France. Lazare, *Rescue*, 267, 311; Cohen and Marrus, "France," 517.

48. Lazare, *Rescue,* 39–40; Cohen and Marrus, "France," 514; Latour, Jewish, 44.

49. Lazare, *Rescue*, 39, 43–45, 88, 137, 153.

50. It also changed its name from the original Russian Society for the Medical Protection of Jewish Populations.

51. Samuel, *Rescuing*, 31; Lazare, *Rescue,* 44, 48, 126, 131; Weill, "Andrée Salomon," 96; Latour, Jewish, 40.

52. Lazare, *Rescue,* 88, 131, 133, 139; Samuel, *Rescuing,* 34, 54. It is well to

remember that the United States and Vichy France maintained diplomatic relations until the U.S. invasion of North Africa in November 1942.

53. Samuel, *Rescuing*, 35, 82; Lazare, *Rescue*, 133, 194.

54. Lazare, *Rescue*, 128, 140, 194; Poznanski, *Juifs*, 474–75; Samuel, *Rescuing*, 87; Hammel, *Souviens-toi*, 197.

55. Poznanski, *Juifs*, 476; Lazare, *Rescue*, 194–95; Latour, *Jewish*, 69–70. It should be mentioned that WIZO, the Women's Zionist organization, was also involved in sheltering children with foster families, and it had about 1,250 children in its charge who were mostly placed with farming families, school teachers, truck drivers, and religious boarding schools. Lazare, *Rescue*, 179–80.

56. Lazare, *Rescue*, 165–66, 194, 201–2; Poznanski, *Juifs*, 485–86.

57. Lazare, *Rescue*, 309.

58. Lazare, *Rescue*, 16–17, 59, 61; Hammel, *Souviens-toi*, 328, 330.

59. Latour, *Jewish*, 30; Hammel, *Souviens-toi*, 330.

60. Lazare, *Rescue*, 56–61, 126–27; Latour, *Jewish*, 30, 37.

61. Lazare, *Rescue*, 62–63, 262; Poznanski, *Juifs*, 477; Hammel, *Souviens-toi*, 332. Fernand Musnik represented the EIF in the occupied zone. Hammel, *Souviens-toi*, 431. Claude Guttman ("Griffon") assumed the EIF operation in Nice. He was arrested on September 23, 1943, and deported. Marrot-Fellag, "Enfants," 10.

62. Hammel, *Souviens-toi*, 331; Latour, *Jewish*, 30–33.

63. Latour, *Jewish*, 37, who notes that the police commissioner did not carry out his threat.

64. Lazare, *Rescue*, 29.

65. Lazare, *Rescue*, 276.

66. Lazare, *Rescue*, 25–26.

67. Latour, *Jewish*, 74–75. The Gestapo remained dumbfounded what the Sixth stood for. Gestapo files released after the war show the confusion in the minds of the Gestapo by this apparently new organization. "The Sixth, the Sixth, what's this?" they asked. It actually stood for the sixth division of the fourth section in the UGIF. To the Gestapo, the Sixth appeared as a sinister organization, never realizing that it was actually the EIF under a different name when it was forced to go underground. Hammel, *Souviens-toi*, 195.

68. Latour, *Jewish*, 75–76; Hammel, *Souviens-toi*, 202; Lazare, *Rescue*, 181, 197–98; Poznanski, *Juifs*, 478.

69. Latour, *Jewish*, 73–78 ; Poznanski, *Juifs* 478, 480; Hammel, *Souviens-toi*, 196, 200; Lazare, *Rescue*, 198.

70. Latour, *Jewish*, 93–97, 99–100.

71. Latour, *Jewish*, 185–89, 192–93; Lazare, *Rescue*, 208, 278–79.

72. Cohen and Marrus, "France," 517; Latour, *Jewish*, 98, 100, 106–7.

73. Lazare, *Rescue*, 65, 68–69; Latour, *Jewish*, 87–88, 90; Poznanski, *Juifs*, 480–81.

74. Poznanski, *Juifs*, 468; Latour, *Jewish*, 87, 91; Lazare, *Rescue*, 225–26; Hammel, *Souviens-toi*, 206; Marrot-Fellag, "Enfants," 9.

75. Poznanski, *Juifs*, 462; Latour, *Jewish*, 89.

76. Latour, *Jewish*, 133; Lazare, *Rescue*, 166–67.

77. Latour, *Jewish*, 131. Rodolphe Furth was another such expert forger. Latour, *Jewish*, 132.

78. Latour, *Jewish*, 131; Lazare, *Rescue*, 167–68.

79. Latour, *Jewish*, 130–31.

80. Latour, *Jewish*, 137.

81. Lazare, *Rescue*, 170; Latour, *Jewish*, 134. The Jewish resistance had attained such professional expertise in the manufacture of false credentials that they were in demand by the general resistance to the extent that, in the estimation of activist Anny Latour, on the eve of the liberation of France, they had become the leading suppliers of fabricated false credentials to the general resistance. Latour, *Jewish*, 137–38.

82. Lazare, *Rescue*, 105–6, 175; Latour, *Jewish*, 120, 122.

83. Lazare, *Rescue*, 145, 176. A year earlier, during the detention of nearly 4,000 Parisian Jews in May 1941, Solidarité organized a demonstration at the camp gates by the wives and mothers of detainees, demanding the right to visit their loved ones and to send them food packages. Lazare, *Rescue*, 108.

84. Lazare, *Rescue*, 81, 110–11, 221, 279–80; Latour, *Jewish*, 180–81. In hindsight, while the military value of shooting isolated members of the Wehrmacht at close range appeared insignificant, the price paid for this was inordinately harsh, for after each assassination, the enemy shot dozens of hostages. Lazare, *Rescue*, 111.

85. Lazare, *Rescue*, 42, 109. These units also sustained severe losses, as the Gestapo was able by 1944 to strongly diminish its effectiveness by seizing 230 combatants. Lazare, *Rescue*, 280.

86. Lazare, *Rescue*, 112.

87. Lazare, *Rescue*, 47, 83.

88. Samuel, *Rescuing*, 114; Hammel, *Souviens-toi*, 206; Latour, *Jewish*, 167–68.

89. Latour, *Jewish*, 168, 171–74; Lazare, *Rescue*, 287–88.

90. Latour, *Jewish*, 169–71.

91. Lazare, *Rescue*, 288; Latour, *Jewish*, 167.

92. Lazare, *Rescue*, 202–3, 205–7.

93. Lazare, *Rescue*, 246–47; Latour, *Jewish*, 198–99. In August 1944, as the Germans prepared to evacuate the area, they planned the massacre of the wretched detainees still in the Drancy camp, but were deterred from this by the Swedish consul, Raoul Nordling, and instead turned the remaining 1,523 internees over to the Red Cross, to await the arrival of the Allied liberating forces. Latour, *Jewish*, 269.

94. Latour, *Jewish*, 245–46, gives the figure of 3,500 soldiers who surrendered. Lazare, *Rescue*, 305.

95. Lazare, *Rescue*, 295–96, 298, 301–4; Latour, *Jewish*, 177, 218–20, 230, 233–34, 242.

96. Siekierski, "Hommage," 142; Latour, *Jewish*, 114; Delpard, *Les Justes*, 178.

97. Paldiel, *Saving*, 286–97; Hammel, *Souviens-toi*, 214; Latour, *Jewish*, 114, 116.

98. Latour, *Jewish*, 115–16.

99. Paldiel, *Saving*, 291.

100. Siekierski interview; Paldiel, *Saving*, 294–95; Hammel, *Souviens-toi*, 213.

101. According to Denise Siekierski, Bass had offered his interrogator a glass of wine in which he secretly added a sedative. Siekierski, "Hommage," 157.

102. Latour, *Jewish*, 118; Siekierski, "Hommage," 157–58.

103. Hammel, *Souviens-toi*, 215. Simone Mairesse-Doise was recognized by Yad Vashem as a Righteous; YVA-M31.2/4012.

104. Latour, *Jewish*, 119, 250–51; Siekierski, "Hommage," 152, 155, 159; Paldiel, *Saving*, 295.

105. Siekierski interview.

106. Paldiel, *Saving*, 286–87.

107. Denise recalled placing one healthy Jewish couple in a mental institution and the terrifying visits to that place from time to time to verify that this couple were well taken care of. "I had nightmares from these visits, for to get to them, I had to pass a hall where various types of seriously deranged persons were held in chains. I was afraid." Paldiel, *Saving*, 287.

108. Paldiel, *Saving*, 288–89.

109. Paldiel, *Saving*, 294.

110. Siekierski interview. Also, when she left for Israel in 1948 and tried to talk about the war, the young people there countered: "We don't want to hear about this. One must turn another page; it is a stain on the Jewish people. One must erase it from history. For not one Jew had the courage to resist; six million Jews allowed themselves to be led to slaughter like sheep. Let us cross out this page from history." Siekierski, "La Résistance," 181.

111. Poliakov, *L'Auberge*, 126, 148–49.

112. L.M. "Armée," 14; Arnon, "Georges Garel."

113. Avni, "Interview," 22; Arnon, "Georges Garel"; L.M., "Armée," 15; Poznanski, *Juifs*, 474.

114. L.M., "Armée," 15; Arnon, "Georges Garel."

115. Marcou, "Responsables," 15–16. Pierrette Poirier was one of the non-Jewish activists in the Garel network in the Châteauroux (Indre) region. She was responsible for 100 children hidden under assumed names and visited them constantly to check on their upkeep. She was honored by Yad Vashem; YVA-M31.2/1484c. Renée Pauline Gaudefroy was likewise honored by Yad Vashem; YVA-M31.2/1038. She enlisted in the Garel network in September 1943 and was in charge of three regions, Haute Vienne, Creuse, and Corrèze, where she placed or kept tabs on 150 hidden children. Arrested by the French Milice on June 11, 1944, in Limoges, she was brutally interrogated, but managed to escape. She later disappeared without a trace. It is possible that she was mistaken by a French underground unit as a pro-German collaborator and shot. Her death is still a mystery.

116. Arnon, "Georges Garel"; Latour, *Jewish*, 72; L.M., "Armée," 15; Samuel, *Rescuing*, 143. In 1943, Georges Garel married Lily Tager (a.k.a. Elizabeth-Jeanne Tissier), and they bore seven children. Arnon, "Georges Garel"; Latour, *Jewish*, 72.

117. Marrot-Fellag, "Enfants," 1–2; Lazare, "Nice."

118. Marrot-Fellag, "Enfants," 2; Landau and Sigaar, *Le Reseau Marcel*, 4, 19.

119. Landau and Sigaar, *Le Reseau Marcel*, 20–21; Marrot-Fellag, "Enfants," 5; Lazare, "Nice."

120. Landau and Sigaar, *Le Reseau Marcel*, 22. In a 1948 interview, Abadi reported addressing the bishop in a more abrasive tone and pleading for his help for children whose parents were still accused by the bishop's religion of complicity in the death of Jesus. Levesque, "Les Chasseurs d'Enfants"; Marrot-Fellag, "Enfants," 6.

121. Latour, *Jewish*, 71; Marrot-Fellag, "Enfants," 6–7. See Paldiel, *Saving*, 282, for a slightly different version of the conversation between Abadi and Rémond. This commitment by the bishop of Nice must have come as a surprise to Abadi and others who knew him, in light of Rémond's earlier staunch support of the Vichy regime. On June 23, 1940, in a sermon from the pulpit, Rémond urged his audience: "You have heard the voice of Maréchal Pétain. . . . That's enough. One must obey." Possibly by 1943, disenchantment with Pétain and his regime had taken hold of Rémond, as for many earlier supporters of the aged World War I hero, although it should be pointed out that Rémond was at the same time an early critic of the racial policies of the Vichy regime. Wolf Brafman, in the Paul Rémond-file; YVA-M31.2/5061.

122. Landau and Sigaar, *Le Reseau Marcel*, 5, 26; Latour, *Jewish*, 71; Paldiel, *Saving*, 283.

123. Landau and Sigaar, *Le Reseau Marcel*, 4, 31; Marrot-Fellag, "Enfants," 7.

124. Landau and Sigaar, *Le Reseau Marcel*, 5, 23; Marrot-Fellag, "Enfants," 7.

125. Landau and Sigaar, *Le Reseau Marcel*, 28; Marrot-Fellag, "Enfants," 10.

126. Landau and Sigaar, *Le Reseau Marcel*, 28; Marrot-Fellag, "Enfants," 11, 13.

127. Marrot-Fellag, "Enfants," 16. These included the Clarisses convent, the institutes of Sainte-Marthe, Maison Blanche, Don Bosco, Saint-Cerno school, and the Notre-Dame presbytery in Séranon. Marrot-Fellag, "Enfants," 13. Don Bosco admitted only boys; girls were sent to the nearby Sisters of the Nazareth school. Landau and Sigaar, *Le Reseau Marcel*, 27. Other girls found safe haven at the convents of Saint-Vincent de Paul or Jeanne d'Arc in Grasse. Landau and Sigaar, *Le Reseau Marcel*, 30; Marrot-Fellag, "Enfants," 16.

128. Marrot-Fellag, "Enfants," 11.

129. Latour, *Jewish*, 72; Marrot-Fellag, "Enfants," 17.

130. Marrot-Fellag, "Enfants," 11; Landau and Sigaar, *Le Reseau Marcel*, 6; Schor, *Evêque*; Paul Rémond file (YVA-M31.2/5061); Paldiel, *Saving*, 283.

131. Landau and Sigaar, *Le Reseau Marcel*, 36.

132. Landau and Sigaar, *Le Reseau Marcel*, 37.

133. Landau and Sigaar, *Le Reseau Marcel*, 40, 41. The harrowing story of her oppressive mistreatment at the hands of the Nazis appears in a book that Odette Abadi published in 1995, *Terre de Dtresse: Birkenau-Bergen-Belsen*.

134. Marrot-Fellag, "Enfants," 19. Landau and Sigaar, *Le Reseau Marcel*, 43. Paldiel, *Saving*, 284.

135. Marrot-Fellag, "Enfants," 20–22; Landau and Sigaar, *Le Reseau Marcel*, 6.

136. Marrot-Fellag, "Enfants," 24; Paldiel, *Saving*, 284; Landau and Sigaar, *Le Reseau Marcel*, 7.

137. Kahn, *l'Oasis*, 31–32. Much of this account is based on Wikipedia's entry on "Angelo Donati."

138. Latour, *Jewish*, 49; Kahn, *l'Oasis*, 32–33.

139. Kahn, *l'Oasis*, 26–27, 32; Latour, *Jewish*, 149.

140. Kahn, *l'Oasis*, 41.

141. Knout, *Contribution*, 42; Latour, *Jewish*, 152–53.

142. Kahn, *l'Oasis*, 55, 61; Latour, *Jewish*, 152; Knout, *Contribution*, 42–43.

143. Kahn, *l'Oasis*, 67.

144. Marrot-Fellag, "Enfants," 8; Kahn, *l'Oasis*, 77–78.

145. Kahn, *l'Oasis*, 79, 133, 150.

146. Kahn, *l'Oasis*, 79.

147. Banitt, "Interview," 18–20.

148. Banitt, "Interview," 20.
149. Duvernoy, "Andrée Salomon," 2, 5, 8.
150. Avni, "Interview," 9, 12–13; Weill, "Andrée Salomon," 97; Weiss, *Joshko's Children*, 98.
151. Latour, *Jewish*, 41; Avni, "Interview," 10.
152. Samuel, *Rescuing*, 78–81.
153. Fellow colleague Georges Loinger planned the first crossings, out of a base in Grenoble, of children evacuated from OSE homes, with the help of members of Sixth, such as Annemarie Kilies and Elisabeth Hirsch.
154. Avni, "Interview," 20; Delpard, *Les Justes*, 194; Latour, *Jewish*, 70.
155. Weill, "Andrée Salomon," 102.
156. Avni, "Interview," 15, 18–19; Poznanski, *Juifs*, 485.
157. Andrée Salomon reportedly met JDC European head Dr. Joseph Schwartz in Marseilles before he moved his base to Lisbon and subsequently dealt with JDC representative Herbert Katzki
158. Avni, "Interview," 21, 23.
159. Weill, "Andrée Salomon," 91.
160. Delpard, *Les Justes*, 195; Samuel, *Rescuing*, 143.
161. Duvernoy, "Andrée Salomon," 27–30.
162. Duvernoy, "Andrée Salomon," 36.
163. Duvernoy, "Andrée Salomon," 37.
164. Duvernoy, "Andrée Salomon," 38, 41, 43.
165. Duvernoy, "Andrée Salomon," 49–51.
166. Duvernoy, "Andrée Salomon," 117–18.
167. Duvernoy, "Andrée Salomon," 119–24; Delpard, *Les Justes*, 196. Vivette's father did not return from deportation, but her mother survived in hiding. Other members of Julien's family also died in deportation. Samuel, *Rescuing*, 129.
168. Patrick, "Madeleine Dreyfus," 13–14, 16–17, 32.
169. Patrick, "Madeleine Dreyfus," 17. In Chambon, Madeleine Dreyfus was in close contact with Magda Trocmé, wife of the town's pastor, André Trocmé, and many non-Jewish rescuers of Jews, especially Léonie Déléage and her daughter, Eva (today, Phillit). Mrs. Déléage was her chief link in Chambon. The two would leave the children at the Hotel May and then make the rounds from farm to farm. Patrick, "Madeleine Dreyfus," 18. They were both honored by Yad Vashem with the Righteous title. YVA-M31.2/3835.
170. Samuel, *Rescuing*, 95. Eugene Paul and Celie Courtial were awarded the Righteous title by Yad Vashem (YVA-M31.2/12367).
171. Patrick, "Madeleine Dreyfus," 20–21.

172. Patrick, "Madeleine Dreyfus," 24–25, 30–31, 33.

173. Delpard, *Les Justes*, 185. Hirsch, "Böszi," 19.

174. Hammel, *Souviens-toi*, 106–7.

175. Samuel, *Rescuing*, 106–8.

176. Hammel, *Souviens-toi*, 107. Hirsch, "Böszi," 19.

177. Lefenfeld, "Marianne Cohn." Information obtained from the archives of the Centre de Documentation Juive Contemporaine in Paris and the archives of the State of Geneva. This account is also based on the testimonies of Sacha Maidenberg (née Racine), Emmanuel Racine, Léon Herszberg, Sam Jacquet, Helen Stein, Rachel Mandelbaum, Frieda Wattenberg, Georges Loinger, Georges Schneck, and Ruth Fivaz-Silbermann, of the State of Geneva archives.

178. The month of May 1944 was very active in children crossing into Switzerland, as attested by the Geneva canton archival documents: May 22: 30 children; May 23: 21 children; May 25: 19 children; May 26: 35 children. Barras Emile, YVA-M31.2/6755.

179. Barras, YVA-M31.2/6755.

180. Joseph Fournier testimony, as well as that of Alice Lentz, in file of Emile Barras. Fournier was honored as Righteous (YVA-M31.2/6755a), as was Barras (YVA-M31.2/6755). Barras was also honored by the U.S. government for having conveyed downed Allied pilots into Switzerland. Lefenfeld, "Marianne Cohn"; Latour, *Jewish*, 162; Delpard, *Les Justes*, 180.

181. Latour, *Jewish*, 165. In the original French, it reads as follows: "*Je trahirai demain, pas aujourd'hui. Aujourd'hui, arrachez-mois les ongles. Je ne trahirai pas. Vous ne savez pas le bout de mon courage. Mois, je sais. Vous êtes cinq mains dures avec des bagues. Vous avez aux pieds des chaussures avec des clous. Je trahirai demain, pas aujourd'hui, demain. Il me faut la nuit pour me résoudre. Il ne me faut pas moins d'une nuit. Pour renier, pour abjurer, pour trahir. Pour renier mes amis. Pour abjurer le pain et le vin. Pour trahir la vie. Pour mourir. Je trahirai demain, pas aujourd'hui. La lime est sous le carreau, La lime n'est pas pour le bourreau. La lime est pour mon poignet. Aujourd'hui, je n'ai rien à dire. Je trahirai demain.*" Latour, *Jewish*, 164.

182. Latour, *Jewish*, 162–63. Yad Vashem awarded the Righteous title to Jean Deffaugt; YVA-M31.2/178.

183. Lefenfeld, "Marianne Cohn"; Hammel, *Souviens-toi*, 451; Delpard, *Les Justes*, 180.

184. Lazare, "Gamzon," 537; Delpard, *Les Justes*, 183; Hammel, *Souviens-toi*, 322–23, 326–27.

185. Hammel, *Souviens-toi*, 328, 330.

186. Hammel, *Souviens-toi*, 330–31; Lazare, "Gamzon," 538.

187. Hammel, *Souviens-toi*, 331–32; Lazare, "Gamzon," 537–38. To help with this type of work, the EIF had a whistleblower, Gilbert Lesage, who headed a Vichy department dealing with foreigners in the country. A Quaker by belief, he alerted Gamzon on any government plans to raid the EIF farming communities to nab those of foreign origin and turn them over to the Germans for deportation. This indeed took place on August 20, 1942, and thanks to Lesage's warning call, many in the EIF communities were given time to get out and hide in the surrounding woods. Gilbert Lesage was honored by Yad Vashem with the Righteous title; YVA-M31.2/3012.

188. Lazare, "Gamzon," 538.

189. Samuel, *Rescuing*, 55, 138.

190. See, for instance, the testimonies of Jacques Samuel Schmelz and sister Amalia-Rosa Perez, both of whom were taken by Loinger in 1944 to the non-Jewish children home Chateau de la Guette in Villeneuve–St. Denis (Seine et Marne), headed by Germaine Hénaff (later, Le Guillant). She was awarded the Righteous title by Yad Vashem. YVA-M31.2/3395.

191. Latour, *Jewish*, 156–57; Samuel, *Rescuing*, 104; Poznanski, *Juifs*, 484.

192. Latour, *Jewish*, 157.

193. Latour, *Jewish*, 158.

194. Samuel, *Rescuing*, 192, 205–6; Latour, *Jewish*, 157–58.

195. Jackson, "Rescue," 3, 25–27, 31; "Le Rav Zalman Schneersohn"; Schneerson, *Shevet Y'hudah*, 4–5.

196. Schneerson, *Shevet Y'hudah*, 9–10; Poliakov, *Mémoires*, 104; Poliakov, *l'Auberge*, 84–85. Also Centre de Documentation Juive Contemporaine, *Activité des Organisations Juives en France sous l'Occupation* 4:43–44.

197. Jackson, "Rescue," 25; Poliakov, *Mémoires*, 103–4. In his postwar memoirs, Rabbi Schneerson went out of his way to praise Roux's friendly disposition and help to the rabbi and his wards. Schneerson, *Shevet Y'hudah*, 10.

198. Poliakov, *Mémoires*, 100.

199. Jackson, "Rescue," 25; Centre de Documentation Juive Contemporaine, *Activité*.

200. Fontan and Robert du Costal, "Enfants," 49–53; Schneerson, *Shevet Y'hudah*, 11. See the moving story of Bertha and Malka Teitelbaum and their stay with Rabbi Schneerson, both in Marseilles and Dému. Teitelbaum-Schwarz, "How Rabbi," 1, 6, 13, 16.

201. Schneerson, *Shevet Y'hudah*, 12; Centre de Documentation Juive Contemporaine, 45.

202. Jackson, "Rescue," 26; Poliakov, *l'Auberge*, 130; Kountrass, 50. May Charretier, a non-Jewish associate of Poliakov's underground cell, helped out

in the evacuation, as she accompanied each group of out of the city. She later helped some of the children to escape to Switzerland. May Charretier was awarded the Righteous title by Yad Vashem; YVA-M31.2/473. Broussard, "Voiron," 15.

203. Jackson, "Rescue," 26.
204. Fontan and Robert du Costal, "Enfants," 56; Broussard, "Voiron," 15; Kountrass, 51–52; Schneerson, *Shevet Y'hudah,* 13–14; Schneerson, Centre de Documentation, 46; Jackson, "Rescue," 27.
205. Schneerson, *Shevet Y'hudah,* 16. His daughter, Hadassa, married Rabbi Eli Haim Carlebach, the twin brother of the famous rabbi-singer Shlomo Carlebach.
206. Schneerson, *Shevet Y'hudah,* 6–18; "Le Rav Zalman Schneersohn en France," 54.
207. Latour, *Jewish,* 22, 127; Samuel, *Rescuing,* 194.
208. Latour, *Jewish,* 46–48; Lazare, *Rescue,* 153.
209. Latour, *Jewish,* 25; Delpard, *Les Justes,* 179.
210. Hammel, *Souviens-toi,* 330; Latour, *Jewish,* 42. In 1967, after hearing French president Charles de Gaulle criticize the Jewish people for having a "dominating" urge, Weill returned the Légion d'honneur as a form of protest. Delpard, *Les Justes,* 200.
211. Latour, *Jewish,* 42–44; Samuel, *Rescuing,* 143.
212. Latour, Jewish, 83; Delpard, *Les Justes,* 178.
213. Samuel, *Rescuing,* 120–22; Latour, *Jewish,* 156, 199.
214. Siekierski, "Hommage," 10–11; Lazare, "Resistance."
215. Hammel, *Souviens-toi,* 334.
216. Personal interview in 1992 with Jacques and Monique Pulver; Delpard, *Les Justes,* 192; Latour, Jewish, 82. In the 1980s, Jacques Pulver served as a member of the Yad Vashem Commission for the Designation of the Righteous, dealing with French rescuers of Jews.
217. Latour, *Jewish,* 34, 202–3; Hammel, *Souviens-toi,* 280, 283, 327.
218. Latour, *Jewish,* 80–81, 83–85. Roger Braun was awarded the Righteous title by Yad Vashem; YVA-M31.2/762.
219. Latour, *Jewish,* 155; Hammel, *Souviens-toi,* 199–200.
220. Hammel, *Souviens-toi,* 196.
221. Latour, *Jewish,* 90; Delpard, *Les Justes,* 184; Hammel, *Souviens-toi,* 424.
222. Hammel, *Souviens-toi,* 422–23, 425–26; Delpard, *Les Justes,* 189.
223. Latour, *Jewish,* 161–62; Siekierski, "La Résistance," 10.
224. Latour, *Jewish,* 90–93, 155.
225. Latour, *Jewish,* 24–25, 102, 204; Delpard, *Les Justes,* 187.
226. Delpard, *Les Justes,* 191.

227. Latour, *Jewish*, 59.
228. Latour, *Jewish*, 98–99; Delpard, *Les Justes*, 192.
229. Delpard, *Les Justes*, 181; Latour, *Jewish*, 125; Hammel, *Souviens-toi*, 198; Bauer, *American*, 256, 258. Each time a Jewish resistance group needed money, Jefoykin's assistant, Maurice Brener, was the man approached, and he proved his mettle. After the war, he stated: "I had considered myself French through and through—not until the persecutions did I realize I was a Jew." Latour, *Jewish*, 126.
230. Latour, *Jewish*, 125; Hammel, *Souviens-toi*, 198; Bauer, *American*, 256, 258.
231. Marcou, "Responsables," 16.
232. Poznanski, *Juifs*, 483; Delpard, *Les Justes*, 189.
233. Delpard, *Les Justes*, 193–94.
234. Delpard, *Les Justes*, 185. The following rescue activists also merit mention: Lucien Fayman ("Hibou"), active in the Sixth, was deported to Buchenwald; he survived. Margot Kahn-Cohn, affiliated with the Yeshurun Orthodox youth movement, was sent by Andrée Salomon to Lyon, where Madeleine Dreyfus assigned her the task of finding safe houses for young Jews, accompanying children to their host families, and visiting the former residents of the children's home, who were now in hiding. Ruth Lambert, a social worker in the Gurs camp, helped to free children from that camp. Lucien Lazare, born in Strasbourg, was first in the EIF, and later joined the Sixth. He also fought within the ranks of the Haguenau Company. Later in Israel, he became a leading member of the Yad Vashem's Commission for the Designation of the Righteous, dealing specifically with French cases of rescue. He authored several studies on rescue in France, including the French-version encyclopedia of Frenchmen honored with the title of Righteous Among the Nations. Rachel Lifchitz, a social worker, assisted the Women Zionist organization (WIZO) to find sheltering places for children, especially in the Chavagnes en Paillers (Vendée) region. Germaine Masour worked for the Garel network in Limoges, accompanying children in groups of eight to twelve to their hiding places. She later wrote *Mes vingt ans à l'OSE* (My Twenty Years in the OSE). Lise Schlanger-Hanau, training as a nurse, was asked by Andrée Salomon in 1942 to hurry to Rivesaltes camp and serve as a nurse for children there. Watching Jews boarding buses for departure to Drancy, she snatched a small boy and hurriedly hid him and two other children and then took them to an OSE-operated children home. Jacques Waintraub, active in Nice in fabricating false documents, also participated in the rescue of children heading to Switzerland. Arrested and tortured, he disappeared without a trace. Simone Weil-Lipman, an OSE social worker,

entered the Rivesaltes internment camp to minister to the sick and despairing. Joining the OSE's Garel network, she was in charge of the Chateauroux region, under the assumed name of Simone Werlin. With a team of several workers she organized the clandestine placement and supervision of some 350 children. Ninon Weyl-Haït was one of Andrée Salomon's volunteers in the Gurs and Rivesaltes camps and participated in various rescue efforts of those interned there. Delpard, *Les Justes*, 181, 187–88, 199; Latour, *Jewish*, 70; Samuel, *Rescuing*, 193; Hammel, *Souviens-toi*, 196–97; Picard, "Lise Hanau," 5–6; http://jwa.org/encyclopedia/article/resistance-jewish-organizations-in-france-1940-1944. Lazare, "Resistance."

235. Hammel, *Souviens-toi*, 267.

236. Duvernoy, "Elie Bloch," 7, 8; Hammel, *Souviens-toi*, 264–70. After Bloch's arrest, his associates Miss Breidick and Miss Rosenbaum continued with Father Fleury to aid Jews. Father Jean Fleury was honored by Yad Vashem with the Righteous title; YVA-M31.2/57.

8. Belgium

1. Michman, "Belgium," 160.
2. Michman, "Belgium," 164.
3. Michman, "Belgium," 164.
4. Michman, "Belgium," 162–63.
5. Michman, "Belgium," 162–64.
6. Michman, "Belgium," 162.
7. Gutman *Encyclopedia*, 1799.
8. An estimated 80,000 non-Jews went into hiding to avoid the forced-labor draft. Some 70,000 people are estimated to have been in the resistance, out of a total population of 8 million. Michman, "Belgium," 165.
9. Michman, "Belgium," 165.
10. Michman, "Belgium," 165, 167.
11. The participants included Abusz Werber, of the Zionist Poalei Zion Left movement, Maurice Mandelbaum (Solidarité Juive), Benjamin Nykerk, Eugene Hellendael, and Albert Rotkel, employed at the AJB, as well as the sole non-Jewish Emile Hambresin, a left-wing Catholic journalist with the FI. Seven of these eight persons represented various factions of Jewish political life in prewar Belgium, with only the Jewish Socialist Bund organization refusing to be a part, since it meant being associated with Jewish communists who were also represented in the CDJ, their most hated rivals. Of the 8 founding members, 6 were eventually arrested and deported (Rotkel, Hellendael, Hambresin, Jospa, Nykerk, Mandelbaum), with only Jospa and Mandelbaum as sole survivors. Steinberg, *Comité*, 69–70.

12. Steinberg, *Comité*, 71, 76.

13. Yvonne Nèvejean was awarded the Righteous title by Yad Vashem; YVA-M31.2/99.

14. Michman, "Belgium," 167; Steinberg, *Comité*, 72.

15. When Heiber was arrested in May 1943, the children's department was taken over by Yvonne (Hava) Jospa, wife of Ghert Jospa; later, by Roger van Praag; then Sala Allard, wife of Prof. Emile Allard. Steinberg, *Comité*, 75; Heiber, "Enfants," 2.

16. Steinberg, *Comité*, 77. These two Yiddish prints endorsed the views of the Zionist-Socialist organizations. Steinberg, *Comité*, 78.

17. Steinberg, *Comité*, 77; Jospa, "Belgian," 4–7.

18. Steinberg, *Comité*, 119–20. CDJ leadership also included Ghert Jospa, Abusz Werber, Eugène Roske (representing the Orthodox community), Eugène Hellendael, Chaim Perelman, Maurice Heiber, Benjamin Nykerk (a Dutch Zionist), Roger Van Praag, Maurice Bolle (Dutch businessman), Maurice Mandelbaum and Richard Volman, of *Solidarité Juive*. CDJ affiliate leaders in others cities were: in Liège—A. Wolf, Idel Steinberg, Jacques Pailloucq; Antwerp—Léopold Flam, Istinne, Mrs. Casterman, and Manaster; and Charleroi—Max Katz, Sem Makowski, Pinkes Broder and Dr. Bejarski. Jospa, "Belgian," 3.

19. Jules Dubois-Pélerin was honored as a Righteous by Yad Vashem, YVA-M31.2/649; Michman, "Belgium," 108; Steinberg, *Comité*, 115.

20. Steinberg, *Comité*. 10–11.

21. Steinberg, *Comité*, 116.

22. Steinberg, *Comité*, 129. Moszek Aron Rakower ("Vladek") the leader of this group was arrested and shot on January 6, 1943. Cécile Glineur, "L'impasse des Représentants Officiels." *Regards*, Brussels, Belgium, No. 467, February 2000, 23.

23. Michman, "Belgium," 167. Of the 26,500 Jews who were deported from Mechelen, the total number of escapees was 571; of these, 539 escaped from transports #16 and #20.

24. Steinberg, *Comité*, 100. Both Andrée Geulen and Suzanne Moens were honored with the Righteous title by Yad Vashem. Geulen, YVA-M31.2/4323; Moens, YVA-M31.2/7474.

25. Heiber, "Enfants," 2–3.

26. Heiber, "Enfants," 4; Steinberg, *Comité*, 83, 87.

27. Heiber, "Enfants," 4.

28. Heiber, "Enfants," 3; Michman, *Encyclopedia*, 136. Christine Hendrickx-Duchaine was awarded the Righteous title by Yad Vashem, also for arranging sheltering places for Jewish children on the run; YVA-M31.2/1840c.

29. Geulen-Herscovici, "Rescue" 1; Heiber, "Enfants," 5; Steinberg, *Comité*, 84.

30. Steinberg, *Comité*, 94–95. Léon Platteau was honored with the Righteous title by Yad Vashem for his role in saving many other Jews from deportation; YVA-M31.2/229. Michman *Encyclopedia*, 209–10. In October 1943, Ferdman again was instrumental in saving the lives of 18 Jewish children held in the Mechelen/Malines detention camp, who were slated for deportation, by paying a substantial ransom to Gestapo officer Erdman, to prevent the children's deportation. Steinberg, *Comité*, 95.

31. According to Lucien Steinberg and Maurice Heiber. Steinberg, *Comité*, 89; Heiber, "Enfants," 5.

32. Steinberg, "Jewish," 606; Wikipedia, "Comité de Défense des Juifs."

33. Jospa, "Belgian," 1.

34. Jospa, "Belgian," 2.

35. Geulen-Herscovici, "Rescue," 1. Steinberg, *Comité*, 86. Before the war, Yvonne Jospa had studied and done social work, especially with refugees of the Spanish Civil War.

36. Steinberg, *Comité*, 34.

37. Steinberg, *Comité*, 35, 37.

38. Steinberg, *Comité*, 38.

39. Steinberg, *Comité*, 40.

40. Steinberg, *Comité*, 41–43, 49.

41. Steinberg, *Comité*, 62.

42. Jospa, "Belgian," 71.

43. Steinberg, *Comité*, 68.

44. Steinberg, *Comité*, 77, 92–93.

45. Steinberg, *Comité*, 74, 100.

46. Steinberg, *Comité*, 67.

47. Steinberg, *Comité*, 116–17.

48. Steinberg, *Comité*, 117–18.

49. Fela Perlman's mother and stepfather, who remained in Poland, were deported from the Łódz ghetto to Auschwitz in October 1941, where they perished. Based on private communication to the author by Noemi Mattis, daughter of Chaim and Fela Perelman.

50. Steinberg, *Comité*, 66–67.

51. Jeanne Daman was honored by Yad Vashem as a Righteous; YVA-M31.2/560.

52. Steinberg, *Comité*, 67, 84, 92, 122. Also, Noemi Mattis to Paldiel.

53. Noemi Mattis to the author. According to historian Lucien Steinberg, Ghert Jospa first turned to Fela when he wanted to enlist her husband to the idea of the CDJ creation, and she seemed to have played a role in persuading Chaim to become involved. Steinberg, *Comité*, 67.

54. Noemi Mattis to Paldiel. Both rescuers of Noemi Mattis—Emile Bleeckx

and Lucie Moniez—were honored with the Righteous title by Yad Vashem, YVA-M31.2/1840b & d.

55. Steinberg *Comité*, 49, 69.
56. In his teachings and writings, Perelman rejected the idea that value judgments are arbitrary and lack rational justification, but upheld that they are rather based on a priori universal principles.
57. Steinberg, *Comité*, 74, 96.
58. Heiber, "Enfants," 6.
59. Heiber, "Enfants," 6.
60. Heiber, "Enfants," 8.
61. Heiber, "Enfants," 9–10.
62. Heiber, "Enfants," 14–15, 19. Steinberg, *Comité*, 142. His wife, Esta Heiber ("Madame Pascal"), also helped out by transferring the funds received by her husband from secret channels to the sheltering families and institutions that needed them. Steinberg, Comité, 99; Heiber, "Enfants," 15.
63. Sterno, "Hiding," 1–3.
64. Sterno, "Hiding," 15.
65. Sterno, "Hiding," 14–15.
66. Sterno, "Hiding," 9–10.
67. In her postwar account, Ida Sterno noted that a medical report of July 1945 found that among 539 children living with their families or with hosts, there were 15 cases of pre-tuberculosis; 61—bowed legs due to vitamin D deficiency; 96—much loss of weight; 30—serious physical weakness; and 6—abnormal curvature of the spine. Sterno, "Hiding," 36.
68. Sterno, "Hiding," 14.
69. Sterno, "Hiding," 28.
70. Sterno, "Hiding," 29.
71. Sterno, "Hiding," 30.
72. Sterno, "Hiding," 32.
73. Sterno, "Hiding," 33–34.
74. Heiber, "Enfants," 18; Steinberg, *Comité*, 49, 75, 124.
75. Steinberg, *Comité*, 75.
76. Heiber, "Enfants," 19; Geulen-Herscovici, "Rescue," 2; Steinberg, *Comité*, 151.
77. Heiber, "Enfants," 19.
78. Steinberg, *Comité*, 149–50.
79. Steinberg, *Comité*, 102, 153–55, 159; Heiber, Enfants," 18. Abbé Joseph André was awarded the Righteous title by Yad Vashem; YVA-M31.2/486. Michman Dan, *Encyclopedia*, 36–37.
80. Steinberg, *Comité*, 118–19.
81. Heiber, "Enfants," 18.

82. Heiber, "Enfants," 18.

83. Jospa, "Belgian," 28–29.

84. Jospa, "Belgian," 30–31.

85. Steinberg, *Comité,* 85, 93, 97–98.

86. Steinberg, *Comité,* 121–22.

87. Steinberg, *Comité,* 91–92; Michman Dan, *Encyclopedia-Righteous;* 194–95. After the war, her married name was Yvonne Feyerick-Nèvejean.

88. Geulen-Herscovici, "Rescue"; Michman Dan, *Encyclopedia,* 128–29. After the war she married Charles Herscovici, a Holocaust survivor. As of January 1, 2016, 1,707 non-Jewish Belgian men and women had been listed by Yad Vashem as Righteous.

89. Steinberg, *Comité,* 105, 107–8, 113, 151.

90. Brachfeld, "Jews," 14.

91. Paldiel, "From," 5.

92. Brachfeld, "Jews," 15, based on Sister Marie-Amélie's statement in YVA 033/6722.

93. Sara-Simone Stolnicki (today Schwarz) was one of the three missing girls. She told Sylvain Brachfeld that she and the two others had been baptized as Catholics, and therefore attended religious instructions outside the convent. Brachfeld, "Jews," 14.

94. Sterno, "Hiding," 25–26.

95. Brachfeld, "Jews," 14.

96. Paldiel, "From," 5.

97. Paldiel, "From," 5.

98. Paldiel, "From," 5.

99. Steinberg, *Comité,* 142.

100. Brachfeld, "Jews," 15.

101. There is some uncertainty on the actual number of children carried off. Holocaust chronicler of Belgium, Sylvain Brachfeld, who corresponded with some of the raiding party and the children, wrote that before the Paul Halter group raided the place, the mothers of two girls (Margot Herbst and Clara Scheinok) had come in a hurry to take them away. Another girl, Sara-Simone Stolnicki, was replaced by her older and adult sister Gutki Stolnicki, who was not on the Gestapo list, and Sara-Simone sped off to her mother's hiding place in Brussels. That would leave twelve girls snatched away to safety. Sister Marie Amélie, Floris Desmedt, Andrée Ermel and her parents, Marcel and Céline Ermel (where one of the children was placed), were awarded the Righteous title by Yad Vashem, YVA-M31.2/9552. Paldiel, "From," 5; Milgram, *Encyclopedia,* 54. In 1978, Father Jan Bruylandts was awarded the Righteous title; YVA-M31.2/1349.

102. Steinberg, *Comité,* 137.

103. Jospa, "Belgian," 13–14.

104. Steinberg, *Comité,* 132–35, 141.

105. Jospa, "Belgian," 15.

106. Maistriau, YVA-M31.2/6174.

107. Jospa, "Belgian," 16–24.

108. Jospa, "Belgian," 25.

109. Jospa, "Belgian," 27; Steinberg, *Comité,* 141; Delpart, *Les Justes,* 203–4.

110. Roger van Praag, of the CDJ, tried to plan another similar attack; this time, targeting convoy number 23, that left on January 14, 1944. He had smuggled into the Mechelen/Malines camp, but the plan had to be aborted because of lack of supporting help. Steinberg, *Comité,* 141. One of the imponderables of Jewish behavior during the Holocaust is the lack of any similar attempt by Jewish combat groups, in France, and Eastern European countries to derail deportations trains, while instead quite active in sabotaging German military convoys and targeting military personnel.

9. The Netherlands

1. Michman, "Netherlands," 1045.

2. Michman, "Netherlands," 1046.

3. Michman, "Netherlands," 1047.

4. Michman, "Netherlands," 1050–51.

5. Michman, "Netherlands," 1049.

6. Michman, "Netherlands," 1048.

7. Michman, "Netherlands," 1051.

8. Michman, "Netherlands," 1052.

9. Michman, "Netherlands," 1053. In an exceptional move, 220 Dutch Jews were exchanged in 1944 for German residents in Palestine, under an agreement with the British.

10. Michman, "Netherlands," 1055.

11. As of January 1, 2016, 5,516 non-Jewish Dutch rescuers were listed as Righteous by Yad Vashem.

12. After the war, the Jewish community contested the Dutch government's decision not to return to the Jewish community some 3,500 orphans who were sheltered by non-Jewish rescuers. After a long and bitter struggle, 1,540 children were restored to their families or Jewish guardianship, while 360 children remained with non-Jewish families. This has remained a stain on the Dutch record, the only postwar country to have gone out of its way to prevent Jewish children from being returned to their people. Michman, "Netherlands," 1056.

13. Schellekens, "Op Zoek," 5.

14. Schellekens, "Op Zoek," 7–9.

15. Walter's two younger brothers, Karl and Alfred, were married to gentile women, and because of Nazi laws at the time for Jews in mixed marriages, they were not deported, and they survived.

16. Schellekens, "Op Zoek," 17.

17. It is estimated that some 100,000 passed through its gates on their way to the death camps. Trains left every Tuesday, with up to 3,000 people on board.

18. Flim, "Omdat," 7, 40n1; Schellekens, "Op Zoek," 25–27; testimony of Lisette Lamon, in the author's file of Süskind.

19. Schellekens, "Op Zoek,"15; Lamon testimony.

20. Schellekens, "Op Zoek," 15.

21. Schellekens, "Op Zoek," 26–27.

22. Schellekens, "Op Zoek," 27.

23. Schellekens, "Op Zoek," 28–29.

24. Hans Heilbut, Leo de Wolff, Hans Steinitz, and Raphäel (Felix) Halverstad are some of the Jews who worked under Sluzker and Süskind. Schellekens, "Op Zoek," 29–32; Flim, "Omdat," 42n54.

25. Johannes Houwink ten Cate and Bert Jan Flim (who made a study of the rescue of Jewish children), in a private communication to the author.

26. Schellekens, "Op Zoek," 33–36.

27. Schellekens, "Op Zoek," 35, based on Grete Weil, *Mijn Zuster Antigone*, 75.

28. Johannes Houwink ten Cate, private communication to Paldiel.

29. Flim, "Omdat," 16.

30. Schellekens, "Op Zoek," 39.

31. Schellekens, "Op Zoek," 39.

32. Schellekens, "Op Zoek," 21–23.

33. Schellekens, "Op Zoek," 34.

34. Schellekens, "Op Zoek," 38.

35. Flim, "Omdat," 17.

36. Schellekens, "Op Zoek," 37.

37. David, "Quiet," 20–38. People helped to escape from the Dutch Theater included Betsy Ehrlich, born 1931, who wrote after the war: "In October 1942, I was arrested with my family. I was held for three weeks at the Theater. To my luck, and thanks to the intervention effort of Mr. Walter Süskind, of the Jewish council, I was freed after three weeks." Her Dutch rescuer, Jan Westbroek, later earned the Righteous title by Yad Vashem (YVA-M31.2/973). Deborah Feivel was saved by Süskind and later hidden by Menno Goudberg, who was also honored by Yad Vashem YVA-M31.2/564). As for Meijer Groen and his wife, Süskind had the S (for *strafe*, punish-

ment) removed from their card before they were moved to Westerbork, thus sparing them from "special treatment," that is, harsher incarceration conditions there. Schellekens, "Op Zoek," 36–37.

38. Schellekens, "Op Zoek," 32–33.
39. Schellekens, "Op Zoek," 45.
40. Schellekens, "Op Zoek," 46.
41. Schellekens, "Op Zoek," 47–50. Joop Woortman was part of a clandestine Dutch organization, NV, created for the single purpose of saving Jewish children. Woortman and others in the NV group were awarded the Righteous title by Yad Vashem. Joop Woortman, YVA-M31.2/2083L.
42. Schellekens, "Op Zoek," 53; Flim, "Omdat," 7–8.
43. Schellekens, "Op Zoek," 53.
44. Schellekens, "Op Zoek," 53–54.
45. Groups such as the Amsterdam student group headed by Pieter Meerburg, or the Utrecht Student Children Committee, and especially the so-called NV group (Ltd)–"Nameless Cooperative Group," formed by the foursome, Joop Woortman, the brothers Jaap and Gerhard Musch, and Dick Groenewegen van Wijk.
46. Flim, "Omdat," 26–30; Schellekens, "Op Zoek," 54.
47. Lamon testimony, Paldiel, Walter Süskind; Ommeren and Scherphuis, "De Crèche," 9–10.
48. Flim, "Omdat," 16–17. Sometimes children would be made to escape when a tram passed by on Plantage Middenlaan, the street that separated the theater from the crèche and blocked the view of the German guard across the street, in front of the theater. A child and resistance worker then jumped on the tram and disappeared. As told by crèche nurse Sammy Glasoog: "When we heard the tram coming . . . we slipped out, each carrying a heavy child. And we ran along the tram so that the guard couldn't see us. At the next corner there was a stop, and we could get in. The whole tram started laughing . . . but no one betrayed us." Flim, "Omdat," 11.
49. Schellekens, "Op Zoek," 55–56.
50. Flim, "Omdat," 14.
51. Eventually, after May 1943, when the crèche became increasingly filled, children from the crèche stayed inside the teacher training college in the afternoon, and beds were brought in for them. This led to the empty classroom in the teacher training college to be used as an escape conduit. Flim, "Omdat," 19–20. Johan van Hulst as well as a host of other non-Jewish rescue activists who cooperated with the Süskind team in rescuing Jews were honored with the Yad Vashem Righteous title. These include Johan van Hulst (YVA-M31.2/588, Joop Woortman (YVA-M31.2/2083L),

Gesina van der Molen (YVA-M31.2/8228), Hester Baracs-van Lennep (YVA-M31.2/2018), Pieter Meerburg (YVA-M31.2/862), Jaap and Gerard Musch (YVA-M31.2/2083a & e); Dick Groenewegen-van Dijk (YVA-M31.2/2083c), Piet Vermeer (YVA-M31.2/2083j), Annie Marie van Verschuer (YVA-M31.2/2083n), Gisela Sohnlein (YVA-M31.2/3853a), Hetty Voute (YVA-M31.2/3853), Nico Dohmen (YVA-M31.2/2878), and Hanna van de Voort (YVA-M31.2/966).

52. Flim, "Omdat," 32.

53. Flim, "Omdat," 2, 4, 39, 44; Schellekens, "Op Zoek," 59; Ommeren and Scherphuis, "De Crèche," 2.

54. Schellekens, "Op Zoek," 60.

55. Schellekens, "Op Zoek," 63; Flim "Omdat," 35.

56. Schellekens, "Op Zoek," 66.

57. Schellekens, "Op Zoek," 70–73.

58. Arnold, "Walter Süskind: Quiet Hero of the Holocaust." *Boston Globe,* October 21, 1990.

59. Benjamin, *They Were,* 4, 8, 9, 10–12.

60. Benjamin, *They Were,* 12–14.

61. Benjamin, *They Were,* 17–19.

62. Benjamin, *They Were,* 21–24, 30–31. A different fate awaited the religious pioneering movement, known as *Bachad,* a movement that strongly opposed dipping in the underground. Most of its 86 members were deported after they dutifully reported to the summons. Benjamin, *They Were,* 25. As for the more religious Agudah pioneering movement, of the 52 members in the Enschede training center, 27 succeeded in finding hiding places for themselves, mostly thanks to the assistance of a Christian underground group led by Reverend Leendert Overduin, and they were also actively supported by several members of the Jewish community in Enschede. Of the 27 in hiding, 15 survived by not being discovered. As for the 25 deported, only 8 survived. Benjamin, *They Were,* 27. Reverend Leendert Overduin was awarded the Righteous title by Yad Vashem; YVA-M31.2/805.

63. "Jewish Resistance in Holland: Group Westerweel and Hachshara;"

64. Latour, *Jewish,* 109–10. After Joachim Simon's death, the Westerweel group added Kurt Reilinger ("Nanno") to its illegal escape team. Reilinger, born in Stuttgart in 1917, had risen to become one the leaders of the Hechalutz movement and had helped a pioneering group from one of its centers to escape to Belgium. He presently worked out of Paris, where he was arrested in April 1944 and deported to Buchenwald, where he survived.

65. The documents were stolen earlier, in an unbelievably risky undertaking,

by Paula Kaufmann, a Hechalutz member who for a time worked as a secretary in the Paris Gestapo office.

66. Lazare, *Rescue,* 169, 285–86; Latour, *Jewish,* 110–12, 173–74.

67. Flörsheim, *He Who,* 31, 42–45, 47–48, 56.

68. "Sophie Yaari Tells Her Story."

69. "Sophie Yaari Tells Her Story."

70. "Sophie Yaari Tells Her Story."

71. "Sophie Yaari Tells Her Story."

72. Joop Westerweel was executed by the Germans on Dutch soil; his wife, Wilhelmina, also arrested, survived the hardships and torments of the Ravensbrück concentration camp. Both were honored by Yad Vashem with the Righteous title in 1963; YVA-M31.2/32.

73. Meyer-Dettum *Max Windmüller.*

74. Leons, *A Mitzwa,* 5, 6.

75. Leons, *A Mitzwa,* 7–8.

76. Leons, *A Mitzwa,* 8.

77. Leons, *A Mitzwa,* 9.

78. Leons, *A Mitzwa,* 13, 14, 42. Leons ran into some trouble when at church services, which he attended like everyone else in the village, the pastor turned to John 1:1–7 in the New Testament, followed by the singing of Psalm 23:1–2 in the Hebrew Bible. Leons felt terribly embarrassed that as a supposedly dyed-in-the wool Calvinist, fully familiar with these passages, he had no inkling where to find them, having never before opened a Bible. Queried by others why he was not joining them in the singing of the Psalm, he answered: "Because they never sing it in my church." It is not known whether that answer stilled their query. Leons, *A Mitzwa,* 13.

79. Leons, *A Mitzwa,* 18–19.

80. Leons, *A Mitzwa,* 16.

81. Leons, *A Mitzwa,* 17.

82. Leons, *A Mitzwa,* 20–21, 41.

83. Leons, *A Mitzwa,* 27.

84. Leons, *A Mitzwa,* 29.

85. Leons, *A Mitzwa,* 30.

86. Leons, *A Mitzwa,* 32.

87. Leons, *A Mitzwa,* 33. There was an additional encounter worth telling that could have ended badly but with good luck and Jewish chutzpah ended well. It happened when Max Leons took an eight-year-old Jewish boy from Nieuw Amsterdam to Nieuwlande, with the boy strapped on the back seat of a bicycle. On the road, Leons heard someone in the car behind him shout, "Halt!" He pretended not to have heard and peddled on. Soon

enough, the vehicle from behind overtook him, and there were four of the pro-German Landwacht militia, armed with shotguns. They kicked up a row, demanding to know why he had not stopped when so ordered? Leons explained that with the unusually heavy wind blowing in his ears at the time, he had not heard them. One of the militiamen shone his flashlight at the boy. "Who is that?" Leons answered, "That's my nephew." As they continued to inspect the bicycle, Leons blurted out, "Gentlemen, you'll have to excuse me. I must go on to be home in Hoogeveen before curfew. Good evening," and he sped off, leaving them a bit bewildered. The trick had worked. It had been another lucky break! Leons, *A Mitzwa*, 36.

88. Leons, *A Mitzwa*, 17.
89. Leons, *A Mitzwa*, 38.
90. Leons, *A Mitzwa*, 39–40.
91. Arnold Douwes, YVA-M31.2/65.
92. Michman and Flim, "Verduin, Leendert," 584.
93. The Holocaust—Lest We Forget, "Westerbork Liberation—Samuel Schrijver."

10. Toward Palestine

1. Ofer, "Rescue," 160–61, 168.
2. Ofer, "Rescue," 99, 100. The German Helmut Wohlthat (who in 1939 negotiated with the American George Rublee on Jewish migration affairs) announced that he had been told in London that Palestine could absorb another million or so Jews. If these were the numbers envisaged by Nazi policy makers, Jewish emigration to Palestine must surely have been taken very seriously by them, at least in 1939. Ofer, "Rescue," 161.
3. *Aliyah*, in Hebrew as a sole word, means "immigration but only to Eretz Israel," then still Palestine. "Bet" or "B" refers to illegal to contrast with legal immigration. Ofer, "Aliya Bet," 22–23.
4. Ofer, "Rescue," 159–60.
5. Ofer, *Escaping*, 101.
6. Ofer, "Rescue," 161–62; Ofer, *Escaping*, 98. In this, the SS was at odds with the German Foreign Office, which warned against immigration to Palestine for fear of creating a Jewish Vatican, the headquarters of a purported Jewish conspiracy to conquer the world. Ofer, *Escaping*, 99.
7. Ofer, *Escaping*, 102.
8. Ofer, *Escaping*, 162–63.
9. Ofer, *Escaping*, 28–31.
10. Avriel, *Open*, 35.
11. Ofer, *Escaping*, 69–70.

12. Ofer, *Escaping*, 11, 13, 16–17. The Zionists, through their clandestine Mossad organizations, and the Revisionists also differed over the composition of the prospective immigrants: quantity or quality; pioneering youth or everyone in need. The Revisionists held on to the principle of *aliyah* "for all who need it"—that is, a nonselective effort, in contrast to the Hechalutz-Mossad, who opted for Zionist-indoctrinated youth. Ofer, *Escaping*, 14, 70–71; Ofer, "Rescue," 160.

13. Ofer, *Escaping*, 72, 79, 81, 85.

14. Ofer, *Escaping*, 86–87; Ofer, "Rescue," 181.

15. Ofer, *Escaping*, 103; Ofer, "Rescue," 163–64.

16. Ofer, "Rescue," 164–65. As a young man Storfer had gone through a certain conversion process to Catholicism, but he was regarded as "fully" Jewish by the Nazis, based on the 1935 Nuremberg laws. Lustiger, "Kommerzialrat."

17. Ofer, "Rescue," 162, 165.

18. Ofer, "Rescue," 166.

19. Ofer, *Escaping*, 105.

20. Ofer, *Escaping*, 106–7; Ofer, "Rescue," 166–67, 169.

21. Ofer, "Rescue," 165–67; Wikipedia, "Berthold Storfer."

22. Ofer, "Rescue," 166.

23. Ofer, "Rescue," 167–68, 170.

24. Ofer, *Escaping*, 46, 108; Ofer, "Rescue," 171.

25. Ofer, *Escaping*, 110; Ofer, "Rescue," 173.

26. Ofer, *Escaping*, 175.

27. Ofer, *Escaping*, 109, 114; Ofer, "Rescue," 164.

28. Ofer, *Escaping*, 115, 117–18.

29. Ofer, *Escaping*, 119.

30. Ofer, "Rescue," 177; Ofer, *Escaping*, 120–21.

31. Ofer, "Rescue," 177; Ofer, *Escaping*, 33–34, 36, 123.

32. Ofer, *Escaping*, 123–24; Ofer, "Rescue," 170, 177.

33. Ofer, "Rescue," 177.

34. Ofer, "Rescue," 177.

35. Ofer, "Rescue," 104.

36. Ofer, *Escaping*, 123–25.

37. Langbein, *People*, 421–422.

38. Avriel, *Open*, 15. Actually, already in 1934 the Hechalutz tried its hand at illegal immigration, when it organized the *Velos* ship that sailed without official Zionist sanction. The boat was refitted to accommodate 340 mostly Polish Jews and arrived in Palestine without being detected. A second sailing proved less successful and was sighted by the British and forced back to sea, where it

wandered from one port to another until the Polish government allowed the people to return. Four years would pass before Hechalutz attempted another sailing of illegal immigrants to Palestine. Ofer, *Escaping*, 10; Avriel, *Open*, 32.

39. Avriel, *Open*, 134–35.
40. Avriel, *Open*, 37–38.
41. Avriel, *Open*, 39, 42, 43.
42. Avriel, *Open*, 44.
43. Avriel, *Open*, 45.
44. Avriel, *Open*, 48, 51–52.
45. Avriel, *Open*, 53.
46. Avriel, *Open*, 55–57, 59, 61.
47. Avriel, *Open*, 67.
48. Avriel, *Open*, 71.
49. Avriel, *Open*, 47.
50. Avriel, *Open*, 72–73.
51. Avriel, *Open*, 74–75.
52. Avriel, *Open*, 76–77.
53. Avriel, *Open*, 86.
54. Avriel, *Open*, 89.
55. Avriel, *Open*, 90.
56. Avriel, *Open*, 91.
57. Avriel, *Open*, 82.
58. Avriel, *Open*, 92–95, 97.
59. Avriel, *Open*, 108.
60. Ofer, *Escaping*, 91, 93–94.
61. Ofer, *Escaping*, 95–97.
62. Ofer, *Escaping*, 73.
63. Ofer, *Escaping*, 82–84. For more on Wilhelm Perl's exploits, see his book, *Four-Front War*.
64. Ofer, *Escaping*, 136; Ofer, "Rescue," 163.
65. Ofer, *Escaping*, 133–35, 139.
66. Ofer, *Escaping*, 77.
67. Ofer, *Escaping*, 77.
68. Ofer, *Escaping*, 240–41.
69. Ofer, *Escaping*, 134–35.
70. Ofer, *Escaping*, 137. Weizmann himself proposed that the refugee boats be intercepted at sea and sent to another colony in order to prevent the deportation of Jews from Palestine itself. Stephen Wise cabled a strongly worded message to the British embassy in Washington: "It would be hell if this happens. . . . The Jews of the USA will feel it an outrage." Ofer, *Escaping*, 141.

71. Avriel, *Open*, 109.

72. Avriel, *Open,* 108–9, 112, 118.

73. Ofer, *Escaping*, 144.

74. Ofer, *Escaping*, 183, 192.

75. Ofer, *Escaping*, 149–65.

76. Ofer, *Escaping*, 218–19, 235–37.

77. Ofer, *Escaping*, 185.

78. Ofer, *Escaping*, 167.

79. Ofer, *Escaping*, 169–72.

80. Ofer, *Escaping*, 50–67; Ofer, "Rescue," 174; Avriel, *Open*, 133–34.

81. Ofer, *Escaping,* 224.

82. Ofer, *Escaping*, 224–26.

83. Ofer, *Escaping*, 175, 187–88.

84. Ofer, *Escaping*, 218, 239, 283–84.

85. Wikipedia, "Jews in Turkey."

86. Ofer, *Escaping,* 211.

87. Ofer, *Escaping*, 229, 250, 277, 284, 286.

88. Ofer, *Escaping*, 195–97, 260, 264; Avriel, *Open*, 170–71.

89. Avriel, *Open*, 118–19, 123, 148, 150–51.

90. USHMM, "Claude Lanzmann Interview with Ehud Avriel," 7–8.

91. USHMM, "Claude Lanzmann Interview with Ehud Avriel," 8, 10–11; Avriel, *Open*, 138.

92. Avriel, *Open*, 159–60.

93. Avriel, *Open*, 141–42.

94. Ofer, *Escaping*, 271.

95. Ofer, *Escaping*, 275–77.

96. Ofer, *Escaping*, 270.

97. Ofer, *Escaping*, 272.

98. Ofer, *Escaping*, 273–74.

99. Ofer, *Escaping*, 277.

100. Ofer, *Escaping*, 280–81.

101. Ofer, "Rescue," 159.

102. Another 1,200 embarked on this journey but never completed it alive, dying on the *Salvador*, the *Struma*, the *Mefkura*, and the small boats. Ofer, *Escaping*, 14, 318.

11. Switzerland

1. Häsler, *Lifeboat*, 20.

2. Friedenson and Kranzler, *Heroine*, 33. According to Friedenson and Kranzler (31), the Jewish population on the eve of the war was 19,000.

3. Yahil, "Switzerland," 1441–42. Also see Häsler, *Lifeboat*, 30–53.

4. Yahil, "Switzerland," 1443–44.

5. Originally, the family name was spelled Mandl, but later an *e* was added.

6. Kranzler "Swiss Press Campaign," 156; Kranzler, *Man*, 9–14.

7. Lévai, *Abscheu*, 11; Kranzler, *Man*, xxii.

8. http://paulonpius.blogspot.com/p/el-salvadors-holocaust-hero-by-john. html; Lamperti, "Paul on Pius"; Kranzler, *Man*, 2–3.

9. Lévai, *Abscheu*, 11; Kranzler, *Man*, 3–5.

10. Kranzler, *Man*, 2, 6.

11. Parkman, *Nonviolent Insurrection*, 28.

12. Lamperti, *Nonviolent*; Kranzler, *Man*, 3. Disturbances in April and May 1944 led to the resignation of Martínez, and he was replaced by General Andrés I. Menéndez, and the foreign minister was the writer Julio Enrique Avila.

13. Kranzler, "Swiss Press Campaign," 157.

14. Lévai, *Abscheu*, 10–11.

15. Lévai, *Abscheu*, 12, 333; Kranzler, *Man*, 7.

16. Kranzler, *Man*, 15.

17. Palestina Amt was headed by Dr. Samuel Scheps and Dr. Chaim Pozner, the Jewish Agency was headed by Richard Lichtheim, the Hehalutz movement was represented by Natan Schwalb, the World Jewish Congress was represented by Dr. Gerhart Riegner, and the JDC by Saly Mayer, who for a time also seconded as head of the Federation of Swiss Jewish Communities.

18. The Bund relayed to the Jewish Labor Committee, its American ideological counterpart, the first major report on the annihilation of Polish Jewry. After the fall of France, the JLC initiated the Emergency Visitors' Visas program, also known as "above-quota visas," approved by the Roosevelt administration.

19. Kranzler, *Man*, 15–16.

20. Kranzler, "Swiss Press Campaign," 157.

21. Kranzler, *Man*, 25.

22. Kranzler, "Swiss Press Campaign," 15; Kranzler, *Man*, 27, 35.

23. Kranzler, *Man*, 35.

24. On December 23, 1942, Mantello wrote to the Polish and Dutch diplomatic representatives in Switzerland, urging them to exert pressure on the governments of Honduras, Nicaragua, and Paraguay, in whose names some 3,000 passports were issued, affecting some 10,000 people, to validate these passports in order to prevent the passport holders from being deported to concentration camps. Kranzler, *Man*, 35–38; Lévai, *Abscheu*, 15, 334–37. In the fall of 1943, the Swiss launched an investigation into the

entire issue of the sale of Latin American papers. The report stated that the Honduras consul had issued 400 passports. The consuls in Switzerland for Haiti, Paraguay, and Peru were dismissed for their behavior in passport sales. Kranzler, *Man*, 33.

25. In 1942 Salvador was still in the hands of General Martínez, and it was not until September 12, 1943, that the Salvadoran government gave its approval. Kranzler, *Man*, 28.
26. Kranzler, *Man*, xxii, 26, 197; Kranzler, "Swiss Press Campaign," 157; Lévai, *Abscheu*, 14.
27. Cohen, "Mantello," 94–95; Kranzler, *Man*, 30.
28. Cohen, "Mantello," 94. Lévai, *Abscheu*, 14. It was Agudah activist Chaim Israel Eiss who introduced Müller to Mantello, who also assisted Eiss in obtaining Latin American papers. Kranzler, *Man*, 31.
29. Kranzler, *Man*, 218.
30. Kranzler, *Man*, 28.
31. Cohen, "Mantello," 98.
32. Cohen, "Mantello," 96.
33. Cohen, "Mantello," 96; Lévai, *Abscheu*, 21. Also Document 6, by Jonas Tiefenbrunner, born Wiesbaden, in 1914, residing in Brussels, and head of a Jewish orphanage; Lévai, *Abscheu*, 343.
34. Cohen, "Mantello," 96.
35. Lévai, *Abscheu*, 24; Kranzler, *Man*, 7.
36. Lévai, *Abscheu*, 25.
37. Kranzler, *Man*, 61, 185; Lévai, *Abscheu*, 26.
38. Kranzler, *Man*, xxi.
39. Based on Brand, *Desperate*, chapter 5; Kranzler, *Man*, 31.
40. Kranzler, *Man*, 205.
41. Kranzler, *Man*, 204.
42. Kranzler, *Man*, 189. Wallenberg also reportedly agreed to house recipients of Salvadoran documents to avoid harm by the Arrow Cross gangs roaming the streets of Budapest. The sheltered Salvadoran group was headed by a certain Dr. Jenö Szilasi, chief physician of the Jewish hospital in Budapest. Cohen, "Mantello," 131.
43. Kranzler, *Man*, 205. On November 3, 1944, the Swiss government, ever suspicious of Mantello's work, consulted with Consul General Castellanos on the legitimacy of Mantello's role as a distributor of the papers, asking whether Mantello was paid a salary. The response by Castellanos was, "I wish to let you know that Mr. George Mantello . . . has waived all payments." Kranzler, *Man*, 207.
44. Kranzler, *Man*, 208; Cohen, "Mantello," 97.

45. Kranzler, *Man,* 83.

46. Kranzler, *Man,* 82.

47. Kranzler, *Man,* 83, 86, 157, 183–84.

48. Kranzler, *Man,* 84–85.

49. Kranzler, *Man,* 86.

50. Based on testimonies of Rudolf Vrba, Alfred Wetzler, Arnost Rosin, and Czeslaw Mordowicz, all Auschwitz escapees.

51. Kranzler, *Man,* 87–88. Lévai, *Abscheu,* 352.

52. Kranzler, "Swiss Press Campaign," 158. According to Lévai, as a supplement to his letter, Krausz attached the Vrba/Wetzler Auschwitz Protocol, as originally recorded when the two escapees arrived in Slovakia. Lévai, *Abscheu,* 352–61.

53. Kranzler, *Man,* 96.

54. Kranzler, "Swiss Press Campaign," 160–61.

55. Kranzler, *Man,* 109, 158. Of all the Swiss theologians, Vogt was the most vociferous in denouncing the atrocities of the Holocaust. Witness his screaming sermon on June 27, 1944: [God asking Christians] "Where, where, where! Where is your brother, the homeless Jew? . . . Where are the homeless Jewish children today? . . . Where are the widows, the orphaned, the hungry, the thirsty, and the strangers? . . . You Christians, tell me, where? Cain gave the classic response to those shirking their responsibility: 'I don't know!' . . . Today, Christians respond in the same classic fashion of irresponsibility: 'I do not know where the Jew is! Nor does it concern me in the least.' Oh Holy God . . . we are not worthy of standing before Thee, because we Christians loved so little and have so little faith, . . . In the midst of our Christendom, godlessness seeks to exterminate the entire Jewish people, and we can no longer prevent it, . . . Have mercy upon the persecuted Jews. Have mercy upon the sorrow-laden Jews!" Kranzler, *Man,* 110–12.

56. Kranzler, *Man,* 123, 172; Kranzler, "Swiss Press Campaign," 162.

57. Kranzler, *Man,* 149. Romanian Jewish leader Wilhelm Filderman reported on his conversation with Manoliu on August 21, 1944: "His Excellency [Manoliu] informed us that . . . his [press] campaign was not initiated by himself but by Mr. George Mantello, alias George Mandel . . . brother of Josef Mandel." Kranzler, *Man,* 83.

58. Kranzler, "Swiss Press Campaign," 161–62, 166; Kranzler, *Man,* 115–17.

59. Kranzler, *Man,* 122–23. On July 17 Maximilian Jäger, the Swiss minister in Budapest, warned Hungarian prime minister Sztójay that Switzerland was toying with the idea of breaking off relations with Hungary. Kranzler, *Man,* 161.

60. Kranzler, *Man*, 151.

61. Kranzler, *Man,* 168. One may also mention two other endeavors by George Mandel-Mantello that did not produce results, not due to any fault by him, but it underlines the man's commitment to the rescue of as many Jews as possible. In late 1943 he wrote to Salazar, the Portuguese head of state, asking him to allow Jews fleeing from persecution in Europe to use the Portuguese colony of Angola as a place of refuge. This act would rebound to the prestige of Portugal and would be a boon to the economy of Angola. Lévai, *Abscheu,* 339. In another rescue endeavor, after the creation of the War Refugee Board, in February 1944 he posted a letter to President Roosevelt asking that U.S. citizenship be awarded to Jews under German domination, an act "that would constitute one of the most beautiful expressions of human solidarity," similar to George Washington's granting of U.S. citizenship in 1792 to a group of Portuguese Masonic members, wanted by the Portuguese Inquisition authorities. Lévai, *Abscheu,* 341.

62. Lévai, *Abscheu,* 27; Kranzler, *Man,* 32, 236.

63. Kranzler, *Man,* 204. In a private communication in December 1945, George Mandel-Mantello wrote bitterly to his wartime colleague Mathieu Muller: "The obstacles that were placed in our way did not come so much from official sources as from Jewish personalities in Switzerland. . . . In our work we had not the slightest financial support from any Jewish organization. We paid virtually all expenses from our own pockets. . . . We also had to defend ourselves against the other Jewish authorities, which caused us great difficulties. . . . Why did these organizations fight against us? They saw in us a dangerous competitor. We were in a position to give something for nothing to thousands of people . . . and we dispensed it without any 'protektzia,' intervention by higher authorities, the slightest distinctions among the recipients. They were afraid that we would end their monopoly. . . . You can judge how much more could have been accomplished had we cooperated with each other. . . . Instead of helping us, they hindered. . . . We were sabotaged and even undermined by informers. . . . And don't think that this campaign has stopped. . . . Thereby making it impossible for me to obtain a visa [to England]." Kranzler, *Man,* 238–39.

64. Kranzler, *Man,* 242–43.

65. Kranzler, *Man,* 246–47.

66. Kranzler, *Man,* 237.

67. Kranzler, *Man,* 234–35.

68. Kranzler, *Man,* 240.

69. Kranzler, *Man,* 242.

70. Lévai, *Abscheu,* 12; Kranzler, *Man,* 249–50.

71. Friedenson and Kranzler, *Heroine,* 26–27.

72. Friedenson and Kranzler, *Heroine,* 29.

73. Friedenson and Kranzler, *Heroine,* 28.

74. Friedenson and Kranzler, *Heroine,* 252.

75. Friedenson and Kranzler, *Heroine,* 253.

76. Friedenson and Kranzler, *Heroine,* 20–22.

77. Paul Grüninger was awarded the Righteous title by Yad Vashem; YVA-M31.2/680.

78. Friedenson and Kranzler, *Heroine,* 37.

79. Friedenson and Kranzler, *Heroine,* 38–39.

80. Friedenson and Kranzler, *Heroine,* 42. At the trial, Recha's defense attorney also pointed out her help to hundreds of Jews who wished to transit through Switzerland, with Swiss visas, after obtaining Chinese end-visas, most likely from the Chinese consul general in Vienna, Feng Shan Ho. Yad Vashem honored him with the Righteous title; YVA-M31.2/8688.

81. Friedenson and Kranzler, *Heroine,* 40–41.

82. Friedenson and Kranzler, *Heroine,* 43.

83. Friedenson and Kranzler, *Heroine,* 35. Police officer Paul Grüninger, who lost his police position due to his assistance to Jewish refugees, was harsh in his condemnation of Saly Mayer. In 1945 he charged Saly Mayer with making Grüninger's rescue work "more difficult." Friedenson and Kranzler, *Heroine,* 36.

84. Friedenson and Kranzler, *Heroine,* 81–82; Kranzler, *Man,* 17.

85. Friedenson and Kranzler, *Heroine,* 44. There were close to 500 yeshiva scholars out of the 20,000 Jewish refugees in Shanghai. Friedenson and Kranzler, *Heroine,* 77.

86. Friedenson and Kranzler, *Heroine,* 45, 47.

87. Friedenson and Kranzler, *Heroine,* 54.

88. Friedenson and Kranzler, *Heroine,* 55–56.

89. Friedenson and Kranzler, *Heroine,* 50. HIJEFS continued to operate for another five years after the conclusion of the war. Friedenson and Kranzler, *Heroine,* 79.

90. Kranzler, *Man,* 26–27. Chaim Israel Eiss and Mathieu Muller of Agudath Israel obtained such documents from the diplomats of Peru, Costa Rica, and Honduras. Friedenson and Kranzler, *Heroine,* 101.

91. Friedenson and Kranzler, *Heroine,* 102–5.

92. Kranzler, *Man,* 20–21; Friedenson and Kranzler, *Heroine,* 87.

93. Friedenson and Kranzler, *Heroine,* 88, 93.

94. Friedenson and Kranzler, *Heroine,* 69–70.

95. Friedenson and Kranzler, *Heroine,* 68, 73. Joseph Friedenson and David Kranzler, in their book on the Sternbuchs, wrote that in 1944, with approval of rabbinic authorities, the Sternbuchs presented Bernardini with the most beautiful gift in recognition of his good deeds, a Torah scroll. Friedenson and Kranzler, *Heroine,* 75.

96. Kranzler, *Man,* 134.

97. Kranzler, *Man,* 134.

98. Friedenson and Kranzler, *Heroine,* 71.

99. Friedenson and Kranzler, *Heroine,* 124.

100. Friedenson and Kranzler, *Heroine,* 125.

101. Bauer, *Jews,* 225.

102. Friedenson and Kranzler, *Heroine,* 126, 131.

103. Friedenson and Kranzler, *Heroine,* 128–30.

104. Friedenson and Kranzler, *Heroine,* 134.

105. On March 6, 1945, Musy in a handwritten note to the Union of Orthodox Rabbis of the United States and Canada placed the blame squarely at the door of Saly Mayer, writing, "Last week I was told in Berlin: 'You may thank Mr. Saly Mayer that no convoy of Jews of German camps reached Switzerland." Friedenson and Kranzler, *Heroine,* 133.

106. Friedenson and Kranzler, *Heroine,* 169.

107. Friedenson and Kranzler, *Heroine,* 167, 173.

108. Friedenson and Kranzler, *Heroine,* 246–48.

109. Friedenson and Kranzler, *Heroine,* 176–77.

110. Friedenson and Kranzler, *Heroine,* 198–99. Pierre Chaillet was awarded the Righteous title by Yad Vashem for his involvement in the rescue of Jewish children during the German occupation of France; YVA-M31.2/1770.

111. Friedenson and Kranzler, *Heroine,* 201–2.

112. Friedenson and Kranzler, *Heroine,* 250, 254.

113. Goldfinger, "Reb Chaim Yisroel Eiss."

114. Shalem, "Remember," 348–49.

115. Shalem, "Remember," 374.

116. Goldfinger, "Reb Chaim Yisroel Eiss."

117. Goldfinger, "Reb Chaim Yisroel Eiss."

118. Shalem, "Remember," 364–65.

119. Shalem, "Remember," 361.

120. Goldfinger, "Reb Chaim Yisroel Eiss."

121. Shalem, "Remember," 377.

122. Shalem, "Remember," 366, 368.

123. Shalem, "Remember," 369.

124. Shalem, "Remember," 377.

125. After his passing, the Agudath Israel designated the Sternbuchs as the Agudah representatives to replace Eiss. Kranzler, *Man*, 19.

12. Concentration Camps

1. Pingel "Concentration," 308–10.

2. Pingel, "Concentration," 310–11.

3. Pingel," Concentration," 309, 312–13, 315.

4. Arad, "Sobibor," 1373–74.

5. Arad, "Sobibor," 1374.

6. Arad, "Sobibor," 1376.

7. Arad, "Sobibor," 1376

8. Arad, "Sobibor," 1377.

9. Arad, "Sobibor." The death toll for Treblinka camp is much higher—870,000 victims. Bełżec, the third camp in the tripartite Nazi Aktion Reinhard camps operation, claimed at least 500,000 victims; but according to historian Yitzhak Arad, the figure for Bełżec may be as high as 600,000 and perhaps even more. Arad, *Belzec*, 127. On August 2, 1943, a breakout was also attempted from Treblinka camp. Of the approximately 750 prisoners who tried to make their escape, 70 survived to see liberation. Arad "Treblinka," 1487.

10. Arad, *Belzec*, 307.

11. Wikipedia, "Alexander Pechersky"; HEART, "Alexander Pechersky"; Arad, *Belzec*, 307.

12. Wikipedia, "Alexander Pechersky"; HEART, "Alexander Pechersky"; Arad, *Belzec*, 307.

13. Wikipedia, "Alexander Pechersky"; Ehrenburg and Grossman, *Complete*, 492–93, as reported by Pechersky, Antokolsky, and V. Kaverin.

14. Wikipedia, "Alexander Pechersky"; Arad, *Belzec*, 307; HEART, "Alexander Pechersky."

15. Ehrenburg and Grossman, *Complete*, 492–93; Arad, *Belzec*, 307.

16. Arad, *Belzec*, 299, 304.

17. Arad, *Belzec*, 299, 303.

18. Arad, *Belzec*, 300.

19. Arad, *Belzec*, 307; HEART, "Alexander Pechersky."

20. Ehrenburg and Grossman, *Complete*, 493–94; Arad, *Belzec*, 307–8; HEART, "Alexander Pechersky."

21. Arad, *Belzec*, 300.

22. Arad, *Belzec*, 302.

23. Arad, *Belzec*, 309–10; HEART, "Alexander Pechersky."

24. Arad, *Belzec*, 302, 304, 310–11; HEART, "Alexander Pechersky"; Ehrenburg and Grossman, *Complete*, 495.

25. Arad, *Belzec*, 310–12; Wikipedia, "Alexander Pechersky"; HEART, "Alexander Pechersky."

26. Arad, *Belzec*, 311–12; Wikipedia, "Alexander Pechersky."

27. Arad, *Belzec*, 316; HEART, "Alexander Pechersky."

28. Arad, *Belzec*, 316–19.

29. Ehrenburg and Grossman, *Complete*, 494; Wikipedia, "Alexander Pechersky."

30. Ehrenburg and Grossman, *Complete*, 497–98.

31. Arad, *Belzec*, 307, 321–22, 315; HEART, "Alexander Pechersky."

32. Arad, *Belzec*, 323–28, 334; HEART, "Alexander Pechersky."

33. Arad, *Belzec*, 329.

34. Arad, *Belzec*, 330–31.

35. Arad, *Belzec*, 329, 331–32, 334; Ehrenburg and Grossman, *Complete*, 499; Wikipedia, "Alexander Pechersky"; HEART, "Alexander Pechersky."

36. Arad, *Belzec*, 338–39; Wikipedia, "Alexander Pechersky"; HEART, "Alexander Pechersky."

37. Arad, *Belzec*, 340, 348; HEART, "Alexander Pechersky"; Wikipedia, "Alexander Pechersky."

38. Arad, *Belzec*, 334–35, 337, 341; Ehrenburg and Grossman, *Complete*, 498–99; Wikipedia, "Alexander Pechersky"; HEART, "Alexander Pechersky."

39. Arad, *Belzec*, 342.

40. Arad, *Belzec*, 345, 347–48.

41. Arad, *Belzec*, 333, 341; Ehrenburg and Grossman, *Complete*, 499; Wikipedia, "Alexander Pechersky," for another estimate.

42. Arad, *Belzec*, 337.

43. Ehrenburg and Grossman, *Complete*, 500; Arad, "Sobibor," 1378.

44. Wikipedia, "Alexander Pechersky"; HEART, "Alexander Pechersky."

45. Wikipedia, "Alexander Pechersky";

46. Buszko, "Auschwitz," 107, 108; Pingel, "Concentration," 312. For a more comprehensive study of Auschwitz, see Gutman and Berenbaum, *Anatomy*.; Langbein, *People.*

47. Buszko, "Auschwitz," 112.

48. Buszko, "Auschwitz," 107, 109.

49. Buszko, "Auschwitz," 108, 113.

50. Pingel, "Concentration," 312; Buszko, "Auschwitz," 109, 114.

51. Buszko, "Auschwitz," 109–10. Of the 405,000 registered prisoners who received Auschwitz numbers, only about 65,000 survived. Buszko, "Auschwitz," 117.

52. Buszko, "Auschwitz," 111–12.

53. Pingel, "Concentration," 313; Buszko, "Auschwitz," 110, 114.

54. Buszko, "Auschwitz," 114–15; Pingel, 312.

55. Buszko, "Auschwitz," 110, 115.

56. The women led by a certain Roza Robota were later apprehended and executed. Buszko, "Auschwitz," 116.

57. Buszko, "Auschwitz," 108–9.

58. Buszko, "Auschwitz," 114.

59. Buszko, "Auschwitz," 115.

60. Buszko, "Auschwitz," 116.

61. Buszko, "Auschwitz," 117.

62. "Alfred (Fredy) Hirsch, February 11, 1916–March 8, 1943." www.holocaust .cz/en/history/people/alfred-fredy-hirsch-2.

63. Keren, "Freddy Hirsch";

64. Keren, "Family Camp," 428.

65. Vrba and Bestic, *Escape*, 228.

66. Keren, "Family Camp," 431.

67. Vrba and Bestic, *Escape*, 229.

68. Keren, "Family Camp," 428.

69. "Alfred (Fredy) Hirsch"; Keren, "Family," 431.

70. Keren, "Family Camp," 428, 431.

71. Keren, "Family Camp," 432.

72. Keren, "Family Camp," 230.

73. "Alfred (Fredy) Hirsch."

74. Brod, "Memoir Kept in the Jewish Museum in Prague"; Keren, "Family Camp," 430–31.

75. Keren, "Family Camp," 433–34.

76. "Alfred (Fredy) Hirsch."

77. Keren, "Family Camp," 434–35.

78. Keren, "Family Camp," 431–33.

79. Brod, "Memoir Kept in the Jewish Museum in Prague."

80. Keren, "Family Camp," 242–43.

81. Keren, "Family Camp," 244–45.

82. "Alfred (Fredy) Hirsch."

83. Keren, "Family Camp," 428.

84. Keren, "Family Camp," 248; Müller, *Eyewitness Auschwitz*, 90–119.

85. Brod, "Memoir Kept"; Keren, "Family Camp," 436.

86. Keren, "Family Camp," 437.

87. Keren, "Family Camp," 439.

88. Keren, "Family Camp," 429.

89. Keren, "Family Camp," 439–40.

90. Keren, "Family Camp," 429.
91. Rosensaft, *Yesterday*, 3, 8.
92. Rosensaft, *Yesterday*, 8, 11, 12, 15, 20, 22.
93. Rosensaft, *Yesterday*, 27–29.
94. Rosensaft, *Yesterday*, 31–32.
95. Rosensaft, *Yesterday*, 32–33.
96. Rosensaft, *Yesterday*, 33.
97. Rosensaft, *Yesterday*, 36.
98. Rosensaft, *Yesterday*, 41–43; Krakowski, "Bergen-Belsen," 185, 187.
99. Rosensaft, *Yesterday*, 43.
100. Rosensaft, *Yesterday*, 44.
101. Rosensaft, *Yesterday*, 44.
102. Rosensaft, *Yesterday*, 44–45.
103. Rosensaft, *Yesterday*, 45.
104. Rosensaft, *Yesterday*, 45.
105. Rosensaft, *Yesterday*, 46–47. This medical intervention is also mentioned in Berkowitz, *Where*.
106. Rosensaft, *Yesterday*, 59–60.
107. Rosensaft, *Yesterday*, 52, 55.
108. Rosensaft, *Yesterday*, 54–55.
109. Rosensaft, *Yesterday*, 59.
110. Krakowski, "Bergen-Belsen," 189, 190. Son of Deborah and Menachem Mendel Rosensaft, Josef (Yossel) was the youngest of six children. Married to Bronka Bajtner, a widow with a daughter, on June 22, 1943, Yossel, his wife and her daughter were deported from Będzin to Auschwitz. He was able to escape through the train car window as three bullets hit him. He made his way back to Będzin ghetto where a doctor removed the bullet from his wrist, but the one in his leg was located too close to a vein to be removed safely. On August 27, 1943, he was again deported to Birkenau and sent to work at a labor camp. In March 1944 he escaped again and returned to Będzin, where he found shelter at the home of a Polish friend for six weeks. He was caught again and returned to Auschwitz, where he was interrogated and underwent terrible tortures. Sent to several labor camps, he finally arrived in Bergen-Belsen on a death march in early April 1945. Rosensaft, *Yesterday*, 61–66.
111. Kochan, "Himmler," 661–62.
112. Fox, "A Jew Talks to Himmler."
113. The rest of this chapter is based on Masur's "Report to the World Jewish Congress: Regarding My Visit with Heinrich Himmler, April 21, 1945."
114. Fox, "A Jew Talks to Himmler."

13. England

1. Tydor-Baumel, Sagi, and Zweig, "Jewish Refugees," 607.
2. Ben-Israel, "Appeasement," 603–4; Holmes, "Fascism," 605–6.
3. Tydor-Baumel, Sagi, and Zweig, "Jewish Refugees," 308.
4. Zweig, "Great Britain," 601.
5. Tydor-Baumel, Sagi, and Zweig, "Jewish Refugees," 607, 609.
6. Tydor-Baumel, Sagi, and Zweig, "Jewish Refugees," 610.
7. Zweig, "Great Britain," 602.
8. Zweig, "Churchill," 300–301.
9. Gurewitsch, "Chance," 12.
10. Licht, "Rabbi," 17.
11. Gurewitsch, "Chance," 12; Kranzler, *Holocaust Hero*, 5.
12. Licht, "Rabbi," 17–18.
13. Kranzler, *Holocaust Hero*, 23–24, 27; Licht, "Rabbi," 17.
14. Kranzler, *Holocaust Hero*, 10, 29–30, 32.
15. Kranzler, *Holocaust Hero*, 19, 30.
16. Kranzler, *Holocaust Hero*, 12, 19, 151; Licht, "Rabbi," 18.
17. In mid-1938 the orthodox Agudath Israel movement established a separate organization called the Emigration Advisory Council, with an office in London, headed by Jacob Rosenheim, president of the World Agudath Israel and a member of Schonfeld's Adas Yisroel congregation. After consultation with Herbert Samuel (formerly the British high commissioner in Palestine) and Chief Rabbi Joseph Hertz, the Chief Rabbi's Religious Emergency Council (CRREC) was created, with Rabbi Hertz as the nominal head and Schonfeld as the executive director. CRREC was to become the primary Orthodox rescue vehicle. Kranzler, *Holocaust*, 51–52.
18. Kranzler, *Holocaust Hero*, 55. In the summer of 1942, Klibansky, his family, and all his remaining charges were deported and killed. Kranzler, *Holocaust Hero*, 55. See Klibanksy story in chapter 1, Germany.
19. Kranzler, *Holocaust Hero*, 38.
20. Kranzler, *Holocaust Hero*, 39.
21. Kranzler, *Holocaust Hero*, 56; Licht, "Rabbi," 18.
22. As told by Dr. Judith Grunfeld, an educator of Jewish religious girls. Kranzler, *Holocaust Hero*, 56, 156–57.
23. Kranzler, *Holocaust Hero*, 193.
24. Kranzler, *Holocaust Hero*, 142.
25. Kranzler, *Holocaust Hero*, 147, 225.
26. Licht, "Rabbi," 19.
27. Kranzler, *Holocaust Hero*, 492.

28. Kranzler, *Holocaust Hero,* 64, 176.
29. Kranzler, *Holocaust Hero,* 177.
30. Kranzler, *Holocaust Hero,* 65, 166, 178–79; Licht, "Rabbi," 19–20.
31. Kranzler, *Holocaust Hero,* 5–6, 54, 148.
32. Licht, "Rabbi," 18.
33. Kranzler, *Holocaust Hero,* 7, 151.
34. Kranzler, *Holocaust Hero,* 152.
35. Licht, "Rabbi," 18–19.
36. Kranzler, *Holocaust Hero,* 20–21, 58.
37. Kranzler, *Holocaust Hero,* 62, 77, 153; Licht, "Rabbi," 20.
38. Kranzler, *Holocaust Hero,* 87–89.
39. Licht, "Rabbi," 21.
40. Sompolinsky, *Britain,* 159; Licht, "Rabbi," 21.
41. Licht, "Rabbi," 21–22.
42. Kranzler, *Holocaust Hero,* 106, 109, 111.
43. Kranzler, *Holocaust Hero,* 98.
44. Kranzler, *Holocaust Hero,* 18; Licht, "Rabbi," 22.
45. Kranzler, *Holocaust Hero,* 204. She reported that during the war, she had wandered from place to place. In one encounter with a group of boys who wished to harm her on Christmas Eve, she pleaded: "You must know you are celebrating the birthday of a Jew," and they let her go. Kranzler, *Holocaust Hero,* 201–3.
46. Kranzler, *Holocaust Hero,* 205–7. See the similar accounts of Joshua Olshin and Judith Alter Kallman (born Mannheimer) of help by Rabbi Schonfeld to get them out of Poland and Slovakia. Kranzler, *Holocaust Hero,* 210–17.
47. Licht, "Rabbi," 21; Kranzler, *Holocaust Hero,* 99.
48. Kranzler, *Holocaust Hero,* 112–13; Licht, "Rabbi," 22.
49. Kranzler, *Holocaust Hero,* 9; Licht, "Rabbi," 18; Taylor, *Solomon Schonfeld,* 59.
50. Licht, "Rabbi," 22.
51. Kranzler, *Holocaust Hero,* xix.

14. The United States

1. Feingold, "United," 1546–47; Feingold, "American Jewry," 40.
2. Such as the antisemitic rantings of Catholic Father Charles Coughlin, who spoke to millions over the airwaves, and auto producer Henry Ford, who publicized the forgery Protocols of the Elders of Zion. Feingold, "American Jewry," 40. Some critics of President Roosevelt's policies used the increasing number of Jews in high positions in the administration to sarcastically call Roosevelt's New Deal a "Jew Deal." Feingold, "United," 1546.
3. Feingold, "United," 1546. For more on the pre–Pearl Harbor mood in the

United States, the reader is referred to the two studies by David Wyman, *Paper Walls* and *The Abandonment of the Jews*.

4. See Wikipedia, "Hillel Kook."
5. Hurwitz, "United," 1545.
6. Feingold, "United," 1547; Hurwitz, "United," 1545.
7. Feingold, "Roosevelt," 1302–4.
8. Feingold, "United," 1547. In 1939 a bill introduced in Congress to admit 10,000 Jewish refugee children outside the quota (the Wagner-Rogers Bill), and reintroduced in 1940, was allowed to linger and lie dormant in a House committee, due to opposition by many nativist organizations (with claims such as "charity begins at home") and the lack of enthusiasm by the Roosevelt administration.
9. Feingold, "Roosevelt," 1303. The Bermuda conference rejected a recommendation that ships with empty holds returning from European to the American shores might be used to transport refugees to safe havens, thereby improving the flow of refugees who had escaped to Spain and Portugal. Negotiating with Berlin for the release of the Jews and a halt to the slaughter was also rejected. So meager were the results of the Bermuda conference that it was decided not to make the results public. Feingold, "United," 1548.
10. Hurwitz, "United," 1545, 1547.
11. Feingold, "United," 1547; Feingold, "Roosevelt," 1302.
12. Merlin, *Millions*, 129.
13. Feingold, "United," 1549. In April 1944, more than 900 predominantly Jewish refugees were admitted and housed in Fort Ontario at Oswego, New York, but this was a symbolic rather than a substantive victory and only demonstrated what could have been done had there been a will to save lives. Feingold "Roosevelt," 1303; Genizi, "Bergson Group," 191.
14. Feingold, Roosevelt," 1302; Feingold, "American Jewry," 38.
15. Hecht, *Child*, 567–68.
16. Feingold, "American Jewry," 38.
17. Feingold, "United," 1547.
18. Nahum Goldmann, one of Wise's confidants, later admitted: "Wise exaggerated his appreciation of Roosevelt. The accusations against Roosevelt are partly justified. No question. And [Wise] was so attached to him and they were buddy-buddy." Rafael Medoff, "Other Views of the Bergson Group," private communication.
19. Feingold, "American Jewry," 37, 39.
20. Feingold, "American Jewry," 38; Silberklang, "American," 35.
21. Silberklang, "American," 35. In April 1943 the AJC agreed to join the Amer-

ican Jewish Conference. However, the conference's September 1, 1943, resolution calling for the establishment of a Jewish commonwealth in Palestine led the AJC to withdraw from the conference in October 1943. In protest, 10 percent of its membership resigned from the AJC.

22. Feingold, "American Jewry," 39.
23. Genizi, "Bergson Group," 190.
24. Feingold, "American Jewry," 25, 40.
25. Hecht, *Child*, 516–17.
26. Wikipedia, "Ben Hecht."
27. Hecht, *Child*, 520–21.
28. Hecht, *Child*, 522.
29. Hecht, *Child*, 519–20.
30. Hecht, *Child*, 524–25.
31. Hecht, *Child*, 536–37.
32. Hecht, *Child*, 538–39.
33. Hecht recalled a lengthy conversation he had with movie producer David Selznick: "'I don't want anything to do with your cause,' said David, 'for the simple reason that it's a Jewish political cause. And I am not interested in Jewish political problems. I'm an American and not a Jew. I'm interested in this war as an American. It would be silly of me to pretend suddenly that I'm a Jew—' . . . 'If I can prove you are Jew, David,' I said, 'will you sign the telegram as cosponsor with ME?' [for the creation of a Jewish army within the ranks of the British army before America's entrance into the war]. 'How are you going to prove it?' he asked. 'I'll call up any three people you name,' I said, 'and ask them the following question—what would you call David O. Selznick an American or a Jew? If any of the three answers that he'd call you an American, you win. Otherwise, you sign the telegram.' David agreed to the test and picked out three names. I called them with David eavesdropping on an extension." The responses were: "'I'd say David Selznick was a Jew,' he said (Martin Quigley of the *Motion Picture Exhibitors' Herald*). Same reply by Nunnally Johnson. Leland Hayward: 'For God's sake, what's the matter with David? He's a Jew, and he knows it.' David honorably admitted defeat. Apparently in everybody's eyes but his own he was a Jew. His name went on the telegram." Hecht, *Child*, 539–40.
34. Hecht, *Child*, 543.
35. Hecht, *Child*, 545.
36. Hecht, *Child*, 546.
37. Hecht, *Child*, 547.
38. Merlin, *Millions*, 41; Hecht, *Child*, 547–48.

39. Merlin, *Millions,* 42.

40. Merlin, *Millions,* 36.

41. Merlin, *Millions,* 179.

42. Merlin, *Millions,* 59–60.

43. Merlin, *Millions,* 106.

44. Merlin, *Millions* , 106; Hecht, *Child,* 577.

45. Hecht, *Child,* 577.

46. Hecht, *Child,* 578.

47. Merlin, *Millions,* 87.

48. Hecht, *Child,* 553–54, 556, 558.

49. Hecht, *Child,* 575–76.

50. Hecht, *Child,* 558.

51. Merlin, *Millions,* 40, 63l; Hecht, *Child,* 576; Wikipedia, "Hillel Kook."

52. Hecht, *Child,* 563, 575–76.

53. Hecht, *Child,* 552.

54. Hecht, *Child,* 564.

55. Hecht, *Child,* 565; Merlin, *Millions,* 64.

56. Merlin, *Millions,* 83–84, 99.

57. Merlin, *Millions,* 87; Hecht, *Child,* 585.

58. Merlin, *Millions,* 90.

59. Merlin, *Millions,* 58–59.

60. Merlin, *Millions,* 157.

61. Merlin, *Millions,* 177.

62. Merlin, *Millions,* 58.

63. Zuroff, *Response,* 258; Wikipedia, "Hillel Kook."

64. Merlin, *Millions,* 92.

65. Zuroff, *Response,* 258–59; Genizi, "Bergson Group," 191.

66. Zuroff, *Response,* 259–60; Merlin, *Millions,* 92

67. Wikipedia, "Hillel Kook."

68. Merlin, *Millions,* 183.

69. Merlin, *Millions,* 64, 183–84.

70. In his gloomy New Year's message in January 1944, Hitler announced his intention to win one great victory—over the Jews! Merlin, *Millions,* 125.

71. Hecht, *Child,* 579; Merlin, *Millions,* 58, 164.

72. Merlin, *Millions,* 95–96.

73. Merlin, *Millions,* 96.

74. Hecht, *Child,* 580.

75. Hecht, *Child,* 582. A month later, while in San Francisco Hecht began writing a play he called "Call the Next Case." The plot concerned Franklin Delano Roosevelt being summoned before the Bar of History to state what

he had done to save the Jews of Europe. But when Hecht learned that Roosevelt had died, he threw the script away. He had been a lifelong supporter of Roosevelt ("he was on the side of the angels"), but by 1945 he was totally disenchanted. "In my mind his chief monument remained—the dead Jews of Europe," Hecht wrote in his memoirs, *Child*, 578–79, 584.

76. Merlin, *Millions*, 71–73; Wikipedia, "Hillel Kook."

77. Feingold, "American Jewry," 40; Wikipedia, "Hillel Kook"; Merlin, *Millions*, 71–72. Years later Seymour D. Reich, former chairman of the Conference of Presidents of Major American Jewish Organizations, wrote: "Wise was deeply bothered by Bergson's success in attracting the support of prominent non-Jews. 'They are a disaster to the Zionist cause and the Jewish people,' he wrote to one colleague in 1944. 'Yet see how many names they capture who are well-meaning and are friendly to the Jews! It is too sad for words.'" Merlin, *Millions*, ix, 123.

78. Merlin, *Millions*, 72; Genizi, "Bergson Group," 191.

79. Merlin, *Millions*, 99.

80. Merlin, *Millions*, 99–101, 104.

81. Merlin, *Millions*, 113. When he began to investigate why the State Department was stalling, Treasury official Josiah E. DuBois Jr. noticed that the U.S. ambassador in Switzerland, Leland Harrison, had been sending frequent reports about the extermination of Jews in Europe. Then for three months Harrison had been virtually silent on the subject. After strenuous research and overcoming State Department obstructions, DuBois learned of a memo by Breckinridge Long to Harrison, instructing him not to send further reports on the extermination of Jews. Merlin, *Millions*, 110. Morgenthau's father, Henry Morgenthau Sr., had been ambassador to Constantinople and had attempted to alert America and the world about the genocide of the Armenians. Merlin, *Millions*, 104.

82. Merlin, *Millions*, 113. A year earlier, Nazi Propaganda Minister Josef Goebbels had noted in his diary, on December 1, 1942: "At bottom, however, I believe both the English and the Americans are happy that we are exterminating the Jewish riffraff." Merlin, *Millions*, 126. An assimilated Jew, aloof from Jewish institutional life, Morgenthau later wrote: "America has no cause to be proud of its handling of the refugee problem. We knew in Washington, from August 1942 on, that the Nazis were planning to exterminate all the Jews of Europe. . . . Officials dodged their responsibilities, procrastinated when concrete rescue schemes were placed before them, and even suppressed information about atrocities in order to prevent an outraged public opinion from forcing their hand." Merlin, *Millions*, 114.

83. Merlin, *Millions,* 115

84. Merlin, *Millions,* 115, 116. Morgenthau had earlier told his aforementioned three aides: "Unfortunately you are up against a generation of people like those in the State Department who don't like to do this kind of thing [to rescue Jews], and it is only by me happening to be Secretary of the Treasury and being vitally interested in these things with the help of you people . . . that I can do it. . . . I will do everything I can, and we will get it done." Merlin, *Millions,* 111.

85. Genizi, "Bergson Group," 191; Feingold, "Roosevelt," 1303.

86. Merlin, *Millions,* 119.

87. Feingold, "United," 1549.

88. Merlin, *Millions,* 119, 125, 128.

89. Merlin, *Millions,* 129, 134.

90. Wikipedia, "Hillel Kook."

91. Zuroff, *Response,* 30–31.

92. Zuroff, *Response,* 32–33.

93. Zuroff, *Response,* 34.

94. Zuroff, *Response,* 35–36.

95. Zuroff, *Response,* 52, 70–71.

96. Zuroff, *Response,* 74.

97. Zuroff, *Response,* 80–81.

98. Zuroff, *Response,* 87–88. Rabbi Jacob Levinson, several months later, argued in the Orthodox journal *Ha-Pardes* that "when we save a brilliant Torah scholar (*gaon* in rabbinic Hebrew) and great sage, we are not only saving a soul but part of our nation, an organ upon which the soul is dependent. . . . We are injecting new blood, live blood into the body of American Jewry." Zuroff, *Response,* 89–90.

99. Zuroff, *Response,* 91.

100. Zuroff, *Response,* 91.

101. Zuroff, *Response,* 92.

102. Zuroff, *Response,* 92.

103. Zuroff, *Response,* 136.

104. Zuroff, *Response,* 151, 186.

105. These last figures are a bit inflated, according to Efraim Zuroff, who made a special study of the Vaad Hatzala. Zuroff, *Response,* 194–96.

106. Zuroff, *Response,* 220.

107. Zuroff, *Response,* 221.

108. Zuroff, *Response,* 221–22. One week earlier, on August 28, Wise had received a communication from Member of Parliament Samuel Sydney Silverman, leader of the British section of the World Jewish Congress,

with a message from Gerhard Riegner, the wJC representative in Switzerland. On September 2, 1942, Wise sent Silverman's cable to Undersecretary of State Sumner Welles, unaware that the State Department already had a copy of Riegner's original message. Welles phoned Wise the next day and asked him not to publicize the information until the State Department could confirm its authenticity. Zuroff, *Response*, 222–23.

109. Zuroff, *Response*, 223.

110. Zuroff, *Response*, 223.

111. Zuroff, *Response*, 224.

112. Zuroff, *Response*, 226–27.

113. Zuroff, *Response*, 227, 229–30.

114. Zuroff, *Response*, 257–58.

115. Zuroff, *Response*, 276.

116. Zuroff, *Response*, 286.

117. Zuroff, *Response*, 286. As an afterthought, Efraim Zuroff adds a critical note that had the Vaad joined forces with the Joint, the overall results would probably have been more beneficial to the Jewish people than those achieved individually by each organization. Zuroff, *Response*, 287.

118. The Bund was a Jewish Social Democratic party that sustained its own network of schools and cultural/fraternal institutions in order to strengthen Yiddish culture and socialist values. It was generally hostile to both Zionist and Communism and was associated with the Social Democratic Second International.

119. Jacobs, "Friend," 392–93.

120. Jacobs, "Friend," 393, 395.

121. Jacobs, "Friend," 395.

122. Jacobs, "Friend," 298, 399, 401. Varian Fry, whose mission was to save intellectuals, mostly Jewish, on the Gestapo wanted list, on behalf of the Emergency Rescue Committee, stayed on until he too was expelled in September 1941. He was awarded the Righteous honor by Yad Vashem; YVA-M31.2/6150.

123. Bauer, *Brother's; Bauer, American*.

124. Bauer, *Brother's*, 27; Bauer, *American*, 21–22.

125. Bauer, *Brother's*, 64.

126. Bauer, *Brother's*, 250; Bauer, *American*, 23, 41.

127. Bauer, *American*, 41.

128. Bauer, *American*, 42, 179, 217

129. Bauer, *American*, 179, 218.

130. Bauer, *Brother's*, 25, 288–89.

131. Bauer, *Brother's*, 303. In Bauer's second book, dealing with JDC help in

wartime years, the figures are slightly different. Between 1933 and 1939, some 244,400 Jews left Germany; 117,409—Austria; 43,000—Czech lands. Bauer, *American*, 26.

132. Bauer, *American*, 35.

133. Bauer, *American*, 36–37, 40, 169.

134. Bauer, *American*, 40, 42.

135. Bauer, *American*, 178, 217.

136. Bauer, *American*, 403, 405.

137. Bauer, *Brother's*, 112, 115.

138. Bauer, *Brother's*, 116.

139. Bauer, *Brother's*, 117, 125.

140. Bauer, *Brother's*, 109, 126; Bauer, *American*, 27, 30.

141. Bauer, *Brother's*, 146.

142. Bauer, *Brother's*, 169. For children heading to America, a guarantee of $500 per year for each child placed with a private family had to be posted. Bauer, *Brother's*, 122. A first group of 53 children arrived in America in November 1934. A total of 433 children came to the United States under this program before the outbreak of the war in 1939. Bauer, *Brother's*, 123; *American*, 66.

143. Bauer, *Brother's*, 154–55.

144. Hitler reportedly supported this idea, as did the U.S. administration, with President Roosevelt personally involved in backing the plan. The advantage of this plan was that it would allow most remaining German Jews to leave the country in an orderly fashion (and release all Jews still held in concentration camps), with support for their rehabilitation abroad. Did the Germans really intend to implement such a large-scale emigration scheme? asked Holocaust historian Yehuda Bauer. His answer is that "on the whole, it seems that the Nazis took this plan seriously and were willing to consider it as a possible solution to the Jewish question." Bauer, *Brother's*, 275–77, 282–84. An open question is whether an opportunity was missed for a successful emigration trial balloon that might have spurred other emigration plans and thus possibly have avoided the Nazis' mass exterminations?

145. Bauer, *Brother's*, 223–24.

146. Bauer, *Brother's*, 228.

147. Bauer, *Brother's*, 225–26.

148. Bauer, *Brother's*, 32, 187.

149. Bauer, *Brother's*, 189–90, 201, 205–6.

150. Bauer, *Brother's*, 244–47; Bauer, *American*, 32.

151. Bauer, *American*, 73, 79–80.

152. Bauer, *American,* 98, 102–3.

153. Bauer, *American,* 95–96.

154. Bauer, *American,* 106, 318, 322.

155. Bauer, *American,* 331–32.

156. Bauer, *American,* 93.

157. Bauer, *American,* 85–86.

158. Bauer, *American,* 86–87. Nominally, the whole JSS operation existed as an agency separate from the ghetto Juderats. Weichert's attempt to intervene and alleviate conditions in the camps seems to have been successful in some cases. By early 1942 JSS claimed to have 412 local committees, of which 56 were in East Galicia. Bauer, *American,* 89.

159. Bauer, *American,* 320.

160. Bauer, *American,* 321.

161. Bauer, *American,* 319.

162. Bauer, *American,* 319–20.

163. Bauer, *American,* 321.

164. Bauer, *American,* 85, 88.

165. Bauer, *American,* 320, 322; Bauer, *Brother's,* 45, 59–61, 63, 67, 81, 98–99, 103, 295, 297–300.

166. Bauer, *American,* 108, 113.

167. Bauer, *American.* 325.

168. Bauer, *Brother's,* 32, 211.

169. Bauer, *Brother's,* 214–15, 336–37.

170. Bauer, *American,* 350.

171. Bauer, *American,* 351.

172. Bauer, *American,* 384. Also Raz, *Days,* 38–39, for JDC assistance to Munkács Jews.

173. Bauer, *American,* 446.

174. Bauer, *American,* 444, 446–47.

175. Bauer, *Brother's,* 269; Bauer, *American,* 62.

176. Bauer, *American,* 147, 277.

177. Bauer, *American,* 283–84.

178. Bauer, *American,* 288, 291–92.

179. Bauer, *Brother's,* 140, 265.

180. Bauer, *American,* 172. Helga Holbeck, a Danish-born Quaker operative active in French detention camps, paid out the funds in accordance with instructions she received orally from Schwartz and, possibly, Jefroykin. She was honored by Yad Vashem as a Righteous among the Nations, also for conveying Jewish children in France to safer places of refuge. YVA-M31.2/2142.

181. Bauer, *American*, 169.

182. Lazare, *Rescue*, 258; Bauer, "Schwartz," 1335; Bauer, *American*, 173, 177.

183. Lazare, *Rescue*, 258, 263; Latour, *Jewish*, 126.

184. The United States and Vichy France still maintained diplomatic relations at that time.

185. Bauer, *American*, 175–76.

186. Bauer, *American*, 260–61.

187. Bauer, *American*, 262.

188. Bauer, *Brother's*, 265–67.

189. Bauer, *Brother's*, 72, 267.

190. Bauer, *American*, 273, 275. For more on Van Tijn's help to Jews in Holland, see Bauer, *American*, 276; Wasserstein, *Ambiguity*.

191. Bauer, *Brother's*, 241, 268.

192. Bauer, *Brother's* 241–42.

193. Bauer, *American*, 180, 218–19.

194. Bauer, *American*, 219–20.

195. Bauer, *American*, 221–22.

196. Bauer, *American*, 223, 225.

197. Bauer, *American*, 224–25.

198. Bauer, *American*, 412–13.

199. Bauer, *American*, 357, 359–60.

200. Bauer, *American*, 359.

201. Bauer, *American*, 362–63.

202. Bauer, *American*, 369.

203. Bauer, *American*, 371–72.

204. Bauer, *American*, 372.

205. Bauer, *American*, 374.

206. Bauer, *American*, 375.

207. Bauer, *American*, 377.

208. Bauer, *American*, 48, 210.

209. Bauer, *American*, 49–50.

210. Bauer, *American*, 47.

211. Bauer, *American*, 50–52.

212. Bauer, *American*, 125.

213. Bauer, *Brother's*, 291; Bauer, *American*, 302, 304.

214. Bauer, *American*, 306–7.

215. Bauer, *American*, 307–8, 314.

216. Bauer, *Brother's*, 288.

217. Bauer, *American*, 203.

218. Bauer, *American*, 199.

219. Bauer, *American,* 287.
220. Bauer, *Brother's,* 286.
221. Bauer, *American,* 137.
222. Bauer, *American,* 140.
223. Bauer, *American,* 140.
224. Bauer, *American,* 142.
225. Bauer, *American,* 142.
226. Bauer, *American,* 120–21, 140–41, 143, 354.
227. Bauer, *American,* 414.
228. Bauer, *American,* 415.
229. Bauer, *American,* 416.
230. Bauer, *Jews,* 226–29. The following story highlights Himmler's desperate attempts to open negotiations with the Western Allies. Sometime in December 1944, he invited Becher and Eichmann to meet with him. According to Becher, Himmler yelled at Eichmann and demanded obedience of him. If he had ordered Eichmann to kill Jews before, Eichmann had done so; if he now ordered him to serve as a nursemaid to Jews, he had to do that, too. Bauer, *Jews,* 237.
231. Bauer, *American,* 416–17.
232. Bauer, *American,* 428.
233. Bauer, *American,* 429–30, 450–51.

Afterword

1. Bauer, *American,* 457.
2. Licht, "Rabbi Solomon Schonfeld," 18; Kranzler, *Holocaust Hero,* 7, 151; Kranzler, *Man,* 238–39; Merlin, *Millions,* ix, 71–73; Genizi, "Bergson Group," 192; Feingold, "American Jewry and the Holocaust," 1:40.
3. Ofer, *Escaping,* 207, 209. The Zionist movement had throughout the 1930s insisted on viewing the fate of Jews as inseparable from the Palestine question and was psychologically not prepared to seriously consider alternative sites for refugee shelters, which might someday pose a serious challenge to Zionism.
4. Ofer, *Escaping* , 201, 203–5, 208–9; Ofer, "Rescue," 163. World Zionist leader Chaim Weizmann also felt that brazenly flouting the law of the land was incompatible with Zionism's nature as a moral force, and he regarded an open confrontation with the British over illegal immigration as rash and ill-advised. Ofer, *Escaping,* 17–18.
5. Merlin, *Million,* ix, 27.
6. Laqueur, *History,* 372; Avneri, *From Velos,* 196, 383; Ofer, *Escaping,* 69.
7. Weizmann, *Trial and Error,* 420.

8. Some of Hitler's pronouncements on the Jews may be found in Fried-
   lander, *Nazi Germany and the Jews,* 18, 81, 132, 136, 166, 203, 238–40, 272–
   75, 278—and more in that study.
9. Weizmann, *Trial and Error,* chapters 40–41.
10. Bauer, *My Brother's Keeper,* 284.
11. Bauer, *American,* 411.
12. Avriel, Ehud, *Open,* 187–88.
13. Ofer, *Escaping* , 213–14, 250.
14. Bauer, *American,* 432.
15. Bauer, *American,* 434
16. Bauer, *American,* 378.
17. Bauer, *Jews for Sale?* 119.
18. Bauer, *American,* 55.
19. Bauer, *American,* 378.
20. Warhaftig, *Refugee,* 385.

Bibliography

Archives/Manuscript Materials/Private Letters

Arnon, Chana. "Georges Garel (Grigori Garfinkel)." JRJ Committee, Jerusalem, 2002.

Avni, Haim. "Interview with Andrée Salomon (Paris), June 8, 1963." Hebrew University, Department of Contemporary Judaism, Oral Testimony Section. Jerusalem, 1963.

Banitt, R. "Interview of Andrée Salomon, on help to Jewish children arriving in France from Germany, Czechoslovakia, and Austria until the start of the war." Paris, December 28, 1965.

Central Committee of Jews from Austria in Israel. March 2000. "Lehitraot Be-Eretz Israel: Maavako shel Aharon Menczer Lehatzalat Yeladim Yehudim Bevina Hanatzit" (See you in Eretz Israel: the Struggle of Aaron Menczer to Save Jewish Children in Nazified Vienna). Yad Vashem Library; catalog number 1000–2592F.

Charcas, Shlomo. "The Escape from the Ghetto: The Story of Rufeisen." YVA-M.49/727.

Drucker, Yeshayahu. Testimony (Hebrew), 1968. YVA 03/3249.

Flim, Bert Jan. Letter to Paldiel, March 29, 1999.

Garel, Georges (Grigori Garfinkel). Born 1909 in Vilnius–died 1979 in Paris (by JRJ Committee—Chana Arnon), March 5, 2002.

Geulen-Herscovici, Andrée. "The Rescue of Jewish Children in Belgium." YVA 02/961.

Heiber, Maurice. "Les Enfants." YVA 029–20.

Houwink ten Cate, Johannes. Letter to Paldiel, December 10, 1998.

Jospa, Ghert. "Belgian Resistance and the Camps of Breendonck and Buchenwald. YVA 02/298.

Kohn-Bankier, Miriam. Private file.

Lamon, Lisette. Testimony. In Mordecai Paldiel's private file on Walter Süskind at Yad Vashem.

Lanzmann, Claude. "Siegmund Forst, Interview by Claude Lanzmann on Rabbi Michael Dov Weissmandl." U.S. Holocaust Memorial Museum, Tapes # 3119–3124. Claude Lanzmann Shoah Collection, rg-60.5004.

Leons, Max (Nico). *A Mitzwa*, 1988. Personal memoirs, sent to Paldiel.

Levin, Dov. Interview with Dr. Zerach Warhaftig, Minister of Religious Affairs (Hebrew), (November 30, 1965). Hebrew University of Jerusalem, Institute of Contemporary Jewry, Oral History Division.

Ochayon, Sheryl. "The Female Couriers during the Holocaust." Jerusalem: Yad Vashem International School for Holocaust Studies, 2010.

Paldiel, Mordecai. Interview with Denise Siekierski, May 19, 1992.

———. Walter Süskind. Private file.

———. Interview with Jacques and Monique Pulver, 1992.

———. Miriam Kohn-Bankier file (in author's possession): a 1949 statement by Isaac Stern and Isaac Salpeter; letter by Milton S. Hirschfeld, New Cracow Friendship Society, Inc., Oceanside NY (2000); Association of Zionists-Democrats, Ichud, Krakow (1949); letter by Bronia Gross-Guns, Forest Hill NY (1998); letter by Solomon (Sol) Urbach, Flemington, NJ (n.d.); letter by Rena Fagen-Schonthal, Boca Raton FL (1998).

Patrick, Henry. "Madeleine Dreyfus: Righteous Jew." Author's collection.

Siekierski, Denis, interview by Paldiel, May 19, 1992.

Sterno, Ida. "Hiding of Jewish Children in Belgium." YVA 02/571.

"Tuvyah Bielski." YVA 03/3607.

Weiss, Robert R. *Joshko's Children.* Zagreb: privately written, 1998. A copy is stored at the U.S. Holocaust Memorial Museum in Washington. It includes accounts by Josef Indig that also appeared in a Hebrew edition.

"Wertheim, Anatol." YVA 03/3861.

Zmigrod, Irène. Testimony. YVA 02/1106.

Published Works

Abadi, Odette. *Terre de Détresse: Birkenau-Bergen-Belsen.* Paris: Harmattan, 1995.

Aderet, Ofer. "The Silent Savior of Germany's Jews." *Haaretz,* February 4, 2011.

"Alfred (Fredy) Hirsch, February 11, 1916–March 8, 1943." www.holocaust.cz /en/history/people/alfred-fredy-hirsch-2.

Arad, Yitzhak. *Belzec, Sobibor, Treblinka: The Operation Reinhard Death Camps.* Bloomington: Indiana University, 1987.

———. "Jewish Family Camps in the Forests." In *Rescue Attempts during the Holocaust: Proceedings of the Second Yad Vashem International Historical Conference, April 8-11, 1974,* edited by Yisrael Gutman and Efraim Zuroff, 333–53. Jerusalem: Yad Vashem, 1977.

———. "Sobibor." In *Encyclopedia of the Holocaust,* 4:1373–78. New York: Macmillan and Collier, 1990.

———. "Treblinka." In *Encyclopedia of the Holocaust,* 4:1481–88. New York: Macmillan and Collier, 1990.

Arad, Yitzhak, Yisrael Gutman, and Margaliot Abraham. *Documents on the Holocaust*. Jerusalem: Yad Vashem, 1981.

Arnold, David. "Walter Suskind: Quiet Hero of the Holocaust." *Boston Globe*, October 21, 1990.

Avneri, Arieh L. *From Velos to Taurus: The First Decade of Jewish Illegal Immigration to Mandatory Palestine (Eretz-Israel), 1934–1944*. Tel Aviv: Hakibbutz Hameuchad, 1985.

Avriel, Ehud. *Open the Gates! A Personal Story of "Illegal" Immigration to Israel*. New York: Atheneum, 1975.

Bauer, Yehuda. *American Jewry and the Holocaust: The American Jewish Joint Distribution Committee, 1939–1945*. Jerusalem and Detroit: Hebrew University and Wayne State University, 1981.

———. *Jews for Sale? Nazi-Jewish Negotiations, 1933–1945*. New Haven: Yale University Press, 1994.

———. *My Brother's Keeper: A History of the American Jewish Joint Distribution Committee, 1929–1939*. Philadelphia: Jewish Publication Society of America, 1974.

———. *Rethinking the Holocaust*. New Haven: Yale University Press, 2001.

———. "Schwartz, Joseph J." In *Encyclopedia of the Holocaust*, 4:1335–36. New York: Macmillan and Collier, 1990.

———. "Why Kook Is Out." *Jerusalem Post*, August 21, 2008.

Ben-Israel, Hedva. "Appeasement of Nazi Germany." In *Encyclopedia of the Holocaust*, 2:603–5. New York: Macmillan and Collier, 1990.

Benjamin, Yigael. *They Were Our Friends: A Memorial for the Members of the Hachsharot and the Hehalutz Underground in Holland Murdered in the Holocaust*. The Association of Former Members of the Hachsharot and the Hehalutz Underground in Holland, Westerweel Group included. Tel Aviv: Hidekel, 1990.

Benshalom, Rafi. *We Struggled for Life: The Hungarian Zionist Youth Resistance during the Nazi Era*. Jerusalem: Gefen, 2001.

Berkowitz, Sarah. *Where Are My Brothers?* New York: Helios, 1965.

Berman, Avraham. "Hayehudim Batzat Haari" [Jews on the Aryan side]. In *Encyclopedia of the Jewish Diaspora, Poland Series*, edited by Yitzhak Gruenbaum, 1:685–733. Tel Aviv, 1953.

———. *Mimei Hamachteret* [Underground days]. Tel Aviv: Hamenorah, 1971.

Biss, Andre. *A Million Jews to Save*. London: Hutchinson, 1975.

Blumental, N. *Entskiklopedyah shel Galuyot*. Jerusalem: Mir Sefer, 1962.

Bogner, Nachaum. *The Zionist Coordination to the Redemption of Jewish Children*. Jerusalem: Yad Vashem, 2000.

Borut, Jakob. "Austria: Historical Introduction." In *The Encyclopedia of the*

Righteous among the Nations, edited by Israel Gutman, xix–xxiii. Jerusalem: Yad Vashem, 2007.

Borwicz, Michal. *Arishe Papiren* (Yiddish). 3 vols. Buenos Aires: Tsentral-Farband fun Poylishe Yiden in Argentina, 1955.

———. *Vies Interdites.* Tournai, Belgium: Casterman, 1969.

Brachfeld, Sylvain. "Jews Rescued Jews." *Hidden Child/ADL* 15 (2007).

Braham, Randolph L. "Hungary: Jews during the Holocaust." In *Encyclopedia of the Holocaust,* 2:698–703. New York: Macmillan and Collier, 1990.

———. *The Politics of Genocide: The Holocaust in Hungary.* Condensed ed. Detroit: Wayne State University Press, 2000.

———. "Rescue Operations in Hungary: Myths and Realities." *East European Quarterly* 38 (Summer 2004): 173–203. Originally published in *Yad Vashem Studies* 32 (2004): 21–51; reprinted with permission from *Yad Vashem Studies.*

———. "Letters." *Yad Vashem Studies* 33 (2005): 481–82.

Brand, Joel. *Desperate Mission.* New York: Criterion, 1958.

Brenner, Lenni. "The Wartime Failure to Rescue." In *Zionism in the Age of the Dictators,* edited by Lenni Brenner. Westport CT: L. Hill, 1983.

Brod, Toman. "Memoir Kept in the Jewish Museum in Prague." http://www.holocaust.cz/en/resources/collections/zm78.

Broussard, Philippe. "Voiron, la rafle oubliée." *Le Monde,* December 2, 1997, 14–15.

Buszko, Jozef. "Auschwitz." In *Encyclopedia of the Holocaust,* 1:107–19. New York: Macmillan and Collier, 1990.

Campion, Joan. *In the Lion's Mouth: Gisi Fleischmann and the Jewish Fight for Survival.* San Jose: toExcel, 2000.

Carpi, Daniel. "Italy: Concentration Camps," and "Aid to Jews by Italians." In *Encyclopedia of the Holocaust,* 2:726–30. New York: Macmillan and Collier, 1990.

Centre de Documentation Juive Contemporaine. *Activité des Organisations Juives en France Sous l'Occupation* (L'Association des Israélites Pratiquants) 4. Paris: Editions du Centre, 1947.

Cesarani, David. *The Final Solution: Origins and Implementation.* London: Routledge, 2002.

Cholawski, Shalom. "Belorussia." In *Encyclopedia of the Holocaust,* 1:169–74. New York: Macmillan and Collier, 1990.

———. "Simcha Zorin." In *Encyclopedia of the Holocaust,* 4:1739–40. New York: Macmillan and Collier, 1990.

Cohen, Asher. *The Halutz Resistance in Hungary: 1942–1944.* Boulder: Social Science Monographs, 1986.

Cohen, Judith. "The Mantello Rescue Mission." *Prism* 4 (Spring 2012): 93–99.

Cohen, Richard, and Michael R. Marrus. "France." In *Encyclopedia of the Holocaust,* 5:506–17. New York: Macmillan and Collier, 1990.

Corbach, Dieter. *Die Jawne zu Köln: Zur Geschichte des ersten jüdischen Gymnasiums im Rheinland und zum Gedächtnis an Erich Klibansky.* Koln: Scriba, 1990.

Crowe, David M. *Oskar Schindler.* Cambridge MA: Westview, 2004.

Dawidowicz, Lucy. *A Holocaust Reader.* New York: Behrman House, 1976.

Delpard, Raphael. *Les Justes de l'Ombre.* Paris: J. C. Lattès, 1995.

Drohobycz-Boryslaw-and vicinity. http://www.drohobycz-boryslaw.org.en.

Duvernoy, Marianne. "Andrée Salomon: Portrait d'une 'Soeur Aînée." *Mémoire Vive.*

———. "Elie Bloch," *Vive Memoire,* 7, 8.

Dwork, Deborah, and Robert Jan Van Pelt. *Holocaust: A History.* New York: Norton, 1990.

Ehrenburg, Ilya, and Vasily Grossman. *The Complete Black Book of Russian Jewry.* New Brunswick NJ: Transaction, 2003.

Encyclopedia of the Holocaust. Edited by Israel Gutman. New York: Macmillan and Collier, 1990.

Fatran, Gila. *Merkaz ha-Yehudim ha-uz* (Hebrew)—*The Jewish Center Ustredna Zidov-uz.* PhD diss., Yeshiva University, New York, 1988.

———. "The 'Working Group.'" *Holocaust and Genocide Studies* 8, no. 2 (Fall 1994): 164–201 and 9, no. 2 (Fall 1995): 269–76.

Feingold, Henry L.

———. "American Jewry and the Holocaust." In *Encyclopedia of the Holocaust,* 1:37–41. New York: Macmillan and Collier, 1990.

———. *The Politics of Rescue: The Roosevelt Administration and the Holocaust, 1938–1945.* New Brunswick NJ: Rutgers University Press, 1970.

———. "Roosevelt, Franklin Delano." In *Encyclopedia of the Holocaust,* 4:1302–4. New York: Macmillan and Collier, 1990.

———. "United States of America." In *Encyclopedia of the Holocaust,* 4:1546–49. New York: Macmillan and Collier, 1990.

Fishman, Joel S. "Jewish War Orphans in the Netherlands: The Guardianship Issue, 1945–1950." *Wiener Library Bulletin* 27, no. 30–31 (1973–74): 31–36.

Flim, Jan. "Omdat Hun Hart Sprak" (Lest we forget). PhD diss., Groningen University, 1995.

Flörsheim, Chanan (Hans). "He Who Dares Wins." Originally published in German. Konstanz: Hartung-Gorre, 2007. www.hassia_judaica.de/chanan floersheim_He_Who_Dares_Wins.pdf.

Fontan, Bernadette, and Alain Robert du Costal. "Les Enfants du Chateau de Seignebon a Dému." *Familles Juives dans le Gers,* 2008.

Forst, Siegmund. "Rabbi Michael Ber Weissmandl: He Struggled with All He Possessed to Save Europe's Condemned Jews." *Jewish Observer*, June 1965, 9–13.

Fox, Frank. "A Jew Talks to Himmler." http://www.zwoje-scrolls.com/zwoje38/text18p.htm.

Fraenkel, Daniel. "The German 'Righteous Among the Nations': An Historical Appraisal." *Leo Baeck Institute Year Book* 48 (2003): 223–47.

———. "Germany: Historical Introduction." In *The Encyclopedia of the Righteous among the Nations: Europe*, edited by Israel Gutman, 1:liii–lxiii. Jerusalem: Yad Vashem, 2007.

Freier, Recha. "Ich wurde von Recha Freier gerettet." http://www.schoah.org/zeitzeugen/givon.htm.

———. *Let the Children Come: The Early History of Youth Aliyah*. London: Weidenfeld and Nicolson, 1961.

Friedenson, Joseph, and David Kranzler. *Heroine of Rescue: The Incredible Story of Recha Sternbuch Who Saved Thousands from the Holocaust*. Brooklyn NY: Mesorah, 1984.

Frieder, Emanuel. *Lehatsil Nafsham: Darko Shel Rav Tsair Bishnot Hashoah* (To deliver their souls: The struggle of a young rabbi during the Holocaust). Jerusalem: Yad Vashem, 1986.

———. *To Deliver Their Souls: The Struggle of a Young Rabbi during the Holocaust*. New York: Holocaust Library, 1987.

Friedländer, Saul. *Nazi Germany and the Jews, 1939–1945: The Years of Extermination*. New York: HarperCollins, 2007.

Fuchs, Abraham. *The Unheeded Cry*. Brooklyn NY: Mesorah, 1998.

Garfinkels, Betty. *Les Belges Face à la Persécution Raciale, 1940–1944*. Université Libre de Bruxelles, 1965.

Gelber, Yoav. "The Origins of Youth Aliyah." *Studies in Zionism* 9, no. 2 (1988): 147–71.

Genizi, Haim. "Bergson Group." In *Encyclopedia of the Holocaust*, 1:190–92. New York: Macmillan and Collier, 1990.

Glick, David. "Some Were Rescued." *Harvard Law School Bulletin* 12, no. 2 (October 1960): 6–9.

Goldfinger, Shoshanna. "Reb Chaim Yisroel Eiss, the Man at the Center of Orthodoxy's WWII Rescue Activities." http://www.chareidi.org/archives5764/REI64features.htm.

Goldman, Shalom. "Meet Brother Daniel: A Jew Turned Christian Convert." *Haaretz English Edition*, August 18, 2011.

Gur, David. *Brothers for Resistance and Rescue: The Underground Zionist Youth Movement in Hungary during World War II*. Jerusalem: Gefen, 2007.

Gurewitsch, Brana. "The Chance to Live: The Kinder and the Rescuers." *Prism* 5 (Spring 2013): 11–16.

———. *Mothers, Sisters, Resisters: Oral Histories of Women Who Survived the Holocaust.* Tuscaloosa: University of Alabama, 1998.

Gutman, Israel. "The Jews in Poland." In *Encyclopedia of the Holocaust*, 3:1151–76. New York: Macmillan and Collier, 1990.

———. "Poland: Historical Introduction." In *The Encyclopedia of the Righteous Among the Nations: Poland,* edited by Israel Gutman, 1:xx–xlvii. Jerusalem: Yad Vashem, 2004.

Gutman, Yisrael, and Michael Berenbaum, ed. *Anatomy of the Auschwitz Death Camp.* Bloomington: Indiana University Press in association with the U.S. Holocaust Memorial Museum, 1994.

Hammel, Frédéric Chimon ("Chameau"). *Souviens-toi d'Amalek: Témoignage sur la lutte des Juifs en France (1938–1944).* Paris: CLKH, 1982.

Häsler, Alfred A. *The Lifeboat Is Full: Switzerland the Refugees, 1933–1945.* New York: Funk and Wagnalls, 1969.

Heart–Holocaust Education and Archive Research Team. "Alexander Pechersky: Leader of the Sobibor Revolt, Testimony." http://www.HolocaustResearchProject.org.

Hecht, Ben. *A Child of the Century.* New York: Simon and Schuster, 1954.

Hilberg, Raul. *The Destruction of the European Jews.* New York: Harper and Row, 1979.

Hirsch, Colette. "Böszi la Rayonnante." *Mémoire Vive.*

Hirschmann, Ira A. *Life Line to a Promised Land.* New York: Jewish Book Guild of America, 1946.

———. *Caution to the Winds.* New York: David McKay, 1962.

Holmes, Colin. "Fascism in Great Britain." In *Encyclopedia of the Holocaust,* 2:605–7. New York: Macmillan and Collier, 1990.

Hurwitz, Ariel. "United States Department of State." In *Encyclopedia of the Holocaust,* 4:1545. New York: Macmillan and Collier, 1990.

Jackson, Harriet. "The Rescue and Resistance Work of Rabbi Zalman Schneerson in Vichy France (1940–1944)." *Hidden Child* 19 (2011): 25–27, 31.

Jacobs, Jack. "A Friend in Need: The Jewish Labor Committee and Refugees from the German-Speaking Lands, 1933–1945." *YIVO Annual* 23 (1996): 391–417.

Jelinek, Yeshayahu, and Robert Rozett. "Slovakia." In *Encyclopedia of the Holocaust,* 1:1364–70. New York: Macmillan and Collier, 1990.

"Jewish Resistance in Holland: Group Westerweel and Hachshara." http://www.thefreelibrary.com/Jewish+Resistance+in+Holland.

Kahn, Madeleine. *De l'Oasis Italienne au Lieu du Crime des Allemands.* Nice: Editions Bénévent, 2003.

Karpin, Michael. *Tightrope: Six Centuries of a Jewish Dynasty.* Hoboken NJ: Wiley, 2008.

Karski, Jan. *Story of a Secret State.* Boston: Houghton Mifflin, 1944.

Keren, Nili. "Fredy Hirsch—Educator in a Concentration and Death Camp." In *Guf Shelishi Yahid*, edited by Ronen Avihu and Yehoyakim Cochavi, 1:287–300. Moreshet: Ghetto Fighters' House and Yad Ya'ari, n.d.

———. "The Family Camp." In *Anatomy of the Auschwitz Death Camp*, edited by Yisrael Gutman and Michael Berenbaum, 428–40. Bloomington: Indiana University Press in association with the U.S. Holocaust Memorial Museum, 1998.

Kermish, Joseph. "The Activities of the Council for Aid to Jews ('Żegota') in Occupied Poland." In *Rescue Attempts during the Holocaust*, edited by Yisrael Gutman and Efraim Zuroff, 367–98. Jerusalem: Yad Vashem, 1977.

Knout, David. *Contribution a l'Histoire de la Résistance Juive en France, 1940–1944.* Paris: Editions du Centre, 1947.

Kochan, Lionel. "Himmler, Heinrich." In *Encyclopedia of the Holocaust*, 1:660–62. New York: Macmillan and Collier, 1990.

"Le Rav Zalman Schneersohn en France." *Kountrass*, no. 95 (May/June 2003): 39–55.

Krakowski, Shmuel, "Bergen-Belsen." In *Encyclopedia of the Holocaust*, 2:185–90. New York: Macmillan and Collier, 1990.

Kranzler, David H. *Holocaust Hero.* Jersey City NJ: Ktav, 2004.

———. *The Man Who Stopped the Trains to Auschwitz: George Mantello, El Salvador, and Switzerland's Finest Hour.* Syracuse NY: Syracuse University Press, 2000.

———. "The Swiss Press Campaign That Halted Deportations to Auschwitz and the Role of the Vatican, the Swiss and Hungarian Churches." In *Remembering for the Future: International Scholars' Conference, Oxford, 10–14 July 1988*, edited by Yehuda Bauer, 1:156–70. Oxford: Pergamon, 1988.

———. *Thy Brother's Blood.* New York: Mesorah, 1987.

Kulka, Otto Dov. "Germany." In *Encyclopedia of the Holocaust*, 2:557–75. New York: Macmillan and Collier, 1990.

L.M. "Une Armée Secrete au Service des Enfants." *Mémoire Vive.*

Lamperti, John. "Paul on Pius: El Salvador's Holocaust Hero." http://www.paulonpius.blogspot.com/p/el-salvadors-holocaust-hero-by-john.html.

Landau, Maria, and Jacqueline Sigaar. *Le Reseau Marcel: Histoire d'un Réseau Juif Clandestin.* Documentary. Paris, 1995.

Langbein, Hermann. *People in Auschwitz.* Chapel Hill: University of North Carolina Press, 2004.

Laqueur, Walter. *A History of Zionism.* New York: Holt, Rinehart and Winston, 1972.

Latour, Anny. *The Jewish Resistance in France (1940–1944)*. New York: Holocaust Library, 1981.

Lazar, Chaim. *Despite It All*. New York: Shengold, 1984.

Lazare, Lucien. "Gamzon Robert." In *Encyclopedia of the Holocaust*, 2:537–38.
New York: Macmillan and Collier, 1990.

———. "A Nice Occupée par les Allemands, Moussa Abadi a Orchestré
le Sauvetage de 527 Enfants Juifs." *Le Monde Juif*, no. 155 (September–
December 1995): 48–57.

———. *Rescue as Resistance: How Jewish Organizations Fought the Holocaust
in France*. New York: Columbia University, 1996.

———. "Resistance, Jewish Organizations in France: 1940–1944." http://jwa
.org/encyclopedia/article/resistance-jewish-organizations-in-france-1940
-1944.

Lefenfeld, Nancy. "Marianne Cohn." *Mishpocha*, Summer 2003.

Lévai, Jenö. *Abscheu und Grauen vor dem Genocid in aller Welt*. New York/
Toronto: Diplomatic Press, 1968.

Levesque, Morvan. "Les Chasseurs d'Enfants." *Journal Carrefour*, November
16, 1948.

Levin, Dov. "Lithuania." In *Encyclopedia of the Holocaust*, 3:895–99. New York:
Macmillan and Collier, 1990.

———. "Lithuania: Historical Introduction." In *Encyclopedia of the Righteous
Among the Nations: Europe*, edited by Israel Gutman, 2:lxi–lx. Jerusalem:
Yad Vashem, 2011.

Licht, Rochel. "Rabbi Solomon Schonfeld: The Singular British Rabbi Who
Saved Jewish Children." *Prism* 5 (Spring 2013): 17–23.

Lustiger, Arnold. "Der Kommerzialrat charterte die rettende Flotte." *Frankfurter Allgemeine Zeitung*, January 27, 2011.

Madajczyk, Czesław. "Poland." In *Encyclopedia of the Holocaust*, 3:1143–51.
New York: Macmillan and Collier, 1990.

Marcou, Léa. "Un des Responsables du Réseau Garel: André Chouraqui."
Mémoire Vive.

Marrot-Fellag Ariouet, Céline. "Les Enfants Cachés Pendant la Seconde
Guerre Mondiale aux Sources d'une Histoire Clandestine: Chapter 1: Le
Réseau Marcel: Sauvetage des Enfants Juifs dans la Région de Nice." http://
www.lamaisondesevre.org/cel/cel5.html, November 13, 2006.

Marrus, Michael R. "Commissariat Général aux Questions Juives (Office for
Jewish Affairs; CGQJ)." In *Encyclopedia of the Holocaust*, 1:306–7. New
York: Macmillan and Collier, 1990.

———. "Statut des Juifs (Jewish Law)." In *Encyclopedia of the Holocaust*,
4:1411. New York: Macmillan and Collier, 1990.

Martin, Dean. "Resistance Plans and Escape from the Mir Ghetto." *Encyclopedia of Camps and Ghetto, 1933–1945*. U.S. Holocaust Memorial Museum. http://www.ushmm.org/wlc/en/article.php?moduleId=10007238.

Masur, Norbert. "Report to the World Jewish Congress: Regarding My Visit with Heinrich Himmler, April 21, 1945." Brookdale Center for World War II Studies and Conflict Resolution.

Meed, Vladka. *On Both Sides of the Wall*. New York: Holocaust Library, 1993.

Merlin, Samuel. *Millions of Jews to Rescue: A Bergson Group Leader's Account of the Campaign to Save Jews from the Holocaust*. Washington DC: David Wyman Institute for Holocaust Studies, 2011.

Meyer-Dettum, Klaus. *Max Windmüller "Cor" (1920–1945)*. Emden: Druckhaus W. Dahlheimer, 1997.

Michaelis, Meir. "Italy." In *Encyclopedia of the Holocaust*, 2:720–26. New York: Macmillan and Collier, 1990.

Michman, Dan. "Belgium." In *Encyclopedia of the Holocaust*, 1:160–69. New York: Macmillan and Collier, 1990.

———. *Belgium and the Holocaust: Jews, Belgians, Germans*. Jerusalem: Yad Vashem, 1998.

———, vol. ed. *The Encyclopedia of the Righteous Among the Nations: Belgium*. Jerusalem: Yad Vashem, 2005.

Michman, Jozeph. "Netherlands, The." In *Encyclopedia of the Holocaust*, 3:1045–57. New York: Macmillan and Collier, 1990.

Michman, Jozeph, and Bert Jan Flim. "Verduin, Leendert." *Encyclopedia of the Righteous Among the Nations: The Netherlands*. Jerusalem: Yad Vashem, 2004.

Milgram, Avraham. *The Encyclopedia of the Righteous Among the Nations: Supplementary Volume 1*. Jerusalem: Yad Vashem, 2010.

Miron, Guy, and Shlomit Shulhani. *Encyclopedia of the Ghettos*. Vol. 1. Jerusalem: Yad Vashem, 2009.

Morley, John F. *Vatican Diplomacy and the Jews during the Holocaust, 1933–43*. New York: Ktav, 1980.

Müller, Filip. *Eyewitness Auschwitz*. Chicago: Ivan R. Dee, 1979.

Neumann, Oskar Y. *Gisi Fleischmann: The Story of a Heroic Woman*. Tel Aviv: Wizo, 1970.

Nodot, René. *Les Enfants ne Partiront Pas!* Lyon: Nouvelle Lyonnaise, 1970.

Ofer, Dalia. "The Activities of the Jewish Agency Delegation in Istanbul in 1943." In *Rescue Attempts during the Holocaust*, edited by Israel Gutman and Efraim Zuroff, 435–50. Jerusalem: Yad Vashem, 1977.

———. "Aliya Bet." In *Encyclopedia of the Holocaust*, 1:22–31. New York: Macmillan and Collier, 1990.

————. *Escaping the Holocaust: Illegal Immigration to the Land of Israel, 1939–1944*. New York: Oxford University, 1990.

————. "The Rescue of European Jewry and Illegal Immigration to Palestine in 1940—Prospects and Reality: Berthold Storfer and the Mossad Le'Aliyah Bet." *Modern Judaism* 4, no. 2 (1984): 159–81.

Oliner, Samuel. *Who Shall Live: The Wilhelm Bachner Story*. Chicago: Academy, 1996.

Ommeren, Anita van, and Ageeth Scherphuis. "De Crèche, 1942–1943." *Vrij Nederland*, January 18, 1986, 2–21.

Paldiel, Mordecai. "From the Hands of the Aggressor: The Rescue of Jewish Children in Belgium." *Yad Vashem Magazine*, April 2003, 5.

————. "The Rescue of Jewish Children in Belgium during World War II." In *Belgium and the Holocaust*, edited by Dan Michman, 307–25. Jerusalem: Yad Vashem, 1998.

————. "Righteous Gentiles and Courageous Jews: Acknowledging and Honoring Rescuers of Jews." In *French Politics, Culture, and Society* 30, no. 2 (Summer 2012): 134–49.

————. *Saving the Jews*. Rockville MD: Schreiber, 2000.

Parkman, Patricia. *Nonviolent Insurrection in El Salvador: The Fall of Maximiliano Harnández Martínez*. Tucson: University of Arizona Press, 1988.

Pauley, Bruce F. *From Prejudice to Persecution*. Chapel Hill: University of North Carolina Press, 1992.

Peleg-Mariańska, Miriam, and Mordecai Peleg. *Witnesses: Life in Occupied Kraków*. London: Routledge, 1991.

Perl, William R. *The Four-Front War: From the Holocaust to the Promised Land*. New York: Crown, 1979.

Perthuis, Valérie. *Le Sauvetage des Enfants Juifs du camp de Vénissieux–août 1942*. Lyon: Editions Lyonnaises d'Art et d'Histoire, 1997.

Picard, Marianne. "Lise Hanau, la merveilleuse infirmiere de Rivesaltes." *Mémoire Vive*, no. 22–23 (June 2001).

Pingel, Falk. "Concentration Camps." In *Encyclopedia of the Holocaust*, 1:308–17. New York: Macmillan and Collier, 1990.

Poliakov, Léon. *L'Auberge des Musiciens: Mémoires*. Paris: Mazarine, 1981.

————. *Mémoires*. Paris: Jacques Grancher, 1999.

Porat, Dina. *The Blue and the Yellow Stars of David: The Zionist Leadership in Palestine and the Holocaust, 1939–1945*. Cambridge: Harvard University Press, 1990.

Porter, Anna. *Kasztner's Train*. New York: Walker, 2008.

Poznanski, Renée. *Jews in France during World War II*. Hanover NH: Brandeis University, 2001.

———. *Les Juifs en France pendant la Seconde Guerre mondiale.* Paris: Hachette, 1994.

"Recha Freier, or the Dream to Save 10,000 children." http://www.berlin-ju dentum.de/englisch/freier.htm.

Rein, Armand. Rapport sur les Événements de 1943 en France Occupée par les Troupes Italiennes: Les Centres de Résidence Assignés en Savoie (March–September 1943). OSE Archives, box 22, August 1944.

Reuveni, Moshe, and Simcha Reznik. "The Wondrous Story of Oswald Rufeisen (Hebrew)." In *Sefer Mir,* edited by Blumenthal Nachman, 313–27. Jerusalem: Entsiklopedyah shel Galuyot, 1962.

Reznik, Simcha. "Rescue and Rebellion of Mir Jews: Oswald Rufeisen (Hebrew)." In *Sefer Mir,* edited by Nachman Blumenthal, 328–46. Jerusalem: Entsiklopedyah shel Galuyot, 1962.

Ringelblum, Emanuel. *Polish-Jewish Relations during the Second World War.* Jerusalem: Yad Vashem, 1974.

———. *Notes from the Warsaw Ghetto.* New York: Schocken, 1974.

Rosensaft, Hadassah. *Yesterday: My Story.* New York and Jerusalem: American Society for Yad Vashem and Yad Vashem, 2004.

Rotkirchen, Livia. *The Destruction of Slovak Jewry: A Documentary History.* Jerusalem: Yad Vashem, 1961. Documents in Hebrew. Letter by Gisi Fleischmann to Istanbul, January 5, 1944, on the deteriorating medical condition of her daughter in Palestine (230); letter by Gisi Fleischmann to Hechalutz, Geneva, September 1, 1943, on the difficulties in aiding fleeing Jewish refugees arriving in Slovakia (231); letter by Rabbi Weissmandl to Hechalutz, not dated, on the importance of ransom to save Jews (236); letter by Rabbi Weissmandl, 1944, on the need to bomb the railways leading to Auschwitz to stop the deportation of Hungarian Jews (237).

———. "The 'Europa Plan': A Reassessment." In *American Jewry during the Holocaust,* edited by Maxwell Finger Seymour, appendix 4–7. New York: Holmes and Meier, 1984.

Segal, Raz. *Days of Ruin: The Jews of Munkacs during the Holocaust.* Jerusalem: Yad Vashem, 2013.

Samuel, Vivette. *Rescuing the Children: A Holocaust Memoir.* Madison: University of Wisconsin Press, 2002.

Schellekens, Mark. "Op Zoek Naar Walter Süskind" (Looking for Walter Süskind). MA thesis, University of Amsterdam, 1992.

Schmalz-Jacobsen, Cornelia. *Zwei Bäume in Jerusalem.* Hamburg: Hoffmann und Campe, 2002.

Schneerson, Zalman. *Shevet Y'hudah: Letters, Part One.* Brooklyn: Empire Press, 1978.

Schor, Ralph. *Un Evêque dans le Siècle: Monseigneur Paul Rémond (1873–1963)*. Nice: Editions Serre, 1984.

Segev, Tom. *The Seventh Million: The Israelis and the Holocaust*. New York: Henry Holt, 1991.

Seligmann, Avraham. "An Illegal Way of Life in Nazi Germany." *Leo Baeck Institute Year Book* 37 (1992): 327–61.

Shalem, Chaim. "'Remember, There Are Not Many Eisses Now in the Swiss Market': Assistance and Rescue Endeavors of Chaim Yisrael Eiss in Switzerland." *Yad Vashem Studies* 33 (2005): 347–79.

Shapira, Anita. *Old Jews, New Jews* (Hebrew). Tel Aviv: Am Oved, 2003.

Shealtiel, Shelomo. *From Birthland to Homeland: Emigration and Illegal Immigration to Palestine from Bulgaria and via Bulgaria in the Years 1939–1949*. (Hebrew) Tel Aviv: Am Oved, 2004.

Shelah, Menachem. "Croatia." In *Encyclopedia of the Holocaust*, 1:323–29. New York: Macmillan and Collier, 1990.

Shepherd, Naomi. *A Refuge from Darkness: Wilfrid Israel and the Rescue of the Jews*. New York: Pantheon, 1984.

Shor, Essie, and Adrena Zakin. *Essie: The Story of a Teenage Fighter in the Bielski Partisans*. Bryn Mawr PA: Mindfulness, 2009.

Siekierski, Denise. "La Résistance juive in France: cette méconnue." In *Cevennes: Terre de Refuge*, edited by Joutard Philippe, Poujol Jacques, and Cabanel Patrick, 175–82. Club Cévenol: Presses du Languedoc, 1987.

———. "En hommage a Joseph Bass ('Monsieur André'), mon Chef." *Mémoire Vive*, ca. 2000.

Silberklang, David. "American Jewish Committee." In *Encyclopedia of the Holocaust*, 1:35–36. New York: Macmillan and Collier, 1990.

Smilovitsky, Leonid. "Jewish Family Camps and Groups in Belarus, 1941–1944." Diaspora Research Center of Tel Aviv University. www.Jewishgen .org/yizkor/belarus/bel119.html.

Sompolinsky, Meier. *Britain and the Holocaust*. Brighton: Sussex Academic Press, 1999.

"Sophie Yaari Tells Her Story." http://www.sorrel.humboldt.edu/-rescuers/book /Pinkhof/yaari/sophie1.html.

Stauber, Roni. *The Holocaust in Israeli Public Debate in the 1950s*. London: Vallentine Mitchell, 2007.

Steinberg, Lucien. *Le Comité de défense des Juifs en Belgique, 1942–1944*. Brussels: Université de Bruxelles, 1973.

Stoltzfus, Nathan. *Resistance of the Heart*. New York: W. W. Norton, 1996.

Taylor, Derek. *Solomon Schonfeld*. London: Vallentine Mitchell, 2009.

Tec, Nechama. *Defiance*. New York: Oxford University Press, 2009.

———. *When the Light Pierced the Darkness*. Oxford: Oxford University Press, 1986.

———. "Reflections on Rescuers." In *The Holocaust and History*, edited by Michael Berenbaum and Abraham Peck, 651–62. Bloomington: Indiana University Press, 2002.

Teitelbaum-Schwarz, Bertha. "How Rabbi Zalman Schneerson Saved the Teitelbaum Sisters, Bertha, Malka, and Bella." *Hidden Child* 19 (2011): 1, 6, 13, 16.

Temkin-Berman, Basia. *City within a City*. New York: International Psychoanalytic Books, 2012.

The Holocaust—Lest We Forget. "Westerbork Liberation—Samuel Schrijver." http://www.holocaust-lestweforget.com/camp-westerbork-liberation-samuel schrijver.html.

Thorne, Leon. *Out of the Ashes: The Story of a Survivor*. New York: Bloch, 1961.

Tomaszewski, Irene, and Tecia Werbowski. *Żegota: The Council for Aid to Jews in Occupied Poland, 1942–1945*. Montreal: Price-Patterson, 1999.

Twersky, David. "The Strange Case of 'Brother Daniel.'" http://www.jewish worldreview.com/cols/twersky080598.html.

Tydor-Baumel, Judith, Nan Sagi, and Ronald Zweig. "Jewish Refugees." In *Encyclopedia of the Holocaust*, 2:607–10. New York: Macmillan and Collier, 1990.

U.S. Holocaust Memorial Museum. "The Bielski Partisans." http://www.ush mm.org (January 6, 2011).

———. "Claude Lanzmann Interview with Ehud Avriel." http://resources.ush mm.org/film (1985).

———. "German Jews during the Holocaust, 1939–1945." http://www.ushmm .org (June 20, 2014).

Vrba, Rudolf, and Alan Bestic. *Escape from Auschwitz: I Cannot Forgive*. New York: Grove Press, 1964.

Warhaftig, Zerach. *Refugee and Survivor: Rescue Efforts during the Holocaust*. Jerusalem: Yad Vashem and World Zionist Organization, 1988.

Wasserstein, Bernard. *The Ambiguity of Virtue: Gertrude van Tijn and the Fate of the Dutch Jews*. Cambridge: Harvard University Press, 2014.

Weill, Georges. "Andrée Salomon et le Sauvetage des Enfants Juifs (1933–1947)." *French Politics, Culture, and Society* 30, no. 2 (Summer 2012): 89–112.

Weissmandl, Michael Dov. *Min Hametsar*. New York: Emunah, 1960.

Weizmann, Chaim. *Trial and Error*. New York: Harper and Brothers, 1949.

Wertheim, Anatol. "With Zorin in the Family Camp." http://www.eilatgordin levitan.com/minsk_pages/min_stories-Zorin.html.

Wiesel, Elie. *Night*. New York: Bantam-Dell, 1986.

Wikipédia. "Union genérale des Israelites de France." October 12, 2012.

Wyman, David. *The Abandonment of the Jews*. New York: New Press, 1998.

——. *Paper Walls: America and the Refugee Crisis, 1938–1941*. Amherst: University of Massachusetts Press, 1968.

Yahil, Leni. *The Holocaust: The Fate of European Jewry, 1932–1945*. New York: Oxford University Press, 1990.

——. "Switzerland." In *Encyclopedia of the Holocaust*, 4:1441–44. New York: Macmillan and Collier, 1990.

Ziemian, Joseph. *The Cigarette Sellers of Three Crosses Square*. New York: Avon, 1975.

Zuroff, Efraim. *The Response of Orthodox Jewry in the United States to the Holocaust: The Activities of the Vaad ha-Hatzala Rescue Committee, 1939–1945*. New York: Michael Scharf Publication Trust of the Yeshiva University; Hoboken: Ktav, 2000.

Zweig, Ronald. "Churchill, Winston Leonard Spencer." In *Encyclopedia of the Holocaust*, 1:299–301. New York: Macmillan and Collier, 1990.

——. "Great Britain." In *Encyclopedia of the Holocaust*, 2:600–603. New York: Macmillan and Collier, 1990.

Index

Figures are indicated by F plus a page number

Ganzenko, Semyon, 95
Garel, Georges, F16, 230–32, 259
Garel, Lily, 505n116
Garel network, 245–46, 263, 504n115, 511n234
Garrett, Walter, 353
Gau, Albert, 216
Gaudefroy, Renée Pauline, 505n115
Gaulstick, Friedrich, 378
Geist, Raymond H., 17, 463n66
Gelblum, Irena, 54–55
Gemmeker, Hermann, 299
General Zionists movement, 140
Geniewski, Otto, 261
Gereformeerde (Calvinist) church, 310
Geulen, Andrée, F20, 269, 277–78, 281
Ghert, Jospa, 267, 271–73
Ghert, Yvonne, 269, 271–72
Gillette, Guy, 423
Giniewski (Ginat), Otto, 217, 261
Ginsburg, Pino, 317
Gitler, Józef, 32
Givon, Kalman (Karl Kleinberger), 10, 462n44
Glaeser, Léo, 211
Glasoog, Sammy, 519n48
Glass House, 158, 170, 491n63, 491n65
Gleitmann, Wolf Lazer, 56
Glick, David, 16–18, 463n63
Gligorijevic, Milan, 166, 493n88
Glovacki, Pius, 81
Goebbels, Josef, 541n82
Goethals, Alphonse, 274, 279
Goglowski, Jacques ("Fat Jacques"), 272, 277–78, 282–83
Goldfarb, Tzvi (Cvi), F9, 167
Goldmann, Nahum, 362, 427, 538n18
Goldstein, Peretz (Franz), 179–80
Golub, Malvina, 187
Gomułka, Władyslaw, 59

Good Shepherd Mission, 492n69
Gordon, Aaron, 464n73
Gordonia movement, 20, 464n73
Gottlieb, Maurycy, 59
Goudberg, Menno, 518n37
Grad Lesno Brdo, Slovenia, 186, 188–90
Grajek, Stefan, 54, 466n41
Green, Wiliam, 423, 435
Griffel, Jakob, 339, 368
Grodzinski, Haim Ozer, 76–77, 474n23
Groen, Meijer, 518n37
Groenewegen van Wijk, Dick, 519n45
Gronowski, Simon, 284–85
Gross-Guns, Bronia, 58
Grossman, Haika, 442
Grossman, Sanyi, 151
Grossman, Vasily, 381
Grosz, Bandi, 171–74
Grósz, David. *See* Gur, David (Endre Grósz)
Groupe d'Action Contre la Déportation, 225
Gruenbaum, Yitzhak, 454
Grumsinger, Germaine, 356
Grünhut, Aaron, 106
Grüninger, Paul, 357, 358, 530n83
Grünwald, David (Coca), 145, 149
Grüson, Max, 119, 126, 451–52
Grynszpan, Yehiel, 380
Guerrero, José Gustavo, 349
Günther, Karl, 65
Gur, David (Endre Grósz), 149, 151, 160–63, 168, 459n3
Gurewitsch, Brana, 406
Gurs camp, 202, 204, 240, 247, 511n234
Gustav V, king, 354
Gutman, Michal, 56
Gutman, Ruth, F27
Guttman, Claude, 502n61

Schumacher, Emil, 378

Schwalb, Nathan, 21, 111, 123, 185, 197, 199, 454

Schwartz, Barry, xv

Schwartz, Isaïe, 501n47

Schwartz, Joseph, F30, 112, 180, 436, 442, 444, 446, 456, 507n157

Schwarz, Heinrich, 101

Schwarzbart, Ignacy, 466n43

Schweizer Rabbinerverband, 347

Schweizerischer Israelitischer Gemeindebund, 345, 445

Schweizerischer Unterstutzungsfonds fur Fluchtlinge, 451

Sebestyen, Arpad, 101, 128

Secours d'Hiver, 269

Secours Mutuel Juifs, 280

Selznick, David O., 539n33

Sendlerowa, Irena, 33, 466n37

Sequerra, Samuel, 448

Serafinowicz, Semion, 97

Sered camp, 105, 118

Sered, Novaky, and Vhyne camps, 101, 123, 136, 479n38

Sereni, Enzo, 5

Seventh Fort, 75

Seweryn, Tadeusz, 470n102

Seyss-Inquart, Arthur, 287

Shaprut, Hasdai bin, 485n2

Sherer, Emanuel, 348

Shertok (Sharett), Moshe, 173–75, 319, 456, 495n131

Sheva Kehillos (Seven Communities), 105, 357

Shevet Yehudah, 258

Shicke, Lon, 409

Shind, Zeev, 319, 339–41

Shlomovitz (Shalev), Eli, 149

Shor, Essie, 88, 90, 93

Sieff, Rebecca, 8

Siegel, Manuel, 449

Siekierski-Caraco, Denise, F12, F13, 223, 227–30

SIG (Federation of Swiss Jewish Communities), 355, 369

Silber, Devorah, 69

Silber, Moshe, 495n13

Silberberg, Marie, 29

Silver, Abba Hillel, 362, 417

Silver, Eliezer, 360, 424, 430, W29

Silverman, Samuel Sydney, 542n108

Simon, Edouard and Charlotte, 219, 247, 260

Simon, Joachim (Shushu), 302–3, 306

Sisters of the Resurrection, 98

Sivák, Jozef, 103, 127–28

Sixth (Sixième), 215–6, 219, 221, 235, 251, 259–60, 502n67

Slachta, Margit, 104

Sluzker, Edwin, 290–93

Snow White and the Seven Dwarfs, 388

Sobibór camp, 25, 122, 144, 288, 371–82

Société Belge de Banque, 269

Solidarité movement, xvii, 210–11, 220, 503n83

Spellman, Francis, 104

Spielberg, Steven, 56, 58

Spielman, Rudolf, 130

Spier-Donati, Marianne, 238

Spitzer, Sime (Simon), 337, 443, 450

Springmann, Samuel, 176

Stanley, Oliver, 338

Stein, Rachel, 32

Steinberg, Lucien, 270, 273, 280, 282, 514n53

Steiner, Andrej, 111–12, 114, 131, 135–36

Steinhardt, Laurence, 342–43

Stella Maris Monastery, 99

Stephens, Dorsey, 448

Stern, Isaac, 56, 58

CPSIA information can be obtained
at www.ICGtesting.com
Printed in the USA
LVOW07*2222020217

523057LV00002B/2/P